OUR BODIES, OURSELVES
A Book By and For Women

Second Edition, Completely Revised and Expanded

The Boston Women's Health Book Collective

A Touchstone Book
Published by

SIMON AND SCHUSTER   NEW YORK

Permission to reprint the following is gratefully acknowledged:

"Billions for Band-Aids," copyright © 1972 by the Medical Committee for Human Rights, San Francisco Bay Area Chapter.

"Child of Mine," Words and music by Gerry Goffin and Carole King, copyright © 1970 by Screen Gems-Columbia Music, Inc., 711 Fifth Ave., New York, N.Y. 10022. Used by permission. All rights reserved.

"Declaration," by Miriam Goodman, first published in Our Bodies, Ourselves, Simon and Schuster, copyright © 1971, 1973 by The Boston Women's Health Book Collective.

Drawings by Betty Dodson, from The New Sex Therapy, by Helen Singer Kaplan, M.D., Ph.D., Brunner/Mazel, Inc., New York, 1974, pp. 404, 406, and 408. Reprinted by permission of Brunner/Mazel, Inc.

"Love Song of a Species," by Cora Brooks, from Heather in a Jar, a book of poems published by Pomegranate Press, Cambridge, Mass., copyright © 1973 by Cora Brooks.

"Our Faces Belong to Our Bodies," copyright © 1972 by It's All Right to Be a Woman Theatre, 146 Sixth Ave., Brooklyn, N.Y. 11217.

Tables pages 185, 189 and 197 used with permission of the Emory University Family Planning Program.

"The Edge," from Firstborn, by Louise Glück. Reprinted by permission of New American Library, copyright © 1968 by Louise Glück.

"The Patients' Bill of Rights," adapted from The Rights of Hospital Patients, by George Annas, Avon copyright © 1975 by the American Civil Liberties Union.

"The Seven of Pentacles" was originally published in Off Our Backs and later appeared in To Be of Use, copyright © 1972 by Marge Piercy; "Bridging" was originally published in The Liberated Guardian and later appeared in To Be of Use, copyright © 1969, 1971, 1973 by Marge Piercy. Reprinted by permission of Doubleday & Co., Inc.

"What Can A Woman Do?," copyright © 1974 by HealthRight, 175 Fifth Ave., New York, N.Y. 10010.

"Where Does All the Money Go?" from HealthRight, vol. I, Issue 3, 1975. Copyright © 1975 by HealthRight, Inc. (New York Women's Health Forum).

A Touchstone Book
Published by Simon and Schuster
A Division of Gulf & Western Corporation
Simon & Schuster Building
Rockefeller Center
1230 Avenue of the Americas
New York, New York 10020
TOUCHSTONE and colophon are trademarks
of Simon & Schuster

Designed by Elizabeth Woll
Manufactured in the United States of America

26   27   28   29   30   31   32

Library of Congress Cataloging in Publication Data

Boston Women's Health Book Collective.
    Our bodies, ourselves.

    Includes index.
    1. Women—United States—Addresses, essays, lectures.
    2. Women—Psychology—Addresses, essays, lectures.
    3. Women—Health and hygiene—Addresses, essays, lectures. 1. Title.
HQ1426.B69 1975   301.41′2′0973   75-25802
ISBN 0-671-22146-9 pbk.

Special thanks to the following for their help with the 1979 update:

Michelle Harrison
Mary Howell
Janet Jones
Freada Klein
Sherry Leibowitz
Jessica Lipnack
Peggy Lynch
Devin Ryder MacQueen
Barbara Menning
Clare Potter
JR Roberts
Jane Hyman Wegscheider
Fran Wiltsie

Thanks to the following people for your information, advice and support:

Herbert Aaron
Phyllis Aaron
Helene Aarons
Alyce R. Adams
Judy Alland
Kathee Allen
Diana Altman
George Annas
Joanne Apter
Elayne Archer
Kathy Babel
Diane Balser
Ruth Balser
Donald Bell
Zachary Bell
Trude Bennett
Alan Berger
Madelene Berkowitz
Lorraine Bethel
Gene Bishop
Andrea Black
Kenneth Blotner
Liz Blum
Diane Bohl
Nancy Bongiovani
Alice Bonis
Cathy Booth
Women in the Boston
    Association for Childbirth
    Education, Inc.
Barbara Brainin
Edward Brecher
Thomas Brewer
Geraldine Bridgeman
Nancy Brigham
Cora Brooks
Jan Bumstead
John Bunker
Dorothy Burlage
Hester Butterfield
Leslie Cagan
Mary Jane Campbell
Barbara Cane
Joanna Caplan
Peggy Carlson
Linda M. Chagnon
Helen Chernoff
Michelle Clark
Peggy Clark
Betsy Cole
Beverly Coleman
Jeanne Collins
Cynthia Cook
Sally Cook
Lee Cooke
Oliver Cope
Thayer Cory
Mary Costanza
Belita Cowan
Laurie Crumpacker
Pauline D'Allesandro

Irene Davidson
Annie Denton
Martin Diskin
Linda Dittmar
Bruce Ditzion
Robert Ditzion
Alice Donaldson
Joan Donato
Sharon Donovan
Benjamin Nathan Doress
Hannah Susan Doress
Irvin Doress
Sheila Dowd
Carol Driscoll
Beverly Edwards
Mary Elizabeth
Joanna Ekman
Helen English
Phyllis Ewen
Tess Ewing
Tom Fallaw
Judy Folkmanis
Rachel Fruchter
Roberta Gannon
Marsha Gerstein
Louise Glück
Donna Gold
Ginger Goldner
Miriam Goodman
Linda Gordon
Emily Graeser
Helen L. Gray
Marian Johnson Gray
Roger W. Gray
Mary Greely
John W. Grover
Doris Haire
Sara Hale
Susie Harris
Florence Haseltine
Pat Haseltine
Andy Hawley
Gina Hawley
Joshua Hawley
Sharon Hennessy
Linda Henry
Meg Hickey
Ellin Hirst
Lucy Horwitz
Mary Howell
Linda Hunt
Roxane Hynek
Patsy Hynes
Leah Jackson
Myla Kabat-Zinn
Laurie Kanke
Marcia Kasabian
Susan Katz
Jane Kaufman
Steve Keese
Jamie Kelem

Claire Keough
Joseph Kerrins
Freada Klein
Grace Kleinbach
Linda J. Knight
Thomas Kosasa
Gale Kosto
Carol Koury
Joan Wexler Kroll
Anne LaCasse
Jim Lakiotes
Louise Lander
Wini Lawrence
Ray Lawson
Margaret Lazarus
Elizabeth Levingson
Jane Levy
Lanayre Liggera
Janis Long
Pamela Lowry
Judy Luce
Florence Luscomb
Peggy Lynch
Jane Mansbridge
Robert Margulis
Joe Marks
Jennifer Marmaduke
Maternity Center Association
Joan Matheson
Mercedes Mattsen
Elizabeth A. McGee
Barbara McHugh
Karen M. Metzler
Lynne Morgan
Robin Morgan
Marilyn Murphy
Merry Muscato
Sheri Mutch
Carole Myers
Linda Neville
Elizabeth Newby
The Staff of the New England
    Free Press
New York Women's Health
    Forum
Karen Norberg
Agnes Norsigian
D. David Nuss
Mary O'Brien
Beth Oglesby
Barbara Orrok
Gerard Ostheimer
Cookee Paul
Karen Pavides
Preterm Inc.
Robbie Pfeufer
Ben Pincus
Ed Pincus
Sami Pincus
Ann Popkin
Gina Prenowitz

Janet Press
Ann Preston
Doreen Querido
Jean Raisler
Allan Rashba
Joanna Reiff
Susan Reverby
Alberta Richmond
Harriet Ripinsky
Nathan Rome
Joanne Rosemont
Kris Rosenthal
Alice Ryerson
Matthew Sanford
John Scanlon
Ted Schocken
Marzi Schorin
Alice Schwartz
Leonard Schwartz
Joseph Schwarz
Barbara Seaman
Kathy Segal
Peggy Shapiro
Nancy Shaw
Diana Siegal
Marilyn Slotkin
Barbara Smith
Somerville Hospital School of
    Nursing Library
Ann Sosne
Sam Stamper
Elizabeth Stein
Sharon Steinick
Roland Stern
Nancy Stokly
Marcia Storch
Pat Sweeney
Sarah Swenson
Dorothy Tennov
Ruth D. Terzaghi
Terry Thorsos
Trudy Trumpy
Maureen Turner
Corrinne Van Alstine
Ann Walsh
Jane Ward
Jane Knowles Webb
Jerry Weinstein
Linda Willner
Marliese Wior
Jill Wolhandler
Karen Wolkoff
Women at the 1975
    Conference on Women and
    Health
Women's Community Health
    Center of Cambridge, Mass.
Women of the Sydney Farber
    Cancer Center
E. Louise Worthington
Phoebe Wray
and especially our families

With special thanks to our editor Alice Mayhew

ILLUSTRATION CREDITS

(All are photo credits except as indicated.)

CONTENTS

PREFACE

A GOOD STORY

The history of this book, *Our Bodies, Ourselves,* is lengthy and satisfying.

It began in a small discussion group on "women and their bodies" which was part of a women's conference held in Boston in the spring of 1969, one of the first gatherings of women meeting specifically to talk with other women. For many of us it was the very first time we had joined together with other women to talk and think about our lives and what we could do about them. Before the conference was over, some of us decided to keep on meeting as a group to continue the discussion, and so we did.

In the beginning we called ourselves "the doctors group." We had all experienced similar feelings of frustration and anger toward specific doctors and the medical maze in general, and initially we wanted to do something about those doctors who were condescending, paternalistic, judgmental and non-informative. As we talked and shared our experiences with one another, we realized just how much we had to learn about our bodies. So we decided on a summer project—to research those topics which we felt were particularly pertinent to learning about our bodies, to discuss in the group what we had learned, then to write papers individually or in groups of two or three, and finally to present the results in the fall as a course for women on women and their bodies.

As we developed the course we realized more and more that we really *were* capable of collecting, understanding and evaluating medical information. Together we evaluated our reading of books and journals, our talks with doctors and friends who were medical students. We found we could discuss, question and argue with each other in a new spirit of cooperation rather than competition. We were equally struck by how important it was for us to be able to open up with one another and share our feelings about our bodies. The process of talking was as crucial as the facts themselves. Over time the facts and feelings melted together in ways that touched us very deeply, and that is reflected in the changing titles of the course and then the book—from *Women and Their Bodies* to *Women and Our Bodies* to, finally, *Our Bodies, Ourselves.*

When we gave the course we met in any available free space we could get—in day schools, in nursery schools, in churches, in our homes. We wanted the course to stimulate the same kind of talking and sharing that we who had prepared the course had experienced. We had something to say, but we had a lot to learn as well; we did not want a traditional teacher-student relationship. At the end of ten to twelve sessions—which roughly covered the material in the current book—we found that many women felt both eager and competent to get together in small groups and share what they had learned with other women. We saw it as a never-ending process always involving more and more women.

After the first teaching of the course, we decided to revise our initial papers and mimeograph them so that other women could have copies as the course expanded. Eventually we got them printed and bound together in an inexpensive edition published by the New England Free Press. It was fascinating and very exciting for us to see what a constant demand there was for our book. It came out in several editions, a larger number being printed each time, and the time from one printing to the next becoming shorter. The growing volume of requests began to strain the staff of the New England Free Press.* Since our book was clearly speaking to many people, we wanted to reach beyond the audience who lived in the area or who were acquainted with the New England Free Press. For wider distribution it made sense to publish our book commercially.

You may want to know who we are. Our ages range from twenty-five to forty-one, most of us are from middle-class backgrounds and have had at least some college education, and some of us have professional degrees. Some of us are married, some of us are separated, and some of us are single. Some of us have children of our own, some of us like spending time with children, and others of us are not sure we want to be with children. In short, we are both a very ordinary and a very special group, as women are everywhere. We can describe only what life has been for us, though many of our experi-

*New England Free Press publications cover a wide range of topics. Contact them for a free literature list at 60 Union Sq., Somerville, Mass.

ences have been shared by other women. We realize that poor and nonwhite women have had greater difficulty in getting accurate information and adequate health care, and have most often been mistreated in the ways we describe in this book. Learning about our womanhood from the inside out has allowed us to cross over some of the socially created barriers of race, color, income and class, and to feel a sense of identity with all women in the experience of being female.

We are eleven individuals and we are a group. (The group has been ongoing for three years, and some of us have been together since the beginning. Others came in at later points. Our current collective has been together for one year.) We know each other well—our weaknesses as well as our strengths. We have learned through good times and bad how to work together (and how not to, as well). We recognize our similarities and differences and are learning to respect each person for her uniqueness. We love each other.

Many, many other women have worked with us on the book. A group of gay women got together specifically to do the chapter on lesbianism. Other chapters were done still differently. For instance, the mother of one woman in the group volunteered to work on menopause with some of us who have not gone through that experience ourselves. Other women contributed thoughts, feelings and comments as they passed through town or passed through our kitchens or workrooms. There are still other voices from letters, phone conversations, and a variety of discussions that are included in the chapters as excerpts of personal experiences. Many women have spoken for themselves in this book, though we in the collective do not agree with all that has been written. Some of us are even uncomfortable with part of the material. We have included it anyway, because we give more weight to accepting that we differ than to our uneasiness. We have been asked why this is exclusively a book about women, why we have restricted our course to women. Our answer is that we are women and, as women, do not consider ourselves experts on men (as men through the centuries have presumed to be experts on us). We are not implying that we think most twentieth-century men are much less alienated from their bodies than women are. But we know it is up to men to explore that for themselves, to come together and share their sense of themselves as we have done. We would like to read a book about men and their bodies.

We are offering a book that can be used in many different ways—individually, in a group, for a course. Our book contains real material about our bodies and ourselves that isn't available elsewhere, and we have tried to present it in a new way—an honest, humane and powerful way of thinking about ourselves and our lives. We want to share the knowledge and power that come with this way of thinking, and we want to share the feelings we have for each other—supportive and loving feelings that show we can indeed help one another grow.

From the very beginning of working together, first on the course that led to this book and then on the book itself, we have felt exhilarated and energized by our new knowledge. Finding out about our bodies and our bodies' needs, starting to take control over that area of our lives, has released for us an energy that has overflowed into our work, our friendships, our relationships with men and women, and for some of us, our marriages and our parenthood. In trying to figure out why this has had such a life-changing effect on us, we have come up with several important ways in which this kind of body education has been liberating for us and may be a starting point for the liberation of many other women.

First, we learned what we learned equally from professional sources—textbooks, medical journals, doctors, nurses—and from our own experiences. The facts were important, and we did careful research to get the information we had not had in the past. As we brought the facts to one another we learned a good deal, but in sharing our personal experiences relating to those facts we learned still more. Once we had learned what the "experts" had to tell us, we found that we still had a lot to teach and to learn from one another. For instance, many of us had "learned" about the menstrual cycle in science or biology classes—we had perhaps even memorized the names of the menstrual hormones and what they did. But most of us did not remember much of what we had learned. This time when we read in a text that the onset of menstruation is a normal and universal occurrence in young girls from ages ten to eighteen, we started to talk about our first menstrual periods. We found that, for many of us, beginning to menstruate had not felt normal at all, but scary, embarrassing, mysterious. We realized that what we had been told about menstruation and what we had not been told—even the tone of voice it had been told in—had all had an effect on our feelings about being female. Similarly, the information from enlightened texts describing masturbation as a normal, common sexual activity did not really become our own until we began to pull up from inside ourselves and share what we had never before expressed—the confusion and shame we had been made to feel, and often still felt, about touching our bodies in a sexual way.

Learning about our bodies in this way is an exciting kind of learning, where information and feelings are allowed to interact. It makes the difference between rote memorization and relevant learning, between fragmented pieces of a puzzle and the integrated picture, between abstractions and real knowledge. We discovered that people don't learn very much when they are just passive recipients of information. We found that each individual's response to information was valid and useful, and that by sharing our responses we could develop a base on which to be critical of what the experts tell us. Whatever we need to learn now, in whatever area of our lives, we know more how to go about it.

A second important result of this kind of learning is that we are better prepared to evaluate the institutions that are supposed to meet our health needs—the hospitals, clinics, doctors, medical schools, nursing schools, public health departments, Medicaid bureaucracies and so on. For some of us it was the first time we had looked critically, and with strength, at the existing institutions serving us. The experience of learning just how little control we had over our lives and bodies, the coming together out of isolation to learn from each other in order to define what we needed, and the experience of supporting one another in demanding the changes that grew out of our developing critique—all were crucial and formative political experiences for us. We have felt our potential power as a force for political and social change.

The learning we have done while working on *Our Bodies, Ourselves* has been a good basis for growth in other areas of life for still another reason. For women throughout the centuries, ignorance about our bodies has had one major consequence—pregnancy. Until very recently pregnancies were all but inevitable, biology *was* our destiny—that is, because our bodies are designed to get pregnant and give birth and lactate, that is what all or most of us did. The courageous and dedicated work of people like Margaret Sanger started in the early twentieth century to spread and make available birth control methods that women could use, thereby freeing us from the traditional lifetime of pregnancies. But the societal expectation that a woman above all else will have babies does not die easily. When we first started talking to each other about this, we found that that old expectation had nudged most of us into a fairly rigid role of wife-and-motherhood from the moment we were born female. Even in 1969, when we first started the work that led to this book, we found that many of us were still getting pregnant when we didn't want to. It was not until we researched carefully and learned more about our reproductive systems, about birth-control methods and abortion, about laws governing birth control and abortion, and not until we put all this information together with what it meant to us to be female, that we began to feel we could truly set out to control whether and when we would have babies.

This knowledge has freed us to a certain extent from the constant, energy-draining anxiety about becoming pregnant. It has made our pregnancies better because they no longer happen to us, but we actively choose them and enthusiastically participate in them. It has made our parenthood better because it is our choice rather than our destiny. This knowledge has freed us from playing the role of mother if it is not a role that fits us. It has given us a sense of a larger life space to work in, an invigorating and challenging sense of time and room to discover the energies and talents that are in us, to do the work we want to do. And one of the things we most want to do is to help make this freedom of choice, this life span, available to every woman. This is why people in the women's movement have been so active in fighting against the inhumane legal restrictions, the imperfections of available contraceptives, the poor sex education, the highly priced and poorly administered health care that keep too many women from having this crucial control over their bodies.

There is a fourth reason why knowledge about our bodies has generated so much new energy. For us, body education is core education. Our bodies are the physical bases from which we move out into the world; ignorance, uncertainty—even, at worst, shame—about our physical selves create in us an alienation from ourselves that keeps us from being the whole people that we could be. Picture a woman trying to do work and to enter into equal and satisfying relationships with other people—when she feels physically weak because she has never tried to be strong; when she drains her energy trying to change her face, her figure, her hair, her smells, to match some ideal norm set by magazines, movies and TV; when she feels confused and ashamed of the menstrual blood that every month appears from some dark place in her body; when her internal body processes are a mystery to her and surface only to cause her trouble (an unplanned pregnancy, or cervical cancer); when she does not understand or enjoy sex and concentrates her sexual drives into aimless romantic fantasies, perverting and misusing a potential energy because she has been brought up to deny it. Learning to understand, accept, and be responsible for our physical selves, we are freed of some of these preoccupations and can start to use our untapped energies. Our image of ourselves is on a firmer base, we can be better friends and better lovers, better *people*, more self-confident, more autonomous, stronger and more whole.

March, 1973.

Some Notes on the Second Edition

When we started to revise *Our Bodies, Ourselves*, we thought it would be a simple two-month job of updating some facts. Now, several months and much hard and exciting work later, we surface for air and rush to get the "new Book" out by February! The revised edition turned out to be over 100 pages longer and more than two-thirds revised, because:

1. We ourselves have grown and changed with two more years of living, as we have worked, loved, played, read, heard from others and shared among ourselves.
2. Readers of the first edition have energetically urged us both by letter and in person, to include more of

certain kinds of needed information—for instance, on menopause, breast cancer, self-help.

3. Much has changed in the health field, including improvements (like the increased availability of first-trimester abortion and the emergence of various woman-generated health-care alternatives), and setbacks (such as increasing medical intervention in normal childbirth).

These three kinds of change have affected nearly every chapter in the book. Some parts have been almost totally rewritten: Sexuality, Common Medical and Health Problems (in Chapter 6), Venereal Disease, Rape, Abortion, Considering Parenthood, Preparation for Childbirth, Some Problems in Childbearing, Menopause and Women and Health Care.

The new book costs two dollars more to cover rising costs of paper and printing. We hope that clinics and other health-care delivery and education groups with IRS tax-exempt status will take advantage of the clinic discount mentioned on the copyright page. (If your group has trouble qualifying for a clinic discount you can write to us.) We have used the royalties from book sales to support health-education work done both by our group and in conjunction with other women's health groups.

We have been together now for more than five years as a work-and-personal-sharing group. Since the book's publication we have experienced some conflict between our work load as authors of a widely selling book and our desire to be a close personal support group for one another. We have been exploring ways of getting our work done more effectively. And we have been learning more about how to ask for help from each other and how to give it. As our interconnectedness grows, we feel increasing love and appreciation for each other.

We feel proud and glad that the book has reached so many people. It has been published in Japan and Italy, and is soon to come out in France, Holland, Sweden, Denmark, Greece and Great Britain. A number of Spanish-speaking women have been working on a Spanish translation for the United States (and possibly other countries) which we hope to have published in 1976.

The book has also been put into seven volumes of braille (Braille No. 2328, Library of Congress No. 301).

The work of redefining health education and health care for women is being carried on, expanded and improved by a dramatically increasing number of groups and individuals in the women's health movement. Many women, both as consumers and as health workers, are making a radical challenge to the health-care system as we have known it. The hardest work is ahead: as the challenge has become more effective, most of the medical world has intensified its resistance to change. We urge you to work for change, in any way that feels right for you.

The experience of finding so much of the 1973 edition outdated less than two years later has made us aware that by the time this edition comes out even some of the "revised" material will not be totally up-to-date. Throughout the book we have tried to list resources for the most current information, and we hope you will find them useful tools as you move to take control of your body, your health, your physical, emotional and spiritual well-being—your life.

Remember the dignity
of your womanhood.
Do not appeal,
do not beg,
do not grovel.
Take courage,
join hands,
stand beside us.
Fight with us . . .

—CHRISTABEL PANKHURST
English suffragette, 1880–1958

From,

Norma	Nancy	Wilma	Wendy
Pam	Paula	Esther	Joan
Judy	Ruth	Jane	

May, 1975

Box 192, West Somerville, Mass. 02144

Our Faces Belong to Our Bodies

Our faces belong to our bodies.
Our faces belong to our lives.

Our faces are blunted.
Our bodies are stunted.
We cover our anger with smiles.

Our faces belong to our bodies.
Our faces belong to our lives.

Our anger is changing our faces, our bodies.
Our anger is changing our lives.

Women who scrub have strong faces
Women who type have strong faces
Women with children have strong faces
Women who love have strong faces

Women who laugh have strong faces
Women who fight have strong faces
Women who cry have strong faces
Women who die have strong faces.

Our love is changing our faces, our bodies.
Our love is changing our lives.

Our sisters are changing our faces, our bodies.
Our sisters are changing our lives.

Our anger is changing our faces, our bodies.
Our anger is changing our lives.

Our power is changing our faces, our bodies.
Our power is changing our lives.

Our struggle is changing our faces, our bodies.
Our struggle is changing our lives.

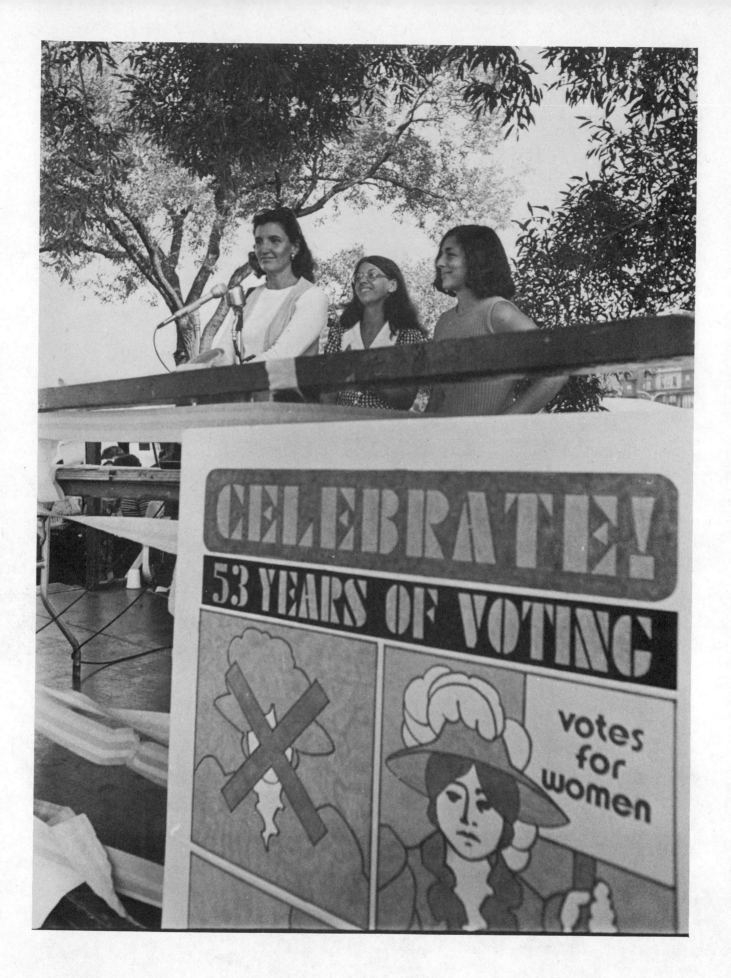

CHAPTER 1
OUR CHANGING SENSE OF SELF

This book was written by many women. Those responsible for seeing its completion form the Boston Women's Health Book Collective. This, in part, is who we are: we are in our mid-twenties to early forties, mostly married or in (or have been in) some long-term relationship with a man. Some of us have had children recently. We are college educated (some of us have gone to graduate school), and all of us have spent a number of years living away from home either with female roommates, with men, alone, or in some varying combination. We have worked or are working. Most of us feel that contrary to what we were promised in childhood, we were not totally fulfilled by marriage (a man), and/or motherhood (a child), and/or a (typically feminine) job. This is not to say that we have not grown a lot within marriages and with our children or in our work. Most of us see these relationships as continuing. But just being wife or wife and mother and viewing our work as secondary was too limiting for us. We needed space to do our own work or find out what work we wanted to do. We also needed space to discover who we were separate from these primary relationships so that we could become autonomous adult people as well as have important relationships with others.

We can talk only for ourselves, although we consider ourselves part of a larger movement of women in the Boston area—a group of great variety. We realize that the development of the ideas presented in this book comes from many women we know from other women's collectives as well as our own.

Coming together with women was exciting. We were individual women coming together out of choice and strength. Since we had patterned and focused much of our life around men, this was liberating. It was also liberating because we were legitimizing our need for one another. Most of us had gone to college, had lived with women, and so had had close friendships with women, but viewed this as a transitional stage leading up to a male-centered life. That was the traditional pattern, and that is what we expected of our lives. We felt that as young adult women we had missed close female friendships. Traditionally, the extended family provided close female contacts—women in unselfconscious ways providing support, sharing experience and wisdom with each other. Most of us were not living in the cities where our families lived, and needed to create for ourselves a place and occasion for women to get together.

Coming together to do something about our lives was scary. It was admitting that we were not completely satisfied with the lives we were leading. We knew we would be standing back and taking a hard look at ourselves, and this aroused anxiety, fear of the unknown. Some of us fantasized that commitment to the women's movement and pressure from the group would weaken our ties with our men, children, jobs, life styles—we would lose control over our lives. We came to realize that this fear was unrealistic. No one could take from us what we did not want to give up. We were coming together out of choice. Our hope was to come to feel ourselves to be fuller, more integrated female persons.

Like most early women's groups, we talked to each other about what life was like for us growing up female. The underlying purpose of this introspection and analysis of our past was to have some basis for figuring out how we wanted to change the ways we thought and felt about ourselves. We could act on this new sense of self in our lives to create a broader understanding of what it means to be female. To do this very personal work we made an accepting environment for ourselves—a place where we could talk and work together and think out loud. Probably the most valuable learning for each of us was learning to feel good about speaking for ourselves and being ourselves.

At first we feared disclosing personal information. We each thought we might be ridiculed, rejected, misunderstood, gossiped about by the others. Many of us were friends before the group began and we were shy about getting into personal discussions about our relationships with men. Our fears of other women were exaggerated. We turned out to have a lot in common as women. And as we related to each other in more direct and honest ways, more genuine relationships were possible. On the other hand, we found it takes a long time to feel comfortable and trusting in a group. If we do not feel comfortable and trusting, there is probably some basis for it.

We also feared rejecting each other. We would see traits in others which we did not want to see in ourselves, which were different from our own, or which we did not like. We realized that as women we had been raised to be nice to everyone, to please everyone, and that we had not allowed ourselves to experience ambivalent feelings about ourselves and others. Facing this allowed us to be more honest with ourselves and others.

One thing that came out in talking together about growing up was that most of us felt we had spent a lot of time and energy in inner conflict during adolescence—trying to become selfless, sweet, passive, dependent children so that our princes would find us and we would live happily ever after. By the end of adolescence most of us had resolved the conflict by learning to conform to the feminine role while suppressing qualities within us inappropriate to that role—independence, activity, anger and pride. These human qualities which would have got in the way of our "femininity" were, logically enough, labeled by our culture "male."

From our beginning conversations with each other we discovered four cultural notions of femininity which we had in some sense shared: woman as inferior, woman as passive, woman as beautiful object, woman as exclusively wife and mother. In our first discussions we realized how severely those notions had constricted us, how humanly limited we felt at being passive, dependent creatures with no identities of our own. As time passed, with each other's support we began to rediscover ourselves. The passion with which we did this came from getting in touch with human qualities in ourselves that had been taboo.

We all went through a time when we rejected our old selves and took on the new qualities exclusively. For a while we became distortions, angry all the time or fiercely independent. It was as though we had partly new selves, and we had to find out what they were like. But ultimately we came to realize that rejecting our "feminine" qualities was simply another way of going along with our culture's sexist values. So with our new energy came a desire to assert and reclaim that which is ours.

In no way do we want to become men. We are women and we are proud of being women. What we do want to do is reclaim the human qualities culturally labeled "male" and integrate them with the human qualities that have been seen as "female" so that we can all be fuller human people. This should also have the effect of freeing men from the pressure of being masculine at all times—a role equally as limiting as ours has been. We want, in short, to create a cultural environment where all qualities can come out in all people.

Changing Our Internalized Sexist Values

When we started talking to each other we came to realize how deeply ingrained was our sense of being less valuable than men.

In my home I always had a sense that my father and brother were more important than my mother and my-

self. My mother and I shopped, talked to each other, and had friends over—this was considered silly. My father was considered more important—he did the real work of the world.

In my home I got a complicated message. On the one hand I was told I was as important and as competent as men. In other ways I was told this was not true. Money was set aside for my brother to go to college but not for me.

In school we learned that we were expected to do well, but our real vocation was to be wife and mother. Boys were being trained for the important work in society. We learned that what our culture labeled important work was not for us, and what we did was not seen as important.

I wanted to be a doctor, but I was told in direct and indirect ways that my ultimate ambition should be marrying a doctor and raising a family. I gave up my dream.

I wanted to be an elementary school teacher, mostly because I had hated going to elementary school and I wanted to make it better for others. Although at first I thought this was important work, I learned not to value it because it was considered second-rate in this culture.

The few of us who did *not* stay out of "male" work suffered the consequences. We had to choose between being a "brain" or being a woman.

For me the evidence of my mental competence was unavoidable, and I never had any trouble defending or voicing my opinion with men, because I beat them in all the tests. Consequently none of them would come near me in my first seventeen years of life.

It was as if to be considered women we had to keep in our inferior place. If we challenged this we were treated badly and came to think of ourselves in negative ways.

Our learned sense of inferiority affected the way we thought about our bodies—our physical selves.

I remember coming home from high school every day and going over my body from head to toe. My forehead was too high, my hair too straight, my body too short, my teeth too yellow, and so on.

And when we evaluated our present situations we found that we still thought in sexist terms. Among our male peers we always found ourselves valuing what men said over what we said, and what men did over what we did.

Every time my husband has free time he sits down and reads a book. We both have a sense that that is really important. When I have free time I sit and crochet or read, and it feels as if I am doing nothing.

I genuinely enjoy loving and raising kids and setting up a home, but I have always felt that it was not important.

I have a lot of talents. I like to paint, dance, and am sensitive to people and their needs, but whenever I demonstrate this I think, Anyone could do this.

I look at the way we have divided up the space in our house. My husband has a little space that is considered his own, and I have no space that is mine. It is as if I exist everywhere and nowhere.

We lived our lives as if there were something intrinsically inferior about us.

What was exciting through all this talking together was learning that what each of us had thought was a personal sense of inferiority was in fact shared by many women. This reflected a larger cultural problem: that power is unequally distributed in our society. Men, having the power, are considered superior, and we, having less power, are considered inferior. What we have to change are the power relationships between the sexes, so that both sexes have equal power and people's qualities can be judged on their own merits rather than in terms of power. Although this problem is not easily solvable, at least the situation is changeable, since it is not based on biological facts. We know we will feel daily tension in recognizing the gap between our ideology and the realities of our everyday life caused by our resistance to change, male resistance and external social structures not supportive of our ideology. Still, we have a direction we want to move in.

We looked at our present lives and realized how we were perpetuating unequal power relationships between ourselves and men. Many of the instances, which are numerous, are explored in this book. We never expected enough time and pleasure in sex; we never respected the questions we asked our doctors; we never expected men to adjust their lives to parenthood, as we bore the child for both of us; we never expected men to take on some of the worry about birth control; we didn't take care of our bodies as if they/we mattered; we never respected the support and comfort other women gave us when we needed it. The list is endless. We began to see our rela-

tionships with ourselves, men, other women and the social institutions in this country in a new way. To be able to see and feel the strength, beauty and potential in women was exhilarating. We began to feel prouder and prouder of ourselves.

We started considering what we had thought of as our weaknesses as our strengths. At the same time we were trying to become separate people. We began to really appreciate our capacity to empathize, to nurture, to be passive and to be dependent. By empathy we mean the ability to identify emotionally with other people and be sensitive to what their life events mean to them. Although this can be bad for us if we only identify with others and have no sense of self, this capacity of ours is valuable and ours to use when we choose. By nurturing we mean taking care of the emotional and physical needs of others—maintaining life. Although in the past we only maintained life and depended on men to do and act and build, this capacity to maintain life is valuable and ours to use. By passivity we mean the ability to sit back. Although in our past we were passive and not able to act when we wanted, now we realize that we can act but that it is nice to choose not to at times. By dependency we mean the capacity to depend on, rely on, another person. Previously we had no sense of self and had to depend on someone else. Now we can choose to be dependent, and we see this as a strength, because intimate relationships are dependent relationships. The list could go on. We are really coming to enjoy our talents and our abilities, who we are and what we do.

Still, as we grow and change we discover things about ourselves that we don't like—our limitations, our imperfections, our mistakes—but we realize that these do not reflect our inferiority, but are part of being human. We are learning to tolerate parts of ourselves that we don't like and to build on what we do.

Rediscovering Activity

Talking to each other, we realized that many of us shared a common perception of men—that they all seemed to be able to turn themselves on and to do things for themselves. We tended to feel passive and helpless and to expect and need men to do things for us. We were trained to give our power over to men. We had reduced ourselves to objects. We remained children, helpless and giving other people power to define us and objectify us.

As we talked together we realized that one of our central fantasies was our wish to find a man who could turn us on, do for us what we could not do for ourselves, make us feel alive and affirm our existence. It was as if we were made of clay and man would mold us, shape us, and bring us to life. This was the material of our childhood dreams: "Someday my prince will come." We were always disappointed when men did not accomplish this impossible task for us. And we began to see our passive, helpless ways of handing power over to others as crippling to us. What became clear to us was that we had to change our expectations for ourselves. There was no factual reason why we could not assert and affirm our own existence and do and act for ourselves.

There were many factors that affected our capacity to act. For one, the ideal woman does less and less as her class status rises. Most of us, being middle class, were brought up not to do very much. Also, the kind of activity that is built into the traditional female role is different in quality from masculine activity. Masculine activity (repairing a window, building a house) tends to be sporadic, concrete, and to have a finished product. Feminine activity (comforting a crying child, preparing a meal, washing laundry) tends to be repetitive, less tangible, and to have no final durable product. Here again our sense of inferiority came into play. We had come to think of our activity as doing nothing—although it was essential for maintaining life—and of male activity as superior. We began to value our activity in a new way. We and what we did were as valuable as men and what they did.

On the other hand, we tried to incorporate within us the capacity to do more "male," product-oriented ac-

tivity. Our motivation to write this book falls into that category. To be more specific: what began as conversation was translated into written papers, was extended into a course based on informal discussion and the presentation of some of the material we had learned, and culminated in the publishing of our papers as a book. During this slow evolution we became more and more motivated to work hard on our ideas—to refine them, to clarify them, and to present them in a form that would be accessible to other women. This sustained work on a tangible product is exciting to us. But throughout this process we have in no way sacrificed the quality of our relationships with each other, as men often do when they work together. We have genuinely collaborated, which meant having good communication as we worked together. We devised our own forms of working and doing within the social context we created.

Along with our more task-oriented activity comes a new sense of wanting to succeed. By succeed we mean getting recognition for what we do. We also mean an inner sense of having done something well. This ties in with our new sense of pride—feeling proud of what we do.

This is new for us. As women, we have been taught to want to fail, or if not to fail, to walk a fine line between

success and failure. We were never encouraged to use our full strength. This new motivation to do and do things well is more risky. It involves taking and accepting responsibility because others are counting on us to come through with what we can do.

I am aware that I am responsible to other human beings—my parents, my husband, my children, my friends. What greater responsibility is there?

It also means that we have to maintain a rather consistent performance, according to our own standards. It involves the strength to stand up for ourselves and what we can do while realizing that others may reject what we do, do it differently, or put us down. Still, it is worth these risks, because these are the risks of living.

With our new sense of strength and activity comes a new sense that it is all right to be passive as long as we choose to be.

In lovemaking I have come to take great pleasure in taking a passive role as long as I actively choose it. I also know that I can be active. It is wonderful to know there is time both to give and receive love and caresses.

We have also come to enjoy physical activity as well as mental and emotional activity. Again, the realm of physical strength is traditionally male; and again we realized that we were active in our own ways, but that we did not value them. As we looked at the details of our lives—the shopping and the cleaning—we realized that we used up a lot of physical energy every day but that we

had taken it for granted and thought of it as nothing. We did avoid heavy, strenuous activity.

I thought that girls did not have to be physically strong. They could do everything they needed with their heads. The fact is that some mental work involves a back-up of physical strength. For example, engineers and architects can become more experienced in their trades if they are physically able and have the strength and stamina to build machines and structures. I now feel that all desirable qualities and abilities are neither male nor female but, rather, human, and I am trying to get the most out of my body, mind and feelings.

We are learning to do new things—mountain climbing, canoeing, karate, auto mechanics.

Rediscovering Anger

As we were changing we found we were frequently feeling angry. This surprised us and embarrassed us. We had grown up feeling that we needed to love everyone and be loved by everyone. If we got angry at someone or they at us, we felt in some sense that we were failures.

We shared memories of our pasts. Nearly all of us had had a hard time expressing anger verbally or physically.

In my family my mother expressed love and my father spanked me. My mother was super-uncritical of me and my father hypercritical. I learned that women are never disapproving or angry.

I have very few memories of fighting. Each time I did I felt guilty and embarrassed.

We did fight a lot at home, but I never made a public display of any anger or aggression. That was unladylike.

We shared perceptions of our current situations.

My husband has this habit of not listening to me when I talk. I get angry at him, but I don't tell him.

I seem to put up with a lot of nonsense from people. It is as if I am always being the accepting, forgiving and accommodating person.

We began to admit that we had felt angry during our lives but that we had been using the anger against ourselves in hating ourselves. There were many ways we had learned to cover up our anger. It had built up for so long inside us that we were afraid we would explode if we let it out. We have come to realize that there are many aspects of our lives and our relationships that make us angry. Until we know and feel our own oppression we are not motivated to try to create constructive alternative ways of being and living. Many have accused us of being shrill. Our mood is far more complex. Our critics hear only the anger, and anger separated from real issues is a distortion. The anger that is in us is a starting point for creative change and growth.

Rediscovering Our Separateness

In our early discussions it became clear that we did not really feel ourselves to be separate, independent people. The men in our lives embodied, or felt they were supposed to embody, freedom and independence. The women in our lives stayed at home, needed company, and were always dependent on those near them. They embodied, or felt they should, dependency, need and connection. As we talked to each other we realized that as children and even as young adults we had never thought it would be possible to live without someone else, particularly a man. We trembled at the thought of being alone. But we realized that we were no longer

powerless, helpless children. We realized that we could survive on our own and that until we felt confident of our ability to feel like separate people and take on the freedom and responsibility of being adults, we were not free to live with another out of choice. We wanted our coming together with another to result from choice and joy and not fear and necessity.

This is not to say that we do not seek relationships out of need and loneliness as well. Some of us who are married have tried to develop the capacity to feel like separate persons within the context of the marriage. Others of us in marriages or long-term relationships have decided to end the relationships or separate. Those of us who were not involved in relationships built up our own strengths. Each of us found her own way to become a separate person. The point was not that one way was better than another, but that it was freely chosen.

During this period of building up our sense of ourselves we tried to find out what we were like on our own, what we could do on our own. We discovered resources we never thought we had. Either because we had been dependent on men to do certain things for us or because we had been so used to thinking of ourselves as helpless and dependent, we had never tried.

It is hard. We are forever fighting a constant, inner struggle to give up and become weak, dependent and helpless again.

I started making batiks again and have become very seriously involved in this craft. It still surprises me that I can create something other than a child. Each time I complete one by myself I feel alone and trembling. Also, each time I have to fight inner voices saying, You are not going to do it.

I went with other women on a trip south almost two years ago. This was the first time I had gone on a trip without my husband. Several things went wrong with the car on the trip. When I came back to Boston I decided that I really wanted to learn how to take care and be in control of a car myself. I learned about auto mechanics. It required a lot of work and discipline. In a way, I identify with the car. There is a connection between my feelings of wanting to take care and control of my life and the feelings of wanting to take care and control of my car.

It feels so good not to have to walk around all the time worrying about what my husband, friends, other people are thinking about me.

Although during the last five years of marriage I have worked in a variety of jobs, my major commitment is to teaching and teacher training. Although I got great pleasure from this work, I never acknowledged to myself that throughout my life I have wanted some work that is my own. I have come to realize that in my marriage my husband and I need separate time and space for ourselves to do our own work, as well as time to be together. This would be more complicated if we had children.

My husband and son have always been important to me, but I found that when my son was a few months old I was feeling unfocused and had low energy a lot of the time and was very unself-confident in relating to people outside my family. I joined with some friends who felt the same way and started a play group (cooperative child care) and began to learn to be a birth-control counselor.

Over the past two years I have found the energy and talent to do this work, and the good people I work with have affirmed me as a person and a counselor. When I am home I am glad to be there. I still feel some conflict between my home-family self and my work self. But hard as it is sometimes, I do not want to give up one for the other.

As we have come to feel separate, we have tried to change old relationships and/or enter new relationships in new ways. We now also feel positive about our needs to be dependent and to connect with others. We have come to value long-term commitments, which we find increasingly rare in such a changing society, just as we value our new separateness.

CHAPTER 2
ANATOMY AND PHYSIOLOGY OF SEXUALITY AND REPRODUCTION

OUR FEELINGS

Our feelings about our physical selves have often been negative. Our hair is too straight or too curly, our noses too small or too large, our breasts too big or too small. We don't like our body hair or odors. Our stomachs are too fat. We are too bony. Our genitals—well, we just try to ignore those parts (our "privates"). They are slightly smutty and unmentionable. And then there are those tiny things too, like the mole two inches below the left ear that drives us mad.

We are always making some comparison, we're never okay the way we are. We feel ugly, inadequate. And it's no wonder! The ideal woman in America is something very specific. She may change over time (for instance, small breasts are "in" these days, large ones "out"), yet there is always something to measure up to. Unfortunately, this is not *our* ideal, not what *we* created. Yet family, friends, school, church, TV, movies and magazines tell us to change in countless ways so we can fulfill this image. We are encouraged to blend together and hide our differences. We are discouraged from appreciating our uniqueness.

We are encouraged to feel as if our bodies are not ours. Our "figure" is for a (potential) mate to admire. Our breasts are for "the man in our lives" to fondle during lovemaking, for our babies to suckle, for our doctors to examine. The same kind of "hands-off" message is even stronger for our vaginas. We expect everyone else to be the final judge of how well we have displayed our "pluses" and minimized our "minuses," though we are somehow sure our "defects" will be noticed and remembered more than our "assets."

We are raised to think of our minds as superior to our bodies. Remember: "Mind over matter," "Use your head." We are supposed to "think rationally" and not respond with feelings.

Having my first child was the first experience in my life in which I felt my physical being was as important as my mind. I related to my total body. I became very unself-conscious. I felt my body was fantastic!

On the other hand, very early we learn that "being emotional" is the weakness that's characteristic of our sex. As a result we can't win. If we react with feelings we are weak, and if we think clearly we are unwomanly. There are no cultural models for combining these conflicting views of ourselves.

Experiences in the women's movement have drastically changed our thinking and feelings about our bod-

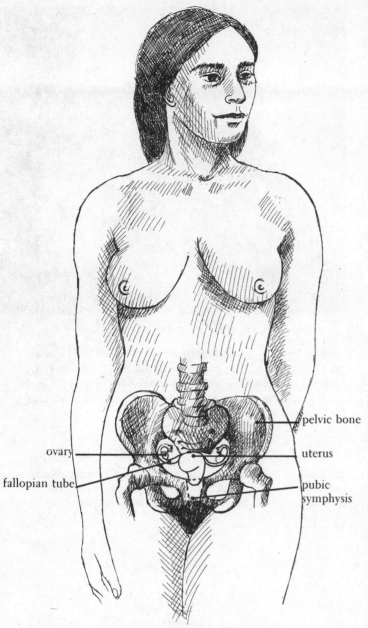

ovary

fallopian tube

pelvic bone

uterus

pubic symphysis

ies. We've described to one another the ways in which we've felt weak, especially in getting medical care, because we knew so little about ourselves. We have given each other support to begin learning about our bodies so that we could act to make some changes.

Recently, as I became more aware of my body, I realized I had pretended some parts didn't exist, while others now seemed made of smaller parts. I also discovered mental and physical processes working together. I realized that when my chest pulled down and felt collapsed I felt unhappy or depressed. When I felt sad my chest would start to tighten. When I became aware of some

of the connections, I could start to change. Gradually I felt a new kind of unity, wholeness in me, as my mental and physical selves became one self.

Until we began to prepare this material for a course for women, many of us didn't know the names of parts of our anatomy. Some of us had learned bits and pieces of information about specific body functions (menstruation, for example), but it was not permissible to find out too much. The taboos were strongest in the areas of reproduction and sex, which is why our book concentrates on them.

The first month I was at college some of my friends were twittering about a girl down the hall. She was having a painful time trying to learn to put in a tampon. Finally someone helped her and found she was trying to put it in her anus.

FINDING OUT ABOUT OURSELVES

Knowing the facts about our anatomy and physiology helps us become more familiar with our bodies. Learning this information has been very exciting for us. It's exhilarating to discover that the material is not as difficult as we once thought. Understanding the medical terminology means that we now can understand the things the doctors say. Knowing their language makes medical people less mysterious and frightening. We now feel more confident when asking questions. Sometimes a doctor has been startled to find us speaking "his" language. "How do you know that? Are you a medical student?" we heard again and again. "A pretty girl like you shouldn't be concerned about that."

But we are. Out of our concerns we are acquiring specific medical knowledge. In response to our questions, many doctors have become aware of women's growing interest in medical issues. Some are genuinely cooperative. Yet many others appear outwardly pleased while continuing to "manage" their patients with new tactics.*

Equally important as learning technical facts, we are sharing our experiences with one another. From this sharing we develop an awareness of difference as well as similarity in our anatomy and physiology. We start to have confidence in our knowledge, and that confidence helps us change our feelings about ourselves.

I used to wonder if my body was abnormal even though

*Valerie Jorgensen, "The Gynecologist and the Sexually Liberated Woman" (editorial), *Obstetrics and Gynecology*, Vol. 42, No. 4 (October, 1973), pp. 607-11.

I didn't have any reason to believe it was. I had nothing to compare it with until I started to talk with other women. I don't feel any more that I might be a freak and not know it.

We realized that we were doing a lot of talking about our sexual organs but that we were not as familiar with their appearance as we were with other parts of our bodies. We found that with just a mirror we could see how we look on the outside. We have been encouraged to look inside at our vaginal walls and cervix (lower part of the uterus) by the women's self-help movement. To do this we use a mirror, flashlight and a clean plastic speculum, an examining instrument which is inserted into the vagina and gently opened up. This is something we can choose to do alone or with others, once or often. With practice we can see how the cervix and vaginal walls change with our menstrual cycle or with pregnancy, and learn to recognize the various vaginal infections. (To get a plastic speculum, contact a women's center or clinic, or a self-help group as mentioned in Chapter 18.)

Some of us have taken a while to get over our inhibitions about seeing or touching our genitals.

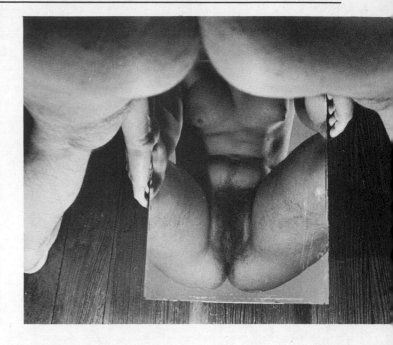

When someone first said to me two years ago, "You can feel the end of your own cervix with your finger," I was interested but flustered. I had hardly ever put my finger in my vagina at all, and felt squeamish about touching myself there, in that place "reserved" for lovers and doctors. It took me two months to get up my nerve to try it, and then one afternoon, pretty nervously, I squatted down in the bathroom and put my finger in deep, back into my vagina. There it was(!), feeling slippery and *rounded, with an indentation at the center through which, I realized, my menstrual flow came. It was both very exciting and beautifully ordinary at the same time. Last week I bought a plastic speculum so I can look at my cervix. Will it take as long this time?*

We still have many bad feelings about ourselves that are hard to admit. We have not, of course, been able to erase decades of social influence in a few years. But we have learned to trust ourselves. We *can* take care of ourselves.

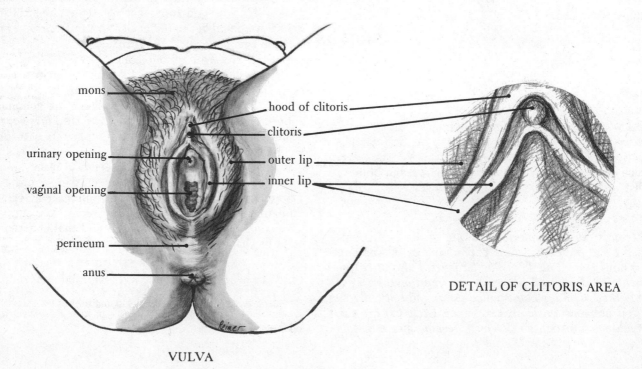

mons
hood of clitoris
clitoris
urinary opening
outer lip
inner lip
vaginal opening
perineum
anus

VULVA

DETAIL OF CLITORIS AREA

DESCRIPTION OF SEXUAL AND REPRODUCTIVE ORGANS: ANATOMY (STRUCTURE) AND PHYSIOLOGY (FUNCTION)

Pelvic Organs

The following description will mean much more if you look at yourself with a mirror while you read the text and look at the diagrams. It is written as if you were squatting and looking into a hand mirror. If you are uncomfortable in that position sit as far forward on the edge of a chair as you comfortably can. Make sure you have plenty of light and enough time and privacy to feel relaxed.

First you will see your *vulva*, or outer genitals.* This includes all of the sexual and reproductive organs you can see in your crotch. Many of us too often confuse the vagina, only one part, with the whole area. Notice the confusion especially when slang is used. The most obvious feature on a mature woman is the *pubic hair*, which starts on the front of the body near the legs. It grows from the soft fatty tissue called the *mons*. The mons area lies over the *pubic symphysis*. This is the joint of the pubic bones, which are part of the *pelvic bones*, or hip girdle. You cannot feel the actual joint, though you can feel the bones under the soft outer skin.

As you spread your legs apart you can see in the mirror that the hair continues between your legs and probably on around your *anus*. The anus is the opening of the *rectum*, or large intestine, to the outside. You can feel that the hair-covered area between your legs is also fatty, like the mons. This fatty area is called the *outer lips*. They surround some soft flaps of skin which are hairless. These are the *inner lips*. They are sensitive to touch. With sexual stimulation they swell and turn darker. The area between the inner lips and the anus is the *perineum*.

As you gently spread the inner lips apart, you can see that they protect a delicate area between them. This is the *vestibule*. Look more closely at it. Starting from the front, right below the mons area you will see the inner lips joining to form a soft fold of skin, or *hood*, over and connecting to the *glans*, or tip of the *clitoris* (klit'-or-is).† Gently pull the hood up to see the glans. This is the most sensitive spot in the entire genital area. It is made

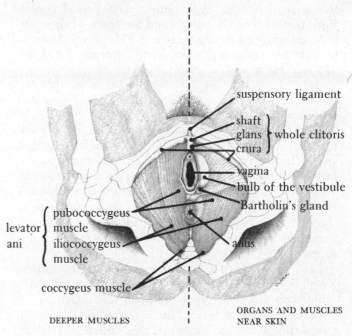

PELVIC FLOOR

DEEPER MUSCLES — ORGANS AND MUSCLES NEAR SKIN

suspensory ligament
shaft
glans } whole clitoris
crura
vagina
bulb of the vestibule
Bartholin's gland
anus
levator ani { pubococcygeus muscle / iliococcygeus muscle }
coccygeus muscle

up of erectile tissue which swells during sexual arousal. Let the hood slide back over the glans. Extending from the hood up to the pubic symphysis, you can now feel a hardish, rubbery, movable cord right under the skin. It is sometimes sexually arousing if touched. This is the *shaft* of the clitoris. It is connected to the bone by a *suspensory ligament*. You cannot feel this ligament or the next few organs described, but they are all important in sexual arousal and orgasm. At the point where you can no longer feel the shaft of the clitoris it divides into two parts, spreading out wishbone fashion, but at a much wider angle, to form the *crura* (singular: *crus*), the two anchoring wingtips which attach to the pelvic bones. The crura of the clitoris are about three inches long. From the fork of the shaft and the crura, and continuing down along the sides of the vestibule, are two bundles of erectile tissue called the *bulbs of the vestibule*. These, along with the whole clitoris and an extensive system of connecting veins throughout the pelvis, become firm and filled with blood (pelvic congestion) during sexual arousal. Some pelvic congestion, giving a feeling of full-

---

*See Betty Dodson's "Liberating Masturbation: A Meditation on Self Love" (New York: Bodysex Designs, 1974) for fifteen beautiful drawings of vulvas, showing how much variety there can be in the proportions of the different parts.

†The glans of the clitoris is commonly referred to as the "clitoris." We will follow that convention, but please remember that the clitoris, referred to here as the "whole clitoris," is really a much more extensive organ, consisting of the glans, shaft and crura, all described in the text.

For a discussion of the history of society's attitude toward the clitoris we refer you to Ruth and Edward Brecher's excellent summary of the Masters and Johnson findings, *An Analysis of Human Sexual Response* (New York: New American Library, 1966). Also see Mary J. Sherfey's *The Nature and Evolution of Female Sexuality* (New York: Random House, 1972).

ness or heaviness in the pelvic region, can occur during the menstrual cycle right before your period comes. Both the crura of the clitoris and the bulbs of the vestibule are wrapped in muscle tissue. This muscle helps to provide tension during arousal and contracts during orgasm, playing an important part in the involuntary spasms felt at that time. The whole clitoris and vestibular bulbs are the only organs in the body solely for sexual sensation and arousal.

Vestibular or *Bartholin's glands* are two small rounded bodies on either side of the vaginal opening and to the rear of the vestibular bulbs. They are important only because they sometimes get infected and swell. You can feel them then. Before Masters and Johnson's work (see Chapter 3, "Sexuality") these glands were thought to provide vaginal lubrication for intercourse, though it is now known that they produce only a few drops of fluid.

Let's return to what you can see with the mirror. Keeping the inner lips spread and pulling the hood back again, you will notice that the inner lips attach to the underside of the clitoris. This is important for sexual stimulation when the inner lips are swollen and pulled, as in penis-vagina intercourse. The clitoris will then be moved and stimulated. Right below this attachment you will see a small dot or slit. This is the *urinary opening*, the outer opening of a short (about an inch and a half), thin tube leading to your *bladder*. Below that is a larger opening, the *vaginal opening*. Because the urinary opening is so close to the vaginal opening, it can become irritated from prolonged or vigorous intercourse and you may feel some discomfort while urinating. Around the vaginal opening, if you have never had intercourse, you may be able to see the *hymen*. It is a thin membrane that surrounds the vaginal opening, partially blocking it

SOME HYMEN VARIATIONS

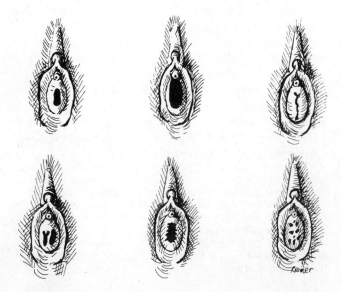

but almost never covering the opening completely. Hymens come in widely varying sizes and shapes. The hymen can be stretched before intercourse by using a tampon, by petting or masturbating with fingers in the vagina, or simply by gentle finger pressure. (See "Sexuality," Chapter 3.) Even when stretched by intercourse, little folds of hymen tissue remain.

Now insert a finger or two into your *vagina*. Notice

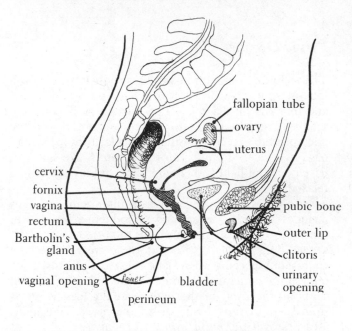

FEMALE PELVIC ORGANS (side view)

how the vaginal walls which were touching each other now spread around your fingers and hug them. Feel the soft folds of skin. These folds allow the vagina to mold itself around what is inside it. This happens around fingers, a tampon, a penis, or a baby. Notice that your finger slides around inside the vagina as you move it. The walls of the vagina may be almost dry to very wet, depending on whether you are in your reproductive years and, if you are, what stage you are at in your menstrual cycle and how sexually aroused you are. These continuous secretions provide lubrication, help keep the vagina clean, and maintain the acidity of the vagina to prevent infections from starting. The secretions taste salty. Push gently against the walls of the vagina all around and notice that only the outer third, which has most of the vagina's nerve endings, is very sensitive. Now try to pull your vagina in around your finger. It might help to do it if you imagine you are stopping the flow of urine. You are contracting the *pelvic floor muscles*. You can feel the contractions about one or two finger joints in from the entrance of the vagina. These muscles hold the pelvic organs in place and provide support for your other organs all the way up to your diaphragm, which is stretched across the bottom of your rib cage. If these muscles are weak you may have trouble having an orgasm, controlling your urine (urinary incontinence), or your pelvic organs—particularly the bladder, lower intestine, or uterus may sag and in extreme cases bulge out of the vaginal opening. These muscles are also important during pregnancy and childbirth. See Chapter 6 for ways to strengthen these muscles.

There is only a thin wall of skin separating the vagina from the rectum, so you may be able to feel a bump on the "bottom" side of your vagina if you have some feces in the rectum.

Now slide your middle finger as far back into your vagina as you can. Notice that your finger goes in toward the small of your back at an angle, not straight up the middle of your body. If you were standing instead of squatting, your vagina would be at about a 45-degree angle to the floor. With your finger you can just feel the end of your vagina. This part of the vagina is called the *fornix*. (If you are having any trouble reaching it, bring your knees and chest closer together so your finger can slide in farther.) A little before the end of the vagina you can feel your *cervix*. The cervix feels like a nose with a small dimple in its center. If you've had a baby the cervix may feel more like a chin. The cervix is the base of the *uterus*, or womb. It is sensitive to pressure but has no nerve endings on its surface. The uterus changes position during the menstrual cycle and during sexual excitement, so the place where you feel the cervix one day may be slightly different from where you feel it the next. Some days you can barely reach it. The dimple you felt is the *os*, or opening into the uterus. The entrance into the uterus through the cervix is very small, about the diameter of a very thin straw. No tampon, finger, or penis can go through it, although it is capable of expanding enough to allow a baby to pass through.

You will not be able to feel the rest of the organs which are described. The nonpregnant uterus is about the size of a fist. This organ has thick walls made of one of the most powerful muscles in the body. It is located between the bladder, which is beneath the abdominal wall, and the rectum, which is near the backbone. The walls of the uterus touch each other unless pushed apart by a growing fetus or by an abnormal growth. The upper end of the uterus is called the *fundus*.

Extending outward and back from the sides of the upper end of the uterus are the two *fallopian tubes* (or *oviducts*; literally, "egg tubes"). They are approximately four inches long and look like ram's horns, facing backward. The connecting opening from the inside of the uterus to the fallopian tube is so small that only a fine needle can penetrate it. The other end of the tube is fimbriated (fringed) and funnel-shaped. The wide end of the funnel wraps part way around the *ovary* but does not actually attach to it. It is held in place by connecting tissues.

The ovaries are organs about the size and shape of

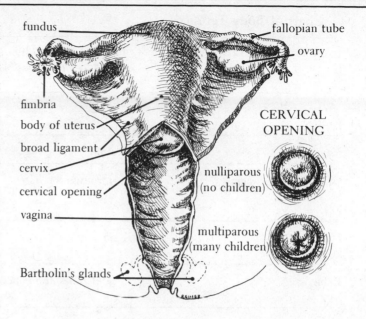

unshelled almonds, located on either side and somewhat behind the uterus. They would be about four or five inches below your waist. They are held in place by connecting tissue and are protected by a surrounding mass of fat. They have a twofold function: to produce germ cells (eggs) and to produce female sex hormones (*estrogen* and *progesterone*). The small gap between the ovary and the end of the corresponding tube allows the egg to float freely after it is released from the ovary. The finger-like ends of the fallopian tube move to set up currents which wave the egg into the tube. In rare cases when the egg is not "caught" by the tube, it can be fertilized outside the tube, resulting in an abdominal pregnancy. See "Ectopic (Misplaced) Pregnancy" in Chapter 16, for more on this.

Development of Pelvic Organs

All female and male organs, including sexual and reproductive organs, are similar in origin, develop from the same embryonic tissue (homologous), and are similar in function (analogous). The following are examples of corresponding organs:

FEMALE	MALE
outer lips	scrotum
inner lips	bottom side of penis
glans of clitoris	glans of penis
shaft of clitoris	corpus cavernosum
ovaries	testes
bulb of the vestibule	bulb of the penis and corpus spongiosum
Bartholin's glands	Cowper's glands (bulbourethral glands)

Chart of Body Terms

COMMON ENGLISH TERMS	MEDICAL TERM (*If not listed here, name used in the text is also common medical term*)	SOME SLANG TERMS	
Vulva Crotch	same	Cunt Pussy	Box Cut
Vagina	same	Snatch	Slit
Opening of the vagina	Introitus	Treasure Furburger Bearded Clam	Hole Twat
Hymen	same	Cherry Maidenhead	Membrane
Pubic hair	(*sometimes also* pubes)	Beaver Bush	
Mons	Mons pubis (*mons* = "*mountain*") Mons veneris (*veneris* = *Venus*)		
Outer lips Major lips	Labia majora (*singular: Labium majus*)	—	
Inner lips Minor lips	Labia minora (*singular: Labium minus*)	—	
Hood	Prepuce of the clitoris	Button Clit	
Glans of the clitoris Glans Clitoris	Glans clitoridis	Man in the boat	
(Whole) Clitoris	Clitoris		
Urinary opening	Urethral orifice Urethral meatus (*the* urethra *is the tube leading to the bladder*)	Peehole	
Anus	Anus *is opening only;* Rectum *is interior part*	Asshole	
Fallopian tubes Oviducts	same	Tubes	
Pubic symphysis	Pubis symphysis	—	
Pelvic floor muscles	*The major muscle involved is the* levator ani, *an important part of which is the* pubococcygeus.	—	
Breasts	same	Boobs Tits Bonkers Knockers	

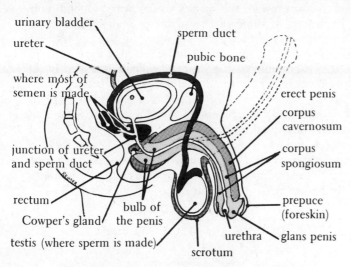

MALE PELVIC ORGANS (side view)

Female and male fetuses appear identical during the first six weeks in the uterus.

Breasts

Let's start with what we can see. "The *nipple* is in the middle of the *areola*, the darker-colored portion of your breast. [During pregnancy the areola becomes even darker.] The nipple may stick out from the areola, it may not protrude at all, or it may sink into the areola. When the nipple is exposed to cold temperatures or when sexually aroused, the small muscles around it contract, causing the nipple to become more erect than usual. [After puberty there] may be a slight secretion which collects periodically in the nipple. This comes from the *ducts* [small tubes for milk inside the breast] and is very normal. . . . You may observe small bumps on the surface of the areola. These are *sebaceous* or *oil* glands which secrete a lubricant that protects the nipple during nursing. It is quite common for hairs to grow around the areola. They may appear suddenly due to normal hormonal changes as you grow older. Many women notice an increase in hair growth during or following the use of birth control pills."* (Italics ours.)

The inside of the breast consists of *fat* and a *milk-producing (mammary) gland.* The gland is made up of milk-producing areas and ducts from these areas to the nipple. With the great increase of sex hormones during adolescence, the glandular tissue in the breasts starts to develop and increase in size. Because sex hormone levels change during the menstrual cycle, when starting and stopping birth control pills, and during pregnancy, there

*From *Your Breasts: Information and Self-Examination* by the San Francisco Women's Health Center (see bibliography), pp. 3–4. This pamphlet will be included in a forthcoming book by them.

can be variations in the amount of glandular tissue in the breast and thus in its size and shape. All women have approximately the same amount of glandular tissue at the same points in their reproductive life cycles. Most of the breast consists of fat over and between sections of the gland. The amount of fat collected in the breasts is partly determined by heredity. This fat is what makes breast size vary so much, and it explains why breast size is not related to the sexual reponsiveness of the breast area or to the amount of milk produced after giving birth. (See Chapter 6 for breast self-examination, and appendix to Chapter 15 for breast-feeding.)

STAGES IN THE REPRODUCTIVE CYCLE

In childhood our bodies are immature. Then during puberty we make the transition from childhood to maturity. In women, puberty is characterized by decreased bone growth; by growth of breasts, pubic and axillary

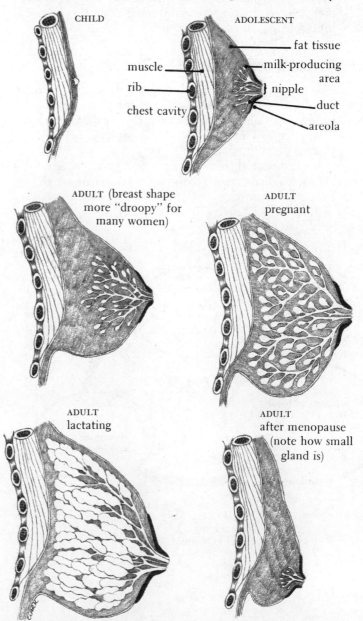

(armpit) hair; starting of menstruation (menarche) and ovulation; and increase of sexual urges. The last stage of the cycle is when we are no longer able to reproduce. The climacteric is the transition between the reproductive and postreproductive stages. Menstruation stops (menopause) and ovulation stops. (Although "menopause" is commonly used to mean the whole transition period, technically this is incorrect.) For more on the climacteric see Chapter 17.

This entire reproductive cycle is regulated by hormones. Hormones function as chemical messengers and initiators in the body. Women have high levels of sex hormones (estrogen and progesterone) during the reproductive period and low levels in childhood and after menopause. The signs and symptoms of the transitional periods are thought to be caused by the changing levels of hormones.

Within the reproductive stage there are hormone-caused cycles of approximately one month's duration. These monthly fluctuations of hormones determine the timing of ovulation and menstruation. This cycle, the menstrual cycle, prepares a woman's body for the possibility of pregnancy every month.

The Ovarian Cycle—Ovulation

The ovaries at birth contain 300,000 to 400,000 *follicles*, which are balls of cells with an immature egg in the center. Only about 300 to 500 of these will develop into mature eggs. The other follicles degenerate before completing development.

Each month during our reproductive years, one follicle (occasionally more than one) matures under the influence of hormones (see Appendix for fuller description of hormones). One of the cell layers in the follicle se-

cretes estrogen. The follicle, with the maturing egg inside, moves toward the surface of the ovary. Ovulation is the process of the follicle and the ovarian surface disintegrating at a particular point, allowing the egg to float out. For some women this can be felt as a cramp on the left or right side of the lower abdomen or lower back, and there may be some discharge, possibly bloody, from the vagina. The cramp is sometimes painful enough to be confused with appendicitis. However, there is no nausea or abdominal tenderness. The phenomenon is called *mittelschmerz* (literally, "middle pain"). If you look at your cervix with a speculum you may notice a drop of clear, stretchy mucus near the os. This happens within a day before and after ovulation.

FOLLICLE CHANGES
DURING MONTHLY CYCLE

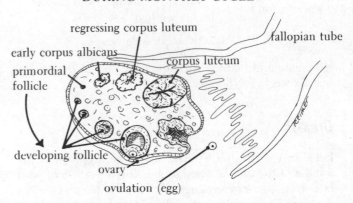

Just before ovulation the same cell layer in the follicle starts secreting progesterone as well as estrogen. After ovulation the follicle is called a *corpus luteum* ("yellow body," referring to the yellowish fat in it). If the woman becomes pregnant, the hormones produced by the corpus luteum help to maintain the pregnancy. If no pregnancy occurs, the follicle degenerates. After several months only a whitish scar remains near the surface of the ovary. It is then called the *corpus albicans* ("white body") and eventually disappears entirely.

After ovulation the released egg is trapped by the funnel-shaped end of one of the fallopian tubes (oviducts) and begins its six-and-a-half-day journey to the uterus, moved along by peristaltic (wavelike) contractions of the tube. Fertilization, the union of an egg from a woman and sperm from a man, takes place in the outer third of the fallopian tube (nearest the ovaries). This is also called conception and usually occurs within one day of ovulation. (See Chapter 13 for the development of the fertilized egg.) There is a slight possibility that the fertilized egg may implant in the fallopian tube while en route to the uterus. It is more likely to happen if the tube is scarred or unusually twisted. This is a tubal pregnancy and requires surgery before the tube ruptures. (See Chapter 16, "Ectopic [Misplaced] Pregnancy.") If

THE MENSTRUAL CYCLE

estrogens and progesterone decrease suddenly

SECRETORY PHASE

MENSTRUATION
surface of endometrium shed; bleeding
(5 days)

estrogens increasing

PROLIFERATIVE PHASE

thickening of endometrium, increased secretions and blood supply due to follicle's manufacture of progesterone

development of egg and repair of endometrium
(9 days)

(14 days)

estrogens reach high level in blood, causing egg release

OVULATION

the egg is not fertilized, it disintegrates or is sloughed off in the vaginal secretions. You won't notice it. This usually happens before menstruation.

The Uterine Cycle—Menstruation

Estrogen, made by the maturing follicle, causes the uterine lining (*endometrium*) to proliferate (to grow, thicken, and form glands that will secrete embryo-nourishing substances). Progesterone, made by the ruptured follicle after ovulation, causes the glands in the endometrium to begin secreting the nourishing substances and also increases the uterine blood supply. The lining is proliferative until the egg is released; after ovulation the corpus luteum secretes progesterone, which changes the character of the lining to secretory. A fertilized egg can implant only in a secretory lining, not in a proliferative one. If all goes well, the egg, after its six-and-a-half-day journey, should find a well-developed secretory lining.

The ruptured follicle, or corpus luteum, will produce estrogen and progesterone for only about twelve days, with the amount dwindling in the last few days, if conception has not occurred. As the estrogen and progesterone levels drop, the arteries and veins in the uterus pinch themselves off. The lining is no longer nourished and is shed. This is menstruation, or the menstrual period. It is like a tree shedding its leaves in the fall. It is possible to menstruate without ovulating (anovulatory period), but this usually occurs only around the time of puberty or the climacteric. Menstruation lasts a week or less. Most of the lining is shed; the bottom third remains to form a new lining. Then a new follicle starts growing, starts secreting estrogen; a new uterine lining grows; and the cycle begins again.

Menstruation starts in about the middle of puberty, generally at the age of eleven or twelve, though any time from nine to eighteen years is normal. It continues until the average of forty-eight or forty-nine, in the middle of the climacteric. The age range for menopause is generally between forty and fifty-five.

ENDOMETRIUM AT FOUR STAGES OF MENSTRUAL CYCLE:
day 5, day 14 (ovulation), day 19, day 1 of new cycle
(day 1 is first day of menstrual period)

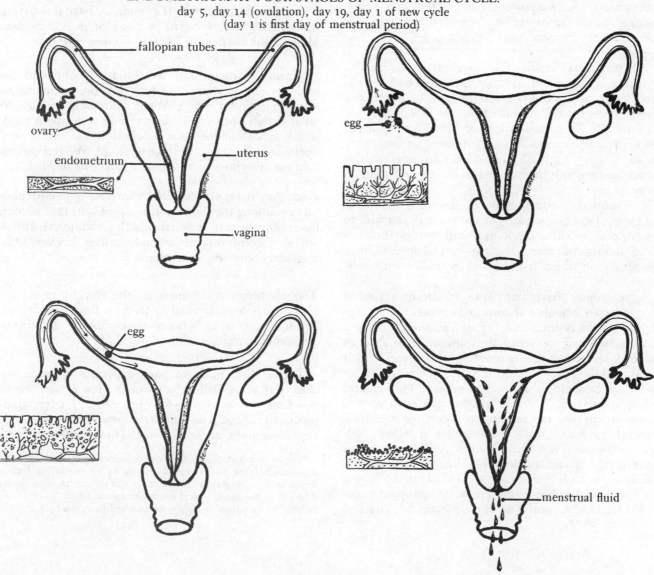

There is no record of a woman with an absolutely regular menstrual cycle. The length of the cycle usually ranges from 20 to 36 days, the average being 28 days. (Menstruation is from the Latin *mensis*, for "month.") There are spontaneous small changes and there can be major ones when a woman is under a great deal of stress (such as a pregnancy scare). A normal period lasts 2 to 8 days, with 4 to 6 days being the average. The flow stops and starts, though this may not always be evident. A usual discharge for a menstrual period is about 4 to 6 tablespoons, or 2 to 3 ounces. Each woman has her own cycle, which really is a more important guideline than the statistics, since the acceptable ranges vary from one medical source to another. Many women feel an increased sexual urge during one part of the cycle. For some it comes around ovulation, for others it comes right before or during the period.

There is no evidence to indicate that you should stay in bed, avoid exercise, refrain from sexual intercourse, or observe any of the traditional taboos surrounding menstruation. Myths have endowed menstruating women with everything from supernatural healing powers to supernatural destructive powers. Too bad they aren't true. If doing something makes you feel uncomfortable, it is only common sense to avoid doing it.

THE MENSTRUAL FLUID. The menstrual fluid contains cervical and vaginal mucus and degenerated endometrial particles as well as blood (sometimes clotted), but this mixed content is not obvious since the blood stains everything red. This regular loss of blood, even though small, can cause anemia. (See "Nutrition," in Chapter 6, for ways to avoid this.) The fluid does not smell until it makes contact with the bacteria in the air and starts to decompose.

The most common method of absorbing menstrual fluid is with sanitary napkins or tampons. If you wish to use tampons and have cervicitis (ask at your gyn exam or notice during your own self-exam—see Chapter 6), then use a tampon which is short and expands mostly sideways.

Some women have started to substitute a natural sponge, often available at cosmetic counters or art supply stores, for commercially made tampons. To use a sponge, tie string or dental floss around it or through one end. Dampen it before insertion. When you think it is full, pull the string to remove. Wash well in cool water and soap. Squeeze in a towel to remove excess water before reinserting. A diaphragm without birth control cream or jelly also can be used to collect the menstrual fluid. Use a little contraceptive cream or jelly or K-Y Jelly on the rim if it is hard to put in. A diaphragm holds more than a sponge or tampon. When you think it is full, remove, wash and reinsert. If it is left in too long it will overflow. Another method is called menstrual or period extraction. A special small tube (cannula), attached to a suction device, is inserted into the uterus when the period starts, and the menstrual fluid is sucked out in five minutes. This same technique can also be used for early abortions. (See description in Chapter 11, under "Endometrial Aspiration.") There is no way of knowing yet whether there are any possible long-range effects on the uterus from regular period extraction. For those of us who feel menstruating is a real burden, the idea of freedom from it is exciting.

FEELINGS ABOUT MENSTRUATION. Many of us were scared or even embarrassed when we first started to menstruate. We grew up with little or no knowledge about where the blood and tissue were coming from and why they came, and why it sometimes hurt. Some of us thought we were dying when we first saw our menstrual blood. Some of us were desperately afraid that a teacher or a boy would notice when we had our period. On the other hand, some of us felt inadequate if we didn't menstruate.

I used to worry about having my period. It seemed that all my friends had gotten it already, or were just having it. I felt left out. I began to think of it as a symbol. When I got my period, I would become a woman.

Starting to menstruate will always be different for each person—welcome to some, just the beginning of inconvenience for others. What we want to be sure to do is to tell both our daughters and sons about menstruation so that they can be comfortable with it and open about it in a way that we were not. We feel we can help our daughters to celebrate a new part of life.

MENSTRUAL PROBLEMS. Uncomfortable or painful periods are among the most common problems that women have. Most women experience at least some menstrual-related discomfort sometime in their lives. Yet very little is known about why it happens.

The day before and sometimes the first day of my period my whole abdominal cavity feels unsettled. It feels like the membranes between my organs are disintegrating and everything is getting mixed up.

The medical term for painful periods is *dysmenorrhea.* Katherina Dalton,* one of the few researchers in this field, divides these problems into two kinds, *spasmodic* and *congestive.* The symptoms of the spasmodic type are cramps, acute pain in the lower abdomen, pos-

*For an excellent discussion of the menstrual cycle, and especially dysmenorrhea, see *The Menstrual Cycle,* by Dr. Katherina Dalton (listed in the bibliography), which treats the subject far more clearly than any of the gynecological textbooks we consulted. Much of the material on menstruation here is summarized from this book.

sibly nausea or occasional shakiness at the beginning of the period. It is most common between the ages of fifteen and twenty-five—usually not later. Dalton believes this is because pregnancy and childbirth clear it up. Since this type of dysmenorrhea seems to occur only, but not necessarily, during an ovulatory cycle, she suggests it can be controlled with birth control pills (see "Birth Control," Chapter 10, pill safety section).

Congestive dysmenorrhea and the related *premenstrual syndrome* are characterized by such symptoms as a heaviness or a dull aching in the abdomen, nausea, water retention, constipation, headaches and backaches, breast pains, irritability, tension, depression and lethargy. The symptoms are often relieved by the heaviest flow of the period. This type of dysmenorrhea can start at puberty and continue until menopause and often gets worse with each pregnancy. The time just before the onset of the period seems to be the most difficult for women with this type of dysmenorrhea. The premenstrual syndrome and congestive dysmenorrhea are real, although doctors are often taught otherwise. There is some evidence that the symptoms are a result of progesterone deficiency. Depression, particularly, may be caused by sodium retention and potassium depletion in the cells, resulting from a lowered progesterone level.*

Dr. Dalton theorizes that both types of dysmenorrhea are caused by a hormone imbalance.† She has found that dysmenorrhea can be induced by giving particular doses of hormones. This can be important if you are taking birth control pills or are having hormone therapy. The spasmodic type is a result of too much progesterone in relation to estrogen, and the congestive type (and also premenstrual syndrome) is a result of too much estrogen for the amount of progesterone. She treats both types with the appropriate hormone therapy.

Another theory about a possible cause of menstrual discomfort is that of Dr. Elizabeth Connell: "We now know that prostaglandins (hormone-like chemical substances) are manufactured by the lining of the uterus—the endometrium—and that shortly before the onset of menstruation there is a sharp increase in the amount of prostaglandins produced. We think, therefore, that perhaps the pain of menstrual cramps may be a result of the presence of too much of the type of prostaglandin that causes contractions."‡ Dr. Connell does not suggest a related form of therapy.

If you have trouble every cycle check with a doctor to find out if you have endometriosis (see Chapter 6).

Another menstrual problem is *amenorrhea* (absence of menstrual periods). Primary amenorrhea is the condition of never having had a period by the time menstruation usually starts (age eighteen), and secondary amenorrhea is the cessation of menstruation after at least one period. There are quite a variety of causes. Some are: pregnancy, a congenital defect of the genital tract, hormone imbalance, cysts or tumors, disease, stress, or emotional factors relating to puberty. Amenorrhea is treated extensively in most gynecological textbooks, since it is a frequent symptom of infertility. In fact, considerably more attention has been paid to amenorrhea than to dysmenorrhea, although dysmenorrhea is by far more common. Doctors once again show more concern for, and do more research on, a dramatic, less common problem than on a less dramatic problem that bothers many more women. Moreover, little attention is paid to the kinds of emotional adjustments we may go through and the kinds of support we need if this happens to us.

COPING WITH MENSTRUAL DISCOMFORTS. Among those women who have menstrual difficulties, the problems are not uniform throughout their lives, nor are they necessarily severe. For those of us who have problems either occasionally or even fairly regularly, it is important to recognize that they exist and to deal with them—arranging schedules so we can get more rest if we need it at that time, planning exams or critical meetings for a time when we are not premenstrual, and so on.

Sometimes expecting to feel premenstrual tension and depression may increase the severity of the depression. We must not forget that the problems we get depressed about are usually there all the time, but perhaps we can't handle them as well at this time, or perhaps we have been ignoring them the rest of the time. A lot of us have found that if we are feeling good about ourselves we don't get depressed, or as depressed, before our period.

A few times when I've been feeling good about myself I got really high just before my period. It was like a drug high, even though I didn't take anything. It came and went, totally unexpected.

Diet and exercise can be used as preventives. "A majority of doctors now believe that not only can women participate in any strenuous activity at any time, but that they actually benefit from it. A 1965 study comparing 65 women swimmers with 138 nonathletic students revealed that the swimmers had far less menstrual difficulty."*

We have also heard that some women have tried to reduce their intake of coffee and refined foods, especially sugar and white flour, with good results. Others use

*The Menstrual Cycle, pp. 60-64.
†Ibid., pp. 44, 46-50, 64-70.
‡Elizabeth Connell, M.D., "Prostaglandins: A New Wonder Drug?" Redbook Magazine (January, 1972), p. 11.

*Ann Crittenden Scott, "Closing the Muscle Gap," Ms. Magazine (September, 1974), p. 55.

dolomite calcium or vitamin C tablets a few days before they expect their periods. Very ripe bananas and fresh orange juice are often prescribed for potassium depletion. Acupuncture treatments may help.

If you already have cramps, you might get some comfort from a pain-killer; from curling up with your knees to your chest or with a hot-water bottle on your stomach or lower back; drinking raspberry-leaf or bancha-leaf-and-tamari (soy sauce) tea (check your health-food store); exercising (see Hilary C. Maddux, *Menstruation*, pp. 128–43, for specific exercises); or from menstrual extraction. Lower back massage can be effective. Marijuana is rumored to be helpful. If your symptoms are relieved by the heaviest flow of your period, try to have an orgasm or take a sauna or steam bath, all of which can speed up the flow considerably.*

Do menstruation and the premenstrual syndrome affect our ability to function effectively and to hold positions of responsibility? During "the last three Olympics, . . . women won gold medals and established new world

*For instructions on how to do a menstrual massage, send a stamped, self-addressed, business-size envelope to: BWHBC, Dept. BB, P.O. Box 192, Somerville, MA 02144.

*Ann Crittenden Scott, "Closing the Muscle Gap," *Ms.* Magazine (September, 1974), p. 55.

records during all phases of the menstrual cycle."* It is amazing that we are denied responsibility on the basis of menstrual cycles, while men, who are much more prone to seriously incapacitating diseases such as heart problems continue in highly responsible positions (the presidency of the country, for example) even after these problems are discovered. There is also some evidence that men too have hormonal cycles.† We are still allowed to work where we are "needed"—at home, in factories, in offices—with no concessions in schedules or routines to take account of our cycles.

APPENDIX: HORMONES OF THE MENSTRUAL CYCLE

During the reproductive part of a woman's life, low levels of all the sex hormones are being continuously produced. In addition to these base levels there are fluctuations which establish the menstrual cycle. The main organs involved in the cycle are the hypothalamus (a part of the brain) and the pituitary and the ovaries (both glands). The hypothalamus signals the pituitary, which then signals the ovaries, which in turn signal the hypothalamus. The signaling is done by hormones secreted by the different organs and carried from one part of the body to another through the blood.

The hypothalamus is sensitive to the fluctuating levels of hormones produced by the ovaries. When the level of estrogen drops below a certain level the hypothalamus releases FSH-RF, follicle-stimulating-hormone-releasing factor. This stimulates the pituitary to release FSH, follicle-stimulating hormone. This triggers the growth of 10 to 20 of the ovarian follicles. Only one of these will mature fully; the others will start to degenerate sometime before ovulation. These are called atretic.

As the follicles grow they secrete estrogen in increasing amounts. The estrogen affects the lining of the uterus, signaling it to grow, or proliferate (proliferatory phase). When the egg approaches maturity inside the follicle that will develop fully, the follicle secretes a burst of progesterone in addition to the estrogen. This combination of progesterone and estrogen probably triggers the hypothalamus to secrete FSH-RF and LH-RF, luteinizing-hormone-releasing factor. These releasing factors signal the pituitary to secrete simultaneously FSH and LH, luteinizing hormone. The FSH-LH peak probably signals the follicle to release the egg (ovulation). Under the influence of LH the follicle changes its function. Now called a corpus luteum, the follicle secretes decreasing amounts of estrogen and increasing amounts of progesterone. The progesterone influences the estrogen-primed uterine lining to secrete fluids nourishing to the egg if it is fertilized (secretory phase). Immediately after the peak that triggers ovulation, FSH returns to a base-line level. LH declines more gradually as the progesterone increases. If the egg is fertilized the corpus luteum continues to secrete estrogen and progesterone to maintain the preg-

THE MENSTRUAL CYCLE—relationship between follicle development, hormone cycles, and endometrial (uterine lining) buildup and disintegration

*Ann Crittenden Scott, op. cit.
†See Estelle Ramey, "Men's Cycles" (listed in the bibliography).

nancy. However, the corpus luteum is stimulated to do this by HCG, human chorionic gonadotropin, a hormone which is secreted by the developing placenta. HCG so far appears to be chemically identical to LH, so it's not surprising it has the same function.

If the egg is not fertilized the corpus luteum degenerates until it becomes non-functioning, then called a corpus albicans. As the degeneration occurs, the levels of hormones from the corpus luteum decline. The declining levels fail to maintain the uterine lining, which leads to menstruation. When the level of estrogen reaches a low enough point, the hypothalamus releases FSH-RF and the cycle starts again.

FURTHER READINGS

Boston Women's Health Book Collective. *Menstruation*. For a copy send stamped, self-addressed, business size envelope to: BWHBC, Dept BB, P.O. Box 192, Somerville, MA 02144. Eight page brochure including information on attitudes, examining your cycle, menstrual sponges, and home remedies for menstrual problems.

Chagnon, Linda M. *Topics in Human Reproduction*. West Haven, Conn.: Pendulum Press, Inc., 1975.
Clear, accurate, up-to-date explanation of the human reproductive system. Written to be a junior-high-school text but valuable for older people too.

Culpepper, Emily. *Period Piece*. (film) 16 mm, color, 10 minutes. For more information write to: Culpepper, 64R Sacramento St, Cambridge, MA 02138 or Insight Exchange, P.O. Box 42594, San Francisco, CA 94101. About attitudes, experiences, and images of menstruation.

Dalton, Katherina. *The Menstrual Cycle*. New York: Pantheon, 1969.
Comprehensive book on menstruation and menstrual problems. Her preferred treatment (hormones) may not be for everyone, but her analysis makes sense.

Delany, Janice, Mary Jane Lupton, and Emily Toth. *The Curse: A Cultural History of Menstruation*. New York: Dutton, 1976.

Frisch, R., et al. "Components of weight at menarche and the initiation of adolescent growth spurt in girls." *Human Biology* 45 (1973) p. 469.

———. "Critical weights, a critical body composition, menarche and the maintenance of menstrual cycles." In *Biosocial Interrelation in Population Adaptation*. The Hague: Mouton, 1976.

Maddux, Hilary C. *Menstruation*. New Canaan, Conn.: Tobey Publishing Co., 1975.
Section on exercise is good, rest of book fair, underlying attitude about menstruation negative.

Netter, Frank H. (illus.) and Ernst Oppenheimer (ed.). *The CIBA Collection of Medical Illustrations, Vol. 2: Reproductive System*. Summit, N.J.: CIBA Pharmaceutical Company, 1965.
Clear illustrations, all in color. Often several views of one area. Color is sometimes strange when used schematically. Easy for lay person to use.

Novak, Edmund R., Georgeanna Seegar Jones, and Howard W. Jones, Jr. *Novak's Textbook of Gynecology*, 8th ed. Baltimore: Williams and Wilkins Co., 1970.
Considered one of the good gynecological textbooks. It's good if you want to find out what the recommended doctor's text is. It is pretty chauvinistic—see Chapter 18, "Women and Health Care," for the type of attitudes expressed. It mystifies medicine by constantly using jargon when simpler words are sufficient.

Ramey, Estelle. "Men's Cycles (They Have Them Too, You Know)," *Ms.* Magazine (Spring 1972), pp. 8-14.
Examines evidence of male cycles; includes some discussion of accepting and working with cycles.

Sabotta-Figge, Frank H. J. *Atlas of Human Anatomy, Vol. III: Atlas of Visceral Anatomy: Digestive, Respiratory, and Urogenital Systems*. New York: Hafner Publishing Co., Inc., 1965.
For medical schools. Clear drawings done from actual subjects. Most medical textbook drawings are copied from other drawings.

San Francisco Women's Health Center. *Your Breasts: Information and Self-Examination*.
Twelve-page pamphlet includes physical description, self-examination, types of lumps and possible treatments. For a copy send 30¢ to San Francisco Women's Health Center, 3789 24th Street, San Francisco, California 94114.

See Chapter 3, "Sexuality," bibliography for:
Brecher, Ruth and Edward, eds. *An Analysis of Human Sexual Response*.
Deutsch, Ronald M. *The Key to Feminine Response in Marriage*.
Dodson, Betty. *Liberating Masturbation: A Meditation on Self Love*.
Hegeler, Inge and Sten. *An ABZ of Love*.
Sherfey, Mary Jane. *The Nature and Evolution of Female Sexuality*.
See Chapter 17, "Menopause," bibliography for:
Weidegar, Paula. *Menstruation and Menopause: The Physiology and Psychology, the Myth and the Reality*.
See Chapter 18, "Women and Health Care," bibliography for:
Frankfort, Ellen. *Vaginal Politics*.

CHAPTER 3
SEXUALITY

In the five years since we first began to work on the material for this chapter we have learned a great deal more about ourselves as sexual beings, and we are still learning. We want to share what we have learned with you.

We grow up in a society that is sexually confused and repressive, especially for women. Magazines and TV are constantly telling us how to make ourselves attractive and sexy, yet at the same time, we learn that "good girls" don't have intercourse until marriage. The focus of sex is genital—intercourse, and especially orgasm. Sexual experiences with other women are inconceivable. If we do have sex before marriage we often feel that we are hiding a shameful secret. If we marry, the men we live with usually are as ignorant as we. Sexually, our roles mirror society's conceptions of male and female: men are to know and we are to learn from them; men lead and we respond. With all these conflicting messages it's no wonder that we all, female and male, learn to listen to others' ideas of how things ought to be in sex rather than listening to the rhythms and responses of our own bodies.

Slowly we are beginning to work our way out of the web of myth, ignorance, confusion and role demands in which society entangles us. We are thankful for the courage of all the women who began speaking openly about their sexual experiences and feelings in small consciousness-raising groups when the women's movement surfaced again eight years ago, and of all who have continued this sharing process. We are deeply indebted to the research of Virginia Johnson and William Masters, and we have been influenced and supported by the growing volume of positive, creative work on sexuality—in a variety of forms, much of it written by women.* (See bibliographies of this chapter and Chapter 4, Relationships.)

Yet the oppression of women has gone on for so many generations we don't know what our optimal sexual lives might be like. This chapter makes use of our personal experiences and the most recent comprehensive research (Masters and Johnson) to go as far as we can in describing our sexual lives right now. However, just as Freud

*See "Women Rediscover Their Own Sexuality" in Edward M. Brecher's *The Sex Researchers* (New York: New American Library, 1971) for a list of important women pioneers in sex research.

and Kinsey were not the final word, neither are Masters and Johnson today. Their study, of present-day American women, reflects the situation of those women. Therefore we do not hold their findings as all-time norms for sexual behavior. Our daughters, granddaughters and great-granddaughters may behave differently than we do today.

For most of us it is difficult to be open about sexuality. Yet as we explore together our sexual experiences, fantasies, questions and feelings, we find that talking about sex gradually gets easier. As we share, we discover we have many of the same concerns. We heartily suggest talking about sexual feelings with friends and in small

women's groups. Here we can free ourselves of sexual inhibition and misinformation by educating and supporting each other. We increase our skill in expressing our own sexuality to others.

We seek an understanding of sexuality that includes a wide range of feelings and actions. Sexuality is so much more than intercourse. Our sexuality belongs first and foremost to us. It is pleasure we want to give and get. It is a vital physical expression of attachments to other human beings. It is communication that is fun and playful, serious and passionate. We are trying to describe a range of sexual experience we as women are beginning to have, and to give legitimacy to a variety of feelings, experiences, and the notion that we can grow.

We seek comfort with our sexual responses, those fantasied as well as those acted upon. We know this is a lifelong process. We believe that as we accept ourselves and support one another, we can learn to express sexual feelings in ways that strengthen our sense of self, deepen our pleasure, and enhance the building and renewing of intimacy with others.

Our feelings about sex are primordial—they go very deep and far back, to Biblical times and before. Sex has the same kind of strength as birth, death and life itself. It is one of the propelling forces of being, and as such has profound meaning. For me it is one of the crucial experiences in life.

SEXUAL FEELINGS

We are our bodies. Our book celebrates this simple fact. Sexual feelings and responses are a central expression of our emotional, spiritual, physical selves. Sexual feelings involve our whole bodies.

When I'm feeling turned on, either alone or with someone I'm attracted to, my heart beats faster, my face gets red, my eyes feel bright. The lips of my vagina feel wet, and my whole genital area feels full. My breasts hum. If I'm standing up I feel a rush of weakness in my thighs. If I'm lying down I may feel like a big stretch, arching my back, feeling the sensations go out to my fingers and toes. These are special feelings whether I do anything to act on them or not.

We may have to learn to let our sexual feelings come without our judgment or control and to accept them as part of ourselves. They have a rhythm and flow of their own. They can't be forced, they come and go. Sensations and emotions simply are. However, when the feelings come we do have some choices—whether to act and how to act—and responsibility for the actions we choose. Though sexual feelings may be simple in themselves, they exist in the context of our society and feel complicated to us. For many of us sex has been confused with a special nurturing—with parental love, attention and acceptance that we needed as children but may never have gotten. We are older in years now, and still there may be that hungry child in us, craving for something. When we recognize that child, then we can begin to sort out what we are asking of others, what we expect from sex.

When I made love with Jack I felt like he was feeding me. I felt full with his penis inside me. When I wasn't with him I would feel hungry again. Often I didn't have

orgasms. I kept coming back to him, though it was an impossible relationship, because I needed to be fed. Later I realized he was mothering me, I was asking him to be my mother. That was a revelation!

Sadly, some of our guilty, self-denying feelings about sex we have accepted for too long.

Our ambivalent feelings about our bodies and conflicted feelings about sex get in the way of sexual enjoyment. We can learn to let go of these feelings and at the same time to enhance the sexual feelings that give us a powerful sense of connection with other people and all of nature.

GROWING UP

I watch my daughter. From morning to night her body is her home. She lives in it and with it. When she runs around the kitchen she uses all of herself. Every muscle in her body moves when she laughs, when she cries. When she rubs her vulva, there is no awkwardness, no feeling that what she is doing is wrong. She feels pleasure and expresses it without hesitation. She knows when she wants to be touched and when she wants to be left alone. She doesn't have to think about it—it's a very direct physical asking or responding to someone else. It's beautiful to be with her. I sometimes feel she is more a model for me than I am for her! Occasionally I feel jealous of the ease with which she lives inside her skin. I want to be a child again! It's so hard to get back that sense of body as home.

We are born loving our bodies.

Our sense of our own sexuality was shaped by numerous childhood experiences and memories. Sex was not talked about, not openly, in most of our families. We learned euphemistic terms for our genitals. From the embarrassed words, from the "don'ts" that came as our fingers naturally started to explore our vulvas, vaginas and clitorises, we came to think of sex as dirty and *those* parts of our body as shameful, with power to harm us.

We learned as much from what wasn't said as what was. Perhaps a younger brother or sister appeared as "a gift from the stork," with no real explanation of our mother's pregnancy. If our parents weren't openly affectionate with each other, if they were careful to keep us from seeing them naked, that taught us something.

When I was six years old I climbed up on the bathroom sink and looked at myself naked in the mirror. All of a sudden I realized I had three different holes. I was very excited about my discovery and ran down to the dinner table and announced it to everyone. "I have three holes!" Silence. "What are they for?" I asked. Silence even heavier than before. I sensed how uncomfortable everyone was and answered for myself. "I guess one is for pee-pee, the other for doo-doo and the third for caca." A sigh of relief; no one had to answer my question. But I got the message—I wasn't supposed to ask "such" questions, though I didn't fully realize what "such" was about at that time.

From the moment we are born we are treated differently from little boys. Adults handled us differently as infants. Our toys were different: dolls instead of erector sets. Our clothes were different: dresses to be kept clean instead of sloppy pants, and skirts that restrict our movements and have no pockets.

Over the years the distinctions between female and male become inequalities and are repeated to us in so many ways that we too come to believe them. We're emotional; they're intellectual. We're dainty; they're clumsy. We're domestic; they're athletic. We can make babies and relationships; they can make ideas and objects. We're going to get married and be mothers; they're going to work and be mail*men*, or doctors, or administrators. If all goes right we will be pronounced man and wife. Thus we learn as children to split the qualities of being human between us. All of us, women and men, lose the genuine freedom to express all of ourselves. This split deeply affects our experience of sexuality.

When we become teenagers our developing bodies are usually a mystery to us. We discover that there is only one norm for beauty—a commercial norm, a Hollywood norm. TV sells us products as we agonize over breasts, hair, legs and skin that will never—ever—measure up. We lose respect for our uniqueness, our own smells and shapes and ways of doing things. We look to others to reassure us that we are, despite all this, okay. We learn to judge ourselves in relation to others and images from the media. The constant comparing leads to a competitiveness that separates us from each other.

Because multiple birth defects (cleft lip and palate, spina bifida) made my body different, my whole being is perceived and related to as different. My body creates feelings of denial, anger, guilt and rejection both within myself and within others. The only people who touched my body were medical personnel, with all their clinical coldness and detachment, and then it was to induce pain. I never thought my body could be itself pleasurable or be a source of pleasure.

In a disabled and disfigured body, I am "desexed" by both society and myself. I was never aware of my sexuality until at twenty-two my emotional and social development put me into relationships where sexual attraction toward me occurred. A thirteen-year-old has greater knowledge, skill, and a sense of her sexuality than I did! I struggled to identify with and accept my "womanness." With no one there to help me, I was forced to go it alone. Always I've asked, "Am I a person despite my physical handicaps?" Now I ask also, "Am I a woman?"

Worst of all, we feel isolated—could anyone else be as ugly, dull, miserable as I? An ad for sanitary napkins reinforces our aloneness and shame: "When you have your period, you should be the only one who knows."

Even if we were told that getting our first period was an exciting event (as well as "the curse"), a signal that we were becoming *real* women, many of us could not celebrate this transition because we had not learned to accept our body processes as normal and desirable.

What did we really learn about sex in a positive way in our teens? We had to wait until our twenties, or thirties, to learn at last that we have the only uniquely nonreproductive human sexual organ, the clitoris. Almost none of us ever heard about that as we were growing up. In spite of all the experiences that taught us to repress our sexuality, we are learning to be proud of it.

As we remember the experiences of our own growing-up years, we want to help our children grow up differently, with healthier feelings about their bodies and their sexuality. We are trying to be more open with our words and affection, more positive when they explore their bodies, more ready with information when they ask for it. But we find it hard sometimes to move beyond our own upbringing. There are few good models, so we need each other's help.

The other day I was taking a bath with my almost-three-year-old daughter. I was lying down and she was sitting between my legs, which were spread apart. She said, "Mommy, you don't have a penis." I said, "That's right, men have penises and women have clitorises." All calm and fine—then, "Mommy where is your clitoris?" Okay, now what was I going to do? I took a deep breath (for courage or something), tried not to blush, spread my vulva apart, and showed her my clitoris. It didn't feel so bad. "Do you want to see yours?" I asked. "Yes." That was quite a trick to get her to look over her fat stomach and see hers, especially when she started laughing as I first put my finger and then hers on her clitoris.

At least I feel that I can have some greater ease and openness about sexuality with my daughter than my mother had with me.

It took us time to develop bad feelings about our sexuality, and we must allow ourselves more time to undo those feelings and develop new and healthier ones.

SEXUAL LANGUAGE

The true language of sex is primarily nonverbal. Our words and images are poor imitations of the deep and complicated feelings within and between us. Unsure of touching as a way of sharing with another, we have let our fear and discomfort limit the rich possibilities for this nonverbal communication. Sexual expression has a power most of us are still just beginning to explore.

Sometimes when we want to talk or even think about sex we need words and we face the annoying dilemma—what words shall we use? For many of us there are no words that really feel right because of the attitudes and values they convey: the clinical, proper terms—vagina, penis and intercourse—seem cold, distant, tight; the street, slang terms—cunt, cock, fuck—seem degrading or coarse; euphemisms like "making love" seem silly and inexact. So we use different words with our lovers, children, friends and doctors. We feel awkward, and this awkwardness convinces us that even if sex is a natural way of expressing ourselves, we have no natural way of talking about it.

Many of us are trying to put together a language with which we are comfortable. We are trying to give old words a more positive sexual feeling. Some of us feel comfortable using words like fuck, cunt, balls, ass, etc., in a new way.

I was dancing with a man I liked a lot. We were feeling very sensual. As we moved our bodies to the music I could feel his cock and balls pressing on me. He whispered in my ear, "I bet your cunt is warm and juicy!"

SEX IN OUR IMAGINATION— OUR FANTASIES

For most of us it is difficult to acknowledge our sexual fantasies.

I never felt the freedom to explore parts of me that might come out in fantasy, dreams at night, daydreams, nonverbalized thinking. I was scared they would take me by surprise, tell me things about myself that I didn't know, especially bad things, and I was having enough trouble dealing with what came up without fantasizing. "Let well enough alone" was my attitude.

I imagined I was sitting in a room. The walls were all white. There was nothing in it, and I was naked. There was a large window at one end, and anyone who wanted to could look in and see me. There was no place to hide. There was something arousing about being so exposed. I masturbated while having this fantasy, and afterward I felt very sad. I thought I must be so sick, so distorted inside if this image of myself could give me such intense sexual pleasure.

We feel we "waste time" when we allow our minds to wander. We feel our self-images are threatened when we think about sex as anything except intercourse with a man. We feel we are disloyal when we fantasize about someone other than the person we are with. Worse, we feel we might be losing our minds when we imagine ourselves doing something we would never dare do in our real world, and then we worry that we will do it.

Everyone has fantasies. They flash as fleeting images or evolve as detailed stories. In talking with each other we have found that it is common to have fantasies that scare or confuse us. It is true that, for a few, fantasies can reflect deep emotional disturbances—if you truly fear that your fantasies will lead to self-harm or hurt to others it may be a good idea to check out those fears with a professional. For most of us, however, fantasies simply reflect our needs, desires and dreams. Our fantasies are depths in us wanting to be known and explored. In them we can be whatever we imagine. Through fantasy we are connected with the collective imagination of womankind and with creative sources that have produced some of the deepest, loveliest expressions of our humanity. Our fantasies are our treasures. They enrich our sense of ourselves and the world.

Enjoying a fantasy is a new and liberating notion for me. I always felt restrained because I thought I might act on my fantasies—whatever they were. Now that I know I don't have to act—now or ever—I can enjoy them.

Our fantasies, like our dreams, tell us about parts of ourselves we have ignored. They allow us to try alternative ways of expressing ourselves, add color and humor to the more mundane moments of our days. Some of us have shared fantasies with lovers and friends, and that has deepened our communication with them.

Here are some of our fantasies.*

A fantasy before I made love to a plumber I know: I was entertaining myself one night by imagining I was dancing with a stillson wrench (the most enormous wrench I ever saw, very businesslike!), and it turned into the plumber. He said, "Well, men are still good for something!" We were fixing the pipe while we were dancing, and the scene changed. We were swimming in a sea of rubber doughnuts (the connector between the tank and the bottom part of the toilet), and the doughnuts got stuck over our arms and legs. The scene changed again, to the beach, where we fell asleep.

One time, just as I was climaxing with Steve, I suddenly saw and felt someone else. I didn't realize until right then that that other person was on my mind.

I've had fantasies of having to drink urine from a man's penis while he was peeing.

When I was a kid, every time I masturbated I imagined my parents spanking me as I climaxed. When I got older it changed to my parents making love, then to my being kissed by someone, then to my making love.

I used to have a recurring fantasy that I was a gym teacher and had a classful of girls standing in front of me, nude. I went up and down the rows feeling all their breasts and getting a lot of pleasure out of it. When I first had this fantasy at thirteen I was ashamed. I thought something was wrong with me. Now I can enjoy it, because I feel it's okay to enjoy other women's bodies.

I fantasize about sleeping with my brother, who is nineteen and groovy and looks just like me. I fantasize sleeping with him because he's the person most like me. I acted on it by sleeping with his best friend.

I had the fantasy of making love with two men at once. I pictured myself sandwiched between them. I acted on this one, with an old friend and a casual friend who both liked the idea. It was fun.

I fantasize making love with horses, because they are very sensuous animals, more so than cows or pigs. They are also very male animals—horse society is very chauvinist.

*Nancy Friday's *My Secret Garden* (New York: Trident Press, 1973) is an exciting book full of women's fantasies.

At the height of making love with a man, I wished he was a woman. I wished he didn't have a penis. I wished he wasn't him but more like me.

Sometimes when I'm making love with myself or someone else, I think about the ocean roar and feel the waves swirling about me. Perhaps this means that I'd rather be floating in the sea than be in my bed. But it's also a way of heightening the experience for me. The fantasy makes me feel loose, easy, fluid. It makes me more relaxed. I usually have the fantasy just before orgasm, and it helps me let go.

VIRGINITY

What does virginity mean, anyway? Maybe virginity is a physical state but, much more important, it's a state of mind. Those of us who grew up in religious families may feel that to lose our virginity before marriage is to have sinned.

I confined my sexual involvement to heavy petting, since the Catholic Church makes intercourse seem like such a sin. The day I left the Church was the day I had an argument in the confessional with the priest about whether having intercourse with my fiancé was a sin. I maintained it wasn't; he said that I would never be a faithful wife if I had intercourse before marriage. He refused me absolution and I never went back.

The sexual revolution of the 1960s and the advent of the pill started to change these feelings about the importance of virginity. Its loss before marriage was less disapproved of if you grew up in the sixties rather than in the fifties. But new problems were created. In the fifties, if a guy was pressuring you to sleep with him and you didn't want to, you could use the virginity bit on him. Or you could use fear of pregnancy as an excuse. In the sixties it became harder to say no; being a virgin was passé, and birth-control methods were more widespread.

The loss of virginity, the loss of the state of purity and innocence, is viewed as a move from childhood to adulthood, a definite breaking away from parents and a move toward more autonomy and independence. Autonomy is surely a good thing, but the cost of sexual exploration should not have to be a sharp, brittle separation if that doesn't seem necessary.

Most of us were taught sex belongs in marriage. The linking of virginity and marriage often forces us into marriage before we are ready, before we know whether it's something we want.

Today the pressure on us to have sex may be as strong as the more traditional pressure to remain a virgin.

Your first sexual experience may not be everything you hoped for or expected. But in most cases, with the right preparation (physical and mental), and despite the mythology,* first intercourse need not be physically painful for a woman. And it may even be fun!

If you haven't had sexual intercourse as yet and feel you are ready for that, it's important that your partner be someone you know, trust and like, and who will help make it a comfortable and joyful experience. You can

---

* The mythology distorts reality to make women seem more helpless and dangerous and men more aggressive than they are, or want to be. Many myths that go far back in time and span different cultures express similar negative attitudes about female sexuality—e.g., the teeth-in-vagina myth, the menstrual uncleanliness myth and so forth.

give yourself time and space and learn about your body* (see Chapter 2 for more detail) when you are alone and when you are together with your partner. This taking of time and space can enhance your lovemaking in the present and set a positive tone for the future. Share your feelings and fears with each other. Read together parts of this chapter that would be helpful (e.g., "Female Sexual Response" and "Sex in a Relationship"). Talk about birth control and decide on a method beforehand. Spend some hours with each other exploring your bodies (looking, touching, smelling, tasting).

Your first experience may not sound like this. If not, don't be disappointed. There are many experiences to come, and intercourse, like anything else, gets better with time and practice. (See "Sex with Intercourse.")

HOMOSEXUAL FEELINGS

When we are born we instinctively do all we can to feel good. We need closeness, warmth and sensual pleasure, and we reach out toward those who offer them. Gradually we are taught to direct these sensuous—and increasingly explicitly sexual—feelings toward the opposite sex. Within each of us, however, the early sensual/sexual feelings we had for both sexes remain.

Society, through our parents, schools and churches, has told us that homosexual feelings are sinful and sick. For many of us these teachings have been very frightening. They have made it hard for us to acknowledge, let alone accept, the sexual feelings we may have for women. They have separated us, through fear, from women who openly act on sexual feelings for other women.

When I was about seven or eight I had this best friend Susan. We loved each other and walked around with our arms around each other. Her older sister told us not to do that any more because we looked like lesbians. So we held hands instead.

---

* A lot of women have questions about hymens. The hymen is a pliable membrane that encircles part or all of the entrance to the vagina and partially covers that entrance. You may have already stretched, or can stretch, the hymen by inserting your fingers or your partner's fingers in your vagina during petting, or by using a tampon or by masturbating. Some of us have hymens that never need stretching. As hymens come in different shapes and sizes, when the penis or finger(s) moves past the hymen there may be a little physical discomfort, or there can be a stretching and a small amount of bleeding. If you do not attempt penetration until you are highly aroused and your vagina is well lubricated, and if your partner moves slowly, most of this discomfort can be prevented. However, we've talked with some women who really bled a lot when they first had intercourse, so this is a possibility even if you are well prepared.

Homosexual feelings need not be denied. Like our fantasies, they are a part of us that we can act upon or not, as we wish. We can enjoy them, explore the dimension they add to our friendships, without ever acting on them if we don't want to. Those of us who do choose to act upon our homosexual feelings want to be able to do so without moral judgment from others. It is our birthright as human beings to explore and express those feelings within us that will not harm others.

In this chapter we have tried to provide information that will be of use to any woman, whoever she chooses as her sexual partner. Labels such as homosexual and heterosexual only divide us. We are all sexual beings.

FEMALE SEXUAL RESPONSE

Our sexual feelings can be affected by sounds, sights, smells and touch. We can be aroused by fantasies, a baby sucking at our breast, the smell of a familiar body, a picture of a bikini-clad model, anal stimulation, a dream, touching our own bodies, a lover's breathing in our ear, brushing against someone, or hearing the person we love say, "I love you." We can express our sexual feelings in an almost infinite variety of ways—writing a poem, rolling down a grassy hill in the sunshine, dancing to rock music, massaging a friend. We can also express them by masturbating or making love with a man or a woman.

No matter how our sexual feelings are aroused or how they are expressed, physiologically our bodies follow a sequence of physical changes called the *sexual response cycle*, and culminating, if we are sufficiently aroused, in *orgasm*. Orgasm is a sudden peak and release of sexual tension, after which our bodies slowly return to their non-aroused state. Sometimes when we become aroused we don't move through the entire cycle because it's not the moment to seek additional stimulation and reach orgasm. We simply let ourselves enjoy the rush of sexual feelings. However, although sexual tension can certainly be released without orgasm, it takes much longer, and sometimes, when we get sufficiently aroused and don't move through the entire cycle, we may feel a painful aching in our genitals which can take hours to subside.

Whether or not we reach orgasm, there are two changes that occur in our bodies in the earlier stages of sexual response: *vasocongestion* and *myotonia*. Vasocongestion is the dilating and filling with blood of the veins, especially in the pelvis and vulva. Myotonia is the tightening of muscles. Orgasm, if and when it occurs, is the sudden, involuntary, almost instantaneous release of pelvic congestion and muscle tension, accomplished by muscle contractions expelling blood from the tissues in the pelvic area. There are also contractions in the vagina, rectum and uterus which sometimes we feel.

Though sexual response follows the same physiological pattern for everyone, subjectively each experience is likely to feel somewhat different to each of us. Every orgasm is physiologically the same, too, but it may not feel that way at all.

Orgasm can be a very mild experience, like a ripple or peaceful sigh; it can be a very sensuous experience where our body glows with warmth; it can be an intense experience with crying out and thrashing movements; it can be an ecstatic experience with momentary loss of awareness.

I have such different experiences with orgasm. Sometimes it takes energy to hold back. The natural thing when I'm particularly loose is to let go and energy is released and I can't go to sleep for hours. Other times I'm aroused but it's not a flowing, effortless experience. I need to expend energy. I feel good and then I want to go to sleep. The two experiences contrast with each other.

The Role of the Clitoris

It is arousing to stroke any part of our bodies, exciting to have our thighs caressed or our necks nibbled or our breasts sucked. However, the clitoris is the part that is the most sensitive and responsive to sexual stimulation. The clitoris has *the* central role in elevating our feelings of sexual tension. Without this buildup of sexual tension we could not have orgasm.

Here is a summary of the role of the clitoris:

The clitoris has three parts: the glans, the shaft and the hood (see Chapter 2 for more detail). The shaft of the clitoris is under the skin. The glans, which is the tip of the shaft, is covered by the hood. With sexual arousal, all of the clitoris fills with blood and swells. The hood becomes so swollen it balloons up, uncovering the glans. When sexual tension reaches a very high level, the glans retracts under its hood.

Stimulation of the clitoris helps produce the pelvic congestion and muscle contraction that are necessary for orgasm. When we are highly aroused, stimulation of the clitoris may bring on orgasm.

All stimulation of the pubic hair-covered mons area, the inner lips and any parts of the clitoris itself is considered direct stimulation. (Since the clitoris is not in a rigidly fixed position, any stimulation in this area will move the clitoris and also may press and rub it up against the pubic bone.) The clitoral area is stimulated directly by touching with a hand, caressing with a tongue, applying a vibrator or pressing someone else's body close. Although some women say that they touch the glans to become aroused, the glans of the clitoris is so sensitive that touching it directly can hurt. Also, if stimulation is focused on the clitoris for a long time, we may lose the sensation and not feel excited any more.

Stroking the skin on the lower abdomen and inner thighs is another effective way to stimulate the clitoris (the tension of abdominal and thigh muscles pulls on the ligaments that attach the clitoris to the pubic bone).

At high levels of arousal, the clitoris retracts under its hood and can no longer be seen or felt. This occurs some time before orgasm, from one minute to perhaps thirty. Also, the clitoris can emerge and retract several times during a sexual experience. During orgasm the clitoris is always retracted; however, retraction doesn't guarantee orgasm, especially if stimulation doesn't continue and increase. To reach orgasm a woman needs continuous, effective stimulation of the clitoris—by penile thrusting, body pressure, or touching of the clitoral area with a hand or tongue. With direct stimulation, retraction will occur at lower levels of sexual excitement than with intercourse alone. With intercourse alone, very high levels of sexual arousal are reached before retraction occurs. This may explain why many of us have orgasm quicker through direct manipulation, and makes it clearer to us that intercourse is not better or worse than direct stimulation, it's just different.

In intercourse there is indirect stimulation of the clitoris. Penile movements and any movements in the vagina provide continual clitoral stimulation by moving the inner lips which, by their connection to the clitoral hood, move the hood back and forth over the glans. In addition, the inner lips become so swollen and firm they act as an extension of the vagina, hugging the penis as it moves back and forth. To reach orgasm most of us need either direct or indirect clitoral stimulation before intercourse, and some of us need direct clitoral manipulation during intercourse. *The distinction between vaginal and clitoral orgasm is a myth.*

Sexual Response

To help us understand how our bodies respond to sexual stimulation, Masters and Johnson separate the process of sexual response into four consecutive phases: excitement, plateau, orgasm and resolution. Together these phases make up the sexual response cycle.* They are for descriptive purposes only: we move from one phase to

---

*Masters and Johnson's big contribution has been a scientific observation of people going through the sexual response cycle and measurement of their reactions. Wilhelm Reich did similar research thirty years ago.

the next without any sense of demarcation. Although generally the first and last phases are the longest, we pass through the phases in differing amounts of time under different circumstances. The amount of stimulation needed or desired for orgasm varies from person to person and for each of us from time to time.

The two fundamental reactions of sexual arousal—vasocongestion and myotonia—lead to that feeling of fullness, warmth and arousal we experience as sexual excitement.

Here is what happens for us during a sexual response cycle (you may want to refer to the description of female anatomy in Chapter 2 while reading this).

Excitement—The Beginning Feelings of Arousal

The vagina becomes moist (lubricated) as the swelling blood vessels around it push fluid through the vaginal walls, making them "sweat." The vagina begins to expand and balloon and eventually the inner two-thirds double in diameter.

The inner lips swell and deepen in color.

The clitoris swells, becomes erect, and is highly sensitive to touch. If there is clitoral stimulation during this time, orgasms of greater intensity are more likely.

The breasts enlarge and become more sensitive. The nipples become erect.

The uterus enlarges and elevates within the pelvic cavity.

The heart rate increases; breathing becomes heavier and faster.

A flush or rash may appear on the skin.

The muscles begin to tighten, especially in the genital area.

Plateau—The Full Feelings of Arousal Necessary for Orgasm

While the inner two-thirds of the vagina continues to balloon, the outer third narrows by one-third to one-half of its diameter. This allows the vagina to hold the penis during intercourse. Some of us fear this narrowing means we are not sufficiently aroused for intercourse, and feel intercourse will be painful. In fact this constriction signals we are physically ready for intercourse. However, too many of us begin intercourse during the excitement phase, when we are only slightly aroused. Intercourse will be most pleasurable and most likely to include orgasm if we don't allow penetration until we are more completely aroused.

Although the upper two-thirds of the vagina is relatively insensitive to touch, following sexual arousal the outer third is quite sensitive to pressure. For some of us, at times, the whole vagina feels responsive.

The entire genital area continues to swell, as do the breasts. (You may become increasingly aware of these areas of your body.)

The uterus elevates fully.

We breathe very rapidly; we may pant.

The muscles continue to contract.

During the plateau phase the clitoris retracts under its hood. Stimulation of the inner lips from manipulation or intercourse moves the hood of the clitoris back and forth over the glans.

Orgasm—The Release of Sexual Tension

For women, if sexual stimulation is interrupted, excitement may decline. This is especially true just before and during orgasm, when we need continuous stimulation. Then direct or indirect stimulation of the clitoris intensifies to orgasm.

Orgasm may start with a spastic muscle contraction of two to four seconds' duration. Orgasm is three to fifteen rhythmic contractions of the muscles around the outer third of the vagina at .8-second intervals, and orgasm is the time of our most intense sexual feeling. The uterus and rectum also contract (the contractions cause the release of the blood trapped in the pelvic veins). Just before orgasm some of us feel a sense of suspension, and after orgasm most of us feel a sense of release and warmth spreading throughout our bodies.

Physiologically, when we are effectively stimulated, we can reach orgasm again and again. (Our multi-orgasmic capacity is one indication of what Masters and Johnson call our "superior physiological capacity for sexual response.") On the other hand, many of us are fully satisfied with one orgasm.*

Resolution—Return to Non-aroused State

For a half hour or more after orgasm, if lovemaking doesn't continue, swelling decreases, the muscles relax, and the clitoris, vagina and uterus return to their usual positions. For those of us who reach plateau but not orgasm, this can take hours and can be uncomfortable. Orgasm speeds the release of pelvic congestion. Without orgasm the congested pelvic feeling can become a painful ache. If we have reached orgasm, this time afterward can be one of great peacefulness.

Male Sexual Response

The male sexual response cycle is similar to ours, with the four phases following in sequence. The fundamental reactions of vasocongestion (blood-engorged veins) and myotonia (muscle contraction) are the components of sexual arousal in men as well as women. Our first reac-

---

*The knowledge that we are physiologically capable of having many orgasms has led many of us to feel that not only must we reach orgasm, but we must have several orgasms. If the old trap was low expectations, the new problem, for women and men, is excessive expectations. We don't know finally what full human sexual functioning is, so in the meantime try to enjoy what feels good to you.

tion to arousal is vaginal lubrication, and a man's is penile erection. These things happen well before either partner is ready for intercourse (especially for those of us who want orgasm with intercourse). For both sexes the peak of sexual excitement is orgasm, which for a man includes ejaculation.

With men, the four phases of the sexual response cycle are less well defined. The first phase, excitement, is shorter, another way of saying we get aroused more slowly. After orgasm a man has a period of a few minutes or even hours (longer as he gets older) when he cannot have another erection. This is called the refractory period.

SEX WITH OURSELVES— MASTURBATION

From the moment we were born we all began making ourselves feel good by touching and playing with our bodies. Some of these experiences were explicitly sexual.

From our parents and, later, our schools and churches many of us learned that we were not to continue this pleasurable touching. Some of us heeded their messages and some of us did not. But by the time we were teenagers, whether we masturbated or not, most of us thought it was bad. If we did masturbate we often felt guilty. If we didn't masturbate, sometimes it was because we felt we had to control our sexual feelings by pushing them away.

Guilt and repression can inhibit and even block our natural sexual responsiveness. For some of us these reactions that we first learned to associate with masturbation are now connected with sex in general. For many of us, learning to masturbate has opened up sex again.

Masturbation allows us the time and space to explore and experiment with our own bodies. We can learn what fantasies turn us on, what touches arouse and please us, at what tempo, and where. We can come to know our own patterns of sexual response. We don't need to worry about a partner's needs and opinions. Then, if and when we choose, we can share our knowledge by telling or showing our partner, by taking his or her hand and guiding it to touch the places we want touched.

Masturbation is a special way of enjoying ourselves. "It is our sexual base. Everything we do beyond that is simply how we choose to socialize our sex life."*

I taught myself to scream while making love (something I was jealous of my friends' ability to do) by letting myself make noises while I masturbated. After a few practice sessions alone, I could let my voice out with my partner.

Women have many ways of masturbating: some of us masturbate by moistening our fingers (with either saliva or juice from the vagina) and rubbing them around and over the clitoris. We can gently rub or tweak the clitoris itself; we can rub the hood or a larger area around the clitoris. We can use one finger or many. We can rub up and down or around and around. Pressure and timing also vary. Some of us masturbate by crossing our legs and exerting steady and rhythmic pressure on the whole genital area. Some of us have learned to develop muscular tension throughout our bodies resembling the tensions developed in the motions of intercourse. Some of us get sexually excited during physical activity—climbing ropes or trees, riding horses. Still other ways of masturbating include using a pillow instead of our hands, a stream of water, or an electric vibrator.

It's exciting to make up sexual fantasies while masturbating or to masturbate when we feel those fantasies coming on. Some of us like to insert something into our vaginas while masturbating— a finger, candle, a peeled cucumber, a vibrator. Some of us find our breasts or other parts of our bodies erotically sensitive and rub them before or while rubbing the clitoris. Enjoying ourselves doesn't just mean our clitoris, vagina and breasts. We are learning to enjoy all parts of our bodies.

Learning to Masturbate*

If you have never masturbated, we invite you to try. You may feel awkward, self-conscious, even a bit scared at first. You may have to contend with voices within you that repeat, "Nice girls don't . . ." or, "A happily married woman wouldn't want to . . ." Most of us have had these feelings too, and they changed in time.

Here are some suggestions for beginning to explore masturbation for yourself:

Read over "Female Sexual Response" and Chapter 2. In a full-length mirror, slowly explore the shape of your body with your eyes and your hands. Find a quiet time when you can be by yourself. Take a long relaxing bath or shower. Afterward rub all of your body with cream, lotion, oil, or anything else that feels good. Experiment with different kinds of touching and see how you feel. Settle yourself into a comfortable spot. Put on a favorite record. Keep the lights soft, light a candle. Have a glass of wine or anything else that makes you feel mellow and easy. Think about the people or situations you find sexually arousing. Let your mind flow freely into fantasy. Let your whole body relax.

---

*Betty Dodson, *Liberating Masturbation: A Meditation on Self Love*, p. 55. We highly recommend this pamphlet. See bibliography.

*Also read *For Yourself, The Fulfillment of Female Sexuality*, by Lonnie Garfield Barbach (New York: Doubleday, 1975).

With some more lotion or oil begin to stroke your body all over. Vary the pressure and timing. Let your sensations come. You may want to borrow or buy a small vibrator to add to your pleasure. (They can be found at local drug or department stores, often sold as body or neck massagers.) Close your eyes and move your fingers around, in and over your entire genital area.

Find your clitoris and focus your attention on stroking it or your inner lips around it or the mons area above it. As you get sexually aroused, your vagina will feel moist. When feelings of sexual tension mount, experiment with what you can do to increase them. Open your mouth, let your breathing be faster, try making noises and moving your pelvis rhythmically to your breathing and voice.*

Explore further those sensations that are the most pleasurable and exciting for you.

As you are getting more aroused you may feel your muscles tighten. Your pelvic area will feel warm and full.

For me the most pleasurable part is just before orgasm. I feel I am no longer consciously controlling my body. I know there is no way I will not reach orgasm now. I stop trying. I like to savor this rare moment of true letting go!

It's this letting go of control that enables us to have orgasms. If you do not reach orgasm when you first try masturbating, don't worry. Many of us didn't either. Simply enjoy the sensations you have. Try again some other time.

If after a month and many tries reaching orgasm is still difficult for you, talk to a friend you feel easy with. It's been hard for many of us to masturbate because we feared we were losing control of ourselves, and we also have trouble allowing ourselves intense pleasure. In talking with friends, we learned these were all too common fears. Once we were aware of them we were able to pay attention to them and sometimes let them go.

Masturbating opens me to what is happening in my body and makes me feel good about myself. I like following the impulse of the moment. Sometimes I have many orgasms, sometimes I don't have any. The greatest source of pleasure is to be able to do whatever feels good to me at that particular time. I rarely have such complete freedom in other aspects of my life.

---

*For specific exercises to help you with your breathing and movements and experience of pleasure see *Total Orgasm* by Jack Lee Rosenberg (New York: Random House/Bookworks, 1973). It's a very helpful book.

SEX IN A RELATIONSHIP

As we move into a relationship with another person, we carry our sexuality—our feelings, our fantasies, our masturbation experiences—with us as part of our whole selves. We can express our sexuality in relation to someone else both as a way of getting sexual pleasure and as a way of communicating loving feelings. Sexual sharing that is satisfying deepens our relationships in a way few other shared experiences can, and good relationships in turn improve our sexual pleasure.

Yet sex in a relationship is as complex as relationships themselves:

I enjoy sex with Mike more than I have with anyone. When we get turned on, we make the most beautiful music together! Still sex often feels difficult for me. When I feel good about myself and close to him and when the pressures of our children and my work and my friends are not demanding a lot of my energy, our sex is very fluid and strong. When I feel angry or sad or depressed or very childlike and needy, or any combination, or busy with other people in my life, I have a hard time being sexually open with Mike. We've talked about this, and he experiences a lot of the same ups and downs and distractions as I do.

Sex in relationships can vary in meaning and intensity for us.

Sometimes I make love to get care and cuddling. Sometimes I am so absorbed in the sensations of touch and taste and smell and sight and sound that I feel I've returned to that childhood time when feeling good was all that mattered. Sometimes I am the tom-girl as we tumble and tease. Sometimes sex is spiritual—high mass

could not be more sacred. Sometimes I fuck to get away from the tightness and seriousness in myself. Sometimes I want to come and feel the ripples of orgasm through my body. Sometimes tears mix with come mix with sweat, and I am one with another. Sometimes sex is more powerful than getting high, and through it I unite with the stream of love that flows among us all. Sex can be most anything and everything for me. How good that feels!

Sometimes a brief encounter can be intensely exciting and can free us to try things we wouldn't with someone we were in a certain pattern with. On the other hand, a brief encounter or an affair we know will end can be unsatisfactory if we don't know or trust our partner well enough to ask for what we want. In a long-term relationship there is an opportunity to learn about each other's bodies over time; to explore different sexual techniques, roles and fantasies; to express deeply our many and varied feelings through sex. Yet some long-term couples get into sexual patterns that fail to satisfy either or both partners. Some of us have had short-term relationships and have been able to use what we've learned in them to get out of unsatisfying patterns with a long-term partner. (Some relationships can last through such changes, others cannot. See Chapter 4 for more detail.)

Whatever kind of relationship we have, good sexual sharing requires trust, clear communication, appropriate technique, a sense of humor, time and privacy. We want relationships based on mutual respect and equality. We want relationships in which our commitment allows us to share our vulnerable places as well as our joyful places. We need to cry and laugh together. We want to spend many quiet, unhurried hours with each other, finding what pleases and excites us.

Sex as Communication

When we asked a group of women and men college students, "How do you let someone know that you want to go to bed with them?" they started to laugh. The laughter expressed, "Well, you know the games, too, so why are you asking?" It was also saying, "It's hard to think seriously and talk openly with each other about sexual feelings."

We pressed on beyond the laughter. One woman responded, "By the eyes—the way you look at each other, you know." A guy said, "I ask her if she wants to come to my room and smoke a joint." Others spoke of how they touched each other—squeeze on the hand, arm on the shoulder—to communicate a desire for sex. "How are you sure that the other person gets the message you intended and wants to have sex too?" More laughter. A guy spoke up. "Well, it's obvious—she got into bed with me." I continued, "Was she aware of how she felt, and if she felt she didn't want sex now, could she have said no comfortably?"

One woman joined in and very clearly said, "I've been in that situation and couldn't say no because even though I didn't want intercourse, I did want to be physically close to someone and be held and touched, and I felt they all go together." Another woman added, "This is the first time I've talked about things like this in a mixed group, and I have not always known what I felt, or if I have, haven't felt I could say it."

A guy continued, "Frankly, there have been times I've felt so horny it didn't matter to me what the other person felt." (Nods from both women and men to this.) "There have been other times I didn't feel like sex— holding hands and a good-night kiss were fine, and yet I felt the girl expected it, and the guys I live with expected it, so I had sex."

This discussion illustrates some of the issues we all face in a sexual situation, whether it's with a date, long-time lover, or spouse: How do I feel at the moment? Do I want to be sexually close with this person now? In what ways? What if I don't know; can I say I'm confused? Then can I communicate clearly what I want, what I don't want? Do I feel comfortable saying it in words or letting him/her know some other way? What are the unspoken rules? Is there enough trust between us, enough caring, for this person to listen to my feelings and respect them if I feel differently from him/her?

These questions come up all the time, and there are no easy or permanent answers. We can try to be as fully aware as possible of our feelings at the moment, and to be honest with ourselves about them. Our first instinct, though, is not to do this:

Gary gives me a good-night kiss and turns over to go to sleep. I feel very sexually turned on and am angry he is tired. I want to rub up against him and try to arouse him. But I don't want to risk an argument. So I'll try to go off to sleep quietly. Yet inside I'm still full of both sexual and angry feelings.

Sometimes we can avoid going to sleep so unsettled if we try to communicate our feelings to the other person in a straightforward, non-accusing, unapologetic way. Here's a rewrite of the scene above:

Gary gives me a good-night kiss and turns over to sleep. I feel very sexually turned on and rub up against him.

"Sue, I'm glad I turn you on, but I'm just too sleepy tonight to have sex."

—*or*—

"Sue, I didn't know you wanted sex. I'm tired and yet would like to hold you and be close."

With either of these exchanges, Sue might not end up getting exactly what she wants sexually, yet having expressed her feelings and had them acknowledged, she could sleep.

Communication about our sexual needs is a continuous process. One woman who had gotten up the courage to talk with her man about their sexual relationship said in frustration, "I feel like I told him what I like *once*, so why doesn't he know now? Did he forget? Doesn't he care?" None of us is a mind reader. Sometimes we can sense what someone close to us wants or needs. Other times we can't. We are aware that our own sexual feelings are different at different times, yet we're not always comfortable telling our lover how we feel from time to time.

I felt passionate and intense last time we had sex. This time I'm feeling mellow and wanting to be physically close and don't care if I have an orgasm. While I'm clear about what I want, I have trouble saying it. The voices in my head say:

—I felt so physically, spiritually and emotionally close that I crave that peak experience again. Anything else is less than that.

—I fear he expects me to want intercourse and an orgasm and he'll feel bad if I don't.

The voices go on. I want to scream, to shut them off. The more I let them go on, the less I feel like any kind of sex.

Letting Tony know what I need at a certain point was not always so simple. I knew that he had grown up believing males are supposed to know more about sex. So even when he told me he wanted to know what made me feel good, I had this feeling that telling him would seem like criticism of what he was doing.

We were both really excited. He began rubbing my clitoris hard and it hurt. It took me a second to figure out what to do. I was afraid that if I said something about it, I would spoil the excitement for both of us. Then I realized I could just take his hand and very gently move it up a little higher to my pubic hair.

Communicating about sex is often awkward at first. Here are some of the barriers that we have felt:

We are afraid that being honest about what we want will threaten the other.

We are embarrassed by the words themselves.

We feel sex is supposed to come naturally and having to talk about it must mean there's a problem.

We aren't communicating well with our partner in other areas of our relationship.

We don't know what we want at a particular time, or we

need to react to something our partner does. The barriers can be within us, not just between us and our partners.

How do we work on better communication in sex? We are discovering that talking about sex with our partner—the sharing of what we feel, of what we enjoy and don't enjoy in our lovemaking—is part of the whole experience. Sometimes it's helpful to talk while we are making love. This can create surprises and add to our excitement. At other times it feels better to wait until later to talk.

Either way, talking can add new dimensions to the experience and can make for a greater sense of closeness and intimacy. Talking about lovemaking can also be painful, because sometimes when our sex isn't as we want it to be, it is clearly reflecting our general inability to connect, and that's disappointing.

Making love is one of the special times when we have more than words to use to reach each other. Taking our partner's hand and putting it in a new place, making the noises that let him/her know we are feeling good, speeding up or slowing down our hip movements, a firm hand on the shoulder meaning "let's go slow"—there are many ways we have of communicating, if we will use them.

We have so many ways of expressing affection, trust and pleasure—touching, hugging, kissing, communicating through words and gestures, teasing, laughing and crying.

I can so clearly remember moving in and around him and him in me, till it seemed in the whole world there was only us dancing together as we moved together as we loved together as we came together. Sometimes at these times I laugh or cry and they are the same strong emotions coming from a deep protected part of me that is freer now for loving him.

With all our old stereotypes about who does what in sex, these kinds of communication don't happen overnight—we move gradually away from the old myth that men know all about sex, women just have it done to them, and no one talks about it. However, more and more of us are finding that telling or showing each other what feels good is not complaining or demanding; it's a profound kind of honesty.

There's More Than Intercourse

The pleasures of sex include a wide variety of feelings and experiences. The categories we learned for sex—foreplay, intercourse, orgasm—confine us. They imply that all sex is the prelude to, culmination of, or substitute for vaginal intercourse. This conception of sex limits the ways we think about and seek pleasure.

We have many ways of getting and giving pleasure. We can touch each other, caress each other, stroke each other to orgasm without intercourse. Sometimes this is called mutual masturbation. It is a particularly good way to learn what kind of touching arouses us and to experience orgasm.

We can suck and lick our partner's genitals to orgasm or as a part of lovemaking that later may include intercourse. This is called *cunnilingus* (the licking and sucking of a woman's genitals; slang: "eating" or "eating-out") or *fellatio* (the licking and sucking of a man's genitals; slang: "blow job," or "going down on" somebody). With our mouths and tongues we can experiment with ways to delight our partners and ourselves.

The anus can be stimulated with fingers, tongue, penis, or any slender object. The anus is highly sensitive to erotic stimulation. However, it is not as elastic as the vagina. Be gentle and careful and use a lubricant (saliva, secretions from the vagina or penis, or a water-soluble jelly, such as K-Y Jelly) if you have anal intercourse—the penis within the anus. Anal bacteria can cause serious vaginal infections, so if you want your partner's penis or finger in your vagina after it has been in your anus, be sure it has been washed first.

We can excite each other with erotic pictures, by sharing our fantasies, with the stimulation of a vibrator. Use your imagination. The possibilities are endless.*

Sex With Intercourse

Sharing intercourse means learning together how to please each other. Sexual equality begins in bed. We want to act on feelings expressing mutuality and personal preference. No longer must we perform by pleasing and men please by performing.

Sex with intercourse includes what is traditionally called foreplay. Giving more importance to intercourse is unnecessary: all sexual pleasures are equal.

Most of the time we want intercourse to lead to orgasm because it feels so good for us and our partner. There are many ways to enjoy ourselves and to come to orgasm; there is no one right way. Sometimes we feel like having intercourse and having an orgasm is not important to us. Then it is a different experience from intercourse with orgasm, not a lesser one.

Here is one experience of sexual intercourse with a man:

We got home late in the evening after a long visit with friends. Bryan and I went straight to bed, both of us feeling very sleepy. After a few minutes of cuddling and good-nights, I began to feel somewhat sexually aroused; but thinking I was too tired to enjoy making love, I

*For further suggestions see *The Joy of Sex*, and *More Joy*, edited by Alex Comfort (listed in the bibliography).

rolled over to go to sleep. Bryan, also feeling aroused, reached around me and began to stroke my body. As I felt his hand on my breast and then on my stomach, I smiled to myself and rolled back toward him. At this point I knew I wanted to make love and was amazed at how quickly my moods could change.

We moved our bodies against one another gently. Neither Bryan nor I was very energetic or passionate, but we were both feeling aroused. I kissed his chest and then slid my cheek along his stomach and thighs. I stroked and held his penis, which had been erect for several minutes, and lay quietly upon his stomach. We touched and kissed each other affectionately, sometimes laughing and biting playfully, sometimes looking into one another's eyes with that very special nonverbal expression of our love.

When I felt ready, I lay on top of Bryan and guided his penis into my vagina. I moved my pelvis slowly back and forth enjoying the familiar, warm sense of fullness of feeling Bryan inside me. The muscles in my vagina began to contract and release rhythmically. At the same time, I began to fantasize about being by the ocean, with the rhythmic sound of waves breaking on the shore. Then Bryan put his hands on my hips and asked me to stop moving for a while—he was close to the point of orgasm and didn't want to come yet.

We lay still for several minutes and talked about the evening with our friends as well as plans we'd made for the following day. I began to move my pelvis again and felt that I wanted to have an orgasm. Though I had nice sensations all over my body, I sensed that I needed to change positions, that my clitoris needed a lot of stimulation before I could have an orgasm. We both knew from experience that at times like this I felt best if Bryan penetrated me from behind and reached around me with his hand to rub my clitoris. Sometimes I liked to do this while lying on my stomach with him on top of me, but this time it felt better to lie with my back to his stomach. Bryan knew from my movements and my breathing when to increase the pressure on my clitoris and when to move his fingers more rapidly. I communicated this nonverbally by rubbing my hands against his thighs: he knew how to match the movement of his fingers with the movement of my hands.

I soon became very excited, experienced tingling sensations all over, and then felt the intense pleasure of those moments just before orgasm, when I seemed to be soaring over the top of a waterfall. My orgasm was a rush of wonderful feelings.

I moved rhythmically for several minutes, enjoying the sense of release and looseness after my orgasm. Bryan said how much he had enjoyed tuning in to my orgasm. (He often likes to hold back from coming himself so that he can share in my orgasm more fully.) He then started to thrust inside me, moving more and more forcefully and rapidly. As he approached orgasm, I be-

came aroused again and started to rub my clitoris. When he came, he moaned softly and kissed the back of my neck (one of my most erotic places). His orgasm was especially arousing for me and I came soon after him. We both felt a warm glow and snuggled against each other for a while. Just before dozing off in our favorite "spooning" position (curled on our sides, Bryan's front to my back), I smiled and whispered to Bryan: "And we were going to go right to sleep. . . ."

For most of us it is quicker, physiologically, to reach orgasm with direct clitoral stimulation by hand or mouth or vibrator than solely with the indirect stimulation of intercourse. Yet many of us also feel that orgasm with a penis in our vagina is pleasurable and emotionally satisfying. Since many of us find it difficult to get sufficient stimulation with a penis in our vagina but want orgasms through intercourse, we have included some suggestions that have helped us reach orgasm with intercourse. (There may also be other reasons for difficulty in reaching orgasm—see "Problems with Orgasm" in the Appendix.)

Take the penis into your vagina only when you are very aroused (see "Masturbation" and "Female Sexual Response" sections). Over time you will learn to know when you are ready to begin intercourse without giving it much thought.

Sometimes when you make love you may be eager for penetration without clitoral caresses, but more often most of us need clitoral stimulation manually or orally for some time before intercourse.

If you are highly aroused when actual intercourse begins, the minor lips around the entrance to your vagina will be swollen and will stimulate your clitoris (see "Female Sexual Response"). You may want additional manual stimulation of the clitoris during intercourse. You or your partner can do this easily if you are sitting on top (female superior position) or the two of you are lying side by side (lateral coital position)—see figures p. 53. For many women the female superior position is the easiest and sometimes the only way to achieve orgasm with intercourse. It is also easier to get breast stimulation in this position. The man on top is not a more "natural" position for intercourse. You can both sit up with your legs over his and his penis in you. Or your man can enter you from behind and use his hands to reach around and stimulate your clitoris. We are all different shapes and need to find the positions that suit us. We can gain a lot of pleasure by trying different positions.

If you are not ready for orgasm and your man is highly aroused when you begin intercourse, you might bring him to orgasm too soon for you if he engages in vigorous penile thrusting and you move your pelvis against his quickly. You can both slow your movements down until you are more excited.

female superior with clitoral stimulation

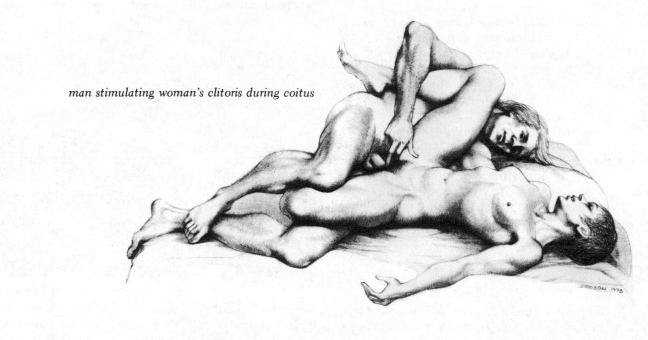

man stimulating woman's clitoris during coitus

self-stimulation during coitus

Sex with Your Lover

It is fun to plan with your lover to spend more hours exploring your own unique patterns of sexual response. Here are some experiences some of us have enjoyed:

Set aside a time to enjoy a good meal, snack, or drink together. Undress each other and sit by candlelight with your favorite music. Take turns rubbing each other with oil or lotion. We need to take time to accept pleasure. Tell or show each other what touches please or arouse you. Don't rush into intercourse.

Do this again and again until you both feel relaxed with nudity, with touching, with caressing all parts of your bodies, with talking openly about your feelings, with the giving and getting of pleasure.

Now begin to explore your own rhythms of arousal. You can learn a kind of mutual pacing so that penetration occurs when you both want it. Be patient—it takes time to learn how to move with another. When you are ready for him to enter you, experiment with holding your bodies still with each other for a time. Then begin to move together slowly. If either of you comes close to orgasm, signal the other and stop moving until you are slightly less excited. Then begin gentle movements again.

With these subtle movements you can hover at the edge of orgasm for a long time, which is exquisitely exciting. Also, you are more likely to both reach orgasm and to do so within minutes of each other. (Simultaneous orgasms are not important—or frequent.) These experiments with moving slowly can help men learn to delay ejaculation, which can make intercourse more pleasurable for both of you.

The first few years we had a great sex life. We were very attracted to each other and I loved sex with Ralph. I didn't have orgasms and I didn't even know what an orgasm was. Then I learned about orgasms, partly by reading some of the new books and articles, and partly by having one while masturbating. It felt so good that I wanted to have it with Ralph. The next two years were awful in bed. We had this goal—my orgasm—and it was like we'd look at our watches and say, "One, two, three, go," and work at it until we succeeded. Now, finally, we're back on an even keel. Usually I come, sometimes I don't. I let Ralph know which way I'm feeling. We can forget that goal and just do what feels good. But I wish I'd known everything I know now back then when our feelings were so intense.

A Lifetime of Sex

Our powers to express ourselves sexually are powers that last a lifetime—from birth to death. For some of us that may be a new notion. Certainly many of us don't see our parents as sexual beings; they are our parents, and many older people haven't felt comfortable sharing that part of themselves with us.

When he was drinking, an old family friend (he's in his late sixties) said to me, "Your generation doesn't believe we had sex before marriage. Well, my wife and I were sleeping together for three years before we got married, and we are still enjoying it!" I drew back for some moments. My response was one of surprise and I said, "Well, how could we know, you never talked about it."

As we start to be more open about sex with the older people in our lives, and they with us, we discover, happily, that there is no age limit.*

Recently I heard this story: The seventy-five-year-old mother of a friend told her daughter that an eighty-year-old man she knew had propositioned her. She was delighted and said, "Walter, you really want to make love with me and I accept!" I was surprised and also excited that sexual loving doesn't end at sixty!

Over our lifetime we can have many changing feelings about our sexuality—how we want to explore it, with whom, etc. Sometimes these changes take us by surprise.

I have trouble talking about sex right now because there isn't much. I feel closeness and deep connection with my husband and still I'm disturbed. We used to always count on being able to make love, no matter what else was wrong. And that just isn't true any more. I feel uneasy.

---

*For more information see "The Effects of Age on Sexuality," Chapter 6, in Helen Kaplan, *The New Sex Therapy* (listed in bibliography).

If we're not having a sexual relationship or not getting what we want in the one or ones we're in, it's hard to accept that sex isn't everything we always thought it would be. We can easily begin to feel deprived, discouraged, less a woman and caught up in what should be rather than what is. If we are at a comfortable place with ourselves about our particular sexual arrangements right now, we can flow with these changes.

I'm feeling this is a space in my life for myself, to explore certain issues I've never allowed myself to explore before. I want male companionship from time to time. Yet I don't want an intense, continuous relationship. That means I have sporadic and spontaneous encounters with men (some sexual, some not)—momentary intimacies. This is a new experience for me, and the newness of it sometimes makes me feel shaky. Most of the time I feel okay.

It helps us feel easier with fluctuation in sexual feelings when we see that while our sexual feelings can go just as they can come, they can also come back again.

I've gotten so angry that I could easier kill him than sleep with him. At first these feelings scared me. Now I know they pass and change and I feel loving again.

There are times in our lives when sex is in the background of a relationship. We go on a business trip for a month, we visit a sick relative and stay awhile, we spend time with a friend.

I'm absorbed right now in figuring out what work I want to do. This is a time of crisis for me, and I need all my energy for myself. I can't relate very intimately to the man I live with. We've been together for several years and I trust this is what is happening right now and will change.

It felt so good to talk to Anne. We've been married about the same time, ten years. I was feeling there was something wrong in my relationship with Steven—we haven't had sex for a month. I was feeling, "What's wrong with us? I need to create some excitement, perhaps go have an affair, do something different to keep the sexual fires burning." She was very reassuring. She said she'd had a similar experience and felt the same way at the time. She said that after that time they began having sex regularly again.

People who have lived together for a long time may feel less energy or urgency for sex.

We have been married for fifteen years. For several years we were passionate lovers, there was a lot of romance in our lives. Now there is less romance and very deep love and friendship. Sex is no longer the most important thing in our lives. We have sex less frequently and yet our lovemaking feels good in different ways than in those early years. We feel very warm, intimate and deeply trusting of each other.

In Bed

Discontinuous we lie
with an old cat asleep
between our backs

where jealous children
used to squirm
wedged in between us.

We grow old, you and I,
to be so equable, lying
back to cat and cat to back.

ALICE RYERSON

For many couples, sex comes to be more meaningful over time:

I didn't marry for love or sexual passion. Sex was something I didn't know much about and neither did my husband. Just in the last two years—after fourteen years of marriage—we've been able to talk to each other about sex. That's mainly because we're not playing games, we're not criticizing and tearing each other apart. We are each more responsible for who we are as individuals. We are not expecting the other to live up to our expectations, to live out prescribed roles. So when we were making love the other night I felt clearest that I was making love as an adult, not a child. We didn't talk at the time—it wasn't necessary. Next morning we both felt the same thing. What I mean by adult is a deep kind of un-crazy passion. When you are in love it's crazy passion—you want to swallow each other up and be swallowed. This, in contrast, is a relaxed openness, anything goes, no hurry, free of guilt. We are more sexually connected than we've ever been in our lives and able just to be with each other.

We look forward to a lifetime of ups and downs and growth and change in how we live our sexuality. We will be fascinated to see how our daughters revise this chapter!

LOVE SONG OF A SPECIES

think of
long tall animals
making love
into themselves
breaking themselves
together
swallowing
each other's air
each other's songs
think of these
animals
not knowing
their species
their strangeness
think of them
trying to tell each other
all day long
with words
think then
of the most
natural
way of
saying
I love you
eyes
mouth
a place
there is a place
that has no thoughts
think of something
of a thing that cannot think
inside a place
that cannot contain thoughts
think of these things together not thinking
think of the most natural way to think of this
then unthink everything that follows from that
then sleep
a sleep
in which all dreams
and these words
are stolen from the dream
you are having

CORA BROOKS

APPENDIX

Sexual Health Care

Sexual health is a physical and emotional state of well-being that allows us to enjoy and act on our sexual feelings. We all need to follow certain procedures of routine care to stay sexually healthy.

A YEARLY GYNECOLOGICAL EXAM (see Chapter 6).   Women need a complete gyn exam each year to make sure we have no physical difficulties that would interfere with our health, including sexual functioning.

CARE OF INFECTIONS (see Chapters 6 and 9).   If you get an infection of the vagina or urinary tract, you need to get it treated immediately. You may have to refrain from intercourse for a while. If you're wanting intercourse, your partner(s) will need to wear a condom each time as long as the infection lasts.

DOUCHING.   Unless you are instructed by a doctor for a particular reason, you never need to douche (wash out the vagina). The vagina has a natural cleansing process. Frequent douching and the use of vaginal deodorants can change the acidic and alkaline balance in the vagina. This change can lead to infections, destroying the vagina's natural protection against infection.

GENITAL CLEANSING.   Rather than douche or use vaginal deodorants, you simply can wash your genital area daily with warm water. Separate the outer lips and pull back the hood of the clitoris to clean away the secretions that collect around the glans. Our body secretions and smells are a natural part of us, and if you are in good health and wash regularly, you smell and taste good. However, some of us like to wash our genitals before sex with another. Do what makes you comfortable.

BIRTH CONTROL (see Chapter 10).   If you do not want to be pregnant and if you are having intercourse, you'll need to discuss with the man involved the use of birth control and who will use the selected method. If you cannot discuss it with him or he won't discuss it with you, perhaps the relationship is not ready for sex. Even if you are not having intercourse, if sperm is deposited anywhere near the vagina (even in the mons area), the sperm can swim into the vagina on vaginal secretions and on up through the cervix to the uterus and fallopian tubes and join with an egg.

ANAL INTERCOURSE (see this chapter, "There's More Than Intercourse").   If you insert anything larger than a finger into your anus, you need to use a lubricant—saliva, a commercial jelly such as K-Y, or vaginal secretions. And be gentle. The anus is a much tighter opening than the vagina. If you wish vaginal intercourse after anal, have him wash his penis to protect you against infection. Some people like to use a rubber for anal intercourse and then take it off before vaginal penetration.

MENSTRUATION.   You can enjoy sex during your menstrual periods if it feels comfortable to you. Some of us have found that masturbating or having sex with a partner relieves menstrual cramps. If you use a diaphragm for birth control, while it is in place it will hold back menstrual blood.

PREGNANCY.   You can be sexually active during pregnancy up to the last few weeks before due date. Some of us feel stronger sexual desire during pregnancy, especially in the second trimester.

In the eighth and ninth months many of us have had to abandon our familiar positions for intercourse since they were no longer comfortable. We've experimented with some new ones. Or, when we haven't wanted intercourse at all, we have used our hands and tongues and vibrators to give each other pleasure (with or without orgasm). (See this chapter, "There's More Than Intercourse"; Chapter 13, "Pregnancy"; and SIE-CUS Guide #6, "Sex in Pregnancy and Postpartum," available from SIECUS, 1855 Broadway, New York, N.Y. 10023.)

Problems with Sex

At one time or another all of us have problems with sex. Read about the causes and treatment for the problem you are having, particularly if it is a severe one. See Helen Kaplan's *The New Sex Therapy*, Chapters 18, 19, 20; and Masters and Johnson's *Human Sexual Inadequacy*, Chapters 8, 9, 10, 11 (both listed in bibliography). Kaplan's book is full of illustrations and information that can be of help to any of us.

Sexual problems in a relationship are relationship problems. In a relationship we contribute to ways of being with each other that are not satisfying. Sexual ignorance is the most frequent cause of sexual problems; poor communication patterns, male and female role expectations, a lack of trust or commitment, or unresolved conflicts between us can also lead to sexual difficulties.

Here are some of the reasons we may have troubles with our sexuality:

We are so concerned with sexual images and goals we cannot think of sex outside the context of success/failure.

We grew up feeling that sex was bad and dirty and deep down we still feel that way.

We fear becoming pregnant.

We are afraid to follow our own feelings—we may not even be sure what they are.

We are ignorant of facts that would help us.

We are too shy and embarrassed to ask for the touching or other sorts of sexual stimulation we would like.

We fear if we ask for something different we will embarrass or threaten our lover, and our lover might leave.

We sleep with someone we are attracted to but do not feel comfortable with.

We always have sex at the end of the day when we are tired.

We make love with someone with whom we are angry.

We have been with one partner for many years and we are stuck in patterns that no longer excite us.

We expect to be instantly free and at ease with people we don't know well or feel very close to.

We don't have any friends with whom we talk about our experiences, feelings and concerns.

We don't have anyone we want to sleep with.

How we think and feel about ourselves and sex powerfully affects how our bodies respond. Guilt, shyness, fear, conflict, ignorance, all can block or inhibit sexual responsiveness. Our problems can take many forms: we have difficulties having orgasms; we show no interest in sex at all (sometimes called *sexual aversion*); we have pain with intercourse (called *dispareunia*); or we have pain with penetration (called *vaginismus*). If any of these is a problem to us, we owe it to ourselves to explore further. We need not be in total agony or the worst on the block to look for help. Sexual problems are common.

Problems with Orgasm

Many of us experience difficulties reaching orgasm—either by ourselves or with a lover. Shame about exploring and touching ourselves keeps us from learning to bring ourselves to orgasm through masturbation. A variety of problems keeps us from having orgasms with another. Here are some of the reasons why:

We don't notice or else we misunderstand what's happening in our bodies as we get aroused. We're too busy thinking about abstractions—how to do it right, why it doesn't go well for us, what our lover thinks of us, whether our lover is impatient, whether our lover can last—when we might better be concentrating on sensations, not thoughts.

We feel ourselves becoming aroused, but we are afraid we won't have an orgasm, and we don't want to get into the hassle of trying, so we just repress sexual response.

We hold our breath the more excited we get and cut off the feeling of our own orgasms.*

We don't know how to coordinate our breathing with the movements of our pelvis.*

We can't tolerate too much pleasure and our orgasms—if we have them—are less satisfying and intense than they could be.*

We are afraid of asking too much and seeming too demanding.

Although we really want to cuddle, we feel we must have intercourse, since he has an erection. We fear it is physically painful for him not to come, although becoming aroused and not having an orgasm is no more uncomfortable for him than for us.

We haven't learned, and often neither has he, that the getting to orgasm is as pleasurable, if not more pleasurable, than orgasm itself.

We find it takes longer for us to get aroused than for him, and we are anxious he'll become impatient for penetration. That anxiety assures our not getting aroused.

We let him enter before we really want him inside us. We rush into it—or let our partners rush us into it. We end up fucking with great intensity—swept off our feet just like in the movies and swept under the rug when it comes to climaxes.

I really love to stroke and kiss and lick Ned! Why can't I trust that he likes to do the same for me, with me, when I know he does? Maybe it's just too good for me to feel it could be true!

We are afraid that if he concentrates on our pleasure we will feel such pressure to come that we won't be able to—and then we don't.

We are trying to have a simultaneous orgasm—which seldom occurs for most of us. It can be just as pleasurable if we come separately.

We are deeply conflicted about, and often angry at, the person we are sleeping with. Unconsciously we withhold orgasm as a way of withholding ourselves.

We feel guilty about having intercourse and so cannot let ourselves really enjoy it.

*For more detail on these points see *Total Orgasm*, by Jack Rosenberg, and also *For Yourself*, by Lonnie Barbach (both listed in bibliography).

I like to do anything that pleases Mick—and yet—sometimes I feel like a prostitute when I am absorbed in exciting him. Sometimes this excites me and sometimes I feel tremendous power over him, and sometimes I feel a kind of disgust that gets in my way of enjoying sex at all.

We don't want to make love in the first place.

Lack of Interest in Sex—Sexual Aversion
Sometimes we find that we have no interest in sex at a particular time.

Sometimes we seem to compete for who can be the most passive. Not just about initiating sex, but about who will make love to whom. If we have to argue about who is going to do what to whom, then I feel like, who needs it?

We can ignore our sexual feelings because we are absorbed in something else, because we are overtired, or because we are angry. We can block our sexual feelings out of anxiety and fear. For a few of us the conflicts about ourselves and sex are so deep we never have any interest in sex. We may even feel an extreme, unpleasant sensitivity to touch, or may feel so ticklish that we can't relax. Our bodies react this way for a reason, and it protects us from sexual experiences we can't handle at the time. This lack of interest in sex gives us a chance to figure out what is bothering us.

Painful Intercourse—Dispareunia
You may experience discomfort, even pain, with intercourse for physical rather than emotional reasons:

LOCAL INFECTION. Some vaginal infections—monilia or trichomonas, for example—can be present in a non-acute, visually unnoticeable form. The friction of a penis moving in the vagina might cause the infection to flare up, making us sting and itch. A doctor can give us medicine to clear it up. (See Chapter 6, for more details.)

LOCAL IRRITATION. The vagina might be irritated by the birth-control foam, cream, or jelly we are using. If so, try a different brand. Some of us react to the rubber in a condom or diaphragm. Many of the vaginal deodorant sprays can irritate the lips of the vagina; if sprayed inside, they can irritate the inside too. If you've been using one of these and intercourse makes you itch, don't switch brands, just stop using deodorant.

INSUFFICIENT LUBRICATION. The wall of the vagina responds to sexy feelings by "sweating," giving off a liquid that wets the vagina and the entrance to it, which makes the entry of the penis easier. Sometimes there isn't enough of this liquid. Some reasons: a) you may be trying to let the penis in (or the man might be putting/forcing it in) too soon, before there has been enough foreplay to excite you and set the sweating action going; b) you may be nervous or tense about making love (e.g., it's the first time, or you're worried about getting pregnant), so there isn't enough liquid; c) if the guy is using a rubber (condom) you may need to add lubrication. Be sure to give the vagina time to get wet. If you still feel dry you can use saliva, lubricating jelly (e.g., K-Y), or a birth-control foam, cream or jelly. (Never use Vaseline to lubricate a condom or diaphragm. It will deteriorate the rubber.) Occasionally, insufficient lubri-

cation is caused by a hormone deficiency. After childbirth (particularly if you are nursing your baby or if your stitches hurt) and after menopause are the two times when a lack of estrogen can affect the vaginal walls in such a way that less liquid is produced. A doctor can give you vaginal suppositories or some kind of hormone therapy. Meanwhile try the lubricants suggested above.

TIGHTNESS IN THE VAGINAL ENTRANCE. The first few times we have intercourse, an unstretched hymen (if we have one) can cause pain. Anyway for a penis to get in easily, our vagina and its entrance have to be relaxed as well as wet. If we are tense and preoccupied the vaginal entrance is not likely to loosen up, and getting the penis in might hurt. Even if we feel relaxed and sexy, timing is important. The vagina gets wet well before the clitoris, vaginal lips and the outer third of the vagina are fully sensitized and ready for orgasm. If we try to get the penis in before we are fully aroused, we might still be too tight though we are wet enough. So don't rush, and don't let yourself be rushed.

PAIN DEEP IN THE PELVIS. Sometimes the thrust of the man's penis hurts way inside. Masters and Johnson say this pain can be caused by: a) tears in the ligaments that support the uterus (caused by obstetrical mismanagement during childbirth, a botched-up abortion, gang rape); b) infections of the cervix, uterus and tubes (such as pelvic inflammatory disease—the end result of untreated gonorrhea in many women); c) endometriosis (see "Common Medical and Health Problems," in Chapter 6); d) cysts or tumors on the ovaries. These can all be treated successfully. Also, if the penis hits the cervix we feel pain. That pain can be relieved by having the man not go in so deeply or by being more fully aroused (which moves the cervix away) before penetration.

CLITORAL PAIN. The clitoris is exquisitely sensitive, and for most of us direct touching or rubbing of the clitoris is painful (many men don't know this until we tell them). Also, genital secretions can collect under the hood, so when we wash we need to pull back the hood of our clitoris and clean it gently.

Painful Penetration—Vaginismus
For a few of us, intercourse is painful and sometimes impossible. While there are physical reasons why we experience this pain (see "Tightness in the Vaginal Entrance," above) we most often experience vaginismus because of strong conflicts and fears about sex, which we express, often unconsciously, by making it difficult for us to have or enjoy intercourse.

If you have vaginismus you experience a strong, involuntary tightening of your vaginal muscles, a spasm of the outer third of your vagina, which makes entrance by the penis acutely painful.

Vaginismus can be your body's defense against a sexual situation you can't handle or don't want to be in. It can also be the result of bad experiences, such as rape. If you think you are suffering from vaginismus, read about it in *The New Sex Therapy*. There is a physical treatment for vaginismus which you can learn to do. For some of us, good psychotherapy can also help change unhappy sexual patterns.

Whatever the cause, if intercourse is at all painful, don't put up with the pain! Find out what is causing it and do something about it. Until the problem is solved, figure out other ways to make love. The power that each of us has, and the power that we have together, to make our lives more satisfying is enormous.

Helping Ourselves

If you are feeling pain in your pelvic, genital, or vaginal area, get a good gynecological exam to find out if there is a physical cause. Unfortunately, many gynecologists overlook all but the most obvious physical problems and say, "It's all in your head, dear." Beyond that, they have not been trained to discuss sexual problems with us. Enlist the help of a local women's group to find a sympathetic and competent doctor.

Despite our knowledge about sex, despite the support of friends and partners, sometimes we cannot work through our difficulties. Counselors are being trained all over the country who can help us with our sexual problems. If you need someone to talk with, call your local women's health center or free clinic, or write the American Association of Sex Educators and Counselors (AASEC, 5010 Wisconsin Ave. NW, Suite 304, Washington, D.C. 20016) for the name of a recommended counselor or therapist in your area. Since there are men and women without adequate training, who call themselves sex therapists, we believe that writing AASEC is better than consulting your yellow pages or, often, your physician.

When there are sexual problems in a couple relationship it is often the woman who seeks help first. This may be because culturally it is easier for us to admit to our sexual concerns. It may also be because we too often assume that if sex is a problem, it's we who are in need of help. Sexual problems reflect or express relationship problems. While each of us may want to work on our part of the problem, both partners need help for a relationship to grow.

You may have a difficult time finding a good doctor or therapist. Those of us who are single or in homosexual relationships have even fewer resources than heterosexual couples. You may need to concentrate on working with friends or your partner or both, after reading the available books. When we have found talented sex therapists or counselors, we have gotten reassurance and help.

A Word About Men

If we are having sex with a man and he's having sexual difficulties, it is hard to share the kind of pleasure both partners would like. Further, his difficulties may complicate our own problems—even create some for us. (For example, if our partner ejaculates prematurely, we will probably not have an orgasm. It is difficult for us to climax with stimulation from penetration alone if he lasts just a few minutes once inside the vagina.) We need to give him the kind of patience and encouragement we want from him if the two of us are to overcome anxieties and establish a satisfying sexual relationship.

Men can suffer problems similar to ours, and for many of the same reasons. The common male sexual problems are: 1) premature ejaculation—the inability to control the ejaculatory reflex; 2) impotence—the inability to maintain, or even be aroused to, an erection; 3) dispareunia—pain with intercourse; and 4) sexual aversion—lack of interest in sex altogether.

Some sexual problems can be worked through with a little knowledge and a caring partner, while others might call for professional help.

There are relatively few men's groups, because men find it more threatening than we do to share sexual anxieties and problems directly. Men we know feel isolated with their concerns. We want to offer our support to them, when we can, around issues that are vital to us all. Books such as *Men and Masculinity*, edited by Joseph H. Pleck and Jack Sawyer (see bibliography), are beginning to pave the way for men to understand themselves.

Sex Discussion Group for Women: Learning Together About Sex

Some of us in women's groups have decided to talk about sex every week for a month or two. Some of us form groups for the express purpose of talking about sex.

In a group, we can discuss factual information; explore our feelings; talk out problems; practice communicating (verbally and nonverbally); get help deciding how, when and with whom to share sexual feelings; and learn alternative ways to get what we want sexually.

Here are some suggestions for organizing a women's sex discussion group:

Either suggest to a group of your friends that you meet weekly for some weeks to talk about sex or propose to your woman's group that you focus on sexuality for some weeks.

Meet together and explore what you are wanting to discuss with each other. Draw up a list of topics and a flexible plan for discussions. Select some members of the group to find out more about local resources you might want to use—films you could see or persons who might want to meet with you and share their specialized knowledge (a woman gynecologist or a Planned Parenthood birth control counselor). Choose other members to consider what materials besides this chapter you might like to read together.

Topics you may want to discuss include: childhood and adolescent memories of sexuality; your feelings about your body; differences in female and male socialization; masturbation; fantasies; the nature of female sexual response; virginity; homosexuality; lovemaking; intercourse; orgasm; feelings about touching and looking at your genitals; sexual health care; birth control; abortion; sexual problems; relationships with yourself, women and men; the sexuality of your children.

This woman's journey through her own sexuality is a stimulating way to begin your discussions. Before your second or third meeting, two of you get together and draw up a list of questions beginning with first memories of sensual pleasure and affection (e.g., "What kind of touching did you get as a child from your parents? How did you feel?"). You will want to include questions about sexual language, your parents' relationship to each other and with you, sex play with siblings and friends (e.g., playing doctor), first menstrual period, dating, petting, intercourse, orgasm, crushes on girl friends, marriage, sexuality as an adult, etc. When you all meet together again, the two of you take the rest of the group on the "journey." Ask each woman to find a comfortable spot and close her eyes. The two of you alternate reading your questions very slowly, giving women time to remember. Leave a minute or two between questions. When the questions are finished leave some more space before joining together to discuss your memories and reactions to them.

Consider activities you think would enrich your talking together. You might: keep personal journals throughout the weeks you meet and share from them at a final meeting; make a collage of sex cartoons at the beginning of one week's meeting; see a porno flick or visit a bookstore that sells pornography; make a group list of all the street and slang terms you know for sex.

Toward the end of your time together you may want to include your men friends and lovers for some hours. You can share with them what you've learned and what you want them to know. You can begin to discuss sex and sexuality together.

FURTHER READINGS

Historical Books on Women and Sexuality

De Beauvoir, Simone. *The Second Sex*. New York: Bantam Books, 1961 (paper).
> This is a classic book about us. Originally published in France in 1949 and in America in 1953, it predates the current women's movement, and was the first book many of us read that made us aware we were oppressed as females.

Freud, Sigmund. *Three Essays on the Theory of Sexuality*. Translated by James Strachey. New York: Basic Books, 1962 (paper).
> No bibliography on sexuality would be complete without an annotation on Freud. This book outlines his basic theories on female sexuality, part of a larger psychoanalytic view that holds we are not whole human beings because we lack a penis. Nonsense, we say! By the end of his life Freud recognized he didn't know everything about women and that more scientific studies were needed. However, many therapists who followed him have held rigidly to his doctrines.

Friedan, Betty. *The Feminine Mystique*. New York: Dell, 1963 (paper).
> One of the popular books about our condition as women in America. Gave impetus to the women's movement in the sixties, and to us. Recommended highly.

Herschberger, Ruth. *Adam's Rib*. New York: Harper & Row, 1970 (paper).
> First published in 1948, before the first Kinsey et al study. Filled with sexual theories, analyses and general discussion of women's oppression, *Adam's Rib* was unread history until discovered by the women's movement in the sixties. For example, she recognized the importance of our clitoris in our sexuality.

Kinsey, Alfred C., Wardell B. Pomeroy, Clyde E. Martin, and Paul A. Gebhard. *Sexual Behavior in the Human Female*. Philadelphia: W. B. Saunders, 1953 (also paper).
———. *Sexual Behavior in the Human Male*. Philadelphia: W. B. Saunders, 1949 (also paper).
> Long studies of human sexual behavior that give lots of information and many experiences, of women in the first book and men in the second. They are historical books because they opened a new era of sex research. Masters and Johnson follow them.

Reich, Wilhelm. *The Function of the Orgasm*. New York: Noonday Press, 1961 (paper).
———. *The Sexual Revolution*. New York: Noonday Press, 1963 (paper).
> Very important and original works on human sexuality. He did pioneering research on sexuality before Kinsey and Masters and Johnson. See *Journal of Orgonomy* for more details.

Sexual Histories

Brecher, Edward. *The Sex Researchers*. New York: Signet Books, 1969 (paper).
> Lively history of discoveries in the field of sex, with information about the women and men who made them. Enjoyable to read.

Ditzion, Sidney. *Marriage, Morals, and Sex in America: A History of Ideas*. New York: Bookman Associates, 1953.
> Fascinating overview of ideas that have influenced our views of marriage and sexual relationships.

Lewinsohn, Richard. *A History of Sexual Customs*. New York: Harper & Row, 1971 (paper).
> The title describes the book. It's full of interesting information. Lewinsohn is sensitive to women as he writes the history. You can see the development of our oppression over time.

Theories of Sexual Development and Psychology Books

Freud, Sigmund. *Beyond the Pleasure Principle*. Trans. by James Strachey. New York: Liveright, 1970.
———. *The Sexual Enlightenment of Children*. New York: Macmillan, 1963.
———. *Sexuality and the Psychology of Love*. New York: Macmillan, 1963.
Harding, M. Esther, M.D. *Women's Mysteries*. New York: Bantam Books.
———. *The Way of All Women*. New York: G. P. Putnam's Sons, 1970.
Horney, Karen. *Feminine Psychology*. New York: W. W. Norton, 1967.
Jung, Carl. *The Portable Jung*. Joseph Campbell, ed. New York: The Viking Press, 1971.
Mead, Margaret. *Male and Female*. New York: Dell, 1968.
Miller, Jean Baker, M.D., ed. *Psychoanalysis and Women*. Baltimore, Md.: Penguin, 1973.
———. *Toward a New Psychology of Women*. Boston: Beacon Press, 1976.
Mitchell, Juliet. *Psychoanalysis and Feminism*. New York: Pantheon, 1974.
Montagu, Ashley. *Touching: The Human Significance of Skin*. New York: Harper & Row, 1972 (paper).
Rogers, Carl, and Barry Stevens. *Person to Person*. New York: Pocket Books, 1971.
Sherfey, Mary Jane, M.D. *The Nature and Evolution of Female Sexuality*. New York: Vintage Books.

Specific Information About Sex and Sexuality

Bach, George, M.D., and Peter Wyden. *The Intimate Enemy: How to Fight Fair in Love and Marriage*. New York: Avon Books, 1968.
Barbach, L. G. *For Yourself—The Fulfillment of Female Sexuality*. New York: Doubleday, 1975.
> Written for the "pre-orgasmic" woman; this guide to female sexuality is excellent reading for us all.

Bell, Alan P., and Martin S. Weinberg. *Homosexualities: A Study of Diversity Among Men and Women*. New York: Simon and Schuster, 1978.
Blank, Joani, and Honey Lee Cottrell. *I Am My Lover*. Down There Press, P.O. Box 2086, Burlingame, CA 94010, $4.50, 1978.
Chartham, Robert. *Sex and the Over-Fifties*. Brandon Books, Inc., 1969.
> From SIECUS: "A very practical, descriptive and graphic book for persons over fifty who wish to maintain a good sex life in their later years."

Comfort, Alex, M.D. *The Joy of Sex: A Gourmet Guide to Lovemaking*. New York: Simon and Schuster (paper).
> If you don't get offended by the cookbook style of this book, it gives encouragement and helpful suggestions for variety in your sex life.

———. *More Joy: A Lovemaking Companion to The Joy of Sex*. New York: Simon and Schuster, 1975 (paper).

Deutsch, Ronald M. *The Key to Feminine Response in Marriage*. New York: Random House, 1968.

> Popularized account of how we can have better orgasms by strengthening our pelvic floor muscles. A how-to book. The last third of the book explores some reasons why women have trouble enjoying lovemaking.

Dodson, Betty. *Liberating Masturbation: A Meditation on Self Love*. Published and distributed by Bodysex Designs, P.O. Box 1933, New York, N.Y. 10001 ($4.00). 1974.

> The title is very descriptive. This book offers suggestions and encouragement for masturbation. Highly recommended.

Friday, Nancy. *My Secret Garden: Women's Sexual Fantasies*. New York: Pocket Books, 1974.

> Finally a book of women's fantasies. It has stimulated many of us to pay attention to our own.

Hegeler, Inge and Sten. *An ABZ of Love*. New York: New American Library-Signet Books.

> A superb book about sex. Written as a dictionary of sex terms by a doctor and a psychologist who have a very open, honest, human view of sexuality and respect for women. Can be used as a marriage manual on feelings, not techniques—it's natural and normal to want to know more about sex and explore your own sexuality.

Hite, Shere, *The Hite Report*. New York: Dell, 1976.

> A nationwide survey involving over 3,000 women which challenges some of the current stereotypes about female sexuality.

Masters, William, and Virginia Johnson, with Robert Levin. *The Pleasure Bond*. Boston: Little, Brown & Co., 1974.

> Emphasizes the emotional elements that enrich the act of sex and create the bond of pleasure that is the source of personal commitment. Not well written but worth the effort.

McCary, James L. *Sexual Myths and Fallacies*. New York: Van Nostrand Rheinhold Co., 1971 (paper).

> A fun-to-read collection of popular myths—followed by the "facts."

Pietropinto, Anthony, and Jacqueline Simenauer. *Beyond the Male Myth (What Women Want to Know About Men's Sexuality)*. New York: Signet, 1977. Survey of 4066 men.

Rosenberg, Jack Lee. *Total Orgasm*. New York: Random House, and Berkeley, California: Bookworks, 1973 (paper).

> Discusses why people have trouble fully enjoying sex and suggests exercises (with illustrations) to do alone and then with a partner to help us have greater sexual pleasure. Highly recommended.

Ruben, Isadore, Ph.D. *Sexual Life After Sixty*. New York: New American Library-Signet Books ($.95) 1965.

> From SIECUS: "One of the few books available which deals with sexual needs, problems and attitudes of older men and women. Emphasizes the need to help the aging deal with these problems which prevent them from finding acceptable expressions of their sexuality."

Rush, Anne Kent. *Getting Clear: Body Work for Women*. New York: Random House, and Berkeley, California: Bookworks, 1973 (paper).

> Like *Total Orgasm*, this is a workbook filled with exercises, experiences, etc., for us to get in better touch with our bodies and ourselves. Written by a sensitive woman who has had experience as a therapist with other women. Fun to use—highly recommended.

Shanor, Karen. *The Fantasy Files: A Study of the Sexual Fantasies of Contemporary Women*. New York: Dell, 1977.

Silverstein, Judith, Ph.D. *Sexual Enhancement for Women*. Jay Publishing Co., P.O. Box 142, Arlington, MA 02174 ($8.95), 1978.

Smith, Carolyn, Toni Ayres, and Maggie Rubenstein. *Getting in Touch: Self-sexuality for Women*. San Francisco: Multi-Media Resource Center, 1972.

Shulman, A. K. "Organs and Orgasms," in Gornick and Moran, eds., *Woman in Sexist Society*. New York: Basic Books, 1972.

> Excellent short essay on female sexuality.

Teeters, Kass. *Women's Sexuality: Myth and Reality*. Women, Inc., Box 32236, San Jose, CA 95132, 1977.

Sex Research

Masters, William H., and Virginia E. Johnson. *Human Sexual Response*. Boston: Little, Brown & Co., 1966.

> A revolutionary book—now sex is a legitimate topic for scientific inquiry. Masters and Johnson's research began to destroy many myths that have kept us down sexually. Important and hard to read.

————. *Human Sexual Inadequacy*. Boston: Little, Brown & Co., 1970.

> Major research on the nature of sexual dysfunction and its treatment. Again, important and hard to read.

Sex Therapy

Belleveau, Fred, and Lin Richter. *Understanding Human Sexual Inadequacy*. New York: Bantam Books, 1970 (paper).

> Shortened and more readable version of the second Masters and Johnson study, without all the clinical details. Can be used as a handbook for those who can't get to a sex counselor and need some help.

Brecher, Ruth and Edward, eds. *An Analysis of Human Sexual Response*. New York: Signet Books, 1966 (paper).

> This is a very readable analysis of the first Masters and Johnson study. Contains sections on other sex research, practical applications of sex research, and sex research and our culture. Wide range of articles and many bibliographical references.

Kaplan, Helen S. *The New Sex Therapy*. New York: Brunner-Mazel (Quadrangle-New York Times Book Co.), 1973.

> Excellent and highly readable discussion of male and female sexual dysfunctions and their treatment. Pictures are particularly fine.

————. *The Illustrated Manual of Sex Therapy*. New York: Quadrangle/The New York Times Book Co., 1975.

Texts

Katchadourian, Heront, and Donald Lunde. *Fundamentals of Human Sexuality*. New York: Holt, Rinehart & Winston, 1972.

> Very fine general textbook on human sexuality as a biological, behavioral and cultural phenomenon.

McCory, James. *Human Sexuality* (second edit., revised). New York: Van Nostrand Rheinhold Co., 1973 (paper—*Human Sexuality: A Brief Edition*).

> Highly readable general discussion of human sexuality.

Books for Children, Teens and Parents

This section is excerpted in part from SIECUS Report (January, 1974), Human Sexuality: Books for Everyone (SIECUS is Sex Information and Education Council of the U.S., 1855 Broadway, New York, N.Y. 10023). Additional material is available from the Multi-Media Resource Center—see listing later in bibliography.

Young Children (4-9)

Ets, Marie. *The Story of a Baby* (revised edition). New York: The Viking Press, 1969.

Fleischhauer, Dr. Helga (text), and Will McBride (photos and captions). *Show Me: A Picture Book of Sex for Children and Parents*. New York: St. Martin's Press, 1975.

Gruenberg, Sidonie Metsner. *The Wonderful Story of How You Were Born* (revised edition). New York: Doubleday & Co., 1970.

Levine, Milton I., and Jean H. Selegman. *A Baby is Born* (revised edition). New York: Golden Press, 1962 (paper).

Mayle, Peter. *Where Did I Come From?* Secaucus, N.J.: Lyle Stuart, Inc., 1973.

Pre-Teens (10-14)

Gordon, Sol. *Let's Make Sex a Household Word: A Guide for Parents and Children.* New York: Johnsay Co., 1975.

Mayle, Peter, *What's Happening to Me?* Secaucus, N.J.: Lyle Stuart, Inc., 1975.

Later Teens (15-18)

Fiore, Evelyn, with Richard S. Ward, M.D. *Sex Facts for Teenagers.* New York: Ace Books, 1971.

Hamilton, Eleanor. *Sex Before Marriage.* Des Moines, Iowa: Meredith Press, 1969.

Lieberman, E. James, M.D., and Ellen Peck. *Sex, Love and Birth Control: A Guide for the Young.* New York: Thomas Y. Crowell Co., 1973.

Mazur, Ronald M. *Commonsense Sex.* Boston: Beacon Press, 1968.

Parents (any age)

Brown, Rev. Thomas E. *Concerns of Parents About Sex Education.* SIECUS, 1971.

Gordon, Sol. *The Sexual Adolescent.* N. Scituate, Mass.: Duxbury Press, 1974.

    For the parent or professional helping teens.

LeShan, Eda. *Sex and Your Teenager.* New York: David McKay Co., Inc., 1969.

Pomeroy, Wardell B. *Young Child and Sex: A Guide for Parents.* New York: Delacorte Press, 1974.

Ruben, Isadore, and Lester Kirkendall, eds. *Sex in the Adolescent Years: New Directions in Guiding and Teaching Youth.* New York: Association Press, 1968.

———. *Sex in the Childhood Years.* New York: Association Press, 1970.

Other Recommended Books

Bengis, Ingrid. *Combat in the Erogenous Zone.* New York: Bantam Books.

Cade, Toni. *Black Women.* New York: Signet Books, 1970.

Chesler, Phyllis. *Women and Madness:* New York: Avon Books, 1972.

Firestone, Shulamith. *The Dialectic of Sex: The Case for Feminist Revolution.* New York: Bantam Books, 1971 (paper).

Greer, Germaine. *The Female Eunuch.* New York: McGraw-Hill, 1970.

Jong, Erica. *Fear of Flying.* New York: New American Library–Signet Books, 1973.

Millett, Kate. *Sexual Politics.* New York: Doubleday & Co., 1970; and Avon (paper).

Morgan, Robin, ed. *Sisterhood is Powerful: An Anthology of Writings from the Women's Liberation Movement.* New York: Vintage Books, 1970 (paper).

Pleck, Joseph, and Jack Sawyer, eds. *Men and Masculinity.* Englewood Cliffs, N.J.: Spectrum, 1974.

Seaman, Barbara. *Free and Female.* New York: Fawcett, 1973.

Solonas, Valerie. *S.C.U.M. Manifesto.* New York: Olympia Press, 1968.

    Strong treatise on female superiority.

Pamphlets and Journals

Much current material is published in this form and in women's newspapers. Here are some pamphlets or journals we used or are aware of.

There are more sources in your own area. See also bibliographies of Chapters 4 and 5.

Allen, Pamela. *Free Space: The Small Group in Women's Liberation.* Times Change Press, c/o Monthly Review Press, 62 West 14th St., New York, N.Y. 10011.

Unbecoming Men: A Men's Consciousness-Raising Group Writes on Oppression and Themselves. Times Change Press, c/o Monthly Review Press, 62 West 14th Street, New York, N.Y. 10011.

Aphra, Box 893, Ansonia Station, New York, N.Y. 10023 ($4.50/4 issues).

The Second Wave, Box 344A, Cambridge, Mass. 02139 ($3.00/4 issues; $.75 plus postage, single issue).

Women: A Journal of Liberation, 3028 Greenmount Avenue, Baltimore, Md. ($5.00/4 issues).

The Female State: We Choose Personhood—A Journal of Female Liberation. No. 4 (April, 1970).

No More Fun and Games—A Journal of Female Liberation. One of the first women's journals. Put out by a Boston group. No. 1 (Spring, 1967), No. 2 (February, 1969); No. 3 (Fall, 1969).

Notes From The First Year (1968). The first feminist journal, put out by a group of women in New York City who were part of the new Women's Liberation Movement. It and *Notes From The Second Year* (1970) contain original source material on, for example, consciousness-raising, the myth of vaginal orgasm, etc. Eds. Shulamith Firestone and Anne Koedt. These valuable resources are out of print, but see *Voices from Women's Liberation*, Leslie B. Tanner, ed., New York: Signet Books, 1971, for some of this material.

Films and Other Resources

Unitarian-Universalist Association puts out two programs on sexuality: 1) *About Your Sexuality*, for junior high and up; includes records, filmstrips, books, etc. 2) *The Invisible Minority: The Homosexuals in Our Society*, also with a variety of materials. Write UUA, Department of Education, Social Concerns, 25 Beacon Street, Boston, Mass. 02108.

The Multi-Media Resource Center is a valuable source for sex-education and sex-therapy films and materials. Send for their annotated bibliography on human sexuality (review of 300 comics, pamphlets, books). Film list comes separately. Write 1525 Franklin St., San Francisco, Calif. 94108.

The Williams and Wilkins Co., 428 East Preston Street, Baltimore, Md. 21202, produces an audiovisual program on human sexuality. Distribution limited to professionals and health-related facilities such as schools, hospitals. Expensive but can be previewed for reasonable fee ($25.00). Contact Mr. Stanley Langsom or Ms. Trudy McCarra, Audiovisual Sales Dept.

For researchers in the field of human sexuality, we refer you to the Information Service, Institute for Sex Research, 416 Morrison Hall, Indiana University, Bloomington, Ind. 47401.

Institute for Family Research and Education, 760 Ostrom Avenue, Syracuse, N.Y. 13210. Send for literature list, especially *Impact*, the journal of National Family Sex Education Week, October 1978. (Send $1.00 for postage and handling.)

CHAPTER 4
LIVING WITH OURSELVES AND OTHERS— OUR SEXUAL RELATIONSHIPS

We experience many different kinds of relationships in our lives—with parents, children, family, friends, people we work with. In this chapter we have chosen to focus on those relationships which are primarily shaped by our sexual feelings. Most of us grow up in families, and it is while we are still living at home that we experience some form of sexual awakening and the beginning of sexual activity with others. Later many of us go on to some other type of living situation, which we may or may not feel is permanent—living away from home, at school, alone, with roommates or in some other group situation. Being on our own, we have more freedom to experiment with various kinds of relationships and ways of living with others. At some point later on, most of us feel that we want to make a long-term commitment to some one person or group of people, and perhaps to a particular life-style.

Our sexual relationships with others in our teen years can be exciting, scary, confusing, embarrassing, funny, fumbly, miserable and wonderful. They also have a lot to do with how we experience our sexual feelings later on. Because of this connection we would like to begin the chapter by talking about some of our early sexual feelings and involvements. The second half of the chapter will move on to the experiences of women in a variety of relationships and life-styles.

FEELINGS ABOUT BECOMING SEXUALLY MATURE AND SEXUALLY ACTIVE

Whether we remember our childhoods as sexual or not (see "Growing Up," in Chapter 3), most of us date the beginnings of our mature sexual lives from our teen years, when physically, hormonally and emotionally we begin the transition to womanhood. Many of us found that it took time for our self-image to catch up with the dramatic changes taking place in our bodies. How we appeared to others and what others expected of us were often very different from how we felt inside. It was often hard to conceive of ourselves as sexual people and potential sexual partners.

At age twelve I was among the first of my friends to begin to menstruate and to wear a bra. I felt a mixture of pride and embarrassment. For all of my life I had been a chubby, introspective child, but a growth spurt of a few inches, along with my developing breasts, transformed me one summer into a surprisingly slim and shapely child-woman. The funny thing was that on one level I had always known this would happen. Yet it was as if a fairy godmother had visited me. I felt turned on, but I was mostly turned on to myself and the narcissistic pleasure of finding I was attractive to boys.

Within a year or so, when we began to have mixed parties, we often played kissing games with no parents present. I didn't really like kissing whoever the bottle spun to or, later, necking with whoever took me out on a date. My parents viewed all sexual expression, even kissing, as signifying pretty strong attachment. Yet at the same time they agreed with me that dating and being popular were very important.

Most of us were expected, quite arbitrarily, at some point in childhood to stop playing with boys and have our friendships exclusively with girls. Then at some point in our teens many of us felt expected magically to feel comfortable with boys, to begin developing relationships with them, and somehow to transfer the close attachments we may have formed with our girl friends to members of the opposite sex.

This is the kind of question that kept coming up for us: Do we feel comfortable with boys right away? Will we "make it" in this new world of boy-girl relationships? Do we want to? Some of us feel confused by our strong feelings for our girl friends.

Here is a friendship that suffered because exaggerated fears about homosexuality had been so well taught:

When I was a junior and senior in high school I had an intense friendship with Jan, a girl in my school. We wrote notes and went on walks and climbed trees, sharing dreams, reciting poems that we liked, and talking about coming back to the school in later years to teach together. We vowed lifelong love and friendship, but physically we could express the energy that was between us only by clowning around, bumping into each other—and once when she was asleep I kissed her hair. The intensity of my friendship with Jan made my family uneasy—I remember comments about seeing too much of one person. Their uneasiness got to me a little, because I was a bit uncomfortable with my strong pit-of-the-stomach feelings about her anyway. I remember being shy about undressing with her in the room, although I undressed with other friends without thinking about it. Then during the summer after we graduated, having not seen Jan for several weeks, I was leafing through a psychology book and found a section that talked about the intense, bordering-on-homosexual friendships of young girls.

Before long I had labeled it as a silly, childishly intense friendship. I made no efforts to see her when we both went to college, for I figured we had nothing in common.

I think our feelings grew more intense as we tried to repress their sexual side. So I pulled away from Jan because I couldn't handle the natural sexual part of my feelings of affection for her.

One of the things we have learned through the women's movement is that our feelings for our women friends include sexual feelings. This makes us look back on some of our teenage friendships with more understanding. It is important to us to realize that there is a difference between having sexual feelings and acting on them, and a difference between having some homosexual experiences and choosing to live as a lesbian. Over our lifetime we have the freedom to choose among a variety of sexual experiences and relationships that meet our needs at different times.

As teenagers, few of us can determine our own lifestyle. We may find ourselves in a school or community where our sexual energy is frustrated by a hypocritical double standard of girl-boy sexual behavior and the feeling that if we want to experiment sexually we have to convince ourselves that we are in love.

When I was a teenager I lived in a small town where the good girl/bad girl idea was totally accepted. Everyone knew exactly what everyone else was doing sexually, so there was no trust or privacy to experiment sexually with someone you liked and to learn about your body and your sexuality that way, let alone to develop any kind of intimacy. I always resented my parents' moving to the suburbs just when I was of an age to enjoy the diversity and anonymity of the city. I was so envious of one girl who had the courage to stay overnight with her boyfriend at a motel. Of course, she was generally regarded as a slut. I really enjoyed what little sex play was considered permissible for a "good girl," but was quite dismayed once when I overheard a boy tell some other boys that I was a "hot one," and you could get away with murder with me.

In high school there was a very clear difference to me between guys I could trust and guys I couldn't trust. If I felt their loyalty to their boyfriends was greater than to me, then I wouldn't be interested at all, because I knew they would blab to everyone. But there were three guys who were really crazy about me. And I convinced myself each time that we were in love. We talked romance and marriage while we experimented with heavy petting. With each one of them, I sort of seduced them, but pretended that it was the first time I had ever done these things and wasn't it great and terrific. One boy was really beautiful. He looked like a movie star. He introduced me to cunnilingus, which he said his brother-in-law told him would drive women wild. I said, "No wonder." The funny thing is, he would never let me touch his penis. He felt that was dirty. All of these boys defined me as the kind of girl they would marry. So they never talked about me even after we broke up. I never shared any of these experiences with my girl friends, either, because I felt they were private. I never had sexual intercourse until I was in college at age twenty, but I had a lot of very pleasurable and valuable sexual experience while still in high school.

As birth control becomes more accessible and society appears to be more accepting of sexuality, we often feel pressure to pretend to be more experienced than we really are. We may feel pressure to have intercourse whether or not we really want to. Yet it is so important that we have the chance to move into our sexual experience gradually, to give ourselves time to explore and become familiar with our own responses and those of our partner(s). (See "Female Sexual Response," "There's More Than Intercourse" and "Sex with Intercourse," in Chapter 3.) It takes most of us years to learn to talk honestly with our partner(s) about what we want and don't want.

The first time I had intercourse, I didn't want him to know I was a virgin. I was seventeen and he was eighteen, but I knew he was more experienced because I knew several girls that he had slept with. I touched his penis because I knew that was the thing to do. Of course I pretended to have an orgasm. I was so busy trying to act sophisticated that I really couldn't pay attention to what I was experiencing.

SOME LIFE-STYLE OPTIONS FOR WOMEN: OUR EXPERIENCES

In this section we present the experiences of a lot of different women. These experiences are not meant to be models. We hope that no woman reading this chapter will feel that these are goals she has to get to someday. We want to share our confusions and regrets as well as the joy and growth we've experienced, so that every woman can be more aware of what her own choices are. Instead of systematically separating the different options for discussion one by one, we have chosen to use poetry, narratives and conversations from the lives of several of us who have passed in and out of one or a number of these options on our way to finding what's best for us.

We have found for ourselves that broadening the scope of our close relationships has been very difficult and has taken a lot of time and energy. The support of other women has allowed us the space to grow in many directions.

The Experience of Being Single

Many Voices: Excerpts from Taped Conversations Among a Group of Single Women in Boston

It is an old belief that heterosexual couples are the only natural and necessary form of existence. Think of Noah's ark. Everything leads up to finding a mate—for love, for intimacy, for economic security, for survival of self, and for the survival of the species. Any other form of adult life is an exception to be pitied (old maid, widow), maligned (homosexual), or possibly tolerated (playboy bachelor, eccentric artist).

We all grew up with these assumptions. People outside our families were defined as "outsiders." We ex-

pected to be inside a couple and inside our own families when we grew up. We might be single women and do exciting things for a while, but that would be just a breathing space before marriage.

It didn't work out that way for us. We are a group of single women in our twenties. We have all had relationships with men that have been important to us, but none of us has ever been married. For the past few years we have all been deeply, personally involved in the women's liberation movement, and our lives have changed drastically. All of us have varying degrees of intimacy with people now, primarily with women. None of us has a primary relationship that defines who we are. Together we are trying to explore our independence and find positive identities for ourselves—not in isolation from other people, but outside of relationships that feel limiting or defining.

We have different fantasies for the future. Some of us want more intimate relationships. But in our lives outside of couples we've felt a lot of strength and joy—alone and as part of a group. What we've learned from being single is much more than the skills of survival in a "transitional" state. And we look forward to new options for women in the future. Here are some of our experiences and thoughts.

ELAINE. As a child I was often told it was impossible for a woman to take care of herself alone in the world, that she needed a man to manage things for her. No one took a woman seriously. I knew a repairman would come immediately if my father called, but it would take my mother many phone calls before he'd finally come around.

JUDITH. I was brought up with the idea that not getting married was the worst thing that could happen to you. If you didn't get married, your life was doomed to loneliness.

My mother had one single friend named Janice. She was the only adult I called by her first name. I remember my mother always trying to fix Janice up with the few eligible men around. There was always the problem of how to include Janice in social situations where there were all married couples. As a result, Janice came to our house alone, usually in the daytime. She was the only adult I had a real independent friendship with.

From junior high school through high school my close friends were mainly women. But after junior high school I stopped having one best special girl friend to whom I could reveal everything. In fact, around fourteen or fifteen I stopped confessing all my innermost feelings to anyone. I remember, in spite of all my girl friends, feeling lonely and thinking that no one understood me.

At this time I started to dream about Prince Charming, though I had few dates and knew very little about sex. Sometimes I would share my fantasies about meeting Prince Charming with a few friends who shared similar dreams, but our actual experiences with boys became more and more private.

I remember when I first started going to parties. Now everyone says they had similar experiences—feeling awkward, ugly and unpopular; no one asking me to dance; not knowing how to start conversations. I kept wondering what was expected of me, what did guys like. I could never talk to anyone about those feelings, and I was always mystified about what did happen between men and women.

DEBORAH. I'll always remember the day I was supposed to go to the movies with my friend Darlene. She called me at the last minute and told me that a boy she knew from camp had called her up and they were going to go somewhere instead. I got really upset. I hung up the phone and said I didn't understand why she had canceled her date with me. I really didn't understand it—I hadn't learned yet. My older sister and my mother said that I shouldn't get upset, because that's what girls do. It's more important for them to be with boys, and I just had to start getting used to it.

In high school I decided it was silly that boys should pay for girls. So I remember saying to my family that I should pay for myself, and my father started ranting and screaming at me, "If you have that attitude, Deborah, boys will never like you and no one will ever take you out and you'll never get married!"

SUSANNE. In high school I found it harder to be without a boyfriend than it is now at twenty-three. All of us were expected to have a rocky time in adolescence, but those of us who didn't go on to get boyfriends and husbands still have a rocky time.

DEBORAH. In college, groups were usually made up of couples. Any activity for couples excluded me, so I felt bad. It seemed like you had to have a boyfriend to go places. It also affected my relationships with the women in the couples, since they shared and talked about their relationships with their boyfriends.

ELAINE. Sometimes I accepted dates to get out of the dorm.

JUDITH. I found that it was hard to just date. Also, women with serious boyfriends often implied that if you weren't with one man consistently you were promiscuous.

I would talk with many of my women friends about careers, but by the time of my senior year I was the only one in my group who wasn't getting married. When I thought about going to graduate school, a male professor told me not to go—that I would become too much like a man and never get married.

Like many other single women, I went to New York after college. I spent months looking for an "exciting" job to meet "exciting" people. Of course I didn't get the ideal job but finally settled for enough to live on.

I came home after the battle in rush hour to eat dinner with my roommates and talk about meeting men. The evening was spent waiting for someone to call for a date or trying to find someone to do something with.

There was one guy I remember who had listings of open parties in all the boroughs.

I went to those parties dressed in my new and most sophisticated attire. I tried to learn the art of cocktail chatter, taking subtle initiatives, looking confident and above it all. Going out on dates was another ordeal. Coolness and dishonesty seemed like the only qualities of the early parts of relationships. Informal socializing over real interests was almost impossible. Then, of course, there were the sex hassles—will you or won't you? What you learn quickly is that New York is filled with lonely people—women petrified that they will never get married, men on the make. I knew that I wasn't ready to get married. There were still so many things I wanted to do—travel, meet people, find exciting work. But I didn't know how long I could last; marriage seemed the only way out. For me the horror of being single was the loneliness, the lack of intimacy and honesty, as well as the lack of commitment between women.

As a single woman I felt a lot of anger and pain in my life. There was no outlet for the feelings, no focus for my anger and disappointment. I wanted freedom and independence, but I also wanted to be loved. Getting both seemed impossible. In retrospect I realize that I chose to be single. I wanted independence and excitement more than marriage. But at that time, I couldn't see it as a choice. It seemed impossible to share my feelings with other women. Everything made me feel ashamed; it must be my fault, there must be something wrong with me if I didn't have a permanent and lasting relationship with a man.

ELAINE. One of the things I hated most was to be around married friends. Seeing their closeness reminded me of my aloneness. Around couples I often felt like a child, that couples were adults and single people were still not grown up.

KATHY. As a single woman I was constantly worried about my image to the outside world. A lot of my married women friends used to romanticize my position and tell me that I should stay single since it was a better and freer life. A lot of times I wanted them to think I was happier than they were.

CAROLYN. When I tried to "make it," become successful in my own right, I became aware of the incredible social stigma put on independent women. It became clear that one could not be seen as womanly and at the same time be successful in the "active work world of men."

DEBORAH. I gained a lot of respect for being politically and intellectually aggressive. But I always felt that men wouldn't see me in a romantic way, although I knew they liked me. My girl friends told me it was great I was direct and honest, but they acted differently around men.

RACHEL. When I got out of college I lived with several men, one after another. I got a lot out of those relationships—love and security and understanding and support. I thought I had what I'd always wanted. But underneath I was terrified. I was very dependent on my sexual relationships, and that frightened me. Instead of feeling nurtured by the sense of "losing myself" in sexuality, I began to feel I was shutting out the world and dying when I made love.

Being out of a couple for several years has let me grow up and learn to function independently in the world. I really feel as if I can rely on myself now. And I feel I want more intimacy and am ready for it, but I don't know if I'll ever want to be part of a couple that develops a lot of dependency.

As a group of women we felt free to talk about our problems and begin to act on our feelings; we began to look at each other differently. We rediscovered a common bond that allowed us to stop judging ourselves and other women by men's standards. We tried to stop competing with one another. We worked to respect our emotions and to support each other's strengths. We learned to take each other seriously.

We joined women's consciousness-raising collectives and worked on various women's projects and organizations. We moved into houses with other women and began to acknowledge our feelings of love toward women. We changed our lives—our expectations, our environments, our definitions of meeting our needs.

Within the women's movement we have found that our interests and our needs sometimes differ from those of married women. At times we have felt excited that single women seemed freest to change their lives. At other times we have felt burdened and saddened by the insecurity of being single. We want to find new ways of relating to men, but we have no models. The possibility of gayness has opened new options for us, but gayness does not resolve the conflicts we feel about couple relationships.

When we tried to summarize the differences that the women's movement has made in our lives, we ended up with a lot of confusion. There is still fear, but also joy and relief about the roles we have grown out of and the possibilities we see ahead of us.

DEBORAH. Basically the difference is that you no longer feel alone. When you're with someone you have the whole women's movement behind you. Last summer I was dancing with a man at a party and he started making a pass at me. I remember thinking at the time that a few years before, I would have sidled away or clung to someone else. Instead I just told him I didn't want to have anything to do with him. It felt so good, and it was so easy.

Now it seems if I wanted a relationship with a man I could get in touch with him, or we'd just decide on a good way to get together and spend time together. Probably what would determine who picked up whom would be who had a car.

ELAINE. Now at most parties I go to, people function independently whether they're in couples or not. There's some sense of community. Your goal at a party is not necessarily to meet someone.

JUDITH. When I felt there was a clear community of women that was autonomous, I think I stopped thinking about myself primarily as a "single" woman and started to think of myself more as a woman.

DEBORAH. Now I don't have to feel second best to a friend's husband or boyfriend. When Susan and I started becoming friends I was able to say that I had fears about becoming friends with her because I knew she had a commitment to her husband. She said she didn't see that as an issue between us.

I realized a year ago that more and more women really wanted to hear what I had to say and considered it legitimate when I chose not to have a boyfriend.

KATHY. I think there has been a growing respect for women who are more aggressive. A woman who is single is now given a certain amount of respect for having the strength to go out on her own. I always liked doing things that were thought of as boys' things, and in the women's movement these have become acceptable for women for the first time. Learning auto mechanics and feeling that people respected me for it has been very important to me.

SUSANNE. Now I really count on other women as being prominent in my life. I no longer feel that I just happen to be there with other women who happen to be there because they aren't married or aren't with men.

KATHY. I still look toward the future with a lot of dread. I'm really scared that it's all going to collapse and I'll still be left alone. I have an absolute fear of what it means to be forty—I mean for me. The fact that many women are going back into couples—some with men and others with women—is what brought that fear back, since I've never related primarily as part of a couple.

DEBORAH. The women's movement opened up to me for the first time the option of not getting married. That's frightening, because it means that I have to create something new; there aren't the old forms of security. On the other hand, I feel better, since those old forms never really seemed quite so secure or didn't really give me the kind of happiness they were supposed to.

In giving up the idea of getting married I gave up one sense of the future. Now it feels as though I'll be making certain decisions for a few years at a time, but I don't have any sense of where my future is headed. Some of that's really good. It allows me to live from day to day and to express my needs for the present. On the other hand, I do need a greater sense of continuity.

I still want some kind of permanent relationship, to feel security and love. I want to have children of my own or share ongoing responsibility for friends' children. Now both those possibilities seem so hard to achieve; I have no models for what I want.

RACHEL. I don't like to think that I would necessarily have to be in a sexual relationship with either a man or a woman to experience trust and commitment. I still feel confused about what a couple is, what needs it meets, and how much it's possible to meet those needs without becoming part of a couple. A woman friend said to me two years ago that she felt there was a part of myself that I really held back because I was waiting for a man. I don't see my life in the last three years as "waiting for a man," but I do feel like I'm waiting for something.

I get scared when I think about the future. The greatest fear I have is of stagnation. I need to believe that my life won't be static and I won't stop working for what I want.

Stephanie: Living with Others as a Single Woman— Communal Families

Since my senior year in college (five years ago) I've lived communally in both rural and urban areas. I've thought a lot about my life-style—my relationships, my physical environment, my work and my play, etc. Living with others has been mostly a good experience. I've learned much about myself—about my strengths and weaknesses, about my needs for both intimacy and aloneness, and about the things I like and don't like.

When I first lived collectively (while still in college), I had little understanding of how much time, energy and commitment it would take to create trusting, loving and caring relationships. I thought that simply our desire for a warm, loving home was enough—that working out conflicts and differences would all happen in time, without too much hassle. We certainly did hassle and struggle, but it took many months of living together for us to realize that we could not work through our conflicts. I learned a lot from that first communal experience. I re-

alized how emotionally draining it could be for me to be close to four or five other people at the same time. I learned that I had important needs for space and time spent alone, needs which I often failed to recognize until I was already feeling very fragmented and pulled away from my "center." It was particularly hard for me to know my own feelings and to find my own pace, since I was so easily sucked into my environment: if others were cheery and playful, then I would be, too; if others were depressed, then I'd feel sad. The people I lived with helped me to become more aware of my feelings—it's now much easier to be around others and to still be in touch with the "me inside."

One of my most intense and growthful experiences was a year of communal living on a farm. We started out as eight adults and two children who had met regularly for almost six months before actually living together. We had "self-selected" ourselves from a slightly larger group of friends and felt a strong sense of family during the first few months of living together. At times, I would imagine that we might all be together for years, though that fantasy came more from my need to create lasting bonds and deep commitments rather than from any realistic perception of the potential of our staying together.

So much happened so fast it's still hard for me to believe that we were on the farm less than a year and a half. Most of us wanted to share an intense process of day-to-day encounter—a commitment to "dealing with feelings" first and foremost. This frequently drained our energies away from other kinds of contact with one another and with people outside the commune. It was also a process that often conflicted with some of our most basic needs for space and time alone.

Though we started out as four couples, most of us were interested in moving away from "coupledom." Some of us became sexually involved with others both in and out of the commune; others felt very threatened by any sexual sharing at all. Sometimes we felt excitement and joy in being sexually intimate with more than one person; other times we felt pain and fear and sadness. Some of us experimented with making love in threes or in fours (though we did not consider it an experiment at the time; it feels that way looking back). On a hot summer afternoon, three of us along with a friend (all women) had our first homosexual experience together. It was loving, playful and sexually arousing in a newly titillating, exciting sense.

We talked about all these experiences, shared our feelings and responses, and became more comfortable with and accepting of our sexuality. We had the most trouble in working out our sexual relationships with each other within the commune, and sometimes we couldn't: one woman left largely because she wanted a monogamous relationship with a man who didn't. Sometimes I think we fooled ourselves into thinking we were more open to and accepting of multiple sexual involvements than we really were (both for ourselves and one another). Given our socialization and the incredible importance that's always been attached to "The Sexual Relationship," it's no wonder that we had trouble radically changing our gut feelings about sexual intimacy. A few of us often did feel comfortable with sexual sharing. I most often felt good about my mate's being involved sexually with another person, though my being sexually intimate with another man usually threatened him, but we almost always worked it out in a good way. We knew that we were taking risks and needed to be especially sensitive to one another. What was important to us was that our risk-taking be a mutual decision.

For most people in the commune multiple sexual relationships were painful (and probably somewhat destructive for a few of us). We weren't going to change any faster or make our guts react any differently just because we wanted to. This is an area where change comes much more slowly and with more difficulty than I think we had realized.

The story of our breaking apart is long and complicated. Our inability to resolve our sexual relationships in a good way is only a part of this story, though I'm not quite sure how big a part. It took almost a year for us to break up; though I would often have a glimpse of this inevitability, I refused to accept it. In my diary at one point I wrote, "Somehow I feel that our love for one another should go beyond our differences, beyond how we'd like each other to be different." Today I'd never write that. There are some things I don't think I'd ever be able to accept in another person, however much love I felt.

During the past few years my sexual relationships have become more fulfilling and more intense, both physically and emotionally. Maybe because of this I've wanted fewer sexual relationships and only with those I could potentially live with. My relationships with women, whether sexual or not, have also taken on a special importance for me. In part this is because I've found exciting, meaningful work and have a wonderful sense of integrating my personal life and political involvements. Because of a unique understanding and connectedness I've felt with women, and only with women, I know I'll probably never live alone with a man—I would always want to have that very special relationship with a woman as part of my family/home experience.

I still want very much to create a home with several people, including men, that I love and feel committed to. I want to build the deep bonds that can come only with time, to have a family including children, and to feel rooted in land I love. All this now seems to be happening in a beautiful way with three of the people (a woman, a man and a child) that I lived with communally on the farm. Possibly another man who has become very important to me will be included. The two of us have a

very fine relationship, and I hope we will eventually feel the same long-term commitment that I feel with the others.

We've all become more patient, accepting and realistic. We've learned to respect our individual needs for space and our different natural paces. We understand that we need to nourish both our relationships with one another and ourselves as individuals. Sometimes this is hard to do and we won't always succeed, but that's okay, too. Whatever happens, I feel like I'm moving in the right direction.

More Voices: Black Single Women on How Their Relationships with Men Have Been Damaged by Racism and Sexism.

JOANNE. As a black professional woman, and especially as an active feminist, I have just about resigned myself to few meaningful relationships with men right now. My friends and I (members of a black women's consciousness-raising group) feel that many black men in the professions have no desire for relationships with females who are their peers. They seem to prefer a "doll," a woman who would provide them with sexual pleasure, run the house by herself, and help them socially in their push for advancement in the white male world of business.

I feel that my relationships with black men have not been very successful. I never could get what I expected on an emotional level. The men I related to seemed peculiarly unable to express deep feelings and caring, perhaps because for mere survival, vulnerability and sensitivity were conditioned out of them by a hostile, white environment.

If black male consciousness is ever raised so that they relate to women as real and equal human beings, things might get better. The extreme suspiciousness that both black men and women have toward the women's movement does not make this change likely in the near future.

It should be kept in mind that because of racist conditions in the United States, there are substantially fewer black men than black women. By the age of eighteen, the ratio of men to women in the black population begins to decline although nearly equal numbers are born. This occurs because a disproportionate number of black men die in wars and other violent circumstances. Also the number of black men in prisons is highly out of proportion to their numbers in the population. This is because they are more likely to go to prison and to get longer sentences than whites accused of the same crimes. Further, racism in employment has undermined the black family and created strains in the relationships between black men and black women.

SANDRA. Even though I am constantly aware of racism, I find that there is nothing altogether unique about my

relationships with black men that is not experienced by all people in this society. Both men and women are given an image to which we expect to make ourselves and our relationships measure up. We lie to ourselves as well as to our partners in order to make our relationships appear like the images in the media. My previous relationships had been based on such pretenses and so could never reap anything but dishonesty—unfaithfulness, possessiveness and jealousy, ending in what is popularly called heartbreak.

After many bitter experiences with men, I decided to purge myself of all qualities and personality traits that were perpetuating inequality and dishonesty in my relationships. I have changed not only my way of thinking and speaking, but the clothes I wear, the way I talk, my hair style, the TV shows I watch, and the company I keep. The relationships I accepted, even sought, one year ago would be totally unacceptable to me now.

MARJORIE. I am an eighteen-year-old black feminist and an undergraduate at a formerly all-male Ivy League college. In my one significant relationship with a man so far, I found myself attempting to deal with feelings that I think black men often inspire in black women, namely the idea that they as black men are fighting battles with racism daily, and that therefore black women should play the role of comforter, consoler and solacer to their black knights. Unfortunately it is not often recognized by black men that black women are up against the very same racism compounded by sexism. As women, we rarely get a situation of mutual consideration from our men. I realize that to some extent all male-female relationships contain an element of protecting each other from the harsh and cruel external world (you and me against the world); but among blacks this protective role has a historical tradition that tends to make it an all-consuming one for the female partner.

I have therefore decided that for the present I will devote most of my time and energy to academic work and consciously refrain from initiating or seeking an emotional involvement with a man. The most difficult part of this change in consciousness for me has been to put aside the fantasy of the one and only true love, to stop waiting passively for my Prince to come and to realize that I can be emotionally fulfilled through a broad range of interpersonal relationships. I especially want to develop and maintain friendships with feminist women.

Margaret: A Middle-aged Single Woman

I've always wanted to have a family, but I wasn't going to get married just to have children. I've never met a man who was a good friend and a good lover, as well as someone who loved to be with children. So now I'm fifty and I'm still single with no children of my own. I feel sad about this sometimes, but since my work has been so fulfilling and involves working with children—I'm a teacher—I still feel that my life has been rich and complete.

Hannah: An Older Single Woman

I am eighty-eight years old. I have never been married, nor have I had sexual relations. I have all my life had fine relationships with men as fellow students, as warm friends, and as comrades and co-workers in various causes and movements. I would like to have had a devoted marriage, but I never considered marrying just for the sake of being married, and I have never met a man whom I loved enough to marry. My philosophy about sex has been that the only justification for sex relations is total mutual devotion, and that it should be a permanent relation, not a mere temporary physical attraction. I believe this mutual love is what constitutes a marriage even if there is no wedding ceremony and that a couple who go through that ceremony merely for other material reasons are really not married.

In my high school and early college years there was a neighborhood group of boys and girls who regularly played together, went on picnics, etc. One of these boy friends was a particular pal of mine. After he graduated from college he got a job in the Midwest. For seven years he wrote to me twice a week, and in every letter he asked me to marry him. Unfortunately I felt a very warm friendship for him, but not the love to warrant marriage.

I have no living relative and, as I have learned from experience, living in an apartment all by yourself is a very inhuman existence. You get up and eat breakfast with no one to speak to; you return at night to dark and empty rooms and cook and eat supper all alone. I have tried it. So for about twenty-five years I have been a member of one or another commune, having anywhere from five to fifteen members, all but one of them including both sexes. I was always the only old member, the others usually being in their twenties or early thirties. It was an approximation of family living—we ate together, shared all the household tasks and expenses, swapped news and views, and often members would go out together to meetings or social gatherings.

The members of all these communes were inclined to leftist opinions, and whenever a vacancy occurred we took care that the new member would have congenial views. So I felt that I had a satisfying substitute for the family relationships that circumstances denied me.

I carried on my soul-satisfying activities in many vital social movements—the peace movement; the women's movement; many civil liberties battles; the struggle for justice to black Americans, Chicanos and Indians, etc. In the last few years I have filled over 150 speaking engagements. So life for me is still interesting and worthwhile.

The Experience of Being Married

We learn from our culture that the relationship of a married woman with her husband is the most intimate and lasting relationship a woman has, and that a woman is always expected to put this relationship before every-

one and everything else in her life. In this chapter (and in our lives), we want to counteract this misleading and confining message. We want to open the definition of marriage and to explore intimate relationships in addition to marriage.

Although in this society the monogamous, nuclear family is seen as the ideal living situation, there are, in fact, other choices we can make about how and with whom we live.

We have no one opinion about monogamous or non-monogamous relationships. We want to express both our good and bad experiences. We want to begin to separate the good reasons for staying in monogamous relationships from the good reasons for leaving. (And remember, monogamy is not limited to just heterosexual relationships.) We want to explore the possibilities of getting love and support from several people, rather than having one primary intimate relationship that is supposed to satisfy all needs. For those of us who decide that marriage *is* a very deep and important relationship for us, our marriage will be far better if we feel that it is our clear choice rather than our only alternative or our life-defining duty.

Mathilde: A Deepening Relationship

Julien and I met when we were very young, eighteen and nineteen years old. We had a fiery, emotional, storybook love affair—read poetry to each other, took long walks in the country, went skiing. We spent whole afternoons, days, weekends in bed, holding and touching each other, bringing each other to orgasm many times, even though we didn't actually have intercourse with each other for over a year. After a couple of years we got married.

The years before we had kids we spent a lot of time together studying, working, traveling and making friends, building up a reservoir of experiences we shared and talked about. They have become a part of us both, have somehow made us part of each other.

Over the past ten years we've had plenty of fights and disagreements, but I've had only one huge trauma. In our third or fourth year of marriage we had a fight over something—I don't remember what—and he wouldn't talk to me for over a week no matter how much I cried. I hated that coldness more than anything else in my life.

When we were first married and had gotten over the first high excitement of early lovemaking, we started talking about how we would handle it if either of us wanted to have an affair. Well, we blissfully thought, that would be easy! We would simply bring the third person into our relationship and all make love together! It actually almost happened once.

We also talked about having sexual relationships with other couples. Both of us had had very little sexual experience before we met each other and wanted to "broaden our love relationships" (though we didn't want to betray each other). I realize now that those things could not possibly have happened the rational way we planned.

The women's movement coincided with my very little babies and with Julien's getting a job for the first time. Before the movement we played traditional roles—I worked from nine to five and did all the things in the house too. It never occurred to me to ask him to cook, clean, or do the marketing. When the kids came, there was a lot more stuff to do in the house, and I didn't want to do it all. There were lots of fights around those things, but he really changed a lot. Now we share much of the child care. But still, he has a full-time job, while I stay home with the kids and work part time.

Julien has always been a good lover, has always wanted to do what I liked. It was a couple of years before I had orgasms during intercourse, but I was never left unsatisfied. Our love affair remained a love affair for a long time after we were married. Then, inevitably, it became more tranquil. But our relationship never lost the closeness, the basic understanding we have of each other: we love each other very much and we tell each other so, often.

That wild sexual excitement of our early lives has been gone for a long time, along with all those wild positions, antics, lotions, honeys. But then we're now much more proficient at lovemaking, and when we do it we do it very well.

We have both made compromises in our lives for each other, for our kids. We have both changed a good deal over the years we have been together. I often think that it was just luck that our individual changes did not make us grow apart but allowed us to draw together. I'm very glad they did.

Sarah: Thoughts and Feelings About Monogamy

After many years of struggle we have reached a plateau of trust together, and these trustful feelings allow us to take risks with each other and ourselves. I also feel less hung up about the traditional roles of male and female, because through our openness and the resulting intimacy I have learned that my husband has many of the same weak feelings, fragile feelings, that previously I thought were female—just as he has learned that I have certain kinds of strengths he doesn't have. This kind of relationship provides a unique opportunity, I feel, for self-exploration and deep understanding of oneself and one's mate. I think the crucial thing here is time, to build up feelings of confidence and trust and comfort and kindness, and time also to foster a special atmosphere that seems to be a combination of closeness and openness which teaches one the confidence to begin to explore, search and grow.

I want to stress that at this point in my life, knowing all the things now I didn't know when I got married, I would again choose monogamy, not for the sake of the children or the family, but for myself, and my husband. I don't prescribe my choice for everyone. I just feel—I have tasted love and it is good.

Marriage and Multiple Relationships

JENNIFER. I have felt as strong, if not stronger, feelings for a certain woman as I have felt for my husband. She was a good friend I had known as long as I'd known my husband. We loved each other very much, and with support from the women's movement, became more comfortable being openly physically affectionate, and this grew into our sleeping with each other. It wasn't just sexual, but deeply emotional too. When I made love to her I felt like I was loving myself in a new way. But just because we were women, it did not mean that we could avoid all the problems of power, control and competitiveness we had experienced in relationships with men. That frightened me. I still have a lot of sexual feelings toward women and feel good about being physically affectionate, but I have chosen for now not to sleep with women.

After the high times of the first year of the women's movement, when we discovered how wonderful women were and believed everything was possible, we came down to earth. The gap between the ideology of sisterhood and the reality became very apparent to me in the second and third years of the movement. In fact I even found that in some instances I got more support and understanding from men friends than from women.

It took me a long time to accept this. (I wanted very

much to believe in the ultimate power of sisterhood, when in fact people are people, and just because someone is a woman it doesn't necessarily mean we're going to be close friends.) I realize now that it makes sense. It is very hard to change the deep patterns of competition between women for men. At least the pattern has begun to change—we've begun to be open, honest and able to cooperate, be supportive to each other. During these changes I've felt a new commitment to women. I also am able to accept men as friends and lovers again. Perhaps this is part of my and other women's growing mellowness and openness to men now as compared to when I had first become involved in the women's movement. ELENA. In the seventh year of our marriage I got involved in the women's movement and began to sort out a lot of issues in my life. I had been at home for several years with two small children, and although I had chosen to become a mother, I found myself overwhelmed by the total responsibility and became deeply depressed. With the support of other women, I began to question the traditional roles we had drifted into since becoming parents. Because I had been so much into myself when I was depressed, for a whole year my husband had been feeling a lot of unmet emotional needs. He began to talk about wanting to have other relationships.

I felt hurt and rejected because our exclusive sexual bond was somehow the price of certain household duties. Some of my women friends, too, had begun to question the validity of monogamy, emotionally as well as sexually. But I had grown used to depending on one person and was fearful of exchanging the security of marriage for the rat race of adolescence, which was my only other model.

At that time there were other areas of my life that I was more concerned with changing; I wanted to put my energy into work, personal development and friendships with women. I was learning that I liked women after all, and was liking myself better too.

I didn't think I wanted other relationships and feared I would drift into having them if my sexual needs were not met by Jim, my husband. I wanted my sexuality to be determined by my own choice and not by fiat. I was feeling very turned off to men at the time and didn't want to be intimate with men I didn't feel emotionally close to just to prove some obscure point about women's rights and equal sexual capacity. Yet who would meet my emotional needs if my husband was intimate with others?

Because I was seeing myself more as a separate person I began to see my husband that way too. I didn't think we should possess each other, so I told him to do what he thought was best for him but not to put pressure on me. During that time, Jim and I became friendly with a couple who turned out to be living with another couple. Both women were in the women's movement. All household chores were shared equally by the four adults. One

of the men assumed a large, possibly major, role in his young son's care. After we became friends they told us they had a group marriage, exchanging marital partners when all four agreed to do so. They proposed that we might be interested in this arrangement. My husband was quite interested. I was frightened and opted out. I was turned off by the "contracting" (to safeguard the basic marital relationship), which meant that if he joined I did too. It seemed to me even more oppressive than conventional marriage.

The next fall we started a couples group. After many weeks of rehashing old hurts—how Lucy always had to cook after both she and John came home from their jobs, etc.—we came to the realization that the nuclear family was somehow tied to the economics of one adult going out to earn money while the other kept the life systems operating at home. Because women earn less for the same work and because part-time work pays less per hour, the option of each partner working half time is not economically feasible for most families. The majority of us were interested in starting a commune, or cooperative household, in which child care and housekeeping duties would rotate, and all adults would work part time (about three days) outside the home—an arrangement impossible to achieve within the confines of the nuclear family.

My husband and Anne were the major proponents of sexual openness. We resolved to be monogamous within the group, keeping open the option of discussing changes of feeling as they developed in group meetings. I was still threatened by Jim's wanting to have a sexual relationship with another woman and thereby rejecting me.

After several months in the house I found myself growing closer to Michael, Anne's husband. We both enjoyed child care and going to community meetings, and so began to spend a lot of time together. We became more and more aware of being attracted to each other and began to touch and kiss more (which was generally accepted). Since both my husband and Anne wanted to break out of monogamy we felt free to develop our relationship, but we realized there could be problems. One evening when I came home from my job, both my husband and Michael kissed me as I came in the house. This seemed really strange to me.

One afternoon while visiting Jim at his office, I made a chance discovery that led to his telling me that he had slept with a woman about a month before while out of town on business. I was hurt and upset and went about with a lump in my throat for days. I was especially upset that he had not told me, and felt it as a breach of trust.

Jim had been having a lot of trouble living with a group. I enjoyed having people around the house during the day. I had more free time than ever, and my life seemed more integrated than before. I could be a "good mother" and still have time for myself. Most important, I was getting a lot of positive feedback from the group

and getting and giving a lot of emotional support.

One evening when I was talking with Michael, an electric current or something almost tangible passed between us. I knew at that moment that I could not continue living in the same house if we did not have a sexual relationship.

We discussed it first with our spouses and then in the women's caucus of the house, and got supportive responses.

When we first slept together it was Christmas Eve. Half the group were away (the pro-monogamy faction). It turned out to be a really fine sexual experience and the beginning of a strong emotional bond. Both our spouses were upset. After we had made love we could hear Jim pacing the halls and taking a shower. Anne was upset because we hadn't told her clearly that we were going to make love that night and perhaps because it was Christmas Eve.

Anne, who had had other relationships before, quickly got over being upset and was supportive of our relationship, as were the other women in the house. The other men were rather noncommittal and just didn't speak of it. Jim continued to be upset and insisted that he had to be out of the house or sleeping with his lover when I slept with Michael.

My preference was to be spontaneous about sexuality and to move in the direction of breaking out of our "coupleness," only sleeping together when we felt like it, and sleeping with others when we were feeling close to them. (The group considered separate bedrooms at several points, but it was never acted upon. The group norm was for spouses to share bedrooms, although occasionally one or another of the women would spend the night in a study or on the living room couch.) Since we lived in an essentially monogamous group, where Michael and I had the only intragroup relationship, I could see the basis for my husband's feelings of isolation and tried to reassure him as much as I could. The new relationship was of greater intensity, but my marriage had a lot of strong ties and was satisfying and comfortable in an entirely different way.

The group broke up for a whole range of reasons, and half the people left for the country.

With the four of us left, Jim became progressively more mistrustful of Michael, whom he had considered his closest friend throughout the year in the house. Anne and Jim had never gotten along too well, and there was some friction which expressed itself as, "Well, I'm not attracted to you, either!" Anne had mentioned once the possibility that she and I might have a sexual relationship, and although this was not followed up much by either one of us, I think Jim felt doubly rejected (excluded) at the thought of the three of us being close sexually.

The four of us who remained were an untenable group because of the emotional dynamics.

My husband and I and our children are living together. We still have an important relationship with the other couple. Michael and I are very close and continue to have a sexual relationship. We would like to live together again in a group, but it is not yet clear how Jim feels about going back to any group-living situation, let alone one with Michael in the group. I may have to choose between my commitment to my husband and my feeling that I can grow more in a group-living situation. I must also sort out the issues of group living and my attachment to Michael. It seems important not to confuse the two.

Laura: Family, Marriage and Separation

I grew up in a progressive, middle-class family: mother, father, sister, brother. I learned by watching, listening, asking my parents what was important to them. Their relationship to one another was special, different from their relationships to other people. Before their marriage they slept with other people, but after marriage they only slept with each other, as far as I knew.

They never put in words that the marriage relationship was sacred, but I knew it; when friends of theirs got divorced there were sounds of "How terrible!" Even when they were feeling miserable and unhappy, it was clear they would "stick it out." I was never afraid my parents would separate, but I had to hold inside me any tensions and negative feelings that they pushed under. For instance, instead of each of them visiting different friends because that's what they felt like doing, they would fight until one won and one lost. And they both went off together—but angry and resentful.

My parents have functioned as a unit for almost thirty-five years. Their marriage has a sense of continuity, a sense of love, caring and security which is not easy to come by in this crazy world. I have a very real respect, even admiration, for much of what grew out of their commitment to one another. But the lack of questioning in their relationship, their failure to meet problems head on, and their idealization of the nuclear family and monogamy—all this I felt was destructive to both of them and to me.

Okay. So I am twenty-nine years old now. Following the only model I knew, I lived with and then was married to my husband for ten years. We had two children together. I separated from him six months ago.

I got married at nineteen. We were both in college, both young, scared and alone. We got together. It was a way to break ties with our parents, to be on our own in a comforting, secure way. For many years we grew alongside each other as friends and as lovers.

As we grew up we felt our differences more too. But we found it hard to see those differences as legitimate, since all our expectations told us that we were a special "unit." If I wanted to spend time with him and he

wanted to read, I felt hurt. If I wanted to visit my friends and he needed to be with me at that time, he felt hurt. If one of us didn't want to make love and the other did, the hurt was worse. At times the hurt turned to anger and resentment.

Being intimate with only one person did not seem to be enough to meet our needs. But it was hard to go outside the marriage for intimacy, since that would break the "contract." Friendship with others was okay, but sexual intimacy was another matter.

At the point that we both reached out for other intimate relationships we were reaching out for ourselves. Friends still referred to us as the Greenways rather than as Laura and Joe. But the need for each of us to feel whole, distinct, separate and centered in ourselves was pressing; it took priority over the marriage.

How do you know when you reach the point when you no longer can change together? When is separation a cop-out? When is it a positive moving forward? These are crucial questions with no easy answers. Many, many couples get to this point, sometimes over and over again. There are different ways of dealing with the impasse—keeping up a marriage of convenience, splitting up angry, splitting up when the kids are less dependent. For me it was very difficult and painful to think about separation and finally separating. Breaking up doesn't have to mean the whole relationship was bad, but deep down the myth is that marriage should be "for always" and we are failures if our marriages come to an end. I still feel the pain of losing the closeness and intimacy that we had built up over ten years. It was hard to give up even when the marriage lacked joy and things between us were clearly sour.

Ungluing our marriage took at least two years. It began with the women's movement, which gave me support to move out on my own, to develop new skills and new relationships. I still felt in contact with my husband on some levels. I was involved in two different relationships during that time—one with a woman, one with a man. They were each long-term friendships that grew more intimate—emotionally and sexually.

During this time my husband and kids and I were living with a group of people. With other people around, we thought we could perhaps be more independent and still live together. It didn't work. For us, more people meant more conflict and tension as well as more resources.

I split for a while. I left the house to sort out my feelings, though I still wanted to live with my husband and kids. I wound up staying away for several months, and finally left for good. The decision to leave was especially painful because I was breaking up a family as well as a marriage.

So where am I now? I feel in many ways I've exchanged one set of problems for another. I live by myself half time and with my kids half time. (Relative to other women, I'm fortunate that my husband and the people he lives with are willing and able to care for the children half time.) I feel much more centered in me than when I was married. Sometimes my center feels warm and strong, other times cold and lonely. My kids are very important to me, especially now. They are a stable, loving element in my life.

And my friends—I couldn't be living alone without support from them. Some of them have lived or do live alone. They tell me, "Keep going, it's good for a time." It's the first time in my life I've had space to focus on me, to love myself more, so that I can deeply love others, whether men or women.

Bridging

Being together is knowing
even if what we know
is that we cannot really be together
caught in the teeth of the machinery
of the wrong moments of our lives.

A clear umbilicus
goes out invisibly between,
thread we spin fluid and finer than hair
but strong enough to hang a bridge on.

That bridge will be there
a blacklight rainbow arching out of your skull
whenever you need
whenever you can open your eyes and want
to walk upon it.

Nobody can live on a bridge
or plant potatoes
but it is fine for comings and goings,
meetings, partings and long views
and a real connection to someplace else
where you may
in the crazy weathers of struggle
now and again want to be.

MARGE PIERCY

Alice: The Experience of Being Widowed after Twenty-six Years of Marriage

I never liked being married, but in spite of my reluctance I was competent as a wife and mother. I never had sexual satisfaction in my marriage, but this wasn't such a problem, since I couldn't miss what I had never experienced. Besides, I was always too busy and too tired and ready for sleep even before I collapsed into bed. I felt overburdened with the responsibilities of raising five children and keeping house for seven people, but my husband felt that his contribution of eight hours a day at the office was sufficient. I guess my resentment about this was one of the hardest things to live with, especially since there was no support from anyone then for changing this situation. We sometimes talked about divorce,

but my husband felt that we couldn't afford it. After he died I grieved for him and suddenly realized that I had in fact loved him. In retrospect, I think that our marriage might have been salvaged if we had arranged for a lengthy separation, for at least a year. I had so much to settle with myself, by myself, that I could not cope with the way we were married. In many ways the state of marriage just goes against the grain. We might have been better mates under different circumstances, but time ran out. Four years ago when my husband died I cried for his life—not for ours together.

Now I like not having to account to a rigid mate, not having to do things and be someone that I'm not. I like to travel, practice yoga, go to concerts and lectures, and read. These are things I could never find time to do before. Though relatives are often critical of my current interests and activities, my children are wonderfully supportive. In return, I can support them in pursuing unconventional life-styles without nagging from me. It's good that my children are near me, since we get along so well now.

I can see many advantages to a compatible mate, though I think such a person is hard to find. Fortunately life is full of adventures that don't have to be shared with just one special mate. As for exploring my sexuality with another person, I've never felt much sex drive, so sex hasn't been important to me. Though my sexual experiences both during and after my marriage have not been very good, there has been one exception, a good friend and lover whom I see once a week. However, even though I enjoy sex with him, I don't feel much sexual energy at other times.

I still feel that I would like to be really alone sometimes for a long period. That's something I've never tried out. Unfortunately I still have difficulty making time for myself—I so often feel that I ought to do things for other people, whether or not they actually ask for help. So I find myself making dinners for my sons and their friends or listening to other people's problems or driving someone to an appointment or working part time, whether or not that's what I really want to do. It's very hard to change this tendency in me and to begin to think more about some of my own needs too.

Declaration

For years I charted my independence
in miles traveled away from you.
You were New York and I a car
fleeing in every artery.
That I made you the center, there is no question.
No question I could rule on
without your opposition. No adventure unless
it wasn't yours. Today I think of Concord grapes,
those little pyramids, depending;
of the bay's water angrily repeating
its leap up the beach. One man's
violent need becomes a woman's service job.
But I don't work for you.
I'm crazy now.

MIRIAM GOODMAN

The Edge

Time and again, time and again I tie
My heart to that headboard
While my quilted cries
Harden against his hand. He's bored—
I see it. Don't I lick his bribes, set his bouquets
In water? Over Mother's lace I watch him drive into the
    gored
Roasts, deal slivers in his mercy . . . I can feel his thighs
Against me for the children's sakes. Reward?
Mornings, crippled with this house,
I see him toast his toast and test
His coffee, hedgingly. The waste's my breakfast.

LOUISE GLÜCK

Some Thoughts on Long-Term Relationships

We are choosing our own priorities now, and because our lives are complex, involving relationships with family, people we work with, women and men friends, we do not always make our relationships with a man our major priority. The old idea that we are the Second Sex, that we will follow a man to the ends of the earth, is giving way to a more balanced and appropriately self-centered orientation. This is reflected in more equitable relationships with men and in our recognition of a wider range of options which are becoming more socially acceptable.

But even when we make work or self-growth our central priority, committed long-term relationships are very important to most of us. For many of us, our most committed and lasting relationships will be with our children or our friends instead of our sexual partner(s).

Good relationships are difficult, if not impossible, when we don't understand ourselves and our own needs. Asking and being given, telling a need and having it fulfilled, frees us to be able to give. This is very difficult when people come together not as equals but as teacher and taught, the admired and the admiring, the assertive and the acquiescent. Good relationships are mutual. They are built on each partner's feeling as competent and in control of her or his life as the other.

The Experience of Celibacy: Times When We Are Not Having Sexual Relations

The dictionary defines celibacy as a state of being unmarried, usually in connection with religious vows, but in general usage it has come to mean abstaining from genital sex in our relationships with others, even if temporarily.

Many of us enter periods of celibacy deliberately, feeling that we have a need for a time not to be in a sexual relationship of any kind. We may want to mobilize all our energy for our work, our children, our friends; we may want to explore our own sexuality without the distraction of another person; or perhaps we just don't feel "sexy."

Yet many of us have entered periods of celibacy with apprehension—we have feared the insecurity of being without a partner. Often this anxiety diminishes because being alone is a very positive experience. It has given us back our integrity, our privacy, our pride.

Of course there is a difference in how we feel when we choose celibacy and how we feel when being without a sexual partner is not our choice. But either way many of us have found that periods of celibacy—a month, a year, or even longer—can be freeing and growth producing. We are freed to explore ourselves without the problems and power struggles of a sexual relationship. We can begin to define ourselves not just in terms of another person.

Sexual relationships often create anxieties and distractions that keep us from getting in closer touch with ourselves. We wonder why we didn't come, or if the other person liked it, or if he or she wouldn't rather be in bed with so-and-so. This takes up lots of psychic energy that could be used for other thoughts and activities.

Not being in an intense, intimate relationship has been good for me. I've had space to learn more about me—my needs, my talents, my potentials, my own natural rhythms. I now feel much more capable of sustaining intimacy with another person in a way that could better meet both my own needs and those of the other person. It's important to me now that I don't "lose" myself in an intimate relationship—some of the time I need to feel whole and complete as an individual, as the person I am apart from the relationship.

I have been celibate for over a year, since the beginning of my involvement with the women's movement, which gave me a lot of support. I work very hard and feel good about working. I have created my own physical environment, building a house, and have provided my own psychological space—a good combination. I masturbate a lot and enjoy it. I feel happy, independent and free to figure out my own expectations of me.

My first reaction to being without a man was frustration and anger. I thought, Well, here I am feeling pretty liberated sexually, and there's no one to sleep with. Over time, I thought less and less about being with a man. I had very relaxed times with my friends and never had to think twice about making plans with them for dinner. I was not asexual during this time. I was masturbating with much pleasure, having different kinds of orgasms— some long and slow and ripply, others short and jerky and tenser. I explored my sexuality in a way I had not with men. It was also easier to work at what I wanted to, because I was my only obligation.

Some of us come out of celibacy deliberately, feeling that we need a sexual relationship. Some of us, feeling isolated and outside the norms of society, give up and flee into the arms of the first person to come along. Some of us may find we feel better being more autonomous.

But for most of us, being celibate has not provided a long-term solution to the problems posed by sexual relationships. There are also some very real drawbacks to long periods of celibacy.

Most of us crave physical contact and physical affection. To be alone, or to receive physical affection only from our children or pets doesn't quite work. We can have fantasies about sleeping with them, but it doesn't feel right to act on them. We need other adult human beings to meet our deeper sexual/sensual needs.

Going without physical affection for long periods can be a kind of starvation. We won't die as we would without food or air, but the effects may still show in our bodies. We may get stiffer and out of touch with our sensuality. Many of us have found that being physically affectionate with family and friends can prevent this from happening during celibate periods.

When celibacy no longer feels good we want to change it—but that's easier said than done. And it feels harder the longer we have been celibate. Coming out of celibacy, we may feel awkward or defensive, or we may feel embarrassed by needs that seem insatiable. Sometimes it's easier to start a new relationship with someone else who is also coming out of celibacy.

One unresolved thought: Do we ever choose celibacy out of fear of any kind of physical intimacy? What does this mean?

It's hard to take on the loneliness, the bad parts of being alone as well as the good parts of getting in touch with ourselves. It's also difficult to explore fully what being celibate can mean to us, since society does not generally accept the idea of choosing to refrain from sexual activity.

The Influence Coming into Play: The Seven of Pentacles

Under a sky the color of pea soup
she is looking at her work growing away there
actively, thickly like grapevines or pole beans
as things grow in the real world, slowly enough.

If you tend them properly, if you mulch, if you water,
if you provide birds that eat insects a home and winter food,
if the sun shines and you pick off caterpillars,
if the praying mantis comes and the ladybugs and the bees,
then the plants flourish, but at their own internal clock.

Connections are made slowly, sometimes they grow
    underground.
You cannot tell always by looking what is happening.
More than half a tree is spread out in the soil under your
    feet.
Penetrate quietly as the earthworm that blows no trumpet.
Fight persistently as the creeper that brings down the tree.
Spread like the squash plant that overruns the garden.
Gnaw in the dark and use the sun to make sugar.

Weave real connections, create real nodes, build real houses.
Live a life you can endure: make love that is loving.
Keep tangling and interweaving and taking more in,
a thicket and bramble wilderness to the outside but to us
interconnected with rabbit runs and burrows and lairs.

Live as if you liked yourself, and it may happen:
reach out, keep reaching out, keep bringing in.
This is how we are going to live for a long time: not always,
for every gardener knows that after the digging, after the
    planting,
after the long season of tending and growth, the harvest
    comes.

MARGE PIERCY

FURTHER READINGS

Fiction

Women and Literature: An Annotated Bibliography of Women Writers, 2nd. ed., Order for $1.50 from The Sense and Sensibility Collective, 57 Ellery St., Cambridge, Mass. 02138.
    A bibliography that is comprehensive and interesting to read in itself.
The Feminist Press, c/o S.U.N.Y. College at Old Westbury, Box 334, Old Westbury, N.Y. 11568. Write for their catalog of new feminist works and reprints.

Books By and About Black Women*

Angelou, Maya. *I Know Why the Caged Bird Sings*. New York: Bantam Books, 1970.

Brooks, Gwendolyn. *Maud Martha*. New York: AMS Press, 1953.

———. *Selected Poems*. New York: Harper & Row, 1963.

Hurston, Zora Neale. *Their Eyes Were Watching God*. New York: Fawcett, 1972.

Jones, Hettie. *Big Star Fallin' Mama: Five Women in Black Music*. New York: Viking, 1974.

Larsen, Nella. *Quicksand*. New York: Collier-Macmillan, 1971.

Lerner, Gerda, ed. *Black Women in White America: A Documentary History*. New York: Vintage, 1973.

Moody, Anne. *Coming of Age in Mississippi* (autobiography). New York: Dell, 1970.

Morrison, Toni. *The Bluest Eye*. New York: Pocket Books, 1970.

———. *Sula*. New York: Knopf, 1974.

Petry, Ann. *The Street*. New York: Pyramid, 1946.

Walker, Alice. *Revolutionary Petunias*. New York: Harcourt Brace Jovanovich, 1972.

———. *In Love and in Trouble: Stories of Black Women*. New York: Harcourt Brace Jovanovich, 1973.

———. *The Third Life of Grange Copeland*. New York: Avon Books, 1970.

Walker, Margaret. *Jubilee*. New York: Bantam Books, 1966.

Biography, Autobiography and Novels

Davidson, Sara. *Loose Change*. New York: Pocket Books, 1977.

De Beauvoir, Simone. *A Very Easy Death*. New York: Warner Paperback Library, 1973.

———. *Memoirs of A Dutiful Daughter*. Cleveland and New York: World, 1959.

———. *The Prime of Life*. New York: Harper/Colophon, 1976.

Flexner, Eleanor. *Mary Wollstonecraft*. Baltimore, Md.: Penguin, 1973.

* Compiled by Barbara Smith.

French, Marilyn. *The Women's Room*. New York: Simon and Schuster, 1977; Jove/Harcourt Brace Jovanovich, 1978 (paperback).

Goldman, Emma. *Living My Life*. 2 vols. New York: Dover, 1970.

Hellman, Lillian. *Pentimento*. Boston: Little, Brown, 1973.

Also see her introduction to Dashiell Hammett's *The Big Knockover*. She talks about their alliance of over thirty years. Though they did not live together, they had a deeply committed primary relationship.

Jong, Erica. *How to Save Your Own Life*. New York: Signet (NAL), 1978.

Lerner, Gerda. *The Grimke Sisters from South Carolina*. New York: Schocken Books, 1971.

Lindbergh, Anne. *A Gift from the Sea*. New York: Pantheon, 1955.

———. *Hour of Gold, Hour of Lead*. New York: New American Library, 1974.

Milford, Nancy. *Zelda*. New York: Harper & Row, 1970; Avon, 1972.

Millett, Kate. *Sexual Politics*. New York: Ballantine, 1969.

———. *Flying*. New York: Ballantine, 1974.

———. *Sita*. New York: Ballantine, 1974.

Piercy, Marge. *Small Changes*. New York: Fawcett Crest, 1972.

Sanger, Margaret. *An Autobiography*. New York: Dover, 1970.

Sarton, May. *Crucial Conversations*. New York: W. W. Norton, 1975.

———. *A World of Light*. New York: W. W. Norton, 1976.

———. *Journal of a Solitude*. New York: W. W. Norton, 1973.

Sewall, Richard B. *The Life of Emily Dickinson*. 3 vols. New York: Farrar, Straus & Giroux, Inc., 1974.

Solomon, Barbara H. *The Awakening and Selected Stories of Kate Chopin*. New York: Signet (NAL), 1976.

Stanton, Elizabeth Cady, *Eighty Years and More: Reminiscences, 1815-1897*. New York: Schocken Books, 1971.

Tillich, Hannah. *From Time to Time*. Briarcliff Manor, N.Y.: Stein & Day, 1973.

Other Nonfiction

Bach, George. *The Intimate Enemy*. New York. Avon, 1968

Teaches couples how to fight fairly and instructively.

Bequaert, Lucia. *Single Women: Alone and Together*. Boston: Beacon Press, 1976.

Caine, Lynn. *Widow*. New York: William Morrow & Co., 1974; Bantam, 1975.

Chesler, Phyllis. *Women and Madness*. New York: Doubleday, 1972.

Falk, Ruth. *Women Loving: A Journey Toward Becoming an Independent Woman*. New York: Random House/Bookworks, 1975.

Greenwald, Jerry. *Creative Intimacy: How to Break the Patterns that Poison Your Relationships*. New York: Pyramid Books, 1977.

Kanter, Rosabeth. *Community and Commitment*. Cambridge: Harvard University Press, 1972.

Communes past and present, why they stay together or break up.

McDonald, Paula and Dick. *Loving Free*. New York: Ballantine, 1973.

Story of one couple's working on their marriage.

O'Brien, Patricia. *The Woman Alone*. New York: Quadrangle, 1973.

Rogers, Carl. *Becoming Partners*. New York: Delacorte, 1972; Dell, 1973.

Women: A Journal of Liberation, 3028 Greenmount Ave., Baltimore, Md. 21218.

Special Issue on "How We Live and With Whom," Winter, 1971.

Separation and Divorce

Bohannon, Paul. *Divorce and After*. New York: Anchor, 1971.

Culpepper, Emily, Hazel Staats Meynees, Diane Miller. *Coming Out of Marriage*. 1973. Coming Out of Marriage Project, c/o Office of Women's Programs, 45 Francis Ave., Cambridge, Mass. 02138 ($1.75).

Despert, J. Louis. *Children of Divorce*. New York: Dolphin.

Gardner, Richard A. *The Boys and Girls Book About Divorce*. New York: Bantam Books, 1971.

Goode, William J. *Women in Divorce*. New York: Free Press, 1965.

Batik by Jane Pincus

Grollman, Earl A., ed. *Explaining Divorce to Children.* Boston: Beacon Press, 1968.

Hallett, Kathryn. *A Guide for Single Parents: People in Crisis.* Celestial Arts, Millbrae, Calif. 94030 ($3.95).
> Based on principles of Transactional Analysis. Good ideas for problem-solving and helpful for examining feelings and concerns though sometimes the TA ideas seem simplistic and preachy.

Hunt, Morton. *The World of the Formerly Married.* New York: McGraw-Hill, 1966.

Jancourtz, Isabella. *The Massachusetts Woman's Divorce Handbook.* Divorce Handbook, 27 Warren Ave., Weston, Mass. 02193 ($2.00).

Klein, Carole. *The Single Parent Experience.* New York: Avon, 1973.
> Interviews with women and men, many of whom choose to be single parents. Interesting and readable.

Krantzler, Mel. *Creative Divorce.* New York: Signet, 1975.

McFadden, Michael. *Bachelor Fatherhood.* New York: Walker & Company, 1974.

Mindey, Carol. *The Divorced Mother.* New York: McGraw-Hill, 1970.

Ostrovsky, Everett S. *Children Without Men.* New York: Collier, 1962.

Sheresky, Norman, and Marya Mannes. *Uncoupling: The Art of Coming Apart.* New York: Dell, 1973.

Steinzor, Bernard. *When Parents Divorce.* New York: Pocket Books, 1970.

Resources for Problem Solving

Boston Women's Collective. *Women's Yellow Pages.* 490 Beacon St., Boston, Mass. 02115 ($1.50).

Eastern Massachusetts Public Interest Resource Group. *How to Sue in Small Claims Court.* 120 Boylston St., Room 320, Boston, Mass. 02116.

Rennie, Susan, and Kirsten Grimstead. *The New Woman's Survival Catalog—A Woman-Made Book.* Coward, McCann, & Geoghegan, 1973; Berkeley Publishing Corp., 1973.

Suid, Roberta, et al. *Married, Etc: A Sourcebook for Couples.* Reading, Mass.: Addison-Wesley Publishing Co., 1976.

Vocations for Social Change. *People's Yellow Pages.* 353 Broadway, Cambridge, Mass. 02138 ($2.00 plus $.50 for postage).

Women's Survival Manual. Women in Transition, 4634 Chester Ave., Philadelphia, Pa. 19143 ($2.95).

Yates, Martha. *Coping: A Survival Manual for Women Alone.* Englewood Cliffs, N.J.: Prentice Hall, 1976.

Poetry*

Anthologies

Bernikow, Louise, ed. *The World Split Open: Four Centuries of Women Poets in England and America, 1552-1950.* New York: Vintage, 1974.

Bill, Elaine, ed. *Mountain Moving Day: Poems by Women.* Trumansburg, N.Y.; Crossing Press, 1973.

Chester, Laura, and Sharon Barba, eds. *Rising Tides.* New York: Pocket Books, 1973.

Goulianos, Joan, ed. *By a Woman Writt.* Baltimore, Md.: Penguin, 1974.
> Mostly prose; some poetry by Margaret Walker, Dilys Laing, Muriel Rukeyser.

Howe, Florence, and Ellen Bass, eds. *No More Masks: An Anthology of Poems by Women.* New York: Anchor, 1973.

Small Presses

alicejames books, 138 Mt. Auburn St., Cambridge, Mass. 02138. alicejames books is a cooperative with publishing emphasis on poetry by women (among others, Marjorie Fletcher, Betsy Sholl, Liz Fenton, Marie Harris, Connie Veenendahl, Jean Pedrick, Patricia Cummings).

* Compiled by Miriam Goodman.

Times Change Press, 62 West 14th St., New York, N.Y. 10011 (Alta).

Some of Us Press, 4110 Emery Place, N.W., Washington, D.C. (Margaret Gibson).

Broadside Press, 12651 Old Mill Place, Detroit, Mich. 48238 (among others, Nikki Giovanni, Margaret Walker, Audre Lourde, Gwendolyn Brooks).

Books

Atwood, Margaret. *The Animals in That Country.* Boston: Atlantic Monthly Press, 1968.

Bogan, Louise. *The Blue Estuaries, Poems 1923-1968.* New York: Noonday Press, 1968.

Dickinson, Emily. *Selected Poems and Letters.* New York: Anchor, 1959.

Jong, Erica. *Half Lives.* New York: Holt, Rinehart and Winston, 1973.

Kizer, Carolyn. *Midnight Was My Cry.* New York: Doubleday, 1971.

Glück, Louise. *Firstborn.* New York: New American Library, 1968.

Piercy, Marge. *To Be of Use.* New York: Doubleday, 1973.

Plath, Sylvia. *Ariel.* New York: Harper & Row, 1965.

———. *Colossus.* New York: Vintage, 1960.

Rich, Adrienne. *Diving Into the Wreck,* New York: Norton, 1973.

———. *Dream of a Common Language.* Poems 1974-77. New York: W. W. Norton, 1978.

———. *The Will To Change.* New York: Norton, 1971.

Rukeyser, Muriel. *The Speed of Darkness.* New York: Vintage Books, 1971.

Sappho. Translated by Mary Barnard. Berkeley: University of California Press, 1958.

Sexton, Anne. *Transformations.* Boston: Houghton Mifflin, 1972.

———. *All My Pretty Ones.* Boston: Houghton Mifflin, 1962.

———. *To Bedlam and Part Way Back.* Boston: Houghton Mifflin, 1960.

———. *Love Poems.* Boston: Houghton Mifflin, 1969.

Wakowski, Diane. *The Motorcycle Betrayal Poems.* New York: Simon and Schuster, 1971.

———. *Smudging.* Los Angeles: Black Sparrow Press, 1974.

———. *Inside the Blood Factory.* New York: Doubleday, 1962.

Clifton, Lucille. *Good News About the Earth.* New York: Random House, 1972.

Sanchez, Sonia. *We A BaddDDD People.* Broadside Press, 12651 Old Mill Pl., Detroit, Mich. 48238. 1970.

Discography*

Contemporary Feminist Recordings

Hazel & Alice (Rounder Records).

At the Present Moment, Peggy Seeger and Ewan MacColl (Rounder Records).

Mountain Moving Day, New Haven and Chicago Women's Liberation Rock Bands (Rounder Records).

Honor Thy Womanself, Arlington Street Women's Caucus (Rounder Records).

Lavender Jane Loves Women (Women's Wax Works).

Loner, Indra Allen (Cell 16).

Hang in There, Holly Near (Redwood Records).

I Know You Know, Meg Christian (Olivia Records).

Full Count, Willie Tyson (Lima Bean Records).

Virgo Rising (Thunderbird Records).

Popular Records: Folk Rock and Motown

We assume most women are familiar with records in the more popular folk and rock idiom. A full listing of women's and general protest records in the traditional genre can be obtained from Rounder Records, 186 Willow Ave., Somerville, Mass.

*Compiled by Lanayre Liggera.

CHAPTER 5
IN AMERIKA THEY CALL US DYKES*

INTRODUCTION

This chapter is a beginning, the beginning of our efforts to define for ourselves what it means to be a lesbian in this society. It is part of a larger beginning, as more and more gay women throughout the country have started to write, argue, sing and shout their message to the world.

A lot of people worked on this chapter. The continuity was provided by a group of about nine women in Gay Women's Liberation who had been meeting together for a number of weeks before they decided to write this chapter, and most of whom had been friends for some time before that. We had no connection with the group writing the rest of the book—except some individual friendships—and in fact we disagreed, and still do, with many of their opinions. However, we took on the project because we thought it was very important for any book dealing with women and sexuality to have a good section on lesbianism, and because we thought that writing it would help us sort out some of our own ideas, feelings and politics around being lesbians in this society.

In addition to the nine of us, another half dozen women contributed pieces they had written; took part in tape-recording sessions; and helped edit and put material together. We write from many different points of view. But we all have in common that we dig being gay; we think it's one of the most positive aspects of our lives.

We want to break down the myths, misrepresentations and outright lies that permit our oppression and exploitation as lesbians and that control not only our lives but the lives of straight women as well. The horror and fear with which others view us have served to ghettoize us, to isolate us not only from the straight world but from each other, since we must stay hidden to survive. The problems of our lives—from medical questions to the difficulties of living in a society that condemns our very existence—are not viewed as legitimate by straight society, which insists that our only problem is that we are queer. The fact that we are lesbians is used to discredit everything that we say and to make us into scape-

goats for everyone else's problems. The irrational fear of lesbianism is used not only to divide us from other women but also to keep all women isolated from each other, to keep women from becoming close friends. It also serves to keep women "in their place": any woman who acts assertive or holds a "man's" job may be labeled a dyke.

This chapter is a beginning—that means there is much more to come. There are many things we have had to leave out because of space limitations or because we do not have the experience to write about them. We have included nothing about lesbianism in the armed forces or about the problems of older gay women. We do not deal as adequately as we would like to with questions of class, role playing, legal problems, and many other subjects. We welcome your criticisms and ideas. Write to us c/o Lesbian Liberation, The Women's Educational Center, 46 Pleasant Street, Cambridge, Massachusetts 02139.

We have included five of our lives so that you may see us as we see ourselves—as real people. We weren't born lesbians. Coming to think of ourselves as gay was part of a process. We went through social conditioning, had experiences with men and women, and made choices, conscious or not. We have always loved some women—friends, mothers, sisters—but that did not make us gay. At some point our love for our women friends found expression in sexual feelings, and we acted on those feelings. For Clyde this happened when she was nine; for Nell, not until she was thirty-seven, married and the mother of three children.

From this point on, we continued to turn to women for love and friendship. Bisexuality might be possible in a healthy society, but it's not possible in this one. Relationships with men in this society have a built-in power imbalance, and few of us who have explored the possibilities of relationships between women would choose again to start with that handicap.

SARAH. I'm twenty-eight, and I "came out" when I slept with a friend four years ago. But it took me about six months to actively assert my gay identity. I understood my reluctance to being labeled "lesbian" after listening

---

*Since the gay collective insisted on complete control over the style and content of this chapter, the Health Book Collective has not edited it. Because of length limitations, however, the gay collective has had to leave out much material that they feel is important.

to a couple of gay women at a gay bar react violently to the word. They saw themselves as human beings, not as labels. But, I thought, that's just not the way people deal with each other in this society. They give you labels whether you take them or not. They reminded me too much of myself ten or fifteen years ago, when I responded similarly to being called a Jew.

From the sixth grade on, I was the only Jew in my school. Everyone informed me of that, and it was no compliment coming from their mouths. I thought of myself as smart, capable, good at science and math. I was going to be another Marie Curie. But I was also intimidated by other peoples' judgments; I had to figure out how to fit in. "No, we don't bury our dead standing up," I would say. I really wanted to have friends, and I did get close to girls and boys. But I was always on the fence; they might always turn around and say "You're a Jew." This explains a lot of my reluctance to identify myself as gay and say "I'm a lesbian."

I thought I could have what people would call a gay relationship with my friend and not have to get into gay women's liberation or see myself as a lesbian. I had the choice not to do that. I knew by calling myself a lesbian I was asking for disapproval, distance and perhaps violence from most people. And since I had gone through it once, why ask for it again? So for a long time I did not identify. Then I realized that while ideally no one wants to be labeled, I do live in a society where people react to each other that way, and I don't have any control over

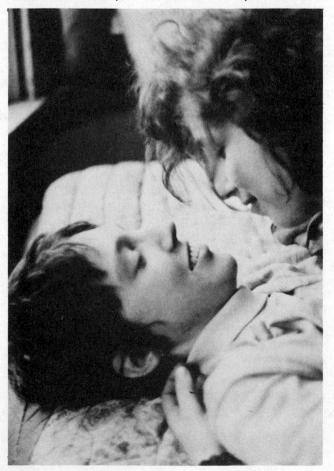

that. I can't deny how people relate to me. Yes, I'm Jewish and I'm a lesbian.

I'm one of those women who "came out" with the women's movement. Women's Liberation made me think about my past, about when I was a kid and liked to play football and baseball. To me the accusation "You throw like a girl" was a terrible put-down—I didn't want to be lumped in the "girl" category. I realized when thinking about my family that my parents had similar expectations for me and my brother—except that I was urged to be nice, considerate, concerned for others in ways my brother was rarely pressed to show.

I thought about how, in junior high, the boys looked at the girls as developing bodies. They would yell, "Pearl Harbor, surprise attack!" as they grabbed our breasts and forced us down on the ground to get the "big feel." I know it scared me then, but how could I deal with my anger and fear when what was so important among girls was to be accepted by the boys? And having a boyfriend was often a protection from those other boys.

In ninth grade a group of girls got close. We used to hug and kiss each other a lot and have slumber parties. Most of us had boyfriends, but we were very important to each other. Once in a while someone would say, "What are you, a homo?" and we'd laugh. It didn't mean anything and it didn't change our behavior in any way.

That's the only reference to homosexuality that I can remember before college. In college I got hit with Freud and latent homosexual tendencies. What did this mean for me, who had always been more emotionally attached to women than to men? In freshman year my roommate and I became very close and dependent on each other, but neither of us could handle the intensity; that happened to me a lot with female friends. In psychotherapy I asked (indirectly of course) if I had "those tendencies." After about fifteen minutes the therapist figured out the question and asked, "Are you wondering if you're a lesbian?" Me: "Not really—ahh, I'm just wondering what you think about those tendencies." "You've given no indications of that," he said. Phew! was my reaction, not knowing what those "indications" were. (That's a story of how expertise has power over people's lives.) So I didn't worry about being a lesbian, but continued to build close friendships with women.

After college I felt the sadness of women friends going in different directions without the question of sharing our lives, as there would be with boyfriends. I went with a guy for three years, but he was never more important to me than two of my female friends. That was to my liking, not his. He wanted to get married, but since marriage wasn't part of any world I could imagine for myself we split up. Sometimes my friendships with women were threatened by their jealous boyfriends. With these feelings, I could no longer ignore the women's movement. I read something another woman had written about her—

and my—experiences. Fantastic! I wasn't alone. I began thinking that men didn't understand friendship, that they were sexual prowlers wanting all the attention focused on them; whereas my relationships with women seemed natural, exciting and intense.

Working with Women's Liberation in Boston meant being with women all the time. A group of us who weren't really close but were friends would hang out together, circle-dance at a bar, play basketball. Diana was one of them. She and I found we could tune into each other's survival tactics. What a relief. We could accept each other without many hurt feelings; we shared a lot of interests and criticisms of the women's movement. Eventually we slept together. That was four years ago.

DIANA. When I was a kid, I was always a tomboy. In seventh grade the situation changed—I went to a private school where I didn't know anyone and all my friends were girls. I never got to know any of the boys and couldn't see why anyone would want to—they were picking on younger kids, harassing women teachers, and so on. It seemed as though you couldn't get to know them as friends, but only flirt with them. I didn't want to flirt, so I didn't go to parties everyone else was going to. I knew of course that when boys and girls grew up they were supposed to mysteriously start being attracted to each other. I thought that would happen to me too, later. But the kids in my class just seemed to be playing at being grown up.

In junior high I started identifying more strongly as a girl. Boys were becoming more and more of an alien group. I still hated stockings and frills, but I certainly didn't want to be a boy any more.

We had dancing classes in junior high. One night between dances a cold breeze started blowing through the open window. I reached over and touched Margaret's knee and asked her if she was getting cold, too. She shrank back in mock horror and said, "What's the matter, Diana, are you a lesbian?" Everyone nearby started snickering. I didn't know what a lesbian was, but I knew I didn't want to be one. Later I found out; there was a lot of joking and taunting among girls in my class about lesbianism, which they viewed as sick and disgusting.

I went to an all-girls boarding school for high school. I was happy to be in an all-girls school because I thought of boys as people you couldn't act naturally with, people who would make the classroom atmosphere tense and uptight. I began to worry consciously about being a lesbian. I knew that wherever I went, women attracted my attention, never men. If I rode on a bus or subway I would watch the faces of all the women. My emotional attachments were all to women, and I had crushes on women friends. But I thought that if my attachments weren't sexual I was okay. I tried imagining sex with one of the seniors and was repelled by the thought. That was a relief. I said to myself that I was attracted to girls'

faces, not their bodies. I told myself, "I just think Kitty's body is beautiful from an *esthetic* point of view, not a sexual one."

I was a tactophobe—a word we invented to mean someone who was afraid of touching people. I was afraid that if I touched other girls I would like it and keep on touching them. So I became repulsed at the idea, to save myself from perversion.

I went to college, and as I began sleeping with boys, I began to lose some of my fear of being a lesbian. I enjoyed sex with boys at first, though I didn't much enjoy being with them otherwise and was always trying to think up reasons not to see my boyfriend. I thought men were boring, and I still felt I had to act very artificially with them.

I began to go on a campaign to become more boy-oriented. I tried consciously to watch more men and fewer women in the subway. I wanted to feel turned on to men, not because it would be enjoyable, but because I was afraid I would not be a complete woman otherwise.

One summer I went to Latin America. There the women are much more physical with each other, walking arm in arm, dancing close together, and touching each other more. I liked this freedom and thought that it showed how culture-bound our definitions of homosexuality are. I got close to one woman, a nurse named Edna. Before I left I spent a day at her house. We were sitting on her bed and she started sucking my finger. I was totally turned on. As I left I thought, Oh, no, there's no denying it any more. I'm a lesbian. Bisexuality did not occur to me as a possibility, although I knew the term. I thought if I was turned on to women, I must accept the fact of being a total queer.

I got into the women's movement and felt an enormous relief that I would no longer have to play roles with men and act feminine and sweet, dress in skirts and heels, and do all the things I'd done on dates. Then I began to feel hatred for men for having forced me into these roles. During this time, I would buy women's papers as soon as they came out and look immediately for articles by gay women. I began to hang out with gay women, who turned out to be regular people, not the stereotypes I had imagined. On a gut level I was beginning to realize that gayness was not a sickness. One night I went out for a long walk, and when I got home I had decided I was a lesbian. For me it was not a decision to become a lesbian. It was a question of accepting and becoming comfortable with feelings that I had always had.

I don't know if I would ever have come out if it hadn't been for the women's movement. The women's movement first led me to question the "naturalness" of the male-female roles that I had always largely accepted. Because I thought that role-playing heterosexuality was "the way it's supposed to be," whenever I rebelled against these roles I was afraid that this meant I was not a complete woman, that there was something wrong with me—not enough sex hormones, no doubt. The women's movement helped me to reject these roles, and with them every reason for struggling to be heterosexual. I realized femaleness was something I was born with; it was not something others could reward me with when I acted "feminine," or take away from me as a punishment.

SHARON. As a black woman growing up in the South in the fifties and sixties, I spent most of my life trying to deal with the racist attitudes in this country. I learned very early that a black woman was supposed to be a passionate and ever-ready bedmate and a tireless drudge. Needless to say, neither option appealed to me a great deal. As a child and adolescent I had always been aggressive and active—with my family's support. Their feeling was that eventually I'd have to face a hostile world, and if I was going to survive I would have to be tough and ready for anything. Ours was a fairly large family and we were poor, so I always knew that I would have to leave home as soon as I could support myself, and once I left, my parents wouldn't be able to help me any more. I would be on my own. My parents were very aware of this and supported my efforts to be as independent as possible, for which I am extremely grateful.

I was never taught that marriage was my only option, and I was encouraged to think in terms of a career for myself. When I reached high school there were a few skirmishes about my unfeminine behavior, but the issue was never pushed too far.

When I was about sixteen I began hanging out with the other kids and pairing off with various guys. We

didn't date then because things were still segregated and there was no place we could go anyway. I had sex with guys off and on, but I was very turned off by the way most guys treated me and the other girls. It was considered perfectly all right for a boy to slap a girl around for next to no reason, and even though the girls objected, they usually put up with it. I hated being hit, and if a guy hit me, or even threatened to, I wouldn't have anything to do with him. The other girls called me stuck-up for this, but I just couldn't tolerate being abused or threatened.

When I went to college there were only two other black students on the entire campus, and they came from comfortable middle-class families. I felt as out of place with them as I did with the middle-class white students. My social awkwardness, combined with the fact that I had to work about forty hours a week to put myself through school, made it really hard to make friends. The people I hung out with were usually other working students, outcasts like myself. It was about this time that I began to become aware of an attraction to women, which I kept trying to suppress. Women struck me as being warmer and more open than men. I was fascinated by the idea of loving a woman but was totally turned off by what I thought lesbians were supposed to be like. I didn't want to be a man nor look like one.

Since I was out of my element socially, I always came on as tough and aggressive to cover up, and people started accusing me of being a dyke. At the time, I was terrified that my fantasies were showing in some way, and I began dating to cover up, to show that I wasn't "like that." Now I realize that the accusations were intended to bring me into line and make me behave "like a lady," and it worked. I knew that being a black woman gave everyone the right to walk on me (or try to, anyway), and I thought that being a black lesbian was some sort of capital crime. I was really afraid of what would happen to me if they could prove anything. I wasn't kidding myself that any of my liberal friends would come rushing to my defense if they thought I was a homosexual. Black and white would avoid me like the plague: a black homosexual woman would be nothing but a liability. It was this more than anything else that made me steer clear of women who showed an interest in me.

My relationships with men have never been very good from my point of view. Though I've known a couple of genuinely good guys, most men share society's view of black women. Guys, both black and white, always expected me to be dynamite in bed, know every trick in the book, and show them a fantastically good time. They'd get angry if I refused to do something they wanted me to. After all, I was black wasn't I? I was supposed to enjoy everything. What right did I have to refuse anything they wanted?

The women's movement came along about the time I

finished college, and at first I was really excited; but I ended up feeling disappointed because the things they were concerned with were not the things that I needed. I had been supporting myself for years, was not dependent on a man, and was very put off by the movement's middle-class way of looking at things. Still, though I never became active, the movement gave me support because I could see other women having the courage to change their lives. Their example gave me the courage to see that I was cheating myself by pretending I was straight, and that if I kept it up I would go on being miserable. I finally did come out sexually with a black woman I met at work. I was scared stiff at first and had to confront my own prejudices about what I thought lesbians were. For the first time, I began to feel the freedom to be whatever I needed to be at the time, and the freedom to be different. I reasoned that if a racist society wanted my head, they'd get it because I was black, and being gay wasn't going to make all that much difference. My life has been much fuller since then, and a lot happier. I still tend to feel more comfortable with other black women, since a lot of white women have the same kind of stereotypes about black women as men have, and I still sometimes get that same pressure to "perform." This can be quite painful and make me feel like a plaything, so I'm still pretty sensitive about it. Generally I feel a lot better having a lesbian life-style, but even though most of my straight friends know I'm gay, I don't foresee coming out of the closet completely. I'm still pretty paranoid about that, but things are still changing. So am I.

SHELLY. I am now thirty-one years old. When I was seventeen I got into a lot of trouble. That wasn't new with me, and my parents felt they could do nothing else, so they took me to court and I ended up in a jail for stubborn children. (In those days there was no place else.) When I got to Framingham Institution for Women . . . that was the change in my life. There were all kinds of people there, and what I became most interested in were the street hustlers, lesbians and pills. I got involved with all.

At that time in my life I had no trouble accepting the fact that I was interested in being with women. A lot of women then, and even now, go through a lot of changes behind these things. Fortunately, I didn't go through that.

One thing happened to me that I will never forget. This one girl came to me in the middle of the night, and it ended up with us having sex for the first time in my life. From that time on, we were close friends. I became close to other women the same way. I assure you, it was quite an experience—being in prison. Well, I don't want to get into all the time I was there. In a way, it was sad to leave all the new and different women I met in my time there.

When I left I looked for the same type of people. I found them. Let me say, I wasn't a very smart person as far as life goes, so I got into things very easy. Like the street life and prostitution. I found it very easy to get into. I not only liked the money and the people, but I liked the fact that I was fooling the men that were paying me. After being out for a few months I met this gay fellow. He was black and very free and a happy person. I liked that because that's the way I wanted to be. We got together.

The first five years were just great. We both made money. We had our thing together, but also he was involved with his men and I with women. We did have a little girl, and that put a stop to a lot of things for a while. I was kind of worried about having a kid in the life I was in. But as far as she was concerned nothing bad came out of it.

Well, things started to go downhill when he got into drugs. I mentioned before that I had gotten into taking pills by this time, but I had had to stop taking as many as I had been. I was at one time very involved with pills, and I was often very high. I had stopped once, when I had my daughter. Well, getting back to him and his drugs . . . he got into heroin. At first I didn't think that he would get a habit, because he had tried it before and had just dropped it. But not this time. He got into it and did it good. I had tried it a few times and liked it, but he wouldn't let me get into it very much . . . for his own reasons, I am sure. As it turned out, I didn't get hung up on it.

It got so bad that all the money we had was going into his arm. We used to buy things for all three of us, but then that stopped. We got into selling it. All this ended when the police busted our house and put us in jail for selling drugs. That was a little over three years ago.

My daughter went to live with my sister, he went to jail for nine to ten years, and I went to a rehabilitation center. Before I got out of there I went through a lot of changes, mostly in groups. Boy, did I get it when I told them I was gay. They went through the whole thing of my being sick to be like that. Most of this came from the men. The women didn't have too much to say about it. The way I thought, either the women wanted to be gay and didn't want to say anything, or they didn't care. Whatever, it really didn't matter to me who liked it and who didn't. I even got accused of trying to make it with one of the girls. I wasn't, but that's how the girl took it. After a while there was no more said about it. I guess they just accepted it as it was.

My stay there lasted fourteen and a half months, and when it was time for me to leave I had no place to go. I didn't want to go to my sister's because that was just too much to put up with. So I called a woman I had met through a place for help. She was there with the help. She took me and my daughter in. I might add that it was really different to live with her, and in a really small town. As a matter of fact, it was difficult for us both. She was used to living alone and being quiet and doing pretty much what she wanted. I was the opposite. Then there was my daughter in between all this. I guess all three of us went through a lot of changes.

Since we have been together she has met a lot of my old friends and I have met hers. They are so different that I have to laugh. We have gotten a chance to meet a new group of people together at a gay club we go to. These people (men and women) are just great. They live in situations close to ours.

I am divorced from my husband now, and I find myself being very happy . . . going to work each day and coming home to my roommate and daughter. I play sports as much as I can. In the summer I play softball, in the winter volleyball. I even go to a theater workshop. It took me a very long time to get my head together and do something for myself and for my daughter. But I did, and it's been three years now. The way things are now is the good way, and I think I'll just keep it like it is.

MIKI. I am a twenty-seven-year-old gay woman who has been into the women's movement for approximately four years. Although I "came out" many years ago, the movement has helped me accept myself as a woman and accept my gayness in a new way.

I was the older of two girls. I always knew my mother wanted a son, and consequently I have always put a high value on achievement (something that is usually more important for sons than daughters). As a young child I played mostly with one boy, because he was the only other Jew around and the other kids were Catholic and didn't want to play with us. From age seven to ten I was a tomboy but lived near other kids, and I had several girl friends and one special friend. I always felt pretty normal—just a little smarter than the others in school. When I was in the sixth grade we moved (still in Queens, New York City), and it was then that I began to feel different. I got crushes on girls, while everyone else had them on boys. My tomboy interests were no longer acceptable, especially to my mother, for I had gotten my period and was now a "woman."

I felt different from girls around me in many ways— they had money and clothes, and their fathers were professionals. They could dance and flirt with boys. I was segregated into special classes in junior high, and thus my social life was confined to bar mitzvahs of the boys in my class, at which we petted and made out. I was increasingly aware of my attraction to other girls. In high school I was placed in a special science class designed to make us all into nuclear physicists. There were forty boys and four girls in this class. I was friends with the girls but developed a really close and important relationship with a boy, M. We talked about many things, and he accepted my feelings toward women as natural. Our relationship was based mostly on intellectual stimu-

lation, since I didn't feel turned on to M. sexually. In a lot of ways I thought of girls as silly and didn't want to compete with them for boys; but I did compete with boys for achievement in school. I wanted to be a boy so that I could have the career that I wanted and also in order to have a girl friend, for I thought that girls only liked boys.

I had my first gay relationship at about age seventeen, in college, with an older woman who looked like a "dyke"—short, greased-back hair, pants, jacket, etc. It made me even more sure that I was gay, but I fought hard to be bisexual.

My years in college were spent with a small group of "druggies" at the beginning of hippie culture. There was a certain level of acceptance of my gayness: I slept with my girl friends, but they were still looking for boyfriends and thought that all I needed was to meet the "right man."

In college there was a woman whom I spent a lot of time with—who taught me to trust, whom I loved very much. When I told her that I loved her and wanted to sleep with her, she said I was sick and she was going to help me with my problem. There was always a certain amount of sexual tension and rejection that I felt from the women that I related to, because they were straight.

Then I went to work for the Welfare Department in the South Bronx. I had my first real affair with a woman and my first taste of reality outside of academia. At the end of that relationship I couldn't deal with my feelings and started shooting heroin. This went on for two years. I didn't get very involved with the people or the realities around me, because it was too depressing. I had one close friend and lover, who fucked me over in a way, because when she got involved with a boy, that was clearly more important to her than our relationship. I got busted twice for dope and kicked my habit. I stayed in Manhattan for a while and was part of the bar scene there and got into cruising and one-night stands.

At that time the women's movement to me meant child-care and abortion demands, which had no relevance to my life as a gay woman. I went to a Radicalesbians meeting because I liked the name, and met a woman from Gay Women's Liberation in Cambridge, who invited me to Cambridge in February 1971. I was really turned on to the feeling of community, and saw so many "freak" gay women that I didn't feel so much alone. Then women from Cambridge and Boston seized a building at Harvard for a women's center. After being at the women's center, I went through a lot of changes and started to accept being a woman, identifying with the women's movement and getting really angry. Only now I had women to help me figure out how to channel that anger. They helped me change the ways in which I was hurting myself and the women I was involved with, because of my former identification with and acceptance of male values.

Now I live my life largely with gay women, and the possibilities for real friendship with women have become a reality. When it's possible, I am open with people about being gay, because I feel good about it. I am learning how to make relationships with women work. I don't feel sick and alone any more, and I have more optimism about the future.

OUT OF THE CLOSET AND INTO THE FRYING PAN

Lesbianism is not a physical characteristic—unlike the quality of being black or being a woman. So most of us have the choice either to be invisible, by passing as straight, or to be open. If we decide to be openly gay we often become vulnerable to physical and psychological harassment. We're labeled sick, sometimes kept away from kids, maybe fired from our jobs. If we keep our gayness hidden we are constantly subjected to the insults and embarrassment of being assumed to be heterosexual: gynecologists want us to use birth control, friends want to "set us up" with boys, men make passes at us. More important, our lives often become filled with the fear that others will find out. We may be blackmailed (though this mostly happens to gay men)—for money if we have it, for favors and information if we don't.

One of the first decisions confronting gay women after they come out is whether to tell their families and friends that they are gay.

HEDY. Sexuality is a very heavy thing with my parents. When my mother found out that I wasn't a virgin any longer she started sobbing hysterically. I think she would rather have heard that I was a mad bomber than *that*. Since I've been more into the women's movement and have come out I've felt much more loving and sympathetic toward my parents, especially my mother. She's noticed that I've been happier when I see her and less hostile. She's also relieved that I'm innocently living with girl roommates instead of with degenerate male lovers. It's scary to think of shattering this—the first real affection between us since I was a kid—by telling her I'm now a pervert. I'm sure she'll accuse me of turning into a lesbian on purpose, in order to torture her. I have to tell them soon, though, because it's getting harder and harder to see my family and feel close to them while I'm still withholding this big secret.

SARAH. The mystique of the family really hits me when I think about telling my parents. I look at my parents as being totally isolated. Who can they talk to about their daughter being gay? (I have my gay friends to talk to.) In this society people make very harsh judgments about gay people, and making a judgment about a kid is also mak-

ing a judgment about the parents. My parents feel that they are responsible for the person I am, and they can get into guilt trips about what they did wrong.

After I came out I really didn't want to be preoccupied with being gay. That was a drag; I'm a regular person too, who has other interests, other things to talk about. Except that when I left this protected gay colony to venture into home-town, family affairs, I was constantly reminded: I'm gay. I'm gay.

For example, at a wedding an aunt let me know that I was expected to be next in line.

"Sarah, come here. I want to talk business."

"Yeah? What are you selling?"

"I'm old, I don't have many years left. Tell me, when can I expect your wedding?"

"I'm too young. I have too much to do."

"Too young? How old are you?"

"I'm twenty-four."

"Twenty-four! I was married for four years when I was your age."

"So you were too young."

She laughed, thank God—and I went to say hello to a cousin.

RITA. Telling my sister was not so difficult and felt good. We have been pretty close most of our lives. She is divorced and has a child, and she has been broadening her ideas about ideal sexuality. I felt that if she could see my girl friend and me interacting—being friends, doing things together—it would break down the idea that we belonged to a secret, erotic, violent underworld, totally removed from other women. Her reaction was a mixture of acceptance because she loves me and confusion because of all her preconceived ideas. I felt that she accepted my gayness too much on the level of sexual preference, rather than understanding the difference in relationships or what it means for me to be gay in a world that is mostly hostile to homosexuality.

It's not just our family and friends whom we have to worry about telling that we're gay. The problem goes beyond that to all the institutions of our society, to our doctors, our psychiatrists, our employers, our teachers, our "friendly" neighborhood cops—all of whom have

the power to make our lives very difficult if they know we're gay, and many of whom don't hesitate to use that power.

Homosexuality is still illegal in most states. Though the statutes prohibiting homosexual acts are almost never enforced against women, they may be used selectively, like drug laws, to punish political undesirables or others whom the Establishment wants out of the way. They may be used as an excuse for discrimination elsewhere, such as on the job. There are also laws in most states against "sex psychopaths," which allow homosexuals to be committed to hospitals for indeterminate periods, from one day to life.

However, most of the discrimination that we face when we come into contact with the legal system is based, not on the laws against homosexuality, but on societal attitudes toward "queers." The police harass us, especially around gay bars. Since it is difficult to prove that anyone has committed a homosexual act, they arrest us for drunkenness or disorderly conduct, charges for which their testimony is usually enough to convict us. In court, lesbians convicted of crimes often get stiffer sentences than straight women. Gay mothers often lose custody of their children. A study of divorce and child-custody cases showed that in most cases in which lesbianism was an issue, the mother lost her kids. The courts seem to want to "protect" our children from us. One of the women working on this chapter lost custody to her husband without even being present in court to defend herself.

Doctors, lawyers, clergy and counselors are others who, because of their position of power over us, can cause us much trouble if they know we are gay. Gynecologists pose a special problem. Often we are forced to tell them we are gay because it affects their diagnosis or the treatment they prescribe for us. However, when we tell them, not only may we be subjected to lectures, snide comments and voyeuristic questions, but we may find that, after all, they are totally ignorant about our problems. Very little research is done on the medical problems of lesbians, and gynecologists often don't bother to acquaint themselves with what is known. One of us went to see a gynecologist because she was hemorrhaging badly. The doctor insisted that she was having a miscarriage although he knew she was gay. A friend of ours was hastily—and wrongly—diagnosed as having gonorrhea by a gynecologist who did not realize that VD is not easily spread from one woman to another.

JODY. I have pelvic endometriosis, a noncontagious disease that women can get from a bad abortion or low progesterone production. The disease isn't very common, and doctors know very little about it. After I found out what I had, I knew I should ask my doctor about making love. He said, "Abstain from sexual intercourse for a while." I didn't have the nerve to tell him I was a lesbian. Besides, I figured that if I told him he still wouldn't have an answer, because homosexuality is something people don't even talk about, let alone do medical research about.

About two months later I figured I'd better find out more, so I asked a gynecologist who I'd heard was fairly sympathetic to women. I was scared to death and felt like I had rocks in my stomach. Instead of answering my question, his face got very stiff and "professional," and he said, "Perhaps you should explain what you do sexually, so I'll have a better idea how it affects you." I just sat there flabbergasted. Here was this medical dude who wanted to know how we "do it." Finally I said, "I don't think that's any of your business. What I need to know is if any form of sex is harmful, or if it's just harmful when there's penetration." He kept pushing me to describe how I made love with women, what it felt like, whether I had been a lesbian my whole life, the whole trip. I got really mad, started yelling at him that we did it with bananas, what did he think—after all, everyone knows that the only reason you're a lesbian is that you want a penis or you're afraid of men. He said, "Your disease is psychological, not medical. I know a very good psychiatrist whom I would recommend that you see. He has cured many homosexuals." I said, "Do you mean that I spent five years in pain, spent months in and out of doctors' offices, and finally had surgery for a psychological disease? Are you telling me that I didn't get endometriosis from a rotten abortion six years ago, that it's all in my head?" He quickly retreated and admitted that he knew I had endometriosis and that that wasn't psychological, then rapidly changed the subject to my abortion with questions like, "Do you think that having that experience was the reason you began to feel hostile toward men?"

By this time it was crystal clear that I wasn't going to get any information out of him that would do me any good. I was crying as I left, and the last thing he said to me was, "I strongly recommend that you see a psychiatrist. You're clearly very emotionally upset because you're a lesbian, and I think it would help you to deal with your disease if you began to work out your feelings about men. You're young, you can change." By that time I wanted to kill him, but I just told him that only a violent feminist revolution would deal with my feelings about men and that he'd definitely be on the top of my list.

Job discrimination, which is a problem for all women, is a big problem for lesbians. We gay women are very dependent on our jobs, since we cannot fall back on husbands for support if we are out of work. Yet in addition to the disadvantages we face as women, lesbians are subject to further job discrimination for being gay. If we are openly gay, we are likely to be the last hired and the first fired. Employers usually need no excuse to justify firing us. If we hide our gayness in order to find a job, we may live in constant fear of being found out.

At the same time, the activities and openness of the gay movement have brought the fight for gay civil rights legislation to many states. While it is still a hard struggle to win such legislative battles, steps are being taken toward granting us our basic civil rights and liberties.

MIKI. I was involved with my supervisor. She would meet me a block away from the office after work and drop me off a few blocks away in the morning, because she was afraid to be seen with me in public. We would not even go to a bar together because she was afraid there would be a raid and she would lose her job.

Despite the risk it entails, many women choose to be open about their gayness on the job—because they don't want to playact all the time, because they don't want to be discovered and fired later, or because they are sick of always being assumed to be heterosexual.

CLYDE. I have worked in many places, mostly factories and plants. When you start a new job it's hard to get to know the people there. The first question I'm always asked is, "Are you married, and how many children do you have?" I just answer, "I have no husband, I have a girl friend." Most of the people in the places I've worked don't have much to say about me being gay. I mean, they're in no position to be worried about my sexuality when they're working in a place like that, because we are both being fucked over by the same people.

THE-RAPISTS: LESBIANS AND PSYCHIATRY

MOLLY. I began to seek psychiatric help when the woman I'd lived with for years committed suicide. I was drinking heavily, couldn't accept her death, and had no idea how to continue my life. When the anxiety became unbearable I checked into a hospital. The interviewing doctor told me they would be able to help me. Oblivious to the fact that I managed to get drunk every day for fifteen months in the hospital, they began to assault my lesbianism: sometimes they assigned me an aide to follow me around the ward; they threw me into "preventive" seclusion; they investigated all my relationships with the other women patients; and on occasion threatened to interrupt friendships with massive doses of tranquilizers.

Doctors have told me I was utterly dependent (love women); had anxiety neuroses (alcohol withdrawal); was borderline schizophrenic (failed to conform to their idea of what a woman's life should be); and had a poor prognosis (I believed in myself more than in their theories about me).

In the few years following, things got worse: the drinking that threatened my life wasn't interesting to them. When I was close to dying, a clinic slip read, "Patient *says* she is alcoholic." But all the doctors were willing to ship me away permanently to the back wards of state hospitals, not because I was harming myself (drinking is just a symptom, they said), but because I lived wrongly. I could feel their need to punish me for not giving in to their opinions of what was wrong with my life—that is, I defended lesbianism as one of the more positive and beautiful aspects of my life. Yet they were so into forcing my life to conform to their theories that while I was literally dying of alcoholism they wanted to know what my lover and I did in bed.

My experience may seem extreme at first, but if we think about it, we can see that their treatment of me was just the logical extension of their theories. The same attitude is always there about lesbians (if they don't have you locked up in a hospital, it doesn't go that far, but it will be simply a milder dose of the same medicine): medicine seeks to undermine, mutilate, and ridicule the lesbian way of life.

Often doctors tell their patients they accept their homosexuality and assure the lesbian that they are able to treat her as a nondeformed being. However, in practice this is rarely the case, since the doctor would have to put aside all of his (her) theories of how women develop in order to truly accept the validity of lesbianism. After all, doctors are people who go through training that lasts up to fourteen years, and training fills their heads with false conceptions about the correct role of women in life. Many students do not come out of such intensive training with an open mind about lesbianism. (Except, of course, for students who are also lesbians.)

A therapist can't provide support in other areas if he or she disagrees with the basic tenets of a lesbian's life. And it would certainly be rare to run into a doctor who had had a lesbian experience and could begin to understand what one was talking about.

I had one resident psychiatrist who assured me that my lesbianism was acceptable to him. However, he told me he was constantly criticized by his supervisors and forced to present a defense of himself for not treating me for my homosexuality, since they insisted that that was at the root of my problems. That therapist subsequently threw me out of a hospital when I wasn't in any shape to leave after I'd discovered that he was a homosexual.

Where does all this leave the lesbian who is deeply troubled and feels in need of help? Obviously the ideal would be to find a therapy group where the members and the leaders were avowedly lesbians. This is rare, although not unknown, as for example the Homophile Clinic in Boston. Second, a number of female clinical psychologists have become part of the movement for women's liberation and are very supportive to women, including lesbians.

A rule of thumb would be to be wary of psychiatrists and analysts—that is, therapists with medical training—as that branch of the psych field is the most reactionary, most grounded in doctrine harmful to women, and its practitioners often give out tranquilizers under the guise of, or instead of, treatment. Psychology is not always better, but the training is shorter—and more flexible—and it is in this realm that radical therapists and young women and men seeking radical, relevant approaches to emotional troubles can be found.

When choosing a group, a lesbian should request that she be put in one with at least some other gay people. She should look for a group in which the leader is also required to participate, not as an inhuman, arrogant authority figure, but as another human being who happens to have a little more information about how people work than the rest of us, and would like to share that knowledge.

And last, one should try to find out whether the orientation of the group is totally in terms of adjusting to society as it is, or whether radical life alternatives are sought and valued.

THE BARS

We need places where we can go to be with other gay women—to meet, talk, dance, relax, be sexual—to be totally ourselves. We need to be able to meet others like ourselves who will understand us when we talk about our lives. Some of us exist secretly where we work and where we live. And each time we are made to feel invisible, insulted, or freakish, we add more anger and hatred to our stored-up frustrations.

Society, knowing that we need someplace to vent our feelings, gives us our bars. Mafia-controlled, they are usually crowded and expensive. If we are lucky, we may have a gay women's bar in our town. Recently one opened up in Boston; it's run by gay women, sometimes has an all-women band, and there are few men. The atmosphere is pleasant and relaxed, but it's still a profit-making enterprise, with high prices and cover charges.

Often, however, gay women, gay men and others of society's outcasts are lumped together in one dingy, crowded little bar—such as the Bottom Rock in Boston. The bar becomes a hustling scene, full of pimps and drug dealers, as well as straight men, often with straight women, who come to get their voyeuristic rocks off on watching us. Booze flows, alcoholism is encouraged, and sometimes fights break out. Then the cops, always hovering nearby, start beating and arresting. Some evening's relaxation that is! And the anger that should be directed toward society is directed toward one another, as it always is when people are ghettoized. We get uptight, jealous and strung-out (emotionally drained and tense) on the destructive bar atmosphere.

Why do we keep going there? Because there is no other place to be with lots of other gay women, open and unashamed, to dance, hold each other close, and try to forget the straight world for a while.

CLYDE. I go to the bar because it's the only place to go, because my friends are there—friends I've been with since I was fifteen—you know, people who taught me to live with myself being gay. Because I was having a hard time putting up with it.

Well, every type of deviant comes in to the bar. I can honestly say I feel as though the people who come in to see the "freaks" (who are us) just come in to get off for the sake of getting off. I mean, we have love and feeling toward one another, where they don't. These dingaling executive guys, who have six kids and a wife, come over and pick up a drag queen on the corner. There's no love, there's no affection, there's no emotional feeling. It's all sexual when they come in. Like among us there're feelings, but like these freaks come into the bar—I mean, *they're* the freaks and come in to see us!

A hopeful alternative to the bars is beginning to appear. Here in Boston weekly lesbian liberation meetings, more and more frequent women's dances and gay dances, a large room and an office for gay women at the Cambridge Women's Center all provide a chance for gay women to get together, rap, dance, vent our anger and frustration and celebrate our joy at being together, ouside the dreary and sick atmosphere of a bar. We control the atmosphere; we set the terms. Nobody gawks at us, insults us, makes money off us.

LOVING

DIANA. One night I gave Sarah a ride home and I went inside to have a cup of coffee and chat for a few minutes. We ended up talking all night long. During the whole time Sarah was jabbing, punching, tugging, wrestling with me. We felt a physical tension but were too uptight to be physically affectionate. Finally, at around five in the morning, we began to nod out and I asked if I could sleep there. She said, "Sure. There're two beds in the living room."

We lay down completely dressed, she on one bed, I on the other. Then she started telling me that hers was much softer than mine. So I got up to try it, lying with my feet to her head. We decided that we'd both sleep on that bed (just because it was the more comfortable, of course).

But suddenly Sarah was afraid that my car might have been ticketed. So she jumped up and ran to look out the window. After she had been standing there for what seemed like fifteen minutes, I said, "Hey, Sarah, what're you doing?"

"Oh, I was just watching to see if the cops would come by to ticket your car."

Finally she came back to the bed and started to lie down again, head to foot and foot to head. I made a sour face and she turned around. At last we were lying together in the same direction. Timidly I put my arm around her. "Hey, Sarah, is this okay with you?" She said "Yeah" and snuggled up to me, putting her leg over mine. Pretty soon we were hugging each other. I tried to get up my nerve to kiss her—I'd bring my face up close to hers, then chicken out and turn away. After about ten false starts I got up the courage to do it—and she seemed to dig it.

That's as far as things went that first night, but soon we were sleeping together every night.

MIKI. My relationship with Daphne started when she was doing my astrology chart. We met and talked for hours, getting to know each other, walking and sitting by the river in the springtime. There is something very earthy, very sensitive, and very warm, kind and understanding about her. She was married and is a mother—that too, and her kids, turned me on. Perhaps being a mother makes a woman more sensitive to feelings in others.

Daphne has had sexual feelings for women all her life, but has always fought them because she was trying to be a good wife and mother. The women's movement gave her the space and support to finally accept her gayness and come out.

That first night by the river we kissed and touched one another hesitantly. For me there's something very exciting about first times, and I too was intoxicated by the freedom and pleasure she felt at finally being able to make love with a woman. For the first time in a sexual relationship with a woman, for me, things were equal. I trusted her, I could relax and enjoy her making love to me, for it was obvious that she got pleasure out of it.

We spent a lot of time together that summer up in Maine, living outdoors—making love under the stars, in open fields at midday, in the woods. We had a very beautiful, very private, special and romantic first few months together. I was happy, secure in loving and being

loved by a woman so beautiful, precious and special to me. I was no longer feeling the confusion of having several relationships at once. I was planning that we could live together, that I would have a family with kids to be a part of my life. I didn't feel lonely, and aside from a few areas in my life I felt Daphne didn't understand or take seriously enough (my past drug problems), I felt that we understood each other and were able to share the pleasures of our love for each other by a passionate, flowing lovemaking and in just being in nature together.

Then the bubble burst—her husband freaked and got custody of the kids just because she was gay. All communication between us was cut off. I've cried a lot.

RONNIE. I've slept with a lot of women. Some people would call this casual sex, but it has involved me in a lot of pain. I took chances sleeping with women I liked, and I have been hurt.

I slept with Lynn long after I first wanted to sleep with her. I had buried my attraction for her because she was in love with June and living with her. One night she was lonely and we had done something together. We kissed goodnight for five minutes. I remember making love with her and being afraid to open my eyes when we were done. I felt like the pauper sleeping with the queen. After making love we talked and laughed until morning, and she became a person like me. I liked her for her energy, her love of herself and life. That day we smiled when we met but did separate things.

The next night we went to the bar. We talked to many other women, extending ourselves because we were high on each other. That night I made love with her in a way you only can with someone whose pleasure you love.

Then I went back to the country. When I saw her next she was torn apart by the ending of her relationship with June. I knew she would feel different about me. She did, worried about what she had gotten herself into. I was angry that she didn't trust my friendship. Didn't she know that I understood her pain with June, that I hadn't intended sleeping with her to change our friendship? We talked and pretty much worked it out. For the rest of the summer there was some closeness between us.

She moved away, and in the fall I went to visit her. I felt scared. I walked instead of driving the last five miles to her house. I spent hours with the other people in her house, seemingly chatting about old times but really being tense. Finally only she and I sat in the kitchen. It wasn't easy. She invited me to sleep in her bed.

Being in bed broke our nervousness. We talked freely, laughed, spoke of our fears and feelings for each other honestly. Secure, we made love. Again I felt a welling up of passion for this incredible she-creature who, with luck, was my lover. Our bodies spoke their own language, but I felt that as I made love to her, I did so with a little less trust than before. Lynn said, "We have something nice. We can talk honestly about sex, and it seems as if we have a relationship with no expectations." I did not feel good with that summary.

When I left she was still sleeping. I was upset. For many months I never contacted her, feeling that each attempt would only create more distance. I saw her again, and again she did not know how to relate to me; she was distant at first, warmer after a while. I resented her caution as well as her warmth. I closed myself to her, saw those things about her which I had never liked, forgot her beauty and my wonder.

Sometimes there is no way you can sleep with someone and come away feeling good about yourself and her. You have to forget something to survive. Casual is not my word. Every time I open myself to someone, I feel love, anger, ripped off, stupid, dulled, released.

June

It just happened one afternoon
As we were walking home
posters in hand
on our way to day care
for Jesse and Raphael

"Do you think you'll ever have children?"
she asked me

My mind swelled with memories of my mother
asking when I wanted to settle down and have a family
memories of teaching retarded children
memories of wanting a baby so he'd stay with me
memories of needing a child to keep the loneliness away
Thinking of my sister alone with her son
Thinking of now
Thinking of who I have become
of whom I live with and whom I love
Thinking of loving women
of loving her (June)

"Do you think you'll ever have children?" she asked me
I felt the dam breaking
flooding my body and mind with warm liquid energy
alive and real

RITA

SARAH. When I first met Diana I didn't feel capable of expressing my thoughts unless someone else said it first. But then Diana and I discovered that we shared a way of relating to the world—our humor, feelings and analyses made sense to each other. And that was really freeing for me. It gave me the strength to be myself, to actively assert myself individually, even without Diana's presence.

Lots of the time we do things separately. On Wednesday nights one of us teaches a French class, the other goes to Lesbian Liberation meetings. We have different schedules at the newspaper.

We spend a lot of time with each other, but we are with other people too. We live with two other women, and there are always lots of people in and out of the apartment. All the things we work on, we do as part of a group. So whenever we get a chance we skip out and snatch a few minutes alone together somewhere beyond reach of visitors and phone calls.

All this is not to say everything's wonderful. We have some basic differences, and we often get into fights.

D. Sometimes I feel like knocking the shit out of her. So I go off into another room and play solitaire for a few hours to cool off. Or I take a walk outside, hoping some man will be foolish enough to try to rape me, so that I can vent my anger in beating the shit out of *him*.

S. Sometimes I feel like I'd like to get a good punch in. But then I don't really want to. So we scream and swear and take swings at each other, and then laugh and hug, all within twenty minutes.

NELL. I've become very afraid of getting closed into any relationship that looks like it might develop into monogamy. Maybe it's because I was married for thirteen years and I need a lot of private space around me. It's not that I don't have the same needs as any other woman. Sometimes I feel very lonely and really want to be intensely in love again, or to be able to just relax and depend on someone else to help me make decisions and share my life intimately. I'm thirty-seven and have three children, and I get tired and scared. But then I look at the lives of my monogamous friends, and I become more and more convinced that there has to be a different way for me to live with and love women. I think that a marriage of two women is better than a marriage between a woman and a man, because a woman will usually take better care of you than a man will. A couple starts off okay, but after a period of time the two people build up a frightening dependency on each other. I don't want to be responsible for someone else's happiness, not even my children's, or feel that she is responsible for mine. I don't want to feel that someone has to know what I'm doing every hour of the day and night. I'd end up lying to her. Even when a monogamous relationship is working well, friends of the couple become secondary.

It is often hard to relate to a tight couple if you are an unattached woman, especially if you're closer to one than the other, and it's not always possible to care for both equally. The other woman will probably resent your friendship with her partner if you're really close, even if it's not sexual. I'm not saying that that's always true, but I think it's common. And then what happens when one partner becomes a little bored with the other or begins to feel trapped? The feelings become unequal, and the pain really starts. If they break up, the process is long and awful. If they decide to loosen up the relationship and start being with other people, they find they can't control their jealousy even if they want to. Or else they agree to keep their thing the primary one and have casual side affairs that don't threaten it. Then these other people may feel second-rate and used. When I talk to my coupled-off friends about this stuff they say, "Maybe so, but no other kind of relationship looks any better." They're right, the way things are now, but I have a vision of what I think could work for me. I want to be very close to several women—live with some of them, sleep with some of them, and love all of them like family. I want the same amount of security and warmth that a couple can give each other, but I want it spread out to more than one woman. If one friendship is having trouble, the other ones can support and help it. If one woman goes away, I won't be totally freaked out and lonely. If I'm sleeping with more than one woman, maybe I can control my jealousy and my desire to own my sexual partners. I know it will be very hard to build free but long-term love relationships among a group of women, but the possibility of that kind of community keeps me going. If it doesn't work, I'll find a nice woman when I'm fifty and settle down.

"BLESSED ARE THE POOR"

As Lesbian Liberation has grown to include more and more women, and more different women, we have come to understand that many of our differences have a class origin. Here two women describe how their backgrounds have affected their relationships with other women and with the movement.

JESSE. I've always felt anxious when movement women started talking about role playing. I suppose because I'm a pretty "butch"-looking dyke, people assume that I am very much into roles. Anyway, the idea of being confronted by a group of middle-class movement women about my "macho" behavior was very intimidating.

In the past I haven't involved myself in the movement to any great extent because I felt intimidated and bitter about that. I have, though, thought a lot about why the movement has isolated me and whether or not it's fucked up, because I want to see the movement grow.

I gradually started to realize I didn't like the way this society set up identities. I didn't like the kind of roles my mother and father played. I liked doing the things my father was free to do, like having the freedom to develop his body. At five or six I was very physically oriented and played basketball and softball. How was I supposed to enjoy wearing skirts when I couldn't climb trees or fight in them? It didn't take me too long to realize I didn't like the role society had planned for me.

When it came time for me to start dating, it intrigued me that this was the way to become accepted. In high school I became bored with boys and related trivialities; wanting a strong mind as well as body, I got into a mind trip.

The mind trip came at about the same time I decided I was queer. The superiority complex I developed as a

defense against middle-class and heterosexual people seemed to me justifiable.

It was justified because they (my schoolmates) with all their middle-class behavior, showed themselves to be totally ignorant. Not only were they ignorant of the kinds of problems I had (an alcoholic father who beat me and a mother made spiritless by him), but they were ignorant of the privileges their social position gave them. They simply took it for granted that some time in their lives they would go to college and to Europe, that a new suede coat would be provided for them in the fall. They never questioned why all these things would be done. They never realized the world was theirs for the asking. They would simply get married, have children, and get a new car every year, and have good Christmases. They'd watch TV versions of poverty and say, "Those poor, underprivileged people."

The only way my relationship with my heterosexual schoolmates changed was that I grew to hate them more. I wanted to isolate myself from them completely, so I joined an all-girls gang. We went around beating up people and shoplifting. I also refused to shave my armpits or my legs, bathe, or comb my hair. Instead of wearing nylons and flats, I wore crew socks and sneakers. I did everything possible to make myself unattractive to my straight schoolmates.

As I approached the end of an ugly high school career and prepared to enter an ugly college career, my feelings of isolation from straight women came more to the front. I became frustrated with my state of forced celibacy. The only contact I had with other gay people was through idiot books I read—like psychology books—which filled my head with all sorts of shit about what gay people were like. It was really hard all my life to keep from thinking I was crazy, because those books and everyone around me told me I was, and often! But I never really thought that.

When I first came to Boston, it was my first real independence and vacation from celibacy. I immediately proceeded into this really dependent relationship—which was fucked up.

Since the books I'd read told me there was a "butch" and a "femme," I identified with the "butch" role, and so I was "butch" in bed, but I really didn't control the relationship. I was tough, but so was she. Now I look on "butch" and "femme" as being the same as "sadist" and "masochist." They have a symbolic relationship in which one is strong and the other weak, and they both get off on it.

After this relationship I slept with lots of women. Finally I began a relationship with a woman who was the first person I've ever trusted. Since the beginning of that relationship she and I have both slept with several other women, so I can't say I'm unfulfilled sexually. I also feel fulfilled emotionally and intellectually, since our ongoing relationship has seen much equal dialogue.

I've explained quite a bit now about where my head is

at. I love lots of women—my sisters. I may act "macho" at times, but I think being "macho" in some ways is right on.

The movement, by insulating itself with rhetoric, which is a middle-class thing, has insulated itself from me. It has no way of knowing who I am. What I want to say to the movement is: "Here I am. I'm a *Woman*, and you have to identify with me because of that. I'm going to trash you if I have to, because I love you."

My sisters have to deal with class and race, especially their own white, middle-class values. They must realize that they still have those values.

The lower (working) class will make the revolution. My sisters must become grassroots, learn to survive, before they can say they believe in themselves as revolutionaries. My sisters must believe in themselves. Only then will they be totally strong. And my sisters need to be totally strong, because they must make the revolution.

MARILYN. *(previously identified as "Clyde")*. I was a girl who liked to do the things boys got to do. I wasn't allowed to do them though, because that wasn't my role as a girl growing up in Amerika. So I rebelled against the straight social structures and was harassed by being called tomboy and queer by my "friends." And I was punished by my folks and other authorities for not being the little lady I was meant to be—punished for the things I wanted and for not accepting their wants of me.

I was created by the very society in which I was brought up. Male-oriented, egomaniac, war-spattered, full-of-hate world; hate for anybody who isn't like them. Therefore I was forced to hide my love for other women by denying myself the truth; *I am a woman!*

So I took on the role of a man in dress and in attitude. It is much easier for men to accept me as one of them than it is for them to try to accept me for myself, a woman in love with other women. This I know just by knowing, and also by being told so by my straight male friends, who treated me like one of the boys.

I have been through a lot of changes throughout my life. The most obvious and best happened since I found the gay left women's movement, which helped me define my anger and stay sober long enough to realize it. (Too bad there aren't more working-class women in it—the intimidation is still there.)

I went to a meeting only because my ego was amazingly macho. I entered the room wearing—get this—a black fur, short-waisted jacket, a Clyde hat, low-waisted beige crepe pants, black patent leather shoes and a V-neck body shirt. "The cat's ass, let me tell you," that was my attitude.

Ever since then I have been realizing that I am a woman and not a butch denying myself my true identity.

I have been gay all my life (twenty-five years). I have hung out with other gay people since I was twelve years old. I picked up my first love in church at age seven, and we still keep in touch. I grew up in a working-class society. A society made up of dope, alcoholism, and the street level of survival.

For people growing up in a middle- or upper-middle-class society the struggle isn't made up of watching their parents trying to make ends meet, street fights, or the sadistic educational system that we are forced into because of our economic status. For middle-class gay women the struggle is not the same, because they can afford to escape the realities of the mafia-controlled bars and the harassment of the heterosexual men who come in to look at and get off on two women together. They have their own bars run by other middle-class people. For a working-class queer to feel comfortable in them is to deny the class differences that exist. They keep close watch on "others" not of their class, expecting fights to break out because they think it is our nature, and they don't realize that this is our way of life and strategy for survival.

We are created by the very society in which we are brought up. Class background has a lot to do with what role you play and how you play it.

If you were brought up in a working-class neighborhood your ideas of male and female roles have gone to the extremes, with all their crude oppressions. If you were brought up middle class your role playing is less crude.

Middle-class women have more possibilities for disguising their gayness and keeping it hidden from the heterosexual world. Theirs are more socially acceptable forms of self-expression. They express themselves in ways that are not considered contradictory to being female, such as being a gym teacher or some kind of professional. The scope of their activities is broader only because their class allows that to be.

The adjustments and changes that we as gay women have made, the numbers and groups in which we move, the patterns we have followed, the effort to deal with our class, gayness and alienation—all will be deeply affected by our strength of numbers in this class-oriented, straight, male society.

LESBIAN MOTHERS

In a society that is afraid of lesbians and tries to shelter children from the fact that women can love women, to be a lesbian mother takes courage. One way or another, after we had already become parents, each of us managed to find the personal strength to stand up against the sexist social pressures to be heterosexual, and declare our freedom to have a choice . . . to love women. But for mothers the decision to be independent of men is not simple. It was difficult and complicated for most of us. Because of concerns about our children's needs (how to protect them from, or help them deal with, possible ridicule from other kids for having a "different" mother; how not to alienate their fathers to the point where they might withdraw their financial or emotional support from the kids), and because of pressures from their fathers and grandparents designed to "guilt-trip" us into conformity "for the sake of the children" ("What will they think of you?" "What will their friends think?"), but especially because of the threat of losing custody of our children if it were ever contested in court, many of us were in conflict before deciding to risk coming out.

For some of us, just getting to the point where we could feel free to define ourselves as lesbians to *ourselves*, let alone to anyone else, involved a process of growth and liberation. But then to act—to end our marriages, lock horns with society, and raise our children as gay mothers—took a level of determination which some of us never knew we possessed. This is particularly true of mothers with older children, who tend to spend more time with their peers and worry more about what their friends think of them than young children do. It is simply a fact that in America children are indoctrinated to be anti-homosexual by the same "brainwashing" devices which feed into other oppressive prejudices—racism, sexism, anti-Semitism, etc.

Through scapegoating tactics, put-down jokes, name-calling, abusive graffiti and society's total refusal to take lesbianism seriously as a legitimate, positive option, children are presented with the picture of lesbians—which we know all too well—as social "rejects," "wallflowers" turned angry. "Faggot" is synonymous with "jerk" these days, and "lesie" is the female equivalent. Obviously this kind of bigoted scapegoating is destructive for everyone (for those who tell the "kike," "nigger," "gook," or "fairy" jokes, as well as for those who are the brunt of them). For sure, the sneering and snickering anti-homosexual mentality, encouraged by our culture, makes the challenge of being a lesbian mother a tough one—especially if your kids go to a conventional school and if you live in a conventional neighborhood.

Many of us are torn between wanting to be free and open, and concern for protecting our children from social reprisals. It is degrading to be an adult and feel the need to conceal an important part of your life. But, in the interest of our kids, some of us "closet" our relationships with lovers to one extent or another, sometimes even in our own homes (where our children's friends come and go). Others of us don't. We feel that our children are able to deal with our nonconformity without any real difficulty, just as other kids have to deal with being from homes that are unconventional in other ways. In either case, it seems to be true that in spite of the "guilt-tripping" which some of our ex-husbands and relatives have tried to put on us for "exposing" our children to our love for women, the kids themselves are comfortable with us as we are!

JOAN. I feel good about being openly gay around my children. They accept my affection for other women very naturally.

NELL. My kids watched my coming out over a year's time. First I went to gay meetings, and then I talked a lot to them about my feelings and fears, and finally I made love with a woman. On the morning afterward, when the kids came in and found us in bed together, one of them whispered to me, "Did you make love?" I laughed and said yes, and she said, "Well—finally!"

They all know that I feel open and proud about being a lesbian, and they accept it. I don't care whether or not they turn out to be gay, but I don't want them to be afraid of homosexuality or think of it as sick or mysterious. (My oldest daughter says, "I don't feel any pressure from my mother to be gay, but I do feel pressure from my father not to be gay.") One of my daughters doesn't want her friends to know I'm gay because she doesn't want to be teased or considered odd. She's thirteen years old and very anxious to fit in at school and with her friends who come from straight and conventional homes. I understand her fears and I try to respect them, but I think it is also important to make it clear that I see lesbianism as healthy, and not something for me, or her, to be ashamed of.

For single gay mothers another challenge is raising sons without men. Nell feels that it is hard to find unoppressive men for her son to be with, but that he needs male company to keep from feeling isolated and lonely in her women's world. However, she doesn't want him to accept oppressive masculine values that most men still cling to.

Nan's year-and-a-half-old son spent the summer with her on a lesbian farm. He seldom saw men. One day he saw two men swimming nude, and he immediately took off his clothes and started playing with his penis. He was clearly identifying as male, and apparently was relieved to find somebody like him.

Many people still think that homosexuals should be kept away from children. Lesbians who want to work with kids are often forced to stay in the closet if they want jobs as teachers, nurses, pediatricians, counselors, baby-sitters, community workers and so on. And sometimes people deny the love and need between children and their mother's female lover. One gay woman helped to raise her lover's child for seven years, beginning with the pregnancy. Once, when the natural mother had to go to the hospital, her parents came at four o'clock in the morning and took the child a thousand miles away so that he wouldn't be left in the care of their lesbian daughter's lover. They kept him for several months. Years later the mother died, and the grandparents again immediately took the child. The mother's lover, who was as close to him as his mother had been, was never allowed to see him after that. If she had been a man, the grandparents could not have treated her in that way or dismissed so coldly the close relationship she had with the boy.

Gay women who would like to have children of their own but don't want to have sex with men find it almost impossible. Artificial insemination and adoption are not permitted to open lesbians, so they are forced to be bisexual. Many lesbians are married to men.

LOLLIE. I'm married, with two kids. Frank and I are good friends. We were never passionate lovers; we were two frustrated lonely misfits who liked each other. I had always been drawn to women but had found only one who wasn't afraid to have a relationship with another woman. I felt terrific with her until she lost interest. Rejections were really getting to me. Frank and I started living together; I eventually got pregnant, and then married him. I'd really wanted to be a mother, and I didn't want to do this alone. Having kids was tremendously absorbing, but now they are older and much more independent, and I'm feeling that maybe I could stop denying my desire to be involved with a woman. But it's so complicated. When I feel attracted to a woman I panic. I'm very doubtful that anything can work out between us. I don't want to mess up the people in my family. I get along well with Frank. We share child care and other jobs. We believe in allowing each other lots of autonomy. The kids seem very happy with things the way they are. I feel really good about that, and I'm scared of changing anything. I have to convince myself that my needs are as important as anyone's in this house.

JOAN. It is hard. But it would have been harder, in many ways, to have stayed in my marriage after deciding that I wanted to share my life with women. For a while I tried to. I felt that my husband needed me and that somehow his needs were more important than mine. But, more and more, my marriage began to seem like a locked cage. Tensions increased over lots of issues—all revolving around sexism in one way or another. Our relationship reached a point where it no longer served either of our needs. Eventually I became strong enough to deal with a separation, in spite of guilt and regretful feelings about the children not being able to live with their father. Since then I have been involved in a lot of the practical struggles divorced women face. Like trying to stand on your own two feet after years of leaning on a man as a financial and social crutch. But the freedom to be myself and to build an alternative life for myself and my kids, on our terms, has been worth all the effort.

I feel sorry for all the gay women who can't find a way to get out of their marriages. So many women stay with men because they can't imagine being able to put together a secure life for themselves and their children without the conventional "front" of having a husband. They may secretly call Daughters of Bilitis once or twice, or attend a meeting now and then (saying that they are going to a friend's house), or even have a lover they see when they can, if she is willing to deal with that! Typically it's another woman in the same situation in her own marriage. Fortunately there are more and more support groups for lesbian mothers. I hope we will all be liberated from these kinds of sexist traps and self-denials before long.

As we said initially, this chapter just begins to offer a picture of what our lives as lesbians are like. There is no one way to describe who we are. Our lives are varied, and each situation brings its own problems and strengths. But as women, as gay women, we have started to find the ways that our lives connect. Slowly we meet each other and begin the process of defining our common needs. At the same time, we define our struggle. It is one that goes on in many forms, and yet we understand that together we can, and do, make the changes we all (gay and straight) need.

FURTHER READINGS

We have tried to list a range of works, including books for and by older lesbians, high-school lesbians, Third World lesbians, middle- and working-class lesbians.

**Highly recommended:

Vida, Ginny, ed. *Our Right to Love—A Lesbian Resource Book* (Produced in cooperation with women of the National Gay Task Force). Englewood Cliffs, NJ: Prentice-Hall, Inc., 1978.
> More than fifty women contributed articles, photographs, and resource lists of groups, bookstores, bars, services, etc., to this long and wonderful book on lesbian identity, relationships, therapy, sexuality, health, activism, visions, religion, parenthood, and more. At $12.95 it's steep, but buy it with your friends and share it around. Its bibliography fills out what this one gives only a taste of.

Poetry

Barnard, Mary, trans. *Sappho*. University of California, 1958.
Bulkin, Elly, and Joan Larkin. *Amazon Poetry*. Out and Out Books, 1975. Anthology of many fine lesbian poets.
Lourde, Audre. *From a Land Where Other People Live*. Broadside Press, 1973.
Rich, Adrienne. *The Dream of a Common Language, Poems 1974-1977*. New York: Norton, 1978.

Fiction

Arnold, June. *Sister Gin*. Plainfield, VT: Daughters, Inc., 1975.
Brown, Rita Mae. *Rubyfruit Jungle*. Plainfield, VT: Daughters, Inc., 1973; reprint ed., New York: Bantam, 1977.
Hall, Radclyffe. *The Well of Loneliness*. New York: Pocket Books, 1974.
Isabell, Sharon. *Yesterday's Lessons*. 5251 Broadway, Oakland, CA 94618: The Women's Press Collective, 1974.
Knudson, R. R. *You Are the Rain*. New York: Dell, 1974, 1978. For and about adolescent women.
Leduc, Violette. *La Bâtarde*. London: Panther Books, 1964.
Miller, Isabel. *Patience and Sarah*. Greenwich, CT: Fawcett Crest, 1973.

Morgan, Claire. *The Price of Salt.* New York: Arno, 1952, 1975.
Nachman, Elana. *Riverfinger Women.* Plainfield, VT: Daughters, Inc., 1974.
Sarton, May. *Mrs. Stevens Hears the Mermaids Singing.* New York: Norton, 1965.
See also authors such as Colette, Ann Bannon (Arno Press), Djuna Barnes, Anaïs Nin, Jane Rule, Gertrude Stein, Monique Wittig. Daughters, Inc., Plainfield, VT 05667, has many great lesbian books.

Nonfiction, General

Abbot, Sidney, and Barbara Love. *Sappho Was a Right-On Woman.* Briarcliff Manor, NY: Stein and Day, 1973.
Covina, Gina, and Laurel Galana, eds. *The Lesbian Reader: An Amazon Quarterly Anthology.* Oakland, CA: Amazon Press, 1975.
Gidlow, Elsa. *Ask No Man Pardon: The Philosophical Significance of Being Lesbian.* Mill Valley, CA: Druid Heights Books, 1975.
Grier, Barbara, and Coletta Reid, eds. *The Lavender Herring: Lesbian Essays from the Ladder.* Oakland, CA: Diana Press, 1976.
Jay, Karla, and Alan Young, eds. *After You're Out.* Links Books, 1975.
———. *Out of the Closet: Voices of Gay Liberation.* New York: Pyramid, 1974.
Johnston, Jill. *Lesbian Nation.* New York: Simon and Schuster, 1973.
Katz, Jonathan. *Gay American History: Lesbians and Gay Men in the U.S.A., A Documentary.* New York: Thomas Y. Crowell, 1976.
Klaich, Dolores. *Woman Plus Woman: Attitudes Toward Lesbianism.* New York: Simon and Schuster, 1974.
Martin, Del, and Phyllis Lyon. *Lesbian/Woman.* New York: Bantam Books, 1972.
Myron, Nancy, and Charlotte Bunch, eds. *Lesbianism and the Women's Movement.* Oakland, CA: Diana Press, 1975.
Rule, Jane. *Lesbian Images.* Garden City, NY: Doubleday and Company, 1975.
Womanshare Collective. *Country Lesbians: The Story of the Womanshare Collective.* 1976. $5.50. Available from Womanshare Books, P.O. Box 1735, Grants Pass, OR 97526.
Wyland, Francie. *Motherhood, Lesbianism and Child Custody.* Toronto: Wages Due Lesbians Toronto and Falling Wall Press, 1977. $1.20. Available from Wages Due Lesbians Toronto, P.O. Box 38, Station E, Toronto, Ontario, Canada.

Health Care and Sexuality

Escamilla-Mondanaro, Josette. "Lesbians and Therapy," in *Psychotherapy for Women*, Edna Rawlings and Dianne Carter, eds. Springfield, IL: Charles C. Thomas, 1977.
Gay Public Health Workers. "Heterosexuality: Can It Be Cured?" 1975. Available from Gay Public Health Workers, 206 N. 35th Street, Philadelphia, PA 19104.
Godiva. *What Lesbians Do.* Eugene, OR: Jackrabbit Women's Printshop, 1975. $4.50. Available from Amazon Reality Collective, P.O. Box 95, Eugene, OR 97401.
A book on sexuality.
Jay, Karla, and Alan Young, eds. Their books, listed above, have articles on lesbians and health care.
Lawrence, John C. "Homosexuals, Hospitalization and the Nurse," *Nursing Forum* XIV (1975).
The Nomadic Sisters. *Loving Women.* 1976. $3.75 Available from The Nomadic Sisters, P.O. Box 793, Sonora, CA 95370 (Add 50¢ for handling).
Nicely illustrated and helpful book on lovemaking.

O'Donnell, Mary. "Lesbian Health Care: Issues and Literature." *Science for the People* 10 (May/June 1978).
Santa Cruz Women's Health Collective. *Lesbian Health Issues.* $1.00. Available from Santa Cruz Women's Health Center, 250 Locust Street, Santa Cruz, CA 95060.
Excellent reading list.
Womanspirit Magazine. Fall 1977.
Contains good articles on nontraditional healing.
Women's Educational Project. *High School Sexuality: A Teaching Guide.* Portland, OR: n.d. $1.00. Available from Amazon Reality Collective, P.O. Box 95, Eugene, OR 97410.
Contains sections on lesbianism.

Bibliography and Reference

Blachmon, Mary K. *Lesbian Mothers' Resource List.* Available in pamphlet form from Leis films, 2130½ Elsinore Street, Los Angeles, CA 90026.
Foster, Jeannette. *Sex Variant Women in Literature.* Oakland, CA: Diana Press, 1975.
Grier, Barbara. *The Lesbian in Literature: A Bibliography*, 2nd ed. $7.00. Available from The Naiad Press, Inc., 7800 Westside Drive, Weatherby Lake, MO 64152.
Task Force on Gay Liberation. *A Gay Bibliography.* 1975. Available from Task Force on Gay Liberation, American Library Association, Box 2383, Philadelphia, PA 19103.

Film

In the Best Interests of the Children. $60 rental, $550 purchase. Available from IRIS Films, IRIS Feminist Collective, Inc., Box 26463, Los Angeles, CA 90026.
Presents social and legal struggles of lesbian mothers. Excellent film.
Word Is Out. Mariposa Film Group, San Francisco. $150/$300 rental. Available from New Yorker Films, 16 West 61st St., New York, NY 10023, tel.: (212)247-6110.
In this excellent film more than 25 lesbians and gay men speak about their lives. Has been shown on public television in some areas.

Periodicals

Azalea: A Magazine by Third World Lesbians. Published quarterly. $4/year, $1.25/copy. Available c/o J. Gibbs, 306 Lafayette Ave., Brooklyn, NY 11238.
Lesbian Connection. $1, suggested donation. Available from Ambitious Amazons, Box 811, East Lansing, MI 48823.
The Lesbian Tide. Published bimonthly. $6/year. Available from 8855 Cattaraugus, Los Angeles, CA 90034.
Sinister Wisdom. Available from P.O. Box 30541, Lincoln, NE 68503.

Organizations

Lesbian Herstory Archives. P.O. Box 1258, New York, NY 10001.
This group is collecting anything by and about lesbians and will send you a Xerox copy of anything in their collection.
National Gay Task Force. 80 Fifth Avenue, New York, NY 10011.

CHAPTER 6
TAKING CARE OF OURSELVES

In the following section we will share basic information which will help you in keeping yourself healthy and in evaluating the medical advice you receive. We've realized that one of the major health problems we face as women is our own passivity—our belief that our health is really being taken care of by the medical profession, and that we are being protected by government agencies such as the FDA or the USDA.* We seem to make two kinds of assumptions about our health. First, we trust that we are leading basically healthy lives, that the way we eat and live are fundamentally all right because "they" wouldn't allow us to be harmed by certain foods or drugs or levels of contamination. Then if we get sick it is somehow our fault. To get well, we seek medical help to "correct" or "solve" the problem; as a result, doctors and modern medicine have become our keys to good health.

Second, we assume that we are very delicate structures that can mysteriously "go wrong" at any moment. We are chronically dependent on doctors for reassurance that we are all right, that we are living well and eating well and free of disease. In between doctor visits we may feel that our health care is the doctor's responsibility, too mysterious for us to understand, clearly "his" job and not ours. If we do become ill or need medical help, all the doctor's decisions and opinions are often accepted without question and become the basis for an even deeper dependency in the future.

Many women believe that our problems in getting good health care are aggravated by both these assumptions, which are usually encouraged by doctors. We live in a society where initiative is often the key to the quality of any experience, whether in education, the marketplace, or the law. If we do *not* take initiative on our own behalf in health care, we may become mere clients or practice material for professional people to study or work out their theories on. This is not to say that health-care professionals are not capable of warmth and caring, but that their training and the structure within which they work virtually force most of them to develop stereotyped expectations of their patients, particularly

*Ralph Nader, Estes Kefauver and many others have shown repeatedly that government agencies provide very poor consumer protection. (See also p. 107.)

women. It is not by chance that most doctors expect women to be passive, whether as patients or coworkers. The term "doctor's orders" applies to nurses and other health professionals with whom the doctor works as well as to women patients. This attitude suggests that doctors are experts in preventive medicine, in nutrition, in exercise and in human sexuality, when in fact we may know as much as they do. (See "Choosing the Doctor" in Chapter 18.)

Working out an adult relationship with health workers and taking initiative and responsibility for our own health care thus become extremely difficult. For many of us it has been part of our "growing up," part of the demystification of medicine and health care, which is one of the areas of American life about which we seem to know least, and which is least acceptable to criticize openly. The "good patient," in the eyes of the health system, is still docile, trusting and incuriously obedient.

Working on this section has reminded us of the many ways in which modern medicine is not very scientific—as when isolated symptoms are treated repeatedly without investigation of systemic causes. Also, modern medicine does not adequately emphasize the preventive measures we can take to keep ourselves well. This failure to encourage people to take active roles in their own health care is not only unscientific but involves a tremendous waste of health-care resources (see Chapter 18). In certain instances, medical and dental practice has stressed prevention as the key to keeping healthy and to preventing fatal illness. Daily dental care, healthy eating, exercise, monthly breast self-examination and getting regular Pap smears are excellent ways to avert serious disease. Eliminating smoking and wearing seat belts also improve our chances of living a longer, healthier life.

There are some leaders among medical professionals and public-health officials who support efforts to encourage patient initiative, but others become angered and offended when patients want to act for themselves in ways not yet widely endorsed by the profession. Their messages are mixed. Doctors want patients to do breast self-examination to detect cancer, but don't want them to get involved in decisions about breast cancer treatment. Doctors want patients to come regularly for Pap smears, but don't want patients to look at their own cervices with a speculum to keep track of normal and abnormal changes. Public-health officials don't want people to smoke or eat junk foods, but they don't publicly oppose advertising and research designed to "prove" that such products are all right. These are only a few examples.

We believe that women who do not take initiative to maintain their own health cannot stay healthy just by visiting doctors regularly (assuming they can find and afford them) or by trusting advice in the media about food and drugs. In order to exercise good judgment and make the wisest independent decisions, when they are called for, we need a certain amount of information. We need to read materials put out by consumer groups and organizations that are not profit-motivated. We need to talk with one another and learn from each other's experiences. This way we can increase our chances of keeping healthy.

We know that many people feel this viewpoint is unduly critical, even hostile, toward medicine. However, more and more doctors, lawyers and other health professionals are agreeing with the idea that patients should take a much more active role in their own health care; it is consistent with good medical practice and probably more effective than any other effort to improve health care. In fact, there are now a number of programs, run by hospitals as well as by women's clinics, designed to teach patients not only about health and illness and patients' rights, but also about basic preventive health-care practices.*

We all have to decide for ourselves how much or how little we want to be involved. Whatever the level of involvement you finally choose, we hope you will at least read what we've written, think about it, and discuss it with other women.

The first section discusses the vital role of good health habits, nutrition and exercise. The second section is designed to help you understand what a good physical exam includes, what an internal exam involves, and how to examine yourself. The third section describes some of our common medical and health-care problems and tells what kinds of treatment are available. A short glossary is included.

*Arlene and Howard Eisenberg, "How to Be Your Own Doctor—Sometimes," *Parade* (February 24, 1974), pp. 11-12. Also, Caroline Rand Herron and Donald Johnston, "Patients and Understanding," *The New York Times* (September 9, 1974).

I. Nutrition, Exercise and Health Habits

While many of us tend to separate our decisions about food from our decisions about exercise, smoking and drinking, we could be making much more effective health decisions if we thought about them all together.

First of all, let's review the leading half-dozen causes of death in the United States (from 1973 data, National Bureau of Health Statistics):

**Leading Causes of Death
(Women and Men)**

1. Heart disease
2. Cancer
3. Strokes (cerebro-vascular disease)
4. Accidents of all kinds (half of these are auto fatalities)
5. Pneumonia and influenza
6. Diabetes

There are wide variations in the ages at which these deaths occur. For example, men die of heart conditions earlier than women do, but women catch up with them after menopause. In countries that consume large amounts of beef, cancer of the colon occurs more frequently than any other cancer.* However, for women breast cancer is the most common cancer and the leading cancer killer. It is the most frequent cause of death among women thirty-seven to fifty-five. While all these death rates are lower for women than for men, there is only one category in which the rate for women is dramatically lower—accidents.

Many of these deaths are preventable; that is, by taking—or not taking—certain actions we can reduce our chances of death and illness. Most of these actions fall into three categories: diet, exercise, and life-style; preventive health-care examinations (done by us or by others); and health habits (such as brushing teeth, not smoking, reducing alcoholic intake, using seat belts).

Studies have shown that Seventh-Day Adventists, who are ovo-lacto-vegetarians (eggs, milk and cheese are the only animal products they eat), and Mormons, who oppose non-herbal teas, coffee, alcohol and cigarettes,† have lower rates of cancer than the general population. It is already well known that heart disease is affected by a combination of health habits: diet (food quality and quantity), exercise and smoking. Psychological stress and life-style also have an important influence. Smoking is probably riskier in terms of heart disease than lung disease, but the incidence of death from lung cancer is

Boston Globe (December 5, 1974), p. 50.
†All of which destroy Vitamin C, incidentally.

Burning Up Calories

ACTIVITIES	CALORIES PER HOUR	ACTIVITIES	CALORIES PER HOUR
Sitting at rest	15	Housepainting	150–180
Standing relaxed	20	Walking slowly (2.6 mph)	115
Writing	10–20	Walking moderately fast (3.75 mph)	215
Dressing and undressing	30–40	Walking very fast (5.3 mph)	565
Ironing (5-lb. iron)	50–60	Running, dependent on speed	800–1300
Dishwashing	50–60	Swimming, dependent on speed	300–1000
Housework	80–180	Rowing, dependent on speed	1000–1300
Carpentry	150–300	Cycling, dependent on speed	150–600

rising sharply and has been attributed to the continued increase in smoking among women, especially since the Surgeon General's warning was first issued ten years ago.* The risks from smoking marijuana are still being investigated but so far appear far less dangerous than those from drinking alcohol or smoking tobacco.† However, there are risks from all smoking, and it's worth keeping track of marijuana risks.

While uterine cancer rates seem to be declining slightly, breast cancer appears to be increasing. Death from these cancers is best prevented by self-examination *and* regular checkups. It is also good preventive practice to question the side effects of drugs and food additives and to avoid any that are unnecessary (see "Breast Problems" and "Uterine and Ovarian Cancer"). Carcinogens (cancer-causing substances) are increasingly implicated in human cancer, yet many known and suspected carcinogens are FDA-approved, such as #40 Red food dye and sodium nitrite.‡

Auto accident fatalities can be reduced by at least four factors: fewer drinkers who drive; slower driving speeds; wearing seat belts; improving public transportation. Driving responsibly and encouraging others to do likewise will help to prevent auto deaths.

As we said earlier, diet, exercise and health habits need to be considered together. Obesity, a serious health hazard for so many of us, is primarily a matter of eating too many high-calorie§ foods and/or getting too little exercise. You might want to compare the calories you burn up and the calories you eat in an average day to see if they are about the same. Above is a list showing about how many calories are used up in some common activities. The importance of adequate regular exercise cannot be overemphasized. See "Women in Motion" for more discussion of this.

Food quality is as important as quantity. Unfortunately, many of us eat quite a lot of poor-quality foods. When we eat such foods instead of—rather than in addition to—more nutritious ones, we do even more harm. Here are some common items in the American diet that we need to reduce.

Take *less* of these calories:

Sugar
In everything: cereals and breads, peanut butter, "juice drinks," yogurt (except plain), soft drinks, candy, mayonnaise and ketchup, etc. (Read the labels; you'll be amazed.)

Fat
Includes eggs, whole milk, ice cream, most peanut butter, most chips and crackers, and most cheeses. Beef is one of the commonest sources in the American diet. Pork is next.

Refined carbohydrates
Most breads, cake mixes and commercial pastries, crackers and chip-type snacks, pizza, pasta and sauces for frozen or canned one-dish meals. Especially beware of *un*enriched white flour products.

Salt
In cold cuts and other cured meats prepared with nitrites; also most commercial baby food, all soft drinks and most "snacks."

*Also, cigarette smoke destroys Vitamin C in the blood, even if the smoke is not yours.

†Edward Brecher, "Marijuana: The Health Questions," *Consumer Reports* (March, 1975), pp. 143-49.

‡Jane E. Brody, "Link to Cancer and Birth Defects Hinted in Tests of 150 Hair Dyes on Bacteria," *The New York Times* (March 18, 1975), p. 26 (possibility of breast cancer link). See also March 21, 1975, *Letters to the Editor*, "On the Safety of Hair Dyes," response written by John Menkart, Vice-President of Clairol, Inc.

§A calorie is a measure of energy often expressed in terms of heat.

While some people may be taking in too much animal protein (meat and eggs), many of us are not getting enough protein or vegetables. If we don't get protein in animal form we must prepare high-quality protein by carefully combining vegetable proteins (see "Nutrition").

Take *more* of these calories:

Fish, liver and chicken
Gram for gram, there's more protein, less fat than in beef—depending upon method of preparation.

Skim milk products
Low-fat or non-fat milk, cottage cheese and other cheeses.

Whole grains, seeds and nuts
(*Very* hard to find fresh.)

Vegetables
All kinds, especially green and yellow, raw and cooked. Best in descending order: fresh, frozen, canned.

One final point about diet: there is evidence that dietary habits begun in infancy (sugar, fat and salt in baby formulas, followed by salty and sugary commercial baby foods, ice cream and soft drinks) may be a factor predisposing Americans to heart and circulatory diseases.* Two common diseases, hypertension (high blood pressure) and diabetes (excess blood sugar), often have dietary components in both cause and treatment. It seems only sensible to begin eating well now to reduce our chances of getting cancer, high blood pressure and strokes, diabetes or other diseases. The best way is by cutting down *and* adding.

In some states there is now pressure to adopt labeling regulations which will identify foods likely to cause diabetes if taken in too great quantities (mostly high-sugar and -carbohydrate products). Also, three drugs, one used to treat hypertension and two used to treat diabetes (see box, "Drugs Women Should Know About," p. 150), have been shown to increase the risks of breast cancer and death from heart disease. In cases where it is possible to control these diseases with drugs, it usually is possible to control them by diet just as well.

The question of labeling leads us to one preventive health skill anyone can learn: to save money and save health, learn how to read labels (see box in "Nutrition" section).

Up to this point we've talked mostly about habits that improve our general health. Certain preventive practices focus on keeping specific parts of our bodies in good shape. Here is a good example:

*Myron Faber, M.D., "The Pediatrician, the Infant and Atherosclerosis," *Birth and the Family Journal*, Vol. 1, No. 1, (1974), p. 22.

Pelvic-Floor (Kegel)* Exercises

You can practice contracting your pelvic-floor muscles to prevent or reduce sagging of the organs and urinary incontinence (losing urine when you cough, sneeze, or laugh), to strengthen your orgasms, and to prepare for childbirth. Practiced regularly, these exercises can help prevent prolapse of the uterus (falling of the uterus into a stretched vagina, which has lost its muscle tone), cystocele (a bulge of the bladder into the vagina) and rectocele (a bulge of the rectum into the vagina).

A good way to locate these muscles is to spread your legs apart while urinating and to start and stop the flow of urine—your ability to do this is one indication of how strong your muscles are. Another method is to try tightening around a man's erect penis during intercourse (this will feel very pleasant to him and can help to enhance your pleasure, too). Or, use one or two of your fingers.

Begin exercising these muscles by contracting hard for a second and then releasing completely. Repeat this ten times in a row to make up one group of exercises (this takes about twenty seconds). In a month's time, try to work up to twenty groups during one day (about seven minutes total). You can do this at any time—while sitting in a car or bus, while talking on the telephone, or even as a "wake-up" exercise. Some of us have noticed improved muscle tone (and occasionally increased pleasure during intercourse) in only several weeks. For more detailed instruction on Kegel exercises, consult your local childbirth group.

*After Arnold Kegel, a pioneering California physician.

NUTRITION

This is a section we have not changed except to add an annotated bibliography and information about reading food labels. For everyone interested in nutrition, we highly recommend *Nutrition Scoreboard—Your Guide to Better Eating*, by Michael Jacobson, and *Food for People, Not for Profit*, by M. Jacobson and C. Lerza (see bibliography).

If you're going to read only one book about nutrition, either is an excellent choice (*Diet for a Small Planet* is also very good—see bibliography). In *Nutrition Scoreboard* Jacobson presents a concise, readable discussion of the poor eating habits of most Americans and the lack of good nutrition education in our country (primarily the fault of the food industry's distorted advertising material and educational literature). He gives a simple, effective way to "score" most of the foods we commonly eat so that we can choose more nutritious foods with a minimum of effort. Along with many useful tables that compare the nutritional value of foods in various categories (including "snacks"), the book outlines the pros and cons of several controversial issues (such as food additives) and offers some very sensible suggestions about what to do until more conclusive nutrition information is available.

It is especially important for us to know about good nutrition. It is one of the basic ways we care for our bodies; it is perhaps the most important preventive medicine; and eating well makes us feel better. Also, as women, we often find ourselves responsible for the diets of others, especially children. To learn more about nutrition and pregnancy see the pregnancy chapters.

Good nutrition isn't just a simple matter of knowing what's good for us and then eating well. There are huge obstacles and problems.

Whenever Jimmy asks me for a marshmallow I feel conflicted about what to do. I don't want to give it to him, since it's bad for his teeth and has so many preservatives in it. But if I say no he cries and argues and puts up a stink for half an hour. Sometimes I just don't want all the hassle. So I'll explain why marshmallows are bad for him, but then let him eat them anyway if he still wants to.

I hear so much these days about chemicals and preservatives and food processing that sometimes I feel that there's nothing healthy left to eat. Everything is either artifically colored or has some huge DDT residue in it or has all the vitamins processed out—I just want to give up. And then I have the problem of liking all these horrible things. If they're all around me and much cheaper than those expensive organic health foods, and they taste good to me, why shouldn't I eat them?

Wintertime is long and full of colds and fevers in my house. I know we and the kids could eat better. But I'm scared to start thinking about good, nutritious foods because planning, shopping and cooking for meals is all up to me in this household, and I don't have lots of time, I've got other things to do, and things like frozen or canned foods are what I already know how to buy and cook. I somehow think it would take so long to relearn all this, it would be expensive, and then I'd have to start persuading my family to go along with the change.

The health-food nuts make me feel guilty all the time about the food my family eats, but I just don't think it would be any fun to live on soybeans and wheat germ. Is it possible to go halfway?

We feel it is important not to condemn ourselves for eating the way we do. Certain changes in our diets would clearly be more healthful, but it's not so easy to make the switch. It helps to find out about foods that are both satisfying and nutritious.

Should we take vitamins and supplements, or are they a waste, maybe even harmful?* How much protein is enough? Is meat protein necessary, or is it even healthy for us? It is important to remember that nutrition is a controversial science and that we will find arguments both for and against many ideas or suggestions.

The Necessary Nutrients

Food gives our bodies the materials for growth and repair, and also provides the energy for all our activities. There are three main food elements that we need: carbohydrates, fat and protein. For body processes, we also need certain vitamins and minerals that are mainly found along with fats and carbohydrates. Although not strictly nutrients, enough cellulose (roughage) and water are also necessary. Individuals require nutrients in differing amounts, and it is difficult to know exactly how much of a certain nutrient we need. It often helps to eat different amounts and proportions to determine what

*Certain vitamins, notably A and D, can definitely be harmful in very large dosages.

suits us best. It is important to eat various kinds of foods, since some nutrients are found only in certain ones.

We often forget that most foods contain a mixture of nutrients. It is a mistake to think of meat as just a protein food—in fact, hamburger contains as much as two thirds fat. And milk is not only a calcium food but also contains fat, carbohydrates, vitamin A, vitamin D, riboflavin and phosphorus. Much advertising distorts this important fact.

The following chart describes some important nutrients and lists their main sources.

NUTRIENT	CHIEF FUNCTIONS	IMPORTANT SOURCES
Protein	Provides nitrogen and amino acids for body proteins (in skin tissues, muscles, brain, hair, etc.), for hormones (substances that control body processes), for antibodies (which fight infections), and for enzymes (which control the rates of chemical reactions in our bodies).	Milk, cheese, yogurt, eggs, fish, poultry, soybeans, lean meats, wheat germ, nutritional (brewer's) yeast and certain vegetable combinations.
Fats	Provide a concentrated source of energy. Carry certain fat-soluble vitamins (notably A, D and E) and essential fatty acids. Provide insulation and protection for important organs and body structures.	Whole milk, most cheeses, butter, margarine, nuts, oils (preferably unsaturated, unhydrogenated). Cholesterol and "saturated" fats are found in eggs, butter, cheap hamburger and ice cream.
Carbohydrates	Keep protein from being used for energy needs, so protein can be used primarily for body-building functions. Also necessary for protein digestion and utilization. Provide our main source of energy. Provide the glucose vital for certain brain functions.	Fruits, vegetables, whole-grain bread, cereals, grains.
Vitamin A (fat-soluble) Extra vitamin A is stored in the liver—that is why animal livers are such a good source.	Helps prevent infection. Helps eyes adjust to changes from bright to dim light (prevents night blindness). Needed for healthy skin and certain tissues, such as the lining of eyes and lungs.	Liver, whole milk, fortified margarine (A is added), butter, most cheeses (especially Swiss and Cheddar), egg yolks, dark-green and yellow vegetables (especially carrots, parsley, kale and orange squash), apricots.
Vitamin D (fat-soluble)	Needed for strong bones and teeth (regulates calcium and phosphorus in bone formation). Essential for calcium absorption from the blood.	*Sunlight shining on bare skin,* vitamin D-fortified milk, fish-liver oil, sardines, canned tuna.
Vitamin E (fat-soluble)	Helps preserve some vitamins and unsaturated fatty acids (acts as an antioxidant). Helps stabilize biological membranes.	Plant oils (especially wheat-germ oil and soybean oil), wheat germ, navy beans, eggs, brown rice.
Vitamin C or ascorbic acid (water-soluble). C is easily destroyed by air and heat. Like many other water-soluble vitamins, it is *not* stored in the body, so we need some every day.	Needed for healthy collagen (a protein that holds cells together). Helps wounds to heal. Needed for normal blood-clotting and healthy blood vessels. Needed for iron absorption. Spares or protects vitamins A and E and several B vitamins. Needed for strong teeth and bones.	Citrus fruits, green and red peppers, green leafy vegetables, parsley, tomatoes, potatoes, strawberries, cantaloupe, bean sprouts (especially mung beans and soybeans).

NUTRIENT	CHIEF FUNCTIONS	IMPORTANT SOURCES
B vitamins (water-soluble) include thiamine (B_1), riboflavin (B_2), niacin, pyridoxine, folic acid, cobalamin (B_{12}), cholene, etc. Folic-acid deficiency is common during pregnancy. It may also be caused by birth control pills. Riboflavin is destroyed by sunlight, so use milk containers that keep out light. Fatigue, tension, depression are often signs of a B deficiency.	Needed for steady nerves, alertness, good digestion, energy production, healthy skin and eyes, certain enzymes involved in amino-acid synthesis, maintenance of blood.	Whole-grain breads and cereals, liver, wheat germ, nutritional yeast, green leafy vegetables, lean meats, milk, molasses, peanuts, dried peas and beans.
Calcium Calcium is more easily digested when eaten with acid foods (such as yogurt or sour milk).	Needed for building bones and teeth, for blood-clotting, for regulating nerve and muscle activity, for absorbing iron.	Whole and skim milk, buttermilk, cheese, yogurt, green vegetables, egg yolk, bone-meal powder, blackstrap molasses.
Phosphorus	Needed to transform protein, fats and carbohydrates into energy in the body. Makes up part of all the body's cells. Needed for building bones and teeth.	Milk, cheeses, lean meats, egg yolks.
Iron Daily intake is important. Children, teenagers, pregnant and menstruating women are especially likely to have iron deficiencies.	Makes up an important part of hemoglobin, the compound in blood that carries oxygen from the lungs to the body cells.	Lean meat, liver, egg yolk, green leafy vegetables, nutritional yeast, wheat germ, whole-grain and enriched breads and cereals, soybean flour, raisins, blackstrap molasses.
Iodine	An important part of thyroxine; helps the thyroid gland regulate the rate at which our bodies use energy. Affects growth, water balances, nervous system, muscular system and circulatory system.	Iodized salt, seafoods, plant foods grown in soil near the sea.
Magnesium	Required for certain enzyme activity. Helps in bone formation.	Grains, vegetables, cereals, fruits, milk, nuts.
Potassium	Needed for healthy nerves and muscles.	Seafood, milk, vegetables, fruits.
Sodium, chlorine, fluorine and other trace minerals. Most of our diets now contain too much sodium, largely because of sodium compounds used in processed foods and excessive use of table salt.	Varying functions, many of them not well understood. Fluorine is especially important from birth to six months. It helps to prevent tooth decay by hardening tooth enamel.	Meat, cheese, eggs, seafood, green leafy vegetables, fluoridated water, sea salt.

NUTRIENT	CHIEF FUNCTIONS	IMPORTANT SOURCES
Water Most people need 6-7 glasses of fluid (water, tea, juice, etc.) a day to keep good water balance in the body.	Not really a nutrient, but an essential part of all tissues. Often supplies important minerals, such as calcium and fluorine.	
Cellulose (Roughage)	Also not a nutrient, but important for stimulating the intestinal muscles and encouraging the growth of certain intestinal bacteria. Keeps teeth clean and gums healthy.	Fruits, vegetables, whole-grain bread and cereals.

About Protein

There is great disagreement about how much protein is necessary. The 1968 revision of the *Recommended Dietary Allowances* of the National Research Council–National Academy of Sciences (NRC–NAS) suggests 55 grams of protein per day for a 128-pound woman or adolescent girl. For a 154-pound man the figure is 65 grams. Many doctors and nutritionists also recommend these amounts, but considerable research indicates that our protein needs may be less.

It is important to know the quality as well as the quantity of the protein we eat. Ideally, protein should be "complete"—that is, it should contain all eight of the essential amino acids* and in the right proportions. Meat, eggs and dairy products (milk, cheese, yogurt, etc.) contain "complete" proteins. Generally, other foods contain "incomplete" proteins, which are lacking in essential amino acids or have poorer amino-acid proportions. Soybeans, wheat germ and nutritional yeast (brewer's yeast), though good protein sources, are "incomplete" in this sense.

There is, however, a simple way to make up first-rate, "complete" protein without using meat, eggs, or dairy products: "By combining different proteins in appropriate ways, vegetable proteins cannot be distinguished nutritionally from those of animal origin."† All we have to do is combine foods so that the essential amino acids lacking in one food are present in another food eaten with it at the same time (amino acids don't wait around for each other and can only work together).

One good protein combination is beans and rice. When eaten separately, 1-1/2 cups of beans and 4 cups of rice provide as much usable‡ protein as 13-1/4 ounces of steak. But when eaten at the same time, as in any common beans-and-rice dish, the same amounts provide as much usable protein as 19 ounces of steak. This represents a 43 percent increase in usable protein, simply because the beans and rice were eaten together! Other good protein combinations are bread with milk or cheese, or lentil soup with non-spongy whole-wheat bread.

When we are trying to lose weight we want to get the most protein for the fewest calories. Fish, cottage cheese and skim milk are especially good for dieting, since they have relatively few calories compared with their usable protein. The chart on page 106 compares the "calorie cost" of different foods.

It is exciting for those of us who must feed both ourselves and others as well as possible on a limited budget to find out that meat isn't necessary for a good diet. We also know that meat protein is a very highly concentrated source of pesticide residue (except for animal livers), and that livestock is a very inefficient protein-maker compared with plant crops.* This kind of eating does require careful planning, however.

Fats and Oils

Today we hear a lot about polyunsaturated fats, hydrogenated products and low-cholesterol foods. Since cholesterol is closely linked to heart disease—a major killer in this country, striking a growing number of women—it is important to understand more about the fat we eat.

First of all, fats and oils can come from either plants or animals. Fatty acids, which make up the main part of fats, are chains of carbon atoms with many hydrogen and fewer oxygen atoms added on. Whenever any of the carbon atoms in these chains are connected by double bonds ($C=C$), the fat is called unsaturated. Fatty acids that have two or more double bonds are said to be

---

*These are the protein "building blocks" our bodies cannot make from other substances and must get directly from the food we eat.

†R. Bressani and M. Béhar, in *Proceedings of the 6th International Congress of Nutrition*, edited by E. and S. Livingstone (Edinburgh: 1964), p. 182.

‡"Usable" protein represents the amount of protein we actually absorb and retain in our bodies. We can "use" anywhere from 50 to 95 percent of the protein we eat, depending upon the food. *Diet for a Small Planet* describes protein usability in more detail.

*This is important when we think about the world food shortage and realize that *half* the good, harvested agricultural land in America is used for crops fed to livestock.

HOW TO GET THE MOST PROTEIN (FOR THE LEAST CALORIES)

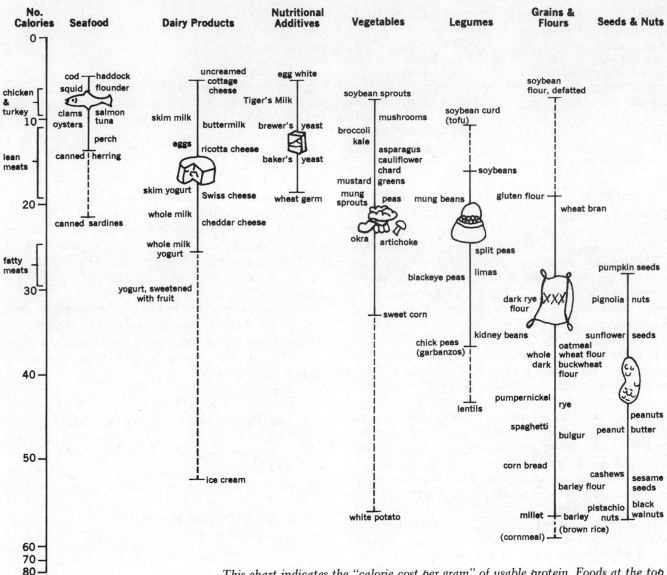

This chart indicates the "calorie cost per gram" of usable protein. Foods at the top have the most protein per calorie.

From *Diet for a Small Planet*.

highly unsaturated, or polyunsaturated. These fats are almost always liquid oils of vegetable origin (such as corn, soybean and safflower oils).

Saturated fats do not have double bonds and harden at room temperature. Most animal fat is saturated (beef, lamb, ham and many dairy products). Saturated vegetable fats are found in many solid shortenings (Crisco and Spry, for example), coconut oil, cocoa butter and palm oil (used in store-bought cookies, pie fillings and nondairy milk and cream substitutes).

Hydrogenation refers to a process of changing liquid, unsaturated fats to solid fats (C=C double bonds are broken by adding hydrogen atoms onto the chain). Some products are completely hydrogenated (hardened), some partially hydrogenated (some table marga-

rines, for instance, and most commercial peanut butters).

One important reason for knowing all this has to do with cholesterol, a waxy substance found in animal fats (in meats, egg yolks and butter) and used in many of our body's chemical processes. Our bodies both make cholesterol and get it from the fats we eat. Everyone needs a certain amount for good health, but too much cholesterol in the blood can cause heart and blood-vessel diseases. Cholesterol deposits can form in the linings of artery walls, eventually blocking off the artery channels completely. When this happens in a major artery of the heart muscle, the result is a heart attack. More and more women now get heart disease, probably because of their diets.

How, then, do we cut down on the cholesterol in our blood? One way is to eat fewer animal fats, especially eggs. Another way is to avoid hardened (hydrogenated) vegetable fats. Probably most important, we should have enough vegetable oils high in polyunsaturated fatty acids. These "essential" acids lower our level of blood cholesterol considerably, though the exact mechanism is unclear. Linoleic acid, the most common fatty acid, is especially abundant in safflower, soybean and sunflower-seed oils.

Apparently, the type of fat we eat may be more important than the total amount. If we want to keep a low cholesterol level our diets should have a high ratio of polyunsaturates to saturated fats. That is, more of the fat we eat should be polyunsaturated, less of it should be saturated. One way of doing this is to substitute polyunsaturated margarines* for butter. Another way is to cook and bake with liquid vegetable oils (except olive oil, which is only mono-unsaturated) instead of margarine and butter.

Carbohydrates (Sugar and Starches)

Along with the little boy at the beginning of the chapter, many of us also want that marshmallow. We Americans eat huge quantities of sugar and spend a lot of money on candy bars and sodas. While some natural sugar is essential, most of us eat too much sugar and from the wrong sources. We may never give up these sources entirely, but it helps to know healthier ways to satisfy our cravings for sugar.

Sugar is necessary for energy, but we get plenty of it naturally from fruits, vegetables and milk. We also get sugar from the breaking down of starch foods such as breads, cereals, grains and legumes. Eating concentrated amounts of sugar (as found in various sweets and beverages)† is harmful to us in the following ways:

It can create a low blood-sugar level by overstimulating our body's production of insulin, which then causes the liver and muscles to withdraw too much sugar from the blood. This sugar is stored as glycogen (a form of starch easily changed back into sugar) or as fat. Thus we may at first feel peppy as sugar rushes into the bloodstream, but after a short while we feel tired out, irritable, even exhausted or nauseated from the resulting low blood-sugar level.

The fat formed from excess sugar creates an extra burden on our bodies and makes us feel sluggish.

Sucrose (ordinary table sugar, also found naturally in some foods, such as honey) causes tooth decay.

Sugar destroys an appetite for other, healthier foods.

*Read the labels! Margarines that are partially hydrogenated are higher in polyunsaturates. Many cheap margarines are completely hydrogenated, and thus contain saturated fats. Some even contain butter.

†This includes raw sugar, honey, molasses and other sweeteners.

Eating lots of sugar foods may cause diabetes in people who would otherwise not develop the disease.

Dental Health

Many of us forget that good teeth are an important part of good health. Poor nutrition can cause dental disease just as it causes other diseases of the body. For example, foods containing a kind of sugar called sucrose cause tooth decay in the following way.

Certain types of bacteria found in almost everyone's saliva can use sucrose to make themselves a protective coating. This coating helps them to cling to our teeth as a sticky substance called dental plaque, which our saliva cannot wash away. These bacteria, tiny organisms known as streptococci, then multiply very quickly and produce large amounts of acids, enzymes, and poisons. These substances drip on or between the teeth, damaging the enamel and irritating the gums.

An important way to prevent this decay is to brush our teeth daily to remove the plaque ("a clean tooth does not decay"). What we eat is equally important. Try to avoid foods with sucrose, especially between meals and at bedtime. Also, try to brush your teeth after eating sucrose-containing foods. Even rinsing your mouth with water is effective. Whenever possible, eat foods that act as a toothbrush (raw carrot sticks, apples, oranges, celery sticks, etc.). In this way your diet can play an important part in dental care.

In addition to sugar, coffee and cigarettes have the same effect on blood-sugar level. Some people try to get rid of their sluggish, low-blood-sugar condition by drinking more coffee or smoking more cigarettes. But every temporary lift is inevitably followed by fatigue, irritability, or headaches.

Try to eat some protein along with the sugar foods you do eat—for example, drink some milk along with a sweet snack. Protein is digested slowly and helps to keep sugar from being absorbed too rapidly into the bloodstream. To feel well throughout the day it is particularly important to have some protein for breakfast. (See the nutrient chart, p. 103, for good sources of protein.)

Problems with the Food and Agriculture Industries

"It's almost impossible to get my kids to eat well with all that advertising on TV for junk foods. If I don't get their favorite sugar-coated cereal, they keep pestering me until I do. Why can't there be more advertising for healthier foods?" The answer is fairly simple. Since the food industry is mainly interested in making more and more profit, it advertises those products that make the most money. Unfortunately, we, as well as our children, have succumbed to this advertising and have in many cases adapted our tastes to the foods best suited for mass production, rapid turnover and longer shelf-life. In other words, we have been conditioned to like the foods that give the food industry the most profit. Since most of us won't suddenly change all our eating habits, the food industry will probably continue advertising as it has been. However, we can learn which highly advertised foods are best (or least harmful) for us and start to buy more of these products. (See "Some Valuable Suggestions," page 109.)

"It's crazy the way food prices are skyrocketing. Pretty soon I won't be able to get enough to eat for me and the kids, let alone get enough nutritious food." The high cost of food is frightening. According to a representative of Merck Chemical Company, it "has been established that 35% of the retail cost of food is being paid by the consumer for convenience features . . . ready-to-eat breakfast cereals, instant foods, soup mixes, cake mixes . . . etc."[*] Many of us are angry about paying thirty-five cents out of every dollar for "conveniences" that often save us only ten minutes and damage our health in addition.

Also upsetting is the fact that we often have to pay twice—first to have important natural nutrients removed from our food, then to have a few of those nutrients restored. (Food companies call this "adding nutrients," but it's really just partially replacing what was originally there and has been removed.) For example, during the processing of white flour, polished rice and refined cereals, the B complex of vitamins is totally removed. Only six of the B vitamins are now being put back in, but we are told by such well-known experts as Dr. Frederick Stare that these are the key vitamins. (Dr. Stare, by the

Food Pollution by Gene Marine and Jay Van Allen.

way, a member of the faculty of the Harvard School of Public Health, wrote a syndicated column on nutrition while serving as a paid consultant to one of the nation's largest food corporations.) In fact, all the B vitamins are key vitamins, and it does little good to restore only six of them.[*]

"I don't understand how they get away with it. Can't the government do anything about all these additives and food colorings and pesticides and chemical fertilizers?" Government agencies such as the Food and Drug Administration (FDA) and the U.S. Department of Agriculture (USDA) have been largely ineffective, mainly because the food industry has so much control over them.[†] Seventy percent of all food standards and regulations are proposed by the food industry itself.[‡] And during meetings when the FDA makes important decisions about food standards, food industry representatives are often the only others present. Because of such industrial control, cola beverages don't have to label their caffeine content (which many people don't know about), some products don't have to label their fat content, and many potentially dangerous chemicals continue to be used. Also, our food is further contaminated by the agricultural industry's use of chemical fertilizers and pesticides.

Even a former commissioner of the FDA (Herbert Ley) has recognized that agency's ineffectiveness: "The thing that bugs me is that the people think the FDA is protecting them—it isn't. What the FDA is doing and what the public thinks it's doing are as different as night and day."[§] This is especially upsetting, since we are discovering more and more that the effects of chemicals are cumulative, that we store up these chemicals over the years until enough is present to affect our bodies seriously.

[*]*Ibid.*, pp. 60–61.
[†]"Economic concentration in the food industry is now so top-heavy that four firms control 90 percent of the breakfast cereals, 75 percent of the bread and prepared flour, 56 percent of all processed meats, 65 percent of sugar, 80 percent of canned goods. . . ." From *Parade* Magazine, August 10, 1975.
[‡]*The Chemical Feast* (see bibliography), p. 64.
[§]Quoted in *The New York Times*, December 31, 1969.

General Foods Plant, Woburn, Massachusetts

How to Read Labels

The first item on the label indicates which ingredient makes up most of the product. The remaining ingredients are listed in order of decreasing percentages. If "sugar" or "water" is the first or second item on the label, you can probably make it cheaper at home, if you really want to have it (examples: many cereals, cocoa mixes, "juice drinks").* In meat products, the words *cereal* and *water* on the same label indicate filler is being used.

Sugar:
  If a label says "brown sugar" or "turbinado sugar," read white sugar plus molasses. There are no superior nutrients in brown sugar of any type, and only a few in certain blackstrap molasses.

Hydrogenated
  means that an oily substance has been hardened into a solid fat (which is what most Americans eat too much of).

Fat:
  Unless it says "vegetable fat" shortening (usually hydrogenated—see above) or "vegetable oil," you can be sure it's animal fat.

Salt:
  We already take in too much salt. If you have a chance to buy unsalted food, buy it. You can always add a little. That way you also can be sure that the salt is *iodized* (important in preventing thyroid problems). Commercially prepared canned or frozen dishes often have high salt contents, as do many baby foods.

Nitrite (sodium nitrite)—remember, this is carcinogenic. Appears in almost all processed meats and is a much more toxic salt compound than ordinary table salt. Try to avoid it.

Wheat Flour
  means *un*enriched wheat flour (unless it *says* enriched), which is practically worthless starch and calories. It is just about impossible to buy a genuine whole-grain cracker made in the U.S., but crackers and cake mixes with enriched flour are still better than plain white-flour products. Many local bakeries use *un*enriched flour!

New labeling is coming which will show percentages of the recommended daily allowances (RDA) of basic nutrients as well as vitamins, minerals and calories. However, labeling regulations vary; some are "required for some foods and optional for others." Consumer Beware.

*One problem is that many stores don't carry "pure and unsweetened" whole-grain cereals or fruit juices. Many consumers foolishly claim they are "expensive," not realizing that they pay inflated prices for water and sugar in the prepared products.

Some Valuable Suggestions

Whenever you can, make your own soups and whole-grain breads. They contain far more nutrients than canned soups and spongy, store-bought breads.

Use cast-iron skillets and pans when cooking. They are an important source of readily absorbed iron, which is needed by women especially.

When cooking vegetables, use only a little water and keep the pot tightly covered. Also, save water in which vegetables have been cooked and use it for stews, soups, sauces, broths and so on. Many vitamins are lost to the air (oxidize) or dissolve in water—save them when possible.

Make sure fresh food is really fresh. Old vegetables may have fewer vitamins than frozen or canned ones.

Read labels to know what you are buying. Even though all the ingredients may not be listed, the ones that are must be listed in order of quantity, the first ingredient being used in greatest quantity.

If you take any supplementing fat-soluble vitamins (A, D and E) it is important to eat or drink some fat-containing food (milk, for example) along with the vitamin. This ensures absorption of the vitamin. If you take iron try not to take vitamin E at the same time.

Do You Know?

Soft Drinks:
  Most soda contains large quantities of salt as well as sugar and sometimes caffeine. When you're counting salt for the day, be sure to include all the soft drinks you drink.

Ice Cream:
  Sad news for ice cream lovers. We often tell ourselves we're eating good food when we eat ice cream, but there is so much sugar, fat and carbohydrates in most ice cream that whatever protein there may be is not really worth it. Enjoy it if you can, but don't think of it as high-quality nourishment. A glass of milk or yogurt (unsweetened) is a far better substitute.

Yogurt and *Cottage Cheese:*
  Unless you buy or make plain yogurt and prepare it with unsweetened fruit, you are eating a lot of sugar in the flavored kinds. If you get a whole-milk yogurt you are also eating some fat. "Creamed cottage cheese" (containing cream) also has fat in it. Ask for 99% fat-free types of both if you are concerned about your fat intake. (Remember though, "97% fat-free" doesn't mean much—whole milk, for example, is 97% fat-free.)

B_{12} is not found in vegetable products (except for certain seaweeds), so vegetarians should eat some eggs or dairy products (or take a supplement). B_{12} deficiency can result in anemia and nerve damage.

If your children pester you for junk foods, try out more nutritious substitutes that might satisfy them equally well. Many children like granola as much as the popular, vitamin-robbed cereals. And popcorn is far better than many sweet snacks, which cause tooth decay as well as provide little nutritional value. Also, one way to avoid buying processed meats (bologna, salami, hot dogs, etc.) is to buy a large ham, bake it, slice it thin, and store it in the refrigerator for sandwich meat.

Conclusion

One very important concern for women is how we relate to food. Often we find ourselves using food as a reward for both ourselves and our children, or we turn to food when we are unhappy, frustrated, tense, or anxious (much as we might turn to cigarettes). Such situations usually involve very complex emotions and would require a much longer discussion than possible here. Also, we feel tremendous pressures from our society to stay "thin and beautiful" and to diet, if need be, to maintain these thin standards. Such standards usually have little to do with our physical and emotional well-being, so we often find ourselves trying to look attractive at the expense of our overall health. Some of us have found it helpful to discuss issues of women and weight with other women, who almost invariably share the same problems. By supporting one another it is sometimes possible for us to resist the tremendous pressures we resent so much. At least we can begin to feel stronger about what we believe in and what we want for ourselves.

For some of us who want to change our eating patterns it is often difficult to find inexpensive alternatives to what is offered in the local supermarket. Most supermarkets carry only hydrogenated peanut butter (with 7 percent sugar added) and foods that are almost always treated with chemicals. To find preservative-free foods we may have to go to a natural-food store, where prices are often high.

We need to make a united demand that our larger stores offer us healthier choices and carry more chemical-free foods. Such foods do not have to be more expensive than other foods. We should also demand that fruits and vegetables not be prepackaged, so that we can examine their quality.

We can also get control of our food selection by joining or starting food co-ops. Co-ops can get good food very cheaply. They can deal directly with natural-food wholesalers to get whole-grain breads, unhydrogenated peanut butter and other preservative-free products. Co-

ops are more likely to get what you want, unlike the local Safeway or A&P. Even a few families in the same neighborhood can work cooperatively by taking turns baking bread for all the families in the group or going to a nearby farmers' market, where foods are sold in bulk. If someone has a back yard, a group of people could plant an organic garden and thus be sure of pesticide-free vegetables.

Putting pressure on our legislators to support strict food-regulation legislation will probably do little to improve the quality of our food. Every now and then a dangerous additive or pesticide might be banned, especially when dedicated groups such as Ralph Nader's or the Environmental Defense Fund win a hard-fought legal battle. But now that DDT is banned the agriculture business will find something else to replace it, and after Citrus Red #40 is gone the food industry will find another harmful red food coloring. Even if the FDA really began to protect us, the food and drug industries would probably not take long to gain control of the agency once again.

Unfortunately, our system hasn't worked and isn't working now. Money seems to rule everything in our economy, including politics. The success we have in making more healthful foods available will not likely come from winning legal battles (at least for a long time) but from joining with others around us to put pressure on local supermarkets, boycott harmful foods (and let the manufacturers know about it), join food co-ops, grow our own gardens, and help spread accurate information about food and nutrition. For all of us, being in control of our bodies also means choosing what we put into them.

WOMEN IN MOTION

How can I explain it? It gets to you, it is you! We have this notion that mind and body are separate—but how can you feel good in the head, really, if your body's like a limp rag? Before, my body would embarrass me—do clumsy things, because there wasn't a lot of muscular control, or it wouldn't do much at all. Now that I exercise I'm happier about my body, it acts and reacts in ways that please me—it's stronger, more real, more energetic. It's like being three-dimensional instead of two-dimensional; it makes me feel more complete, more whole.

We all know the need for good nutrition, enough rest and regular exercise. They keep our body systems functioning in good order; tone our muscles (including the heart) and improve flexibility; protect our bodies better against injury and disease, especially as we age. A healthy body also helps keep our minds balanced and alert, and vice versa. The well-known symptoms of nervous tension—headaches, insomnia, indigestion—have affected most of us at one time or another. Yet instead of using natural preventives like exercise and healthy food, we rely heavily on artificial means which may be harmful—aspirin, tranquilizers, antacid.

In the United States the President's Council on Physical Fitness and Sports estimates that one child in six is "So weak, uncoordinated, or generally inept that he or she is physically underdeveloped."* Equally upsetting is the fact that, according to a recent medical study, American women begin their physical decline at twelve years of age!† The need for exercise is clearly pressing.

Why We Don't Get the Exercise We Need

In agricultural societies and rural areas the concept of exercise is fairly meaningless.‡ The substance of people's lives is strenuous physical labor, with women doing as many (or more) of the heavy tasks as men. Today in America most people live in urban or suburban areas. Here working-class people—especially blacks and other third-world people, but whites too—do the hard physical labor. But a growing majority of jobs, and not just middle-class ones, require little physical effort although they may be extremely tiring.

Women, even more than men, tend to use energy in a way that leaves us exhausted. Our lives are busy, even frenetic, yet the moving around we do is often repetitive motion that doesn't use our bodies completely. Think of how we spend our time:

As houseworkers doing repetitive household chores;

As mothers chasing around after kids;

At jobs—in offices or factories, in stationary positions requiring painful ways of bending and/or endless hours of sitting that often result in poor posture and back trouble, or as hospital workers or waitresses on our feet all day.

Getting the exercise we need is in many ways harder for us than for men. When men decide to get exercise (if they have the time and money) they can usually find facilities—a gym or YMCA, private clubs, steam baths, or athletic leagues. In contrast, the facilities available to

*The Physically Underdeveloped Child, The President's Council on Physical Fitness and Sports, Wash., DC, U.S. Govt. Printing Office, 1977, p.1.

†Lace Wertenbaker, "I Was Probably What You Call a Tomboy," *Yankee*, Nov. 1976, p. 123.

‡Physically active games and dance, however, have been a part of almost every society from the beginning of human life. Most of them were "religious or utilitarian in origin," but as time went on, some were performed "primarily for relaxation and recreation" (Deobold B. Van Dalen and Bruce L. Bennett, *A World History of Physical Education: Cultural, Philosophical, Comparative*, Englewood Cliffs, N.J.: Prentice-Hall, 1971, p. 5).

women are much more limited. Many cities don't have YWCAs, and even schools sometimes lack gyms for women—the girls have to use the boys' gym. Jill's story is typical: "A group of us were looking for a place to play basketball occasionally. We couldn't find any public place. School gyms close at night—or are reserved for league competition—and college gyms are restricted to their students or faculty."

Even when facilities are available, they are often not free. You have to pay to join a health club, a suburban country club, or a city Y. If you're a mother you often have the additional cost of child care. Most cities do have free parks, but as one of the girls in our neighborhood complained, "The boys take over, and if we're lucky they'll let us play once in a while." Then, too, with parks you may have a hassle getting equipment, and you always have to worry about the weather.

Finally there's a problem of time. Over forty percent of American women (or 39 million females) are a part of the labor force. Many also have families and therefore another job waiting for them when they get home. For a mother it is especially difficult to make time for some form of regular exercise, unless, of course, it's done with her kids. "Exercise tends to get tacked on," says Mimi, a mother of three. "When my life gets very busy it's often the first thing to go, even though I feel better when I'm exercising." In this respect single women have it easier.

Many women do not have the luxury of asking, "Do I get enough exercise?" These are the women who are too poor and too run-down from many pregnancies, long work hours, bad food and poor medical care to ever think about exercise. Black, Spanish-speaking and other minority women may have all these problems and then face racial discrimination at their local recreation center on top of everything else.

Still, when time, money and opportunity exist, a strikingly small number of women incorporate vigorous exer-

cise into their daily lives. There are reasons other than the ones we've listed. Social reasons. Many of us have to fight against the prejudiced ideas that women can't do certain things and that we shouldn't do certain things.* How many of us have had more than one of the following comments hurled at us?

"Strong women aren't feminine—muscles will scare away the boys."

"Well, aren't *you* a little tomboy!"

"Sweating is unladylike."

"The boys won't like you if you beat them at baseball."

"Hey, that one with the knee guards looks like a dyke."

"Ah, you throw like a girl."

From early childhood on, many women are discouraged, subtly and sometimes not so subtly, from participating in strenuous physical activities. We get the idea from our parents, our schools, our neighborhoods, our whole society. From infancy on, baby girls are pampered and treated more delicately than boy babies. A woman we know sometimes introduced her baby girl as Danny. The adults who met "Danny" encouraged her to play actively without worrying about a few bumps or even tears. But when she was introduced as Sara, people were more protective of her. No wonder many girls grow up scared to try out things with their bodies. In a recent questionnaire directed to women studying karate, many wrote that as little girls they had been encouraged to go outside and run around, or to dance or swim during the summer, but rarely to do athletics seriously.

In schools, especially in the past, physical education programs often weren't required for women. When they were, less was expected. Our team sports often had softer rules—a women's regulation basketball court was formerly one-third the size of a men's standard court, which made for a much slower game. Some gym programs for girls bog down into a needlessly boring routine of exercise. Other sports, such as ice hockey, weren't available to women in any form in many places. Even neighborhood streets are usually the boys' turf. Growing up to believe that physical coordination is a male characteristic, boys will teach each other athletic skills but won't do the same with girls. Joanne told us: "Sometimes the boys would let me join their stickball games, but if several of us girls wanted to play, they would chase us away." And organized sports is mostly a male world—from the professional level down to neighborhood Little Leagues. Most men want to keep it that way, for sports is one area where they can assert their "masculinity" by showing off their strength, skill and aggressiveness, or by identifying with and idolizing those who do.

As we pass into and through adolescence, the pressures on us to be "popular with the boys" reach epidemic proportions and often squelch any remaining desire to exercise strenuously. We're warned not to compete with boys or they won't like us, so we become cheerleaders to the boys' teams. We give up learning athletic skills in favor of learning to swing our hips. We're taught that popularity depends on "femininity": muscles on a woman are considered unattractive—to men, of course. The only encouragement we get from them is for exercises that improve our gracefulness or "take inches off the hips and waistline, while developing our 'busts.'" Alice told us: "When I started studying karate my boyfriend got real upset: he was afraid I'd get muscular and not be his slim little lady any more. But that's his problem. I feel good now, and I'm not so afraid of a bruise or two."

For some women the threat of being unpopular with the boys or looking "unfeminine" is an empty one. Those women tend to grow up active and tough. But for most women who have been brought up to consider male approval primary, such threats are intimidating, and they prevent many of us from developing our physical potential. Cheryl's example is not unusual: "I was real good at ball games. The boys fought to have me on their team. When I got married—at sixteen—Jim was jealous of the other men and wouldn't let me play ball anymore. So I just sat around."

Those of us who resist buying into the myth of our physical inferiority and actually pursue athletics are usually teased, ridiculed and often forced to pay a heavy price for our success, or are made to feel so clumsy that we may give up before ever getting very far.

There's also the threat that we'll injure ourselves if we try to do something too strenuous. A female dance student was frightened that a leg-lifting exercise might damage her uterus. Many women have been taught that physical activity during menstruation is dangerous.* Both untrue! Women in fact can do all kinds of heavy work without injury to our reproductive organs or any other part of ourselves. Nell described arguments she had with her husband: "Peter gets angry at me for moving furniture. 'You'll hurt yourself,' he says. He doesn't know how many heavy things I lift—like our thirty-pound son! I think he's scared that my being stronger

*These prejudices affect American women of different classes and cultures, even though pre-capitalist and capitalist exploitation has never seen anything wrong with physically driving black and other working-class women as hard as men. Sojourner Truth's famous outburst makes that abundantly clear: "The man over there says that women need to be helped into carriages and lifted over ditches, and to have the best place everywhere. Nobody ever helps me into carriages or over puddles or gives me the best place . . . and ain't I a woman? Look at my arm! I have ploughed and planted and gathered into barns, and no man could head me . . . and ain't I a woman? I could work as much and eat as much as a man when I could get it—and bear the lash as well . . . and ain't I a woman?" (From a speech to the Women's Rights Convention, Akron, Ohio, 1851.)

*For more discussion see Barbara Ehrenreich and Dierdre English, *Complaints and Disorders: The Sexual Politics of Sickness*, Old Westbury, NY: The Feminist Press, 1973.

will make me less dependent on him." It is lack of muscular development that makes some activities or jobs risky for women, *not* some inherent weakness in the female body. With routine, sensible exercise we can depend on our bodies to be more powerful and flexible, quicker and less prone to injury.

A final deterrent to doing vigorous exercise is the clothing that we're expected to wear, which constricts and abuses our bodies in some pretty striking ways:

High heels damage our feet permanently. Our entire foot is meant to hit the ground—our arches are shock absorbers, and that function can't be carried out if half our foot is in the air. High heels also force our weight forward, making balance difficult, which is awkward as well as dangerous. Tight shoes of any kind cramp our bones and prevent our feet from breathing. The paper-thin soles on many women's shoes not only give our feet no protection against the cold in winter, but the lack of cushioning between the hard ground and our feet causes tired legs.

Tight belts and collars, corsets and girdles, overly snug panty hose and other restrictive garments impede our breathing, circulation and digestion. Bras of course fall into this category—they are restricting, but for some women necessary. The breasts consist of glandular connective tissue with muscle behind it. Exercise can strengthen these pectoral muscles but not the breasts themselves. Many small-breasted women will enjoy the comfort and freedom that comes from not wearing a bra, whereas larger-breasted women may always need to wear one for support or because it's painful without. Some women may find a bra helpful while exercising, especially at times of the month when the breasts can be particularly tender. If and when you wear a bra (and it may be just to protect yourself from hassles with men) it makes sense to choose comfort over fashion: be sure it allows you to breathe and move freely.

Other clothing is functionally limiting, though not necessarily damaging:

Very short skirts make it difficult to be active without worrying that this might lead to lecherous comments or even attack.

Very long skirts bind one's legs and make it difficult to move or run.

Many bikini bathing suits are impractical except for lying passively in the sun: the straps are often cutting or break easily. The bottoms may tend to slip down.

Things Are Beginning to Change

Some of this is beginning to change. Changes are apparent in the area of clothing. In recent years many women have become as concerned with comfort and practicality as with style and appearance. Increasingly, women wear pants; they're easier to move in, warmer in cold weather, and greater protection against the eyes of men every-

where. Even in secretarial or receptionist jobs, for example, where women are expected to look "ladylike," the right to wear pants has been won. Women have begun to design and make our own clothes—clothes that are right for our bodies, comfortable, useful, often colorful. More and more, we are rejecting the ridiculous outfits (and postures) of the predominately male fashion world, outfits that have encouraged us to mistreat our bodies. A woman we know designed a pair of pants for hiking and camping which had a zipper going from the front to the back of the crotch. You just unzip the pants and pee standing up—no need for the whole awkward, and sometimes humiliating, production of taking your pants down!

There are similar trends in footwear—away from the binding, high-off-the-ground variety, toward healthier styles: sandals, moccasins, sneakers, running shoes and boots, all of which keep the feet closer to the ground and allow them to live. (Go barefoot when and where possible and stay off the platforms!)

There has been a general increase in public athletic facilities—more public swimming pools, skating rinks and even tennis courts. YWCA and college and public-school programs for women are being improved. The new U.S. Department of Health, Education and Welfare (HEW) regulations allow the department to withdraw federal funds or take court action against schools that discriminate against women in any area of activity, including athletics. These regulations fall under Title Nine of the Education Amendments Act of 1972, which requires that *all* schools receiving federal aid offer comparable sports programs to males and females, with either separate teams or one team open to all—but they don't have to fund the programs equally. This is a dangerous loophole, so we will have to be very aggressive in getting our fair share. (For all the details of this act and/or how to file a discrimination charge, write to HEW in Washington or contact the nearest local office.)

Title Nine is helping, but most important is that all over the country women from girls in grade school to older women in community softball leagues are organizing to get the space, equipment and coaching they need. As usual, poorer cities, towns and ghetto areas will have a harder time meeting these increased demands because there is so little money and space for recreation of any kind. Not until we have an economic-social system that puts people before profit will everyone be able to participate. *Meanwhile, however, what is available should go equally to men and women.*

Rules for organized sports have been changed too, as the various authorities have recognized that women can play a harder, faster game than they had believed possible. For example, women now use the same regulation-size basketball court as men do.

Crucial to all this is the growing interest among women in more physical activity. It's no longer unusual to see as many women as men jogging along tracks where only men used to run. Althea Gibson, Billie Jean King and other female tennis pros have encouraged lots of women to grab a racquet and ball; and after a terrific battle, girls have at long last broken through into Little League baseball. In almost every area of sports from boxing to ice hockey or shot put, women are seriously developing strength, confidence and ability. We are beginning to be able to follow our own sports. Newspapers and magazines are including women's events on an occasional basis (and not *every* article starts with how cute we are), but there should be much more coverage. Then we could read about our current favorites as well as reclaim another part of our history and learn about earlier women greats such as Babe Didrikson Zaharias, who did just about everything—the javelin throw, the 880-meter hurdle, high jump, basketball, golf—superbly, winning countless medals and championships. Or Florence Chadwick, an American who swam the English Channel three times, both ways—in 1950, 1951 and 1955—and many, many others.*

In recent years many of us have begun to recognize our own physical potential. We are interested in, even inspired by, the women who excel at sports. But given the American world of athletics—based as it is on the most aggressive, at times even brutal, dog-eat-dog patterns of male competitiveness and greedily engaged in marketing the successful athlete like any other product

*Sportswoman and *WomenSports*, which began publishing in 1973 and 1974 respectively, are now out of print. Despite lots of good pictures and some good articles, the overall tone of both magazines was depressingly commercial and competitive. We hope a new and better women's sports magazine will be along soon.

in our society—we do not want to see women triumphing over women in ugly, masculine ways. Instead of turning talented people into superstars, we favor providing opportunity and encouragement for all. The Chinese (in the People's Republic), who are very sports-minded, try to involve everyone in *playing*—not "spectating." In their games the Chinese put friendship first, competition second. Like them, we feel it essential that we develop ourselves to be the best we can, each and every woman. We want to be concerned with how we feel, not just how we look. That means a healthy, glowing body that uses its resources well.

Choosing an Exercise: Some Guidelines and Some Benefits

We can learn to throw a ball or swim or climb a tree. Physical skills are *not* a matter of innate male ability, despite what many of us have been taught. Nor should we be discouraged by people saying all the time that men have larger, heavier bones, more muscle mass and so forth, though it may well be true. The real point for us is that as more and more women get into exercise and sports, we will see what we can do and what we want to do. With so many myths to work through, we are just beginning to understand our bodies in terms of our potential strength, coordination, balance, flexibility, speed and capacity for endurance. We need lots of observation, experimentation and *unbiased* research in this area (which should also deal with questions of race and comparisons with other societies past and present).* Mostly we must be encouraged by what is becoming clear:

• Women excel where skill and good reflexes are involved: watch our new jockeys, like Robyn Smith, for instance, or a 120-pound woman throwing a 200-pound man. Not to mention a superb female gymnast or dancer.

• Our endurance: it has been proved statistically that women are healthier from birth, and our average life span is five years longer than men's. A study of long-distance drivers showed that the women's capacity for alertness increased by 10 percent with time, whereas the men's fell off by 11 percent. As for exercise, women can definitely build up endurance to become really outstanding in swimming, hiking, track and so forth. No one needs to doubt that we often have an incredible determination to last even if it means a lot of pain. The American cyclist Sheila Young finished a world championship race in Spain with a "deep 9-inch laceration in her head"† clamped together so she wouldn't have to

**For example, is there as large a size difference between women and men in other parts of the world as there is in the United States? (And there are many more questions.)
†"Women in Sports," *Newsweek* (June 3, 1974), pp. 50-51.

Wilma Rudolph equaling her world record in the indoor 60-yard dash.

take time out for stitches. She went on to win the gold medal.

• Due to a low center of gravity, our balance is good. Another asset is our flexibility. Even that extra fat on our bodies can pay off in terms of buoyancy and resistance to cold in the water.

• Strength will vary from woman to woman as it does from man to man, but with a new attitude toward good muscular development we'll all get a lot stronger.

So what's important now is forging ahead and finding the kind and amount of exercise that's right for each of us, for our bodies, our minds. This will vary, of course, but here are some general criteria:

Select exercises that stretch and strengthen the entire body—arms, legs, torso, neck.
Pick activities that feel good, that give pleasure. All mammals need to play, and humans are no exception.
Select something that allows you to pace yourself, with which you can work at enlarging your own capacity, both in the frequency and intensity with which you do it.
For some of us it'll be important to find activities that can be done at home.

The total exercises, such as running or swimming, are the best because they use and therefore develop many different muscles; they keep bodily systems healthy as well as expand their working ability. Forty to 50 percent of body weight is muscle. Bulging muscles alone won't create good health, but the more solid yet supple the muscle—not loose and flabby—the better. Good back muscles reduce the likelihood of back problems; strong abdominal muscles are also necessary for a healthy back, as well as for holding internal organs in place, for good blood circulation and elimination, and they usually make childbirth and menstruation less painful. In general we'll sit or stand straighter and feel better; everyday tasks will be easier and less tiring. For women who need to rely on men to lift heavy items or even open jars, our new strength will give us a lot more independence.

A total exercise will help your breathing. The exertion of it should make you pant. One woman we knew was afraid that panting meant her body was breaking down. In fact the opposite is true. Working harder, you'll begin to breathe more slowly, deeply, and more regularly. Your lungs will develop a larger capacity for air. With vigorous exercise, blood that is ordinarily pooled in the organs of the body is drawn into circulation; the heart has to pump this increased amount of liquid around faster; over time this means that the heart, a muscle, will strengthen and be able to pump out a greater volume of blood with fewer beats. The contractions and relaxations of the muscles, especially in the legs, which have

been called a second heart, will squeeze the veins, helping the blood return upward to the heart. Good circulation ensures that all the muscles and organs get a continually fresh supply of blood, which is essential to their survival and well-being.

Total exercise also helps our attitude toward food and improves our digestion. It regularizes eating habits: we eat more if we need to, but it helps curb the compulsive eating that is a problem for so many women. The movement of the body and its muscles speeds up the peristaltic (wavelike) action of the digestive organs and therefore the elimination processes as well. People who exercise regularly are less prone to constipation and kidney stones.

Obviously, physical activity will alleviate certain kinds of tension and depression. Our mental and physical states are intimately related. Exercise will help both body and mind relax and enjoy life. We are not suggesting exercise as a cure-all, as a substitute for changing this oppressive society into a human one we can live in, but we are saying that we need it to relieve the harmful effects of all the frustration, anxiety and anger we experience daily. Exercising regularly will help you sleep better (as long as you don't jog a mile just before bedtime). If your body has good tone and doesn't slouch, your mind will surely function better. Learning and practicing many sports is not only a physical exercise but also mentally stimulating since it requires concentration, memorization and creative thinking about how to move the way we want to.

Jogging, as we have said, is one of the best forms of exercise. A several-mile run in the morning will make you feel better all day. Do it anyplace—in the country, along a river, in parks, around the block. Wear comfortable, loose-fitting clothes and sturdy, flexible shoes.

Especially in the city, try to run in the early morning or late evening, when the air is least polluted by traffic and industry. We realize this may be a problem, especially at night because of dangerous streets. Find company to run with if you can—it is safer and more fun.

Build up slowly: start at a slow pace and gradually increase speed and distance. At first walk, then jog, then walk again. As you get stronger, vary periods of slow running with periods of sprinting. This alternation is very good for circulation. Running also helps varicose veins by pumping the blood up from the legs.

Move your feet naturally (heel-toe action with toes pointing straight ahead, though) and let your arms swing, the left arm moving with the right leg and the right arm with the left leg. Try to relax, especially your neck and shoulders, and keep a good body posture.

Stay off pavements (or run lightly) and wear well-cushioned running shoes because the shock of your feet constantly hitting such hard surfaces may result in inflammation of the muscle tissue or cause the calf muscles to be torn away from the bone.

If you can't run outside, do it inside—you can run in

women's volleyball team

place even while doing other things, such as talking on the phone. Some people enjoy running to music. One woman we met jogs while watching TV: "You can run right through a movie once you get into it," she told us.

If you don't feel strong enough to try running, then begin to build up strength by walking daily. Get off the bus one stop sooner on the way to work or shopping and use stairs instead of elevators. Move briskly, with strong strides, using your entire leg. Hiking, in season, is also great—it can be a moderate outing or a real challenging climb.

Bicycling is fine exercise, especially for the legs. Replace as many car trips with a bicycle (or a walk) as time and distance will allow.

Skiing is another vigorous activity that uses the entire body while improving control and balance. And it's tremendously exhilarating as well. There are disadvantages, however: it's both seasonal and expensive. Cross-country skiing is more accessible, cheaper and more of a total-body sport than the down-hill variety. You can also try ice skating. Once you get the hang of it (which demands you work on your balance) it's wonderful fun and really good for the legs.

Swimming is another excellent general conditioner. Try to swim at least several times weekly. Start each session with one, four, or ten laps, whatever feels comfortable, and build up by pushing yourself to do at least one more lap than you think you can.

Group sports are also terrific exercise if done regularly. Basketball, hockey, tennis, baseball, handball and other ball games will build coordination and endurance and improve agility. Team sports can be a great way to meet and get to know other people, to work together on something everyone enjoys. A fast, hard game is good for the spirit as well as the body.

Self-defense arts are increasingly popular with women. Judo, aikido, jujitsu and karate teach us how to defend ourselves and can be excellent forms of exercise. Warm-ups for these skills can include running, stretching, weight lifting, while the various techniques (punching, kicking, throwing) rely on timing, speed and accuracy rather than brute force, which makes them ideal for women. The self-defense arts improve balance, coordination, control and of course strength and endurance; they sharpen your mental capacities—you learn to be decisive, to develop a series of responses quickly, both offensively and defensively. (See also Chapter 8.)

Yoga is not just for Eastern mystics and American hippies. The various yoga exercises have been developed over many, many years to stimulate or, conversely, take the pressure off your internal organs as well as to improve muscle tone and control, limberness and flexibility. With focus on proper breathing, yoga helps you tremendously to relax and sends healing energy to all parts of your body. After a session of it you will feel revitalized and integrated—mind and body together. In our tense and aggressive society, yoga's total lack of competitiveness is a wonderful release.

Tai chi also stresses rhythmic, flowing body movements performed in a noncompetitive way. It is a healthy system of exercise to develop your balance, coordination, flexibility and mental concentration. At a more advanced stage, it can be used for self-defense.

Dance can also be a strenuous and exhilarating form of exercise, especially when done regularly and in a disciplined way. Any form of dance will strengthen and stretch your muscles, teach you muscular control, and improve coordination and balance. As a creative art it also encourages physical expression—without words—of emotions and moods.

Working at home, there are many exercises you can do to develop strength and flexibility. Some suggestions:

Strengthening exercises include push-ups, leg lifts, sit-ups. For a wide assortment of wonderful exercises that will stretch and build up every part of your body, buy or borrow a copy of Maggie Lettvin's *The Beautiful Machine* (see bibliography). She has something for everyone, from people who are bedridden right up to people in serious athletic training. Each exercise is clearly explained and illustrated. Her enthusiasm for keeping the body in motion is very infectious, but she is also careful to include cautions for people with different physical problems.* There are other good exercise books available at your local bookstore or library that will provide variety and get to a lot of different muscles. When you're beginning to get in shape, try some elementary gymnastic stunts (headstand, cartwheel—there are hundreds) or moving to music to keep the pure exercise routine from boring you to the point of abandoning it. Having goals to work toward is great incentive, and there is no end to the challenges for your body.

Use dumbbells to build up arm, shoulder and torso muscles. There is a series of exercises to be done with three-pound weights (available in most sporting-goods stores). Do them faithfully and vigorously for best results. Weight lifting with an adjustable barbell strengthens trunk and leg as well as arm muscles, and is more exciting. Find out how many presses you should begin with and work up.

Jumping rope is excellent exercise and doesn't take up much room. Try to jump steadily for a minute, pause to catch your breath, and jump another minute. Repeat three or four times. Kids and boxers know all kinds of foot-rope patterns and develop good leg muscles, endurance and coordination from this activity. Or try doing the jumping-jack exercises.

Reassess the physical work you do during the day and make each motion using muscles so as to develop but not strain them. Try to build up both sides of your body equally; don't favor the strong side. This can apply to a lot of us, whether we are doing housework or are among the relatively few who have broken into traditionally male trades such as carpentry or machine-shop work.

What about the home exercisers being sold now? Chin-up bars, hand grippers, stationary bicycles can be fun and useful. But why spend a lot of money on gimmicks when there are ways of using just your body to get the same benefits? It's better to save your money for healthy foods or real athletic facilities or camping trips or decent running shoes.

None of these physical activities is an either-or proposition. Running is a total exercise because it is so good for all your body systems and your leg muscles, but you may want to supplement it with a dumbbell routine to develop your arms. Stretching is very necessary, too. You

*See also *Maggie's Back Book: Healing the Hurt in Your Lower Back*, Boston: Houghton Mifflin, 1976. She also has health materials on overweight, dieting, pregnancy, aging, multiple sclerosis and much more. Write for publications list to: Maggie Lettvin, Athletic Dept., MIT DuPont Athletic Center, Cambridge, MA 02139.

want flexible muscles as well as strong ones—throughout your body. Joints freeze if you don't keep them moving in all the directions they are designed to move. Whatever you do, you should do it regularly at least 3 or 4 times a week. Short, frequent periods of practice are better than fewer longer ones.

Suit the exercise to your day—if you've had a physically exhausting one, pick something quiet and relaxing, like yoga, for instance. If you've been stationary and feel draggy or restless, let yourself go and get into something really active. For the endless numbers of women who bend or lean over all day—on the assembly line, at a sewing machine or typewriter—you need to find some exercises that help relax the neck, shoulder and back muscles, straighten out your whole upper body, and then strengthen the muscles you hardly ever use. Some gentle waking-up exercises every morning are a good idea. If lunch or coffee breaks permit, do a few stretches or whatever to get the blood moving and the kinks out.

As you're thinking about what to do, you'll have to decide whether to work alone or in a group. If in a group, then with all women or a mixed group? Many forms of exercise or sports can be practiced alone: running, swimming, karate, working out at a gym, yoga, dance. Many of us lack the discipline to work by ourselves, at least at first, or we get lonely and bored. Others find that moving our bodies vigorously becomes addicting after a very short time.

Especially in the initial learning stages of many skills, some organized instruction is necessary. In addition to providing technical information, a group can also provide support and encouragement. Women we know studying yoga agreed that they needed the discipline of a class situation when they began; as their skills and confidence grew, they found it easier to practice alone. In women's groups we can be more open, less self-conscious about our awkwardness or the shapes of our bodies. There we aren't intimidated by male standards or humiliating comments from men who are either threatened by women's becoming stronger or are only interested in us as sexual objects. It's exciting to work together as women, to encourage one another to grow stronger together.

On the other hand, some women cite the advantages of mixed groups. A women's college athletic director said she likes her teams to scrimmage with men—it makes the team play better and harder. Some female karate students found the experience of sparring with men valuable—it was realistic and prepared them better for an actual encounter.

Some Final Advice

Now that you're about to begin your exercise program, here is some final advice, and a few cautions:

Start slowly and build up, in general and during each session. Muscle growth comes from pushing each muscle involved slightly beyond what you forced it to do the previous time. Stretching (for flexibility) is based on the same principle. But take care. When you're stiff and out of shape you can tear a ligament or even permanently damage a muscle by driving it too violently (this is *always* so). If you want to get into an activity that puts a lot of stress on joints, be sure that the muscles around them are strong (and coordinated) enough to support them; otherwise you may do real damage.

Taper off any period slowly. Never flop down from an energetic run, for example, without some transitional activity such as walking. Your body needs time to adjust its heartbeat, breathing and temperature; it needs to keep up good circulation in order to remove the wastes that have accumulated in the muscles during the run and to bring them fresh supplies of oxygen, glucose and protein. Sudden relaxation may cause dizziness and nausea.

Don't race out into the cold after exercising—that will cause undue stiffness. A hot bath or shower is ideal: it will relax your body, keep circulation up, and clean your body after all the sweating. A hot bath before exercising will increase flexibility. If you have access to a sauna or massage, that's a wonderful treat.

Don't eat heavily before or after exercising. The stomach requires a large blood supply to digest food, and exercise diverts blood from the stomach to other muscles. The stomach's attempts to function actively with less blood than it needs may cause pain. Make sure to eat a variety of *healthy* foods (see "Nutrition") to meet the demands of greater physical activity. Except under extreme conditions, you don't need to take salt pills. At the same time try to cut down on junk food, cigarettes, alcohol and harmful drugs.

Wear exercise clothes that allow your body the full range of motion—never anything too tight or binding. In cold weather especially, wear an outfit (such as sweat pants or long underwear) that keeps the heat in to prevent unnecessary stress or injury to joints and muscles.

Get plenty of rest. You'll probably need more once you start working your body harder, and you'll probably sleep better too. See if you can sleep or rest on your back or side on a moderately hard, flat surface, using a pillow when on your side (to keep your spine and head in a straight line).

Expect some stiffness. If you're really pushing your muscles they're bound to hurt the following day. But don't pamper yourself and stop. The best remedy is moderate exercise: this will increase circulation, which will help carry away the accumulated lactic acid causing the stiffness. Moist heat and massage applied to a particular muscle are also helpful. They are relaxants and they also dilate the blood vessels, bringing fresh nutrients and speeding waste removal. As you keep exercising, your body will gradually become accustomed to working harder and the discomfort will disappear. You'll be amazed at how much progress you'll make. Occasionally, though, you will overdo it and stretch the ligaments of a joint too far, maybe even tear them (a *sprain*) or pull a muscle or a tendon in much the same way (a *strain*). Unless the injury is severe, you can treat it yourself. Elevate the injured part and apply cold to it as soon as possible, for 24 to 48 hours. This minimizes pain and swelling. After 24 hours or so, you can switch to moist heat. Rest it until it feels better; then when you are ready to begin exercising again, bind it evenly (not too tight) for support* and take it easy. As you start getting in touch with your body you'll be able to sense what you can cure by yourself and what may need professional help.

Just as you sort out natural soreness from real pain, you need to use judgment about sickness. Never be put off from exercising by psychosomatic symptoms. Many a headache, nervous stomach and fatigue that comes from tension or boredom or unhappiness has been driven off by some exhilarating physical activity. It won't hurt a cold either, but if you're really ill—with fever and other such symptoms—of course you shouldn't push yourself. After a long illness or surgery you need exercise. Plan a reasonable program. In fact, if you have any physical problem it would be wise to check with a knowledgeable doctor, chiropractor or acupuncturist; you might also get useful suggestions from a physical therapist, gym teacher, trainer, etc., or want to experiment carefully on your own.

Unless you have excessive bleeding, nausea, vomiting, bad cramps and so on, you can always exercise during menstruation—as much and as hard as you desire. In fact, the more active we are, the less the premenstrual syndrome and menstruation itself will interfere with our lives. A study of female track and field competitors reported that 63 percent of the women interviewed felt their performance during menstruation was not affected at all; 29 percent claimed they did their best during menstruation; while only 8 percent thought they did below par.† Men as well as women have definite hormonal and mood cycles, so everyone should stop putting negative emphasis on one of ours.

Exercise during a normal pregnancy is excellent. You'll feel better all the way through and the actual labor will be easier. If you haven't exercised much before getting pregnant, build up sensibly, as you would anyway, but don't worry about jiggling the fetus loose. Even a contact sport like basketball is all right until the eighth month.‡ Then swim! (For exercises specifically

for labor, see Chapter 14.) Exercise is very important afterward too.

Women with special physical problems are often left out of sports or are made to feel so awkward they don't even want to try. We hope this will change. All of us are responsible for helping these women to develop the potential they do have. We know one woman with cerebral palsy who does a lot of swimming and has worked up a really strong punch with her good arm in a self-defense class. Wilma Rudolph had several debilitating diseases and could hardly walk until she was eight years old! The November, 1974, issue of *WomenSports* (pp. 19-22) has an exciting report on members of the National Wheelchair Athletic Association. Our handicapped sisters compete in all kinds of sports, from basketball and track events to swimming and Ping-Pong.

A word about age. In our youth-oriented sexist society the line "Life begins at forty" appears to be a cruel joke to many women. We may feel more that life ends at forty. In terms of physical activity, it is never too late. If you are over thirty and haven't exercised for a long time, begin gradually. At any age you can build up strength, endurance, flexibility and coordination—it just will take a little longer, but it will come, provided the determination is there. Remember that marathon champions have their best years between thirty-five and forty-five (as opposed to sprinters, who peak at a much younger age). A fifty-year-old woman we know jogs five miles a day. A sixty-two-year-old woman we met recently began doing yoga and loves it: "I haven't felt so young and energetic in years!" she told us. "My over-all health is much better, and it's such a welcome relief from housework."

Be patient! It will be hard work and perhaps discouraging at first. You may come home exhausted and dripping wet from jogging one block. You may be frustrated by not being able to make your muscles work the way you want them to at the beginning.

But exercise can help change our lives. It has already given many of us new energy, new confidence and greater independence. "I have more respect for my body. It belongs to me now." "Dance has developed my muscles and stretch. It's beautiful to become aware of my capabilities, to grow." "Karate has made me feel stronger, more alive, more independent. I can run and dance and even climb a tree. Some days I feel like I could fly."

We have in the past accepted limitations on what our bodies can do. But we women are beginning to take our lives into our own hands in countless other ways—for example, demanding job equality, free child care and abortion, nonsexist advertising and education, and for some of us, coming out as lesbians—and that means also demanding better neighborhood athletic facilities free to all and well-rounded programs for girls in our schools.

We need to love our bodies and treat them well. Where would we be without them?

---

*A first-aid manual such as the *Emergency Medical Guide* (see bibliography) has pictures showing how to do this and gives useful information about other kinds of injuries.

†From a report by J. Kral and E. Markalous, cited in *Injury in Sport*, by J. R. Armstrong and W. E. Tucker (London: Staples Press, 1964), p. 118.

‡Ellen Weber, "The Three Great Myths of Sex and Sport," *WomenSports* (January, 1975), pp. 33, 59-60. The second part of the article, on menstruation, is interesting, too.

II. Glossary/Examinations and Tests

GLOSSARY OF SELECTED COMMON MEDICAL TERMS

acute   Sudden and short-lived.

adenoma   A tumor, usually benign, which develops beneath the skin.

aspirate   To treat by aspiration, the removal of fluids or gases by suction; also, to draw in, as in drawing fluid or solid matter into a syringe, or into the lungs (a complication of anesthesia).

benign   Noncancerous.

biopsy   The removal of tissue for laboratory analysis. To diagnose the presence of cancer cells by: removing fluid with a needle; cutting out a whole tumor; or cutting into the tumor and removing part of it. The fluid may be analyzed; the tissue may be frozen and examined under a microscope immediately (frozen section) or prepared for later examination. Results of biopsies are expressed as either benign or malignant.

carcinoma   A malignant new growth made up of cancerous cells which infiltrate the surrounding tissues and are capable of *metastasis* (spreading to other parts of the body).

cauterize   To burn, either with chemicals or with an electrically heated instrument, an area which is inflamed (often discharging) and does not heal.

CBC   Complete blood count, a method of counting the proportion of red blood cells to white to detect a possible illness with which the system may be coping. (Abnormal cells can also be located this way.) Usually done as part of a complete physical exam. The blood samples are drawn from a vein (most often in the arm) and usually sent to a lab.

cervical intraepithelial neoplasia (CIN)   Abnormal development of cells on and slightly below tissue surface (not necessarily pathological or cancerous).

chronic   Long-term, frequently recurrent.

clean voided specimen   A urine sample collected in a sterile jar immediately on arising in the morning. It is laboratory-tested for a variety of conditions.

colposcopy   A special procedure for visually examining the vaginal walls and/or cervix to detect the presence of cancerous cells.

cryosurgery   The destruction of tissue by the application of extreme cold.

culdoscopy   Visual examination of the pelvic organs by placing an endoscope into the upper end of the vagina.

culture   A sample of a discharge or other body fluid, such as urine, that is incubated in a laboratory to allow organisms in it to multiply and be identified.

cyst   A sac in any part of the body, usually filled with fluid or semisolid material (most often benign).

D & C   Dilation and curettage, a procedure to open the cervix (dilation or dilatation) and scrape off the lining of the uterus with a sharp instrument called a curette (curettage). See p. 147 for illustration.

dysplasia   Abnormality of development (not necessarily pathological or cancerous).

endoscope   An instrument for the examination of the interior of a hollow organ, such as the bladder.

fibroadenoma   A tumor containing fibrous tissue.

fibroid   A myoma of the uterus.

generic   A term applied to the original substance from which a drug is derived (genus). Prescriptions of generic drugs are usually much cheaper than trade names; only in very rare instances are there any special properties to name brands (e.g., aspirin bought generically is usually much cheaper than any brand name and *just* as effective; look for USP, for U.S. Pharmacopoeia, on the label).

hematocrit   A measure of blood quality based on volume percentage of red cells in the blood.

hemoglobin   The oxygen-carrying compound in red blood cells. (See p. 123 for hemoglobin test.)

hysterectomy   Removal of the uterus by surgery. Complete hysterectomy involves removal of the cervix but not tubes or ovaries (see salpingectomy and oophorectomy).

iatrogenic   Disease(s) caused by medical treatment itself.

infection   An invasion by bacteria or other organisms.

laparoscopy   A special procedure for examining the inside of the abdomen by inserting a long, narrow tube through a tiny incision. The term is sometimes also used for a method of sterilization involving the laparoscope. (See "Sterilization" in Chapter 10.)

malignant   Cancerous.

mastectomy   Removal of the breast by surgery (see "Breast Problems" for its variations).

metastasis   The transfer of disease from one part of the body to another part not connected to it; the growth which results from this transfer. Plural, *metastases*. These terms usually refer to the spread of cancer.

morbidity   The state of being diseased; also the rate of occurrence of an illness.

myoma   A tumor made up of muscular elements.

neoplasm   Any new and abnormal growth, usually a tumor.

oncology   The sum of knowledge concerning tumors; the study of tumors. (Oncology is a cancer specialty.)

oophorectomy   Removal of one or both ovaries by surgery.

palpation   Examination by touch.

Pap smear   Short for Papanicolaou (after the doctor who developed it) smear. Tissue is gently scraped from the cervix and tested in a laboratory for cancer and other abnormal conditions. Do not douche on the day a Pap smear is taken or the day before. If you have a vaginal infection, treat it first. Since menstrual blood makes cervical cells impossible to analyze, don't schedule an exam then. (See p. 143.)

pH   A measure of acidity and alkalinity. A pH of 7.0 is neutral; the stronger the base (alkaline), the higher the pH. Most tap water is very slightly acid.

polyp   A growth protruding from any mucous membrane, notably the inner lining of the uterus near the cervix.

pus   An accumulation of white blood cells (one of the body's weapons in fighting infections), bacteria and dead cells.

radiation   Rays given off from special sources (X ray, cobalt), which may be used to detect conditions on short exposure or to treat them on long exposure. Capable of causing as well as stopping malignancy.

radical   Directed to the cause; going to the root or source of a morbid condition, as in radical surgery. Now often used to refer to the radical mastectomy (e.g., "She had a radical"). Sometimes applied to a woman who wants to change the health-care system.

salpingectomy   Removal of one or both fallopian tubes.

smear   Any test in which cells or discharges are "smeared" on a slide for microscopic examination.

systemic   Affecting the body (system) as a whole.

tumor   Any abnormal growth, not usually cancer, which is new tissue persisting and growing independent of its surrounding tissue, and which has no function. *Most* tumors are benign (not cancerous).

urinalysis   A test done on a few drops of urine to detect any major changes in the body's handling of sugar or protein.

THE PHYSICAL EXAM AND BASIC TESTS*

We should expect the following as part of any physical exam:

- Thyroid palpation
- Breast exam, including, if necessary, directions for doing a breast self-exam
- Careful listening to the heart and lungs with stethoscope in several positions
- Blood-pressure, weight and height measurements
- Abdominal and pelvic exams (including speculum, bimanual and recto-vaginal exams)
- Complete blood count (CBC), including blood test

*Ask to have a written copy or record of all test results.

for cholesterol and triglyceride levels *or* hemoglobin test at a bare minimum

- Urinalysis, and clean voided specimen if there are cystitis symptoms
- VD tests
- Pap test
- Other tests as may be necessary for our individual health needs.

The Internal (Pelvic) Exam

When we go for our annual checkup (biannual, if we take birth control pills or are over thirty-five) we should expect the following as part of the internal (pelvic) exam:

INSPECTION OF THE EXTERNAL GENITALS (THE VULVA). The physician or nurse practitioner will check for irritations, discoloration, bumps and swellings, lice, irregular hair distribution, size and/or adhesions of the clitoris, skin lesions and unusual vaginal discharge. You will be checked internally (usually with a finger) and asked about cystoceles and rectoceles (see p. 101), stress incontinence (you will be asked to cough to see if urine will involuntarily flow), presence of pus in Skene's glands, presence of Bartholin's cysts, and strength of pelvic-floor and abdominal muscles.

SPECULUM EXAM. With the speculum inserted in place (if metal, it should be pre-warmed), holding open the walls of the vagina, the examiner will look for lesions, unusual discharge and inflammation of the vaginal walls, unusual discharge from the cervix, signs of infection, damage or growths and abnormal mucous membrane color.

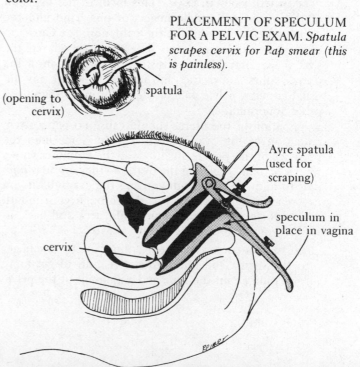

PLACEMENT OF SPECULUM FOR A PELVIC EXAM. *Spatula scrapes cervix for Pap smear (this is painless).*

(opening to cervix)

spatula

Ayre spatula (used for scraping)

speculum in place in vagina

cervix

S/he will then obtain a scraping of tissue from around the cervix for a Pap test (for cervical cancer). This does not hurt, though too much pressure applied against the cervix during the scraping (only a couple of seconds) may be uncomfortable. In addition, a smear of discharge for microscopic examination and for a culture to test for gonorrhea should be taken at this time. (Speculum should have only water lubrication for this test.)

Many examiners keep a hand mirror around for women who would like to see their own cervices. If you are curious and have not yet tried a self-exam, ask for help to position a light and mirror so that you can see yourself. Also ask for a demonstration of how to use the plastic speculum (a few doctors will do this) if you are interested. (Also see "Self-examination Techniques.")

BIMANUAL PELVIC EXAM

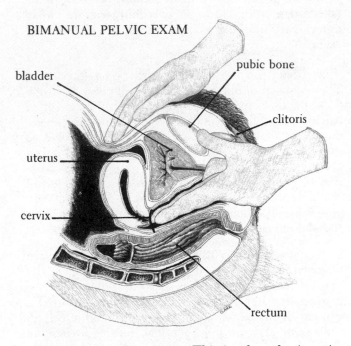

bladder

pubic bone

clitoris

uterus

cervix

rectum

BIMANUAL VAGINAL EXAM. This involves the insertion of the index and middle fingers of one hand into the vagina and, on the outside, the palpation (see Glossary) of the lower abdominal wall. The examiner will feel the size, shape, movability, consistency and position of the uterus, tubes and ovaries and will try to locate any unusual growths, pelvic pain, evidence of inflammation or other abnormalities.

Palpation of the uterus should cause no pain; often, palpation of the ovaries hurts a little (sometimes the presence of this pain is the only way the examiner knows s/he is actually touching the ovaries—they are *very difficult* to find). It helps both you and the examiner if you can relax; it may help to breathe through your mouth and to focus on relaxing your hands, neck and back, as well as your abdomen. See figure above.

RECTO-VAGINAL EXAM. The examiner inserts one finger into the vagina and one into the rectum to get more information about the tone and alignment of the pelvic organs and adnexal region (includes ovaries, tubes, and ligaments of the uterus); about rectal lesions; and about the tone of the rectal sphincter muscle. This can be an unpleasant procedure for some women—talking about any discomfort you may have usually helps. Also, you may feel as though you are having a bowel movement as the examiner's finger withdraws from the rectum, but this will not happen.

There are wide variations in the skill and sensitivity of those who give internal exams; there are also differences in the ability of individual women to relax, which can make the same technique feel very different. You can do Kegel exercises (p. 101) and practice inserting a tampon or a speculum in advance of an internal, to help you learn relaxation.

Self-examination Techniques*

You need for self-examination:
Directional light (a strong flashlight)
Speculum (plastic ones are inexpensive and easier to
   obtain)
K-Y Jelly (or similar lubricant)
Long-handled mirror
Firm bed or table, or floor

It's a good idea to have your own plastic speculum to prevent the transfer of infection. Be sure to wash it in warm water and an antibiotic soap after each use. You should go through the motions of opening and locking the speculum before you actually examine yourself.

1. When you are familiar with manipulation of the speculum, position yourself comfortably on the bed or table, sitting or lying down with knees bent and feet placed far apart. You may want to prop yourself up on a pillow.
2. Lubricate the speculum with a small amount of K-Y Jelly. Holding the speculum closed, gently insert it sideways into your vagina, at the same angle you would hold a tampon.
3. When it is in all the way, slowly turn it so that the handle points up.
4. Then grasp the handle and firmly push the shorter, outside section of the handle toward you. This will open the blades of the speculum inside you.
5. Now, steadily holding the part of the handle next to your pubic hair, push down the outside section until you can hear a click. The speculum is then locked open.
6. If you have never done this before, or are in an awkward position, your vagina may tend to reject the speculum. Also, you may have to move the speculum around or reinsert it before the cervix pops into view. Sometimes a friend can be very

*Adapted from *Second Wave*, Vol. 2, No. 3 (Summer, 1973).

helpful here, particularly if your cervix is off to one side (a common occurrence).

7. It is often easier to have the light pointed at the mirror and the mirror held so that you can see into the tunnel that your speculum has opened up. This pink area, which looks much like the walls of your throat, is your vagina. At the end of the tunnel is a pinkish, bulbous area that you'd think was surely the head of a wet penis. That is your cervix. If you don't see it, then gently draw out the speculum and push down with your stomach muscles. This usually causes the cervix to pop into view.

8. To remove the speculum, keep it open and slowly pull it straight out.

When I first saw another woman's cervix, I thought that it was pretty gruesome, and why were all these women in the clinic getting so excited about it? Then, when I saw my own, I couldn't believe that now I actually had access to it. I could even see the string of my IUD! It was coming out of the very opening that my child would come from. It was, indeed, a passageway to life!

I became overwhelmingly awed, and even spiritual! Recovering from the spiritual part of this pretty quickly, I realized that by regular examination I too could have some part in keeping myself healthy.

By examining ourselves regularly we can learn more about our normal discharges, about the amount and type of mucus our bodies secrete at different stages in the menstrual cycle. If something goes wrong, we are more likely to find out about it early and to get medical attention sooner rather than later. Depending on an annual visit to a physician, who only sees our cervices at this time, cannot compare in protection. We need both. (See also "Breast Self-examination," p. 126.)

III. Common Medical and Health Problems, Traditional and Alternative Treatments

ANEMIA AND HYPERTENSION

As women, we often find ourselves affected by anemia and hypertension, two conditions which are systemic (affecting all parts of the body) and which may cause serious health problems if not cared for soon enough. Frequently we don't recognize the symptoms of these conditions and, as a result, don't do anything about them until we're very obviously sick. Sometimes we think that only medical treatments of some kind can help, when in fact there are many useful health habits we can practice on our own.

Many male doctors who are bored by the frequency and sameness of symptoms women commonly experience often attribute these symptoms to some psychological disorder. Consequently they give superficial exams and may tell a woman that there is no physical problem when in fact anemia or hypertension may be present. Always remember to ask for blood-pressure and iron-deficiency test results (in writing preferably). It also helps to know and to develop some of the preventive health habits described below.

Anemia

One common condition women, particularly menstruating women, need to anticipate is iron-deficiency anemia, which results from a shortage of red blood cells. The symptoms may include extreme fatigue, dizziness, short-

ness of breath and occasionally bone pain. The best preventive is an iron-rich diet—foods that contain iron (liver, eggs, dried fruits, brewer's yeast, some shellfish)—and getting enough folic acid (primarily from leafy green vegetables). If you can't eat enough iron-rich food, you may want to consider supplements. There are many expensive iron products for sale, so ask for the generic name—*ferrous sulfate*, or *ferrous gluconate* or *fumarate*—to get the most for your money.

A CBC (complete blood count, a lab test done on blood removed from a vein in your arm) is the only accurate way to detect anemia and to determine its cause. But there is one crude, simple test, called a hemoglobin test, which can be done in two minutes in an office without going to an expensive lab. It won't help much if you're borderline, but it will quickly pick up more serious anemic conditions. A drop of blood from a prick on the finger or ear is absorbed on special paper and then compared with a chart showing a range of samples. This is a good way to decide whether a further, more expensive test is really needed.

Hypertension

Hypertension is the medical term for high blood pressure. In a recent *Time* article it was called "The Quiet Killer" because even though just having high blood pressure doesn't kill you immediately, it can, if untreated, lead to heart disease and strokes, which *are* the leading killers of both men and women in the United States. For example, if you have untreated high blood pressure you are four times as likely to have a heart attack or stroke and twice as likely to develop kidney disease. (However, some theorize that kidney disease is the cause of high blood pressure rather than the other way around.)

Even younger women and babies are showing signs of hypertension. We do not yet know how early hypertension in women thirty-five and under affects life expectancy. This unknown factor is becoming more important as larger numbers of women who are, or have been, on the pill move into this age range, since about 25 percent of women who use the pill develop hypertension. We know of many, many women who were examined prior to having the pill prescribed but never examined again afterward to check for any side effects. Their prescriptions were simply refilled. Still others have been given the pill with no examination at all. Insist on finding out your blood pressure both before and after a few months on the pill. If it is initially high or rises over a few months, it's wise to choose another contraceptive.

Hypertension may be accompanied by warning symptoms such as headache, dizziness, fainting spells, ringing in the ears, etc. However, the only way to get a sure diagnosis is to take periodic blood-pressure readings. (Sometimes specialized blood tests may be necessary.) Taking blood pressure is a simple procedure that can be learned by almost anyone. In fact, many doctors now believe that this basic skill should be taught to everyone, particularly those of us who have hypertension or have it in our families.

"Essential" hypertension is the name given to 95 percent of all cases of high blood pressure (those not caused by specific glandular or hormonal abnormalities). Causes other than the pill are still being investigated; they fall under several broad categories:

1. Diet
2. Obesity (excess weight)
3. Stress (from both emotional and life-style factors)
4. Hereditary links
5. Water supply

In this list heredity and life-style are perhaps the hardest to change. Diet, which is often linked to life-style, can play a key role in reducing and controlling hypertension. Excess salt, in particular, can contribute to high blood pressure. The balance of protein and carbohydrates in our diets is another important factor. Finally, the role of trace elements in the American diet is only now being seriously investigated. Cadmium, which is strongly linked to hypertension, is of specific interest.

Recent studies have demonstrated a remarkable correlation between high rates of hypertension and geographic areas where the water is soft. Hard-water areas seem to show significantly fewer cases of hypertension. It is not yet fully understood whether this is because of something beneficial in the hard water or something harmful in the soft water. Present evidence suggests that the acidity of soft water is the problem—that acid water attacks surrounding earth and rocks to extract trace elements, such as cadmium, which is linked to hypertension. Although more research is needed, soft water is clearly much more significantly related to hypertension than are such factors as socioeconomic background, education, stress, or smoking (all repeatedly investigated in the past, though with less significant results). Also, cadmium is one of the prominent trace minerals in refined white flour products. It may be that the combined amounts of cadmium in soft water and in white flour products have become harmful for many of us.

As we suggested earlier, eating carefully *before* we become hypertensive is good prevention. So is getting together with other people in our community to investigate the water.*

Such preventive efforts have taken on new importance in recent months as more and more commonly prescribed drugs are being found to have serious side effects. Reserpine, a well-known drug used to treat hypertension, has now been shown to increase the risk of breast cancer two to three times. This does not mean, however, that women must risk getting either hypertension or breast cancer. Hypertension that can be controlled by drugs may also be controlled by diet.

Other kinds of self-help for hypertension have also shown some success—specifically, "biofeedback" (which involves a special machine that illustrates bodily responses and can be used to teach control over them) and meditation (which has been shown to benefit many bodily functions).

The greatest tragedy about hypertension is the possibility that it is truly a disease of malnutrition and poverty. The fact that blacks, especially women, appear to be more susceptible than whites may simply mean that too many black people have tried to live too long on inadequate protein and protein substitutes. Foods that are high in fats and carbohydrates are often cheapest, so poorer people, of all races, have learned to survive on them; women usually feed themselves last. Often malnutrition results because so much pleasure is associated with eating many non-nutritious foods. It can be difficult to give up high-salt and high-sugar foods that are giving so much (sometimes the only) pleasure in life to isolated and restricted people like the poor and the elderly.

Unfortunately, most hypertension programs do not deal with these cultural and economic realities.

BREAST PROBLEMS

When we first begin to develop breasts most of us are

---

*See *Consumer Report's* continuing series on drinking-water safety—June, July, August and October, 1974; January, March, etc., 1975.

preoccupied with how they look, because they not only change how we feel about ourselves and our body image but they become a message to the rest of the world that we are becoming women, whether we want to be treated that way or not. In this country breasts seem to have an exaggerated sexual significance to both men and women, so it's hard to outgrow the early self-consciousness we feel about them, even after we are older. Breasts are displayed provocatively (but never fully exposed) in ads as a way of titillating male consumers into buying everything from cars to whisky. Topless waitresses and dancers are the final step in this process. Hundreds of women have breast-enlarging operations each year, hoping to appear more desirable to men or more like the stereotyped images of women society as a whole approves.

Going braless is for some of us an attempt to deal with this kind of sexist exaggeration and objectification—to say to the world, "This is my natural woman shape and I like it and I'm not going to push it into some distorted line or hide it just because it's 'unfashionable.'" But the braless look now has its own place in fashion, and for some men it has made breasts more titillating than ever. Meanwhile we as a country can still be weirdly puritanical about breast-feeding in public.

As we live with our developing sexuality we often discover that our breasts can be intensely pleasurable to us as well as to those who look at us or with whom we make love, although this response varies tremendously from woman to woman. Some women can even experience orgasm from breast stimulation alone, and mothers sometimes report orgasm while nursing their infants. This sexual context makes it hard for us to think about breasts as functional parts of our bodies that need health care and attention from us. It also makes breast problems particularly disturbing.

Beginning with going braless, there are short-term and long-run problems that are unique to us as women because we have breasts. Young breasts can probably go unsupported for a year or so without any long-range ill effects, but the sheer laws of physics will eventually cause a breast of any size to begin to sag. This may not matter to you now or ever, but it's hard to be sure of that in advance. If your breasts are large or clearly stand away from your body, you may also find it uncomfortable to dance or be active in sports without a bra. For women with small breasts this is less of a problem. There is also a myth that breast-feeding causes breasts to sag, while it is just the failure to support the extra weight with a good bra.

Premenstrual Tenderness and Swelling

The most common problem some of us have to deal with once our menstrual cycles are fully established is the monthly swelling and painful tenderness (*mastody-*

nia) that often precede a period. Wearing a bra can be helpful, especially one of the stretchy types. Avoiding excess salt, sugar, coffee, tea, alcohol and refined carbohydrates seems to help some women to reduce the overall feeling of premenstrual tightness and puffiness, of which breast tenderness is just a part. Once the period is over, however, we usually don't think about it again until the next period is near; then it may not happen again for a while.

As we get older, however, many of us find that this kind of swelling can become chronic and often includes a kind of lumpy texture. Sometimes after our period is over, some of the lumpiness remains. In fact, a certain amount of lumpiness is normal in breasts. If we have not been in the habit of examining our breasts each month after our period—and even if we have—we may suddenly discover what feels like a distinct lump that wasn't there before. There are no adequate words to describe the feeling of panicky anxiety that follows. Cancer is the first thought that flashes into our minds, along with a lot of wild, confused thoughts about why this should be "happening to me." Hundreds of women rush immediately to the nearest doctor, particularly since Betty Ford and Happy Rockefeller have had their breasts removed because of cancer. Hundreds of other women may live silently with their lumps, afraid to go to a doctor because they are sure it *is* cancer and they can't face the thought either of having the disease or of having to undergo the treatment of mastectomy, which is so often involved.

We will talk more about cancer in the next section, but first it is important to look more carefully at the

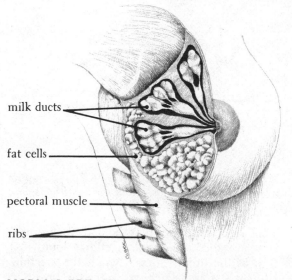

milk ducts

fat cells

pectoral muscle

ribs

NORMAL BREAST, *showing structure of fat and milk ducts*

problem of swelling and lumpiness which affects so many of us, particularly in our childbearing years, when cancer is much less likely to be the cause.

In its chronic, recurring state, this lumpy condition may be either *fibroadenosis* (multiple tiny nodules) or (chronic) *cystic mastitis,** sometimes called "fibrocystic disease." A lump may be a *fibroadenoma* (a solid benign tumor). The label "chronic disease" has a scary sound, which may make it hard for us to cope with it or live with it comfortably. One reason it is called a disease is that not all women have it, and also because it represents a failure or an inability of our systems to deal with the buildup of fluid and congestion each month.

One way to think about the problem is to compare the breast with the uterus. As we explained in Chapter 2, the monthly buildup of the lining of the uterus in response to hormones, particularly estrogen, is a preparation for pregnancy. When that doesn't happen, the lining is sloughed off and the cycle starts over again. However, after a great many cycles the uterine lining may begin to thicken and may build up fibroid tumors (see p. 142).

In a way, the same thing happens to the breast. It builds up fluid and fibrous tissue in preparation for pregnancy. However, when there is no conception, there is no convenient way for the breasts to get rid of these extra substances. While there is a lymph system into which the breasts drain (see figures below and pp.

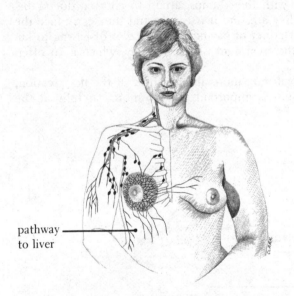

pathway
to liver

THE LYMPHATIC SYSTEM OF THE BREAST, *showing drainage to nodes under the arms, under the breastbone, and pathways to the liver and neck*

130-131), the process requires that the body reabsorb all of this extra substance rather than shedding some of it immediately, as the uterus does. (Lymphatics are thin-walled vessels that form a network from the breast to certain glands called *lymph nodes.* These vessels drain tissue fluids from the breast.)

*Mastitis is an infection which results from a plugged milk duct in a breast-feeding mother, and is not to be confused with cystic mastitis.

As months and months go by without conception, it is harder and harder for the system to do this.

Without pregnancy, some congestion may become more or less permanent (pregnancy usually clears this up). Fluids get trapped in the ducts to form sacs called cysts, which are rarely harmful, or lumps called fibroadenomas, which virtually never become cancers. Most of these benign lumps are approximately round, move around freely under the skin, and don't seem to be attached to the chest beneath. There is often an accompanying tenderness to the touch, though not always.

In over 80 percent of all cases one of these two benign conditions causes the "lumps" which prompt women to rush off to their doctors and onto the operating table in fear of cancer, only to find out that they really are benign after the anguish, cost and risk of hospitalization, anesthesia, biopsy and recovery. Fibroadenomas are more common than cysts but don't usually disappear with pregnancy. Like cysts, they are less frequent with advancing age, becoming rare in our forties. However, both are tricky in that if they don't disappear they must be distinguished from cancer by some type of biopsy. Fibroadenosis is also not serious and tends to disappear with pregnancy.

In other words, these common conditions are usually not cancer, and are really a sort of side effect or by-product of our controlling our reproduction during the years when our systems are most ready for us to conceive, give birth and lactate.

Breast Self-examination

Once we understand this, it can become easier for us to look for *lumps* without the fear of thinking we are necessarily looking for *cancer*. Breast self-examination (BSE) should be done very frequently (possibly every few days) when you first begin to do it so that you can learn the characteristics of your breasts over the course of a month or two, in all phases of your cycle (see p. 127 for BSE and how-to). Later you can do it once a month, about a week after your period ends, when your breasts are at their quietest stage. As one cancer specialist said, "The patient is the best monitor of her own lumps."* In this way you can begin to realize that most lumps you find will probably tend to get suddenly larger before your period and then go down or even disappear altogether a week afterward. These are almost certainly cysts, because only fluid could disappear so rapidly. If you find a small discrete (separate) lump for the first time, you can probably wait one more cycle, and then if it hasn't disappeared, go to a doctor.

Since your breasts will be different at different times

*Dr. Val Donahue on Channel 4, WBZ-TV, Boston, January 28, 1975.

in your menstrual cycle, examine them at the same time each month. A few days after menstruation is good— they will then be at minimum fullness, and it will be easier to detect any unusual lumps. After a few examinations you will become quite familiar with the shape and texture of your own breasts and will probably be able to detect an abnormality better than many doctors, who have to take into account the wide variation in the breasts of different women, which they examine only once or twice a year at most.

First stand in front of a mirror and view your breasts with your hands at your sides; then with hands raised above your head; with hands pushing firmly on your hips, or with your palms pressed together. Good lighting will make the examination easier. You should look for differences in shape (not size) of the breasts: for a flattening or bulging in one but not the other; for puckering of the skin; for a discharge from a nipple when it is gently squeezed; and for a reddening or scaly crust on a nipple. You should also be suspicious when one nipple is particularly hard or inelastic, or when the two nipples point in asymmetric directions. Many nipple asymmetries are not due to cancer, but it is better to check. Make sure a sore on a nipple is investigated for cancer before assuming it is merely a skin disorder.

Next, lie down on a bed or couch. (Or you may want to perform this part of the exam in a bathtub, with soapy fingers.) As you examine each breast, have the arm on that side raised above your head or the hand under your head and the elbow lying flat. A small pillow or large folded towel placed under your shoulder will distribute the breast tissue more evenly. Also examine each breast with the arm lying along your side or hanging over the edge of the bed.

Feel your breast gently and systematically with the flat of the fingers of the opposite hand. Move your fingers in small circles or with a slight back-and-forth motion, covering the entire breast with a broader motion. The most common location of tumors is between the nipple and armpit, so give special attention to that area.

General thickening, pain, or tenderness are likely to occur normally just before or during your periods. A discrete, round, hard lump is probably a noncancerous cyst or fibroadenoma but should still be checked by a doctor if it doesn't go down. Cancer often causes a thickening in a specific area. This irregular, spreading thickening is what gives cancer its name (the crab).

For films and literature on breast self-examination, write the American Cancer Society. (National office: 219 E. 42nd St., New York, N.Y. 10017; telephone: 212-867-3700.) Also, the National Cancer Institute in D.C.*

Whenever you do go to a doctor be sure to demand both a breast exam *and* instruction in BSE, since the vast majority of physicians do not even do breast examinations or discuss self-examination with their patients on checkup visits.† Also, once a physician has examined your breasts, DO NOT ASSUME THAT THIS IS ADEQUATE PROTECTION UNTIL YOUR NEXT SIX-MONTH OR ANNUAL VISIT TO A PHYSICIAN. Your health is not in your doctor's hands, it is in your hands. BSE must be practiced by you, and it must be practiced monthly to be truly useful. Studies show that women are much more likely to practice BSE faithfully if their doctors show them how and explain what to look for, rather than just examining them.

Remember, women usually discover their own lumps. We believe that women who learn BSE in groups with other women will be more likely to continue the practice than women who only read about it or see it in a film and then try to do it by themselves. Ideally, a group of women who know one another well, who are in a consciousness-raising group or a self-help group, might meet with a physician and learn together, and then later help other women to learn.

When to Begin BSE

BSE should begin whenever you have a breast to exam-

*See bibliography for details.
†Gallup Survey, "Women's Attitudes Toward Breast Cancer," 1973.

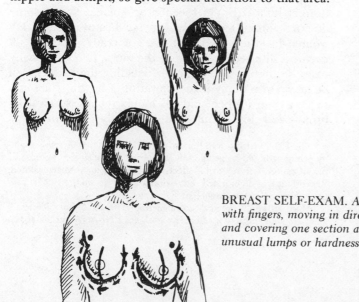

BREAST SELF-EXAM. *Applying pressure with fingers, moving in direction of arrows, and covering one section at a time, feel for unusual lumps or hardness.*

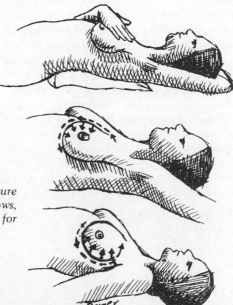

ine, in your teens, or as soon as your menstrual cycle is at all regular. While cystic mastitis is rare and cancer even rarer in these early years, they do sometimes occur. The important thing, however, is not so much looking for cancer as getting into the habit and knowing your own breasts as well as you can by examining them regularly, much the same way as you keep up your dental health by brushing your teeth regularly. Then if anything unusual does occur, you will know it right away and will be in the best position to take action without panicking. Those of us who learn BSE later in life may have to try to overcome lifelong attitudes about touching ourselves at a time when we are at increasing risk of more serious diseases. Whatever your age, start now.

If You Find a Lump

Now that we've said what most lumps turn out to be, the big question is, "What if I do find a lump that doesn't disappear in one more cycle?" Remember, most such lumps are *not* cancerous, but it is important to be sure. Neither you nor your doctor will be able to tell for certain simply by feeling (although your description should help in distinguishing what it's likely to be). Only a pathologist's microscopic examination of cells from the lump (a *biopsy*) is certain. However—and this is crucial—you do *not* necessarily have to undergo hospitalization, anesthesia and surgical biopsy right away in order to find out. Let's go back a step.

Screening Tests

First

Assuming you have found a lump that doesn't go away and you go to the doctor, what can you expect? A doctor's response will depend on many factors. First, it will depend on his or her training and experience. If the training has been primarily surgical in orientation, and surgical biopsies are a routine operation for him or her, you can expect a certain amount of impatience with any other approach. In most cases a doctor will order one or another type of screening examination such as: *mammography*, similar to the type of X ray used by dentists but developed especially for breasts; *xerography*, or xeroradiography, a newer type of test done with smaller doses of radiation and producing a picture of the underlying breast tissue which is easier to "read"; *thermography*, in which a heat-sensing device produces a "picture" of any area where a high level of cellular activity is going on (this method is more likely to produce a positive test when there is nothing wrong, though it eliminates the radiation and picks up problems which can be missed by the other methods).

If you have never had one of these tests and are in the latter half of your childbearing years you might want to have it done, whatever you decide to do next. You will be the one paying for the test and can request it from your physician's files later if you move away or decide to go to another doctor. Meanwhile it will provide some baseline information against which to compare any future developments. On the other hand, you may feel strongly about wanting to avoid all radiation unless there is clear justification for it, particularly if you know or suspect you have been exposed to too much radiation in the past. (Federal standards and enforcement for X-ray equipment have been very uneven in the last ten years.)*

Second

Another factor in what happens next will be how well your doctor knows you and what his or her attitude is toward patients in general. Most doctors are trained to discredit what patients, particularly women, report about themselves.† You may be disappointed when your careful records of self-examinations and changes throughout your menstrual cycle are ignored. You may be reprimanded for not coming in sooner and then be put under a lot of pressure to rush immediately to a cancer specialist if your doctor does not have specialized training in cancer. Be sure to ask about his or her training (see also "Choosing and Using Health and Medical Care," in Chapter 18). Though this is rare, some cancer specialists will offer reassurance and send you home without doing any tests at all.

Needle Biopsy

It's important for you to realize that some pressure may arise from the physician's own anxiety and his or her very strong need to be absolutely positive. Nevertheless, DO NOT ALLOW YOURSELF TO BE STAMPEDED INTO SURGERY. Unless you have nipple discharge, gross underarm swelling, or other unusual symptoms which require emergency care, it is possible to have a "needle biopsy" on a distinct lump right in the doctor's office. While some doctors administer a shot of Novocaine first, many women have reported that it's not really necessary. A needle is inserted directly into the lump. In a great many cases the lump then collapses, yielding fluid which can be drawn into the syringe (aspiration), showing the lump to be a cyst. (Other kinds of lumps require surgical biopsy—see below.) This fluid, which also contains some

*The FDA issued a warning on April 24, 1975, that X rays—mammography—should be avoided by women under thirty-five because of risk of cancer, and relative ineffectiveness of test on younger women. Recently it was determined that women under 50 should not be routinely X-rayed in the absence of symptoms.

†Mary Howell, "What Medical Schools Teach About Women," *New England Journal of Medicine*, Vol. 291, No. 6 (August 8, 1974).

cells from the wall of the cyst at the point of entry, can be analyzed in a laboratory for the presence of any abnormal cells (though these are rarely found). While it is of course possible for some cancerous cells to be present in another part of the cell wall, this is extremely unlikely, particularly if there are no other signs or symptoms, or any history of pathology.* There is also a technique of shining light through the breast, which can also be done in the office, to help somewhat in indicating what the lumps are likely to be.

Every woman should at least ask her physician why a needle biopsy is *not* being performed first as a very simple means of identifying a cyst, should that be what it is, and of avoiding the cost and trauma of surgical biopsy as a first step. Needle biopsy may also help in the decision to avoid X-ray examination. Again, these are joint decisions between a woman and her doctor. A physician cannot proceed in treating you without your informed consent; you have every right to know *why* each decision is made and what the risks, benefits and cost will be—both of taking a particular step and also of *not* taking it (see "Our Rights as Patients," in Chapter 18).

Third

Another factor in what happens next is the hospital with which your doctor is affiliated. In some states regulations are being proposed which would require any hospital treating cancer patients to meet a whole series of standards for good care, including the ability to offer all three standard forms of cancer therapy: surgery, radiation and chemotherapy (drug treatment), either on the premises or at an affiliated hospital. Obviously if your doctor is affiliated with a specialized hospital (unless it is a cancer hospital) it is less likely that a choice of treatments will be available, and this in turn will probably affect the screening techniques he or she chooses to identify lumps. Do not agree to a surgical biopsy if your doctor is not a cancer specialist capable of treating the disease. Again, ask about the hospital as well as the doctor. (See "The Hospital," in Chapter 18.)

Surgical Biopsy

If the needle biopsy does not collapse the lump and reveal it as a cyst, it is probably a benign tumor, or fibroadenoma. In order to be positive it is not cancerous, a section of it must be carefully examined under a microscope by a pathologist. The pathologist's examination should not be done too quickly if it is to be accurate. The whole lump and a bit of surrounding tissue must be removed. This type of open, surgical, excisional biopsy is now one of the commonest operations performed on women, over 500,000 every year. As we said earlier, 80 to 90 percent of the lumps are benign.

*When in doubt, you can have a physician re-examine a drained cyst via air injection followed by a new mammogram.

Unfortunately most biopsies are performed under full anesthesia, with all of its attendant risks,* and in addition, the laboratory examination is done as quickly as possible (by frozen section) so that if cancer cells are found the breast can be surgically removed while the woman is still anesthetized. Apart from the dangers of anesthesia and diagnostic error, the psychological risks of this procedure are only now, after fifty years of use, being questioned. Two separate stages are increasingly being recommended, particularly since cancer treatment may not necessarily involve surgery.

If after a thorough explanation and discussion you agree with your doctor that a surgical biopsy must be performed, you will probably want to ask that:

1. The biopsy be done as an end procedure—that is, that no plans be made for further treatment until the results are known (be very careful to read the wording of any papers or permission forms you are asked to sign);
2. The possibility of the biopsy with local anesthesia be considered (ask for any reasons why the risk of full anesthesia and the problems of recovery from it cannot be avoided).†

The advantages of doing the biopsy under local anesthesia are several:

1. Considerable savings in hospitalization and anesthesia costs. Much less sophisticated equipment and many fewer trained personnel are needed for local anesthesia. Fewer hours are required in the hospital beforehand and a whole day can be saved afterward, thus possibly reducing the total hospitalization time to less than one full day.
2. The procedure can even be performed on an outpatient basis, though only a handful of hospitals and clinics make surgical suites or operating rooms available for outpatient procedures, and medical specialty societies vary in their evaluation of outpatient procedures. (The financing and politics of health insurance programs are part of the reason

*Risks with general anesthesia include such complications as cardiac arrest, brain damage from aspiration, postoperative pneumonia and lengthened recuperation, among others. To this list, an NIH study has recently added a very strong indication (though not absolute proof) that general anesthesia may, in and of itself, inhibit the body's immune response system. (AP News Release, October 4, 1972.)
†The argument that this procedure might "knock" cancer cells into the system is no longer considered a valid excuse for the simultaneous procedure. See George Crile, Jr., "Possible Role of Uninvolved Lymph Nodes in Preventing Metastasis from Breast Cancer," *Cancer*, Vol. 24, No. 6 (1969), p. 1283; I. D. Bross, Jr., "Is There an Increased Risk of Metastasis When Biopsy and Operation Are Separated?" *Surgery, Gynecology and Obstetrics*, Vol. 134 (1972), p. 1000; A. S. Earle, "Delayed Operations for Breast Cancer," *Surgery, Gynecology and Obstetrics*, Vol. 131 (1970), p. 291; J. E. Deritt, "Unnecessary Morbidity from Breast Surgery," *Canadian Medical Association Journal*, Vol. 106 (1972); W. P. Maier, "Needle Aspiration of Breast Cysts," *Consultant* (April, 1972), p. 106.

for this, since full hospitalization is often covered, while outpatient-care coverage may be restricted or disallowed.)

3. The average woman, whose lump is benign, will suffer the minimum of psychological and physical trauma and inconvenience. She can return to full activity almost immediately.

4. The woman whose lump is malignant can adapt to her diagnosis in two stages, absorbing the reality and adjusting to it while she considers all the possible treatment alternatives with her doctors (more than one, we recommend) and with family members before making a decision.

Those of us with benign breast conditions can repeat the steps described, many times if necessary, with a minimum of trauma and disruption of our lives. But to do this we must believe that the major responsibility for our health and decisions about it belong in our own hands. We cannot leave it for the occasional physician visit. This is no less true if our breast conditions are not benign.

Breast Cancer

If you turned to this section first, we hope you will go back to the beginning of the "Breast Problems" section and read from there. If you ever do have a breast cancer diagnosis following biopsy, you will be much better able to cope with it and to decide what to do next if you have done some reading and thinking beforehand. (See bibliography, under "Breast Cancer.")

No one yet knows exactly what causes breast cancer. There are virus theories and immune-system-breakdown theories for cancer in general. In the case of breast cancer, many causal theories have been discarded along with old wives' tales, and only three or four lines of investigation seem at all promising. As to the discarded theories, we now know:

Cancer is not caused by sexual intercourse, childbirth, or nursing, nor by blows, bites, or bruises.

Cancer cannot be caught from another person like an infection.

Breast-feeding does not protect against breast cancer.

Among the possibilities:

Diet or environment—since women from Japan and other low-incidence countries who come to the U.S. begin to show a pattern like ours after a generation or two. Breast cancer incidence is highest among women in the U.S., Britain and Northern Europe; also among Jewish women.

Heredity—since the *susceptibility* to breast cancer (not necessarily occurrence) seems to run in fam-

ilies (though the presence of other cancers in the family does not seem to relate to breast cancer incidence).

Age at which a woman bears her first child—women who give birth very early in their childbearing years appear to gain some protection even if they have no more children.

Virus particles in breast milk—in animal studies definite virus transmission has been demonstrated. Among Parsi women in India such a process is suspected, but this has not yet been proven in any human group. Since so few American women breastfeed, this can hardly be a major cause in the U.S.

Hormone levels*—of the several different types of estrogens normally circulating in women, some are carcinogenic. When these predominate, breast cancer seems to increase. But no one yet understands what determines the higher proportions of carcinogenic estrogens in American women. The earlier the ovaries are removed, for example, the better the protection against breast cancer. (See "Fibroids, Polyps and Ovarian Cysts," p. 142, and "Uterine and Ovarian Cancer," p. 146.) It is not yet known for sure whether giving synthetic estrogen afterward helps or hinders the start of breast cancer. (See "D&C and Hysterectomy," p. 147.)

Breast cancer takes at least three or four different forms. Because the different types grow at different rates, a small lump may be either a slow-growing tumor which is containing the cancer, or the fastest-growing type which may have spread (metastasized) throughout the body by the time the lump is discovered. In between there are slower-growing cancers which may have spread into surrounding tissues, but not to other body systems. Cancer of the breast usually spreads into the lymphatic system before it reaches the bloodstream.

The lymph nodes first affected are near the armpit, under the sternum, or along the upper spine. Until recently, only metastasis in the armpit (axillary) nodes was considered important. However, it has become clear that the nodes under the sternum and along the spine are also important places for metastasis to occur. Adequate treatment of breast cancer must consider all these areas. (See illustration, p. 126.)

*The long-range impact of synthetic hormones in developing cancer is still under intensive investigation. DES (diethylstilbestrol) definitely played a part in the development of vaginal cancer. (See "Vaginal Cancer," p. 146; also box, "Drugs Women Should Know About," p. 150.) The Pill may turn out to be either carcinogenic or, in certain formulations, protective against breast cancer (see Chapter 10). Also, new tests have been developed which can help determine whether a cancer is sensitive to hormones. Called estrogen receptor assay, this test can make treatments more effective with hormones or chemotherapy. High quality laboratory work is *essential*, however. Call CIS for help (see bibliography).

Enlarged nodes under the arm may or may not be cancerous and, as with breast lumps, only biopsy can tell for certain. Currently it is being suggested that retaining the axillary nodes may be possible, treating them with radiation if necessary (if they are not enlarged) when cancer is found in a breast lump.*

From these facts we can see how mysterious breast cancer is and why it is one of the deepest fears we women have. While it is not the commonest killer disease among women (that is heart disease) it is the commonest cancer killer and the leading cause of death of all women aged thirty-seven to fifty-five. (See boxes on breast cancer, pp. 131 and 135, and on causes of death, p. 99.) Since breast cancer takes many different forms and spreads through the body in different ways, it is becoming harder to believe that any one treatment would be best for all of them. In England and Scandinavia there is no longer one standard method, but in the United States radical mastectomy is still preferred by the majority of doctors. Ninety-five percent of breast surgery is radical surgery. We will explain the different types.

Traditional Surgery

Simple removal of the breast, by increasingly sophisticated surgery, was the treatment for breast cancer until a little less than 100 years ago, when an American surgeon named William Stewart Halsted perfected the radical mastectomy. Since it seemed to show an improved survival rate compared with simpler mastectomies, it was established as the method of choice by 1910. Although various modifications of the radical were introduced, it was not until 1960 or so that the unchanging breast cancer death rate stimulated investigation by some doctors of alternative procedures being reported in Canada, England and Scandinavia. The traditional treatments have been:

*Cardiff and Edinburgh trials. (See Kushner in bibliography.)

SIMPLE MASTECTOMY: *removal of entire breast tissue, leaving pectoral muscle intact. Some nodes may or may not be removed under the arm. Surgery may be followed by radiation.*

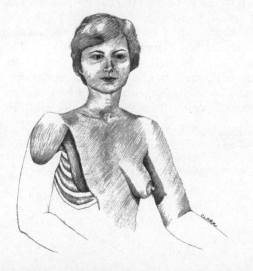

Who Is at Risk?

One way of approaching the problem is the Breast Cancer Risk Profile,* which all doctors could use in deciding how closely to watch particular patients. Women can use it, too. Here's how it works. Compared to women in general:

If you are the daughter of a breast cancer victim, you have twice the risk.

If you are a sister you have two and a half times the risk.

If you are infertile, you have one and a half times the risk (of a fertile woman).

If your first full-term pregnancy came after age 25, you have twice the risk (of women who got pregnant sooner); after 31, three times the risk of the women pregnant before 21.

If you began menstruating very early and have been menstruating for a long time, you have twice the risk.

If you have fibrocystic disease there is also twice the risk (though doctors disagree strongly on this point, since the apparent link may be only statistical).

Your risks are also somewhat greater if you eat large amounts of fat; have earwax that is wet rather than dry; have a hypothyroid (underfunctioning thyroid) condition; live in a cold climate; or have relatively high socioeconomic status. One woman in fifteen will develop breast cancer, and this rate *may* be rising. (The risk is lowest under the age of 30 [10 per 100,000], rising as we get older [e.g., at age 70 it is 200 per 100,000]. The earlier the menopause, whether artificial [via surgery] or natural, the lower the risk.)

*Adapted from Dr. H. P. Leis, Jr., New York Medical College, in a report to the International College of Surgeons, San Diego Meeting, 1974.

SIMPLE MASTECTOMY removes only the breast, leaving everything else, including axillary nodes and all muscles. Halsted's study of the superiority of his radical method over simple mastectomy was based on exactly 133 women, 75 of whom were followed up for three years, yet it has taken ninety-two years to successfully challenge his figures!

RADICAL MASTECTOMY involves taking all of the breast, all the axillary nodes, and the pectoral muscles under

RADICAL MASTECTOMY: *this operation removes the breast, the entire pectoral muscle and the armpit nodes. Swelling of the arm and restriction of movement must be treated after surgery. The lungs remain vulnerable throughout life.*

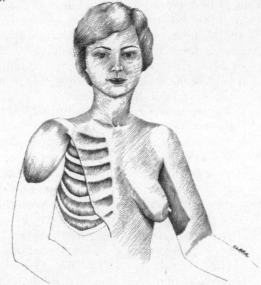

the breast (which also support arm function), in the belief that this is the best way to prevent recurrence.

SUPER-RADICAL MASTECTOMY involves removal of the breast, all the armpit glands, the underlying muscles of the chest wall, and the nodes under the sternum. This operation is fairly risky, since the chest wall must be opened. Only reluctantly, when it began to seem that the upper spine nodes were sometimes implicated in metastasis as well, were the ever-more-radical surgical experiments brought to an end here.

MODIFIED RADICAL MASTECTOMY takes less of the chest muscles that connect the arm, and leaves some nodes.

PECTORAL MUSCLES *provide support for the breasts and are necessary for many arm movements.*

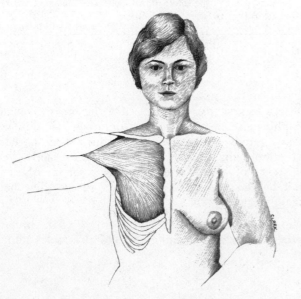

Less disabling, it has also shown longer survival rates than the radical in some studies. Radiation of remaining nodes may follow.

PARTIAL MASTECTOMY removes the lump and enough of the surrounding tissue to be sure there is no cancer beyond. One breast will be smaller than the other afterward, but modern FDA-approved silicone or saline envelope implants are a possibility.

SUBCUTANEOUS MASTECTOMY involves removal of the inner breast but leaves the outer skin and nipple. Silicone or saline envelope-type implants are then possible.*

Following is a list of the kinds of breast cancer and modern treatment alternatives.

Different Breast Cancers and Their Alternative Treatments†

STAGE O. The cancer is very small (microscopic) and is usually found accidentally, in biopsy of a lump which is predominantly not cancer but in which a few cancer cells are found. This type does not infiltrate (invade) breast tissue and is called *in situ* (in place) cancer. Therapy has ranged from biopsy to total mastectomy. The problem is that women with this sort of cancer are at risk of having similar small (microscopic) deposits of cancer cells in other parts of the same breast and/or in the other breast. The concern is that in time (2 to 25 years later) a percentage of these women will develop a palpable lump all of which is cancerous and therefore more serious. The figures range from 10 to 30 percent over a lifetime. Currently there is controversy about whether mastectomy is too much surgery. Some surgeons advocate simple biopsy and very careful medical follow-up, since most women (70 to 90 percent) will *not* develop such "infiltrating" cancers.

STAGE I. This stage refers to a cancer mass (lump) which is usually palpable (can be felt) but is still small (less than 2 cm.). These cancer cells do invade breast tissue. Sometimes (rarely) they also invade beyond to nodes. Occasionally the lymph nodes in the axilla (armpit) are felt to be enlarged, sometimes not. Only biopsy of such lymph nodes can tell for sure whether cancer has really spread there.

The treatment of this stage of breast cancer is very controversial. Some doctors think that a small lump, particularly when located on the outer side of the breast, can be adequately treated by wide excision or excision followed by radiation therapy. Others suggest simple mastectomy. Still others feel radical or modified radical

*For help, write: AFTER, 99 Park Ave., N.Y., NY 10016. Many surgeons are unaware of reconstruction possibilities.
†Courtesy of Dr. Mary Costanza, Department of Oncology, Tufts New England Medical Center, Boston.

mastectomy is the correct way. At the present time there is no difference in survival (or cure) rate of women with Stage I cancer whether they have had radical mastectomy or simple mastectomy or excision and radiation therapy.

STAGE II. In this case the cancer is larger (2 to 5 cm.) when diagnosed. More frequently the axillary lymph nodes are infiltrated with cancer (indeed there is a positive relationship between the size of the cancer lump and the chances that the lymph nodes will be involved).

There is much controversy about how such disease should be treated. So far no "best" way has been proven. Treatment can be of four sorts:

1. Wide local excision plus radiation therapy to the breast and lymph node areas.
2. Simple mastectomy plus radiation therapy to the same areas.
3. Modified radical mastectomy with or without radiation therapy.
4. Radical mastectomy with or without radiation therapy.

Depending on the type of surgery, lymph nodes may or may not be removed. If they are removed, the pathologist can tell if cancer has affected them. The chance of cure depends in great part on whether and how many lymph nodes are involved.

There is no firm evidence that if lymph nodes are in fact involved removing them (radical or modified radical mastectomy) will improve survival or chances of cure. A study now in progress is testing which therapy (modified radical or simple mastectomy plus radiation therapy) is better. Another study is currently being conducted to see if giving chemotherapy (drugs) to women with cancer in nodes will improve their chances of cure or survival. In neither case is the answer yet known.

STAGE III. In this instance, when breast cancer is diagnosed it is large (greater than 5 cm.), and lymph nodes are almost always involved. The chances of cure by any therapy are not good. Nevertheless there are therapies which can help local control and even survival. Simple mastectomy or radiation therapy may be used to control the local breast disease. Chemotherapy may be used to try to forestall cancer recurrence and hence prolong survival.

STAGE IV. In this case, when first found, the cancer in the breast is usually quite large (greater than 5 cm.), the lymph nodes are usually enlarged, and most important, there is evidence that the cancer has already spread via the bloodstream beyond the breast and lymph nodes to other parts of the body. At this stage the cancer is not curable, but there are still many things that can be done to improve survival.

Such therapies include removal of ovaries (for menstruating women), removal of adrenal glands (for post-menopausal women), hormone administration and/or chemotherapy. Advances are being made in extending useful, symptom-free survival time for women even when they have extensive disease.

As you can see, there's a great deal that is *not known* about the best way to treat breast cancer in its different stages of presentation. It is therefore most important that you be able to discuss openly with your surgeon or internist the various alternatives, his or her prejudices, and the possibility of a second opinion. No doubt, in the next five or ten years certain questions will be answered. In the meantime, be sure your doctor is up-to-date with current evidence and study results, has experience with many breast cancer patients, and is willing to discuss and learn about the different therapies.

One thing, however, seems clear. The sooner a breast cancer is discovered, the smaller it usually is, and hence the chances of complete cure (by whatever method) are much, much better. It is for this reason that breast self-examination, regular checkups and mammography, xerography, or thermography are so important (see footnote, p. 128).

Radical Mastectomy as Breast Cancer Treatment

There are many national experts who now believe that at our present state of knowledge there is no longer any justification for any version of the radical mastectomy. Tentative findings from the National Cancer Institute have already shown no difference in effectiveness between radical mastectomy and simple mastectomy.* In other words, there is nothing that radical mastectomy can accomplish that cannot be achieved as well by simple mastectomy, local excision, partial mastectomy, or radiation. It is almost certain that only radiation and drugs could affect those cancer cells out of reach of the surgeon's knife, no matter how radical the mastectomy. So why are radical mastectomies usually done? We have to come back again, as we have in many other sections of our book, to the training, temperament and beliefs of physicians, in this case those who treat cancer, the vast majority of whom are male surgeons.

The fact that the radical mastectomy is one of the oldest operations in the history of modern medicine gives it a kind of sacredness that many doctors are reluctant to challenge. It is part of modern Western medicine's broader belief in "the surgical answer" to human problems, the mechanistic approach of removing the offending or affected *part* without considering how the body system as a whole affects the part or is affected by it (to say nothing about how emotional or spiritual factors may be involved).

The New York Times (September 30, 1974), p. 26.

However, it is also true that the newer approaches have not been in use long enough to prove that they are any *better* than radical mastectomy. And since radical mastectomies have been done on so many women for so many decades it will be a long while before any such statement can be made. Meanwhile, the major argument for trying the newer methods is that radical mastectomy has not reduced the death rate from breast cancer in over thirty years. The worst thing that can be said about these newer methods is that results are no better and no worse than with radical mastectomy, and that they have not been practiced long enough for a proper judgment to be made.

If You Have Had a Mastectomy

Of the thousands of women who have had mastectomies, some of them famous, many have adjusted quickly and gone on to lead busy, active lives almost as if nothing had happened. Many have been helped by a program of the American Cancer Society, called Reach to Recovery,* started by a former mastectomy patient named Mrs. Terese Lasser. Volunteers who have undergone mastectomy visit new mastectomy patients in the hospital and help them with practical questions and offer psychological support and a living example of confident recovery.

Unfortunately, physicians still control the communication among mastectomy patients, deciding whether women may see Reach to Recovery volunteers and whether the volunteers are "suitable" visitors. Any woman who has had a mastectomy should make every effort to contact other women with similar experience, with or without the permission of doctors or the Cancer Society. You can start such a group by asking friends to put you in touch with such women or through personal newspaper ads. We believe strongly that women can offer one another unique help through sharing experiences, and they have a need and a right to do this.†

There are many reasons why this kind of help is important. The first and most crucial is that very few women ever receive adequate preparation for the reality of mastectomy—from anyone, even their surgeons. The Reach to Recovery program would probably be several times as effective if the volunteers could visit mastectomy candidates *before* the surgery. Then prospective patients could learn in advance what to expect during the first hours, days and weeks afterward. They would know about the painful arm swelling that almost always follows complete axillary lymph node removal; the impairment of arm mobility and function that may accom-

pany the radical; and the therapies which attempt to improve both.

They could also discuss in advance, both with the other women and with their husbands, the doubts and fears about how the loss of a breast may affect their marriages and the sexual desire of both partners. They could be helped to anticipate the depression or grief that seems to be a normal human response to the loss of any body part, but particularly such a uniquely feminine part as a breast. Deeper depression and rage may also be involved—rage at the disease itself, or at fate for "choosing me," or at the outside world for not caring more or doing more research. The depression may stir up normally hidden and controlled feelings of low self-esteem and convince us that we are forever unlovable.

Programs like Reach to Recovery and surgeons who perform mastectomies do not choose to publicize "unsuccessful" mastectomy patients or encourage any serious research on how widespread such cases are. Obviously, if you already have a full, active life, a good marriage, generous hospital coverage, well-adjusted children and/or an interesting job (and are famous besides), your chances of making a good adjustment to mastectomy would be fairly high. But like other crises in life, a mastectomy can also put the maximum stress on your resources when they are less than ideal or downright inadequate, and that's the case with most of us. Most women may need much more help than is ever offered.*

As with hysterectomy and other serious surgery, women deserve a chance to explore all the possibilities and prepare for all the outcomes *in advance*. The fact that so many women who have had mastectomies do feel mutilated and unlovable afterward, and sometimes feel hostility and resentment toward women who have challenged the mastectomy mystique, indicates that many women have not had a chance to work through all the feelings that mastectomy stirs up. The fact that doctors so often use words like "silly" and "sensible" to describe women's differing attitudes toward mastectomy suggests that they know very little about the psychology of women and have not been very interested to find out.

All of this is changing, but only because we as women ourselves are changing, demanding options and psychological care to meet our needs. Some doctors are now recognizing that fear of treatment may cause delays in seeking medical help.

This controversy about treatment is one of the most bitter and heated in medical history. Since it erupted into the popular press (*Woman's Day*, November, 1970) women *and* doctors have gotten into the battle.† Since the Ford and Rockefeller operations the controversy has

*Coordinated from ACS headquarters in New York (see "Breast Self-examination").

†New group programs of the YWCA, called "Encore," are starting in many cities. Write to Encore/National Board YWCA, 600 Lexington Ave., N.Y., NY 10022.

*Incidentally, one of the outrages is that Blue Cross/Blue Shield does *not* pay for breast prosthesis in many states, classifying it as "cosmetic."

†See also Rosamond Campion's *The Invisible Worm* (New York: Macmillan, 1972).

intensified, with many doctors quietly suggesting that the more radical procedure may not have been necessary, referring to the National Cancer Institute's report.* The American Cancer Society, however, continues to take the conservative view that the more radical operation is still the surgery of choice until something better is proven by experience.

How Can Women Decide?

When doctors disagree as much as they do in this case, they are usually poor sources of objective advice. Since they are all trained differently, they will have a certain loyalty to their own specialty's views or even to the views of particular schools of opinion established by one or two famous men or prestigious hospitals. In a case like this we women really make the final choice, because the kind of treatment we end up with depends on whom we choose to treat us. If keeping your breast is of vital importance to you, there are highly reputable doctors who can help to plan treatment which may permit that. Once you have read this chapter and the supporting materials

The New York Times (September 30, 1974), page 26, "Breast Cancer Study Finds Radical Surgery Has No Advantage over Simple Mastectomy."

you can ask *why* a doctor wants to perform a particular procedure or whether another would be any better or worse (see "Our Rights as Patients," in Chapter 18). Again, be sure to get a second opinion. If you are a very high-risk patient, you can decide how you want to fight your battle against breast cancer, which approaches would give you the most will and strength to cope with the disease. This is rarely the same from woman to woman, and we need to be helped to demand the choices that will give us the greatest sense of confidence. Again, do not expect this type of support from your physician (although it *may* be there), but get it from somewhere. You deserve it; it's your breast and your life.

CRABS, OR PUBIC LICE

PHTHIRUS PUBIS is a roundish, crablike body louse that lives in pubic hair and occasionally in the hair of the chest, armpits, eyelashes and eyebrows. You can "catch" them by intimate physical contact with someone who has them, or from bedding or clothes that person has used. They are bloodsuckers and can carry such diseases as typhus. The main symptom of crabs is an intolerable

Key Facts About Breast Cancer for Women Consumers

1. Women are still their own best protection against a fatal breast cancer. We are in the best position to find suspicious lumps, through breast self-examination, and to report them. Over 90 percent of diagnosed breast cancers are found by women, not doctors.
2. Most lumps are benign, close to 90 percent of those biopsied. Lumps that don't disappear in one or two menstrual cycles are probably benign, but without tests neither you nor your doctor can tell for sure by examination alone.
3. A biopsy should be performed and the results carefully explained to you before any treatment decision is made. General anesthesia is not always necessary for a biopsy. Be sure your physician is qualified to treat you.
4. Cancer is not the leading cause of death of women in the United States, but breast cancer kills more women than any other cancer—over 33,000 annually—and it *is* the leading cause of death for all women age thirty-seven to fifty-five. Many of these deaths are preventable through early diagnosis and treatment.
5. Radical mastectomy (removal of the breast) is not the only treatment for breast cancer and has yet to be proven better than other treatments. Breast cancers are not all the same and call for individual treatment or, increasingly, for combined treatments (surgery, radiation and chemotherapy).
6. Whenever removal of a breast (or any other organ or body part) is recommended it is wise to seek another opinion, from a specialist in breast cancer, in this case, preferably affiliated with a different hospital than your doctor. A university (teaching) hospital staff physician's opinion should be available to you before you decide anything.
7. You have a legal right to be told all the advantages and disadvantages of any treatment recommended; what all the alternatives and known outcomes are; and what the risks may be, including those of having no treatment.
8. You have a right to refuse any treatment or procedure at any time.
9. Make sure you have someone with whom you can talk out your feelings. Most doctors and nurses are too busy and may have different ideas from yours about what is important. If possible, get someone you trust to act as an advocate for you. Even the strongest of us needs familiar support at a time of crisis.

itching in the genital area; they are easily diagnosed because crabs are visible without a microscope. The cure is a simple but expensive white cream (Kwell), which works very quickly and effectively (normal soap will *not* affect crabs). After treatment you should use clean clothing and bed linen. Crabs will die within twenty-four hours after separation from the human body, but the eggs will live about six days. Previously used bedclothes, towels, etc. are safe after a week without use. Anything dry cleaned or washed in boiling water can be used immediately.

HERPES AND VENEREAL WARTS

HERPES is a common viral disease which has recently reached epidemic proportions, particularly among women. It is usually (but not necessarily) spread by sexual intercourse. It is caused by a virus known as *Herpes simplex*, type 2, which is closely related to *Herpes simplex*, type 1, the cause of cold sores or fever blisters. Type 2 seems to appear below the waist and type 1 above, although there is an estimated 10 percent crossover, probably resulting from oral-genital sex. The way it is transferred and its incubation period are unknown. A woman who has Herpes may increase her risks of getting cervical cancer and, if pregnant, may miscarry or deliver early. Also, if a baby gets Herpes while passing through the birth canal where there is an open Herpes sore, s/he may die or suffer severe brain damage.

Herpes appears as painful sores which look like blisters or small bumps. These sores may be inside the vagina, on the external genitals, thighs, in or near the anus, or on the buttocks. Sores also appear on the cervix, where they are not painful. The blisters can rupture to form open sores, or ulcers, which are often very painful. While the sores are open the Herpes virus is thought to spread very easily to other people. The open sores are also subject to infection by other bacteria. Other possible symptoms are fever, enlarged lymph nodes and flu-like symptoms. The sores sometimes heal by themselves in anywhere from a week to a month. The virus then enters a latent stage during which it is not contagious. A new eruption can occur at any time, although it often appears to be related to stress, either physical or emotional. For some women the outbreaks recur after prolonged intercourse or are connected with their menstrual cycles. There does not seem to be a limit to the number of outbreaks, although for many people the first one is the worst.

Men's symptoms look like women's. However, they usually appear somewhere on the penis or near the anus.

Diagnosis is often determined by the appearance of the sores. A more accurate diagnosis can be made by microscopic examination of a smear taken from the base of the sore and/or from the cervix. A serum test for antibodies can also be done.

There is no known cure for Herpes. There is some symptomatic treatment, though. Surface anesthetics and oral pain-killers can be used. If the labia are irritated they can be separated with a lubricated tampon for some relief. There are several dyes which may be applied to the sores and then exposed to fluorescent light. Although these dyes usually make the sores go away, there is some question as to whether the dyes themselves may be cancer-causing.

Sulfa creams may be used to prevent infection of the sores. It is also a good idea to have open sores examined by a medically trained person to make sure they have not become infected by harmful bacteria. When condoms cover the affected area, they may help to keep Herpes from spreading. Probably the best way to prevent infection and recurrence is to be in good physical condition, to eat good food (see "Nutrition," in Chapter 6), and to get enough exercise and rest.

VENEREAL WARTS, or *Condyloma acuminatum*, are very common. They are caused by a virus and may look like regular warts. Though they may be spread in other ways, sexual intercourse helps to transmit them. The warts, which don't hurt, appear one to three months after contact with an infected person, usually on the bottom part of the vaginal opening. They are also found on the vaginal lips, inside the vagina, on the cervix, and around the anus. When small, they look like little pieces of hard, raised skin. If they become large they can develop a cauliflower-like appearance. Warmth and moisture seem to help them grow.

On a man the warts usually occur toward the tip of the penis, sometimes under the foreskin, and less often, on the shaft of the penis or the scrotum.

Diagnosis is usually made by appearance. If the warts are small they can be dried up with an application of podophyllin, a dark ointment or liquid. (It is important to wash this chemical off after six hours so that you do not get burns from it.) Several treatments may be necessary. Podophyllin should not be used during pregnancy. Small warts can also be frozen off (cryotherapy) with solid CO_2 (dry ice). This hurts very briefly. If the warts are large they must be removed surgically. If all the warts are not removed at the same time, the ones left will usually spread again. If you want to get rid of them completely, make sure all the warts, including those inside the vagina and on the cervix, are removed. Even after apparently thorough treatment the warts may reappear. You can also catch them again if your sexual partner is not treated at the same time. If the warts are located only on the penis or inside the vagina, using a condom can help keep them from spreading.

VAGINAL INFECTIONS

All women secrete moisture and mucus from the membranes that line the vagina. This discharge is transparent or slightly milky and may be somewhat slippery. When dry, it may be yellowish. When a woman is sexually aroused this secretion increases. It normally causes no irritation or inflammation of the vagina or vulva. If you want to examine your own discharge, collect a sample from inside your vagina—with a washed finger of course. It is easiest to see if you smear it on a glass.

Many bacteria grow in the vagina of a normal, healthy woman. Some of them help to keep the vagina somewhat acid and keep yeast, fungi and other harmful organisms from multiplying all out of proportion. In large amounts, the waste products secreted by these harmful organisms may irritate the vaginal walls and cause infections to develop. At such times we may experience an abnormal discharge, mild or severe itching and burning of the vulva and chafing of the thighs, and occasionally frequent urination.

Some of the reasons we get vaginal infections are: a general lowered resistance (from lack of sleep, bad diet, another infection in our body, and similar factors); too much douching; pregnancy; taking birth control pills, other hormones, or antibiotics; diabetes or a pre-diabetic condition; cuts, abrasions and other irritations in the vagina (from childbirth, from intercourse without enough lubrication, or from using an instrument in the vagina medically or for masturbation).

Prevention

Here are ways to prevent vaginal infections:

1. Wash your vulva and bottom regularly. Pat your vulva dry after bathing and try to keep it dry. Also, don't use other people's towels or washcloths. Avoid irritating sprays* and soaps (use special non-soap cleansers for skin very sensitive to plain soap).
2. Wear clean, cotton underpants. Avoid nylon underwear and panty hose, since they retain moisture and heat, which help harmful bacteria to grow faster.
3. Avoid pants that are tight in the crotch and thighs.
4. Always wipe your anus from front to back (so that bacteria from the anus won't get into the vagina or urethra).
5. Make sure your sexual partners are clean. It is a good practice for a man to wash his penis daily, especially before making love. Using a condom can provide added protection.
6. Use a sterile, water-soluble jelly if lubrication is needed during intercourse (something like K-Y Jelly, for example, *not* Vaseline). Also, recent

*"Feminine hygiene sprays" may damage the delicate skin of the vulva. They are at best unnecessary and often harmful. The FDA has suggested and may soon require that all "feminine hygiene sprays" carry a warning on the label.

studies have shown that birth control jellies slow down the growth of trichomonas and possibly monilia. Using these jellies for lubrication and/or general prevention is a good idea, especially with a man you may not know very well.

7. Avoid sexual intercourse that is painful or abrasive to your vagina.
8. Try to keep down your sugar and refined-carbohydrate intake (diets high in sugars can radically change the normal pH of the vagina).
9. Some women have found that applications of plain (not flavored) yogurt in the vagina help to prevent infections and to cure mild symptoms. Unpasteurized yogurts also contain lactobacilli, "good" bacteria normally found in the vagina and often destroyed when we take antibiotics (yogurt sometimes replenishes the supply of these bacteria).
10. Some women occasionally douche with a solution of 1 or 2 T. vinegar in 1 qt. warm water. This is mildly acidic, like yogurt, and can help to prevent infections. Other women have found that douching with plain water or a solution of baking soda and water has helped them to prevent vaginal infections. Remember to douche with great caution.
11. "Don't put anything in your vagina you wouldn't put in your mouth," as the McGill Birth Control Handbook says.

It's a good idea to continue most of these practices even after we get an infection.

Yeast Infections (Also Called Candida, Monilia, or Fungus)

CANDIDA ALBICANS, a yeast fungus, normally grows in harmless quantities in your rectum and vagina. When your system is out of balance, yeastlike organisms may grow profusely and cause a vaginal discharge that is thick and white, may look like cottage cheese, and may smell like baking bread. If a woman has a yeast infection when she gives birth, the baby will get yeasts in its digestive tract. This is called thrush and is treated orally with nystatin drops or gentian violet.

Candida grows best in a very mildly acidic environment. The pH in the vagina is normally more acidic than this (4.0 to 5.0), except when we take birth control pills or some antibiotics, when we are pregnant, when we have diabetes, and when we menstruate (the pH rises to 5.8 or 6.8 because blood is alkaline). Obviously, we often find ourselves with a vaginal pH favorable to monilia, so preventive measures are especially important. Acidic douches (2 T. vinegar to 1 qt. water) or boric acid suppositories (you can make your own by filling size 00 capsules with boric acid crystals) can often keep monilia from developing. (However, once a yeast infection has started, such procedures usually won't cure it.) For most of us, reducing sugar and refined carbohydrate intake can be an extremely effective preventive.

Once monilia sets in, treatment usually consists of some form of nystatin (e.g., Mycostatin) taken as a suppository. Suppositories have fewer side effects than nystatin taken orally, and they can be used during pregnancy, but they may not be strong enough to cure severe yeast infections. Other methods of treating monilia include various prescription creams and painting the vagina, cervix and vulva with gentian violet. This is bright purple and it stains, so a sanitary pad must be worn. This messy procedure really helps, except in occasional cases when there is a severe reaction to gentian violet.

Some of us have had success with the following home remedies: yogurt douche (daily); goldenseal-myrrh douche (simmer one Tb. of each in 3 cups water, then strain and cool); and garlic suppositories (peel, but don't nick, a clove of garlic, then wrap in gauze before inserting).

For a long time I felt as though I were on a merry-go-round. I would get a yeast infection, take Mycostatin (a brand of nystatin) for three weeks, clear up the infection, and then two weeks later find that the itching and the thick white discharge were back. Finally, once while on medication I also douched with Lactinex* and carefully watched my sugar intake. This worked for me and the monilia has not recurred in many months.

Trichomoniasis

TRICHOMONAS VAGINALIS, or trich, is a one-celled parasite that can be found in both men and women. At least 50 percent of all women have trich organisms in their vaginas, though often without symptoms. Usually women with trich have a thin, foamy vaginal discharge that is yellowish-green or gray in color and has a foul odor. If another infection is present along with trichomoniasis, the discharge may be thicker and whiter. Trich can also cause a urinary infection. It is most often contracted through intercourse (thus trichomoniasis can be a venereal infection) but can be passed on by moist objects such as towels, bathing suits, underwear, washcloths and toilet seats.

Trich grows best in an alkaline environment, so acidic douches may eliminate a trich infection if applied early enough. Since blood is alkaline, we may be even more prone to getting trichomoniasis when we menstruate. At these times a vinegar douche may have preventive value. Unfortunately, acid douches usually won't clear up an infection if monilia is also present.

Although trichomoniasis is usually treated with oral

doses of metronidazole (Flagyl), an expensive drug (only G. D. Searle makes it!), WOMEN SHOULD AVOID THIS DRUG. In various tests, metronidazole has caused gene mutations in standard test systems; birth defects in animals; and cancer in rats and mice (in at least seven different studies!).* Its safety is clearly questionable, as is that of a similar drug, tinidazole (which may soon be marketed by Ortho Pharmaceutical, despite protests by such groups as Nader's Health Research Group in Washington, D.C.). In no case should Flagyl be taken orally by pregnant women or by anyone who has peptic ulcers, another infection elsewhere in the body, a history of blood diseases, or a disease of the central nervous system. Also, anyone taking Flagyl should avoid alcohol, as the combination may cause headache, nausea and other side effects.

Frequently, vaginal suppositories (such as Floraquin) or vaginal gels can provide adequate treatment. There have been better results with short-term, low-dose Flagyl (to be avoided, though certainly less harmful than high doses of Flagyl), but recurrence of the trichomonal infection occurs in about 30 percent of the women receiving this treatment. To avoid such recurrences, one trichomonas specialist† recommends the following: tub bathing throughout the menstrual cycle, nightly use of Floraquin suppositories (or a similar product), loose clothing (since exposure to air destroys the parasites, or "trichomonads," causing the infection), and avoidance of tampons, ordinary douches, and vaginal sprays.

Nonspecific Vaginitis

Other vaginal infections are often called nonspecific vaginitis. The discharge may be white or yellow and possibly streaked with blood. The walls of the vagina can be cloudy, puffy with fluid, and covered by a thick, heavy coat of pus. The first sign of an infection may be the appearance of cystitis-like symptoms (see p. 139). There may be lower back pain, cramps and swollen glands in the abdomen and thighs. It is usually treated with sulfa creams or suppositories (Vagitrol, Sultrin, AVC Cream). Other treatments are available for people allergic to sulfa.

One kind of vaginitis formerly diagnosed as nonspecific is now believed to be caused by the bacterium *Hemophilus vaginalis*. The symptoms are similar to those of trichomoniasis, though the discharge tends to be creamy white or grayish and especially foul-smelling after intercourse. Although the bacterium is fairly easy to recognize on a "wet mount" (mixture of vaginal secretions and saline solution observed under a microscope), it is sometimes diagnosed incorrectly. Hemophilus is of-

---

*This and similar products are sold over the counter and help to produce the lactic acid favorable to growth of the friendly bacilli.

*Letter to FDA Commissioner Schmidt from Dr. Sidney Wolfe and Anita Johnson of Nader's Health Research Group. See also *Medical Letter*, June 20, 1975.
†Dr. Jane E. Hodgson, University of Minnesota.

ten a venereal infection (transmitted by sexual intercourse), so treatment of both partners is necessary. Nitrofurazone (Furacin), in a suppository or cream, or sulfa suppositories are usually prescribed for women and tetracycline or ampicillin for men. In many areas *Hemophilus vaginalis* is becoming more common than trichomoniasis or monilia.

CYSTITIS

Cystitis is an inflammation and/or infection of the bladder. Sometime in her life nearly every woman gets it, and it can be hard to eradicate permanently. It usually means that intestinal bacteria, such as *Escherichia coli (E. coli)*, useful in the digestive tract, have gotten into the bladder. Trich can also cause cystitis. The symptoms can be really frightening, but it is not a serious condition. If you suddenly have to urinate every few minutes and it burns like crazy even though almost nothing comes out, you probably have cystitis. There may also be blood in the urine (hematuria) and pus in the urine (pyuria). You may have pain just above your pubic bone, and sometimes there is a peculiar, heavy urine odor when you first urinate in the morning.

If these symptoms develop, you should see a doctor, although the infection may disappear without treatment. You can help relieve the symptoms before you see the doctor:

1. Drink *lots* of water, enough to pour out a good stream of urine every hour. It really helps!
2. Avoid coffee, tea, alcohol and spices; they irritate the bladder.
3. Soak in hot tub two or three times a day.
4. Try a hot-water bottle or heating pad on your abdomen and back.

I had recurring bouts of cystitis for several months, always precipitated by intercourse but not attributable to any specific cause that could be found by a urologist. The first few times I had an attack my distress seemed drastically out of proportion to the actual physical pain. I did not really "hurt," but the physical discomfort, especially at night, triggered a terrible restlessness and panic. Talking to other women in the hospital emergency room, I discovered that this kind of psychological reaction is commonly associated with the physical symptoms for many women. Other women described the feeling that they were "climbing the walls" or "climbing out of their skin" all night. Knowing what to expect, I began to relax more when I had an attack and stopped feeling ashamed of "overreacting" to the symptoms. I found that I was most uncomfortable lying down and preferred to lose sleep when I felt a need to be active or distracted at night.

The doctor will ask for a urine sample, so take a drink of water before your visit. If it is during your period you may be catheterized (have a tube inserted in your urethra) to get a clean specimen. Treatment may begin immediately with Gantrisin (a sulfa drug), although it is often delayed a couple of days until the offending bacteria and the drugs they are sensitive to can be identified. Tetracycline, nitrofurantoin (get a generic prescription), and ampicillin are also commonly used.

Full treatment may take two weeks, but the symptoms should disappear in a day or so. If they don't, return to the doctor. Some bacteria are resistant to, and even thrive on, some of the drugs. You may be asked to control the pH of your urine by drinking cranberry juice or taking vitamin C (both are acid). This is important, since some drugs do not work well when the urine pH is not in the right range. Vaginitis and some digestive upset are common side effects of the antibiotics and sulfa drugs. Nausea may be decreased by taking the medication with meals.

Many women have found that taking cranberry juice alone (about 4 oz. every four hours) can clear up cystitis. Some women drink cranberry juice regularly as a preventive measure.

Like vaginitis, cystitis is more likely to occur when your resistance is low. Damage to the urethra from nearby surgery, childbirth, or intercourse may also make you more susceptible to infection. Women who urinate infrequently and people who are catheterized for a long period or frequently (such as diabetics) often develop cystitis. If your cystitis keeps recurring consult a urologist, as a serious abnormality may be present.

Cystitis is sometimes, though not always, sex-related. The first time you have intercourse with a particular man or have intercourse after a long period of abstinence, you may get a sudden attack of urethritis (inflammation of the urethra), often called "honeymoon cystitis." In some cases this can lead to true cystitis.

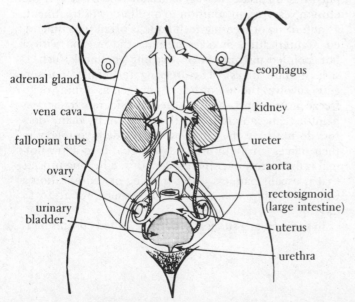

adrenal gland

esophagus

vena cava

kidney

fallopian tube

ureter

ovary

aorta

urinary bladder

rectosigmoid (large intestine)

uterus

urethra

If you have chronic cystitis and expect to be distant from medical help, you can get a prescription for Pyridium. It relieves the symptoms, though it does not affect the bacteria. It makes your urine bright orange, and a stain is permanent, so guard against drips.

Women sometimes have bacteria in their urine (bacteriuria) without any symptoms, so you should have a urine test with your gynecological exam. An ordinary urine analysis is not sufficient to test for cystitis—make sure your doctor takes a "clean voided specimen." If cystitis and bacteriuria are not treated, kidney infection and such complications as high blood pressure or premature births may result.

For prevention, follow the suggestions given on page 137, and drink enough to urinate several times a day. Some intercourse positions (such as penetration by the penis from the rear) put excessive pressure on the bladder and may rupture newly healed skin. To prevent possible reinfection after a case of cystitis is cured, avoid these positions until the bladder is completely healed and no longer tender.

After several months of nearly continuous cystitis attacks, my urologist slit a narrowed area in my urethra to help drainage (internal urethrotomy). I had only one infection in the next three years; then the same story began all over. My second operation did not help at all.

I consulted another doctor, who, while recognizing the importance of checking for serious abnormalities, also stressed the benefits of drinking lots of water. I now drink enough to urinate every hour or two (ten glasses a day, sometimes more). Ten glasses! Impossible, I thought. But it is better than drugs and not too hard if you work up to it. Take a drink whenever you urinate. I also wash my vulva every day and keep my urine pH at about 5.0 to 5.5 to inhibit bacterial growth. [Use phenaphithazine paper, available in drugstores, to check it.] In the year since I began this program I have had only two infections—when I slipped up on precautions—and nipped a minor one by using these tactics.

If you suffer from chronic cystitis you should also make sure the hands and penis of your sexual partners are clean, and avoid stretching or traumatizing the urethra during intercourse. Finally, get a urine culture every three to six months.

Sometimes chronic cystitis will involve the Skene's glands (at the opening of the urethra). In such cases you may think you are cured, then the glands are squeezed (as in intercourse, for example) and release some pus, which starts the cystitis symptoms all over again. Sometimes the Skene's glands are removed (meatotomy) to solve this problem, though specialists disagree about the need for this operation (which takes about a month to recover from).

One form of cystitis—interstitial cystitis, or Hunner's ulcer—is not associated with bacteria. It is found mostly in post-menopausal women and may be related to genital and hormonal changes that alter the mucus of the lower urinary tract; or it may be psychosomatic. It is very difficult to treat.

UTERINE AND OVARIAN PROBLEMS

Cervical Erosion and Cervicitis

CERVICAL EROSION refers to a large or small sore (benign lesion) that may develop on the cervix beside the cervical opening. It is usually pinkish-red and sometimes rough-looking. It is estimated that 95 percent of all women of childbearing age have cervical erosion at some point. This is probably because estrogen, which reaches its highest rate of production during this period, stimulates erosion by causing rapid growth of the cervical cells.

Cervical erosion has few symptoms and causes little discomfort. The commonest symptom is a whitish discharge (leukorrhea), which may have an unpleasant odor. When the erosion is irritated, a bloody discharge may also appear. Usually the erosion is not discovered until a woman has a pelvic exam.

The first step in diagnosis is a Pap smear. If abnormal cells are present, some of the cervical tissue is removed and examined under a microscope (a biopsy). A biopsy will distinguish cervical erosion from cervical cancer. There is controversy over the treatment of cervical erosion. Some doctors think it does no harm and should be left alone. Others think that if a cervical erosion is not treated it may become chronic and possibly lead to cervical cancer. It is also thought that untreated cervical erosion may affect a woman's fertility.

If the erosion is not severe you may choose not to treat it or to treat it with a sulfa cream (e.g., Sultrin Vaginal Cream, AVC Cream, or Vagitrol), which is applied well up inside the vagina, usually twice a day. If the erosion is severe, in addition to a sulfa cream treatment, a cauterizing or freezing technique is often recommended. Cauterization involves burning the erosion with a hot, pointed instrument or a strong chemical (such as silver nitrate sticks). The freezing technique (cryosurgery) involves the use of liquid nitrogen as a spray or to freeze instruments, and is often considered to be less painful than cauterization. (Unfortunately, many doctors do not have the facilities to provide cryosurgery in their offices.) In both methods the goal is to allow normal cells to grow over the eroded area, a healing process that is usually painless. After freezing or cauterization a woman should not have sexual intercourse for 10 to 14 days.

In some cases a surgical procedure called *conization* is

recommended. This requires hospitalization and involves removal of a cone of the cervical tissue affected by the erosion (a "coring-out"). A D&C (see p. 147) usually accompanies this procedure. (If you choose to do this, remember that it is probably not necessary to be "put out" with a general anesthetic—a local anesthetic is almost always sufficient. You should ask about the methods used in your hospital. See p. 144.)

CERVICITIS is an infection of the endocervical glands. Cervical erosion may or may not be present at the same time. Treatment for cervicitis is usually a sulfa cream, as described above.

Endometritis

Endometritis is an inflammation of the utcrine lining. Its main symptoms are pelvic pain and a tender uterus (when you have a bimanual exam); however, endometritis is sometimes without symptoms. A speculum examination often reveals a thick, foul cervical discharge.

The cause of endometritis is often an IUD which has irritated the uterine lining. In the beginning you may not feel this irritation.

Treatment usually includes ampicillin or tetracycline (for about one week), lots of bed rest, and no sex for two weeks. As with PID (see below), a culture and sensitivity test (if not originally taken) is required if the symptoms persist.

Endometriosis

The endometrium is a special kind of tissue that grows in the lining of the uterus each month for the nourishment of a fertilized egg. If no egg gets implanted, the endometrium is sloughed off (this is menstruation). Endometriosis results when endometrial tissue grows somewhere other than in the lining of the uterus—usually in the genital, urinary, or intestinal organs. Doctors disagree about why this happens. Endometriosis is quite common during the childbearing years, particularly the thirties.

The symptoms of endometriosis vary, depending on the location of the extra endometrium. Menstrual pain is the most common symptom, although other pains may occur. Diagnosis is hard in the early stages, and the condition is not usually suspected unless there is menstrual pain or an endometrial cyst large enough to feel. Endometriosis is a serious disease in that it is progressive and frequently results in infertility. Present treatment methods do not guarantee cure.

I had been having painful menstrual cramps and went to the university health service. A doctor there, without giving any physical examination, told me my cramps were psychosomatic and implied they would go away when I got married and settled down and lived according to the conventional woman's role and conventional sexual morality.

Two years later the cramps had gotten very much worse, and my periods were lasting eleven days. I asked friends about private gynecologists and one was recommended. He found I had endometriosis. I suggest that all women troubled by painful cramps and/or unusually long periods ask to be checked for this condition. Untreated endometriosis can lead to sterility, which can be prevented by early, proper treatment.

Many women have told us of experiences similar to the one above, so we should listen to this woman's advice and not ignore very painful and repeated menstrual cramping.

If endometriosis is diagnosed and you are planning to have children, you may want to have them as soon as possible, since some doctors believe that the ovaries or tubes may become blocked, depending on the location of the extra tissue.

Endometriosis will go away by itself at menopause or when the ovaries are removed, if no estrogen compounds are taken. Estrogen, produced by the ovaries during the childbearing years, is responsible for the building of the endometrial tissue. Treatment of endometriosis may involve removal of the endometrial cyst or some part of the affected organ; sometimes hormones are given. Although the removal of certain pelvic nerves (presacral neurectomy) is sometimes recommended in the case of severe pain, this is a highly controversial procedure.

Before making any decision about treatment, you should investigate the risks of any treatment you are considering.

Pelvic Inflammatory Disease (PID)

PID refers to a group of several pelvic infections including parametritis (affects the uterus), salpingitis (affects the tubes), and salpingo-oophoritis (affects the tubes and ovaries). It can be caused by gonorrhea, certain bacteria, or certain viruses. Symptoms of PID can include pelvic pain, increasing pain with intercourse and/or menstruation, irregular bleeding (spotting or flooding or passing clots) and occasional chills and fever. (These same symptoms also occur in an ectopic pregnancy, so a pregnancy test is a good idea whenever they are present.) Some women who have PID in its early stages (subacute) also report a sharp abdominal pain at the time of ovulation, a pain they don't usually have.

Treatment of PID can include either tetracycline or ampicillin (for about 10 days), lots of bed rest (complete rest for at least one full week is strongly advised), *no sexual intercourse for at least 2 weeks* (this allows the infected area to heal), and a well-balanced diet (it's a good idea to have friends cook for you, so you can stay in bed). Symptoms should clear up somewhat within a few days. If they don't, you will probably need a culture and sensitivity test, if this was not already done at your first exam. In this test, a smear of your cervical discharge is cultured on a plate to determine exactly what organism is causing the infection. That way you can know if you are taking an antibiotic that effectively destroys the organisms infecting you. Sometimes you will have to try a different drug to treat PID successfully.

Some women have trouble curing PID and/or problems with recurrence. Sometimes a woman may have to be hospitalized, especially when she is unable to get adequate bed rest at home. When the tubes are involved and become sufficiently scarred, infertility may result. Also, scarred tubes may increase the chance of an ectopic pregnancy.

My pelvic inflammatory disease (PID) was caused by my IUD, according to my doctor, though the IUD gave me no pain and I had no medical history which would predict trouble. The first episode of infection was cleared up by ampicillin. That was over ten months ago and I'm not well yet. When the infection came back I went through one antibiotic after another, living in terrible pain, fever and misery for over two months, while the doctor assured me that this medicine would surely cure me. Then they hospitalized me for intravenous antibiotics, looked in with a laparoscope, decided not to operate, and sent me home. Two more months later the infection flared up again. This time they took out my tubes, leaving my ovaries, since they seemed all right. After I recovered from the surgery my abdomen was swollen. I had a lot of pain and enormous fatigue, and the fever prevented me from functioning very well mentally. Everything has been complicated by the fact that I took no extra time off from work and have two toddlers, and my husband is out of town four days a week. Today, four months after the surgery, I still have intermittent pain caused by inflammation in my ovaries and uterus and by adhesions, internal scar tissue binding my organs together. I have learned not to wear trousers or do much

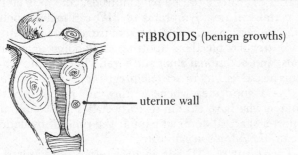

FIBROIDS (benign growths)

uterine wall

bending and to get extra rest; intercourse no longer hurts so much, but orgasm sometimes still does. I'm waiting for improvement now but don't know if this is wise, since there's no cure and some doctors say I may get better while others predict I'll end up with a total hysterectomy even if I wait six more months. It's a pretty dreadful disease.

Fibroids, Polyps and Ovarian Cysts

Fibroids

One out of four or five women of childbearing age is apt to get fibroids, which are almost always benign and slow-growing. Only a very small percentage are cancerous, and these usually can be diagnosed early with a Pap test. As cycle after cycle goes by without a conception, the uterus is less able to slough off the entire build-up of muscle-like tissues and lining each month. One possible result is that fibroids (myomas of the uterus) may develop.

Fibroids usually appear a few at a time. They can interfere with pregnancy in a young woman, either by blocking the tubes or by making a normal delivery difficult; however, most fibroids are usually too small to cause problems. Later, in older women, they can get large enough to cause menstrual irregularities—either bleeding between periods or an excessive flow. Fibroids may also push against the rectum or bladder or cause urinary tract infections. They rarely cause pain, though they may produce a feeling of heaviness in the abdomen. (See illustration.)

When women who are past childbearing age get fibroids there is usually nothing to worry about, particularly since menopause usually makes fibroids shrink or even disappear.

If fibroids become large enough to cause problems, they can be removed by myomectomy, a surgical procedure which leaves the uterus intact. However, some women, and their doctors, feel that if childbearing is over, the uterus should be taken out. There is controversy on this point (see "D&C and Hysterectomy," p. 147).

Polyps

Polyps are protrusions that grow from a mucous membrane. In women they may appear inside the uterus (endometrial polyps) or along the canal of the cervix, where they grow out of the glands lining the canal. Endometrial polyps are more common. A polyp appears long and tubelike. It is small, but easily noticeable by the redness at the tip.

If you have had suspicious bleeding or menstrual flow that seems irregular, it may be caused by polyps. Aside from an abnormal menstrual cycle, bleeding at other times—between periods or right after intercourse—may indicate that there is a growth inside the uterus. This should be checked. A gynecologist very often will discover a polyp during a regularly scheduled examination. A D&C may be done to remove polyps, and further tests may be suggested to ensure that the specimen is not malignant. Sometimes polyps can be removed in the doctor's office. (They are almost never malignant.)

Ovarian Cysts

Ovarian cysts are relatively common and often don't give any symptoms or discomfort. They are found by a bimanual pelvic exam and usually don't require any treatment at all (they disappear by themselves), though some types of cysts may have to be removed.

A cyst develops when a follicle has grown large—as one does every month during ovulation—but has failed to rupture and release an egg (see Chapter 2). Most of these cysts fill with fluid; others become solid tumors. Cysts may be accompanied by certain symptoms such as a disturbance in the normal menstrual cycle; an unfamiliar pain or discomfort at any point during the cycle; an unexplained abdominal swelling.

To determine whether a cyst requires treatment, simply waiting a cycle or two for it to disappear is one method. At one time abdominal surgery was the only way to tell whether a cyst that didn't disappear was benign, or a cancerous tumor which needed removal. Today laparoscopy or culdoscopy (see Glossary) may enable the doctor to make this examination with a minimum of interference and trauma so that unnecessary abdominal surgery can be avoided. Be sure to ask which procedure will be used and why.

Cervical Intraepithelial Neoplasia: Dysplasia and Cervical Cancer

Every woman should have a Pap smear (cervical smear test to detect presence of irregular or "abnormal" cervical cells) regularly. For certain women (e.g., DES daughters, older women), six-month intervals are urged.

The Pap smear is a useful method of screening, distinguishing normal from abnormal cells (see box, p. 144). The recommended treatments for various kinds of abnormal cells detected by Pap smears remains a controversial subject among physicians, so it is important for us to understand some basic facts about Pap tests and our options for treatment in the event of abnormal ("positive") smear results. (See p. 121.)

A positive Pap smear does not usually mean either a

Reproductive Tumors

The word "tumor" is very scary to most of us. It is part of an older language of illness that was used by many of our grandparents, both patients and doctors, to disguise the mention of cancer. Actually tumors are growths of cells which serve no purpose; however, over 90 percent of all tumors are benign and harmless. No one knows exactly why the human body produces them (they have been known since ancient times), but fat consumption and metabolism have been linked to tumor production.

When we have tumors anywhere in our reproductive organs we are almost always afraid it is cancer. The chance of malignancy (cancer) increases with age, particularly after menopause. Reproductive cancers in women occur, in order of frequency, in the breasts, the cervix, the ovaries, the body of the uterus itself and the vagina.

As mentioned elsewhere, hormones, carcinogenic substances and the malfunctioning of the immune system have all been linked to cancer, which takes many different forms but remains mysterious despite extensive research. Our fear of this disease sometimes keeps us from learning even simple facts and habits which could help us to prolong our own lives or the lives of others. This same fear makes us vulnerable to suggestions of violent and dangerous treatments, many of which are not necessary, and keeps us from exploring our options and alternatives. Throughout this section we've tried to show ways our knowledge of both health and disease can free us from the trap of letting others make decisions for us.

cancerous or even a precancerous condition. Cells that are not "normal" are not necessarily malignant. A Pap smear is not a definite diagnosis. Rather, it is an indication that some cells are changing in nature, or have changed, and that some kind of further attention is necessary.

If you have an abnormal, or positive, result, there are several steps that can be taken. First, it's a good idea to double-check a positive smear result, either by following it up with a second smear or by having a tissue (punch) biopsy done, because doctors and labs can differ in interpreting smear and biopsy results. Tissue classification can give different results from Pap smear classification. A Pap smear shows individual cells, while tissue biopsies show the "architecture" of cells—how they are put together.

There is no need to panic or be afraid when smears or biopsies show Class 2, 3 and even 4 conditions. Don't

What Are Pap* Smears?

The primary descriptions are "negative," meaning no abnormal cells are present, and "positive," meaning some abnormal cells are present. There are basically five classifications for the results of Pap smears. They are:

Class 1: all clear

Class 2: inflammation, irritation, infection, or mild dysplasia

Class 3: borderline dysplasia (non-malignant abnormal cell growth), or pre-malignant, or both

Class 4: highly suspicious for malignancy or carcinoma in situ—that is, the cells have malignant properties yet are confined to one area of one level of tissue. Twenty percent of diagnosed carcinomas in situ become invasive carcinoma in 7 to 10 years.

Class 5: positive for malignancy

It's very important to understand that both laboratories and doctors vary in describing or naming these classifications. Often the distinctions between the different kinds of cells are unclear. The quality of lab work is very uneven, and some labs are not as meticulous as others.

*Pap is short for Papanicolaou, the physician who developed the test.

rush (or be rushed) into thinking that you must have a hysterectomy (removal of the uterus) or that you are about to get cancer.

If you have a Class 2 Pap smear, you might have some sort of cervical infection or irritation which causes cells to change in character. Treatment can be merely watching (Pap smears every 3 to 6 months) or some form of appropriate medication. Sometimes the condition disappears by itself.

If you have a Class 3 Pap smear, it is wise to have a tissue biopsy done. The abnormal cells may be only on the surface and can often be cauterized away. While you are statistically unlikely to develop "invasive" cancer— that is, the cells will probably not become malignant and attack other cells—it is not known whether or not dysplasia becomes carcinoma in situ. Some women might even prefer to do nothing—what's wrong with having abnormal cells if they are not in themselves malignant?—and just wait and keep watch for changes.

One current treatment for Class 3 condition is a new method of cauterization called "cryosurgery," which "freeze-burns" (cold-cauterizes) away the abnormal cells.

This is an office procedure that takes about ten minutes and is painless except for cramping afterward. Many traditional doctors believe that a Class 3 diagnosis calls for "conization," or cone biopsy (see illustration). (Cone bi-

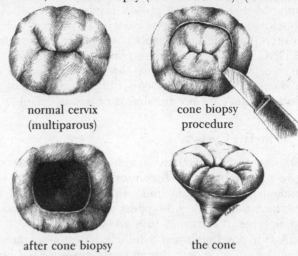

normal cervix (multiparous) cone biopsy procedure

after cone biopsy the cone

cone biopsy

opsy is a cone-shaped excision of the affected area of the cervix, and is considered a serious procedure, requiring hospitalization and anesthesia.)

If you have a Class 4 Pap smear, you might have severe dysplasia that is not malignant at all, or you might have carcinoma in situ. Cone biopsy is usually done to diagnose a Class 4 condition more accurately. Because it removes the affected area, it can turn out to be a successful form of treatment as well. Other treatments are various forms of excision and, finally, hysterectomy. Hysterectomy can be a welcome relief to some women.

Cone biopsy is also the diagnostic tool and sometimes the treatment for Class 5 malignancy, or invasive cancer, if the area affected is *very limited*. Hysterectomy, however, is the treatment most satisfactory to doctors (see "Hysterectomy," p. 147). There are cases where the malignancy has spread from the cervix to surrounding glands and tissues. This kind of development is extreme.

Just because we have the technology available for diagnosis and treatment, does that mean we have to rush into treatment? Medical controversy rages around treatment of both Class 3 and Class 4 conditions. Many doctors believe that treatment for carcinoma in situ should be immediate hysterectomy. Others believe that it is acceptable not to intervene right away. If a woman who has not yet had children and wants them develops carcinoma in situ, she can conceive and bear a child or two. The condition warrants careful watching; women who make this choice do so with the possible risks in mind.

There's also a disagreement among doctors as to whether dysplasia is an intermediate step in the development of malignancy. Does dysplasia predispose cells toward malignancy? Does dysplasia cause malignancy? Some doctors believe that though there might be a statistical correlation between dysplasia and malignancy, many cases of dysplasia do not result in malignancy and thus should not be treated as though they might; the condition would be watched closely but not immediately interfered with. Other doctors would disagree with any waiting, and treat cases of abnormality right away just in case they might fall into the percentage of dysplasias which do become malignancies. It is not known why some dysplasias become malignant. Because these different medical opinions and attitudes determine the kind of treatment we receive, it is important for us to become aware of them.

The cause of cervical cancer is not known. It is connected with intercourse. Some people believe that *early* intercourse increases one's chance of getting it; others say that *frequency* of intercourse is also a factor. Having numerous sexual partners might also increase one's chances of getting it. Cervical cancer is thought by some to be caused by a virus—genital herpes is one virus suspected. In general, the incidence of cervical cancer has gone down since 1920, perhaps because our vaginal hygiene is better, or simply because more people have bathrooms and running water (it is easier to keep clean if running water is available). Yet it's a fact that among women who are economically poor and do not have access to good preventive medical care the incidence of carcinoma in situ and invasive cancer is high, usually occurring at a much earlier age than in middle-class women.

This March I went for my routine gynecological checkup. I felt in perfect health and was not expecting anything to be wrong. Three days later the clinic notified me that my Pap smear was "positive," or abnormal. I made an appointment to see my doctor again.

For several minutes I was powerfully, irrationally terrified. (This reaction is common to many women because we know so little about what an abnormal Pap smear means.) Then I called a friend, we talked, and I felt calmer. Still, I remained upset.

During the following weeks, as I spoke with other women, I was amazed to find out that many women have positive Pap smears. I also found out the crucially important fact that "positive" does not necessarily mean either cancerous or precancerous.

When I went back to the clinic, my doctor stained my cervix and looked at it through a magnifying glass called a colposcope. I saw my cervix in a mirror he held up. He then took cervical "punch" biopsies (small pieces of tissue) from three parts of the affected area, which looked small, and sent them to a lab for analysis. Results came back a week later and showed I had a level 3 classification.

Cryosurgery was done in the examining room. The doctor explained the procedure carefully. It was painless *except for slight uterine cramping as my uterus contracted from the cold. The process took ten minutes. Afterward, for three or four weeks as the area healed, I leaked fluid vaginally and had to wear a tampon. I wasn't supposed to have intercourse for two weeks, and for the two following weeks my partner had to wear a condom to prevent infection. Eight weeks after the cauterization a second cauterization is necessary. (Some doctors prefer to do one cautery right after the other.) Then, for a year, I will have a Pap smear every three months. It is possible that the abnormalities will disappear for good. It is also possible (a 10 percent possibility) that they will recur.*

My moods were low during those first few weeks. I felt angry that something was physically wrong with me. I was angry and sad that my new-found feelings of sexuality were undermined by (1) my awareness of this problem and (2) the fact that I couldn't have intercourse for a while. I feared irritation or infection if I had it too soon. To top off my depression, when I could finally make love, I got a urinary tract infection. A possible side effect of cryosurgery seems to be that the acid balance of our vaginal secretions is changed, that the dead cells create more chance for bacteria to collect, and we are more susceptible to urinary tract infections.

As a positive move, I have begun to gather information about cervical cell abnormalities. It is a complicated and sometimes controversial subject. Yet there are some basic facts we can all easily understand.

In several days I'll have my second round of cryosurgery. I've been told by a cytologist and by several doctors that it is the "best" treatment for Class 3 dysplasia. I wonder if that's true. I vacillate between wanting to trust my doctor and his treatment and questioning it. My eight weeks between cauterizations are up; I have just begun my learning, and I've made the decision to complete this round of treatment. Hopefully no more will be necessary. I definitely don't feel in crisis. Yet I have a "hurry-up-and-get-it-over-with" urge that I think is exaggerated in many of us and compels us to submit to more radical treatment than is appropriate. Why do we have this fear, this crisis reaction? The suggestion of a threat of cancer is upsetting, even when we hear that cervical cancer takes ten to fifteen years to develop. Why the hurry? Part of our upset is fostered by the medical profession. This crisis training often orients a doctor toward less careful analyses of test results and more radical, hurried solutions than are necessary in some cases. (Many unnecessary hysterectomies have been performed because of mistakes in diagnosis.) I respect doctors' skills, yet I urge them to share their knowledge with us, discuss alternative diagnoses and treatments, and help educate us away from irrational and inappropriate fear toward intelligent, patient and careful attention to the problems we have.

Uterine and Ovarian Cancer

CANCER IN THE LINING OF THE UTERUS, or endometrium, is quite rare, but is most common in women who have undergone menopause. Bleeding is the most common symptom, and a D&C is usually done first. If cancer is present, a hysterectomy is usually done, although some doctors prefer to use an internal radium treatment first. Synthetic estrogen is also a factor. (See Ch. 17.)

Post-menopausal, obese and diabetic women are especially prone to cancer of the corpus (body) of the uterus. This condition tends to run in families, and *delayed menopause, with irregular bleeding, is sometimes associated* with it. Such women should watch closely for abnormal bleeding, since a Pap smear often fails to detect this form of cancer. Treatment is the hysterectomy.

OVARIAN CANCERS are relatively rare, about 1 percent of all cancer cases, and are more common in older women, especially those between forty and fifty. There is also an increased risk of ovarian cancer for infertile women and for women who have ectopic pregnancies which result in ectopic endometrial tissue. (Women with IUDs may have a slightly higher rate of ectopic pregnancies.)

While removal of the ovaries (*oophorectomy*) has been suggested and even carried out in order to prevent ovarian cancer, the possible risks and side effects of this operation may not justify it. For example, oophorectomy increases the risk of hypertension and arteriosclerosis. (See "D&C and Hysterectomy" for major operative risks.)

Vaginal Cancer

Until 1970 vaginal cancer was one of the rarest human cancers, virtually unknown in women under fifty. Since then, it has been identified in almost 400 young women (including some preadolescents), almost all of whose mothers were given diethylstilbestrol (DES) during pregnancy to prevent miscarriage. Tragically, it was known as early as 1953 that DES, a synthetic estrogen, did not prevent miscarriage; but many obstetricians continued to prescribe it for this purpose, even after the first link between DES and vaginal cancer was demonstrated in 1970. Vaginal clear-cell adenocarcinoma is fundamentally a new, iatrogenic, disease in world history.

If you were born after 1940, you may be a DES daughter, and that possibility should be investigated. Check the records of your mother's obstetrician or pharmacist, and contact the hospital where you were born to see if records remain. Your pediatrician might also verify a DES exposure. In most states your legal right to your medical record in a clinic or hospital has been thoroughly established, but you may have difficulty getting it. Legal pressure may be needed to obtain records from private physicians. (See "Our Rights as Patients," in Chapter 18.) Since these records may be lost, destroyed or falsified, a practitioner experienced in working with DES daughters can usually detect whether exposure was likely. Though malignancy has not yet appeared in males, DES sons may be at increased risk for sterility and other less serious genital abnormalities, such as epididymal cysts. A urologist's exam might reveal these changes in males.

Diagnosis

There is great disagreement on the proper type of follow-up exam for DES daughters. A Pap smear alone will not detect DES exposure or vaginal adenocarcinoma. In *addition* to the routine pelvic examination and Pap smear, a good DES exam will usually include colposcopy. The vaginal and cervical area is often painted with an iodine stain (Schiller or Lugol test) which highlights some types of abnormal cells.

Although very few DES daughters are expected to develop cancer, the DES-exposed must be examined regularly throughout their lifetimes. The oldest DES offspring are in their mid-30s, and we have no way to know what risks might be posed throughout the whole life cycle.

For most DES daughters, a proper exam will detect benign (noncancerous) conditions that are quite unusual in non-DES-exposed women, but which may be considered almost "normal" for DES daughters. Among these conditions is *adenosis*, in which the glandular cells usually found inside the cervix grow onto the outer cervix or in the vagina. Many DES daughters have extra folds of tissue around the cervix, sometimes called "rings," "hoods," or "collars."

Treatment

Since DES conditions are so new and poorly understood, all treatments are by definition experimental. Unless a DES daughter has actually developed cancer, she probably needs no treatment. Still, some doctors are using various techniques and technologies on benign conditions in the hope of preventing possible future cancers. Laser therapies and cauterization *may* be useful for some women. Other treatments, such as surgical excision, radiation, and progesterone suppositories, have serious side effects and are of questionable value. Some doctors believe that contraceptive jellies provide a more acidic, "healing" environment for a DES-exposed cervix.

Obviously DES-exposed daughters should avoid unnecessary exposure to DES or related synthetic estrogens, and should insist on receiving regular exams by knowledgeable practitioners. DES daughters who demand their rights to information and medical care, and who look out for their general health (see section I of this chapter) have an excellent chance to *remain* healthy. It is often helpful to seek support from other DES-exposed women.

D&C AND HYSTERECTOMY

Dilatation and Curettage (D&C)

A D&C may be performed for many reasons. As a method of abortion, it has been largely replaced by the suction method. It may be performed for infertility (some doctors question its usefulness) and to prevent the spread of infection following an incomplete abortion or delivery. Some doctors perform one routinely before most major gynecological operations. It is also used to diagnose cancer of the uterus and fallopian tubes, the cause of abnormal uterine bleeding or discharge, or a pregnancy outside the uterus. Sometimes a cone of tissue from the cervix is also removed (conization). This may lead to complications in future pregnancies.

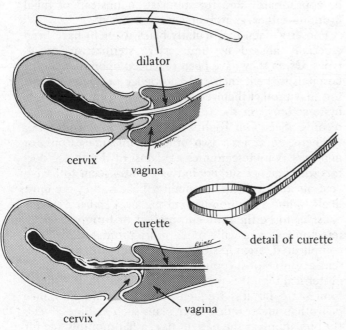

dilator and curette, instruments for a D&C

In a D&C the cervical opening is first enlarged (dilated) by inserting several probes of increasing size. Care must be taken to keep from puncturing the uterus. The womb is then gently scraped with a curette, a metal loop on the end of a long, thin handle. If possible, avoid general anesthesia. Recuperation takes from six hours to two days. During this time there may be some bleeding.

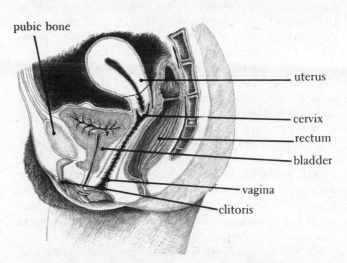

PARTIAL HYSTERECTOMY (*uterus tipped to show line of surgical incision; ovary hidden*). *After surgery the cervix and the stump of the uterus remain, requiring regular Pap tests.*

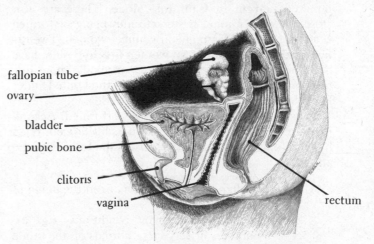

COMPLETE HYSTERECTOMY. *Removal of complete uterus, including cervix (ovaries and tubes are attached to top of vagina).*

Hysterectomy*

Hysterectomy means surgical removal of the uterus. As women, we use the term a lot, without being exactly sure whether it also means removal of the ovaries and tubes (that is *pan-hystero-salpingo-oophorectomy*, not a "complete hysterectomy," as it is sometimes wrongly called). Look at the diagram above, the uterus being removed but the cervix remaining. This is a "partial hysterectomy." The ovaries and tubes are left, and the woman continues to ovulate each month, but there are no more menstrual periods. Another procedure also removes the cervix.† In a more extreme procedure, called "radical

*An excellent new pamphlet, *Hysterectomy*, by Suzanne Morgan, is now available (see bibliography).

†Whether or not the cervix is left, a Pap test every six months is still important.

total hysterectomy," the cervix and upper portion of the vagina are also removed. (This usually is done only in the case of cervical disease.) Hysterectomies may be done by abdominal incision, or through the vagina, which eliminates an abdominal scar. This latter procedure has a much higher rate of complications, however.*

Hysterectomy is major surgery, and its long-term effects on the health and life expectancy of women are not known. Like other procedures involving the removal of a body part and with the long-term outcome unknown, it should only be done after consultation with another doctor and serious discussion with supportive friends or family. When both ovaries are removed along with the uterus, a course of hormone therapy is usually prescribed. The long-term effects of this type of treatment are also unknown (see "Estrogen Replacement Therapy" in Chapter 17).

Within the medical profession there is now tremendous controversy over hysterectomy. In part, this is because the incidence of hysterectomy has risen so dramatically within the last five years—as much as several hundred percent in California alone. There are now close to half a million hysterectomies being performed each year, and increasingly on younger women. Twenty-five percent of all American women fifty and older have had one. Doctors' wives have proportionally more hysterectomies than any other group, and the United States has twice the rate of England and Sweden.

When should a hysterectomy be performed? According to many respected physicians (possibly a majority), a hysterectomy is probably necessary in the following situations:

1. A local malignancy of the cervix or in the lining of the uterus itself.
2. Symptomatic non-malignant conditions—e.g., excessive numbers of very large fibroids on the inside of the uterus (see "Fibroids," p. 142).
3. Excessive bleeding that does not respond to hormone treatments or D&Cs (see above), or in such cases when these treatments may not be appropriate for a particular woman.
4. Diseases of the tubes or ovaries which also require removal of the uterus.
5. Cancer of the uterus itself.
6. Catastrophe during childbirth (which requires removal of the uterus for the woman's survival).

Today many hysterectomies are being performed (especially on younger women) in the absence of these medical indications. In fact, several excellent studies on hysterectomy have found that at least one-third were clearly unnecessary and another 10 percent or more could probably have been avoided; the more recent studies have shown that rate rising close to 50 percent

(see bibliography). This rate of increase roughly corresponds to the rate of the decline in births.

Why are there so many more hysterectomies? In part, this is because a whole new group of gynecologists has begun recommending the procedure for sterilization, calling it "hysterilization." But their underlying argument is more subtle:

Dr. Ralph C. Wright, a Connecticut gynecologist and perhaps the most outspoken advocate of routine hysterectomy, views the possibility of cancer as fundamental. "When the patient has completed her family," Wright contends, "total hysterectomy should also be performed as prophylactic procedure. Under these circumstances, the uterus becomes a useless, bleeding, symptom-producing, potentially cancer-bearing organ and therefore should be removed. . . . To sterilize a woman and allow her to keep a useless and potentially lethal organ is incompatible with modern gynecological concepts. Hysterectomy is the only logical approach to surgical sterilization of women"*

More specifically, hysterectomies are often performed unnecessarily in the following instances: for the removal of small fibroids (instead of a myomectomy, which removes the fibroids and leaves the uterus); for an abortion (in cases where a saline or suction abortion would be appropriate); and for sterilization (instead of tubal ligation—either laparoscopic or traditional).

Poorer women (particularly black women) have been especially abused by unnecessary sterilization of all types. Often they have been practiced upon in teaching hospitals without their full knowledge or consent. Doctors may protect themselves by writing "Patient *requests* hysterectomy" in the record. Ask to see your medical records. (See "Our Rights as Patients" in Chapter 18.)

There are at least two other significant reasons for unnecessary hysterectomies: (1) Most of the 75,000 doctors who practice surgery in this country seem to have a "cut out the problem" mentality. That is, they are most likely to find a solution by "cutting away" whatever they consider to be the problem, present or future. (2) Hysterectomies are usually much more profitable than less complicated, often less dangerous procedures and represent a source of income to compensate for the loss of obstetrical fees. It is probably no accident that hysterectomies are far less frequent under prepaid insurance plans than under indemnity† plans such as Blue Shield. (In prepaid plans the patient pays a flat monthly fee for a full range of medical services, with neither doctor nor hospital profiting from individual services. See "HMOs," p. 347, and "Group Practice," p. 347, in Chapter 18.) Hysterectomies are expensive operations, in terms of both physician's fees and hospital costs, since

---

*E.g., a ureter can be accidentally severed—see p. 148.

*Quoted in "The Greening of the Womb" by Deborah Larned in *New Times* (December 27, 1974).
†Indemnity means coverage for a certain set of specific conditions for a flat annual fee (similar to fire, theft and accident insurance).

both anesthesia and surgery are involved. The average cost varies from $1500 to $2000, about five to seven times the cost of a tubal ligation.

A look at these figures shows that most hysterectomies are being performed as part of private practice, where the decisions are made between the doctor and the woman alone; often no other physicians are involved. We have to ask why women are so willing to risk their lives in surgery and what arguments their doctors use to persuade them to accept such surgery.

Risks and Reasons

First, just knowing that so many other women are having or have had hysterectomies is probably comforting to many women. What most women do not know is that the death rate from hysterectomy is fairly high, about 1 in every 1600 each year. We are playing an enormous gambling game, assuming that we will not be the ones who will die unnecessarily from either the complications of anesthesia or the shock or hemorrhage which can accompany major surgery. (For anesthesia risks see footnote, p. 129.)

Although the lure of avoiding cancer is often held out to a woman by doctors to persuade her to consider a hysterectomy, there is rarely any mention that the death rate from hysterectomy in any year is *ten times* that from uterine or cervical cancers (which can often be prevented through regular checkups and Pap smears).* (See "Neoplasia" under "Uterine and Ovarian Problems.") Sometimes hysterectomies are praised as a 100-percent-effective sterilization method. However, the complication rate in hysterectomies is ten to twenty times the complication rate in tubal sterilizations (which have a failure rate of only 1 to 2.2 percent).

One of the more common complications of a hysterectomy is that a ureter may be accidentally severed. If repaired during surgery, the ureter is somewhat narrowed and may cause urination problems. However, if this mistake is overlooked, after surgery urine will pass into the abdominal cavity.

Probably many women consent to hysterectomies because there are so many risks, side effects and problems with almost all methods of contraception. Also, many of us are told by obstetrician-gynecologists that we are at "high risk" of complications and birth defects if we become pregnant past a certain age. This age has dropped from thirty-five to thirty, and some doctors even discourage younger women from having children.

The most difficult risk to measure is the psychological outcome of hysterectomy. All human beings react to the loss of any part of the body, even though some handle this kind of loss better than others. Losing those parts of our bodies that are uniquely ours as women, such as our breasts or uteruses, is bound to have an impact, whether or not we are as prepared as we might be. Some women

*It is important to understand that the risk of hysterectomy death is in any given year, whereas the risk of cancer death is in your lifetime.

seem to experience nothing but relief, especially if the hysterectomy has eliminated some serious problem or pain. Others express a feeling that they are not themselves, or have been robbed of something. It also matters how a woman has lived with her body; how she feels about menstruating, birth control and childbirth; and what her fears of cancer are. Sometimes a hysterectomy looks like an answer to all these problems at once, both to a woman and to her doctor. Afterward it may become clear that only physical frustrations have been eliminated. Women who have a variety of roles in life seem to be less devastated than women whose sole role has been wife and mother.

Recuperation

I personally was delighted to part with my uterus, but I wonder about women who are still interested in more children or who equate fertility with personal worth. When these women have hysterectomies and then find themselves on the same floor in a hospital with new mothers and babies, how do they feel? This seems to be general hospital practice, and while probably practical, it strikes me as cruel.

While women are frequently depressed by hysterectomy, their symptoms are not always recognized promptly. Only a few are referred for psychiatric help, usually after some time. As with natural menopause, doctors often prescribe tranquilizers (or even more habit-forming drugs) routinely, but rarely encourage supportive psychotherapy at the same time, which should be regarded as poor medical practice. Tranquilizers taken together with estrogen therapy may produce side effects, yet many physicians routinely prescribe both. Also, many women are unprepared for the physical pain of recovery (which pain-killing drugs cannot completely control).

While it evidently has not occurred to the medical profession, it would be an excellent mental-health precaution if a visit to a social worker or women's discussion group were prescribed before surgery rather than afterward. It is important to learn the facts and discuss the issues *before* a decision must be made.

Recovery generally involves a four- to six-week period during which it's usually not possible to return to work. Some women seem to be ready sooner. The longer time periods may in some cases reflect depression.

Many women fear sudden changes in their looks or changes in sexual responsiveness following hysterectomy. For women whose uteruses have an active role in their sexual response, a hysterectomy may affect sexual sensations. If hormone therapy is carefully planned when ovaries are removed, there should be no dramatic changes (such as vaginal atrophy) due to reduced estrogen levels. In many cases, however, women show lowered estrogen levels even when the ovaries remain intact.

DRUGS WOMEN SHOULD KNOW ABOUT

Before we decide to take certain drugs we should know the following information, not always readily available to us:

PENICILLIN. Between 2 and 10 percent of people treated with penicillin or related antibiotics, such as *ampicillin*, have some degree of allergic reaction to them. You may develop an allergy to penicillin while you are taking it. If you have hay fever, bronchial asthma, or eczematous dermatitis, you are more likely to experience side effects. When starting treatment, if in an office or clinic, remain there 20 or 30 minutes. Otherwise have a friend handy who can help you if you have trouble. If you have any unusual symptoms after the treatment, especially if your throat or face begins to swell, immediately notify your doctor or clinic. You also have a 1 in 3000 or 4000 chance of having a "bad trip" for twenty or thirty minutes from procaine penicillin, the kind injected (but not from the other kinds). If this happens, you become agitated and excited and resist efforts to restrain you.

If you are allergic to penicillin, tell your doctor to use another antibiotic such as tetracycline.

TETRACYCLINE. This antibiotic can cause tooth discoloration and bone lesions in a fetus if used after the fourth month of pregnancy. Erythromycin can be used instead. Don't eat—and especially avoid dairy products, antacids, and iron—an hour before or after taking tetracycline. *Doxycycline*, a related drug, is also interfered with by antacids and iron.

Both *tetracycline and penicillin* can produce conditions that allow flare-ups of monilia, so preventive measures are a good idea while taking these antibiotics (see p. 137).

SULFA DRUGS OR PROBENECID. If you are of African or Mediterranean ancestry you may have an inherited deficiency called glucose-6-phosphate-dehydrogenase (G-6PD). It is found mostly among Italians, especially Sardinians, Greeks and Sephardic Jews. If you have this deficiency and take sulfa drugs or probenecid, you can develop hemolytic anemia, which may be fatal. The simple test to detect this deficiency should be given to you, if you are in this category, *before* you accept treatment with sulfa drugs or probenecid. In many cases ampicillin can be used instead, if you are not allergic to penicillin.

LIBRIUM (CHLORDIAZEPOXIDE HYDROCHLORIDE) AND EQUANIL OR MILTOWN (MEPROBAMATE). Both of these drugs apparently cause six times the normal number of birth defects when taken during the first six weeks of pregnancy.* Unfortunately these tranquilizers are too often given without sufficient medical reason—make sure you know why they are being prescribed and whether there are any alternative treatments. If you decide to take either of these drugs, make sure you also consider some type of counseling, therapy or a support group at the same time.

DES (DIETHYLSTILBESTROL, THE "MORNING-AFTER PILL," OR SYNTHETIC ESTROGEN). Since 1940, DES has been prescribed to prevent miscarriage, even though it has since been proven ineffective for this purpose. As we have discussed on p. 146, a small number of young women have developed vaginal or cervical cancer resulting from their prenatal exposure to DES.

DES is also used to suppress lactation for women who do not choose to nurse their babies. Despite numerous attempts to ban DES in cattle feed, it is still used to fatten and stimulate growth in animals raised for food. (Since DES residues collect primarily in the liver, pregnant women are warned not to eat beef liver.)

"Morning-after" prescriptions, whether given as pills or injections, contain DES or some related synthetic estrogen. Do not take morning-after contraception if you have ever had breast or genital cancer, or if you have taken it before. Exposure to synthetic estrogens probably involves significant risk for you if (1) there is a history of breast or genital cancer in your family, or (2) you have been exposed to other estrogens, as in birth control pills. Many researchers question whether morning-after prescriptions, despite their wide use, are truly effective contraceptives. As an alternative to DES, you may wait and see if you really are pregnant and then consider an abortion. In making your decision, consider your chances of becoming pregnant from one act of unprotected intercourse, and think of the known and unknown risks involved with synthetic estrogens.

RESERPINE. Long-term administration of reserpine to women with hypertension is associated with an estimated two- to threefold increase in the risk of developing breast cancer (see *Lancet*, September 21, 1974). It is wise to avoid this drug, to demand help with dietary control, and if necessary, to use instead other anti-hypertensive drugs which have not as yet been connected with cancer.

DEPO-PROVERA (MEDROXYPROGESTERONE ACETATE, A SYNTHETIC PROGESTIN). This drug has been used as an injectable, long-acting contraceptive (only for women unable or unwilling to use other contraceptives) and for various

*L. Milkovich and B. J. van den Berg, "Effects of Prenatal Meprobamate and Chlordiazepoxide Hydrochloride on Human Embryonic and Fetal Development," *New England Journal of Medicine*, Vol. 291, No. 24 (December 12, 1974), pp. 1268–71.

gynecologic and obstetric problems, such as endometriosis, although its effectiveness is questionable. Because it may be cancer-causing and may produce permanent infertility, we should carefully consider its risks before taking it.

ORAL DIABETES DRUGS—ORINASE (TOLBUTAMIDE), DBI OR MELTROL (PHENFORMIN), TOLINASE (TOLAZAMIDE) AND PYMELOR (ACETOHEXAMIDE). These drugs, often used in the treatment of diabetes, can trigger heart disease and even death. Orinase is the most widely used. Even though studies of these drugs are quite conclusive and an article in the *Journal of the American Medical Association* has recommended that they be dropped, many doctors still continue to prescribe these dangerous drugs, despite the fact that there is alternative treatment. Proper diet alone can usually control the level of diabetes for which these drugs are prescribed. (For more serious cases insulin must be used.)

CLEOCIN (CLINDAMYCIN) AND LINCOCIN (LINCOMYCIN). These are widely prescribed drugs which may cause bloody colitis (diarrhea and bowel inflammation), and in some rare cases, even death. According to Dr. Sidney Wolfe of Nader's Health Research Group,* most of the six million prescriptions for clindamycin in 1973 were for colds, sore throats, acne, ear infections and other conditions for which either no antibiotic works or a less dangerous, more effective one would be better.

FLAGYL (METRONIDAZOLE). This is frequently prescribed orally for trichomoniasis. *Women should avoid this drug.* In various tests, metronidazole has caused: gene mutations in standard test systems, birth defects in animals, cancer in rats and mice (in at least 7 different studies!). Its safety is clearly questionable along with a similar drug, tinidazole (which may soon be marketed by Ortho Pharmaceutical despite protests from Nader's Research Group in Washington, D.C.).* In no case should Flagyl be taken orally by pregnant women, or by anyone who has peptic ulcers, another infection elsewhere in the body, or a history of blood diseases or a disease of the central nervous system. Also, anyone taking Flagyl should avoid alcohol, as the combination may cause serious side effects.

FINALLY: Remember that there is *no* drug or anesthetic which is without some risk or harm to the fetus in utero, and most drugs cleared by the FDA for use during pregnancy or during childbirth have been tested on adult males rather than unborn fetuses, or on childbearing women themselves. See "Obstetrical Medications," in Chapter 14.

*2000 P St., NW, Washington, D.C. 20036. Contact this group for more information about drug risks that may concern you.

It is unclear whether this is due to the effects of unrecognized depression or to some unknown factor in the uterus's contribution to the estrogen level. (Also, the adrenals are assumed to be the sources of estrogen after a certain age—the significance of this also is still to be determined.)

In our research on hysterectomy we've become very conscious once again of how difficult it is for women to question the judgments and pronouncements of their doctors, how deeply most of us internalize their values about us and about our bodies. It is important to consider carefully whether or not to have a hysterectomy. More than one doctor (ideally of different specialties) should be consulted.

I'm in my thirties, married, have two adopted children, and although we don't have the birth control hassle, I have experienced the hysterectomy hassle—i.e., an M.D. urging a hysterectomy for what seemed insufficient reasons to me. I was lucky enough to find another M.D. who spelled out my choices to me and let me make my own decision (the diseased ovary alone was removed). I feel very strongly about patients' participating actively in their own medical decisions and treatment.

It is also critical that any man with whom you are living be aware and involved in the decision. An amazing variety of negative feelings toward hysterectomy have been reported from men of all kinds of backgrounds and ages. It would be very helpful if couples would visit together at least two doctors when a major operation is being considered. (This is often done in planning for a childbirth or other major life disruptions involving money and a time of recovery.) When there is no mate, it is a good idea for a close woman friend to go along on these visits.

If you have had a hysterectomy and feel good about it, we hope you will understand why we feel it is still vital for women to think and discuss what we've written here before they make any decisions.

FURTHER READINGS

Nutrition

Books

Duffy, William. *Sugar Blues*. Radnor, PA: Chilton Book Company, 1975. Excellent discussion of effects of sugar on our health.
Goodwin, Mary. *Creative Food Experiences for Children*. $4.00. Available from Center for Science in the Public Interest, 1757 S Street, NW, Washington, DC 20009.
A unique source book of activities for children.

Hall, Ross Hume. *Food for Nought: The Decline in Nutrition.* New York: Vintage Books, 1976. In paperback.

Excellent discussion of problems resulting from increasing high-technology food production.

Hightower, John. *Eat Your Heart Out: Profiteering in America.* New York: Cowan Publishers, Inc., 1975.

Howard, Sir Albert. *The Soil and Health: A Study of Organic Agriculture.* New York: Schocken Books, 1972.

Important report on why organic techniques improve plant quality and health. Good critique of chemical fertilizer testing procedures.

Lansky, Vicki. *Feed Me, I'm Yours: A Recipe Book for Mothers.* Wayzata, MN: Meadowbrook Press, 1978. Spiral binding.

Natural-food recipes for infants and children.

Lappe, Frances Moore. *Diet for a Small Planet.* New York: Ballantine Books, 1971; revised ed., 1975.

Gives excellent evidence that meat is an inefficient, sometimes dangerous, source of protein. Tells how to produce high-quality vegetable protein and includes many good recipes.

Lerza, C., and M. Jacobson, eds. *Food for People, Not for Profit.* New York: Ballantine Books, 1975.

Samuels, Mike, M.D., and Hal Bennett. *The Well Body Book.* New York: Random House, 1973.

Oriented toward preventive medicine, with an excellent 15-page chapter on food, "Eating Becomes You."

Science for the People (Health and Nutrition Collective). *Feed, Need, Greed— Where Will It Lead?* $1.00. Available from SFP, 897 Main Street, Cambridge, MA 02139.

Good high-school curriculum unit on world hunger and population growth.

Turner, Mary Dustin and James. *Making Your Own Baby Food.* New York: Workman Publishing, 1977. Paperback.

Verrett, Jacqueline, Ph.D., and Jean Carper. *Eating May Be Hazardous to Your Health.* New York: Simon and Schuster, 1974.

Williams, Dr. Roger. *Nutrition Against Disease.* New York: Bantam Books, 1973.

Excellent, well-documented (113 pages of reference notes) book about the relationship between nutrition and disease.

Winick, M., ed. *Nutrition and Aging.* New York: Wiley, 1976.

Articles, Pamphlets, and Other Resources

Adams, Carol. "The Inedible Complex: The Political Implications of Vegetarianism," *The Second Wave,* Summer/Fall 1976, pp. 36–42.

Bread and Law Task Force. *Tube Food: How T.V. Affects Children's Choices.* 1976. Available from the Task Force, 3 West Street, Montpelier, VT 05062. (Send $1.00 to cover postage and handling.)

Center for Science in the Public Interest. 1755 S Street, NW, Washington, DC 20009.

Send for extensive literature list on food and nutrition. Very useful materials for both adults and children.

Diet for a Small Planet. Bullfrog Films, Inc. Box 114, Milford Square, PA 18935. $295/purchase; $10/rental.

Feeding Ourselves. 1972. $1.00. Available from the Berkeley Women's Health Collective, 2908 Ellsworth Street, Berkeley, CA 94705.

Food Research and Action Center, 2011 Eye Street, NW, Suite 700, Washington, DC 20006.

Activist advocacy group. Monitors federal legislation and regulations and puts out regular newsletter.

Nutrition Survival Kit. $.50. Available from Action for Children's Television (ACT), 46 Austin Street, Newtonville, MA 02160.

Good pamphlet for children; encourages them to snack on healthy foods rather than junk. ACT, a nonprofit group, has been working to eliminate commercialism from TV, especially TV advertising.

Self-Help Action Center. 1742 W. 87th Street, Chicago, IL 60620.

Send for information on how to form direct farmer-consumer links. Their program bypasses wholesalers and retailers, bringing produce to the inner city and other areas at prices beneficial to both farmer and consumer.

U.S. Government, Consumer Information. Pueblo, CO 81000.

Send for lists of literature on food and nutrition.

Weekly Report. Community Nutrition Institute, 1146 19th Street, NW, Washington, DC 20036.

Good up-to-date resource on nutrition, especially government activity in this area.

Exercise

Henderson, John. *Emergency Medical Guide,* 4th ed. New York: McGraw-Hill, 1978. Paperback.

A very good first-aid book. If you can't locate it, the American National Red Cross *Advanced First Aid & Emergency Care* (New York: Doubleday, 1973) is fine.

Lettvin, Maggie. *The Beautiful Machine.* New York: Alfred A. Knopf, 1972; paperback, Ballantine, 1975.

Exercises for everyone, with sections on exercise for special physical problems such as varicose veins, bad necks and backs, stiff joints, etc. See also fn. p. 117.

Rush, Anne Kent. *Getting Clear: Body Work for Women.* New York: Random House, and Berkeley: Bookworks, 1973. Paperback.

This is a book for women on how to open ourselves up through therapy and role-playing, massage and relaxation.

Bookstores and libraries are overflowing with books on exercise and various sports—especially jogging. Be selective. If you settle on Joan Ullyot's paperback *Women's Running* (Mountain View, CA: World Publications, 1976), supplement it with strengthening and stretching exercises from a good fitness, dance, or yoga manual or *Exercises for Runners* (*Runner's World* Magazine, Mountain View, CA: World Publications, 1973. Paperback). Kathryn Lance's *Running for Health and Beauty: A Complete Guide for Women* (Indianapolis: Bobbs-Merrill, 1977) is also good and includes a section on exercise. Paperback.

Common Medical and Health Problems

General

Buchman, D. D. *The Complete Herbal Guide to Natural Health and Beauty.* New York: Doubleday, 1973.

Bunker, John, et al. *Costs, Risks, and Benefits of Surgery.* New York: Oxford University Press, 1977.

Center for Medical Consumers and Health Care Information. 237 Thompson Street, New York, NY 10012.

Publishes excellent bimonthly newsletter. Back issues available on breast cancer, drugs, tooth care, hypertension, X-rays and other topics. Subscription: $5/year.

Cowan, Belita. *Women's Health Care: Resources, Writings, Bibliographies.* 1977. $4.00. Available from the author, 3821 T Street, NW, Washington, DC 20007.

Howell, Mary. *Healing at Home: A Guide to Health Care for Children.* Boston: Beacon Press, 1978. Paperback available. If not in bookstore, write Beacon Press, 25 Beacon Street, Boston, MA 02108.

Jackson, Mildred, and Terri Teague. *The Handbook of Alternatives to Chemical Medicine,* 1975. $4.95. Available from Handbook, Box 656, Oakland, CA 94604. (Add $1.00 for postage; make checks payable to the title.)

National Women's Health Network. 2025 Eye Street, NW, Suite 105, Washington, DC 20006.

Publishes nine resource guides on various topics ($3 each). Send for list.

O'Donnell, Mary. *Lesbian Health Care: Issues and Literature.* $1. Available from Santa Cruz Women's Health Center, 250 Locust Street, Santa Cruz, CA 95060. Send for complete literature list.

Popenoe, Cris. *Wellness.* $5.25. Available from YES! Bookshop, 1035 31st Street, NW, Washington, DC 20007.
> Extensive annotated bibliography (1500 books) of alternative healing modes.

Prensky, Joyce. *Healing Yourself.* $2 (plus 50¢ postage). Available from Healing Yourself, Box 752, Vashon, WA 98070.
> Excellent guide to nontraditional home remedies for many problems.

Sakti Distributors, 320 State Street, Madison, WI 53703.
> Send for list of homeopathy books, many of them English and Indian.

Werner, David. *Where There is No Doctor: A Village Health Care Handbook.* $5. English and Spanish editions available from The Hesperian Foundation, Box 1692, Palo Alto, CA 94302.
> Much useful information, especially useful in rural areas.

Women's Health Collective of the Washington Free Clinic. *Help Your Self: An Introduction to Women's Self-help.* 1978, 16 pp.
> Simple, clear discussion of self-exam, home remedies for vaginal infections, and more. Send $1 to Washington Free Clinic, 1556 Wisconsin Avenue, Washington, DC 20007.

Breast Cancer

"Breast Cancer Study Finds Radical Surgery Has No Advantage over Simple Mastectomy." *The New York Times,* 30 September 1974, p. 26.

Cancer Information Service. Toll-free number: 1-800-638-6694. (Government-sponsored number.)

Cope, Oliver. *The Breast: Its Problems—Benign and Malignant—And How to Deal With Them.* Boston: Houghton Mifflin, 1977; paperback, 1978.
> Helpful guide. Discussion of controversies; emphasizes doctor/patient relationship.

Frennings, D. H., et al. "Correlation of estrogen receptors and response to chemotherapy in advanced breast cancer," *Proc. Am. Soc. Clin. Oncol.* 19 (1978): 347.

Gjorgov, A. N. "Barrier Contraceptive Practice and Male Infertility as Related Factors to Breast Cancer in Married Women," *Onocology* 35 (1978): 97–100.
> Preliminary results of study testing hypothesis that reduced exposure to human seminal factors in the early reproductive life of a woman is a risk factor in breast cancer.

Greenberg, Daniel S. "Breast X-Rays: Files Yield a Disturbing Tale," *Science and Government Report* 6 (No. 16, October 1976).

The Joint Committee on Cancer Staging and End Results Reporting. "Clinical Staging System/Cancer of the Breast," *CA-A Cancer Journal for Clinicians* 12 (1962): 195. Available in reprint, no. 0331.

Juret, P., et al. "Sex of First Child as a Prognostic Factor in Breast Cancer," *The Lancet,* 25 February 1978.

Kushner, Rose. *Why Me? What Every Woman Should Know About Breast Cancer to Save Her Life.* New York: Signet, 1977 (paperback).
> The best single book about breast cancer.

Lasser, Terese, and William K. Clarke. *Reach to Recovery.* New York: Simon and Schuster, 1972.

Lippman, Marc, and Joseph Allegra. "Estrogen Receptor and Endocrine Therapy of Breast Cancer," *New England Journal of Medicine* 299, No. 17 (26 October 1978).

Lythgoe, J. P., et al. "Manchester Regional Breast Study: Preliminary Results," *The Lancet,* 8 April 1978.
> Compares women treated by simple mastectomy and postoperative radiotherapy with women treated by simple mastectomy alone.

Macdonald, Eleanor. "Ethnic and Regional Considerations in the Epidemiology of Breast Cancer," *Journal of the American Medical Women's Association* 30, No. 3 (March 1975): 105–113.

MacMahon, Brian, M.D.; Philip Cole, M.D.; and James Brown, Ph.D. *Etiology of Human Breast Cancer: A Review.* Department of Epidemiology, Harvard School of Public Health, and Department of Obstetrics and Gynecology, University of Melbourne, Melbourne, Australia, July 1972.

Meyer, Alfred, et al. "Carcinoma of the Breast," *Arch. Surg.* 113 (April 1978).
> Clinical study finding no difference in five- and ten-year survival rates of women undergoing simple, modified radical, or radical mastectomies.

Napoli, Maryann. "Mammography for Women with No Symptoms," *Health Facts* 1, No. 3 (15 May 1977). (See Bibliography, last chapter.)

National Cancer Program, National Cancer Institute, US DHEW. *Cancer and Estrogen Use.* Special Communication, 22 May 1978. Available from the Institute, Bethesda, MD 20014.

"Review Unit Confirms Needless Mastectomies," *Washington Post,* 24 October 1978.

Siiteri, P. K., and P. D. McDonald. "Estrogen receptors and the estrone hypothesis in relation to endometrial and breast cancer," *Gynecological Oncology* 2 (1974): 228–238.

U.S. Senate, Health Subcommittee of the Committee on Labor and Public Welfare. *Breast Cancer,* 1976, hearings on 4 May 1976. Available from the Subcommittee and/or U.S. Government Printing Office, Washington, DC 20402.
> Includes extensive testimony on treatments, risks, costs, etc.

Wolfe, Sidney, and Rebecca Warner. *Mammography: A Case for Informed Consent.* November 1976. $2. Available from Health Research Group, 2000 P Street, NW, Washington, DC 20036.
> Report on radiation-exposure data received from the 28 Breast Cancer Detection Demonstration Projects.

Zalon, Jean. *I Am Whole Again.* New York: Random House, 1978.
> Personal account of reconstruction after breast surgery.

Vaginal Infections and Herpes

Corey, Lawrence, et al. "Ineffectiveness of topical ether for the treatment of genital herpes simplex virus infection," *New England Journal of Medicine* 299 (3 August 1978): 5.

H.E.L.P. (Herpetics Engaged in Living Productively). C/o American Social Health Association, 260 Sheridan Avenue, Palo Alto, CA 94306.
> A clearinghouse for lay and professional information on herpes through a newsletter, *The Herper.* $5/year, tax-deductible.

"Herpes Treatments," *The Hot Flash,* August/September 1978. Newsletter of the Santa Fe Women's Health Services, 316 E. Marcy Street, Santa Fe, NM 87501.

Kagan, Julia. "Herpes: It Can Be Treated—But Not Cured," *Ms.,* January 1978.

Kunin, Calvin M. "Sexual Intercourse and Urinary Infections," *New England Journal of Medicine,* 9 February 1978.

Phiefer, Terrence, et al. "Non-specific Vaginitis," *New England Journal of Medicine* 298, No. 26 (29 June 1978).

Santa Cruz Women's Health Collective. *Herpes.* 1977. $1. Available from the Collective, 250 Locust Street, Santa Cruz, CA 95060.
> Excellent, comprehensive booklet (20 pp.).

Thin, R. N., et al. "How Often is Genital Yeast Infection Sexually Transmitted?" *British Medical Journal,* 9 July 1977.

Cervical, Uterine and Ovarian Problems

Cryosurgery in Gynecology: Implementation and Implications. Mead Johnson Laboratories, Mead Johnson and Co., Evansville, IL 47721. February 1975.

Derbyshire, Caroline, and Robert C. Knapp. *What to Know About Dysplasia, Very Early and Invasive Cancer of the Cervix.* Available from Communications Office, Sidney Farber Cancer Institute, 44 Birney Street, Boston, MA 02115.
> Clear, informative brochure.

Fathalia, M. F. "Factors in the Causation and Incidence of Ovarian Cancer," *Obstetrical and Gynecological Survey* 27 No. 11 (1972): 751–764.

Knapp, Robert C. and Ross S. Berkowitz. "Gynecologic Cancer: Guide to Diagnostic Approach," *Hospital Medicine*, March 1978.

Hysterectomy

Braun, P., and E. Druckman. "Public health rounds at the Harvard School of Public Health, elective hysterectomy—pro and con," *New England Journal of Medicine* 295 (1976): 1–3.

Fried, John J. "Viewpoint on Hysterectomy," *Playgirl*, September 1974, pp. 135–144.

Green, J. "Emotional Aspects of Hysterectomy," *Southern Medical Journal* 66, No. 4 (April 1973): 442.

Larned, Deborah. "The Greening of the Womb," *New Times*, 12 December 1974, pp. 35–39.

Morgan, Susanne. *Hysterectomy*. 1978. 75¢. Available from the author, 2921 Walnut Avenue, Manhattan Beach, CA 90266. Also available from HealthRight, 175 Fifth Avenue, New York, NY 10010.

> The best source of information on hysterectomy to date. Covers all aspects.

Parrott, Max H. "Elective Hysterectomy," *American Journal of Obstetrics and Gynecology* 113 (15 June 1972): 531–540.

Rogers, Joann. "Rush to Surgery," *New York Times Magazine*, 21 September 1975.

Drugs and Substance Abuse*

Bottled-Up Women. $2. Available from Prudence Crandall Center for Women, Box 895, New Britain, CT 06050.

> Packet of materials on and for women alcoholics, from feminist perspective.

Brecker, Edward M., and the editors of *Consumer Reports*. *Licit and Illicit Drugs*. Boston: Little, Brown, 1972.

Burack, Richard. *New Handbook of Prescription Drugs*, rev. ed. New York: Ballantine, 1975.

> Good guide to prescription drugs and prices.

DiCyan, Erwin, and Lawrence Hessman. *Without Prescription*. New York: Simon and Schuster, 1972; paperback, 1973.

> Gives basic information about ingredients and cautions indicated, and lists side effects of certain ingredients of medicines sold over the counter without prescription.

DO IT NOW Foundation. Box 5115, Phoenix, AZ 85010.

> Publishes excellent newsletter and many fine brochures and booklets covering topics of drugs, alcohol, smoking and substance abuse in general. Send for literature list.

Graedon, Joe. *The People's Pharmacy*. New York: St. Martin's Press, 1976; Avon, 1978 (paperback).

> Good information on prescription drugs, brand-name medications, and home remedies.

Gray, Nancy. *Chemical Use/Abuse and the Female Reproductive System*. 1976. 35¢. Available from the DO IT NOW Foundation (see above).

> Covers effects of legal and illegal drugs during pregnancy (includes alcohol, aspirin, tranquilizers, etc.).

Johnson, Anita. "The Risks of Sex Hormones as Drugs," *Women and Health*, July/August 1977.

*See also childbearing section bibliography.

Lasagna, L. "Herbal pharmacology and medical therapy in the People's Republic of China," *Annals of Internal Medicine* 83 (1975): 887–893.

Long, James W., M.D. *The Essential Guide to Prescriptive Drugs: What You Need to Know for Safe Drug Use*. New York: Harper & Row, 1977.

Sandmaier, Marian. *Alcohol Abuse and Women: A Guide to Getting Help*. 1975. 55¢. Available from the National Institute on Alcohol and Alcohol Abuse, U.S. Government Printing Office, Washington, DC 20402.

Seaman, Barbara, and Gideon Seaman, M.D. *Women and the Crisis in Sex Hormones*. New York: Rawson Associates, 1977; Bantam, 1978 (paperback).

> The complete work on the topic. Includes excellent sections on "getting off" hormones and onto alternatives.

Women and Drugs: An Annotated Bibliography. October 1975. Available from National Clearinghouse for Drug Abuse Information, 11400 Rockville Pike, Rockville, MD 20852.

DES

Belden, Nancy. "The Plight of the DES Daughter: Suggestions for Government Action," *Diethylstilbestrol (DES), A Health Resource Guide, Number* 6. Available from National Women's Health Network, 2025 Eye Street, NW, Suite 105, Washington, DC 20006. (Member/ $2.00; nonmembers/$3.00).

Bibbo, Marluce, et al. "Follow-up Study of Male and Female Offspring of DES-Exposed Mothers." *Obstetrics and Gynecology* 49, No. 1 (January 1977): 1–8.

Brudney, Karen, and Naomi Fatt. "D.E.S.," *HealthRight*, Summer 1977.

Coalition for the Medical Rights of Women. *D.E.S.* Available from CMRW, 4079A 24th Street, San Francisco, CA 94114.

Greenwald, Peter, et al. "Prenatal Stilbestrol Experience of Mothers of Young Cancer Patients," *Cancer* 31 (March 1973): 568–572.

Herbst, Arthur L., et al. "Age-Incidence and Risk of Diethylstilbestrol-Related Clear Cell Adenocarcinoma of the Vagina and Cervix," *American Journal of Obstetrics and Gynecology* 128, No. 1 (1 May 1977): 43–50.

———. "Clear-Cell Adenocarcinoma of the Vagina and Cervix in Girls: Analysis of 170 Registry Cases," *American Journal of Obstetrics and Gynecology* 119, No. 3 (1 July 1974).

Mattingly, Richard F., and Adolf Stafl. "Cancer Risk in Diethylstilbestrol-Exposed Offspring," *American Journal of Obstetrics and Gynecology* 126, No. 5 (1 November 1976): 543–548.

Saber, Fay. "The DES Problem: Fashioning a Physician's Duty to Warn," *Journal of Legal Medicine*, March 1977, pp. 25–30.

Schwartz, Ruth W. "Psychological Effects of Diethylstilbestrol Exposure," *Journal of the American Medical Association* 237, No. 3 (17 January 1977): 252–254.

Testimony before the U.S. Senate Health Subcommittee—November 1971; February 1973; February 1975; December 1975. Available from U.S. Government Printing Office, Washington, DC 20515; also available from Room 4228, New Senate Office Building, Washington, DC 20515.

Weiss, Kay. "Vaginal Cancer: An Iatrogenic Disease," *International Journal of Health Services* 5, No. 2 (1975): 235–251.

CHAPTER 7
RAPE*

WHAT IS RAPE?

Webster says that rape is the "illicit carnal knowledge of a woman without her consent, effected by force, duress, intimidation, or deception as to the nature of the act." Rape is a crime against women and children (far more children are victims of rape than most of us realize), a crime which might be viewed as the ultimate expression of negative attitudes toward, and contempt for, women of all ages.

Although most of us think of rape as a clear-cut, unjustifiable sexual act forced on a woman against her will, many people, especially men (but not only men), have misconceptions about what rape is and what it isn't. In their minds "rape is rape" when it happens in an alley, when it's committed by a stranger, or when there are bruises and signs of physical violence; but for them rape is not really rape when it happens in a bed, when it's committed by a friend or acquaintance, or when a woman appears not to be physically harmed. Many of us women know that these latter rapes are just as much "real rape" as the former. More men need to understand this too.

Rape is an exaggerated acting out of some of our society's conventional ideas toward women. Women are supposed to "belong to" a man, so they often are considered "fair game," or to be "asking for it," if they are not visibly protected by a man. Women are often viewed as passive sex objects, "there to be violated." We hope that as attitudes like these change we will begin to eliminate rape and to have better treatment for rape victims—better law enforcement approaches, better medical and psychiatric care and more humane courts.

WHO GETS RAPED:
WHEN, WHERE, BY WHOM AND WHY

Children as young as six months and women as old as ninety-three years have been raped. Rape can happen to any woman—rich, poor, young, old, of any racial or ethnic background. Even the "good girl" (long a destructive stereotype in our society) can be raped.

*See end of this chapter.

The woman is nineteen, a resident counselor in a girls' dorm at a coeducational university. It is about two o'clock in the afternoon and she is in an isolated part of one of the school buildings. Her attacker is a young married man who is a lecturer at the university.

The woman is seventeen, a high-school student. It is about four o'clock in the afternoon. Her boyfriend's father has picked her up in his car after school to take her to meet his son. He stops by his house and says she should wait for him in the car. When he has pulled the car into the garage, this thirty-seven-year-old father of six rapes her.

The woman is thirty-nine, separated from her husband, the mother of five children. Her attacker breaks into the house in the middle of the night. He turns out to be a friend's husband, the father of several children.

The woman is twenty and has recently been hired for a new job. The boss asks her to come in on a holiday to help with the inventory. When she arrives, there is no one else there. Her boss, a man of about thirty, rapes her.

The woman is sixteen, a high-school student. She has a date with a college student she knows fairly well. He drives her to an isolated area and rapes her.*

As more of us realize that rape is a problem for *all* of us, we are increasingly concerned in our daily lives with preventing rapes and finding out what to do in case we or our friends should ever be raped.

As the experiences above suggest, rape doesn't usually happen in a dark alley late at night. According to statistics from the Washington, D.C., Rape Crisis Center, 50 percent of all rapes are committed in the home (over half of these cases involving forcible entry into the house). But it can occur almost anywhere—on the

*Andra Medea and Kathleen Thompson, *Against Rape*, p. 16. (See bibliography.)

street, on highways, in subways, on campus, in public buildings. Although dim lighting and isolated places may increase the danger, rape has happened at midday with people around, sometimes even watching the crime. This is just one indication of how the rape problem extends far beyond rapists: there are many who themselves would never commit a rape, but who continue to condone or accept others' rape crimes. They often blame the victims, and they see no need for significant changes in law enforcement procedures, the hospitals, or the courts. In addition, most men realize at some level that the existence of rape tends to keep women dependent on them for "protection." Unfortunately, many of these men wish to perpetuate such dependence.

We are only beginning to find out how many women actually get raped. Officials estimate that only 10 to 25 percent of rapes are reported. When estimates of the number of rapes that go unreported are combined with the rising rape rate, we find that as many as *1 out of every 3 women in the U.S. will be raped during her lifetime.* In fact, recent household surveys and those in progress have confirmed this alarming statistic. Clearly, rape has become a major social issue as well as a personally traumatic experience.

Who are the rapists? For the most part, rapists look and act like other men, so there's no easy way to tell them apart. Many are married and have regular sex lives. The rapist often knows his victim and usually plans the rape (he is not, as one of the current myths would have it, "in the grip of an uncontrollable sex drive"). Several studies have indicated that 60 to 70 percent of rapes are premeditated. Although some researchers have attempted to categorize rapists,* a great deal more needs to be learned. Some psychological testing of rapists has indicated that they tend to express more violence and rage than the "average" male, but their sexual personalities do *not appear to differ from the average male.* If true, this only makes it harder for women to identify who might be a rapist. According to one New York psychologist,

By virtue of their sex, you could say that all men are potential rapists, but that's a blanket statement. It's "normal" [our quotation marks] for men to think and fantasize about rape, but for the normal man, rape stays a fantasy. It's apparent the rapist isn't satisfied with the fantasy.†

What is it about our culture that produces so many men who rape?

What makes a young man attack a woman old enough to be his mother? Why do some rapists use brutal force in addition

*E.g., Menachim Amir (*Patterns of Forcible Rape*); The Institute for Sex Research; Murray Cohen (et al.)—see bibliography.
†Carol V. Horos, *Rape,* p. 18.

to sexually humiliating their victims? What would possess a man to rape a child?*

Many rapists and non-rapists have similar fantasies about rape, but there is an important difference between having a fantasy and acting on it. We are angry that so many men feel free to act on their rape fantasies. This is another example of how rape reflects a much bigger problem than the act itself—it reflects a prevalent social attitude toward women that continues to undermine more humane relationships between men and women.

Rapists seem to have many different motives. More studies of rapists are increasing our knowledge about why men rape. We hope such information will help to prevent rapes. Here, one rapist speaks of his own motives:

"Other people think they know why I do the things I do.
"One witch doctor [psychiatrist] I talked with told me that I rape women because I fear them and cannot adequately cope with the games they play. Another said that I am incapable of having normal sexual relationships because I view sex as nothing more than an energy release and not as a means of expressing/sharing my love for a particular woman. Another put forth the theory that I used rape to strike back at my mother.
"There's truth in what they say. I often quote them when the need arises to justify/rationalize my behavior. But there's a thing which most people, including the witch doctors, overlook. The main reason why I do the things I do is that I find rape enormously stimulating and very exciting.
"It's fun."†

There is also evidence of a significant (not surprising) relationship between alcoholism and rape. In one study at a treatment center for convicted rapists, 35 percent of the rapists were alcoholic and 50 percent had been drinking before the rape offense.‡

Some rapists need to feel powerful; some need to prove their "manhood" to themselves or to their peers; some need to "violate" another man's "property"; some need to be physically violent in order to achieve sexual satisfaction; some feel that they are simply taking their "due" from girl friends, dates, or acquaintances. None of these reasons can justify the act of rape. We look forward to a time when there are fewer men with such distorted needs.

SOME OF THE PROBLEMS, A FEW OF THE SOLUTIONS

Usually a woman gets little or no support after she is

*Ibid.
†June Bundy Csida and Joseph Csida, *Rape, How to Avoid It and What to Do About It If You Can't,* pp. 32-33.
‡Rapists may plan their attack and *then* drink as an excuse for their violence. This pattern is true for battering husbands.

raped. If she goes to the police, they may be unsympathetic or insulting. When she seeks medical treatment, especially in a city hospital, it will often be insensitive or inadequate. And the laws and courts may only further humiliate a rape victim by implying that it was somehow all her fault to begin with. In some places the picture is not so bleak, especially since the creation of many rape crisis centers,* but we still have a long way to go. In addition to better treatment of rape victims, we want a society in which we can live our lives without fear or threat of attack.

Police

Many police still believe that women want or ask for rape. And they often are insensitive to the rape victim.

Two patrolmen came and asked me to tell them what happened. I could tell they were skeptical because they remarked, "Well, things certainly seem to be in order here now, what was the problem?" They treated me like a criminal; they kept asking me, "What were you wearing, were your pants tight?" They were oblivious to how upset and scared I was. I had to cry before they took me seriously.†

Everyone seemed to believe that I was lying or exaggerating. I was beginning to realize that when you open your front door to a man, it is the same as inviting him to rape you in the eyes of the police and society.‡

Some detectives view rape charges as a woman's revenge: "If she thinks she's pregnant, she'll go for a rape charge," or, "The prostitute's check bounced, so she claims she's been raped . . . ho, ho, ho."

When a woman doesn't resist, but instead succumbs to being raped in order to avoid being beaten as well, she may be assumed to have consented. In one case we know about, a detective took the woman aside to proposition her himself.

Fortunately some police departments are creating rape units staffed by specially trained police (often women), who are more sensitive and supportive toward rape victims. These units sometimes work in connection with a local rape crisis center or women's rape group to ensure the best possible treatment for every rape victim.

The Hospitals

The hospital experience, especially the pelvic exam (a "second rape" for many women), can be as upsetting to the rape victim as the crime itself.

"I waited two hours in the emergency room before anyone

*A listing of rape crisis centers all over the country may be obtained from the National Center for the Prevention and Control of Rape. See bibliography for address.
†From *Freedom from Rape*, publication of the Women's Crisis Center, Ann Arbor, Mich. See bibliography for address.
‡*Ibid.*

would talk to me. I was so upset I couldn't stop crying to answer the nurse's questions. When the doctor came in, he said, 'Oh, just another rape case—let's see if we can get this one out of the way fast.' His disinterest seemed inhuman—I didn't want him to come near me."

Very often a woman is seen and examined by an intern or resident who has had little training in the gentle art of being humane to rape victims. Sometimes the number of cuts and bruises on a woman's body is the doctor's personal criterion for judging if the woman has been raped.*

Again it's important to say that things are changing in a few places. Many rape groups and individual women have pressured hospitals to create twenty-four-hour rape units and to provide better, more sensitive medical care to rape victims. Also, more and more rape victims are going to the hospital with someone along who can give them valuable support. We look forward to a time when we shall have high-quality medical care and more sympathetic doctors.

The Courts

It is important to report rape to the police or to a rape crisis center, so that our communities, and especially women, know its frequency. But prosecuting is difficult and often humiliating. Sometimes a woman may wish to prosecute, but the district attorney decides that she does not have a "good case" (i.e., evidence of physical brutality in addition to the rape). Since the state (not the woman) officially brings the charges, the district attorney can choose not to prosecute despite a woman's wish to do so.

A woman who wants to prosecute for rape can usually expect little help from the courts. Often in rape trials the defense tries to show or suggest that a woman has a "bad reputation"—to put her character on trial rather than the offense of the defendant. (Imagine the absurdity of something similar in a robbery trial, for example.) She will often be assumed to be lying; she will have to face the rapist again; and she will have to relive the rape.

I think the trial was the worst part. When I walked into the courtroom with the detective and the prosecutor, the rapist smiled at me and called me by name. I hated the sight of him and of the jurors who were impressed with his show.

Then I described the details of what took place in my living room. It was hard to remember them because it happened so long before, and it was hard to talk because the defense attorney ripped apart everything I said and made it look like I invited and wanted the rape. Since I knew the rapist previously and had been friendly with him, I guess the jury decided that I was his property and he could do *whatever* he wanted with me. He was acquitted.†

*Horos, p. 86.
†*Freedom from Rape.*

In court, one lawyer tried to prove that no woman could be raped against her will by trying to penetrate a spinning Coke bottle with a pencil.

The laws and courts are slow to change. The laws still don't recognize that a woman can be raped by her husband. Even a woman who is separated from her husband cannot always prosecute if he forces her to have sex. Fortunately, new rape laws and/or amendments have been passed in at least 35 states.* One kind of amendment eliminates the previous requirement of medical evidence (e.g., bruises or semen) to corroborate the rape victim's testimony; another prohibits the introduction in court of evidence concerning a rape victim's previous sexual conduct, unless the victim herself offers such evidence or it is considered "vital" in a closed hearing before a judge; another "staircases" sexual offenses so that rapists will be sentenced according to the severity of their crime (many of us are reluctant to prosecute if the rapist may be sentenced harshly). Such changes in our laws not only will encourage more women to prosecute when they are raped, but also will help to change general attitudes toward rape.

PROTECTING OURSELVES AND EACH OTHER

Someday, as our society's attitudes toward women and sex change, we will have fewer rapists. Someday we will be able to send rapists to rehabilitation centers, not prisons, or to stop them from raping us by hurting them back. By developing our self-defense skills and becoming physically stronger (see Chapters 6 and 8) we will be better able to defend ourselves from most attacks. In a few places women have formed rape squads for protection. These groups may patrol the streets as a deterrent to rape; they may assist women who are being raped by fighting off the attackers; or they may help women who have already been raped. But if there are as yet no such anti-rape groups in our area, what can we do for now?

Being mentally and physically prepared may help us not to panic. Talking with other women about their experiences and getting together to practice on-the-spot fighting, running and screaming may be useful. Thinking in advance about what we would do may really help a lot (Would I try to talk to the guy? About what? Should I call the police? Would I fight?).

Some women have tried talking to their attackers, have tried somehow to make human contact. Sometimes such efforts save us from being raped or being badly hurt.

Here are some precautions against rape by a stranger, used by many women:

*See bibliography for how to obtain information on each state's rape laws from New Responses, Inc.

• We can get together with other women in the same neighborhood or apartment building. We can establish a signal (e.g., a special whistle) as a call for help, exchange phone numbers, find out those times we can accompany each other while walking on the streets at night, and think of any ways we can help one another to avoid situations where rapes might occur.

• If we live alone we can list only our first initials in the phone directory and on our mailboxes. Also, we might add the names of fake roommates or housemates to our mailboxes.

• On all outside doors, we can use dead-bolt locks that are harder to jimmy. We should be sure we know who we are letting in *before* we let them in.

• We can keep our windows locked, especially at night, and obtain special iron grids for windows on the first floor (this is particularly important for windows that we want to keep open).

• We should keep all hallways and entrances brightly lit. (Sometimes we need to pressure our landlords in order to get adequate lighting.) Also, we should try to have our keys ready before we reach the door.

Knowing ways to fight gives us confidence and helps us defend ourselves. Too often we don't feel able or aren't willing to hurt another person. We experience paralysis instead. One woman who was being choked saw a knife within reach but couldn't bring herself even then to stab the man who was trying to kill her. On the other hand, another woman fought off an attacker who had succeeded in killing other women, and she survived many stab wounds.

Some hints from *Stop Rape*,* a booklet put out by a women's group in Detroit: If you're being attacked in an apartment, building, or hotel, don't yell "Help," yell "Fire." If you're in an elevator, press the emergency button. If you're being followed on the street, go up to a nearby house (break a window if necessary).

Learn to recognize cars and license plates. Avoid hitchhiking, but if you have to, make sure the doors have handles on the inside and know how to get out of the car quickly. (Many of us, especially when we travel alone, no longer hitchhike, since the chances of being raped are so great.)

Knives are dangerous to use against someone stronger than you, since they can be turned against you. But if you want to use one, hold it down around your hips and use it underhand, not overhand. Practice kicking—you can reach farther with a kick. If you have one punch to land, make it count. Try distracting the attacker's attention first—throw something, a tissue or a glove. *Don't be afraid to hurt someone who's hurting you.*

Stop Rape may be obtained from Women Against Rape, 18121 Patton Street, Detroit, Mich. 48219. $1.00.

WHAT TO DO IF YOU HAVE BEEN RAPED

Medical Considerations

If you have been raped, your first instinct may be to go home, take a shower, and pretend it didn't happen. But you should get immediate medical attention. If possible, call a friend or the local rape crisis center, if one exists. This is a time when you need a supportive person near you, someone who can accompany you to a hospital.

At the hospital you have two basic concerns: 1. medical care, and 2. the gathering of evidence for a possible prosecution (you can refuse this if you are absolutely sure that you will not want to prosecute). Remember not to sign any release forms for medical information that is not directly relevant to your medical exam after the rape. Your immediate concerns are:

Injuries. There should be a checkup even if you don't feel hurt, because of the possibility of internal injuries.

Pregnancy. You can wait until six weeks after your last period, get a pregnancy test, and arrange for an abortion if necessary. Less anxiety is involved if you take estrogen, which, if taken within 48 hours of intercourse, will prevent implantation of the fertilized egg. But if you choose to take estrogen (diethylstilbestrol is the form most commonly prescribed), make sure you read Chapter 10 and the drug box in Chapter 6 to learn about the serious risks involved.

VD (see Chapter 9). You should have VD tests taken both immediately after the rape and again six weeks after.

Legal Considerations

If you wish, you can report the rape anonymously (several rape crisis centers have established this procedure with their local police departments). If you want to prosecute, it is advisable to call the police as soon afterward as possible (a friend, or sometimes the hospital, can call for you). Don't change clothes, take a shower, or douche. You should be prepared for the "investigative" experience (see above). Fortunately, new rape protocols and specially trained rape staffs are becoming more common; and as more rape crisis centers work with police rape units, police should become more sensitive to rape victims. It is often wise to check out the local courts and rape laws before deciding whether to prosecute. It can help to talk with other rape victims and sympathetic lawyers who have had previous experience with your local courts.

If you decide to prosecute, here are a few ways to improve your chances in court:

- As soon as possible, write down all the details for yourself, but don't tell anyone about this except your prosecutor.*

- Make it clear to the police, as soon as you are sure, that you want to prosecute.

- Don't be afraid of contacting the police and/or the prosecuting attorney to know about the current status of your case. If your case is going to trial, call your prosecutor for a pre-trial conference *before* the day of the trial.

- Be sure to emphasize the force used—don't be tentative. Say "I don't remember" if you are shaky or unsure. Never use the term "consent." If you were threatened with a weapon, even though not actually physically harmed, be sure to emphasize that you were "forced to submit."

- Rehearse your story thoroughly to make sure that your memory is clear and correct. It is important not to contradict yourself at different points in your testimony. Since you may not see your prosecutor till the day of the trial and may not spend more than fifteen minutes with him (it's rarely a "her"), be clear about all the details of your story ahead of time.

- Don't use words like "vagina" or seem too knowing about your anatomy (many jurors equate such knowledge with sexual promiscuity). Let the prosecutor say these words in leading you.

Emotional Considerations

A rape is usually traumatic. It is important to have supportive friends and/or counselors to talk to about your feelings. Sometimes women feel too embarrassed or humiliated to speak about their rape experience—this can be a difficult burden to carry alone. Women who have been raped and have talked about it afterward are apt to feel less guilty and ashamed, because they were able to express their anger and discuss the crime as something that happens to many women. We must remember that rape is *not our fault*. Because rape violates our self-respect, anger is a most appropriate response. We need to help one another to feel and express our anger about rape, since we can suffer a lot from turning these feelings inward. One woman who was raped was severely depressed for six months, until she could finally express her rage at what had been done to her. Many women have joined anti-rape groups to use their angry energy in positive ways.

A rape victim, and often her family, will need follow-up counseling to cope with difficult feelings. Humiliation, embarrassment, guilt, disgust, horror and anxiety—these are all possible reactions to rape. Sometimes

---

*Your lawyer (prosecuting attorney), usually someone from the district attorney's office, who tries to prove your case in court.

Counseling group at a rape crisis center

a close friend has the skills and ability to help a rape victim express and work through her feelings, but in some cases a woman should see a counselor, ideally someone who is experienced with the needs of rape victims. Hospital psychiatric departments are sometimes helpful. Rap groups, often organized by local rape crisis centers (let's start more of them!), can be a good way for rape victims to share their experiences and support one another. Women who have been raped and have had the opportunity to work through their feelings can be especially helpful to a recent rape victim. We cannot overemphasize the importance of talking to an understanding person.

The reactions of friends, lovers and family are critical for a rape victim. She needs support and understanding for what may be the first traumatic experience in her life, especially if she is a younger woman. Many fathers, boyfriends, husbands and lovers feel violent anger toward the rapist, often because they see the rape as a personal violation of themselves (this is especially true of men who view women as their "property"). When this reaction to rape is not accompanied by sympathy and support, it can be demoralizing for the rape victim. Other men are more casual and insensitive to the seriousness of the act ("Why are you so upset? After all, he didn't hurt you"). Fortunately, more and more men (and women) are beginning to understand the serious consequences of rape and are learning to be supportive and sensitive to the rape victim regardless of what their own reactions may be. In at least one area (Philadelphia) men have even organized to help stop rape (MOAR: Men Organized Against Rape). These men can help to break down myths about rape and can provide support for rape victims by talking to their male friends, their lovers and family—and also to rapists and potential rapists.

Very young rape victims have special needs. A little girl may not understand what has happened to her or that the rape was somehow a "bad thing." Her reactions depend in large part on the reactions of those around her: if everyone gets very upset, then she will be very upset; if others express strong anger toward the rapist, she may feel that this anger is directed toward her or somehow her fault—this response to anger is common in children. Whatever our own feelings about the rape of a child, we must try not to express them in ways that will only add to a child's fear and trauma.

Teenage rape victims often feel tremendously embarrassed and/or guilty. Sometimes they keep the rape a secret for many years, until they finally feel okay about sharing the experience or can no longer bear the burden alone. They often feel that they will be blamed for what happened or that "no boy will ever come near them again." Parents must try to be sympathetic and supportive to teenage rape victims, even though other feelings, of anger, dismay and self-pity, may make this difficult to do (especially for fathers).

Through the efforts of women's anti-rape groups, many significant changes in laws, social attitudes, institutional practices and community prevention programs have taken place in recent years. Finally the silence surrounding rape is being broken. In addition, the links made between accepted social behaviors and rape have spurred investigation of, and activism against, all forms of violence against women. Violence against women takes many forms—individual and institutional—and is reinforced through the media, advertising, and sex roles. For example, women are battered by husbands and lovers, and are sexually harassed at work to the point of endangering their jobs and physical safety. Clearly, all male violence against women is rooted in common factors and needs to be combatted with an understanding of the whole web.

One important thing to remember: although they can help, the police, the courts, or men will not finally stop rape. Women will stop rape.

RECOMMENDED READINGS AND RESOURCES

Books and Articles

Brownmiller, Susan. *Against Our Will.* New York: Simon and Schuster, 1975. Paperback, $2.75.
    The best documentation of the history of rape.
Burgess, Ann Wolbert, and Linda Lytle Holmstrom. *Rape: Victims of Crisis.* Bowie, MD: Robert J. Brady Company, 1974. Paperback, $6.95.
    Good discussion of women's reactions to rape and to the attitudes of the police, the courts, medical personnel, family and friends. Describes innovative Victim Counseling Program at Boston City Hospital and is especially helpful to those counseling rape victims.
Cohen, Murray, et al. "The Psychology of Rapists," *Seminars in Psychiatry,* Vol. 3, No. 3 (August 1971).
    Interesting paper which attempts to identify different character patterns among rapists. Also discusses varying responses of rapists to different rehabilitative procedures.

Connell, Noreen, and Cassandra Wilson. *Rape: The First Sourcebook for Women*. New York: New American Library, 1974. $3.95.

Contains women's personal testimony, some good essays analyzing various aspects of rape, several action proposals, and two bibliographies.

Griffen, Susan. "Rape: The All-American Crime," *Ramparts* Magazine, 10 (September, 1971), pp. 26-35.

An excellent article which explores rape in its political and social context.

Horos, Carol V. *Rape*. Tobey Publishing Co., Box 428, New Canaan, CT 06840, 1974. $2.95.

Available from the publisher and in many bookstores. A special 70% discount is available to non-profit, tax-exempt groups; books so purchased must not be resold. Good, but lacks discussion of rape as a product of our society's values. Includes rape myths, recent studies of rapists, ways to avoid rape, self-defense techniques, and the various aspects of the rape experience. The last section, with a list (somewhat outdated) of rape crisis centers, describes how to start such a center.

Russell, Dianna E. *Politics of Rape: The Victim's Perspective*. New York: Stein & Day, 1975. Paperback, $3.95.

Sutherland, Sandra, and Donald Scherl, M.D. "Patterns of Response Among Victims of Rape," *Journal of Orthopsychiatry*, Vol. 40, No. 3 (April, 1970).

Thompson, Kathleen, and Andra Medea. *Against Rape*. New York: Farrar, Straus & Giroux, 1974. $2.25.

This is an excellent, comprehensive book written by two women involved in a rape crisis center. It covers all aspects of the prevention and treatment of rape, and describes how societal values are the basic cause of rape.

Yale Law School—anonymous author. "Rape Corroboration Requirement—Repeal Not Reform," *Yale Law Journal*, Vol. 81, No. 7 (June 1972), pp. 1365-91.

Examines traditional arguments in defense of the requirement that the testimony of an alleged rape victim in a rape trial must have independent corroboration to sustain a conviction. Article concludes that this requirement is unjustified and should be abandoned.

Materials from Groups

Aegis: A Magazine on Ending Violence Against Women, c/o FAAR, Box 21033, Washington, DC 20009. Excellent bimonthly on all issues of violence against women—rape, battering, sexual harassment at the workplace, racism, sterilization abuse, etc. Subscription $8.75/year.

Fuller, William. *Rape—Cause, Elimination, Motivation*. Available from FAAR, Box 21033, Washington, DC 20009, 50¢ per copy. Includes personal and political analysis of rape from a founder of Prisoners Against Rape.

National Center for the Prevention and Control of Rape, NIMH, Room 10003, 5600 Fishers Lane, Rockville, MD 20857.

Center funds rape research, including development of bibliographies, directory of rape crisis centers, and guides to educational materials on rape. Write for publication list.

New Responses, Inc., 752 9th St., SE, #202, Washington, DC 20003. *Sex Offense Statutes by State*, 1978, $4.25. Categorical review of content of each state's criminal statutes pertaining to sex offenses, through Jan. 1, 1979; includes glossary of terms.

Bibliography: Child Sexual Abuse, 1978, 5 pp., $2. Most comprehensive to date; includes books, articles, handbooks, films, pamphlets and kits.

Self-Defense for Children: Teaching Techniques and Concepts, 1978, 85¢ per copy. Outline for programs of instruction in public schools.

Rape Crisis Center, Box 21055, Washington, DC 20009. *How to Start a Rape Crisis Center*, 1977, $4.75 per copy, bulk rates available.

Excellent, comprehensive guide for starting a new center; also covers important issues for existing rape projects, such as community education, structure, and fund-raising.

Women Against Rape, Box 02084, Columbus, OH 43202. *Freeing Our Lives: A Feminist Analysis of Rape Prevention*, 85¢ plus 40¢ shipping. Bulk rates available.

Links short-term individual prevention tactics with long-term societal change. Good discussion of importance of neighborhood organizing and group action.

Women's Crisis Center, Box 7413, Ann Arbor, MI 48107. *How to Organize a Women's Crisis Center*, $2 per copy; *Freedom from Rape*, 50¢ per copy; *Sexual Assault Counselors' Training Manual*, 45 pp., $5 per copy; *Content Outline for Sexual Assault Workshops*, $2 per copy; *Rape Education Bibliography*, 25¢ per copy. Bulk rates available.

Women's Transit Authority, 306 N. Brooks St., Madison, WI 53715. First anti-rape women's transportation service in the country; Outreach Manual in progress, including how the service was organized.

Films

If It Happens to You, Rape. EDC Distribution Center, 39 Chapel Street, Newton, MA 02160.

Rape Culture (35 min., color). Excellent film by Margaret Lazarus and Renner Wunderlich. Includes material on how men are socialized to become rapists, and on how women are socialized to become rape victims. Contact Cambridge Documentary Films, Box 385, Cambridge, MA 02139.

Rape Prevention: No Pat Answers. Convivia Enterprises, 740 Ash Street, Lawrence, KS 66044.

We Shall Not Be Beaten (40 min., b&w). Transition House Films, 120 Boylston Street, Boston, MA 02116.

A film on wife abuse.

CHAPTER 8
SELF-DEFENSE*

Developing a healthy body makes us happier, more complete women. In this violent society, learning to protect ourselves from attack is an integral part of our physical and psychological health. A *reported* rape occurs every seven minutes in America—at about the same frequency as births of baby girls. Many women must face regular beatings by their husbands, boyfriends, fathers at home. Then there are the sex murders, many more than the sensational ones by men like the Boston Strangler or Richard Speck. Every woman—whether or not she is the victim of one of these vicious crimes—knows the fear of dark, deserted streets, strange noises in the middle of the night, obscene phone calls, and the everyday humiliation of dirty remarks and gestures. Older women are the particular prey of handbag thieves, and untold numbers of children are sexually molested every year.

LEARNING TO PROTECT OURSELVES

For too long most of us have had to rely on men, money, or luck for a limited kind of "protection." Some of us, particularly working-class women, learn how to take care of ourselves while growing up—we have no choice. We're often exposed to more physical violence than middle- and upper-class women and sometimes forced into situations where we learn to use our arms and legs and to take pain—at home, in school, on the streets. Many others of us are reared in protective environments where girls are discouraged from learning to fight. As a result, we feel helpless, vulnerable, afraid, and even go so far as to question our right to defend ourselves.

We believe it's essential that women begin to take the right of self-defense seriously. Chapter 6, "Women in Motion" dealt with the need to build up and maintain strength and endurance and discussed ways to accomplish this. That strength alone, however, will not equip us to fight. Most women are afraid of pain and violence. We don't know how much we can take; many of us panic at the mere suggestion of being hit. On the other hand, we have little sense of the potential power in our own bodies—we don't know our own strength or how to

*This chapter should be read together with the ones on exercise and rape.

use it to protect ourselves, to really strike out when necessary. The physical and mental togetherness that comes from exercise and self-defense training not only teaches us this but also gives us added confidence in all areas of our lives. You find, for instance, that you can stand up for your feelings and ideas with much more assurance and determination when you know you can't be pushed around bodily.

SELF-DEFENSE TRAINING

We encourage women to learn some basic techniques of self-defense that include actual fighting. There are several possibilities. If you have time and money you can get formal instruction in a school. Check the yellow pages under "Judo" or "Karate" for schools in your area. These are almost always male-run, but you'll have a lot more female company now than a couple of years ago. Try to find one that takes women seriously. Many men instructors give women a watered-down version of karate that allows no body contact or stresses getaway gimmicks. Others cruelly say, "If you think you can do this as well as a man, try this . . ." and are physically brutal. Watch out also for ugly competitiveness, where only the best get better, women are played off against each other, or are turned into pets. To deal with the problems of the male school, it could be helpful to arrange an extra weekly (or so) women's class to work on techniques that are particularly hard or useful for women and to discuss ways of coping with the day-to-day sexism you face. There are, of course, advantages to a co-ed setup: you learn how to fight men and see that they have weaknesses, too. A lot of male instructors know a ton of useful stuff about how women can effectively fight men, and if it's a good school they should teach it to you in a decent way as fast as you want to absorb it. It may be possible to find a formal school run by a woman—a few exist now. If you decide on an Eastern fighting style such as kung-fu, for example, you may find yourself getting very excited by all the various aspects of the martial art—not just the techniques that are immediately applicable for self-defense. If, on the other hand, you are looking for a basic set of self-defense techniques, find a class that will provide them. Some YWCAs have such classes (ask for one if yours doesn't), meeting once or several times a week. These are usually less expensive than the commercial schools. In many areas women's groups have set up cheaper classes wherever they could find a good space; and, of course, you can start your own at work or in your community. If at all possible, these classes should be taught for women by women who understand where we are coming from physically and emotionally, as well as where we have to go. This is an ideal way to begin physical training—with emphasis on getting strong, limber, quick, and then learning sound self-defense skills in a supportive atmosphere—to begin building your confidence even if after a while you want to go on to the rigors of a formal school. Some older women may need classes especially designed to go at the pace best suited to them; others will feel fine in any of the classes just described. One woman we read about started at the age of sixty-two and at seventy-two had two black belts—in judo and aikido! Girls, of course, should be taught from the earliest years how to take care of themselves and then should join a class that's right for them when they are ready. The public-school system must begin taking responsibility for their training.

If there are no opportunities for you to go to a class, get a couple of books on self-defense (see bibliography) and learn some techniques from the pictures and descriptions. Try to find company to do it with.

It should go without saying that when child care is needed, everyone should help arrange it so all women can have a chance to learn self-defense. So far, this skill is much too often accessible only to young, single, white, middle-class women.

If you want to study the martial arts (and women have, in the East, since ancient times), you have many to choose from. The following outline just gives a few hints. Ask around about the different styles and schools before settling for one. Watch a class or two before signing up, and make sure the money arrangements are clear from the start. (You can always switch if you don't like it, but that is expensive and time-consuming.) Rather than recommending any one particular style, we suggest you pick the commercial school or women's class with the best attitude toward its students and the learning process.

Judo utilizes throwing, grappling, wrestling and choking techniques. It's good for dealing in close with an opponent.

Aikido is similar to judo in that it relies on the motion of the attacker. You wait for the attack and use the attacker's aggressive body motion against him by pulling, twisting, throwing, followed by locks and holds. It is a purely defensive art based on patterns of circular moves, and also emphasizes release of tension to allow a person's inner strength and energy to flow.

We have found *tae kwon do* (Korean karate), or any type of karate like it, a satisfactory form of self-defense for women. It teaches us to mobilize our entire body as effectively as possible, using a variety of striking techniques with special emphasis on kicks. That is important, since most women's legs are more developed than our arms, and we can kick farther than we can punch. Tae kwon do always combines a defensive motion (such as a block) with a fighting technique (a kick, punch, or strike) that allows you to control a sphere around you. As you learn the techniques, you can begin to use them in sparring—controlled fighting situations. The general body conditioning will build up your leg muscles tremendously, so you move solidly, with new self-assurance, in itself a deterrent to men on the prowl.

Jujitsu and some other martial-art styles train you to use combinations of judo, aikido and karate techniques in confrontation situations. This approach seems ideal, but it may not be available where you are, so if you're studying a mostly kick-punch or throwing form, try to swap a few basics with someone doing the other, if only to learn how to protect yourself against their strategy.

SOME THINGS YOU CAN DO

Whether you enroll in a formal class or set up informal training, begin right now to think about self-defense. It is a skill that can be learned, although this is a long process that will require discipline, regular practice and some physical and emotional strain—even pain at times—for most people.* It is also a matter of common sense, knowing your own strengths and weaknesses, and learning to think strategically. Practice with friends. Think through possible situations. Develop a mental image of yourself doing an effective, forceful move. What would you do if someone came up and grabbed you from behind? How would you respond if someone approached you while you were in a telephone booth? Suppose a man's hand started creeping up your knee on a subway. Take turns playing the attacked and the attacker. Work at breaking out of holds or wrestling on the floor. It is also important to spar with each other—punching and kicking (not too hard) to help break down some of the fears and inhibitions women have about striking out and getting hit. Cheap boxing gloves are wonderful for punching—you can hit to the head and get hit without fear of injury. But then don't neglect your legs—kicks to the shins, knees, groin are essential; they surprise and they hurt. Practice into a hard pillow or stuffed laundry bag. If you're not used to yelling at men, nailing them with a devastating remark or express-

---

*Building up resistance to stress and pain is an integral part of this skill, but it should progress within tolerable limits. To ensure this, keep in good shape and warm up thoroughly before each workout. If injuries occur, take care of them—see "Women in Motion," Chapter 6, "Some Final Advice." To help prevent them, warm up thoroughly before each workout.

ing your anger verbally when you would like to, do some of that—it relieves a lot of tension. To get into it, have your partner make some obscene comment, and you retort. (On your own, you can turn an object such as a pillow into a person who upsets or angers you, and tell it *exactly* how you feel and why; then go on and beat it up.) If you work out repeatedly with a friend you'll be much less likely to panic in a real attack situation, since you will have prepared yourself and built up some confidence in your ability to fight back. Fear is a deadly emotion that may keep you from remembering what you can do.

And here are a few things you can do (for a more complete list of self-defense measures, see bibliography):

On the street, especially at night and in unfamiliar surroundings, be alert at all times. Look as if you're together, even aggressive—never helpless or scared. If a threatening situation develops, don't try to ignore it as we've often been taught to do. Start assessing it as you move along quickly with an air of calm determination and direction. If things get worse, the safest response is to run, unless you're *really* confident that you can defend yourself. Head for a store, building, or lighted area where people are likely to be.

If you're caught by surprise or have nowhere to run,

you can fight off an attacker in a number of different ways. He comes at you from the front: you kick his knees (or shins), *hard*. If he grabs you before you can kick, ram your knee up into his groin. If your arms are free, use them: chop or punch at his head—temple, eyes, right under the ears, mouth, nose. If not, you can spit or bite. If he grabs you from behind, move your hips so that you can drive your elbow back into his solar plexus (the sensitive region of the stomach, under the breast bone and between the first ribs), then finish him off with a blow to the groin with the back or side of your fist. Some people advocate grabbing his balls instead, and pulling them down sharply. If this is impossible, kick back hard into his knee with your heel, then slide down the shin and stomp on his instep. Be prepared with more than just one technique—it may take a series of accurate hits to be successful. Be calm but quick, make your hand or foot *tight*,* and put your whole body into the blows while keeping your balance. Remember, in dangerous situations we often respond with a power we didn't know we had, because the level of adrenalin in our bodies

*For good fist-making as well as other hand and foot positions, check in a book with self-defense techniques or get someone who is studying a martial art to show you. The same goes for the vital body areas to aim for.

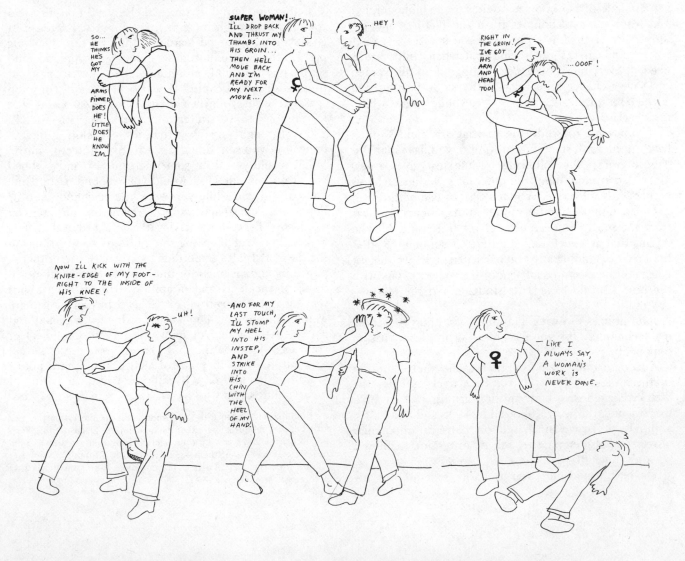

rises, speeding up our reflexes and giving us an unbelievable spurt of strength and energy.

Some women like to carry for ready use (not tucked away in the depths of a handbag or knapsack) a pepper shaker, an artificial plastic lemon filled with lemon juice, vinegar or some other burning substance, or a deodorant spray. The problem with all these is that you have to be really speedy to use them. If you hesitate, the attacker has time to disarm you and may use the object against you. Nevertheless, we know women who have warded off attacks with a spray. It is also possible to use (depending on what's available) an umbrella, handbag, brick, bottle, hammer, baseball bat, hair pick, or the like as a weapon; but this is tricky, so you should know exactly what you intend to do with it. At home, don't be embarrassed to sleep with a weapon nearby if it makes you feel better. Certain weapons, such as knives and guns, definitely require training to be used safely and effectively; check your state laws—they will probably limit your right to carry certain weapons on your person or to keep them in your apartment or house. Whatever kind of counterattack seems best, do it with a yell—not a scream for help, but a loud, blood-curdling battle cry. This will give you a psychological boost and will scare your attacker, throwing him off guard and improving your chances for escape. Once you're free of his grasp, don't hang around to see how he is. Run, fast. If you're at home call friends to help, or the police. If necessary call from next door.

Unfortunately there may be more than one attacker, and then you really have to keep your cool. Break away through the weakest link in their approach and run. As we said in Chapter 7, yell "fire" rather than "help," knock on someone's door, or throw a rock through a window to attract attention. Verbal tactics sometimes work: one friend of ours talked off a bunch of guys by telling them very matter-of-factly about how shitty her day had been and now here they were bothering her to top it all off. Another friend went into a "crazy" act and got rid of two men following her. Of course it's safer to travel in twos or groups, but nothing is foolproof, so discuss with your companions what you might do together in a crisis. Fighting in pairs or more has to be planned and practiced, too.

Your use of these techniques depends upon your being able to move quickly and effectively. Clothes often inhibit movement. It's easier to defend yourself if you're wearing pants (not too tight) and shoes that stay on your feet when you kick and run. Clothes like these attract less of the kind of attention that may lead to attack and will also give you more confidence in your ability to take care of yourself.

Hitching is dangerous. If you absolutely have to, much of the same general advice is applicable. Avoid late-night hitching, or do it in pairs; and try to steer clear of sparsely populated areas. Be careful. Don't get into the back seat unless there's a back door. Be cautious about cars that have more than one man and no women. Remember, you can refuse rides, and you absolutely should if your instinct tells you that an offer may lead to trouble. If trouble develops, you can hit with fists, elbows, knees; scream, cause lots of commotion, grab the ignition key and then try to get out of the car. Assess the situation—the car speed, the amount of traffic—and do what you decide is best—quickly. Hitching hassles could be cut way down if women with cars would pick up their sisters!

In all bad situations you have to decide how aggressive or defensive you want to be. Legally you have the right to stop a physical attack (after trying to escape)—not, though, to injure the attacker beyond what is necessary to stop him from injuring you. But since the law does not concern itself with the anger of oppressed people or our lack of fighting skills, it rules against the force we may feel compelled to use against the brutal, degrading and low-level harassment that endlessly comes our way. In some situations you can pick your time and place. Be aware of resources the man might have to find you later and retaliate, of who else is around, and so forth. It's one thing to let loose at a single stranger in a park miles from home, if you're feeling confident of your ability to handle him, and quite another to take on a gang of neighborhood boys or your drunken husband. Other times there will be no choice: you do what you have to do—as best you can—no matter how it turns out. Women who fight back, as some always have and more and more are starting to do, are forcing the white, male court system to deal seriously with our right to meet violence with violence in our own defense. One woman, Inez Garcia, despite her brave determination to struggle and the support of women's and other progressive groups, was sentenced to jail for five years to life last October (1974).* More recently (August, 1975) the trial of Joan (pronounced Jo-ann) Little, a poor black woman in North Carolina, had a surprising and encouraging end.† Although the state threw the book at her—including a first-degree murder charge and a bail of over

*Since this was written, Inez won a retrial and was acquitted in 1977!

†Joan's ordeal has been something of a phenomenon for everyone concerned with social change, bringing to a head as it does the issues of sexism, racism, poverty and prison conditions in this country. She was originally arrested and convicted of a minor burglary charge, locked up in a small county jail in North Carolina—the only woman there. One night very late, a white jailor came with an icepick to collect on the sexual favors he thought she owed him. In the ensuing struggle, she managed to grab the weapon from him, stab him repeatedly, and escape. Just as the state was about to declare her an outlaw, she turned herself in. The unbelievably high bond was set and the murder charge leveled, which would, if she was convicted, place her on death row under the current state law! The case against her was so flimsy it took the jury (half black) only a little more than an hour to pronounce her innocent. She isn't the first or last woman who may very probably have been shipped off to an out-of-the-way jail purposely for the prison guards' pleasure. (See also Chapter 7).

$100,000—she was acquitted. Her own strong, courageous personality coupled with the efforts of many people, collective and individual, black and white, helped make the outcome what it was. While such victories are exciting and, we hope, precedent-setting, it's a big war we're fighting. We must continue to help support women in these situations in all ways possible.

Not all violence comes from men. Women do, of course, fight one another, and we will as long as we are angry, frustrated, afraid, confused and separated from each other. People lash out most often at someone they can hurt without fear of reprisal—in the case of women, that usually means other women and children. Middle- and upper-class women can also sometimes use their economic and social status against men of other classes and races. All responsible self-defense training should include political education to help us figure out where our anger should *really* be aimed, so that power and fighting skills won't be used in destructive ways.

Self-defense for women should never become only a matter of individual skill at a martial art, useful as that is. The more women get together and develop collective ways of supporting each other, the safer our lives will become. In our communities, we can join together to demand (as some already have) better street lighting; good, frequent public transportation; the right to keep dogs in our apartments; the best locks for doors and windows, installed at the landlord's expense (which should be a part of the housing code in every town and city); good self-defense classes; shelters for battered women; and rape crisis centers. In addition, we must get to know the women in our neighborhoods and perhaps then make up a telephone chain for our apartment building or block so that in case of danger we can band

Karate demonstration at International Women's Day, March, 1973

together to expose any men who are preying on women. Going places in pairs and groups is a lot better than going alone. Older women could pressure the city to provide escorts to the bank on pension-check day. (Never carry your money in your handbag, anyway, always in your clothes.) At work we can demand that union and management take our protection seriously and take responsibility for self-defense classes and special transportation, particularly for women who work late hours or graveyard shifts. The police and courts can be pressured to become more understanding of our problems—but we must *never* rely on them for our ultimate protection. Third-world women, of course, have always known that they usually get more trouble than help from racist, as well as sexist, police and judges. Most violence to women comes from men they already know, especially men they live with. For these women the most important and courageous act of self-defense is to contact a counseling group or refuge for battered women.

At every opportunity we should point out the ways our society encourages men, from boyhood on, to make sex and violence an inseparable pair, and to see women as sex objects up for grabs, as helpless victims, or as bad, wayward and sometimes uppity creatures who have to be punished and kept down. If men must be taught a whole new sense about human relationships, we women must grow up to be strong and self-reliant people aware of our needs and resources, ready to stand up for ourselves and each other, anytime, anywhere.

READINGS AND RESOURCES

Belden, Jack. *Gold Flower's Story.* Somerville, Mass.: New England Free Press. Reprints from Jack Belden's book *China Shakes the World,* 1949, now available in new ed. from Monthly Review Press, 62 W. 14th St., New York, NY 10011. Paperback.

    Gold Flower is the sad but totally inspiring story of how, during the early days of the Chinese Revolution, Gold Flower and other peasant women like her banded together through Women's Associations and began to liberate themselves from their oppressive families—in particular from the endless abuse of their cruel fathers, husbands and fathers-in-law.

Sanford, Linda Tschirhart, and Ann Fetter. *In Defense of Ourselves: A Rape Prevention Handbook for Women.* Garden City, N.Y.: Doubleday, 1979. Paperback.

    This is an excellent self-defense manual for women. It combines clear pictures (with text) of physical self-defense techniques, with very useful exercises in such areas as self-concept, "what if," body language, eye contact, tone of voice, and verbal response. The authors analyze the violence against women in our culture and how we are socialized to be victims of it. There are short chapters specifically about women of different ages and races, lesbians, battered women and others.

    If your local bookstore doesn't have it, get them to order it. This book is especially great for women wanting to begin some kind of self-defense training but it is also informative for those of us long into it.

Women's Martial Arts Union, Box 879, New York, N.Y. 10024.

    Write to them for good material on (1) how to choose or set up a self-defense class or a martial arts course; (2) basic self-defense information, such as precautions for home and on the street, on public transportation, in your car, etc., and self-defense techniques to use if necessary; (3) any new material they may have out on self-defense.

CHAPTER 9
VENEREAL DISEASE

INTRODUCTION

There is at the present a venereal disease (VD) epidemic so widespread that the incidence of the most common of these diseases is second only to the common cold. The possible complications, especially for women, are serious. We want to talk about more than the bare facts that most public sources of information give. We want to help people to confront their problems in facing what VD is and in dealing with it. Therefore, we must explore why VD is still difficult to face and talk about. We need to know how our feelings about sexuality, our conventional morality, and our social problems interfere with coping with the problem of VD. In addition to pointing out problems involved in getting treatment, we will offer suggestions for changes as well as things we can do right now. There are simple ways we can help prevent the spread of VD.

Since VD is hard to talk about, it's sometimes difficult to find information about it. Until recently VD, like sex, was a hush-hush subject. Even now, if we can get information, we still aren't always confident we know enough about it.

Nowadays kids are finding out everything. I was kind of slow about learning things, so I asked my girlfriend about it. And then I asked my mother if it was true. And what did I get? A slap in the face! That's all I got, because she didn't want to answer me.*

So what does it mean to confront VD? It can be awkward, scary, depressing, troublesome, upsetting, embarrassing, confusing. Few people enjoy thinking about unpleasant things, especially diseases. Most of us have heard at least one scary story about it. VD is particularly difficult because of the way it ties in with sex. It's one of those telltale signs, like pregnancy. Say what you want, you had to get pretty close to catch it. If we have difficulty talking about sex or facing our sexuality, we will certainly have difficulty talking about VD.

*YWCA, National Board, *Attention Is Needed, Action Is Called For: Teen Women Tell About Their Needs,* 1974, p. 26. Available from YWCA Resource Center on Women, 600 Lexington Ave., New York, N.Y. 10022, for $2.

One day while I was getting my car fixed by my regular mechanic I realized that I was feeling horny. I hadn't slept with anyone for a long time. I got up my courage and propositioned him. When we got into bed I noticed his penis looked a little funny, but I couldn't really tell because the light wasn't very good. The thought of VD flickered through my mind but it was just casual and I didn't want to be bothered. I wanted some sex, not a lot of hassle.

I slept with this guy one night and a few days later thought I might have gotten gonorrhea. I was a little frightened about what to do. It was awfully hard for me to believe I had VD even though I had symptoms. My old fears came up about being a bad girl if I wanted to have sex and being punished with VD or pregnancy.

It's hard to know, if we want to talk to a sex partner, if s/he will accept our concerns as legitimate or perhaps

Beware of Chance Acquaintances

"Pick-up" acquaintances often take girls autoriding, to cafès, and to theatres with the intention of leading them into sex relations. Disease or child-birth may follow

Avoid the man who tries to take liberties with you He is selfishly thoughtless and inconsiderate of you

Believe no one who says it is necessary to indulge sex desire

Know the men you associate with

AMERICAN SOCIETY FOR SOCIAL HYGIENE 1926

will ridicule them or look down on us. VD has had so many dirty, sleazy overtones. Even those of us who are comfortable with sex still often feel "nice people don't get VD." If we got it, we wouldn't want anyone to know we had it.

Women come to this clinic all the time to get tested because they have a vaginal discharge. They're usually relieved if it's not VD. It doesn't matter that their discharge may have resulted from their having sex.

VD is just like the chicken pox or German measles. It should be dealt with like a disease and not as a moral thing. That's why kids don't like to admit they got it. They're embarrassed.*

If one person in a supposedly ongoing monogamous couple gets VD it often serves as a dramatic focus for any problems the couple might have.

I've been so upset these last few days. My husband told me he'd slept with someone else and might have gotten VD. I didn't know what to do. How could I call up my regular doctor and expose myself? If I asked any of my friends what to do, they would be mortified. I saw an ad yesterday for a VD hotline, and after a lot of hesitation I called. It was such a relief to get some information without anyone knowing who I was.

My husband and I, our toddler and sixteen-year-old baby-sitter went to the country at the end of the summer. When we returned home I started having a vaginal itch. Then my husband started itching, too. I asked him if he had slept with anyone else recently. He admitted to me he had slept with the baby-sitter. Otherwise he would never have told me.

How serious a problem the revelation of extra-couple sex becomes depends on how close and how committed you've been feeling about each other.

No matter how comfortable we may be with facing the problems we have talked about, if there is a possibility that we have VD it still makes trouble for us. We will need to spend time and money hassling with the health care system just to get an examination. This is discussed more fully on p. 178.

What Is VD?

"Venereal" means "relating to sexual intercourse."

"Venereal disease" is a term used to describe a group of diseases which are passed from person to person

*Attention, p. 26.

through sexual contact. The two most common venereal diseases are gonorrhea and syphilis. For an explanation of the nature, symptoms and treatment of gonorrhea, see page 173. For syphilis, see page 176.

How Are Venereal Diseases Spread?

People catch VD only through intimate contact with other people who have one or more of the diseases. Intimate here means the contact of infected mucous membrane with other mucous membrane or the contact of an open venereal lesion to skin. There are many false notions of how VD is spread. Stories of VD being picked up from toilet seats, doorknobs, towels, dishes, or other objects are not true. VD is not caused by straining or by lifting heavy objects or by being dirty. Nor can animals transmit the diseases to humans. Sexual contact with a person who has VD provides ideal conditions for the transferral of it. The organisms that cause the two major venereal diseases, gonorrhea and syphilis, live best in warm, moist environments, such as the linings of the genitals or the throat. Outside the body the organisms die in less than a minute. This explains why most of the superstitions about VD are not true.

Heterosexual, penis-vagina contact is *not* the only way VD is spread. Syphilis can be transmitted if someone touches the infectious chancre sores of another person. (See "Symptoms of Syphilis," p. 176.) Syphilis organisms can go through the pores of the skin. Both syphilis and gonorrhea can be spread through anal and oral intercourse. For gonorrhea, in oral intercourse the organism can be spread from a man's penis to his partner's pharynx (upper part of the throat) but not from the vagina to the throat. The discharge from the vagina or the penis caused by gonorrhea carries enough bacteria to spread the disease via the hands, especially to the eyes. It is less readily spread from the vaginal discharge than the penile discharge.

Curing VD does not provide immunity against future infections.

How Likely Am I to Get VD?

HETEROSEXUAL. If you have intimate contact with another person and don't use any means of VD prevention you have a reasonably good chance of catching it from your partner if he is infected. For women it is estimated that for one exposure to gonorrhea you have a 40-to-50-percent chance of catching it if you use no protection. The pill or IUD probably do not increase your chances of catching it.*

*A. B. Hewitt, "Oral contraception among special clinic patients with particular reference to the diagnosis of gonorrhea," British Journal of Venereal Disease, Vol. 46, No. 106, 1970; L. Juhlin and S. Liden, "Influence of contraceptive Gestogen pills on sexual behavior and the spread of gonorrhea," British Journal of Venereal Disease, Vol. 45, No. 321, 1969; M. A. Kramer, "Contraception and gonorrhea among established and suspected contacts," unpublished memo to James Curran, February 22, 1978.

For syphilis, if you have skin contact with a chancre (first stage) you have about a 20-percent chance of getting it within 30 days. In the secondary stage you have less chance for each exposure.* If you use some method of prevention (below) you can reduce your chance of catching VD.

LESBIAN. In the past it was thought that gonorrhea could not be transmitted by vaginal discharge. Consequently, lesbians have been assumed not to be able to catch gonorrhea from each other. We question this because evidence to prove or disprove it has not been gathered. Recently some clinics have started to ask the sexual partners of infected lesbians to be tested for gonorrhea. However, workers in clinics sympathetic to the lesbian community often report that they see few lesbians with gonorrhea. Syphilis is spread as easily among lesbians as among heterosexuals, though it is also rarely seen among lesbians.

How Big Is the Problem?

The incidence of gonorrhea is extremely high among people of all ages and social classes. In 1977 the United States Public Health Service (USPHS) figures showed about 1,000,000 reported cases of gonorrhea, about the same as the previous year. It estimates 1.6–2 million actual cases. There were about 20,000 new cases of syphilis reported in 1977. This is a decrease from 1976. Estimates of the actual total are as high as 80,000.† The discrepancies stem mostly from two causes. First, private physicians report only 10 percent of their cases even though they are required by law to report them all.‡ Second, many people feel uncomfortable getting medical help or do not have or recognize symptoms.

If you think you may have had contact with someone who had VD turn to p. 178.

PREVENTION

Methods for Reducing the Spread of VD

WHY. Despite the fact that most of the literature on VD stresses treatment and cure, this is not an effective method for controlling and reducing the diseases in this country. Prevention is the only hope for doing so. The diseases can be transmitted to others before we know we have them ourselves, and many who are infected do not have or do not recognize symptoms.

This box shows the extent of the problem:

Gonorrhea — % of people who *have no early symptoms*
    Women: 80%*
    Men: 5–20%†

Syphilis—% of people who *misinterpret* or *remember seeing no primary symptoms*
    Women: 90%‡
    Men: 40–60%§

---

* Lawrence K. Altman, "Gonorrhea Tests Urged for Women," *The New York Times* (December 20, 1971), p. 19.

† This is the most commonly accepted figure. ASHA quotes 12 to 20 percent in their VD bulletin, p. 13. One study shows figures as high as 68 percent. This includes incubating cases, some of which would have developed symptoms in a few days. (H. H. Hansfield, T. O. Lipman, J. P. Harnisch, E. Tronca and K. K. Holmes, "Asymptomatic gonorrhea in men: Diagnosis, natural course, prevalence, and significance," *The New England Journal of Medicine*, Vol. 290, No. 3 [January 17, 1974], pp. 117–23.)

‡ *Venereal Disease*, MEDCOM, Inc. (division of Pfizer, Inc.), 1972, p. 46.

§ *Ibid.*

It's one thing to talk about "being responsible about VD" and a much harder thing to do it at the very moment. It's just plain hard to say to someone I am feeling very erotic with, "Oh, yes, before we go any further, can we have a conversation about VD?" It is hard to imag-

---

*Generally accepted percentages given by the Center for Disease Control, Atlanta, GA.

†See *VD Fact Sheet 1977*, USDHEW. See also *Today's VD Control Problem* (annual bulletin), American Social Health Association (ASHA). All subsequent references to ASHA bulletin are for 1974 edition.

‡Theodore Rosebury, *Microbes and Morals*, pp. 207-208.

ine murmuring into someone's ear at a time of passion, "Would you mind slipping on this condom or using this cream just in case one of us has VD?" Yet it seems awkward to bring it up beforehand, if it's not yet clear between us that we want to make love with each other. Now that I know which birth control creams and jellies will help protect me against VD, I can use one of them the first time and then bring up the subject afterward for us to consider together.

We are not going to make a dent in the epidemic levels of VD without using preventive measures simultaneously with treatment and cure.

EACH OF US IS IMPORTANT. Many of us do not yet fully understand our roles as individuals in the spreading of VD. Let's look at the present situation with gonorrhea. Even if someone has and recognizes symptoms, s/he may have sex with someone else before being cured.

Let's take a hypothetical situation of ten infected people. On the average, as a group, they will give the infection to at least another ten people before being cured. (In reality, one person may give it to several people, and another may not give it to anyone.) We can stop this chain if each of those ten people uses some preventive measure in addition to being cured. *Even if the preventive measure is only 25 to 30 percent effective there will be a dramatic reduction in the number of people who will transmit the disease.* The original ten will transmit it to only seven people instead of ten. The seven newly infected people will pass it on to only five, these five to only three, etc. So as more preventive measures are used, the number of people who have the disease is reduced, and each uninfected person is less likely to have contact with an infected one.*

HOW. There are a number of preventive measures we should all know about. Some have been or are being field-tested; some have been shown effective in the laboratory.† No method is 100 percent effective, but using any of them should considerably reduce your chances of getting gonorrhea or syphilis.

The accompanying box shows some of the most easily used methods:

[Note: The products listed in 1 and 2 may be good for

*Based on a paper by J. C. Cutler, et al., "Potential impact of chemical prophylaxis on the incidence of gonorrhea," *British Journal of Venereal Diseases*, Vol. 48, No. 5 (October, 1972), pp. 376-80.

†Edward M. Brecher has compiled a summary of methods tested plus an extensive bibliography on prophylaxis. See *Journal of Sex Research*, Vol. 11, No. 4 (November 1975), pp. 318-328. See this article for much more documentation than we list. For a popular summary of the methods, see Brecher's "Women: Victims of the VD Rip-off," *Viva*, Nos. 1 and 2 (October and November, 1973). Also see J. C. Cutler, et al., "Vaginal Contraceptives as prophylaxis against gonorrhea and other sexually transmissible diseases," *Advances in Planned Parenthood*, Vol. 12, No. 1, *Excerpta Medica*, 1977, pp. 45-56.

VD prevention in *anal sex* also. But the absorption rates in the anus are different from those of the vagina, and as far as we know no tests have been done using these products in the anus. If you are having anal sex as well as vaginal sex, be sure to put the cream, foam, or jelly in both places. A small amount over the urinary opening may help prevent VD infections in the urethra and bladder.]

---

1. *Certain birth control products** used during vaginal intercourse (for anal intercourse see note above). Most can be used with a diaphragm. See Chapter 10 for more information.
Available in local drugstores or beauty-aid stores:

Delfen Foam	Certane Vaginal Jelly
Emko Foam	Preceptin Gel
Cooper Cream	Milex Crescent Jelly
Koromex A-II Vaginal Jelly	Ortho-Gynol Jelly
	Ortho Cream

2. *Other products* good for VD prevention but not for birth control:
Lorophyn Vaginal Suppositories†
Progonasyl (by prescription only—see #4 below)‡

3. *Condoms§* (rubbers, safes) used during vaginal and anal intercourse. The condom must be put on before the penis touches the partner's vagina or anus. Of course, a condom doesn't protect against infection from syphilis sores that are not on the genitals.

*B. Singh, J. C. Cutler, and H. M. D. Utidjian, "Studies on the development of a vaginal preparation providing both prophylaxis against venereal disease and other genital infections and contraception. II—Effect *in vitro* of vaginal contraceptive and non-contraceptive preparation on treponema pallidum and neisseria gonorrhoeae," *British Journal of Venereal Diseases*, Vol. 48 (1972), pp. 57-64. This list of products, changed from that given in the study, represents the most recent unpublished research.

†*ibid.*

‡H. Porter, B. Witcher, and C. Knoblock, "Social diseases at the cross roads," *Journal of the Oklahoma State Medical Association* (February, 1939). Also, W. M. Edwards and R. S. Fox, "Progonasyl as an anti-VD prophylactic," paper presented at the First National Conference on Methods of Venereal Disease Prevention, Chicago, November 16-17, 1974.

§R. Cautley, G. W. Beebe, and R. Dickinson, "Rubber sheaths as venereal disease prophylactics," *American Journal of the Medical Sciences* 195 (1938), pp. 155-63.

These are additional methods, not necessarily widely used:

4. Progonasyl is an oil containing an organic iodide antiseptic, used in the vagina. It is available in the U.S.

by prescription. Although developed for VD prophylaxis, and effective, it is officially labeled for treatment of vaginal infections.

5. The "short arm" inspection.* This technique, known by prostitutes and in the military, involves examining the penis *before it becomes erect* (before the man is sexually aroused). Wash the penis and genital area with soap and water. Make sure to get in the creases. In a good light, examine the genitals and surrounding area for sores, reddened areas and warts (see "Symptoms of Syphilis," p. 176; "Herpes and Venereal Warts," p. 136). Don't forget to look in the creases in the groin and around the scrotum (balls), around the anus, and on the buttocks. If the man is not circumcised, pull back the foreskin all the way and look there too. Next hold the penis firmly with your fingers and pull the loose skin up and down, as if "milking" or masturbating the penis, then spread apart the skin on the sides of the opening in the tip of the penis and check to see if there is any kind of discharge. A drop or two of cloudy liquid indicates the presence of an infection. It may be gonorrhea or nonspecific urethritis (see "Gonorrhea": "What to Look For in a Man"). Since these drops can be confused with the first drops of semen that may come out when the man first gets aroused, you need to know how to distinguish between the fluids. Obviously, if there are symptoms, you don't touch sores or have sex. Since people can have gonorrhea while showing no symptoms, it makes sense to use a condom or vaginal spermicide for your complete protection.

6. Washing genitals before and especially right after sex. Also, urinating right after sex. Have men wash with soap and water.† *For women this method is questionable.* You can use a douche‡ of warm water and vinegar (1 T. vinegar to 1 qt. water). Use little pressure; hold the bag of liquid no higher than waist level. Otherwise the force of the liquid may mechanically cause pelvic inflammatory disease or cervicitis (see Chapter 6). The same pressure may force the bacteria into the uterus, helping the infection. Frequent douching destroys the natural protective mechanisms of the vagina to prevent other infections. *Do not use* if your birth control method involves contraceptive foam, jelly, or cream used alone or with a diaphragm (douching is *not* a method of birth control). *Less desirable than other methods.*

7. Penigen* is a foaming vaginal tablet containing antibiotics. It was developed and tested in Japan but is not available in this country because safety and efficacy tests have never been filed with the Food and Drug Administration.

8. The "morning-after pill" for VD (different from the morning-after pill for birth control). The pill probably needs to be taken 8 hours or less from the time of exposure. It provides an adequate amount of penicillin† or one of the tetracyclines‡ to prevent the contraction of VD immediately after exposure to an infected person. This dosage is much smaller than the amount needed to cure an established infection. You need a prescription for this and may have trouble finding a doctor who is willing to provide such prevention for VD. If you are convinced this is the method you wish to use, a free clinic might be a good place to find such a doctor. This method has serious drawbacks. Each time we use an antibiotic we increase our chances of becoming allergic to that particular family of antibiotics. Once we become allergic we cannot then use that antibiotic for another illness for which it may be the most effective treatment. Prophylactic doses of antibiotics for VD do *not* contribute to the increased resistance of VD to antibiotics. Syphilis has never developed any resistant strains. Gonorrhea has developed resistant strains as a result of much higher but inadequate treatment doses of antibiotics. Also, prophylactic doses are not large enough to mask symptoms should the disease develop anyway.§

> If you think you have been exposed to VD, even if you are using some kind of protection, get a test. Don't have sex until you know you don't have it or until you know you are cured.

SOCIAL PROBLEMS

THE MEDICAL SYSTEM. VD education for doctors has been ignored by medical schools for the past twenty-five years and is only now being reinstated. Doctors who got

---

*See "Women: Victims of the VD Rip-off."

†M. A. Reasoner, "The effect of soap on treponema pallidum," *Journal of the American Medical Association*, 68, 973 (1917). G. Luys, *A Text-Book on Gonorrhea and Its Complications* (New York: William Wood and Co., 2nd revised edition, 1917), pp. 4-5, 270.

‡J. M. Funes and A. Luz, "Marpharsen-Orvus solution in the prophylaxis of gonorrhea in women," *Boletin de la Oficina Sanitaria Panamericana*, 33 (1952), pp. 121-25. Also, M. Hart, "Gonorrhea in women," *Journal of the American Medical Association*, 216 (1971), p. 1610.

*T. Ohno, K. Kato, M. Nagata, N. Hattori, and H. Kenekawa, "Prophylactic control of the spread of venereal disease through prostitutes in Japan," *Bulletin of the World Health Organization*, 19 (1958), pp. 575-79.

†R. W. Babione, L. E. Hedgecock, and J. P. Ray, "Navy experience with the oral use of penicillin as a prophylaxis," *U.S. Armed Forces Medical Journal*, Vol. 3 (1952), pp. 973-90.

‡H. Smartt, G. Bograd, and R. Dorn, "Prophylaxis of venereal diseases with doxycycline," paper presented at First National Conference on Methods of Venereal Disease Prevention, Chicago, November 16-17, 1974.

§Babione, et al., *op cit.*

their medical education during that period may not know enough about diagnosing and treating VD. Since doctors and health workers in clinics that regularly serve VD patients learn on the job, they probably have the best and most up-to-date VD information. Unfortunately, they are rarely informed about the preventive methods that women can use.

Priorities in our health care system are oriented toward crisis intervention medicine, not prevention. (See Chapter 18.)

EDUCATION AND MORALS. Here, as in so many areas of health, medical personnel do not sufficiently inform people about alternatives. Current information on the relationships between the different kinds of birth control and a person's susceptibility to VD is not widely disseminated. Consequently, the popularity of the Pill and the IUD have aided the spread of VD, since they do nothing to prevent it as some of the other methods may do. The Pill is often blamed as the primary cause of the recent VD upsurge, but no consideration is given to the lack of information about its drawbacks.

Another example involves the national VD hotline, Operation Venus, which is funded by the U.S. Public Health Service (USPHS). It says that condoms are the only effective preventive besides abstention. In spite of evidence for the effectiveness of other methods—especially certain female contraceptives—the USPHS claims that there is not enough scientific evidence to show they work. Some of these methods have been known for several decades. This bias may be a holdover of the stereotype that men are naturally promiscuous and will need protection, whereas a woman with more than one sex partner is not deserving of help.* Our culture has needed the fear of VD to limit sexual activity outside of marriage. With the advent of widespread birth control, which eliminated the fear of pregnancy, fear of VD became the last effective deterrent to complete "sexual license." Until recently, many people were morally opposed to contraception, so foams, creams and jellies, which were probably also good VD preventives, were not displayed openly.

If we had a comparable epidemic of a disease not associated with sex, doctors and public health officials would consider it their ethical duty to inform everyone about how to avoid getting it, as well as to advertise the best known cure. The medical profession seems to feel that it is okay to treat VD, but is reluctant to deal with it in a larger way. If pressed, their recommendation is usually to abstain sexually. People at all levels of responsibility, too moralistic or too ashamed about sex, have blocked research into improved methods of prevention

and curtailed the spread of information about available methods of prevention and cure.

MONEY. One measure of official support (or nonsupport) for VD control is the amount of public money allotted for it and the way this money is spent. In 1977, $32 million was federally appropriated in grants to the states. The state and local governments spent altogether another $60–90 million. At this writing, the amounts spent in 1978 have not yet been compiled, but they are not expected to have risen significantly. In addition, about $6 million is being spent for research of *all* the venereal diseases. Compare the $98–128 million spent on VD control with the $800 million spent, much of it privately, for the estimated total cost of treating complications resulting from gonorrhea alone.* At the same time, about $126 *billion* is spent for "defense," with $1 billion going for each Trident submarine. This money, by helping to supply and support wars and warring countries, creates conditions for the upsurge of VD as well as many other diseases. Outbreaks of venereal disease are clearly related to war zones—where normal life has been disrupted; where many women are forced to earn a living through prostitution; where medicines are of unreliable strengths and can be obtained only on the black market; where men do not feel the constraints of their own social patterns and feel no qualms about raping or maltreating the "enemy." U.S. servicemen have returned from these areas with more highly resistant strains of gonorrhea.

Most of the money used to be allocated for syphilis case-finding (tracing the sexual contacts of infected people). Case-finding can be moderately, though never completely, successful because syphilis develops relatively slowly. More money is now being spent on routine cervical and anal culture tests that screen women for gonorrhea. About 5 percent of the women tested this way are found to be infected.† The screening, however, reaches only those who seek out some sort of medical help to begin with. In Saskatchewan, Canada, the provincial government recently had a trial program to distribute women's self-administered gonorrhea tests (Gonax kits).‡ Until recently, gonorrhea was not treated as a dangerous epidemic because those in authority were reluctant to put money toward eliminating a disease that most severely affected the poor.

There are several other areas where more money should be spent. Most important, money should be spent to determine the effects of existing products on the spread of VD. No money in the VD budget is allo-

---

*See E. R. T. Clarkson, ed., *The Venereal Clinic* (London: John Bale, Sons, and Danielson, Ltd., 1922), for a description of an early program to distribute leaflets to men wholesale, while requiring women to write individually for the same information.

*Personal communication with Paul Weisner.
†ASHA bulletin, p. 9.
‡The program has been phased out because of lack of response, in spite of publicity. Most people preferred to get tested *free* at clinics paid for by provincial health insurance. For more information on kits, write: Dept. of Health, 3211 Albert St., Regina, Saskatchewan, Canada.

cated for this. We need better and easier diagnostic tests for gonorrhea. There is some work being done with blood and urine tests. More must be spent on basic research to lay the groundwork for vaccines against VD.

Changes We Can Make Now

The limited research on VD that has been done in this country has emphasized the development of bigger and better technology to wage war on VD. Although some people heading VD programs feel that in this country "no communicable disease has ever been eradicated unless there was a preventive vaccine to do so,"* we can contain the disease now. Tuberculosis is a notable example of a disease contained and virtually eliminated without the use of a preventive vaccine. We can reverse the trend toward an increased resistance of gonorrhea to antibiotics. This has been done in Greenland,† Saigon,‡ Denmark and Norway.§ In China‖ and Cuba# VD has been essentially eliminated by first educating the people about the symptoms, treatment and the importance of getting rid of VD, and then making it easy to get tests and treatment. We can reduce the number of people who have VD without restricting sexual activity. This has been done in Sweden.**

In order to use what tools we now have, we first have to change the official stance that seems to view VD as a punishment for "immoral" sex. In Western culture this bias goes back a long way. Even before its sexual nature was ascertained, VD was considered a just punishment for blasphemy, once a much more serious crime than any sexual transgression.*** It is not likely that there will be any change in the public attitude until many more of us start to feel comfortable talking about VD. We can change the official attitude by demanding and initiating more public education that is without moralistic overtones. There are some nonjudgmental films, pamphlets and brochures (see bibliography), though few deal with preventives women can use. We can push to have them distributed in public places such as libraries, social centers, schools, movie houses, health facilities. We can support women's centers in their work of body, sex, and health education. We can talk with friends, parents, children, and make sure they have as much accurate information as possible.

Testing and treatment must be made easier and cheaper. Screening must be increased. Some states now require a premarital gonorrhea test. Minnesota and Maryland have stopped requiring a premarital syphilis test. Many people have difficulty making arrangements to get tests and treatment. Programs need to be brought to more places where there already are large groups of people, as schools and business places. Self-testing kits could be distributed to those otherwise unlikely to get tested, or they could be used on a regular basis—e.g., once per month—by those who are in non-monogamous situations. More paramedics and lay community people need to be involved in running the screening programs so that the tests become more accessible to all economic and social groups. We can each ask for routine screening tests for syphilis and gonorrhea when we go for health care, whether it be to a clinic, private doctor, or hospital. Health workers are more likely to include these tests automatically if a good number of clients request them.

We as individuals can use preventive measures to reduce our own chances of catching and spreading VD.

VENEREAL DISEASE SYMPTOMS AND TREATMENT

There is more information available about tests, drugs, and how venereal disease affects men than we include in this chapter. To get this information see the *VD Handbook*. It can be obtained from many Planned Parenthood or sex counseling centers free of charge. If you cannot find it, send 35 cents in coin directly to VD Handbook, P.O. Box 1000, Station G, Montreal, 130, Quebec, Canada.

Gonorrhea

Gonorrhea is caused by a bacterium shaped like a coffee bean, called a gonococcus, which works its way gradually along the passageways of the genital and urinary organs. This disease can be transmitted to another person at all stages. In women the disease is more likely to persist and spread than in men, because the cervix becomes inflamed. The endocervical glands (lining the cervical canal) drain poorly, not allowing the bacteria and pus to be passed out of the body readily.

*W. H. Smartt, M.D., quoted in *Newsweek*, Vol. 74, No. 4, (January 24, 1972).

†"Rural gonorrhea: less sophisticated than city cousin," *Infectious Diseases*, Vol. 4, No. 12 (December, 1974), pp. 7, 22.

‡ASHA bulletin, pp. 49, 53.

§R. R. Willcox, "A world-wide view of venereal disease," *British Journal of Venereal Disease*, Vol. 48, No. 163 (1972), p. 172.

‖Victor W. Sidel and Ruth Sidel, *Serve the People: Observations on Medicine in the People's Republic of China* (New York: Josiah Macy, Jr., Foundation, 1973). Joshua Horn, *Away with All Pests: An English Surgeon in People's China 1954-1969* (New York: Monthly Review Press, Modern Reader Paperback Edition, 1971). Committee of Concerned Asian Scholars, *China! Inside the People's Republic* (New York, 1972), pp. 55-59.

#Word of mouth. No published material yet.

**ASHA bulletin, pp. 48, 52. Sweden has extensively promoted the condom.

***Theodore Rosebury, *Microbes and Morals* (see bibliography), p. 151.

If untreated, the disease's most common complication is a painful infection of the pelvic area, pelvic inflammatory disease (PID—see Chapter 6). Seventeen percent of the women known to have gonorrhea develop PID. Of these women, 15 to 40 percent may become sterile after one episode with it. Also, about 5 percent of the women with PID in this country are surgically sterilized.* A less common complication is proctitis, inflammation of the rectum. Blindness can also occur if the eyes are infected. Rarer but very serious problems occur when the bacteria travel through the bloodstream and cause infection in the valves of the heart, acute arthritis, meningitis, or even death.

Remember: using preventive measures is especially important since a woman usually does not have early symptoms. By the time she has sufficient pain to prompt her to see a doctor her infection has spread considerably. A woman who has had a hysterectomy can be infected in the cervix (if it is left), the anus, urethra, or throat. The IUD may make it more difficult for you to be cured. The IUD seems to locally inhibit the action of the antibiotic. The IUD should be removed before treatment, and then reinserted when treatment has been successful.

*U.S. Department of Health, Education and Welfare: Public Health Service, *VD Fact Sheet 1973*, edition 30, p. 2.

Also, the IUD increases your chance of getting a serious case of PID.

Symptoms of Gonorrhea

Gonorrhea is usually asymptomatic (without symptoms) in women. The minority (20 percent) who do develop symptoms do so anywhere from two days to three weeks after exposure. The cervix is the most common site of infection. The vagina is not affected after puberty. (The vaginal walls are made of cells different from the cervical cells.) You develop a cervical discharge which is the result of an irritant released by the gonococci when they die. You may attribute first symptoms to other routine gynecological problems or to the use of birth control methods, such as the Pill. The urethra may also become infected, possibly causing painful urination. As the infection spreads it can affect the Skene's (on each side of the urinary opening) and Bartholin glands and the rectum. The rectum is infected by the vaginal discharge, which can easily get into it, or through anal intercourse. Symptoms include anal irritation, discharge and painful defecation. As the disease spreads up the uterus and fallopian tubes you can have pain on one or both sides of your lower abdomen. You may also have vomiting and fever. Your menstrual periods may become irregular.

WHERE VD SYMPTOMS SHOW UP

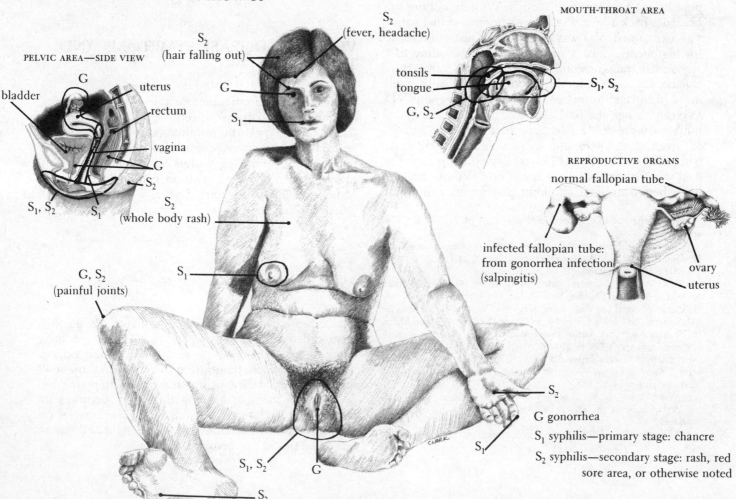

PELVIC AREA—SIDE VIEW

bladder
G
uterus
rectum
vagina
G
S$_2$
S$_1$, S$_2$
S$_1$

S$_2$
(hair falling out)
G
S$_1$

S$_2$
(fever, headache)

S$_2$
(whole body rash)
S$_1$

G, S$_2$
(painful joints)

S$_1$, S$_2$
G
S$_2$

MOUTH-THROAT AREA
tonsils
tongue
G, S$_2$
S$_1$, S$_2$

REPRODUCTIVE ORGANS
normal fallopian tube
infected fallopian tube:
from gonorrhea infection
(salpingitis)
ovary
uterus

S$_2$
G gonorrhea
S$_1$
S$_1$ syphilis—primary stage: chancre
S$_2$ syphilis—secondary stage: rash, red sore area, or otherwise noted

The more severe the infection, the more severe the pain and other symptoms. These symptoms may indicate PID. One type of PID is salpingitis. This is scarring and infection of the fallopian tubes, which can lead to sterility if the tubes become blocked. It is more likely to happen if your birth control method is an IUD. The discharge from the infection can irritate surrounding tissues. Another kind of PID is peritonitis, inflammation of certain abdominal tissues. You may need a hysterectomy to remove a severe infection. Acute pelvic infections can be fatal. The disease can be treated at any stage to prevent further damage, but often damage already done cannot be repaired.

Remember that gonorrhea can also be spread from a man's penis to a woman's *throat*. You may have no symptoms, or your throat may be sore or your glands swollen. The *mouth* does not provide the right environment for gonorrhea bacteria to grow.

What to Look For in a Man

A man usually will have a thick milky discharge from his penis and usually will feel pain or burning when he urinates. Often gonorrhea in a man is confused with a common disease called nonspecific or nongonococcal urethritis (NSU or NGU), which also produces a discharge. Women may be affected by this disease, and they also may act as carriers. It is important to find out which it is because usually different drugs are used to cure each of them.

Testing and Diagnosis of Gonorrhea

It is important to be tested before taking medication because a test done while treatment is being given is not accurate. If you had sex with a man who had a discharge from his penis, you want to know if it is gonorrhea or NSU. Try to get him to come for a test at the same time or soon after you. His discharge can be tested and diagnosed in the same day. If he does not have gonorrhea then you will not have to take unnecessary medication.

Don't douche right before getting a test because you can wash the *accessible* bacteria away, giving a false negative result.

Two types of tests for gonorrhea are currently used: the gram stain and the culture. For a woman, they can be done during pelvic examination (see p. 121) or a throat exam. Although the gram stain is still the only method used in many places, it is practically worthless for women and asymptomatic men. In the gram stain test a smear of the discharge is placed on a slide, stained with a special dye, and examined for gonorrhea bacteria under a microscope. Other organisms in the vagina can easily mask the gonococcal bacteria. There may not be sufficient discharge for an asymptomatic male to insure accuracy. This method is 99 percent reliable for symptomatic men. It is a quick way for a man to tell if he has

gonorrhea or NSU. The second test—the culture test—is more reliable. It can be done any time during your menstrual cycle.* The culture test involves taking a swab of the discharge, rolling it onto a special culture plate, and incubating it under special laboratory conditions for 16 to 48 hours to let the gonorrhea bacteria (if there are any) multiply. This allows the bacteria to be detected more easily.

It is important to emphasize that even the culture test can be inaccurate. Accuracy of the culture test depends greatly on which sites are chosen for testing. If both the most commonly affected sites—the cervix (*not* vagina) and anal canal—are cultured, there is a 92 to 94 percent chance of finding any infection. Ask to have both done. The swab from the cervix is the best single test, 88 to 93 percent accurate. About 50 percent of infected women have an infection in the anal canal.† If you have had a hysterectomy, ask for a urethral culture too. If you have had oral-genital sex, request a *gonococcal* throat culture. Ask what kind of medium is used for culturing. Thayer-Martin is best.

There are several explanations for the insensitivity of the culture test. Sometimes the test is done while the bacteria are still incubating. This can be as long as 3 to 5 days. Sometimes as the disease moves from the cervix up into the uterus and tubes, few bacteria stay near the original site of infection. You can have a discharge and get a negative result if the discharge contains only dead bacteria; they don't grow when cultured. Sometimes the swabs are not rolled over the culture plate properly or the culture medium is not good. There may be too much oxygen around the bacteria, or temperature variations may be too great between the time the culture is taken and the time it is read. All these factors as well as human errors contribute to the unreliability of the test.

The unreliability of present diagnostic devices is another impediment to any successful control of gonorrhea in this country. Unreliable tests for gonorrhea mean the disease can go undiagnosed and therefore untreated until serious damage is done.

If you have any doubt as to how good your test was, try to have someone else do one or come back within a week or two, the sooner the better.

*P. E. Dans and F. Judson, "The establishment of a venereal disease clinic: II. An appraisal of current diagnostic methods in uncomplicated urogenital and rectal gonorrhea," *Journal of the American Venereal Disease Association*, Vol. 1, No. 3 (March, 1975), pp. 107-12.

This is not true of tests for monilia, trichomoniasis or a Pap test (see p. 121). The menstrual discharge makes these tests harder to interpret. About half the women with gonorrhea also have a trichomoniasis infection. Many women, though, have trichomoniasis infections without having gonorrhea. Also, we have heard but not been able to confirm that if you have a Pap test done within two months after you have had gonorrhea you may get a false diagnosis of abnormal cells. Wait two months and then get another Pap test.

†J. D. Schmale, J. M. Martin, Jr., and G. Domescik, "Observations on the culture diagnosis of gonorrhea in women," *Journal of the American Medical Association*, Vol. 210 (October, 1969), pp. 312-14.

Treatment for Gonorrhea

Often treatment is given before the diagnosis is certain. Many doctors will prescribe medication before the culture test is ready to be examined. (The culture test must incubate before it gives any results.) They do this usually for any of three reasons: the tests are not always accurate; the doctor is not sure you will come back; the sooner gonorrhea is treated, the easier it is to cure. On the other hand, there are places that will refuse to treat you even if you are very certain you are infected based on circumstantial evidence (e.g., a man you slept with has been positively diagnosed as having gonorrhea and you have a discharge). One argument in favor of waiting for positive diagnosis is that you should not take antibiotics unnecessarily. As we noted, after repeated doses of antibiotics you may develop an allergy to them, and then you will not be able to take them when you really need to. This is a particularly strong point when you consider that NSU is often confused with gonorrhea unless a test is done. NSU is treated with tetracycline rather than penicillin. Women should also be treated if they have been exposed to NSU and not to gonorrhea. If you decide to wait until your culture test is read, you must consider how easy it is going to be for you to return for possible later tests and treatments.

The normal treatment for gonorrhea is high-dosage injections of penicillin. This has the fewest side effects for most people, and the dose for gonorrhea can also cure a syphilis infection still in the incubation stage. Oral probenecid (1 gram) is recommended in addition, to reduce the urinary excretion of penicillin and allow the penicillin to remain in the bloodstream in a high enough concentration to effect a cure. Tetracycline and other "mycin" drugs can be used by those allergic to penicillin. Some do not work against syphilis. Ask. See box, "Drugs Women Should Know About," Chapter 6, and the *VD Handbook* for more information on drugs and their possible side effects.*

Gonorrhea has required increasing doses of penicillin or other drugs to cure. New strains seem to have developed since the introduction of penicillin, and the more virulent strains are the only ones that survive the dose given for treatment. This trend can be reversed by using sufficient doses to kill all possible strains. The USPHS has increased its recommended dose of penicillin four times in the past ten years, recommending now the maximum amount injectable at one time (4.8 million units). In New York City the standard dose is 6 million units. The total dosage required, however, is still far lower than those commonly used for several other kinds of infection.

*Those of African and Mediterranean ancestry, check note on sulfa drugs and probenecid, p. 150. Pregnant women, check note on tetracycline, p. 150.

Test for Cure of Gonorrhea

It is important that every woman treated for gonorrhea have two negative culture tests, including a rectal culture, a week or two apart before being considered cured. (The culture test, as mentioned before, is not totally reliable.) If cultures remain positive, retreatment is another drug or double the initial dosage of penicillin. Pockets of infection in the reproductive organs or rectum may be particularly difficult to cure. Reinfection may occur soon after cure if your partner has gonorrhea, resulting in a "ping pong" effect.

Pregnancy and Gonorrhea

A pregnant woman with untreated gonorrhea can infect her baby as it passes through the birth canal. In past years many babies became blind right after birth because of gonococcal conjunctivitis. All states now require the eyes of newborns to be treated with silver nitrate or penicillin drops in order to cure this disease if it is present.

Syphilis

Syphilis is caused by a small spiral-shaped bacterium called a spirochete. Once these bacteria have entered the body the disease goes through four stages.

Symptoms of Syphilis

PRIMARY. The first sign is usually a sore called a *chancre* (pronounced "shanker"). It may look like a pimple, a blister, or an open sore. It is usually painless. It probably will show up any time from nine to ninety days after the bacteria enter the body. This sore ususally appears on or near the place where the bacteria enter, usually the genitals. However, it may appear on the fingertips, lips, breast, anus, or mouth. At this primary stage it is very infectious, since the chancre is full of bacteria which can easily be spread to others. Sometimes the chancre never develops or is hidden inside the body, giving no evidence of the disease. This is particularly true for women, in whom the sore frequently develops inside the vagina or is hidden inside the folds of the labia. Only about 10 percent of the women who get these chancres notice them. If you examine yourself regularly with a speculum you are more likely to see one if it develops. (See Chapter 6, p. 122, "Self-examination Techniques.") In any case, the sore goes away in one to five weeks with or without treatment—but the bacteria are still in the body, increasing and spreading. The preventive methods explained before work only if the chemical or physical barrier covers the infectious sore.

SECONDARY. The next stage occurs anywhere from a week to six months later. It usually lasts three to six months, but sometimes the symptoms of this stage can come and go for several years. By this time the bacteria have spread all through the body, and there are many possible symptoms. A rash may appear over the entire body or just on the palms of the hands and the soles of the feet. Sores may appear in the mouth. Joints may become swollen or painful, and bones may hurt. There may be a sore throat, mild fever, or headache (all flu symptoms). Patches of hair may fall out. An infectious raised area may appear around the genitals and anus. Any sexually active person who is not monogamous or whose partner(s) is (are) not monogamous should watch for any of these symptoms. If any appear, s/he should get a routine test for syphilis. During the secondary stage the disease can be spread by simple physical contact, including kissing, because bacteria are present in the open syphilitic sores which may appear on any part of the body. The bacteria are smaller than the average pore size and can easily pass through pores. This is also the stage in which syphilis imitates other diseases. Sometimes the symptoms are so mild that they go unnoticed. Again, the symptoms disappear, but the bacteria remain active in the body.

LATENT. During this stage, which may last ten or twenty years, there are no outward signs. However, the bacteria may be invading the inner organs, including the heart and brain. The disease is not infectious after the first few years of the latent stage.

LATE. In this stage the serious effects of the latent stage appear. Depending on which organ the bacteria have attacked, a person may develop serious heart disease, crippling, blindness, or mental incapacity. With our present ability to diagnose and treat syphilis, no one should have to reach this stage.

What to Look For in a Man

The symptoms are similar to a woman's. The most common place for the chancre to appear is on the penis and scrotum. It may be hidden in the folds under the foreskin or under the scrotum or where the penis meets the rest of the body. In the primary stages men are more likely than women to develop swollen lymph glands in the groin.

Diagnosis of Syphilis

Syphilis can be diagnosed and treated at any time. Early in the primary stages a doctor can look for subtle symptoms, like swollen lymph glands around the groin, and examine some of the discharge from the chancre, if one has developed, under a microscope (darkfield test). Do not put any kind of medication, cream, or ointment on the sore until a doctor examines it. Otherwise the syphilis bacteria on the surface are likely to be killed, making the test less accurate. Spirochetes will be in the bloodstream a week or two after the chancre has formed. They will then show up in a blood test, which from then on, through all the stages, will reveal the infection. If you have been treated for gonorrhea with medication other than penicillin you should arrange for four tests one month apart to cover the possible incubation period of syphilis. Some drugs used to treat gonorrhea do not cure syphilis. Remember, incubation can be as long as ninety days. A good description of the different blood tests used is in the *VD Handbook.* If you are sexually active, request the syphilis blood test if it is not given routinely during your regular health checkups. It should also be given yearly for school children past puberty or on admission to a hospital.

Treatment and Test for Cure of Syphilis

The treatment for syphilis is penicillin, or a substitute such as tetracycline for those allergic to penicillin. It may be one long-lasting dose or a series of smaller doses. Since people sometimes have relapses or mistakes are made, it is important to have at least two follow-up blood tests as checks to be sure the treatment has been complete. The first three stages of syphilis can be completely cured with no permanent damage, and even in late syphilis the destructive effects can be stopped from going any further. Again, see Chapter 6 and the *VD Handbook* for more information on drugs.

Syphilis and Pregnancy

If a pregnant woman has syphilis she can pass the bacteria on to her fetus. The bacteria attack the fetus just as they do an adult, and the child may be born dead or with important tissues deformed or diseased. But if the mother's syphilis is treated before the sixteenth week of pregnancy, the fetus will probably not be infected at all. (Even after the fetus has gotten syphilis, penicillin will stop the disease, although it cannot repair damage that has already been done.) It is important that every pregnant woman get a blood test for syphilis as soon as she knows she is pregnant. Thus, if she has the disease, she can be treated for it before she gives it to her fetus. She should have the test repeated during pregnancy any time she thinks she may have been exposed to syphilis.

Other Venereal Diseases

Other diseases generally considered venereal are chancroid, lymphogranuloma venereum (LGV) and granuloma inguinale. The last may not be venereal. None has been well studied. However, each is treatable with antibiotics. See *VD Handbook* for more information on these diseases.

Other vaginal infections, yeast, trichomoniasis, nonspecific vaginitis and cystitis (bladder infection), as well as crabs, herpes, venereal warts and cervical cancer are discussed in Chapter 6 under "Common Medical and Health Problems: Traditional and Alternative Treatments." Hepatitis also can be spread during sexual intercourse because of the close physical contact.

WHAT TO DO IF YOU THINK YOU HAVE VD

Gonorrhea and syphilis are easy diseases to cure. The biggest difficulty comes in wading through the medical system to get care.

Problems with the Medical System

Even if we knew all we could, we might still be hassled in trying to get treatment. It is important not to let this discourage us from taking care of ourselves.

Private doctors tend to dismiss the possibility of VD in their patients and often don't test for it when they should.

The first time I asked a gynecologist for a routine gonorrhea culture, he smiled with a comradely look in his eye. "But I'm sure no man you'd be involved with would have gonorrhea!"

On the other hand, doctors in clinics in poor areas can be overly suspicious of the possibility of VD in their patients.

Every time someone comes into the clinic they just send them up to the "L" [VD] clinic. No matter whether they've got a pain in their stomach or a sore throat or a fever. So you go up there and everybody's sitting around and you ask them what's wrong and they each tell you a different thing, but they've all been sent to the "L" clinic for VD.*

Too many doctors and medical personnel in private practice or clinics impose a moral judgment about sex on their patients. Most doctors, because of the times in which they grew up and were trained, believe that you get VD by doing something you shouldn't, and respond to you with that prejudice. This attitude can be upset-

**Adapted from *Taking Our Bodies Back*, a film by Cambridge Documentary Films Inc., 1974. Available from them at P.O. Box 385, Cambridge, Mass. 02139.*

ting if you already feel conflicted about sex or are feeling nervous about getting health care.

After a man I slept with told me he had gonorrhea, I went to the college health service for a VD test. I was already a little nervous and embarrassed, but the doctor's attitude made the whole experience a lot worse. He asked me how many times I had had intercourse with my "infected friend" and whether or not I usually slept with lots of different men. I felt that it was none of his business and that many of his questions were irrelevant. The whole time I felt he was more interested in giving me a lecture on morals and in prying into my sex life than in giving me good health care.

You may not feel up to checking out every detail of your treatment. It's a good idea to bring along a friend to help you if at all possible. There's a lot of uncertainty about getting treatment: the tests may not be accurate, the treatment may not work. That means more visits to the clinic or doctor, and that can mean a lot of time and money. You might have to switch birth control methods if you have an IUD. The treatment for gonorrhea can be painful: two or four big shots in the buttocks. But the alternative, not getting treatment, can be worse (see complications under each disease, p. 179). It can be scary either way. That fear itself sometimes makes us procrastinate in getting treatment.

Given all this, doesn't prevention make sense?

What to Know

If you think there is the slightest possibility you have VD, get medical attention as soon as you can.

1. For more information on *symptoms*, read the *VD Handbook* (see p. 180 for where to get it), or call a local hotline, the national VD hotline (Operation Venus—telephone toll free 1-800-272-2577), Planned Parenthood, your state's Division of Public Health: VD Division or Department of Communicable Diseases, or a local VD clinic. Clinics are often in a hospital and might be called "skin clinic" or "L" clinic ("L" stands for "luetic," another name for syphilis).

2. For information on where to get *treatment* try any place listed to *call* in 1. Call several places if you wish to find the best one for you. Some places that treat VD are nonjudgmental and try to help their clients understand how and why they got VD, what to do about it, and how to reduce their chances of getting VD in the future. You don't need to give your name just to get information. Ask about charges. Often tests are free, but the doctor or clinic or both may charge just for the visit. Ask for a place where you can get free or cheap treatment if you need to. If you are a minor and don't want your parents notified or sent the bill, ask about policy on this. Confidentiality for minors is not protected by law.

	GONORRHEA	SYPHILIS
Other names:	Clap, drip, a dose, a case, strain, whites, morning dew, gleet.	Siff, pox, lues, bad blood, Old Joe.
How you catch it:	Sexual intercourse (vaginal, anal, oral-genital) with someone who has it;	Sexual intercourse (vaginal, anal, oral-genital) with someone who has it;
	In eyes, from contact with discharge of infected person;	If fluid·from syphilitic sore or rash gets on your skin;
	Infant's eyes infected in birth canal of infected mother.	Fetus infected in womb of infected mother.
	Not spread by towels, toilet seats, objects.	
How to tell you have it:	Symptoms appear 1–14 days after sexual contact.	Symptoms appear 9–90 days after sexual contact.
	No symptoms for 80% of infected women, 5–20% of infected men.	Primary: Chancre (painless sore) appears at spot where syphilis bacteria entered body, disappears 1–5 weeks without treatment.
	If there are symptoms: Women—greenish or yellow-green vaginal discharge, irritation of vulva; Men—painful urination, urethral discharge; Both—after fellatio, sore throat or swollen glands (sometimes no symptoms).	Secondary: rash, flu-like symptoms, mouth sores, patchy balding. Symptoms will disappear after some months even if you are not treated; disease then attacks internal organs in 1/3 of untreated cases.
	Anal gonorrhea: irritation of anus, discharge, or painful defecation.	
How to find out for sure:	If you have symptoms or have had sexual contact with someone who might have gonorrhea: Women—culture test (80-90% reliable); be sure culture taken from cervix, anus (and throat if necessary); Men—quick gram stain test is often enough. If no symptoms, need culture test: swab of secretions from inside urethra. Be sure to have anus, throat checked if indicated.	If you have symptoms or have had sexual contact with someone who might have syphilis: Tests are— examination of fluid of chancre; blood test (after 4-6 weeks); lumbar puncture (later stages).
Treatment:	Penicillin, or, if allergic, a substitute.	Penicillin, or, if allergic, a substitute.
Follow-up:	After treatment, have a weekly culture test until two are negative.	Blood test one month after treatment, once every three months for a year.
	No sexual intercourse from first suspicion until you know you're cured.	No sexual intercourse from first suspicion until you know you're cured.
	Tell you sex partner(s) immediately!	Tell your sex partner(s) immediately!
Complications if untreated:	Severe inflammation of reproductive organs. Eventual sterility. Arthritis. Blindness.	Muscle incoordination. Deafness. Insanity. Paralysis. Heart Disease. Death. Blindness.

3. Minors can be examined and treated without parents' permission except in Puerto Rico. (It may change policy soon.) The law does not prevent the doctor from telling the parents.

4. Know what problems you might have with medicines (see Chapter 6).

5. Try to find out if the person you had sex with thinks s/he has been exposed to VD. This can help indicate how likely you are to have caught it.

6. Once you think you have VD don't have sex with anyone until you are sure you don't have it or are sure you are cured (indicated by two consecutive negative follow-up tests).

7. If you have VD, inform *all* your recent sex part-

ners, either personally or through a case-finder. (You will probably be asked who your partners were when you get treatment.) Your partner(s) may have no symptoms. VD can have serious consequences if not caught early.

8. For gonorrhea, make sure you get a culture test (see p. 175 for tests). A gram stain (smear) is practically worthless for women. Cultures should be taken from the cervix, not vagina, and from the anus. For a woman with a hysterectomy, include the urethra. If you had oral-genital sex, get a culture test from your throat. If there are any doubts about a negative result, have another test within a week. If a test is ever positive, you are not considered cured until you have had two consecutive tests with negative results.

9. Get a syphilis test at the same time.

10. Don't let the doctor or staff dissuade you from asking questions and finding out answers. If you are not getting a satisfactory response, find another doctor (or clinic). Some doctors and personnel aren't careful enough, especially when treating people on an assembly-line basis. It's your life, not theirs.

11. If you are cured, you can get VD again.

READINGS AND RESOURCES

Organizations Having Bibliographies/Information

American Foundation for the Prevention of Venereal Disease, Inc.: 93 Worth St., New York, NY 10013.

Planned Parenthood: Your local office is listed in the white and yellow pages of phone book.

Institute for Family Research and Education: Syracuse University, College for Human Development, 760 Ostrum Ave., Syracuse, NY 13210. Tel.: 315-423-4584. Subdivision: Family Planning and Population Information Center.

Ed-U-Press: 760 Ostrum Ave., Syracuse, NY 13210. Ordering tel: 800-327-0173, ext. 555 (FL: 800-432-0151, ext. 555).

Venereal Disease Branch, Communicable Disease Center: U.S. Department of Health, Education, and Welfare, Atlanta, GA 30333.

Public Health Department, Venereal Disease Division (state level): Listed in white pages of phone book.

Visual Material

VD: The Hidden Epidemic. Encyclopaedia Britannica, 425 N. Michigan Ave., Chicago, IL 60611. 16mm. film, color, 23 min. 1972.
High school and up. Reasonably good. Mentions prophylaxis—condoms and unspecified methods for women.

VD Questions, VD Answers. BFA Education Media, 2211 Michigan Ave., Santa Monica, CA 90404. 16mm. film, color, 15 min. 1971.
For younger people. Animated.

V.D. Blues. Modern Talking Picture Services, 1212 Ave. of the Americas, New York, NY 16mm. film, color, 1 hour. 1972.
———. 3M Video Learning Systems, Bldg. 236-1N, 3M Center, St. Paul, MN 55101. Video, with instructor's and students' guides, pre- and post tests.

VD and Women. Perennial Education, 477 Roger Williams, Box 855, Ravinia, Highland Park, IL 60035.

Focuses primarily on gonorrhea and herpes. Includes excellent discussion of prevention.

Literature

American Foundation for the Prevention of Venereal Disease, Inc. *The New Venereal Disease Prevention for Everyone.* Free. (Address above.)
Excellent pamphlet on prevention.

American Social Health Association. *Today's VD Control Problem.* For a copy send $2 to 260 Sheridan Ave., Palo Alto, CA 94306.
Annual bulletin with a lot of information on trends. Voice of the establishment.

———. *Women and VD.*
Concise information on five diseases. A little on prevention.

Blue Cross of Southern California. *S.T.D.: Sexually Transmitted Diseases: What They Are/How to Prevent Them.* For a copy send to P.O. Box 70000, Van Nuys, CA 91470.
Pamphlet has short section on prevention.

Boston Women's Health Book Collective. *Preventing Venereal Disease.* 1976. For a copy send a stamped self-addressed business-size envelope to Dept. BEP, P.O. Box 192, West Somerville, MA 02144.
Stresses prevention.

Brecher, E. M., "Prevention of the sexually transmitted diseases," *Journal of Sex Research,* Vol. 2, No. 4 (Nov. 1975).

———. "Women—Victims of the VD Rip-off," *Viva,* Oct. and Nov. 1973.
Best popular article on prevention.

Cherniak, D., and A. Feingold. *VD Handbook.* 1972. For a copy send 35¢ to VD Handbook, Box 1000, Station G, Montreal 130, Quebec, Canada.

Chico Feminist Women's Health Center. Packet of information on lesbian health care including material on VD. For a copy send $1.50 plus postage for 3 ounces to 330 Flume Street, Chico, CA 95926.
One of the few pamphlets for lesbians.

Commonwealth of Massachusetts. *The Facts About VD* and *Los Datos Sobre Ev.* For a copy in either English or Spanish write to Dept. of Public Health, Div. of Communicable Diseases, 600 Washington St., Boston, MA 02111.
Prevention information mentions condom and diaphragm.

Gordon, S. *Facts About VD for Today's Youth.* New York: The John Day Co., 1973.
Good for teenagers. Includes prevention.

Gordon, S., and R. Conant. *VD Claptrap.* 1972. For a copy send 30¢ to Ed-U-Press (address above).
Wonderful comic book. Even mentions prevention, stresses condoms. Has summary in Spanish.

Grover, J., with D. Grace. *The ABC's of VD.* Englewood Cliffs, NJ: Prentice-Hall, 1971.
Chatty, comprehensive, positive. Mentions female and male preventives. Only a few minor slips into moralism; skip the foreword.

Lieberman, E. J., and E. Peck. *Sex and Birth Control: A Guide for the Young.* New York: Schocken Books, 1973.
Has chapter on VD. Tone is good. Only preventive method mentioned is condoms.

Pennsylvania Dept. of Health. *Common Sexually Transmitted Diseases.* For a free copy write P.O. Box 90, Harrisburg, PA 17120.
Concise chart of 13 venereal diseases with brief pertinent information. Nothing on prevention.

Rosebury, Theodore. *Microbes and Morals: The Strange Story of Venereal Disease.* New York: Viking Press, 1971; Ballantine Books, 1973.
Excellent historical look at VD, including examination of theories of origin and spread.

Wear, Jennifer, and King Holmes. *How to Have Intercourse Without Getting Screwed.* Seattle: Madrona Publishers, Inc., 1976. Address: 113 Madrona Place East, Seattle, WA 98112.
Has very good chapter on sexually transmitted diseases.

CHAPTER 10
BIRTH CONTROL

INTRODUCTION

Let's say we want to have sexual intercourse with a man and we don't want a baby. We want to be able to enjoy sex without worrying about pregnancy. We don't want to spend anxious days every cycle waiting for our period. We need birth control—an effective, safe, comfortable, cheap, reversible and easily available method of avoiding pregnancy. Today we are better able to plan and prevent pregnancy than at any other time in human history, yet we still too often get pregnant when we didn't want to or mean to. There is no perfect method, and there are obstacles in both society and ourselves which keep us from making the best possible use of the existing methods. This introduction will outline some of the obstacles that we run into in trying to choose, to obtain and to use a birth control method that will work for us.

Birth Control and Sex Information

Information on birth control and sex is restricted in this country because of persistent anti-sex attitudes and the puritanical shame about sex that still has a hold on so many of us. Although in the past decade many restrictive laws have been changed and some good sex education programs started, the laws, medical practices and public school policies in many areas still keep us from getting the information and services we need, especially when we are young.*

Contraceptives and information about contraceptives are just not available to all of us who want them. Extensive birth-control services do exist for many poor women but usually in the absence of other services essential for basic health care needs. We must challenge the coercive nature of selectively making available various publicly funded alternatives. A low-income woman does not

really have a choice, when sterilizations are 90% publicly funded while abortions receive no public funds at all.*

The Politics of the Birth Control Movement

Effective birth control is both fundamental to our struggle for equality and part of a larger struggle to control our bodies and our lives. It is sometimes difficult for poor and minority women to accept birth control information because some of the most influential people in the birth control movement in the United States have shown a deep though possibly unconscious prejudice against the "lower classes," and sought to control their growth through birth control. In the population control movement which dominates the field of birth control today, both here and in third world countries, the very group of people who control governments and economies also seek to control who has children and how many.

Fear of overpopulation has led to some extreme suggestions, such as contraceptive medication in the water supply. We have already seen cases of involuntary sterilization of welfare mothers or poor women with more than a certain number of children. These trends violate the right of each of us to choose voluntarily whether to have children. Methods with substantial risks and side effects are tolerated, even espoused:

The dangers of overpopulation are so great that we may have to use certain techniques of contraception that may entail considerable risk to the individual women.†

(See Chapter 18 for an examination of the attitudes implicit in a statement like this.)

We don't wish to minimize the dangers of overcrowding the environment. But we believe the problems of population growth and world hunger require the United States not to spread birth control as a substitute for changing its exploitative economic and political actions around the world. Thus, even though the anti-population-growth forces help individual women by pushing for

---

*Remember the myth that giving teenagers birth control information would make them "promiscuous"? It has been completely disproved by a careful national survey. See *Adolescent Sexuality in Contemporary America*, by Robert C. Sorensen (New York: The World Publishing Company, 1973).

*For more on this important issue see Toni Cade's anthology, *Black Woman* (New York: Signet, 1970).

†Dr. Frederick Robbins as quoted by Barbara Seaman in *The Doctors' Case Against the Pill*, page 45.

better access to birth control information and services, we oppose their underlying purposes as we see them.

The Health Care System and Birth Control

Our society is not working with us to assure us control of our bodies. Drug companies, doctors and clinics have a lot of control over our choice and acquisition of birth control methods, yet they frequently are more concerned with their profit and control than with our well-being. See Chapter 18, "Women and Health Care," for a more general critique of the American health care system.

Much of the available information about effectiveness, safety, possibility of side effects, and reversibility of the different contraceptives is researched and published by the drug companies, who are interested primarily in sales and tend to put profit above truth in advertising. So we have to be careful about where we get our information.

What about the doctors? Many of us, unable to get enough trustworthy information about birth control, have depended on doctors to choose for us. But while knowing full well that there is no perfect method, many doctors just push their pet method or brand on us without inviting us to consider our individual needs. It is alarming how much doctors depend on drug company literature and salesmen for their information. Often they do not learn all the up-to-date information from unbiased sources themselves, and what they do know they do not take the time or the trouble to tell us. A Boston gynecologist, witness for a major birth control pill manufacturer (G. D. Searle) at the 1970 congressional hearings on the pill, testified that he didn't tell his patients of all the pill's potential side effects because, "well, if you tell them they might get headaches, they will get headaches."*

Unfortunately, women all over the country are walking out of clinics and doctor's offices with methods of birth control that we have not really thought about or clearly chosen, and are not sure how to use. No wonder so many of us get pregnant when we don't want to, even when we are supposedly practicing birth control!

And the prices are high. Doctor or clinic visits and drugstore prescriptions cost *too much* in our profit-making health care system. Unreasonable prices keep many of us from getting the birth control we want.

Abortion and Birth Control

The great need for abortion will diminish when birth control methods are improved and made universally available. Until then, however, we must have abortion for when contraception methods fail and when, for

*Health-Pac *Bulletin* (March, 1970), p. 12. Published by the Health Policy Advisory Center, Inc., 17 Murray St., New York, N.Y. 10007. See Chapter 18 on women's rights to information about side effects.

some of the reasons outlined here, we don't use birth control effectively or at all. Since legal early abortion procedures carry very little medical risk, barrier methods of birth control (e.g., condom and diaphragm), with abortion as backup in case of method failure, offer the lowest risk of death combined with 100% effectiveness (see Table 2, p. 189). However, even for those of us who would not consider having an abortion, we should remember that consistent use of the condom plus foam (i.e., no "chances" taken) is as effective a birth control method as the pill. Of course, we each have to consider many complex factors in deciding whether barrier methods, with or without abortion backup, are acceptable: what would it mean for me to become pregnant? Would abortion as backup be acceptable? What about moral and religious beliefs? What about factors such as convenience, cost and esthetics?

Unfortunately, current research tends to emphasize the more risky hormonal and IUD methods, rather than the barrier methods. Pressure from women must change this. Clearly, what we need are both safe and effective birth control methods which do not require abortion as a backup.

Men and Birth Control

The men we are sexually involved with have a lot to do with how well we use birth control and how we feel about it. Both men and women in this society at present seem to assume that the burdens of birth control should fall on women. One reason for this is that we women have a more personal interest in preventing pregnancy than men do, for we bear the children, and in this culture we are in large measure responsible for raising them. As a result, most of today's popular methods of birth control are for us. When we ask a man to use a rubber even as a temporary alternative, he often resists: condoms are a drag, he tells us—he can't feel intercourse fully with a condom on.

Ironically, the burden of total responsibility for birth control is a recent one. For centuries before the invention of the diaphragm in 1882, women had to depend on men (condoms, withdrawal) to keep them from getting pregnant (and on crude abortion and infanticide as frequently needed backup methods). The diaphragm was a breakthrough because it was an effective method that *we* could use. With the diaphragm we were more in control of our bodies than ever before.

Yet *total* responsibility for birth control is a burden for us. We must make the arrangements, see a doctor, get examined, go to the drugstore, and usually pay for the supplies. With the pill or IUD, it is our bodies that feel the side effects, and, more seriously, our bodies that take whatever risks are involved. Total responsibility means that if we don't have some kind of birth control and we are pressed to have intercourse, it is up to us to say no: if we have sex without birth control it is our fault if we get pregnant. Our total responsibility for birth control often means that the man can relax more than we can in lovemaking. Total responsibility often creates angry and resentful feelings that can't help but get in the way of our loving feelings.

Many of us do not talk much about birth control with our partner. We worry that he may get turned off, or choose someone else. Yet a man who truly sees his share in the responsibility for preventing pregnancy gains our respect—we feel better about our relationship, and we use birth control better, too. When there is no good method available at the moment, a supportive partner will join us in exploring ways of lovemaking without intercourse. He can use condoms, and not just when we remind him to. He can help pay the doctor and drugstore bills. He can share in putting in the diaphragm and cream or jelly, or in inserting the foam. He can, if it is a long-term relationship where no children or no more are wanted, get a vasectomy. His attitude counts: two people prevent pregnancy a lot better than one.

If you are having trouble talking with your partner about birth control, you may, as we have, find it helpful to talk with your women friends.

Women and Birth Control

Many of us have found that some of the most stubborn resistance to our use of birth control comes from ourselves. Growing up amid repressive attitudes toward sexuality has made it difficult for us to own our sexual feelings and to accept responsibility for our sexual behavior, including using birth control when we don't want to become pregnant.

Here are some of the personal reasons why we sometimes have trouble using birth control or don't even use it at all:

- We are embarrassed by, ashamed of, confused about our own sexuality.

- We cannot admit we might have or are having intercourse because we feel (or someone told us) it is wrong.

- We are romantic about sex—sex has to be a passionate, spontaneous sharing, and birth control seems too premeditated, too clinical, and often too messy.

- We hesitate to inconvenience our sex partner. This fear of displeasing him is a measure of the inequality in our relationship.

- If we are using natural birth control we sometimes have a hard time abstaining during our fertile days because we fear our partner will get angry and find sex elsewhere.

- We feel, "It can't happen to me. I won't get pregnant."

- We have questions about birth control and sex and don't know whom to talk with.

- We hesitate to go to a doctor or clinic and face the hurried, impersonal care or, if we are young or unmarried, the moralizing and disapproval that we feel likely to receive.

- We don't recognize our deep dissatisfactions with the method we are using and begin to use it haphazardly.

- We want a baby and can't admit it to ourselves. Or we feel tempted to get pregnant just to prove to ourselves that we are fertile, or to try to improve a shaky relationship.

What Can We Do?

Facing these many obstacles to our using birth control effectively, what can we do? First, we can learn for ourselves and teach one another about the available methods. By speaking openly and by carefully comparing experiences and knowledge, we can guide each other to workable methods and good practitioners. We can learn to recognize when a practitioner is not thorough enough in examinations or explanations, and support each other to ask for the attention we need. By talking together we can also get a better handle on the more subtle personal hassles we have with birth control. We can begin the long but worthwhile process of talking with our men about birth control, so that they can no longer comfort-

ably ignore their share in the responsibility. We can learn to be more accepting of our sexuality and join proudly together to insist that legislatures, courts, high schools, churches, doctors, research projects, clinics and drug companies change their attitudes and practices so that we can enjoy our sexuality without becoming pregnant. We can work to create self-help clinics and other alternative health care institutions where our needs for information, discussion and personal support in the difficult choice of birth control will be better met. Whatever we choose to do, we can act together.

Birth Control and Sexual Availability

The increased availability and effectiveness of birth control methods can bring pressure on us to have intercourse whenever a man suggests it, or with our husband or lover any time he wants to. Being protected, however, does not mean we always want intercourse. It is important for us to feel confident in not choosing intercourse if our feelings say no. We used to be able to say, "No, I can't, I might get pregnant." Now we have to be more honest and say, "No, I don't want to." This takes a strength and self-possession which we don't have all the time. We look forward to the time when both men and women can say, "No, I don't feel like having intercourse right now," without being apologetic and scared, and without the other person feeling threatened, insulted or furious.

Conception—the Process to be Interrupted

During sexual intercourse, sperm are ejaculated through the man's penis into the woman's vagina. If uninterrupted, some of the sperm swim through the cervical opening, through the woman's uterus and into the fallopian tubes. It is also possible for sperm deposited in or near the lips around the vagina during sex play to swim into the vagina and follow the route to fertilize the egg.

(This is possible even if the woman has an intact hymen or has never been penetrated!) If the sperm encounter an egg in the outer third of the fallopian tube, a sperm may penetrate the egg (fertilization). The process of an egg and a sperm uniting is called *conception*. The fertilized egg then takes 4–5 days to travel down the fallopian tube to the uterus, where after 1–2 days it implants in the uterine lining and develops through the next nine months into a baby.

THE EGG. Chapter 2 describes the cycle in which the egg ripens inside the ovary and is released, and during which the woman's uterus prepares a lining of tissue to nourish a fertilized egg. The egg leaves the ovary (*ovulation*) *approximately two weeks before the beginning of the next menstrual period.** It can be fertilized for only about twelve to twenty-four hours. Although it is unusual, *a woman can get pregnant from having intercourse during her period*, especially if she has an occasional short cycle (less than 27 days). (See "Fertility Consciousness," p. 207).

THE SPERM. Sperm are made in the man's testicles ("balls"). Sexual stimulation makes blood flow into erectile tissue inside the penis, causing the penis to get stiff, hard, erect. Many sperm are contained in the drops of liquid that may come from the penis soon after the erection occurs. Continued sexual stimulation can cause the man to have an orgasm. As his orgasm begins, the sperm travel up the sperm ducts, over the bladder, and through the prostate gland into the urethra. Here the sperm are picked up by about a teaspoonful of seminal fluid (from the prostate and seminal vesicles) and are propelled out of the urethra by rhythmic contractions which are very pleasurable to the man. This is called ejaculation. (See diagram on p. 31 in Chapter 2.)

*A common mistaken assumption is that the egg leaves the ovary at midcycle, halfway between menstrual periods. This is only true when the cycle is 28 days long.

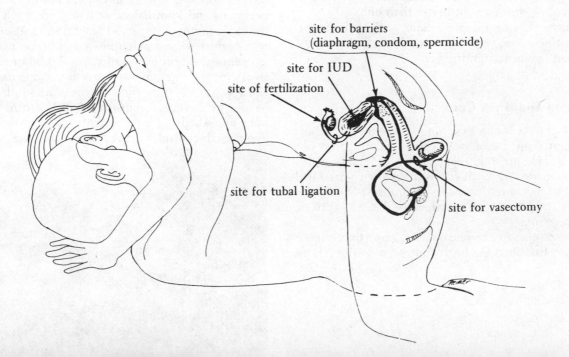

site for barriers
(diaphragm, condom, spermicide)
site for IUD
site of fertilization
site for tubal ligation
site for vasectomy

MONTHLY FERTILITY CYCLE

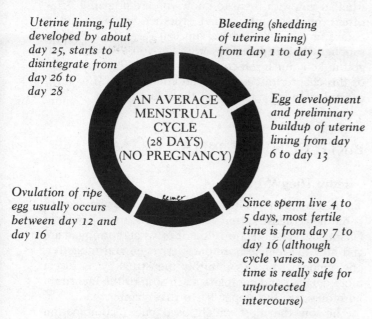

Uterine lining, fully developed by about day 25, starts to disintegrate from day 26 to day 28

Bleeding (shedding of uterine lining) from day 1 to day 5

AN AVERAGE MENSTRUAL CYCLE (28 DAYS) (NO PREGNANCY)

Egg development and preliminary buildup of uterine lining from day 6 to day 13

Ovulation of ripe egg usually occurs between day 12 and day 16

Since sperm live 4 to 5 days, most fertile time is from day 7 to day 16 (although cycle varies, so no time is really safe for unprotected intercourse)

About 300–500 million sperm come out in one ejaculation. So many will die on the long hard trip up to the egg that this great number is needed to ensure that reproduction can occur.

Sperm come out fast, usually headed straight for the entrance to the cervical canal. They swim fast too—an inch in eight minutes—so a sperm may reach an egg in as little as thirty minutes. Sperm can move more quickly in the few days around ovulation because of the nature of the cervical mucus at that time. See "Natural Family Planning" for details.

The acid environment of the vagina is hostile to sperm, so sperm in the vagina die in about eight hours. Once sperm get to the uterus, however, they can live for four to five days.*

Choosing Your Birth Control Method

At first glance, choosing a method of birth control to suit us best looks easy. We may imagine ourselves carefully surveying the choices, learning all about each method and selecting the one which perfectly fits our life-style, our feelings and our bodies. Unfortunately, for most of us the perfect contraceptive has not (yet?) been invented. Each of the currently available methods has disadvantages as well as advantages. Some methods we find to be a nuisance, others may make us sick. Many may have long-term dangers still unknown. The choice usually involves deciding where we are willing to make a compromise. We can weigh whether effectiveness, safety, or convenience matters more to us, and most important, what method we feel the most comfortable with and which one we will use the most consistently.

*For more information, see *Conception, Birth and Contraception*, by Demarest and Sciarra (listed in bibliography), and *Boys and Sex*, by Wardell Pomeroy (New York: Dell, 1968).

We will choose differently according to where we are in our lives—no one method is likely to be satisfactory enough to carry us all the way through our fertile years.

Effectiveness is one of the first things we consider in choosing a method of birth control. When looking at

Approximate Failure Rate (Pregnancies per 100 Woman Years)*

	THEORETICAL FAILURE RATE	ACTUAL USE FAILURE RATE
Abstinence	0	?
Hysterectomy	0.0001	0.0001
Tubal Ligation	0.04	0.04
Vasectomy	0.15	0.15+
Oral Contraceptive (combined)	0.34	4[a]–10[b]
I.M. Long-Acting Progestin	0.25	5–10
Condom + Spermicidal Agent	Less than 1[c]	5
Low Dose Oral Progestin	1–1.5	5–10[b]
IUD	1–3	5[a]
Condom	3	10[a]
Diaphragm (with spermicide)	3	17[a]
Spermicidal Foam	3	22[a]
Coitus Interruptus	9	20–25
Rhythm (Calendar)	13	21[a]
Lactation for 12 months	25	40[d]
Chance (sexually active)	90[e]	90[e]
Douche	?	40[a]

Note: Extensive references, often conflicting, are available on the complicated subject of contraceptive effectiveness.

*Emory University Family Planning Program, *Contraceptive Technology* 1978–1979 (see "Readings and Resources" for ordering details).

[a]Ryder, Norman B., "Contraceptive Failure in the United States," *Family Planning Perspectives* 5:133–142, 1973.

[b]Oral contraceptive failure rates may be far higher than this, if one considers women who become pregnant after discontinuing oral contraceptives, but prior to initiating another method. ORAL CONTRACEPTIVE DISCONTINUATION RATES OF AS HIGH AS 50-60% in the first year of use are not uncommon in family planning programs.

[c]Data are normally presented as Pearl indices. For conversion to the form used here, the Pearl index was divided by 1300 to give the average monthly failure rate n. The proportion of women who would fail within one year is then 1-(1-n).

[d]Most women supplement breast-feedings, significantly decreasing the contraceptive effectiveness of lactation. In Rwanda 50% of non-lactating women were found to conceive by just over 4 months postpartum. It might be noted that in this community sexual intercourse is culturally permitted from about 5 days postpartum on (Bonte, M., and van Balen, H., *J. BioSoc. Sci* 1:97, 1969).

[e]This figure is higher in younger couples having intercourse frequently, lower in women over 35 having intercourse infrequently. For example, MacLeod found that within 6 months 94.6% of wives of men under 25 having intercourse four or more times per week conceived. Only 16.0% of wives of men 35 and over having intercourse less than twice a week conceived (MacLeod, *Fertility and Sterility* 4:10-33; 1953).

EFFECTIVENESS OF BIRTH-CONTROL METHODS

PROBABILITY OF AVOIDING PREGNANCY,
ON BASIS OF PAST USAGE

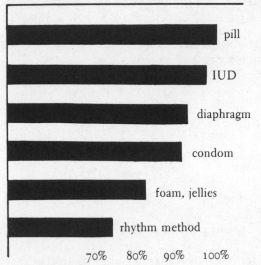

pill

IUD

diaphragm

condom

foam, jellies

rhythm method

70%   80%   90%   100%

Foam and condom used together are up with the pill and
IUD in effectiveness.*

the effectiveness statistics in books and magazines, keep
in mind that there is a difference between the *theoretical failure rate*, which is based on hypothetical perfect
use of the method, and the higher *actual failure rate*,
based on records of actual use of the method over time.
Actual failure rates include accidents such as forgetting a
pill, failing to put on the condom for the first entry of
the penis into the vagina, removing the diaphragm
within six hours of intercourse or leaving it in the drawer
instead of using it. Drug company literature tends to
present only the theoretical rate, which can be misleading. The actual failure rate will give you a more realistic
idea of how effective the method is, and will invite you
to consider the crucial question of how effectively *you
and your partner* will use it.

The table on page 185 gives both actual and theoretical rates. A 5 percent pregnancy rate, or failure rate,
which is the same as a 95 percent effectiveness rate,
means that studies in the past have shown that 5 women
out of 100 using that particular method have become
pregnant in one year. Note that, in comparison, sexually
active women using no method at all have an 80 percent
pregnancy rate.

Besides effectiveness, there are many other factors to
consider. The cost of the different methods. How comfortable you feel touching your genitals, having preparations leak out of your vagina, or taking chemicals into
your system. How much risk you believe there to be, and
how much you are willing to take. How you feel about
using abortion as a backup method. How much you wish
to involve your partner(s) or how much responsibility

*For effectiveness of natural birth control methods (other than the
Rhythm Method) see "Fertility Consciousness," p. 207.

you wish them to have. Whether you trust them,
whether you wish them to know you are prepared. How
often you have intercourse, whether you have intercourse in a location where you can store contraceptive
supplies. Your personality—whether you tend to be forgetful, how much self-control you have. The remainder
of this chapter discusses the different methods of birth
control, with reference to all these factors.

BIRTH CONTROL PILLS

How They Work

To understand how birth control pills work, you need to
know how menstruation works, which is explained in
Chapter 2. That section describes what hormones are
and how the female hormones, estrogen and progesterone, guide a woman's monthly menstrual cycle. For a
more detailed and complete discussion of the menstrual
hormones, see the Appendix to that chapter.

The way the most widely used pills ("combination
pills") work to prevent pregnancy is outlined in the chart
on p. 187, which puts an average menstrual cycle and the
pill cycle side by side. It shows how the pills interrupt
your menstrual cycle by introducing synthetic versions
of the female hormones.

Combination birth control pills prevent pregnancy
primarily by inhibiting the development of the egg in
the ovary. During your period, the low estrogen level
normally indirectly triggers your pituitary gland to send
out FSH, a hormone that starts an egg developing to
maturity in one of your ovaries. The pill gives you just
enough synthetic estrogen to raise your estrogen level
high enough to keep FSH from being released. So, during a month on the pill your ovaries remain relatively
inactive, and there is no egg to be fertilized by sperm.
This is the same principle by which a woman's body
checks ovulation when she is pregnant: the corpus luteum and placenta put estrogen into her blood, thereby
inhibiting FSH. So in a way, using much lower levels of
hormones, the pill simulates pregnancy, and some of the
pill's side effects are like those of early pregnancy. If
ovulation occurs, it is because your body needed a
higher dose of estrogen than your pill gave you to inhibit
FSH, or because you have missed one or more pills.

Synthetic progesterone, called progestin, is used differ-

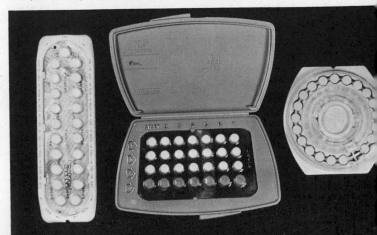

ently in the different kinds of pill. The *combination pill* combines estrogen and progestin for the entire 20 or 21 days. Progestin provides two important extra contraceptive effects: increased thickness of cervical mucus, and improper development of the uterine lining (see chart). The *progestin-only* pills depend on these two effects and do not inhibit ovulation. They are therefore not as effective in preventing pregnancy. A third kind of pill, the *sequential* pill, uses estrogen alone for several days and then a combination of estrogen and progestin. Less effective than combination pills, and with more risks and side effects than the other two, sequentials are not and should not be used except in rare cases (see discussions of the three kinds of pill, below).

Woman's Menstrual Cycle and the Way the Combination Birth Control Pill Affects that Cycle to Prevent Pregnancy

Normal Menstrual Cycle*	With the Pill
DAY 1. Menstrual period begins.	DAY 1. Menstrual period begins.
DAY 5. An egg in a follicle (pocket, sac) in one of your ovaries has begun to ripen to maturity. The egg starts developing in response to a hormonal message (FSH) from your pituitary gland, which in turn has been triggered indirectly by the low level of *estrogen* (an ovarian hormone) at the time of your period.	DAY 5. Take your first pill. In the pill, you take two synthetic hormones every day: *estrogen* and *progestin* (synthetic progesterone).
DAYS 5–14. The follicle in which the egg is developing makes first a little, then more and more *estrogen*: 1. *Estrogen* stimulates the lining of your uterus to get thicker in preparation for pregnancy. 2. As *estrogen* increases, it slows down and then cuts off FSH.	*Estrogen:* The pill contains more *estrogen* than there usually is in your body on Day 5—enough to stop the usual message from your pituitary gland (FSH) for an egg to develop. By taking this amount of *estrogen* every day for 21 days, you prevent an egg from developing at all that month. Therefore there is no egg to be fertilized by the sperm.
DAY 14. Ovulation: *estrogen* peak and a spurt of *progesterone* occurring during days 12–13 indirectly trigger ovulation. Ripe egg is released from ovary, starts 4-day trip down fallopian tube to uterus. Fertilization by sperm from the man must occur in first 24 hours.	*Progestin:* A little *progestin* every day provides two vital back-up effects: 1. keeps the plug of mucus in your cervix thick and dry, so sperm have a hard time getting through; 2. keeps the lining of your uterus from developing properly so that if an egg does ripen (if *estrogen* level of pill is too low for you, or if you forget a pill) and sperm do make it through the cervical mucus and fertilize the egg, the fertilized egg will not be able to implant.
DAYS 14–26. The ruptured follicle, now called *corpus luteum* ("yellow body"), makes two hormones for about 12 days: *Estrogen* continues. *Progesterone* increases and peaks about day 22: 1. makes your cervical mucus (plug of mucus in cervix) thick and dry, a barrier to sperm; 2. stimulates the glands in lining of your uterus to secrete a sugary substance and further thickens the lining.	DAYS 6–25. Continue taking one pill a day.
DAYS 26–27–28. If pregnancy did not occur, *corpus luteum's* manufacture of *estrogen* and *progesterone*, slows down to a very low level. The lining of your uterus, which needs the stimulation and support of these hormones, starts to disintegrate.	DAY 26. Take your last pill.† DAYS 27–28. Sudden drop in *estrogen* and *progestin* makes the lining of your uterus start to disintegrate.
DAY 29–DAY 1. Menstrual period begins. Low level of *estrogen* (see Day 26) will begin indirectly to stimulate pituitary's egg-development hormone (FSH) to start a new cycle.	DAY 29–DAY 1. Menstrual period begins. Your period is lighter than normal, because of effect #2 of progestin in the pill.

*This is a simplified version of the menstrual cycle. See the Appendix to Chapter 2 for a more thorough description.
†With the 28-day combination pill, you take pills without hormones in them from day 27 to day 5.

Combination Pills

Effectiveness

With the three contraceptive factors described (p. 186), the combination pills have the very low theoretical pregnancy rate of 0.5 percent. In actual use they show a failure rate of 2 to 5 percent (see Table on p. 185). Pregnancy can occur if you forget to take your pill for two or more days; if you try to juggle your pill schedule; if you don't use a backup method of birth control for your first two weeks of pills in the first packet, and occasionally when you change from one brand of pill to another (in this case use an extra method for two weeks to be safe).

Reversibility

If you want to become pregnant, stop taking pills at the end of a packet. It may be several months before your ovaries are functioning regularly, and your first non-pill periods may be a week or two late, or missed completely. It is probably a good idea to use another method of birth control for a few months after you go off the pill to allow your body to return to normal before you try to get pregnant. (See "The Pill and Your Children," p. 190.)

There is no agreement at present as to whether there is a higher rate of temporary or permanent infertility or a higher number of miscarriages among women who have taken the pill. Most women do have successful pregnancies after they go off the pill. Some women, especially those who menstruated irregularly before taking the pill, have difficulty conceiving after they go off the pill, but they may have been sterile or subfertile already. Clomiphene citrate (Clomid) is one treatment which you can request to induce ovulation if it has not resumed within one year, although this does not always work and can occasionally result in multiple births. (Pergonal, sometimes used, produces multiple births more frequently than Clomid.)

Safety

Many of us are uneasy about taking a hormone-affecting medication every day for months and years when its effects have not been conclusively tested and it has been in wide use for only fifteen years. Yet some of us choose to take whatever risks are involved because we absolutely don't want to get pregnant. What price do we pay for near-perfect protection against pregnancy?

There is a great deal of information on adverse effects of the pill, and a lot of it is contradictory. We are confused and alarmed by "pill scares," such as the one caused by sensational press reports of the 1970 Senate hearings on the pill. Increasingly, however, studies are emerging to document the serious side effects of the pill.

For a full discussion of these hazards see *Women and the Crisis in Sex Hormones*, by Barbara and Gideon Seaman (Bantam paperback, 1978). Barbara Seaman, who expanded upon the pioneering work of Morton Mintz (see *The Pill: An Alarming Report*, New York: Fawcett, 1969), continues to be a vocal opponent of the pill. Earlier, in *The Doctors' Case Against the Pill* (1969), she cited many case histories in which the pill can be suspected of having caused injury and death. In most of the cases the woman who died or suffered had not been examined carefully enough by the doctor who prescribed pills for her; had not had checkups while taking the pill; or had not been told that there was some risk involved in taking it. Others had too long ignored pains that were in fact warning signals, and had sought help too late. But some of the deaths were unpredictable and unpreventable.

Following are two tables comparing mortality statistics for pregnancy and childbirth, legal abortion, and different birth control methods (from: *Family Planning Perspectives*, V. 9, #2, Mar/Apr 1977):

Table 1. Mortality associated with pregnancy and childbirth, legal abortion, use of oral contraceptives (by smoking status) and IUDs, by age

AGE GROUP	PREGNANCY AND CHILD-BIRTH*	LEGAL ABOR-TION†	PILL‡ NON-SMOK-ERS§	SMOK-ERS§	IUDs‡
15–19	11.1	1.2	1.2	1.4	0.8
20–24	10.0	1.2	1.2	1.4	0.8
25–29	12.5	1.4	1.2	1.4	1.0
30–34	24.9	1.4	1.8	10.4	1.0
35–39	44.0	1.8	3.9	12.8	1.4
40–44	71.4	1.8	6.6	58.4	1.4

From comparative death rates, it can be argued that taking the pill is safer than risking pregnancy. The death rate due to blood clots in women on the pill is estimated at 3 per 100,000; the death rate during pregnancy and delivery is 14 to 17 per 100,000. But this argument is both misleading and not entirely reassuring. The figures are misleading. The risk of death in childbirth is not the same for every woman, and varies with social class, race and age. These mortality figures are not stratified. For

*Ratio per 100,000 live births (excluding abortion), U.S. 1972–1974.
†Ratio per 100,000 first-trimester abortions, U.S. 1972–1974.
‡Rate per 100,000 users per year.
§Estimates by A. K. Jain "Mortality Risk Associated with the Use of Oral Contraceptives," *Studies in Family Planning*, 8:50, 1977; —, "Cigarette Smoking, Use of Oral Contraceptives, and Myocardial Infarction," *American Journal of Obstetrics and Gynecology*, 126:301, 1976.

Table 2. Annual number of birth-related, and total deaths associated with control of fertility per 100,000 nonsterile women, by regimen of control and age of woman

REGIMEN OF CONTROL AND OUTCOME	AGE GROUP 15 TO 19	20 TO 24	25 TO 29	30 TO 34	35 TO 39	40 TO 44
No control						
Birth-related	5.6	6.1	7.4	13.9	20.8	22.6
Abortion only						
Method-related	1.2	1.6	1.8	1.7	1.9	1.2
Pill only/ nonsmokers						
Birth-related	0.1	0.2	0.2	0.4	0.6	0.5
Method-related	1.2	1.2	1.2	1.8	3.9	6.6
Total deaths	1.3	1.4	1.4	2.2	4.5	7.1
Pill only/smokers						
Birth-related	0.1	0.2	0.2	0.4	0.6	0.5
Method-related	1.4	1.4	1.4	10.4	12.8	58.4
Total deaths	1.5	1.6	1.6	10.8	13.4	58.9
IUDs only						
Birth-related	0.1	0.2	0.2	0.4	0.6	0.5
Method-related	0.8	0.8	1.0	1.0	1.4	1.4
Total deaths	0.9	1.0	1.2	1.4	2.0	1.9
Traditional methods only						
Birth-related	1.1	1.6	2.0	3.6	5.0	4.2
Traditional methods, plus abortion						
Method-related	0.2	0.2	0.3	0.3	0.3	0.2

some women the risk of death from the pill may be as great as the risk of death from childbirth. Further, as one woman wrote us from New York, "I have trouble with the comparison of death rates. I don't think that most women choose a birth control method with death rates in mind. And the fact that the risk of death is indeed a consideration is indicative of just how lousy the situation is." A further consideration here is that death rates are no indication of the significant number of women who have been hospitalized with crippling strokes or other non-fatal blood clots, who develop diabetes on the pill, or who become debilitatingly depressed (see below).

In trying to decide whether to express ourselves as pro-pill or anti-pill, our collective has set up the following reasoning: birth control pills are dangerous for some women, and in quite a number of other women can cause side effects that range from nuisances to major complications. Although many women have taken the pill with no major immediate side effects, long-term effects on women and their post-pill children will not be known for many decades. Yet effective protection against pregnancy is a very important tool for us as we start to take control of our lives. Some women therefore will continue to use the pill. Our choice for ourselves is to use other methods whenever possible, if we feel we can use them effectively.

We feel that every woman deserves to be able to make, and must make, an "informed decision" about using birth control pills. She must know the risks, and she must know about other birth control methods that she could use. If she chooses the pill, she must be able to see a responsible physician who is well acquainted with birth control pills. (See "How to Get Pills," p. 193, for an idea of what the doctor should ask and check before giving you pills.)

How Long To Take the Pill

If you are not now experiencing too many side effects, you may feel you want to enjoy the freedom of the pill indefinitely. Yet if you take the pill for many years at a time, you are in a sense part of a huge experiment on the long-term effects of daily hormone ingestion in healthy women. Doctors disagree on how long a woman should stay on the pill. Some suggest two- or three-year intervals with three-month breaks in between; others say in some cases it is safe to take it for ten years without stopping. Your decision depends on a lot of factors. If a pregnancy would be physically dangerous to you, you may choose to stay on the pill. If you want to have a baby at some point later on, you may choose not to stay on the pill for more than two to four years at a time. Keep in mind that some of the side effects, such as depression and decreased sexual energy, are thought to increase over time.

It is a sad fact that many women get pregnant in the first few months after going off the pill, because they do not easily get into using another method of birth control. We are "spoiled" by the simplicity of the pill. Yet we must face the fact that it is *not* a method we can use forever. We need discussion, information and support in making a switch to another method.

Complications and Side Effects

A fairly comprehensive listing of complications and side effects caused by the pill is included in the new (1978) patient package insert required in all pill packets. Ask your druggist or doctor for a copy.

Complications are considered to be potentially life-threatening, whereas side effects vary from major to minor nuisances. It is not surprising that the pill can have many effects: it is a medication that enters your bloodstream and travels around your body, affecting many tissues and organs just as natural estrogens and progesterone do. Hormonal contraception is still in its experimental stage, and many of the effects the synthetic hormones have on the various parts of your body are unknown.

Undoubtedly some of the side effects are psychosomatic. The doctor who said "If we tell women they might get headaches, they'll get headaches" was insulting women by implying that we react to the pill in a mindless, hysterical way and conjure up side effects. There is a tendency, however, to blame mental and physical problems we experience on something concrete, such as the pill, especially if there has been a lot of publicity about the pill or if we aren't sure we want to be taking it. We have the right to know all the possible side effects of the pill, but we must keep in mind that many women notice no side effects other than some nausea at the beginning. Also, most side effects are reversible—they will stop when the pills are stopped. You may decide to put up with mild side effects rather than choose a less effective or less convenient contraceptive. If you get an unpleasant side effect from one brand of pill, you can switch to a different brand and the effect may disappear (see "Differences Among the Several Brands of Pills," p. 195). If you do change brands, use an additional birth control method (foam, condoms) for the first two weeks on the new brand.

THE PILL AND BLOOD CLOTS. A number of studies* have established that women who take the pill run a considerably greater risk of incurring blood clots which can lead to pain, hospitalization and sometimes (in less than 3 per 100,000 women per year) death. The increased incidences include blood clots most often in the leg (venous thrombosis, or phlebitis); blood clots in the lungs, which have usually traveled from the leg (pulmonary thromboembolism); and blood clots or hemorrhage in the brain (stroke). Studies vary in their estimates of what exactly is the increased risk of such problems among women on the pill—from highs of 11 and 9 times greater risk, middle estimates of 5 and 6 times, to lows of 2, 1 and even 0. At worst this means that of women who suffered blood clotting disorders, eleven were taking the pill to every one who was not. But what the risk is for you is totally unpredictable; the great majority of women on the pill do not encounter problems with blood clotting. Taking smaller doses of estrogen (50 mcg) may help guard against clots. Incidences of blood clots are also higher in general among all women over thirty-five years of age, and among smokers.

If you choose the pill, be sure you are carefully examined before you begin and while you are taking pills; have your susceptibility to blood clots checked as thoroughly as possible. The signs which may indicate blood clots are severe headaches, sudden blurring of vision, sensation of flashing lights, severe leg or chest pains, or shortness of breath.

THE PILL AND HEART ATTACKS. A July-August 1975 FDA bulletin warns that two recent British studies "strongly suggest" that women on birth control pills run a higher risk of heart attack (coronary thrombosis) than non-users. This risk seems to be higher for women over forty years old. (See p. 193, under "Who Can Use the Pill Conditionally.")*

RISE IN BLOOD PRESSURE. The pill will cause small increases in blood pressure or outright hypertension in a certain percentage of users. The incidence of high blood pressure tends to increase with increased duration of pill use and with age, and seems to be correlated with estrogen dosage. It is therefore very important to have your blood pressure checked every six months to a year when you are taking birth control pills. Switching brands can eliminate this side effect for some women.

THE PILL AND CANCER. There has been no proof that the pills cause cancer. The pill does cause polyps (nonmalignant tumors) to grow in the lining of the cervix in some women, and causes changes in the cervical cells of others. The pills do cause increases in the number of cells in the ovaries, uterus and breasts; these conditions are thought not to be precancerous, but many doctors feel that not enough long-term studies have been made to prove absolutely that such effects are not an indication of precancerous conditions. It is known that estrogen can aggravate existing cancer, so for your safety be sure you are carefully checked—pelvic and breast examinations and Pap smear—before you start taking pills and every six to twelve months while you are taking them. A family history of breast cancer is not usually considered a contraindication to the pill. In fact, some doctors believe that a progestin-dominant pill may even have a protective effect. It is always important, however, to examine your own breasts every month for lumps.

THE PILL AND YOUR CHILDREN. It has not yet been proved that the pill either directly or indirectly causes infant abnormalities or birth defects. Recently, however, it has been suggested that there may be an association between ingestion of sex hormones in the first trimester of pregnancy (or just before) and congenital limb reductions (absence of a limb or parts of limbs). Such cases

---

*Boston Collaborative Drug Surveillance Program, "Oral Contraceptives and Venous Thromboembolic Disease, Surgically Confirmed Gallbladder Disease, and Breast Tumors," *The Lancet*, Vol.1 (1973), p. 1399. Also, Royal College of General Practitioners, *Oral Contraceptives and Health* (Manchester, England: Pitman Publishing, 1974).

*The New York Times, August 27, 1975, p. 1. See also Samuel Shapiro, M.R.C.P., "Oral Contraceptives and Myocardial Infarction," *New England Journal of Medicine*, Vol. 293, No. 4 (July 24, 1975), pp. 195-96.

have been reported in increased incidences among babies of mothers who were taking the pill while pregnant (including 50 mcg. doses of estrogen); who had taken hormones to help maintain their pregnancies; who had been given progestin as a pregnancy test; or who had become pregnant within three months of stopping the pill.*

There also may be a higher rate of neonatal jaundice among infants whose mothers had taken the pill before pregnancy.

Children who find pills and eat them might become nauseated. We do not know what harm this may cause. You should call your doctor if more than a few pills are swallowed.

HEADACHES. Around 5 percent of women on pills develop bad migraines or other frequent headaches.

Migraines are throbbing headaches which result from a problem in the circulation of blood to the brain. Migraines are painful. Further, migraines *can be a warning signal for impending stroke*, and should cause a woman to switch to a lower-dose estrogen pill or to stop taking pills altogether.

DIABETES. In some women, the pill, like pregnancy, can precipitate diabetes. See p. 193, under "Who Can Use the Pill Conditionally."

DEPRESSION. Possibly one in four women experience increased irritability or a tendency to feel depressed on the pill. These symptoms often continue instead of improving with succeeding cycles, and can grow on you without your being aware that the pill is causing them. Switching to a pill with a *less* potent progestin may help. Also vitamin B_6 supplementation can be very helpful (see "Readings and Resources").

CHANGE IN INTENSITY OF SEXUAL DESIRE AND RESPONSE. Many women experience an increase in sexual desire as soon as their fear of pregnancy is removed. But increasing numbers of women on progestin-dominant, low-dosage estrogen pills are complaining of lack of sex drive, lack of vaginal lubrication, decreased sensitivity in their vulval tissues, and decreased ability to have orgasms. One Boston doctor told us that 25 to 50 percent of his patients who are on low-estrogen, progestin-dominant pills experience these side effects to some degree. This doctor often prescribes a higher-dosage estrogen pill, such as Ovulen, for women who feel these side effects, being sure to tell them that the higher dose of estrogen means a higher risk of thromboembolism.

NAUSEA. A common early side effect of the pill. The estrogen in the pill might irritate your stomach lining or make you feel sick at your stomach just as a pregnant woman feels while her body is getting used to the high levels of estrogen that the placenta puts into her blood. Nausea usually goes away after two months; antacid tab-

*See Harlap and Heinonen citations, under "Readings and Resources"; see also Chapter 13.

lets or taking the pill with a meal or just before bed usually give relief.

FATIGUE. Another common symptom of pregnancy that can affect pill users is tiredness and lethargy. Fatigue usually lasts only two or three months while your body gets used to the different hormone levels.

VAGINITIS AND VAGINAL DISCHARGE. Vaginitis is a vaginal inflammation that may be caused by infection with a fungus, trichomonas, bacteria, or virus. The pills change the normal environment of the vagina and provide excellent conditions for rapid growth of micro-organisms. It does not always occur, but any of the pills could make the vagina more susceptible, particularly to the yeast monilia (*Candida albicans*). Vaginitis is treatable, but if it persists you may have to go off the pill. Increased vaginal discharge is fairly common, can be due to estrogen, and does not necessarily indicate infection—though if it is bothering you, you should have it checked.

INCREASED SUSCEPTIBILITY TO VENEREAL DISEASE. It has been suggested that the pill makes the vagina more susceptible to the gonococcus (organism responsible for gonorrhea), just as the pill makes us more susceptible to monilia (yeast infection). However, the Center for Disease Control in Atlanta now says that this is not true, i.e., that the pill does not increase our chances of getting gonorrhea. It should be emphasized, though, that *the pill provides no protection* from getting gonorrhea, whereas the condom and diaphragm *do* provide some protection. If you are taking pills and either you or your sex partner is having intercourse with more than one person, try to protect yourself. Wash carefully (both of you), use condoms and spermicide (see list under "Diaphragm") for protection against VD, and get yourself checked regularly by a doctor (you usually have to ask for VD tests). See Chapter 9.

THE PILL AND SMOKING. Women who smoke should avoid the pill, especially women over 30. *Women over 40 definitely should not take the pill* (see Tables, pp. 188 and 189).

URINARY TRACT INFECTION. In addition to increased vaginal infections, women on the pill tend to have more infections of the bladder and urethra, the tube which leads urine out of your body. The infection rate is higher with higher estrogen doses.

CHANGES IN MENSTRUAL FLOW. Your periods will be lighter with most pills (estrogenic pills cause more normal flow). Occasionally your flow will be very slight or you will miss a period. Make sure you are waiting a week between pill packages (unless you have a 28-pill package). Missing a period when you haven't missed a pill does not necessarily mean you are pregnant; sometimes it is due to taking pills for a long time or taking pills high in progestin. If you miss two periods in a row, consult a doctor.

BREAKTHROUGH BLEEDING—that is, vaginal bleeding or staining between periods. If there isn't enough estrogen or progestin in the pill to support the lining of your uterus at a given point in your cycle, a little of the lining will slough off. (This may also occur if you miss a pill.) It usually happens in your first or second pill cycle and often clears up after that as your uterus gets used to the new levels of hormones. If breakthrough bleeding doesn't stop after a few months see a doctor to find out whether you need to try a different brand of pills or whether you may have another problem. Breakthrough bleeding does not mean that the pill isn't working as a contraceptive.

BREAST CHANGES. Increased breast tenderness might occur, but it usually lasts for only one or two cycles.

WEIGHT GAIN. Progestin-dominant pills, such as Ortho-Novum, Norlestrin, or Ovral, can cause appetite increase and permanent weight gain because of the build-up of protein in muscular tissue. If you want to gain weight, this is helpful. Estrogenic pills (Enovid, Oracon, Ovulen) can cause fluid retention because of increased sodium. This effect is temporary and usually cyclic. It can often be reversed by changing your brand of pill. Some people who retain fluid take a diuretic drug to stimulate their urine production, but diuretics have their own risks and side effects (rob body of potassium, for instance), so use them sparingly if at all.

SKIN PROBLEMS. The pill may be associated with skin problems such as eczema.

CHLOASMA, or changes in skin pigmentation, sometimes described as "giant freckles." Very rare. Occasionally permanent, but usually disappears or fades after pills are stopped.

ACNE. A progestin-dominant pill can cause or increase skin oiliness in some women. An estrogenic pill can decrease acne.

GUM INFLAMMATION. The pills, like pregnancy, foster the development of gum inflammation. Women on the pill should brush their teeth extra carefully, use dental floss regularly, and see a dentist every six months to a year.

LIVER AND GALL BLADDER DISEASE. The pill is associated with an increased incidence of gall bladder disease and of liver tumors (both benign and malignant). Jaundice may be an early symptom of liver complications, so women taking the pill should stop doing so at the first sign of jaundice. (In rare cases, liver tumors have resulted in death.)

EPILEPSY AND ASTHMA. A higher incidence of new cases of epilepsy occurs among women taking the pill. In addition, the pill can aggravate existing epilepsy and asthma. Low-estrogen pills should be used, and the woman should stay under close medical supervision.

VIRUS INFECTIONS. An increased incidence of chicken pox and other viral infections among pill users suggests that the pill may affect your body's immunity.

VITAMIN DEFICIENCIES. Pill use has been linked to deficiencies in vitamins such as B_6, B_{12}, C, E, and folic acid. B_6 deficiency can cause depression (see "Further Readings").

OTHER COMPLICATIONS. The pill also has been linked to: pleurisy; suppression of bone growth in young women; arthritic symptoms (swelling of joints); visual disturbances; ulcers in the mouth; bruising; antagonism with rifampin, a drug for tuberculosis, so that neither works as it should; lupus erythematosus, a disease of unknown origin which may be caused by an allergic reaction; and abnormalities in the cervix of the uterus. There may be no conclusive proof that the pill causes these effects. But you should know of the mere possibility, and if you should encounter one of these problems, consider that it might be connected with taking the pill.

Beneficial Side Effects

A list of symptoms connected with the pill would not be complete without the possible beneficial results of taking it (besides freedom from pregnancy). Menstrual disorders such as premenstrual tension and cramps tend to be decreased. Iron deficiency anemia is less likely, probably because of the decreased menstrual flow. Benign breast growths are seen less frequently among women on the pill. And in case you are bothered by ear wax, the pill may clear that up.

Warning Signals

Any side effect that lasts more than two or three cycles should be reported to the doctor. More serious symptoms of adverse reactions are: severe pain or swelling in the legs, bad headache, blurred vision. These should be reported immediately, for they are signs of incipient thromboembolism and mean that you should stop taking the pill. (Note on leg pain: some leg cramps might be caused by fluid retention induced by the estrogen in the pill. Don't confuse this with the severe leg pain of thromboembolism, but also don't hesitate to call a doctor if the leg cramps become painful.)

Who Should Not Use the Pill

The pills are dangerous for certain women. To help the doctor in screening women who want to use the pill, the FDA requires drug companies to publish a list of contraindications, or conditions that prohibit the use of the pill. The doctor should check a woman for each one of these contraindications:

ANY DISEASE OR CONDITION ASSOCIATED WITH POOR BLOOD CIRCULATION OR EXCESS BLOOD CLOTTING: bad varicose veins, thrombophlebitis (clots in veins, frequently in the leg), pulmonary embolism (blood clot which has traveled to the lung, usually from the leg), stroke, heart disease or defect.

HEPATITIS OR OTHER LIVER DISEASES. As it is the liver that metabolizes the sex steroids (progesterone and estrogen), no one with liver disease should take pills until the disease is cleared up. Use a good alternative method of contraception, because pregnancy can be a great strain on the liver. A woman who tends to get jaundice during pregnancy should not use pills.

UNDIAGNOSED ABNORMAL GENITAL BLEEDING.

CANCER OF THE BREAST OR OF THE REPRODUCTIVE ORGANS. (See p. 190, "The pill and cancer.")

LACTATION. Nursing mothers should not take the birth control pill for two reasons. First, the pill may dry up the mother's supply of milk, especially if administered soon after she gives birth. Even if it does not dry it up, the pill decreases the amounts of protein, fat and calcium in the milk. There is also suspicion that some estrogen will come through into the milk. At present this is a controversial subject; most nursing mothers are advised not to take the pill.

CYSTIC FIBROSIS. Definitely no pills.

SICKLE-CELL ANEMIA. Women with sickle-cell anemia should not take the pill, because of the increased risk of intravascular blood clotting with both sickle-cell anemia and the pill.

PREGNANCY. Hormones in the pill may affect fetal development. (See p. 190, "The Pill and Your Children.")

Who Can Use the Pill Conditionally

Women with the following disorders or ailments can use the pill but should do so only under *close medical supervision.*

DIABETES OR PRE-DIABETES. Sugar metabolism is extensively altered in women on the pill. The progestin in the pills tends to bind the body's insulin and keep it out of circulation, which increases a diabetic woman's insulin requirement. If you are a diabetic, or if close relatives are diabetic, you should have regular periodic blood tests if you go on the pill. Many doctors do put diabetic women on the pill because pregnancy is especially hazardous to a diabetic.

MIGRAINE HEADACHES. See p. 191, under "Complications and Side Effects."

EPILEPSY AND ASTHMA. See p. 192.

MENTAL RETARDATION.

CIRCULATORY CONDITIONS. A woman with high blood pressure (hypertension) or mild varicose veins must take pills with caution.

CARDIAC OR RENAL DISEASE.
UTERINE FIBROMYOMATA.
TENDENCY TO SEVERE DEPRESSION OR ANY SERIOUS PSYCHIATRIC PROBLEMS. See p. 191.

CHLOASMA. See above.

SICKLE-CELL TRAIT. Black women planning to go on the pill should have a sickle-cell test. If it is positive for sickle-cell trait you should discuss with your doctor the possible hazards of your taking the pill.

AGE. Women over thirty-five run a statistically higher risk of thromboembolism and other complications when taking the pill. Since such risks also increase during pregnancy, women over thirty-five should consider a combination method, such as the diaphragm and condoms, or sterilization—tubal ligation for you or vasectomy for your sex partner.

In August, 1975, the FDA advised that women *over forty* not use the pill because of increased risk of heart attack. (See p. 190, "The Pill and Heart Attacks.") Women over forty who smoke absolutely should not take the pill.

How to Get Pills

As we have seen, certain physical conditions would make taking birth control pills very dangerous, so it is in our vital interest to have a doctor prescribe our pills. Don't borrow them from a friend. Be sure the doctor examines you carefully, including an internal pelvic exam, breast exam, eye exam, Pap smear, and blood-pressure, blood and urine tests. The interview should include questions about you and your family's medical history of breast cancer, blood clots, diabetes, migraines and so on. *Too many doctors prescribe birth control pills hurriedly; it's up to you to make sure you are carefully checked for each one of the contraindications.* When you are on pills you should see a doctor every six months to a year for the same tests and examinations.

How to Use Pills

Combination pills come in packets of 21 or 28 pills. With 21-day pills you take one pill a day for 21 days and then stop for 7 days, during which time your period will come. With 28-day pills, which give you 21 hormone pills followed by 7 different-colored placebos (without drugs), you take one pill a day with no pause between packets. Your period comes during the time that you are taking the 7 different-colored pills. The 28-day pill is good if you feel you would have trouble remembering the on-and-off schedule of the 21-day pill. There is no medical difference between them.

Most pill regimens start the first pill on the fifth day after your period starts, counting the day you start your period as day one. (Some pills start on the first Sunday after your period comes.) Take one pill at approximately the same time each day. If you feel nausea, take the pill with a meal or after a snack at bedtime. Here is an almost foolproof schedule: Take a pill at bedtime; check the packet each morning to make sure you've taken a pill the night before; and carry a spare packet of pills with you in case you get caught away from home or lose pills. *Read the directions carefully.*

If you forget a pill

Take the forgotten pill as soon as you remember it, and take the next pill at its appointed time, even if this means taking two pills in one day. If you forget two pills, take two pills as soon as you remember, then take two pills the next day to catch up and use an additional method of contraception (foam, condoms) for the rest of that cycle. You may have some spotting. If you forget three pills or more, withdrawal bleeding will probably begin, so act as though you are at the end of a cycle. Don't make up the missed pills; stop taking your pills; start a new package after you have been off for 7 days. Use an extra method of birth control from the day you realize you forgot the pills through two weeks of the next cycle. If you miss a pill or two and skip a period, get a pregnancy test. If you've been taking your pills correctly and you skip a period, it is unlikely that you are pregnant, but you may need a different brand of pill.

Protection

Your first packet of pills may not protect you perfectly, as an egg may have started to develop before day 5. To be safe, use another method of birth control for at least the first two weeks. After your first month on pills you will be protected against pregnancy all month long, even during the days between packets.

Responsibility

Birth control pills are primarily the woman's responsibility. You see the doctor, get examined, remember to take the pill, feel the side effects, and run the risks. Hopefully, the man you sleep with understands this, is supportive, and agrees to use condoms or put up with a less invisible means of birth control if you want to stop taking pills.

Advantages and Disadvantages of the Combination Pill

Advantages

Almost complete protection against unwanted pregnancy.

Regularity of menstrual cycle—a period every 28 days.

Lighter flow during periods. This effect pleases most women, bothers some.

Relief of premenstrual tension.

Fewer menstrual cramps or none at all.

An estrogenic pill will clear up acne for some women.

The pill often brings a sense of well-being and a new enjoyment of sex because the fear of pregnancy is gone.

Taking the pill has no immediate physical relationship to lovemaking. This is especially relaxing if you are just starting to have intercourse and have a lot to learn about your body and his. Later on when you are more comfortable with sex and more able to communicate openly with your partner, a diaphragm or foam and condoms will not seem like such interruptions.

Disadvantages

Most of the disadvantages have been described under the section on side effects. The only one to add is that you do have to remember to take a pill every day. Some women are too forgetful, or live lives that are too chaotic for them to remember to take a pill every day. Younger women who live at home and feel a need to hide their pills from their parents sometimes leave them behind or are unable to take them on time.

Sequential Pills

Sequential pills should no longer be prescribed, sold or used. These pills use estrogen alone for the first part of the cycle and then combine estrogen and progestin for the last 5 or 6 days. Sequential pills are both *less effective* and, because of higher estrogen level, *more dangerous* than combination pills.

Although the FDA ordered sequential pills off the market in 1976, some pharmacies still have them in stock and some physicians may still be prescribing them. If you are currently using a sequential such as Oracon, NorQuen or Ortho-Novum SQ, you should get your prescription changed to a combination pill or else use a different form of birth control. (If you switch brands of pills, remember to use an extra method for the first two weeks of the first packet of the new brand.)

Progestin-Only Pills

Progestin-only pills are sometimes called "mini-pills," but this term will not be used here in order to avoid confusion with the "low-dose" estrogen combination pill and with a pill that was taken off the market several years ago.

Description (Progestin-Only Pills)

These pills contain small doses of the same progestins available in combination pills. Micronor and Nor-Q-D each provide 0.35 mg. norethindrone, and Ouvrette provides 0.075 mg. norgestrel. They contain no estrogen. You take one a day continuously, starting on day one of your period, at the same time each day (particularly important), without stopping during your period.

It is unknown how they work, but contraceptive actions which have been proposed for progestins are: changes in cervical mucus that make it hard for sperm to get through; inhibition of the travel of the egg through the tubes; partial inhibition of the ability of the sperm to penetrate the egg; partial inhibition of implantation; and possible inhibition of ovulation.

Effectiveness (Progestin-Only Pills)

The theoretical pregnancy rate is 1 to 4 percent, higher than the combination pill. The actual failure rate is of course higher than this. The pregnancy rate may be lower for women who switch from the combination pill to the progestin-only pill than it is for women who have never taken the combination pill. Pregnancy rates are highest in the first six months, so using an alternative method of contraception during this period is recommended.

Possible Side Effects (Progestin-Only Pills)

The progestin-only pills were developed in part to avoid estrogen-associated complications and are being used particularly among women who had estrogen-related problems on the combination pill. However, some of the side effects seen with the combination pill are being reported for the progestin-only pill. Effects which have been reported are change in weight, cervical erosion and change in cervical secretion, jaundice, allergic skin rash, chloasma, depression, gastrointestinal disturbances, breast changes. A common complaint is that menstrual bleeding is very irregular in amount and duration of flow and length of cycle. (If you don't have a period within 45 days of your last one, get a pregnancy test.) These pills have not been used long enough for any conclusions to be drawn about their desirability. You may feel safer taking them knowing they have no estrogen and a very small dose of progestin, and that they may have about the same rate of effectiveness as an IUD. On the other hand, the irregular cycles may get you down, or you may not wish to be one of the testers of a very new pill.

Differences Among the Several Brands of Pills

If you choose to take the birth control pill, how do you and the doctor determine which pill you should take? We should be aware that different pills have different kinds, strengths and quantities of synthetic estrogen and progesterone in them. The first and firmest guideline for choice has been suggested by the British Committee on Safety of Drugs, which warns us that high-estrogen pills are more likely to give us blood clots. The committee advises that only products containing 50 mcg. or less of estrogen be used; that products containing 75 mcg. or more of estrogen are associated with a higher incidence of thromboembolic disorder. Pills with 50 mcg. of estrogen are: Ortho-Novum 1/50, Norinyl 1 (same as Ortho-Novum 1/50), Demulen, Norlestrin 1, Norlestrin 2.5, Ovral and Zorane 1/50. Pills with more than this recommended dose of estrogen are: Ortho-Novum 1/80, Ortho-Novum 2, Ovulen, Enovid-E, Enovid 5, Norinyl 2, and all sequential pills.

In the past two years several pills with doses of synthetic estrogen lower than 50 mcg. ("low-dose" pills) have come on the market. These are Loestrin 1.5/30, Loestrin 1/20, Zorane 1.5/30, Zorane 1/20, Logest 1.5/30, ModiCon and Bevicon. You may wish to try these, especially if you are having trouble with estrogenic side effects. These pills may produce more spotting between periods, and the pregnancy rate, especially of the lowest doses, may be a bit higher.

Many doctors are still prescribing high-dosage estrogen pills, either because they don't know about the British report or because they disagree with it. Others prescribe higher-dosage estrogen pills if a woman has had bad side effects from a higher-dosage progestin pill or if there is an indication that she will have them (see below). In these cases the doctor must be sure to inform the woman of the higher risk of blood clots.

The kind of side effects that a particular pill is likely to have is directly related to the amount and potency of the progestin relative to the estrogen in that pill. There are several kinds of synthetic progesterone (progestins). Certain progestins, such as norethindrone and norethindrone acetate (used in Ortho-Novum, Norlestrin, Norinyl, Norquen, Loestrin, Zorane), tend to produce *androgenic* ("male") effects—for example, hairiness, scanty periods, acne, permanent weight gain. With pills in which the estrogen dominates (Enovid, Demulen, Ovulen), either because of a lower progestin-to-estrogen ratio or because of the use of a less potent progestin, the effects tend to be what are called *estrogenic*, or "female," such as heavier periods, fluid retention, breast swelling and tenderness.

It is not always possible to predict the estrogen or progestin potency by the dose because the synthetic compounds vary. There are two kinds of synthetic estrogens, ethinyl estradiol and mestranol, which are offered in equivalent doses but may not be equal in strength. Some studies have suggested that ethinyl estradiol is more potent than mestranol and that it is also implicated more often in side effects such as strokes and urinary infections. It is interesting to note that all the "low-dose" estrogen pills (below 50 mcg.) use ethinyl estradiol. Progestins in some pills have an estrogenic effect; others appear to have an anti-estrogenic effect.

The exact effects that a given pill will have on your body, if you experience side effects at all, depend on your normal estrogen and progesterone levels. These levels are hard to test accurately, but you and the doctor can judge them in a general way. For instance, if you have a lot of body hair and scanty menstrual periods, you can guess that in your normal non-pill body chemistry there is a predominance of progesterone over estrogen. A low-dosage estrogen pill is likely to accentuate your progesterone-related characteristics, and you might experience one or more of the progestin-excess symptoms—scant menstrual flow, changed sex drive, poor vaginal lubrication, susceptibility to monilia vaginitis, appetite increase and permanent weight gain, acne, depression, or fatigue. A more estrogenic pill would be likely to balance your natural excess of progesterone, although it might increase your risk of blood clots.

On the other hand, if you have heavy periods or large breasts that get tender before your period, or if you tend to retain fluid and often feel bloated, you are probably estrogen-sensitive or have a natural overbalance of estrogen in your system. A low-dosage estrogen or high-potency progestin pill would be good for you, whereas a high-estrogen pill would be likely to give you nausea, bloating, breast tenderness, leg cramps, chloasma (see p. 192), irritability and heavy periods.

Since it is not yet possible to predict side effects in any given case, use these guidelines when you can. Show them to the doctor; but if a doctor whom you trust believes that a certain pill will be right for you, try it. You can switch if one of these effects shows up.

IUD, OR INTRAUTERINE DEVICE: COIL, LOOP AND SHIELD

Description

Most IUDs are small white plastic devices of different shapes and sizes. They are placed inside the uterus by a trained person—in this country usually a doctor or a nurse practitioner. One or two strings extend from the uterus into the upper vagina so that you can check that the device is still in place by feeling for the threads. Once the IUD is inserted, nothing needs to be done other than checking, unless there are problems or you want to get pregnant. Removal should be done by a doctor or nurse practitioner.

How the IUD Works

No one is absolutely sure how the IUD works to prevent pregnancy. Centuries ago, when camel drivers in the Middle East started out on a long journey across the desert, they would insert pebbles into the uterus of a female camel to keep her from becoming pregnant on the trip. A foreign body in the uterus seems to prevent pregnancy most of the time.

It was formerly believed that the IUD worked by speeding up the peristaltic waves by which the fallopian tube moves the egg down toward the uterus, but this theory is no longer accepted. Currently the IUD is believed to cause a local inflammatory reaction inside the uterus. A fertilized egg might not be able to implant in a lining which has not been able to develop properly. Also, the white blood cells which are present in inflammatory reactions may ingest or be toxic to the sperm and/or the egg, or they may interfere with implantation of a developing egg. The inflammation which occurs is a reaction to a foreign body (the IUD) and to irritation and does not necessarily mean there is an infection, even when there is an increase in vaginal discharge. The copper IUDs seem to have an additional contraceptive effect: small amounts of copper released from the copper wire into the uterus are thought to alter the functions of the enzymes participating in the implantation process and may also interfere with intrauterine sperm transport.

Some people find it a little unsettling that no one knows exactly how the IUD works. Others, uneasy with the pill's more generalized effects and the pregnancy rates of other methods, choose the IUD. However, the effects of IUDs are not just local—for example, infections caused by IUD use can affect the whole pelvic area, and even the whole body.

The Different Types of IUD

Insert devices (e.g., the Lippes Loop and the Sat-T-Coil) and plastic devices with a copper sleeve (e.g., the Cu–7) are the most commonly used IUDs in the United States. In 1977, the Cu–7 was especially popular.

The Dalkon Shield* was one of the IUDs designed to be better tolerated by women who have never been pregnant. A never-pregnant woman can have a hard time tolerating the IUD: a uterus that has not been stretched by pregnancy tends to react to one of these devices with cramping, backache and expulsion. The stainless-steel Majzlin Spring successfully reduced expulsion rates in never-pregnant women, but was soon withdrawn from the market because it tended to become imbedded in the lining of the uterus, making removal very difficult. When first introduced, the Dalkon Shield was widely publicized to have lower rates of pregnancy, expulsion, and other complications—and was quickly adopted by many family-planning programs. It has since been found to cause increased infections and occasional severe pregnancy complications, and even several deaths.

Some of the so-called "second-generation" IUDs which have been developed are slightly smaller plastic devices with an active substance, usually copper, added

---

*No longer in use (see "Further Readings").

to increase their effectiveness. The Cu-7 or Copper-7, now in use, has copper wire coiled around a small plastic device. Also on the market are two T-shaped devices, one with added copper wire (Cu-T) and one containing progesterone, which is released gradually inside the uterus over the period of one year (the "Progestasert"). The long-term effects of these small amounts of copper and progesterone on a woman's body are unknown. At first, the Progestasert was advertised by its manufacturer (Alza Corp.) as having "all the contraceptive features you want in one." In 1977, the FDA required Alza to discontinue its promotional campaign (judged "misleading" by the FDA) and to publish remedial advertisement. Moreover, *The Medical Letter* (July 30, 1976) concluded that the Progestasert "appears to be no more effective than other IUDs, may cause pain on insertion, and must be removed and replaced every twelve months."

Effectiveness

Pregnancy rates for the currently used types of IUD vary from 1 to 7 percent. The published rates are not entirely comparable because they are based on studies of different quality. (Drug company representatives tend to give a lower failure rate for their devices.) Approximate pregnancy rates for the large (Size D) Lippes Loop and the Safe-T-Coil are 3 percent. So far, the copper devices, especially the Copper-7, have lower pregnancy rates, but they have not been tested very extensively. Pregnancy rates are lower among women over 30 and those who have given birth. For 100 percent protection it is good to use contraceptive foam, cream, jelly, or condoms with

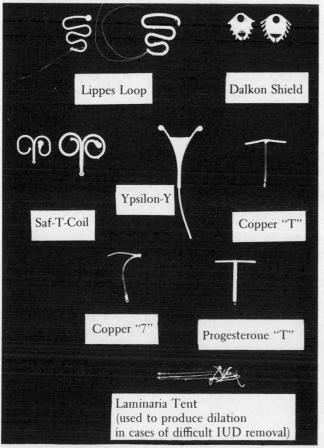

Lippes Loop

Dalkon Shield

Ypsilon-Y

Saf-T-Coil

Copper "T"

Copper "7"

Progesterone "T"

Laminaria Tent
(used to produce dilation
in cases of difficult IUD removal)

the IUD, all the time if you feel particularly fertile, or for 7 to 10 days at mid-cycle (see "Fertility Consciousness," p. 207). Many Planned Parenthood clinics advise women to use a supplemental birth control method for the first three months with an IUD, as that is the time when conception seems to take place most often and when the IUD is most likely to be expelled. Some doctors feel responsible for an IUD failure to the point that they will give you an abortion if this happens. Question your doctor on this point. If you do become pregnant with the IUD in place, a miscarriage can be caused from 25 to 50 percent of the time simply by having the doctor remove the IUD.

MEDICATIONS AND IUD EFFECTIVENESS. Observations of IUD failures over the past few years have given rise to evidence that both *aspirin* and *antibiotics* (e.g., penicillin, tetracycline) may *lower* IUD effectiveness. Aspirin may hamper the action of contraction-causing prostaglandins (see p. 214) stimulated by the IUD's presence in the uterus. Antibiotics may interfere with the contraceptive effect of the IUD's irritation of the uterine lining. If you have an IUD, you may want to avoid taking aspirin and to use extra birth control (foam, condoms) while taking antibiotics.

Reversibility

Because of increased chances of infection (e.g., PID), IUDs may cause sterility in some women.

Safety and Side Effects*

PERFORATION. Perforation of the uterus, occurring in 1 out of about 1,000 women, is sometimes the result of faulty insertion. Occasionally the IUD will slip out through a perforation into the abdominal cavity, where it can cause dangerous inflammation or adhesions, so it is important to check the strings and report their absence to the doctor.

INFECTION. Infection is second only to bleeding and pain as a reason for IUD removal. PID (Pelvic Inflammatory Disease) occurs in 2-4 percent of all women with IUDs, often resulting in hospitalization. Should you choose to get an IUD, remember that the greatest chance of infection (usually caused by improper insertion or the presence of gonorrhea) is during the two weeks following insertion.† One user in twelve develops an infection during this time. Major signs of infection are fever, abdominal or cervical soreness, and a foul discharge.

*See Roberts, Katherine, "The Intrauterine Device as a Health Risk," *Women and Health*, July/Aug. 1977.

†See Targum and Wright, "IUD and Pelvic Infection," *American Journal of Epidemiology*, Vol. 100, No. 262 (1974). This article reports a study which links IUD use with pelvic infection even a long time after insertion. (See also "Further Readings.")

Ten IUDs now in use or being tested in the U.S. (Dalkon Shield now off the market.) Laminaria tent, bottom, may help in cases of difficult IUD removal (see p. 233).

If you feel abdominal tenderness or pain with deep intercourse (when the penis goes in deep) report it to the doctor. If you catch gonorrhea while the IUD is in place, there is a chance that you won't be able to be cured until the IUD is removed, and the effects of the infection may be aggravated.

LONG-TERM EFFECTS. In some cases an imbedded IUD (not removable by ordinary means) will require a hysterectomy, thus resulting in sterility. IUD-related infections may also produce sterility. Tubal abscesses may be another long-term effect.

IUD AND PREGNANCY. If you get pregnant with an IUD in place, chances are about 50 percent that it will cause a miscarriage which may be accompanied by infection. It is now recommended by most physicians that a pregnant woman with an IUD have it removed immediately, because there are increased risks of pregnancy complications, infections, uterine perforations, intestinal obstructions, and hemorrhage. In some cases, spontaneous septic (infected) abortions have resulted in death. Also, the effects of copper (from the copper IUDs) on a developing fetus are as yet unknown. *If you do get pregnant* with an IUD in your uterus, notify your doctor, even if your period is only a week late: you may want to consider an abortion.

Recent research indicates that the rate of ectopic pregnancy among IUD users is 1.2% in the first year of use, and rises to 3% by the second year. The rate remains higher than the norm even after IUD removal. (Normally, .2-.5% of pregnancies are ectopic.) One theory suggests that "ascending infection" caused by an IUD might account for this increased rate. It is possible that the "hostile" uterine environment produced by the presence of a foreign object contributes to the likelihood of a fertilized egg implanting somewhere other than in the uterus. In any event, this is a serious problem. Frequently, ectopic pregnancy is misdiagnosed, so IUD users should be aware of possible symptoms of ectopic pregnancy (see Chapter 16).

EXPULSION. A major drawback of the IUD is the expulsion rate, which is about 4 to 8 or 13 to 19 percent, depending on the study. The IUD is usually expelled, if at all, in the first three months of use, and usually during the menstrual flow. It often comes out without your knowing it or feeling it, so check your tampon or sanitary napkin every time, and be sure to feel for the strings at the entrance to your cervix a few times a month, especially after your period.

BLEEDING AND CRAMPING. Some women experience little discomfort with the IUD; others experience considerable pain and bleeding. Some experience a lot of bleeding, cramping and/or backache for the first days after insertion. Check with your doctor if it goes on for more than a couple of days. Different doctors and clinics report that from 5 to 20 percent of IUDs are removed because of pain and bleeding. The bleeding may be heavier during menstruation, or occur between periods; periods may be irregular. Prolonged menstrual cramps are possible, or cramping and back pain may occur between periods. These symptoms are usually more intense during the first 3 to 6 months of using the IUD and then tend to decline. The following is a subjective account of a probably rare occurrence; but you never know, because such reports rarely get into the literature.

For about four months after I had my IUD inserted I felt that a white-hot wire was cutting through my uterus whenever I got aroused or had orgasms. I told the doctor who inserted it about this occurrence of pain, and he replied "impossible." I knew three other women who had gone to him for a Dalkon Shield, and they all said that they had felt foolish and hadn't mentioned that symptom to anyone, but they certainly felt it, too.

OTHER POSSIBLE EFFECTS. The possible side effects of the copper in the Copper-T and the Copper-7 are unclear. Reports suggest it may produce an allergic skin reaction, and there is some question as to how it might affect a developing fetus. One investigator has suggested that the copper may have an inhibitory effect on gonorrhea, but don't count on it.

There is no evidence that the IUD can cause cancer, but polyethylene (the material of most IUDs) is known to be a weak carcinogen (cancer-inducing substance) in the rat, and the IUD has not been studied long enough to know its long-term effects (cancers usually take 10 to 20 years to appear after initial exposure).

It has been suggested that the IUD causes tubal pregnancies (fertilized ovum implants in fallopian tube). Then this idea was discredited with the argument that the IUD does not prevent tubal pregnancy as effectively as it does uterine pregnancy, so it only *seems* to cause tubal pregnancies. More recent reports are bringing up the subject again, suggesting that IUD-associated infections may cause tubal blockage resulting in tubal pregnancy. This has not been proved. If you have an abortion because of an IUD-failure pregnancy, be sure to have the uterine contents checked for fetal material.

Who Should Not Use the IUD

IUDs should not be used by anyone with the following conditions: pregnancy, endometriosis, venereal disease, any vaginal or uterine infection, pelvic inflammatory disease, prohibitively small uterus, excessively heavy menstrual flow and/or cramping, bleeding between periods, large fibroids, uterine deformities, use of anticoagulants, cardiac disease, liver disease, anemia and sickle cell disease.

How to Get an IUD

Because of the risk of perforation, the IUD must be inserted by a well-trained person. Choose a doctor or nurse practitioner who has experience with IUDs and find out in advance which device she or he uses. Be sure you have a full medical, pelvic and breast examination, Pap smear, and pregnancy and VD tests. The doctor does a sounding of the uterus which measures its depth, shape and position. The IUD can be put into a tipped uterus. If the uterus is small, as it is if you have had no pregnancies, you'll get a small IUD—(unless your uterus is too small, and you can't be fitted with an IUD at all). Just before insertion, the Saf-T-Coil, Lippes Loop and Copper-7 are straightened out in a plastic tube like a straw; remember, the diameter of the cervical opening is the size of a thin straw. The doctor gently puts the tube into the vagina and up into the uterus through the cervix. Then the IUD is pushed through the tube and, being made of "memory plastic," springs into shape within the uterus.

The process can hurt, sometimes a lot, because the uterus is stretched and irritated by the device. You may have cramps during the insertion and for the rest of the day. Bring a friend with you if you can; if you feel you need to, you might choose to take aspirin or a tranquilizer, or try shallow panting to take your mind off it. The plastic IUD can stay in place for years but you should have it checked every six months to a year, at the time of your regular gynecological examination. The copper IUDs must be replaced every two to five years because the copper wire dissolves or gets brittle and breaks off.

When to Get an IUD

Insertion while you have your period or just afterward is preferred because (1) the opening of your cervix is a little larger at that time; (2) bleeding and cramping from the IUD are masked by your period; and (3), most important, doctors and clinics want to be sure you aren't pregnant, as an IUD insertion can cause a septic miscarriage.

Checking Your IUD

At first, you'll want to check your IUD before intercourse (you may want to ask your partner to do it) and after each period. After three months or so, once after each period is enough.

Squat, to shorten the length of your vagina, bringing your bottom down near your heels, and reach into your vagina with your longest (clean) finger. The bathtub or shower is a good place. Bearing down while you are sitting on the toilet will also bring your cervix within reach. You might be confused by the folds of your vagina, but when you reach your cervix you will know it, as it is harder and more substantial than anything else you'll touch. Find the dimple in your cervix; this is the entrance to your uterus, and the strings of the IUD should be sticking out a little way. Some days your uterus will be tipped in such a way that you can't reach the cervix or find the hole; try again the next day. If you cannot find the strings for a few days, or if you feel a bit of plastic protruding, call your doctor or clinic. Some

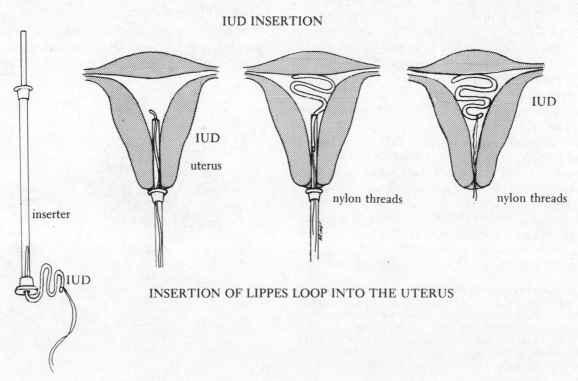

IUD INSERTION

INSERTION OF LIPPES LOOP INTO THE UTERUS

women become so conscious of their IUDs they can tell if the string length has changed—much shorter may mean the IUD has moved· up; much longer means it is moving down or coming out.

Responsibility

The woman sees a doctor for insertion and at least once a year afterward. She experiences the insertion and any side effects. The woman or her partner must check the strings periodically.

Cost

An IUD can be expensive to get but costs nothing afterward except for a visit to the doctor once every six months to a year. The initial charge is $35 to $50 by a private doctor in Boston, $50 to $100 in New York. If there are private doctors who do it more cheaply, your local Planned Parenthood association will have their names. Many clinics charge as little as $10, and in some places there is no charge at all.

DIAPHRAGM* AND SPERMICIDAL JELLY OR CREAM

A lot of people make a face when a diaphragm is mentioned. "It's messy. . . . It's a hassle. . . . It fails all the time." This current disdain is a little ironic, because in 1882, when invented, the diaphragm was a major breakthrough in the liberation of women from unwanted pregnancies. Until the 1960s, when the pill and the IUD started to remove birth control from the scene of intercourse, the diaphragm was the safest precaution women had—at one time one-third of American couples practicing birth control used the diaphragm.* Many of our mothers used it for thirty years without a slip. Whether our mothers *enjoyed* using it is a different question. Today our more positive feelings about our sexuality, and our increasing ability to communicate openly with the men we sleep with, make us more able to use the diaphragm happily. If you are just starting to have intercourse you may not want to add a diaphragm to your sex life immediately, but in a few months, when you are more easy about sex, you may be glad to get off the pill or the IUD for a method that is effective if you use it well and that has no side effects at all.

The diaphragm is not used as much as it could be in this country, partly because it requires a doctor's pre-

*Diaphragm Alert! The 86,000 Koro-Flex diaphragms bearing the serial numbers F6, G6, H6, or I6, were *recalled* in May, 1977, because 1% of them are defective. They have pin-prick size holes along the rim. If your diaphragm is Koro-Flex (n.b. Koro-Mex devices are not included in the recall) and contains one of these four serial numbers on the rim, bring it to the doctor or clinic where you got it, or to a Planned Parenthood clinic, for replacement or refund.

scription—and doctors often have not included time in their schedules for fittings, instruction, etc. Also, doctors frequently assume the IUD or pills are "better" and that

*J. Peel and M. Potts, *Textbook of Contraceptive Practice*, p. 63. (See bibliography.)

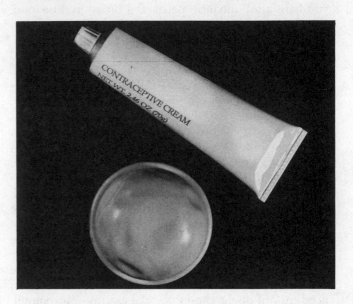

you wouldn't want to "mess" with the diaphragm every time you have intercourse. (Sometimes a doctor's attitudes on sexuality can affect his/her attitudes on certain methods of birth control.)

Description

A diaphragm, *which must always be used with spermicidal cream or jelly*, is made of soft rubber in the shape of a shallow cup. It has a flexible metal spring rim.

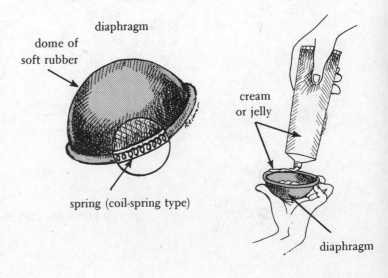

When properly fitted and inserted, it fits snugly over your cervix, locked in place behind the pubic bone and reaching back behind your cervix. It comes in a variety of sizes measured in millimeters (mm.), ranging from 50 to 105 mm., or 2 to 4 inches, depending on the size of your upper vagina.

How It Works

When the diaphragm is in place, holding spermicidal jelly or cream up to your cervix, the sperm cannot make it into your cervical canal. The sperm that swim up around the rim of the diaphragm run into the cream or jelly, which kills them. The sperm that remain in the vagina die in eight hours, as the vagina is a hostile environment to sperm. Some people also smear jelly on the outside of the diaphragm to help kill sperm remaining in the vagina. Never use the diaphragm without cream or jelly: they are the important contraceptive, and the diaphragm exists only to hold them in the proper place.

Effectiveness

A study among more than 2000 young women in New York City* showed that the diaphragm *can be* 98.1 percent effective with careful instruction. The main point in using a diaphragm is to use it *every time*, always with cream or jelly. Also crucial are proper fit and care, and the effectiveness of the spermicide (see "Brands," page 203). Failures do occur about 2 percent of the time even when the diaphragm is properly used. Masters and Johnson found that the upper vagina expands during intercourse, so that the diaphragm moves around a bit (see Chapter 3). The Montreal *Birth Control Handbook* lists other reasons for possible slippage: frequent insertion of the penis, lovemaking positions in which the woman is on top.

The diaphragm can be combined with the natural birth control methods. If a condom is used with the diaphragm on your fertile days, the effectiveness of your method is substantially increased. (See page 204.)

Reversibility

The diaphragm doesn't affect your fertility at all. Simply don't use it if you want to become pregnant.

Safety and Possible Side Effects

The diaphragm is perfectly safe. The only risk you run is that of getting pregnant—and if you use it well, that risk is low. Some of us have at some time felt scared that the diaphragm would slide up inside us and disappear, but as we got to know our anatomy better we realized that the

*Mary E. Lane, et al., "Successful Use of the Diaphragm and Jelly by a Young Population: Report of a Clinical Study," *Family Planning Perspectives*, Vol. 8, No. 2, March/April 1976.

vagina stops about an inch beyond the cervix, and the diaphragm (or tampon) has no place to disappear into.

A particular cream or jelly might irritate your vagina or the man's penis. Check the brand list on p. 203 for different ones to try. Some brands of jelly and cream sold in the U.S. at one time contained mercury. As a result of Japanese studies showing that it could cause kidney damage, the mercury was removed. It may still be found in some jellies or creams sold outside the U.S.

Some women find that the diaphragm irrates their urinary tracts, and may therefore be a contributing factor in bladder infections.

Who Shouldn't Use the Diaphragm

A woman with a severely displaced uterus (severe prolapse, for instance) cannot use a diaphragm. If your uterus is tipped forward or backward slightly, the doctor can choose one of the three kinds of metal spring rim (arcing, coiled, or flat) to fit your particular anatomy. A woman with protrusion of the bladder through the vaginal wall (cystocele) or other openings in the vagina (fistulas) cannot use this method.

If you don't feel comfortable touching your genitals and do not think you can get used to it *at this time*, you would most likely have trouble using a diaphragm effectively and should choose a different method. You can buy a diaphragm inserter if your diaphragm has a flat spring; but you will still need to check whether the diaphragm is covering your cervix, and you have to remove it without the inserter. (You may feel very squeamish and embarrassed the first time you put your finger into your vagina, but as you get used to it and realize that your body is yours to touch, you should get over any uneasiness about inserting the diaphragm.)

How to Get a Diaphragm

The size of diaphragm you should use depends on the size and contour of your vagina. In this country it is usually a doctor who measures you ("fits" you) for a diaphragm. But this is not a hard thing to learn and is one of the tasks that doctors are starting to share with nurses, midwives, or paramedical assistants. You should have a full gynecological examination at the time you get fitted for a diaphragm if you have not had one in the past year.

Very important: When you have been measured and fitted, you should practice putting in the diaphragm right there so the doctor or assistant can tell you if you have put it in right. (Or go home, practice, and come back in a few days with the diaphragm in place.) You can reach in and feel what it feels like when it is in right, and get help right then if you have problems, so that when you actually use it you won't be "experimenting." Some doctors neglect this important step. The doctor will probably give you a prescription for the proper size of diaphragm, and if your local drugstore requires one, a prescription for a good spermicidal cream or jelly.

How to Use a Diaphragm

Somebody said once that if someone handed you a toothbrush with no instructions and you had never seen one before, you might not use it very well for a while. The diaphragm is also a tool, and like any tool, it is simple to use once you've practiced with it. Putting it in the first time might feel awkward, but it will become easier and quicker with every insertion.

Who should put it in. There's a part of all of us that feels that we should go off into the bathroom, insert the diaphragm, and appear like a diaphanous angel ready for spontaneous sex. But there's also a part of us that resents that role. It seems that many of the people who are happiest with the diaphragm insert it as part of sexual foreplay—the man and the woman do it together. This sharing seems to work best in a long-term relationship. One woman told us she prefers to put it in in the bathroom because she wants to be able to wash the cream off her hands. And if you are a couple that gets carried away with sexual intensity, it's probably best to put the diaphragm in in advance. But for many women putting it in together with the man is a much less burdensome and more enjoyable way of using the diaphragm.

When to put it in. The diaphragm must be put in within six hours* before intercourse, since the creams and jellies may start to lose their spermicidal potency in the body after that time (the most conservative estimates say it should be put in as close to intercourse as possible).

Preparation and insertion. Put about one teaspoonful to one tablespoonful of cream or jelly (three-quarters of an inch if it comes in a tube) into the shallow cup, or on the dome side, whichever side you put up against your cervix. Spread the cream around. (Some books say to put the cream on the rim also; others say that cream on the rim makes the diaphragm slip. An effective compro-

*This is a change from the previously recommended time, two hours. We are quoting new information from the latest *Contraceptive Technology* 1978-1979, p. 82. Barbara Seaman's book *Women and the Crisis in Sex Hormones* also reports six hours as an acceptable time frame.

mise might be to put cream around the inside of the rim and not on the top of the rim.) Then squeeze the cup together by pressing the rim firmly between your thumb and third finger. If you have trouble doing this with your fingers, you can buy a plastic inserter (good only with a diaphragm with flat spring). You can squat, sit on the toilet bowl, stand with one foot raised, or lie down with your legs bent. With your free hand spread apart the lips of your vagina, and insert the diaphragm up to the upper third of your vagina, with the cream or jelly facing up. If you have not used tampons or reached into your vagina before, remember it angles toward your back. Push the lower rim with your finger until you feel the diaphragm lock into place. You should then reach in to make sure you can feel the outline of your cervix through the soft rubber cup. For more protection, insert a little extra cream or jelly with an applicator when the diaphragm is in place. When it's in right, and fits properly, you should not be able to feel the diaphragm at all, nor should the man. (Some men notice that the tip of their penis is touching soft rubber instead of cervical and vaginal tissue, but this is not painful or bothersome.) Never use Vaseline with a diaphragm, as it corrodes the rubber.

Leave the diaphragm in for at least 6 to 8 hours after intercourse, because it takes the spermicide that long to kill all the sperm. You can leave it in up to 24 hours. Douching is unnecessary, but if you want to douche you must wait 6 or 8 hours.

Subsequent intercourse. If you have intercourse again within the six hours, you *must* add more cream or jelly with an applicator. Put it into your vagina, leaving the diaphragm in place.

Care. Wash the diaphragm with mild soap and warm water, rinse and dry carefully, dust it with cornstarch if you wish (but never talcum powder), and put it in a container (away from the light). Don't boil it. *Check it for holes* every so often by holding it up to the light or filling it with water and looking for leaks, especially around the rim.

Life of Product

Get your diaphragm size rechecked every year or two. You may need a new size if you gain or lose ten pounds and after a pregnancy, abortion, or miscarriage. The diaphragm will last a couple of years with proper care.

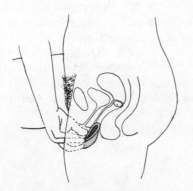

INSERTION OF DIAPHRAGM

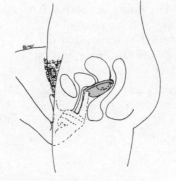
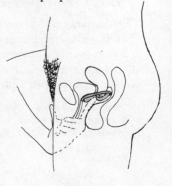

CHECKING OF DIAPHRAGM

Brands of Jelly and Cream

In choosing one brand over another, you should consider factors of effectiveness, smell and taste (for oral-genital play), and any allergic reaction of yours or the man's. If you don't like the brand you're using, feel free to change. Some spermicides are made for use with a diaphragm, while some of them are for use alone. The *Consumer's Union Report on Family Planning* (New York, 1966) lists the following creams and jellies for use alone, in descending order of spermicidal effectiveness: Delfen Vaginal Cream, Koromex N Vaginal Jelly, Preceptin Vaginal Gel. Some of the brands listed for use alone or with a diaphragm are: Certane Vaginal Creme, Contra Creme, Creemoz Vaginal Creme and Lactikol Vaginal Jelly.*

Cost

A diaphragm costs about $7.50. The medical examination for this starts at $35 at private offices, less at most clinics. Jellies and creams vary in price, costing about $3 to $4 per tube (there are about 10 applications in a 3¼-ounce tube).

Advantages and Disadvantages of the Diaphragm

Advantages

A good method if you have intercourse infrequently, or with a regular sex partner who is cooperative and helpful about using it.

No side effects or dangers.

Very effective if well used.

The diaphragm is helpful if you want to have intercourse during your period and don't want a heavy menstrual flow to interfere. It will hold around twelve hours' menstrual discharge, depending on your flow.

Using the diaphragm can be a good kind of body education. If you are unfamiliar with what your vagina feels like, using a diaphragm will teach you! And in the long run, the more familiar you are with your body, the more you will enjoy sex.

Although a doctor's prescription is necessary to obtain a diaphragm, you do not have to be fitted by a doctor; experienced women health workers or nurse practitioners, when available, are often more competent at fitting and teaching the use of diaphragms than physicians.

Cream or jelly reduces your chances of getting VD. (See Chapter 9.)

Disadvantages

Must precede intercourse. If either you or your partner feels that sex must be absolutely spontaneous, with

*The following contraceptive jellies and creams are also effective in helping to prevent VD (see "Venereal Disease" chapter for more details): Certane Vaginal Jelly, Cooper Cream, Milex Crescent Jelly, Ortho Creme, Ortho Gynol Jelly, Preceptin Gel.

no interruptions, putting in the diaphragm will seem like a hassle.

You must remember to use it every time, be sure not to run out of cream or jelly, be sure to have it with you when you need it.

The discharge of cream or jelly can be a nuisance, although it does not stain. Try different brands and, if necessary, use a tampon, pad, or Kleenex for leaking after intercourse.

Some women have mentioned that they experience less cervical stimulation during intercourse when they use a diaphragm. Some like this, others don't. Since most people are not aware of cervical stimulation anyway, this will not be a factor for everyone.

Responsibility

The woman goes to be fitted. After that the responsibility can be shared, although a lot of women do the whole thing themselves.

CONDOM (RUBBER, PROPHYLACTIC, "SAFE")

Description

Condoms were worn by Egyptian men in 1350 B.C. as decorative covers for their penises. The condom was

Plain-ended condom

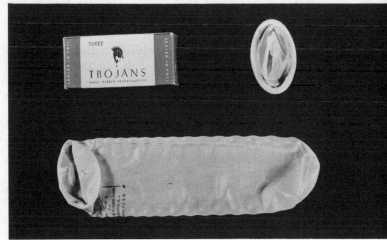

popularized for protection against conception and VD in the 18th century. It is a sheath, usually made of thin, strong latex rubber, designed to fit over an erect penis to keep the semen from getting into the woman's vagina. A condom usually comes rolled up, unrolls to about 7 1/2 inches; the open end has a 1 3/8-inch-diameter rubber ring around it to help keep the condom on the penis, and the closed end is either plain or tipped with a little nipple that catches the semen and helps to keep the condom from bursting. "Skin" condoms (made of lamb membrane) are more expensive but tend to cut down less on sensation. Lubricated rubber condoms minimize the risk of tearing, but these tend to slip off the penis more easily and have to be used extra carefully.

Effectiveness

Used every time as directed, a good-quality condom is 97 percent effective; but in actual use the effectiveness is around 80 to 85 percent, depending on how carefully it is used. We suggest combining condoms with a spermicidal foam, cream, or jelly for close to 100 percent protection. Good with IUD or diaphragm for extra protection at ovulation.

Reversibility

Perfectly reversible. To get pregnant, just don't use condoms.

How to Use

The man or woman unrolls the condom onto the erect penis before intercourse—*not* just before ejaculation, since long before ejaculation the male may discharge a few drops with enough sperm for pregnancy to occur.

Cautions

Leave space at the end of the plain-ended condom for the semen: a half inch of air-free space between the end of the penis and the condom will keep the ejaculate, which comes out fast, from bursting the condom. Catching air in the end may also cause bursting.

If you do not use a lubricated condom, use a lubricant to prevent tearing—spermicidal foam, cream, or jelly, or K-Y Jelly, but *never* Vaseline. Saliva is always available but may increase your chances of developing a monilia infection. Apply the lubricant after the condom is on the penis.

The man or woman must hold the rim when he withdraws his no-longer-erect penis after ejaculation; otherwise the condom might slip off, and sperm could get into the vagina.

In case of accident, use cream or jelly or foam as quickly as possible. Do not douche.

Responsibility

This is the only effective temporary means of birth control that the man can use. As with the methods that are primarily the responsibility of the woman, use of the condom is much more enjoyable if both partners join in putting it on as part of the sexual foreplay. For a couple who sleep together more than a few times, condoms are a good way for the man to share the burden of birth control. In a shorter-term relationship, in which you may not know whether you'll be having intercourse or not, condoms can be very convenient. But if you expect that the man will have a condom in his pocket, you may be disappointed. If you don't know the man well enough to trust that he'll have a condom with him, it makes sense for you to carry something to protect yourself. Ideally, you could carry condoms with you, although for many of us, at least today, it would be hard to pull out a rubber and suggest that the man use it.

Advantages and Disadvantages of the Condom

Advantages

It is fairly cheap, easily available, and easy to use.

It is a method of birth control that gives some protection against VD. It helps to prevent the spread of gonorrhea and syphilis through penis-to-vagina contact, when used in *every instance* of penis-to-vagina contact. It also prevents partners from infecting and reinfecting each other with an infection such as trichomonas.

If the man tends to ejaculate too quickly, a condom can decrease the stimulation of his penis enough to help him delay ejaculation and prolong intercourse.

A condom catches the semen, so if the woman wants to go somewhere right after intercourse, she won't feel drippy.

Disadvantages

The condom has to be used right at the time of intercourse. For some couples this ruins the spontaneity of sex, unless the woman puts it on the man and makes it part of sex play.

It often cuts down on the man's sensation, as his penis is not directly touching the vaginal walls. Many men resist using condoms for this reason, forgetting the effects that women's birth control methods can have on a woman's enjoyment of sex. Pills can decrease her desire for sex; an IUD may make her bleed and have cramps for more days of the month than is normal for her; a diaphragm, if not put in by both partners, can reduce her enjoyment, and so on.

The condom eliminates one source of lubrication for intercourse (the drops of fluid that come out when the man gets an erection), so it can irritate a woman, especially during the entrance of the penis into her vagina. Use of the lubricants mentioned above can help eliminate this problem.

How to Get Condoms

Since cheap condoms sold in vending machines in men's rooms, etc., are more likely to be defective, condoms should be obtained only in drugstores or at family-planning agencies. Many men say they were embarrassed the first time they bought condoms, particularly if the druggist asked, "What size?" and the man didn't know he was referring to the size of the package. Condoms are made in a standard size; they come in packages of three or twelve; and they cost about $1.50 for three rubber ones and $1.75 for three lubricated rubber ones. Some high-quality condoms are: Ramses Rubber Prophylactics, Trojans Rubber Prophylactics, Trojan-Enz Rubber Prophylactics. A wide variety of good-quality condoms can be obtained at reasonable prices (in unmarked envelopes!) from Adam and Eve, 403 Jones Ferry Rd., P.O. Box 400, Carrboro, N.C. 27510 (919-929-2146).

Life of Product

Condoms have a shelf life of two years if kept away from heat. If you carry them around, use a kind sealed in foil; even so, a condom kept in a wallet or a pocket for very long will deteriorate. A high-quality condom can be used five or six times if properly cared for. Put it in a bedside glass of water temporarily, then wash it, dry it, dust with cornstarch and reroll.

"THE FOAM"— AEROSOL VAGINAL SPERMICIDE

Description

Foam is a white aerated cream which has the consistency of shaving cream and contains an effective sperm-killing chemical. It comes in a can with a plunger-type plastic applicator.

How Foam Works

Deposited just outside the entrance to your cervix at the top of your vagina, foam keeps the sperm from entering the cervix and kills them as well.

Effectiveness

Recent studies indicate that foam used alone may be as effective as a condom used alone, or as a diaphragm used with cream or jelly. Because foam spreads more evenly through the vagina, it is more effective than cream or jelly used alone. However, *we strongly recommend using foam in combination with a condom*; when used together, their effectiveness approaches that of the Pill. Foam is also very effective when used as a supplement for the first months of pills, or as an extra precaution with an IUD.

When foam is used alone, problems with effectiveness arise from using too little foam, from not realizing that the foam container is almost empty, from failing to shake the foam container enough, from not inserting the foam correctly, or from inserting the foam after intercourse has already begun.*

How to Use Foam

Insert no longer than fifteen minutes before intercourse. *Shake the can very well*, about twenty times—the more bubbles the foam has, the better it blocks the sperm, and the spermicide tends to settle in the container, so it must be mixed. Put the applicator on top. When the applicator is tilted (Delfen) or pushed down (Emko), the pressure triggers the release valve and the foam is forced into the applicator, pushing the plunger up. Lying down, use your free hand to spread the lips of your vagina, insert the applicator about three to four inches, and push the plunger. If you have never used tampons you may want to practice inserting the applicator. You'll find that your vagina angles up and toward your back, not straight up in your body. Your aim is to deposit the foam at the entrance to your cervix, not beyond. Use two applicators full. Wash the applicator with mild soap and warm but not boiling water before putting it away. (You don't have to wash it immediately.)

Cautions

Put in more foam every time you have intercourse again, no matter how soon.

Leave the foam in for 6 to 8 hours. If you want to douche, you must wait.

Keep an extra can on hand. (Delfen comes out of the can more slowly, but otherwise doesn't indicate when you're running out.)

Use foam with condom for maximum effectiveness of both.

Side Effects

Foam irritates some vaginas and some penises. Delfen, which is thought to be most effective, also tends to be most irritating.

Responsibility

Basically the responsibility is the woman's. But either you or the man can put it in.

---

*The Encare Oval, a suppository containing a foaming spermicide, has been heavily advertised by its manufacturers as having a 99% effectiveness rate. Women's health activists and consumers became concerned when the studies released by the manufacturer in support of these claims appeared questionable. The May-July 1978 issue of the *FDA Drug Bulletin* states that the FDA considers the claim of 99% effectiveness to be unsupported. *We strongly recommend that women who use the Encare Oval use it in combination with a condom.*

HOW TO INSERT SPERM-KILLING FOAM, CREAM, OR JELLY

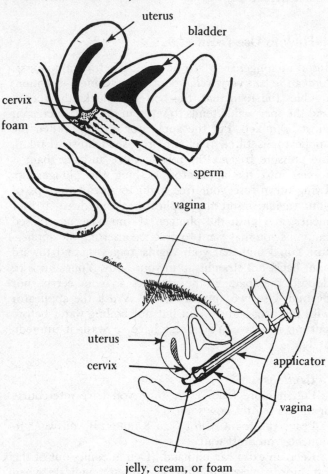

jelly, cream, or foam

Advantages and Disadvantages of Foam

Advantages

It is an easily available stopgap method until you can get to a doctor to be examined for a more effective means of birth control.

It is quick, taking about 30 seconds to use.

It is less drippy than cream or jelly.

Foam is effective in helping to prevent VD (see Chapter 9).

Disadvantages

Using it can be a (brief) interruption of sex if the couple does not treat it as part of the sex play.

Many people think it tastes terrible; it must usually be inserted after oral sex play.

How to Get Foam

Foam can be bought in a drugstore without a prescription. If one druggist gives you trouble or refuses to sell it to you because you are "too young," try another. Better yet, order it from Adam and Eve (see p. 205,

under "How to Get Condoms," for their address), and at the same time order some condoms to be used with the foam. Even though you don't have to see a doctor to get the foam, it makes sense to have a checkup yearly (more often if there's a chance that you've been exposed to VD).

Cost

Foam costs about $3.25 for a medium-sized can (with an applicator), which contains enough for use about twenty times.

Brands

The most widely used brands are Delfen, Emko and Dalkon. Their ingredients differ; if one brand causes irritation, you may find that another is satisfactory.

JELLIES AND CREAMS FOR USE ALONE (WITHOUT A DIAPHRAGM)

How They Work

Spermicidal cream or jelly comes in a tube with a plastic applicator. Jellies are clear and may be less irritating; creams are white. When deposited outside the cervix just before intercourse, cream or jelly (1) forms a film or coating over the cervix which blocks the sperm's entrance into the cervical canal, and (2) kills the sperm by chemical action.

Effectiveness

Creams and jellies alone are not even as effective as foam and have a high failure rate, so please don't depend on them. Cream or jelly used with a diaphragm is more effective than foam alone, as the diaphragm holds it right up to the cervix, where it should be. If you must use cream or jelly alone, get your partner to use a condom. Must be used before any penis-vagina contact.

How to Use Them

As short a time as possible (under 15 minutes) before intercourse, fill the applicator, insert into your vagina, and push the plunger. (See p. 206, for insertion details.) Do this *twice*. Use an additional full applicator for each additional act of intercourse. Leave the jelly or cream in for 6 to 8 hours; if you want to douche, you must wait.

Possible Side Effects

The stronger, more effective creams and jellies tend to be more irritating to the vagina and penis than the others.

Reversibility

Just don't use it if you want to get pregnant.

Responsibility

Responsibility is primarily the woman's, but you both can put it in.

Advantages and Disadvantages of Cream or Jelly

Advantages

The only advantage is that they can be bought at a drugstore without a prescription and no medical examination is necessary, so you can get them on short notice. Certain brands are effective in helping to prevent VD (see p. 170 in Chapter 9).

Disadvantages

There can be problems of leakage, allergy, or reaction to the smell or taste. Jelly tends to be gooier than cream.

Purchase, Cost and Brands

Creams and jellies are available at all drugstores. See "How to Get Foam," p. 206, for purchase hints and mail-order source. See p. 203 for prices, and names of most effective brands.

FERTILITY CONSCIOUSNESS: NATURAL BIRTH CONTROL

Birth control which is free of chemicals and controlled by women is an exciting and powerful concept to many of us. Most of us have heard of the Rhythm Method, notorious for its high failure rate. The Rhythm Method tries to predict what a woman's cycle will be like, based on information from past cycles. However, since no one has absolutely regular cycles all the time, it fails frequently.

Bad experiences with Rhythm have caused many women to discount so-called natural methods of birth control; yet natural methods that work have been developed and their scientific basis is well documented. In using natural methods, a woman learns to observe and understand the changes in her body caused by changes in the levels of her reproductive hormones as she moves through the cycle. The major changes are in the amount and quality of vaginal discharge and in body temperature. Because she is observing what is actually happening in her body at that moment, a woman can accurately decide whether she may be fertile (able to conceive) or infertile on a day-to-day basis. It takes only a few minutes to make and record the observations.

The implications of fertility consciousness are far-reaching: this is the first access many of us have had to knowledge, control, and the ability to listen to the messages of our bodies. Because it teaches us to know when we are fertile and when we are not, we can use the information to avoid or achieve pregnancy. Using fertility consciousness as a method of birth control means that we must learn about and "read" the changes in our fertility signs each day; it means that we must be willing to be honest about interpreting those signs and willing to explore alternatives to unprotected genital contact on fertile days. It means a commitment to increased communication with our sexual partners; many women find that the natural birth control methods have a great potential for shared responsibility. Using natural methods also requires a willingness to examine our attitudes toward sexuality and our motivation to avoid or achieve pregnancy. Above all, using natural methods means taking responsibility and making an informed choice about our actions.

The only risk of using natural birth control is pregnancy. As with all other methods, there is no guarantee of 100-percent effectiveness. If we do not learn the method correctly, if we stop using it, if we allow ourselves to be pressured into unprotected intercourse when we know we are fertile because we are afraid our partners will be angry or hurt—then we are taking a real risk of pregnancy. When used correctly, however, some forms of natural birth control have a very high effectiveness rate (see "Effectiveness").

Description

Fertility consciousness depends on a woman's recognition of body signs which indicate to her whether she is in a fertile or infertile phase of her menstrual cycle. During the fertile time (the time when she is able to conceive), she avoids genital contact with male sexual partners and therefore avoids pregnancy. As natural methods become more widely known, some women are choosing to use barrier methods of birth control, such as the diaphragm, during the fertile time. It is important to understand that no effectiveness studies have been done on this. Some women may find that jelly or foam in the vagina at this time may mask indications of fertility and make it impossible for them to tell whether they are still fertile; other women report no problems in combining a barrier method with fertility consciousness. However, *all the effectiveness rates quoted here on natural birth control methods refer to studies done on women who were willing to avoid all genital contact on fertile days.*

Fertility depends on three factors: a healthy egg, healthy sperm, and favorable cervical mucus. The cervical mucus is necessary because without it the sperm cannot live long enough to reach and fertilize the egg. A woman ovulates once each cycle (if there is a second ovulation, as in the case of dissimilar twins, it occurs within 48 hours of the first ovulation); the egg lives 12 to 24 hours and then disintegrates if not fertilized. Under favorable cervical mucus conditions, sperm can survive as long as five days within the body. Therefore, it is possible to have intercourse up to five days before ovulation and still get pregnant. The actual length of time a woman is fertile varies from woman to woman and from cycle to cycle.

All the effective methods of natural birth control stress the importance of woman-to-woman teaching and daily charting of observations. It is *not* advisable to try to learn a method just by reading a book (for instance, we will *not* present enough information here for you to learn it). Learning from another woman who correctly understands and has used the method herself for a while is the only way to begin to use it. Although a number of books in the bibliography can be very helpful and are recommended, books cannot give you the personal feedback, support, and experience-sharing needed. Check your local women's center for information about groups. If you are willing to hear Catholic morality mixed in with information, most Catholic hospitals or churches can help you find a teacher (see bibliography).

The Ovulation Method (Awareness of Mucus)

You may already be aware that you normally have a discharge from your vagina which changes consistency at different points in your menstrual cycle. You may notice nothing for several days and then suddenly begin to experience a sensation of having a discharge from your vagina—a bubbling sensation or a stickiness or a feeling of being "wet." This is mucus coming out of the vagina; it is made in the cells of the cervical canal in response to your hormonal changes. Two Australian doctors named Evelyn and John Billings have studied these changes in discharge for over 25 years and have developed the Ovulation Method, which explains how to use the sensation and quality of the mucus discharge, according to a set of rules, to determine whether you are fertile or infertile. Here is a brief outline of the relationship of mucus to fertility (see charts of the menstrual cycle pp. 32 and 36, for hormones):

a. Menstruation. A cycle begins on the first day of your period. Since menstrual discharge may mask mucus discharge, the menstrual period is not necessarily safe for unprotected intercourse.

b. In some cycles, as menstruation stops you may feel "dry," i.e., there is no sensation of discharge. No mucus is present at the vaginal opening, nor is there any discharge noticeable on your underwear. Since there is no mucus present, sperm will not be able to survive in the acid vagina. These days are considered infertile and therefore safe for unprotected intercourse. (Note: you will almost always find something resembling mucus if you look *in-*

side your vagina. The mucus that promotes sperm survival is fluid enough to flow to the *outside* and should be checked outside only.)

c. As you begin to approach ovulation, your body produces enough mucus at the cervix to flow down and "coat" the vagina with a protective covering that promotes sperm survival. It is fluid enough to flow out of your vagina. When you begin to feel a sensation of discharge from the vagina, or see a discharge on your underwear, or wipe some mucus off with toilet paper, your fertile time has begun. The mucus may start off as whitish or yellow, tacky, crumbly, or creamy; it usually becomes more fluid, clearer, or thinner as ovulation approaches. It also has a very characteristic slippery or lubricative feel when ovulation is near. Some women even notice that they can take a sample and stretch it between two fingers. The last day of mucus with any of these characteristics is called the Peak Day; ovulation usually occurs on the day *following* the Peak Day. Women who use the Ovulation Method know that they are fertile from the time the mucus first appears until the fourth day after the end of the peak symptom. The number of fertile days varies from cycle to cycle and from woman to woman.

d. At ovulation, your mucus will undergo a distinct change from the peak symptom; you may become dry again, or you may develop a thicker discharge. In either case a change is evident. Your period will start 11 to 16 days after the Peak Day (this is one way to know that you have correctly identified ovulation). From the fourth day past the Peak Day until your period begins, you are infertile. Every woman's mucus pattern is slightly different from this "classic" description we have given—*but every woman can learn to recognize her own pattern.*

The Sympto-Thermal Method

This method combines the mucus observations with other changes in a woman's cycle, such as: cervical changes, breast changes, ovulatory pain and spotting, past cycle history, and changes in basal body temperature. The change in temperature which occurs after ovulation has been used for years by many women as an indication that ovulation is past. By taking your temperature on a basal body thermometer (about $5 at a drugstore) each morning at the same time and recording it on a chart, you will see that your temperature will rise slightly following ovulation and will stay high until menstruation begins (it falls as your period starts and stays low until the next ovulation). A $4/10$ degree rise *sustained* over at least three days indicates that ovulation has occurred (several books in the bibliography will help you learn how to chart and interpret temperature). Temperature method by itself is of no use in determining which days *before* ovulation are fertile or infertile.

Effectiveness of Natural Birth Control

Key factors in effectiveness of the natural methods are personal motivation, correct information, and a commitment to observe and chart physical signs faithfully. Many health professionals rate all natural methods of birth control as very poor; in most cases they have confused the word "natural" with the word "Rhythm." Recent studies indicate that the Ovulation Method or Sympto-Thermal Method can be extremely effective when used correctly.

A two-year study on the Sympto-Thermal method by Dr. Claude Lanctot* showed a rate of 1.1 conceptions per 100 woman-years in women desiring to *prevent pregnancy* (as compared with the rate of 14.9 conceptions per 100 woman-years for those intending only to *space* their next conception). A two year clinical study by Dr. Hanna Klaus on the use-effectiveness of the Ovulation Method showed a total conception rate of 1.3 pregnancies the first year, and 1.896 the second year. When Dr. Klaus subtracted the user failures from these rates, the actual failure rates of the method itself were 0.072 for the first year and 0.517 for the second year. Several other studies have been done on these methods, and more are in progress.

Fertility awareness can be used to *increase* the effectiveness of another birth control method, such as the IUD, diaphragm with cream or jelly, or the condom/foam combination.

Reversibility

Excellent reversibility. Just have intercourse on fertile days!

Responsibility

Can be shared by partners; requires cooperation from the male partner.

Advantages and Disadvantages of Natural Family Planning

Advantages

1. No side effects.
2. Many of us enjoy being more aware of our body's cycles.

*Presented by Claude A. Lanctot, M.D. (Associate Professor of Community Medicine, Faculty of Medicine, University of Sherbrooke, Sherbrooke, Quebec, Canada) in a paper at the 25th Congress of the Federation of French-Speaking OBS-GYN Societies, Montreal, September 26, 1974.

3. Relationship. In certain relationships the cooperation that is necessary in this method brings understanding and closeness between the partners.
4. Can lead, during unsafe days, to exploration of other ways of giving and receiving sexual pleasure—such as mutual masturbation and oral sex (be sure to avoid *all* penis to vagina contact).

Disadvantages

1. Major disadvantage: risk of pregnancy if you do not practice it diligently.
2. It takes time (2-3 cycles at least) to learn these methods and feel confident.
3. It may be impractical for anyone not in a committed, cooperative relationship with her sex partner.
4. If abstention is practiced, it can be sexually frustrating for those who want to have intercourse when they feel like it and who do not feel comfortable with alternate forms of sexual activity.

(The bibliography lists resources for more information on natural family planning.)

BIRTH-CONTROL METHODS THAT DON'T WORK VERY WELL

Withdrawal (Coitus Interruptus, or "Taking Care," or "Pulling Out")

Description

Withdrawal of the penis far away from the vagina just before ejaculation ("coming"), so that the semen is deposited outside the vagina and away from the lips of the vagina as well.

Who Uses Withdrawal

Worldwide, this is the most universally used of all methods, a folk method that is practiced without medical initiative and passed on from one generation to the next. It is not so widely used in the United States in general, but is depended on by quite a number of United States couples who don't have access to good birth control information and care—many teenagers, some college students, people who can't afford medical fees.

Effectiveness

Withdrawal is not highly effective because the drops of fluid that come out of the penis right after it becomes erect can contain some sperm, enough to cause a pregnancy. Also, withdrawing at the last minute can be difficult, and the man cannot always get out in time to avoid contact, not only with the vagina, but also with the vaginal lips (sperm have been known to swim all the way from the vaginal lips up into the fallopian tubes). Multiple acts of intercourse in a short period of time increase the likelihood of failure, since more sperm are mixed in with the lubricating fluid. Withdrawal has a pregnancy rate of 20 to 30 percent.

Responsibility

The man is responsible for withdrawal. The woman is dependent on his control over his ejaculation and must trust him greatly in order to be free of anxiety.

Disadvantages of Withdrawal

Withdrawal is the only last-minute method other than abstinence, but it has a number of drawbacks in addition to its high failure rate. The man must keep in control and therefore cannot relax and lose his self-consciousness. When used over a long period, it may lead to premature ejaculation by the male. Withdrawal can also be hard on the woman: the man might have to withdraw before she reaches orgasm, interrupting the flow of her sexual response; also, a part of her consciousness is wondering whether he's going to make it out on time, so that she, too, cannot entirely relax into her sexual feelings. Some couples who have used withdrawal for a long time have been able to work out these problems.

Vaginal Tablets and Suppositories

Description

Drugstores sell tablets, two or three times the size of aspirin, and suppositories with a glycerogelatin or cocoabutter base, both of which contain sperm-killing chemicals that spread around the cervix (tablets dissolve and suppositories melt) 15 minutes to one hour after insertion deep into the vagina. They are to be put in before *each* time of intercourse, and left in (not washed out by a douche) for 6 to 8 hours afterward.*

Effectiveness

There is a high failure rate. Spermicidal tablets and suppositories are not as effective as creams or jellies, and much less effective than foam, because the spermicide does not get evenly distributed through the vagina.

*Information on the Encare Oval, a heavily advertised foaming suppository, may be found on page 205, under "Foam."

Why People Use Them

Some women probably use them because they are cheap, can be bought in a drugstore with no trips to the doctor involved, and because they seem less messy than foam or jelly or cream. (The high pregnancy rate of tablets and suppositories should outweigh these conveniences.) Also, many women use these products because they are the only methods they know about. Magazines and other publications rarely advertise pills, IUDs, or diaphragms (such advertisements are illegal in many places), but the tablets and suppositories are widely advertised as a "solution to your most intimate marital problems." What is most confusing is that these same magazines carry ads for such feminine-hygiene products as Norforms; the ads are worded in the same suggestive way, leaving many with the impression that the hygiene products *also* prevent pregnancy, which they do not.

Remember, Norforms are not birth control methods.

NON-METHODS

Douching

Some women douche with water or other special solutions immediately after intercourse—trying to remove semen from the vagina before sperm enter the uterus.

Douching does not work. Sperm swim fast, and some will reach your uterus before you've reached the bathroom; and the douche, which is liquid squirted into your vagina under pressure, will push some sperm up into your uterus even as it is washing others away.

Douching is the least effective of all methods, and it puts the burden exclusively on the woman, who must hop up to the bathroom immediately. Don't use it!

Avoidance of Orgasm by the Woman

Some people think that in order to conceive, a woman must have an orgasm. One theory says that at the time of orgasm a woman's uterus or vagina releases a liquid similar to the man's seminal fluid, which helps the sperm up toward the egg. This is all false. One of the major differences between men and women in reproduction is that a man must have an erection to cause a pregnancy, whereas a woman can conceive without any sexual arousal. Avoiding orgasm won't prevent pregnancy!

ABSTINENCE

There is nothing wrong with abstinence. In fact sometimes it is just what we want. It is the most effective form of birth control, has been used for centuries, and is still very common. It has no physical side effects as long as prolonged sexual arousal is followed by orgasm to relieve pelvic congestion.

Sex play such as mutual masturbation, in which you and your partner stimulate each other manually or orally until you both reach orgasm, can be pleasurable and satisfying. Take care that sperm do not get near your vagina, as they can move inside and go on to fertilize.

AFTER UNPROTECTED INTERCOURSE— "THE MORNING-AFTER PILL"

The morning-after pill is a series of very high dose synthetic estrogens which must be started *within 3 days* of unprotected intercourse. The most common treatment is 250 mg. of diethylstilbestrol (DES) taken over a period of 5 days (two 25 mg. pills a day). The effectiveness in preventing pregnancy has not been determined, perhaps in part because of the relatively low rate of pregnancy involved: about 4 out of 100 women who have a *single* act of unprotected intercourse during the month get pregnant.

In 1971 it was first reported that 220 daughters of women who took DES during pregnancy (supposedly to prevent miscarriage) have developed a rare form of vaginal cancer or, in some cases, cervical cancer, as young as eight years old. (See DES bibliography in Chapter 6.)

Because of this link between DES and vaginal or cervical cancer in female offspring, and because there has not been adequate study of long-term effects of even one-time use of DES on the user, DES should be considered *only in an emergency, if at all*. Amid pressure from a number of women's groups to ban the use of DES altogether, the FDA has recently approved its limited use as an emergency medication in such cases as rape or incest. The problem is that since DES has been used as a morning-after pill for several years, doctors might continue to prescribe it as such.

The side effects are the same as those of the estrogen in birth control pills (see "Combination Pills" on p. 188). Some of the common side effects are severe nausea and vomiting, headache, menstrual irregularities and breast tenderness. In addition, women taking DES should be on the lookout for the symptoms of blood-clotting disorders: severe headaches, blurring or loss of vision, severe leg pains, chest pain, or shortness of breath. If any of these occur, the pills should be stopped immediately and a doctor notified. The *doctor should examine you* before prescribing the morning-after pill, to check for contraindications to the use of synthetic estrogen (see "Who Should Not Use the Pill," p. 192).

If you have had unprotected intercourse in mid-cycle and do not want to have a baby, you may prefer not to use DES but to wait to see whether you are pregnant (chances are only 4 in 100) and then have an abortion if you are in fact pregnant. Although abortion is more expensive and a more difficult thing emotionally in the short run, it may be safer in the long run. If you do take DES as a morning-after contraceptive and you become pregnant anyway, you should seriously consider having an abortion because of the potential of vaginal or cervical cancer in daughters.*

WHEN YOU ARE THROUGH HAVING CHILDREN—STERILIZATION

Sterilization is fast becoming the most popular method of birth control among married couples in the US (1978). However, many women are choosing this procedure without adequate information about the possible risks and consequences involved. Space does not permit full discussion here—please refer to Readings and Resources section for further materials.

Sterilization is a virtually 100-percent-effective, usually irreversible form of birth control, available for both men and women. It is legal in all states, although many hospitals and doctors are conservative about it and require the person to be a certain age, have a certain number of children, have the spouse's signed consent, etc. If you can't get information on how to get a sterilization in your community, you can call your local Planned Parenthood or Zero Population Growth. Whenever possible, seek guidance and advice from a women-run health center—generally your most dependable source of information.

Choosing to get sterilized is a big decision. You have to deal with other people's possible adverse reactions as well as your own deeply internalized feelings.

The week before my sterilization I was very nervous, irritable and jumpy. I'd yell at my husband. I tried to pull out of myself all my fears about having an operation: I would die, there'd be a mistake, I'd be out of control, I'd get the wrong anesthetic; and fears about this particular operation: my husband would think that I wasn't a real woman any more, he'd leave me for a fer-

tile woman, I'd get all dried up and wrinkled. I felt angry at my husband for not wanting to deal with his feelings of loss of manhood by having a vasectomy (though that was a little irrational on my part, for his vasectomy couldn't give me my sexual freedom if I wanted to make love with another man).

Now, almost two years later, I am glad I made the choice I did. I feel much freer when I make love, and I am healthier in general. I am interested to discover that most of the sexual problems I had, had little to do with my use of birth control.

A life change like being sterilized must be carefully thought about, and it must be voluntary. Black women in the South are all too familiar with the "Mississippi Appendectomy," in which their fallopian tubes are tied or their uterus is removed without their knowing it. Some medical services, especially in ghetto areas, have been only too willing to sterilize black and poor women, sometimes without their knowledge, sometimes threatening to have their welfare payments cut off. A well-publicized case involved two black minors, twelve and fourteen years old, who were sterilized without the informed consent of themselves or their mother. One reason given to justify the procedure was that they are alleged to be mentally retarded, yet the medical service was not required to produce any evidence on this. Our right to *choose* sterilization must be protected!

There are a number of different sterilization procedures for women. *Hysterectomy* for sterilization purposes alone is an inappropriate procedure, involving unnecessary risk and cost. In November 1978, after much pressure from activist groups such as CESA* and the National Women's Health Network†, the Dept. of HEW issued regulations expressly forbidding the federal funding of hysterectomies for the sole purpose of sterilization. Unfortunately, many hysterectomies continue to be performed for this purpose alone.

The most widely used procedure is *tubal ligation.* There are two ways to perform a tubal ligation. In one, a fairly large abdominal incision is made, a piece of each fallopian tube is cut out, and the two ends are tied off and folded back into the surrounding tissue. This method is now used most commonly postpartum (immediately after childbirth). Tubal ligation can also be done entering the body through the vagina, although this method is somewhat less effective and has a slightly higher complication and death rate (both are much low-

*For more information on sterilization abuse and efforts to stop it, contact the Committee to End Sterilization Abuse (CESA), P.O. Box A244, Cooper Station, New York, NY.

†NWHN, 2025 Eye St., NW, Suite 105, Washington, DC 20006.

er than for hysterectomy). The method of anesthesia for both types of tubal ligation can be either local, conduction (like a spinal in which the lower part of the body is anesthetized), or general, although general or conduction is usually preferred.

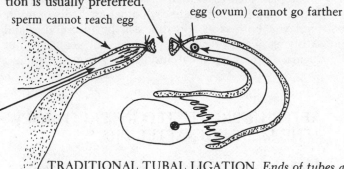

sperm cannot reach egg   egg (ovum) cannot go farther

TRADITIONAL TUBAL LIGATION. *Ends of tubes are actually folded back into surrounding tissue. Tubes cauterized (burned) during endoscopic sterilization look different from those in this drawing.*

A more recent development is the *endoscopic technique,* in which a tube with mirrors and lights is inserted and the fallopian tubes are visually located and then cauterized (burned) with a small instrument. These methods have three names, depending on which route the instrument enters the body: *laparoscopy,* which enters through an abdominal incision; *culdoscopy,* which enters through the vagina; and *hysteroscopy,* in which the instrument enters the uterus through the vagina. The burning instrument is sometimes entered through a different incision or may be attached to the endoscope. The endoscopic techniques have a fairly low complication rate and a somewhat variable effectiveness rate. They are frequently done with a local anesthetic on an out-patient basis, although some doctors are beginning to think they should be treated as a more major procedure than first supposed, due to complications that have arisen. Because it involves less time in the hospital, the endoscopic technique is usually cheaper than traditional tubal ligation.

Even more recently, experiments have been done in which a clip or ring is put on the fallopian tube to hold it closed and to cause the tube to become fibrous.

Sterilization does not affect a woman's hormone secretions, ovaries, uterus (excepting hysterectomy), or her vagina. Her menstrual cycle continues. An egg ripens in and bursts out of an ovary every month but stops part way down the tube, disintegrates, and is absorbed by the body. Her sexual response, which depends on her hormones, clitoris and vagina, is not lessened at all, and in fact usually improves when she no longer fears pregnancy.

Sterilization for the man, called a *vasectomy,* is usually done in a doctor's office or in a clinic. The whole procedure requires about three visits—a preliminary visit (which often includes the wife), the operation, and a follow-up visit weeks later for a test of the sperm count. The operation takes about half an hour. The doctor applies a local anesthetic (such as Novocaine), makes one or two small incisions in the scrotum, locates the two vas deferens (tubes that carry sperm from testes to penis), removes a piece of each, and ties off the ends. Experimental operations have been done in which a piece of plastic was put into the tube to plug it up temporarily so that if the man later wanted to have a child he could have the plug taken out. Several valves have also been tried which can be implanted in the tube and turned back on if the man wishes to regain fertility. These techniques have not yet been successful, but when improved, they may provide reversible "sterilization" for a majority of users.

Vasectomy leaves the man's genital system basically unchanged. His sexual hormones remain operative, and there is no noticeable difference in his ejaculate, because sperm make up only a small part of the semen. Some men, even knowing these facts, are still anxious about what a vasectomy will do to their sexual performance. Talking with someone who has had a vasectomy can help allay such anxieties. For fuller discussion of the choice to have a vasectomy, see the books on vasectomy in "Further Readings" at the end of this chapter.

In some men, antibodies to their own sperm can be found after vasectomy. This finding has led to the suggestion that vasectomy may lead to certain diseases of the immune system. Yet many fully fertile men also have such antibodies, and so far this suggestion is without support.

FUTURE METHODS OF BIRTH CONTROL

Male Contraceptive Research

A few years ago a birth control pill was developed for men, but in addition to its contraceptive effect of decreasing sperm production, it interfered with a man's ability to have an erection. Now researchers in Sweden and California are working on a sperm-incapacitation pill which would stop the sperm's ability to penetrate the egg. There is also a new small-scale study on a pill with synthetic androgen which causes reduced sperm counts. Other methods of male hormonal contraception have been suggested—such as a silastic implant injected under the skin which would release hormones slowly—but none of these methods has reached serious clinical trial.

Two methods which might be used by either a man or a woman but which are far from development are (1)

somehow causing the person to produce antibodies to sperm, rendering them dysfunctional; and (2) placing soluble films with spermicide over the glans of the penis or inside the vagina.

Compared with efforts directed at women, very little research is being done on contraceptive methods for men. Many women have been talking about lobbying for more research on male methods. We suspect that male scientists and doctors would be unwilling to offer men a contraceptive that exposed them to as many side effects and potential risks as the pill or IUD does to women.

But what if there were a pill or shot for men? Not all of us are in situations in which we can absolutely trust our sex partners to keep us from getting pregnant. As part of the active-passive, pursuer-pursued, predator-prey, male-female stereotypes that we act out in sex, men say many persuasive things to women to get us into bed. If the man lied about taking birth control pills, the woman would still be the one to get pregnant. Even in a marriage a man might not have the incentive to remember his pill that the woman has: the threat of unwanted pregnancy and responsibility for child care. Getting men to share the burdens of birth control involves a lot more than finding methods for them to use. For now, many of us prefer to keep the control in our own hands.

Female Contraceptive Research

With current means of birth control as unsatisfactory to us as they are today, it is clear that extensive research must be done to develop methods that are both safer and more effective. Drug companies do a lot of research, but we question whether they have our interests as a top priority. Because we are women and the people who fund and do research are often men, and because no preventive health care is valued very highly in this country, adequate research will not be done unless we join together in effective ways to insist on it. None of the methods listed below is free of side effects.

PREVENTION OF OVULATION, IMPLANTATION, OR SPERM ENTRANCE INTO UTERUS BY USE OF HORMONES. These experimental methods are just variations on birth control pills in that they introduce synthetic hormones into the woman's body:

Subdermal (under the skin) implants of capsules containing progestin that would leak into the blood a little every day, achieving the same effects as the progestin-only pill.

Once-a-month-pill with estrogen and progestin in particular compounds that store in fatty tissue and are slowly released.

Post-coital progestin pill—one progestin pill to be taken after each act of intercourse, preferably within three hours. It seems to work like the once-a-day progestin-only pill, since the method is more effective the more frequently a couple has intercourse.

Progestin-coated vaginal ring that would fit like the rim of a diaphragm. The ring releases enough progestin every day to suppress ovulation. The ring is removed for seven days once a month to allow cyclic bleeding to take place.

An injection of 150 mg. of medroxyprogesterone acetate (Depo-Provera) every three months to suppress ovulation. Side effects are irregular bleeding, no real menstrual period, and most important, a delay in the return of fertility, sometimes permanent. The FDA has not approved this drug for general use as a contraceptive, but has announced its intention to approve marketing it with the instructions that the drug have a limited use, including women who "refuse or are unable to accept the responsibility demanded by other contraceptive methods, are incapable or unwilling to tolerate the side effects of conventional oral contraceptives, or have used other methods of contraception which have repeatedly failed." Black congresswomen have protested that this "limited use" means "minority women, poor women, or retarded women."

NEW IUD DESIGN—in addition to the progestin-coated IUD, an IUD filled with saline (salt water) is being developed. It is non-rigid, and the saline is injected after the device is placed, supposedly to "custom-fit" the uterus.

THE PROSTAGLANDINS. These substances cause uterine contractions and are now used to induce labor and to cause second-trimester abortion. Another use is to put them in a vaginal tampon so that they can act locally to make the uterus contract, bringing on a period, or early abortion if the woman is pregnant. The success rate is still relatively low, and the side effects are still considerable, including nausea, cramping and diarrhea.

READINGS AND RESOURCES

General

Ed-U-Press. 760 Ostrom Avenue, Syracuse, NY 13210.
Send for literature list, including birth control materials for teens.
Emory University Family Planning Program. *The Joy of Birth Control* and *The View from Our Side* (by and for men). Order from the Program, Attn: Educational Materials Unit, 69 Butter Street, SE, Atlanta, GA 30303.
Hatcher, Robert, et al. *Contraceptive Technology 1978-79*, 10th rev. ed. New York: Irvington, 1978.
Impact, the journal of National Family Sex Education Week, October 1978. Available from Institute for Family Research and Education, 760 Ostrom Avenue, Syracuse NY 13210. (Send $1 for postage and handling.)
Includes articles on teenage pregnancy, Margaret Sanger, the cur-

rent backlash against homosexuality, high-school censorship and more.
Origins (Salem Women's Health Collective). *A Part of Our Lives*, 1978. $3. Available from Origins, 140 Washington Street, Salem, MA 01970.
Discussion of birth control and sexuality by and for young women. Written by three teenagers.
Seaman, Barbara, and Gideon Seaman. *Women and the Crisis in Sex Hormones*. New York: Rawson; Bantam, 1978.
Excellent resource on pill, IUD, barrier methods and more.

The Pill

Beral, V. "Mortality Among Oral-Contraceptive Users. Royal College of General Practitioners Oral Contraceptive Study," *Lancet*, 8 October 1977.
Boston Collaborative Drug Surveillance Program. "Oral contraceptives and venous thromboembolic disease, surgically confirmed gall bladder disease, and breast tumors," *Lancet* 1 (1973): 1399-1404.
Briggs, M., and M. Briggs. "Oral contraceptives and vitamin requirements," *Medical Journal of Australia* 1 (1975): 407.
Cowan, Belita. Testimony on the Morning-After Pill Before the U.S. House of Representatives, 15 December 1975.
Evrard, J. R., et al. "Amenorrhea following oral contraception," *American Journal of Obstetrics and Gynecology* 124 (1976): 88.
Fasal, E., and R. S. Paffenbarger. "Oral contraceptives as related to cancer and benign lesions of the breast," *Journal of the National Cancer Institute* 55 (1975): 4.
Heinonen, O. P., et al. "Cardiovascular birth defects and antenatal exposure to female sex hormones," *New England Journal of Medicine* 296 (13 January 1977).
Jain, A. K. "Cigarette smoking, use of oral contraceptives, and myocardial infarction," *American Journal of Obstetrics and Gynecology* 126 (1976): 301-307.
Janerich, D. T., et al. "Fertility patterns after discontinuation of use of oral contraceptives," *Lancet* 1 (1976): 1051-1053.
Lake, A. "The pill: what we really know after 15 years of use," *McCalls*, January 1975, p. 119.
"Liver Tumours and the Pill," editorial, *British Medical Journal*, 6 August 1977.
Mann, J. I. and W. H. W. Inman. "Oral contraceptives and death from myocardial infarctions," *British Medical Journal* 2 (1975): 245-248.
Mintz, M. "Annals of Commerce: Selling the Pill," *Washington Post*, 8 February 1976.
"Oral Contraceptives," *Population Reports*, George Washington University Medical Center, Washington, D.C. (1) Series A, No 4, May 1977: "Debate on Oral Contraceptives and Neoplasia Continues; Answers Remain Elusive." (2) Supplement to Series A, No. 4, May 1977: "U.S. Morbidity and Mortality Trends Relative to Oral Contraceptive Use, 1955-1975, and Danish Morbidity Trends, 1953-1972."
"Patient skin changes may be indication for discontinuing OC," *OB/GYN News*, 15 April 1976.
Seaman, Barbara. *The Doctor's Case Against the Pill*. New York: Peter Wyden, 1969; rev. ed., New York: Dell, 1979 (pb.).
"Searle Concedes Bribe Payments," *The New York Times*, 6 January 1976.
"Serious Adverse Effects of Oral Contraceptives and Estrogens," *Medical Letter*, 27 February 1976.
Toddywalla, V. S., et al. "Effect of contraceptive steroids on human lactation," *American Journal of Obstetrics and Gynecology* 127 (1977): 245.
Vessey, M. P., et al. "A long-term follow-up study of women using different methods of contraception—an interim report," *Journal of Biosocial Sciences* 8 (1976): 373.
Zahran, M. "Effects of contraceptive pills and intrauterine devices on urinary bladder," *Urology* 8 (1976): 567.

IUD

Bevia, Maria, and Gordon Myron. "Common Complications from IUDs," *Resident and Staff Physician*, June 1976.

Cates, W., et al. "The Intrauterine Device and Deaths from Spontaneous Abortion," *New England Journal of Medicine*, 295 (1976): 1155.

Dowie, Mark, and Tracy Johnson. "A Case of Corporate Malpractice," *Mother Jones*, November 1976. Whole issue available from *Mother Jones*, 607 Market Street, San Francisco, CA 94105. (Send $1.)
> Story of the Dalkon Shield.

Faulkner, W. I., and H. W. Ory. "Intrauterine devices and acute pelvic inflammatory disease," *Journal of the American Medical Association* 235 (1976): 1851-1853.

Katz, Barbara J. "The IUD—Out of Sight, Out of Mind?" *Ms.*, July 1975.

"Progestasert—A New Intrauterine Device," *The Medical Letter*, 30 July 1976.

Roberts, Katherine. "The Intrauterine Device as a Health Risk," *Women and Health*, July/August 1977.

Sterilization

Ad Hoc Women's Studies Committee Against Sterilization Abuse. *Workbook on Sterilization and Sterilization Abuse*, 1978. $1.75. Available from Women's Studies, Sarah Lawrence College, Bronxville, NY 10708.

CARASA. Box 124, Cathedral Station, New York, NY 10025.
> Activist group working on abortion rights and against sterilization abuse. Publishes *CARASA News*, $5/year.

Chase, Allan. "HEW policies on hysterectomy, consent rapped," *Hospital Tribune*, 5 September 1977.
> One article in an excellent series by Chase on sterilization abuse (appeared also in the *Medical Tribune*).

Committee to End Sterilization Abuse (CESA). *Sterilization Abuse: The Facts*, 1977. Available from CESA, Box A244, Cooper Station, New York, NY 10003.

Dreifus, C. "Sterilizing the poor," *The Progressive* 39 (1975): 13-18.

Herman, J. "Controlling third world populations: forced sterilization," *Sister Courage*, February 1976.

Mueller, R. L., et al. "Puerperal laparoscopic sterilization," *Journal of Reproductive Medicine* 16 (1976): 307-309.

Rothchild, Alice. Testimony on Proposed HEW Sterilization Regulations. Testimony of National Women's Health Network. (See bibliography, Chapter 18.)

Stamm, Karen, and Suzanne Williamson. "The Sterilization Connection," *HealthRight*, Winter 1978.
> Covers sterilization abuse, federal guidelines, role of population-control organizations.

Winston, R. M. L. "Why 103 Women Asked for Reversal of Sterilization," *British Medical Journal*, 30 July 1977.

Wortman, J. "Vasectomy—what are the problems?" *Population Reports: Sterilization*, Series D, No. 2, 1975, p. D-25.

Wynn, Karen. "Second Thoughts About Sterilization," *Sister*, 1977. Available from *Sister*, 250 Howard Avenue, New Haven, CT 06519. (Send 25¢.)

Barrier Methods

Belsky, R. "Vaginal contraceptives: a time for reappraisal," *Population Reports: Barrier Methods*, Series H, No. 3, January 1975, p. H-40.

Bernstein, G. S. "Conventional methods of contraception: condom, diaphragm and vaginal foam," *Clinical Obstetrics and Gynecology* 17 (1974): 21-33.

Brillman, Judith. "The Cervical Cap." Unpublished paper available from Boston Women's Health Book Collective, Box 192, W. Somerville, MA 02144. Send self-addressed, stamped envelope plus 40¢ in stamps.

Dalsimer, I. A., et al. "Condom: an old method meets a special new need," *Population Reports: Barrier Methods*, Series H, No. 1, 1973, p. H-1.

Dumm, J. J., et al. "The modern condom—a quality product for effective contraception," *Population Reports: Barrier Methods*, Series H, No. 2, 1974.

Klein, Diane. "Update on Birth Control," *Modern Bride*, April/May, 1978, pp. 16ff.

Lane, M. E., et al. "Successful use of the diaphragm and jelly by a young population: report of a clinical study," *Family Planning Perspectives* 8 (1976): 81-86.

New Hampshire Feminist Health Center. Information packet on the cervical cap. Send $3 to the Center, 38 S. Main St., Concord, NH 03301.

Redford, M. H., et al., eds. *The Condom: Increasing Utilization in the United States*. San Francisco: San Francisco Press, 1974.

Vessey, M., and P. Wiggins. "Use-effectiveness of the diaphragm in a selected family planning clinic in the United Kingdom," *Contraception* 9 (1974): 15-21.

Wortman, J. "The diaphragm and other intravaginal barriers—a review." *Population Reports: Barrier Methods*, Series H, No. 4, January 1976.

Natural Birth Control

Note: These are some of the publications or resources currently available. Please understand that they are NOT meant to take the place of a group in which these skills are shared on a woman-to-woman basis. We do not recommend that you use the information for contraception until you have participated in such a group.

Billings, John and Evelyn, and Maurice Catarinich. *The Atlas of the Ovulation Method*. Published in Australia. Available from: WOOMB-USA, Room 119, 1750 Brentwood, St. Louis MO 63144, for $10. This is a teaching manual, written by the Billingses, which can also be very helpful to women who want to learn the method. Well worth the money.

Department of Health and Hospitals, 1400 W. 9th Street, Los Angeles, CA 90015. Large resource center for the ovulation method. Slides and cassettes in English and Spanish, a newsletter and a teacher's guide.

Garfink, Christine, and Hank Pizer. *The New Birth Control Program*. New York: Bantam, 1979. Paperback. Good account of sympto-thermal method. Their information about mucus is not very good; emphasis is on temperature.

Gillette, Nealy, ed. *The Ovulation Method Newsletter*. Published quarterly. $3/year from: The Ovulation Method Teachers Association, Box 14511, Portland, OR 97214.

Guren, Denise S., and Nealy Gillette. *The Ovulation Method: Cycles of Fertility*. Published by the Ovulation Method Teachers Association, 4760 Aldrich Road, Bellingham WA 98225. $2.95 plus 30¢ postage and handling (discounts available for bulk orders). Clear, concise, and without moral or religious overtones. Emphasis on the ovulation method. Best book we've seen yet.

Kippley, John and Sheila. *The Art of Natural Family Planning*. Couple-to-Couple League, Box 11084, Cincinnati, OH 45211. 1975. $4.95. Emphasis on sympto-thermal method. A good book, but much Catholic morality mixed in.

Lacey, Louise. *Lunaception*. New York: Warner Books, 1976. $1.75. How to regulate irregular cycles. A very useful book, although her mucus information is not up-to-date and we would *not* recommend using lunaception for contraception, as she does.

CHAPTER 11

ABORTION

INTRODUCTION

One of our most fundamental rights as women is the right to choose whether and when to have children. Only when we are in control of that choice are we free to be all that we can be for ourselves, for children we already have or may have in the future, for our partners, for our communities. Birth control is the single best tool for implementing this choice, but as Chapter 10 makes painfully clear, today, in 1978, birth control methods are just not effective enough for us to be able always to avoid unwanted pregnancy. And our society's attitudes toward sexuality, sex education and health care make it hard for many of us, especially the very young and the poor, to choose, obtain and use methods of birth control that will work for us. So right now, for many of us, a second indispensable tool for taking control of our fertility is *abortion*, the termination of a pregnancy by medical means.

The decision to have an abortion is rarely free of conflict. Even though a pre-twelve-week abortion performed by a trained person takes only 10 to 15 minutes and is medically very safe, most of us would much rather *prevent* a pregnancy than end one. But when an unwanted pregnancy does occur, many of us feel that giving birth to a baby we cannot properly care for would be a greater grief than abortion, both for us and for the child. So we in our collective believe that women must be free to *choose* abortion. We want all abortions to be legal, inexpensive (ideally free, as all health care should be), voluntary and safe, done in a supportive atmosphere with sufficient information-sharing and counseling.

Abortion is now legal in the United States. In 1973, after several years of research and pressure at all levels by women's groups, family planning organizations and civil liberties groups, the United States Supreme Court legalized abortion performed by doctors up through twenty-four weeks of pregnancy (with minor regulation by the states only after twelve weeks of pregnancy). Today any of us who so choose should be able to end an unwanted pregnancy with a safe and relatively inexpensive abortion in a clinic, hospital or doctor's office. Unfortunately, this is not always the case. In many parts of the country abortion is *still* less available than it should

be, more expensive than it needs to be, and a more negative experience than it ought to be. And the Supreme Court decision is under attack by a small but powerful anti-abortion movement. We have come a long way from the time of nightmarish illegal abortions, but we also have a long way to go.

We know that a number of women and men believe sincerely that abortion is wrong. To them, abortion violates the "right to life" of an unborn fetus; it "kills" an actual person; it is another unacceptable act of violence in a violent society. We cannot agree with them that an unborn fetus has more rights than the pregnant woman who is carrying it. Further, many of us who choose abortion believe that the quality of life we offer our children—which includes our emotional and situational readiness for a child or another child—is as important as the life itself.

We defend any woman's right *not* to end a pregnancy if she feels abortion is wrong for her.* But some who are against abortion for themselves want to restrict others' freedom. We believe they are wrong to try to impose their beliefs on us. The "Today" section of this chapter will describe some of the tactics of the anti-abortion movement and ways we can defend our newly established legal right to abortion.

History of Abortion Laws and Practice

The anti-abortionists sometimes argue that abortion violates an age-old natural law. But for centuries abortion in the early stages of pregnancy was widely tolerated. In many societies in Europe and later in America it was used as one of the only dependable methods of fertility control. Even the Catholic Church took the conveniently loose view that the fetus became animated by the rational soul, and abortion therefore became a serious crime at forty days after conception for a boy and eighty days for a girl. (Methods of sex determination were not specified.) English and American common law,

---

*Because this is a chapter on abortion, it inevitably seems that we are advocating abortion as the "right" or the "best" or "most liberated" thing to do. We do not believe that everyone with an unplanned pregnancy "should" have an abortion. We give so much space to abortion information here because it has been so unavailable in the past and because it is an issue that so many are confronted with.

dating back to the thirteenth century, shows a fairly tolerant acceptance of abortion up until quickening, the moment sometime in the fifth month when the woman first feels the fetus move.*

Most of the laws making abortion a crime were not passed until the nineteenth century. In 1869 Pope Pius IX declared that all abortion was murder. By the 1860s, in this country, new legislation outlawed all abortions except those "necessary to save the life of the woman."

There were reasons why abortion suddenly became a "crime." The first was quite legitimate: abortion was a dangerous operation—methods crude, antiseptics scarce, the mortality rate high. It was in part the mid-nineteenth-century wave of humanitarianism that brought in abortion laws to protect women. Secondly, it was during this time that medical care for women passed out of the hands of midwives, who had almost certainly performed abortions as part of their services, into the realm of male doctors, who did not necessarily respect a woman's right to end a pregnancy. Thirdly, new understanding of the biology of conception and pregnancy made it clear that the fetus is alive before its movements can be felt, so an abortion before quickening became for some a more serious matter. Fourth, just at a time when women's increasing understanding of conception was helping them to avoid pregnancy, certain governments and religious groups desired continued population growth to fill growing industries and new farmable territories. Abortion laws saw to it that women took their place alongside the other machines of a developing economy. Last and perhaps most insidious, a highly moralistic group obsessed with banning "sex for pleasure" struck up a campaign against both abortion and birth control. Sex was for marriage and marriage was for making babies. Sex outside of marriage was immoral; pleasurable sex inside marriage was somewhat immoral; and unwanted pregnancy was the punishment for such indulgence.

These mid-nineteenth-century abortion laws did not succeed in curbing our strong natural sexuality. But history has shown that women will seek abortion whether it is legal or not, and the new laws made increasing numbers of women have to get abortions illegally. The trauma of illegal abortion is a part of our collective history as women that deeply agonizes and angers us. There was a high rate of complication, infertility and even death among women who desperately tried to abort themselves, or who were forced underground for dangerous illegal operations. There were illegal profits to back-street abortionists, who charged high prices for non-medical procedures done in unsanitary conditions. There was blatant discrimination against poor women, who had to risk back-street abortions while their wealthier sisters could often find and pay a cooperative doctor. And those unable to end their unwanted pregnancies too often found their lives, and those of the children born, twisted by the hardships involved.*

In the mid-1960s some angry and concerned women and men began to organize to try to change the existing abortion laws. We were opposed by those who saw abortion as the taking of life; by those who saw abortion as a threat to sacred notions of sex for marriage and marriage

*For full discussion of the history of abortion law and practice, see Lawrence Lader's *Abortion*, cited in bibliography.

*A Swedish study of children of women denied abortion twenty years earlier revealed them to be (as compared to a control group) in poorer health, with histories of more psychiatric care, and with a higher rate of alcohol use. Hans Forssman and Inga Thuwe, "One Hundred and Twenty Children Born After Application for Therapeutic Abortion Refused," *Acta Psychiatra Scandinavica*, 42 (1966), pp. 71–88. See Garrett Hardin's *Mandatory Motherhood*, pp. 105–133, for sections of this study.

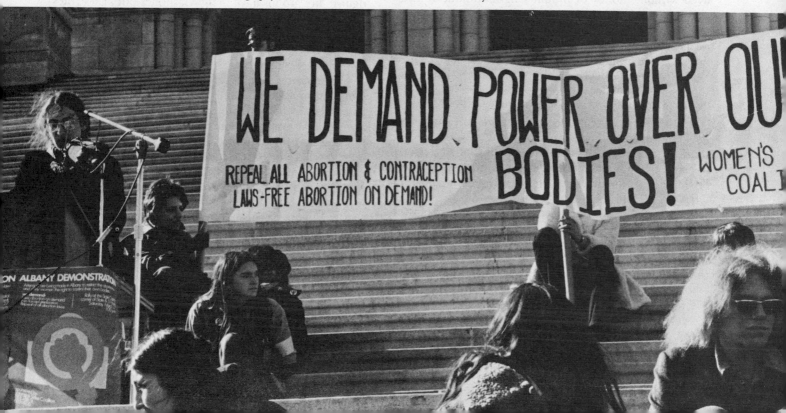

for children; by doctors wishing to maintain their control; and by the profiteers for whom illegal abortion was a lucrative racket.

The first success was the "liberalization" of abortion laws in a few states (Colorado and California, for example). These "reformed" laws allowed women to apply for abortions in certain specific instances but left the decision up to doctors and hospitals. Medical red tape and high costs combined with society's overall nonacceptance of abortion to let only a very few women, mostly wealthy ones, benefit from the reform. In 1969, when a few states had somewhat liberalized their laws, 75 percent of the women who died from abortions (most of them illegal) were non-white, while 90 percent of the year's legal abortions were given to white private patients. The terrible discrimination continued.

Finally in 1970 New York State passed not a mere "reform" but a "near repeal" abortion statute, allowing abortion up through 24 elapsed weeks from the last menstrual period, if it was done in a medical facility by a doctor. By 1972 Alaska, Hawaii and Washington State had passed statutes which approached allowing abortion on request of the woman. In many other states feminist, family-planning and civil rights groups had court cases pending which challenged restrictive laws.

For two years women who could afford it flocked to the few places where abortions were legal. In New York City alone, 223,000 abortions were reported in 1972, 61.8 percent of these being for women from out of state (data from New York City Health Department). We learned from the New York experience that parts of the medical community were willing to respond to the need for abortion. Safety and efficiency of abortion services improved each year. But we knew that for every woman who managed to get to New York there were others who lived without money or mobility in communities where abortion was still an unmentioned word, who were forced underground for abortions in the same awful way as in preceding years. From observation of the proven safety and demand for legal abortion services in New York City, witnesses in a number of cases before the U.S. Supreme Court urged the repeal of all state laws limiting access to abortion.

Then in January 1973 the U.S. Supreme Court made its decision affirming that the "right of privacy . . . founded in the 14th Amendment's concept of personal liberty . . . is broad enough to encompass a woman's decision whether or not to terminate her pregnancy." The Court held that through the first trimester (12 weeks) of pregnancy, the decision to have an abortion may be made solely by the pregnant woman and her doctor. Following approximately the end of the first trimester, a state's power to regulate abortion is limited to the establishment of rules governing where and by whom an abortion may be performed. "It is only when the fetus has reached a point of viability (from 24 to 28

weeks of gestation) that the state may go so far as to proscribe abortion . . . except when it is necessary to preserve the life or health of the mother."

Today

Now we know that the Supreme Court decision was just the first step toward securing the right to decent abortion care for all women. Of course the situation has been much improved by the Court's decision. Most women in the first trimester of pregnancy (through 12 elapsed weeks from last menstrual period) who choose abortion can get one fairly close to where they live, although for a woman in the second trimester of pregnancy (over 12 up through 24 weeks) it is often very difficult to find abortion services. Many under-12-week clinics have opened. Some, such as Planned Parenthood clinics, are non-profit, but too many are profit-oriented, and most are not truly woman-oriented. A few women-run clinics like the Woman's Choice clinics in California are developing models of non-profit, woman-oriented health services that every health care facility in the country stands to learn from.

If legalization of abortion was just a first step, what remains to be done? First, we must counter a strong anti-abortion movement which threatens to undo the legal progress we have already made. Second, the quality and availability of abortion services vary tremendously and need our constant attention. We will discuss these two challenges separately.

The Anti-Abortion Movement

There is a vociferous, powerful and well-monied minority opposed to abortion. Known by such names as Birthright, the National Right to Life Committee, the Celebrate Life Committee, Life Lobby and similar titles, the right-to-life groups have many Catholics but also Protestants and Jews as members. They seem to have the backing of the Catholic hierarchy (U.S. Catholic Conference), the Catholic Hospital Association and the Knights of Columbus.*

The basic right-to-life argument is that the fetus is a person from the moment of conception, and, as such, has a right to be protected from "murder." Abortion at any point is considered murder. These groups are not satisfied that the Supreme Court decision forces no one either to have or to perform an abortion. They want to make sure no one even has the choice. Some go so far as to oppose abortion even in cases where the mother's life is in danger.†

Right-to-life groups appeal to legislators' emotions with slides and pictures of mangled fetuses (when in fact

*Women's Lobby Quarterly, Vol. 1, No. 3 (November, 1974); 1345 G St., Washington, D.C.

†For a thorough discussion of these issues from a pro-choice point of view, see Garrett Hardin's *Mandatory Motherhood*, listed in the bibliography.

Statistics confirm that voluntary legal abortion is improving women's physical and psychological health. The Joint Program for the Study of Abortion* and New York City Department of Health statistics† show that during the first four years of New York's new law:

- the infant mortality rate dropped
- abortion-associated deaths dropped
- hospital admissions for incomplete (illegal) abortions dropped
- mortality and complication rates of legal abortion dropped steadily
- the mortality rate for early abortion was well below that for full term pregnancy and delivery.

Studies on the psychological effects of legal abortion consistently show that women feel more happy than sad, more relieved than depressed, after having a voluntary legal abortion.‡

Who is getting abortions? The typical candidate has been a young, single, white woman, pregnant for the first time. However, of all women seeking legal abortions:

- a relatively high proportion are older women nearing menopause*
- 32% of women who obtain abortions are non-white*
- a slightly higher proportion than their percentage of the population are Catholic women†
- 26% of women who obtain abortions are married.*

These figures show us that all kinds of women get abortions. They also show that too many of us are not getting effective enough birth control, or, for a whole range of reasons both personal and societal, are not able to use it well enough. (See Introduction to Chapter 10.)

*Center for Disease Control, Atlanta, Georgia.
†*The Abortion Experience*, Howard Osofsky, M.D., ed. (New York: Harper & Row, 1973).

*Joint Program for Study of Abortion reports can be found in *Studies in Family Planning*, a periodical of The Population Council, 245 Park Ave., N.Y., N.Y., 10017.
†J. Pacter, M.D., Director, Bureau of Maternity Services, New York City Department of Health, cited in *Effects of New York State's Liberalized Abortion Law*, pamphlet prepared and issued by Abortion Rights Association, Inc. (National Abortion Rights Action League), 250 W. 57th St., New York, N.Y. 10019.
‡Joy D. Osofsky, Ph.D., and Howard H. Osofsky, M.D., "The Psychological Reaction of Patients to Legalized Abortion," *American Journal of Orthopsychiatry*, Vol. 42, No. 1 (January, 1972); Kenneth R. Niswander, M.D., Judith Singer, Ph.D., and Michael Singer, Ph.D., "Psychological Reaction of Therapeutic Abortion," *American Journal of Obstetrics and Gynecology*, Vol. 114, No. 1 (September 1, 1972).

an early abortion removes fetal tissue that is at most 3/4 to 1 inch long). Their huge letter-writing campaigns have Congressional mail well stacked against abortion. Even though a 1977 survey revealed that 64% of the persons believed that regardless of morality, a woman should be legally free to have an abortion if she wants one,§ the 64-percent majority is quieter and tends to be busy with other issues. The right-to-life minority—single-minded, angry and persistent—makes itself seen and heard.

On the federal level, right-to-life forces have pushed unceasingly for constitutional amendments which would overturn the Supreme Court decision, and for limitations on funding bills which would prohibit use of federal funds for abortion services or payments.

On the state level, anti-abortion pressure has brought in many laws which try to restrict freedom of choice or

§*Washington Post* 8/9/78. Survey by Yankelovitch, Skelly and White.

availability of abortions. These laws violate the Supreme Court ruling that the states have no authority over first-trimester abortion, and only certain regulating authority over second-trimester abortion. States have passed "performance requirements," specifying where abortions are to take place; "consent laws," which require consent from parents or spouse; and "conscience" clauses, which permit hospitals and other health care establishments to refuse their facilities for abortion. Some states have challenged whether Medicaid (welfare) has to pay for abortions.‡

If you want to work on the federal level to combat this movement against your freedom of choice, you can join or support the work of the National Abortion Rights Action League, the National Organization for Women (NOW) and the American Civil Liberties Union.§ Write often to your legislators. We must, through letters, phone calls, every kind of communication, let legislators at all levels know they cannot support anti-abortion legislation and be re-elected.

‡In June of 1977 the Supreme Court ruled that the states and other local governments could choose to finance or not finance abortions. This ruling and the Hyde Amendment, which cut off federal Medicaid funds for abortion, have made it difficult if not impossible for many women to obtain abortions.
§NARAL (National Abortion Rights Action League), 825 15th St. N.W., Washington, D.C. 20005; NOW (National Organization for Women) National Office, 1957 East 73rd St., Chicago, Ill. 60649; ACLU (American Civil Liberties Union)—Women's Rights Division, 22 East 40th St., New York, N.Y. 10016.

In Akron, Ohio, a city ordinance has been passed which requires abortion counseling to include such facts as fetal development, and complications of and alternatives to abortion. Abortion clinics around the country have been burned, their employees and clients attacked, harassed and physically endangered. In Kentucky, a young woman was arrested and tried for performing an abortion on herself. This woman was reported by a physician who treated her, and acquitted on grounds of temporary insanity. When, in a country with legal abortion, a woman is arrested for solving her problem because abortion is unavailable to her, the struggle for abortion rights is intensified.

The lobbying and court cases take a considerable amount of time and money, money which pro-choice groups could better use to improve abortion services.

The Medicaid cutbacks and the harassment of women, health workers and abortion providers is part of a large movement to prohibit abortion for all women.

If you want to work at the state level to combat anti-abortion forces in your state, you can get local references from any of the national organizations mentioned above, or contact your local women's center, Planned Parenthood, Civil Liberties Union chapter or NOW chapter.

Improving Abortion Services

We have learned that legalization does not guarantee decent abortion services. Locally there is a lot that we need to do. Existing abortion services vary, and there are too many rip-off referral agencies and clinics that put profit above care. Women's groups have in some places been effective in *monitoring* present services—mobilizing, for instance, to push for lower costs, for doctors who are more sensitive to women, for adequate counseling staff. Often the best way to do this is to provide *referrals* and guidelines for choice, so that women get the best possible services, and the doctors and clinics that treat women best get more business. If you want to start such a project, you can get an idea of what's possible from the Washington Area Women's Center's pamphlet *Abortion—A Woman's Right to Choose: A Guide to Abortion in the D.C. Area* (write 2452 18th St., N.W., Washington, D.C.).

We must try to influence working conditions and choice of staff in existing abortion facilities. The nurses, counselors, doctors who provide abortion services understandably have the same mixed feelings about abortion as we all do. We must press abortion facilities to choose their personnel with the utmost care, trying to find people who are both fully convinced of a woman's right to end a pregnancy and able to handle their own emotional reactions to seeing or doing a lot of abortion procedures. We must urge facilities to arrange counseling sessions or discussion groups in which the staff can ventilate and work through their feelings. Further, nursing and counseling staff should have more decision-making power than they do at present in most places: they deserve to be able to shape their working conditions.

Where local services are nonexistent or inadequate, we need to pressure local (public) health care facilities to provide abortions—the law is not on our side.* But this is a long and frustrating task. It often seems better to develop our own clinics to provide needed services and to demonstrate what kind of care we want. Starting a clinic is a big job, but it has been done or is being planned in a number of places. For advice on starting a clinic you can contact the Feminist Women's Health Center, 746 South Crenshaw, Los Angeles, California, which has opened three woman-controlled Woman's Choice clinics in that state.

In the struggle for free choice about abortion, we have tested and proven our ability to join together as women in order to start to get our needs met. Let's not forget that the abortion services we are pressing for are only a part of the overall health care system we need. We must work for a system that provides good health education and birth control services in an atmosphere which is accepting of people's sexuality. With such health care, freely provided, there will be fewer unwanted pregnancies and consequently less need for us to have to choose abortion at all.

IF YOU THINK YOU ARE PREGNANT

As soon as I missed my period I knew that I was pregnant. I felt differently than I ever had before. There was the going to the bathroom, of course. I have always had a very weak bladder, but it was now weaker and more sensitive than ever. My energy seemed to be dwindling.

I sometimes miss my period anyway, or it comes really late. So when it didn't come this time I didn't even notice for a while. Then when I did notice, I thought, "That couldn't happen to me." So I ignored it awhile longer. [These words, from a sixteen year old, could also come from a woman nearing menopause.]

The most common sign of pregnancy is a missed menstrual period. Nausea and vomiting, breast tenderness, frequent urination, tiredness—these can be signs too,

*The Supreme Court ruled in 1977 that hospitals do not have to provide abortions!

even in early pregnancy. Since none of these signs always means pregnancy, and since the uncertainty and wondering are so agonizing, the first thing to do is go get a pregnancy test. (Getting a test does not mean you chose to have an abortion—it is also the first step in prenatal care.)

Verifying a pregnancy takes two procedures: a laboratory test which checks the urine for a hormone, chorionic gonadotrophin, made by your body during early pregnancy; and a pelvic examination by a trained person to check for relevant changes in your cervix and uterus.

The instructions for collecting and submitting your urine are simple. Drink no liquids after dinner the night before, then as soon as you wake in the morning, collect about half a cupful in a clean, dry, soap-free jar. Cover it and keep it refrigerated until you take it to a laboratory. To find out where to get a urine sample tested, you can call a women's center or women's clinic, a local Planned Parenthood office, a local hospital's gynecology clinic, a doctor (more expensive) if you have one you would feel comfortable telling about a possible pregnancy, or a laboratory listed in the Yellow Pages under "Pregnancy Tests" or "Laboratories—Testing" (some labs won't give results directly to you, so check this before you leave your urine sample with them). Some abortion clinics and pregnancy counseling groups do urine testing inexpensively or free, with no obligation to use the abortion service.

The most common urine test is the two-minute "slide" test, which starts to be effective 42 days from the *first* day of your last menstrual period ("42 days LMP"). The slide test is more accurate a week or so later. A more sensitive (and more expensive) urine test is the two-hour "test tube" test, which is quite accurate by 35 days LMP. See p. 258 for description of a new blood test, not yet widely available, which works even sooner.

You can go to a doctor for a dose of progesterone, which will bring on your period within 10 days if you are not pregnant. This is not an abortion. We do not recommend it, as there is growing suspicion that it may be harmful to a developing fetus.

A pregnancy test can be either "positive" or "negative." A "positive" means that you are almost certainly pregnant and should see a trained medical person to verify the pregnancy with a pelvic exam. False positives are very rare and may mean the onset of menopause. A "negative" may mean that you are not pregnant, but false negatives are fairly common. A false negative could be the result of: urine that got too warm on its way to the lab; urine that wasn't concentrated enough; contamination of urine by soap, aspirin or whatever was in the bottle you took it to the lab in. If you take the specimen too early in your pregnancy there may be an insufficient amount of the hormone. If it's too late in the pregnancy, after about three months, the test may also be falsely negative.

If you have a negative test and your period doesn't come, you should have another test in a week—*and keep using birth control,* for if you aren't pregnant you can get pregnant! After two or three negative tests, you'd better have a pelvic exam, as some pregnancies *never* give positive test results.

DECIDING WHAT TO DO

If you are pregnant, it is first important to determine how far along you are in pregnancy. It may come as a shock to learn that medical people calculate the weeks of pregnancy from the first day of your last menstrual period and not from the day(s) you think you conceived. For example, if your period is two weeks overdue and your menstrual cycle is about 28 days long, you are considered *six* weeks pregnant even though it has probably been only four weeks since you conceived. Thus when we say a "pre-twelve-week abortion," we mean an abortion done within twelve weeks from the first day of the woman's last menstrual period (twelve-weeks LMP), or possibly ten weeks since she became pregnant.

If you are even considering terminating your pregnancy, remember that there is a time limit for your decision. *The earlier an abortion is done, the safer it is!* Also, the less painful and expensive it will be for you. Complication rates for early outpatient (not involving an overnight stay) procedures, while all low, do become higher with each week of pregnancy. The second trimester induction procedure (16 through 24 weeks) carries three to four times the risk of earlier abortions. Also, as the fetus becomes more developed, abortion becomes more emotionally upsetting both for you and for the medical and counseling staff (see "Having a Second Trimester Abortion by the Induction Method," p. 232).

So, eight to ten weeks LMP should be your outside limit for a decision and immediate action.

If you are pregnant and it is still early in your pregnancy, you have some time—not a lot, but some—to make your choice about what to do. You can:

1. go ahead with the pregnancy and keep the baby;
2. go ahead with the pregnancy and give the baby to another family either temporarily (foster home) or permanently (adoption);
3. terminate the pregnancy by having a legal abortion at a medical facility.

For many women this is a painfully difficult choice to make.

Feelings About Being Pregnant

Most of us experience a powerful mixture of feelings when an unwanted pregnancy is confirmed. We may

fear that our families will find out and punish us; fear that we won't be able to figure out what to do; fear that we'll be all alone in trying to decide; fear the prospect of motherhood. We may also fear abortion even though we know it's legal and safe: Will it hurt? Will it cost more than I can pay? Will I be punished by having some dreadful complication and maybe even be made sterile? Will I feel guilty? Will I later wish I had the baby?

We feel a lot of anger too. We may feel angry with ourselves or our partners for not being careful enough about birth control. Often, however, we have been using birth control and it has failed:

When I found I was pregnant, I was frightened and angry that my body was out of my control. I was furious that my IUD had failed me, and I felt my sexual parts were alien and my enemy. I felt I was being punished for my femaleness.

We may be angry and sad that we don't have the money, relationship, or living situation that would allow us to go ahead and have a baby. We are angry that all the consequences of sexual intercourse fall on us. If we do not have the support and understanding of our lover or husband, we feel betrayed. We feel anger and confusion if we are pressured by our parents or friends or sexual partner to do something that we don't want to do, whether it be to have an abortion or to continue the pregnancy. And we feel angry if there are laws and procedures that restrict our right to choose freely what we will do.

We also almost always feel ambivalent. No matter what we choose to do, we will have some conflicting feelings. It helps to realize that our ambivalent feelings about the pregnancy are natural. If we decide we most want to go ahead with the pregnancy, we will still have moments of resentment and fear and uncertainty. On the other hand, if we choose abortion there are also opposing feelings within us. Even if our strongest and clearest feeling is "I cannot have a child right now," if it is a first pregnancy, it may feel exciting to know that our body "works"; even when we absolutely don't want a child, there is a feeling of pride in our body processes that may confuse us if we don't know how natural it is, and make us question our decision for abortion. If we already have children, there's the feeling that we know what a child of ours would be like, and it feels cruel to say no to that possibility. We may feel selfish, especially in the face of our society's emphasis on motherhood or our children's or husband's desire for a larger family. We may feel guilty, especially if our religion disapproves of abortion or if we feel morally opposed to ending life. And there are wishes, too, that make us feel ambivalent. Maybe, married or unmarried, we or our partner or both are filled with romantic feelings that having a baby would "make everything all right" in our relationship.

With all these mixed feelings and not much time, deciding what to do with an unplanned pregnancy can feel like an impossible task. It may help somewhat to know that after you make a decision, the ambivalence and mixed feelings tend to subside. Whatever we decide, it is important for us as women to make an *active* decision, one which is ours, rather than passively slipping into one choice or another. There are a few things we can do to help ourselves make decisions that we will be able to live with.

FIND SOMEONE TO TALK WITH. Many of us have found that it really helps to talk out our feelings about being pregnant, about having to make a choice, about the decision itself, with someone who cares about us. We have often been surprised, once we speak, at the supportiveness of the very friend or relative we had been scared to tell. But sometimes there is no one close to us whom we feel we can trust to be *calm* about the pregnancy, and not to try to talk us into what they think we should do. Even then it is both possible and important to find someone to talk with. You can call a local women's center, Planned Parenthood, United Community Services, the Clergy Consultation Service (often listed in local directory; national number is 212-254-6230; see page 227 for description), or a guidance counselor, dean, or favorite teacher at school. You deserve a chance to "think out loud" about your feelings before you act on any decision about the pregnancy.

For many of us it feels important to involve the man we got pregnant with. If we do not share with him the hassle and pain of the unplanned pregnancy, we allow him to avoid his responsibility or even prevent him from assuming it. We also deprive him of the opportunity to share his feelings and to give us support. Of course some men will not face their involvement, and either leave us or withdraw emotionally. This is when we have to turn to a friend or counselor for all of our support. It is perhaps hardest when our partner disagrees with what we feel we need to do. His feelings are important, but it's our body, and in this society the parenting will be primarily up to us—so the decision must finally be ours.

CHECK THE ALTERNATIVES, if you have any doubts at all. For some of us, continuing the pregnancy and then offering the baby up for adoption is a real alternative. Planned Parenthood, United Community Services, or your state's Department of Public Welfare can refer you to adoption and foster home agencies, as well as to homes in which you can live during your pregnancy if you feel you cannot stay where you are living. Anti-abortion groups such as Birthright will give you all the information but will also probably try to persuade you not to terminate the pregnancy. Adoption of an infant—once no sure thing, for non-white babies especially—is more dependable now that there are so few infants up for adoption relative to the number of people who want to adopt. This would be something to ask a local adoption agency about. Offering a baby for adoption can be a very difficult experience emotionally, with a sense of loss that can last for years. But for some of us it may be the least upsetting and most positive of the three alternatives.

If you are single and considering raising a child by yourself, be sure to speak with single mothers to learn something of what it is like, what's hard, what kinds of support you would depend on from family and friends.* Some of the groups mentioned above, including Birthright, will help you prepare for single parenthood by putting you in touch with sources of financial assistance, counseling and so on. Reading Chapter 12, "Considering Parenthood," may be helpful.

FIND OUT ABOUT THE ABORTION EXPERIENCE. Sometimes not knowing what happens in an abortion—what the risks, procedures, prices are—can keep us from making a clear decision for or against it. Any of the groups mentioned under "Agencies That Can Help You Find an Abortion," p. 227, can give you the factual information you need. Try to get an idea of what to expect by talking with someone who has had an abortion recently.

MEDICAL TECHNIQUES FOR ABORTION

When you are deciding whether to have an abortion, or choosing where and how to have it done, you have a right and a need to know just what procedures are used at each stage of pregnancy and what risks, if any, are involved, as well as what the cost should be. In this section we will outline these.

*See *The Single Parent Experience* by Carole Klein (New York: Avon Books, 1973).

In pregnancy, the woman's fertilized egg attaches itself to the lining of her uterus about one week after conception (see Chapters 2, 10 and 13 for discussion) and continues to grow. When the embryo is one month old (about 6 weeks LMP) it is a pea-sized mass of tissue. A mass of tissue called the placenta is developing to nourish the embryo. By the end of the second month (10 weeks LMP) the growing embryo, by this time called a fetus, is about one inch long and is beginning to assume human shape. A three-month fetus (14 weeks LMP) is about three inches long. A fluid-filled sac, the *amniotic sac*, surrounds and helps to protect it. By about the 20th week, the fetal heartbeat can be discerned with proper instruments, and the mother can start to feel the fetus move. Sometime between the 24th and 28th weeks the fetus reaches the point that it might live for at least a short while under intensive hospital care if the mother had a miscarriage.

In an abortion, the contents of the uterus (fetus, placenta and built-up tissue on the lining of the uterus) are removed, leaving the uterus in an unpregnant state. Different methods are used, depending on how large the fetus has grown. These are outlined below. Since improvements are being made in abortion procedures, keep in mind that some of the information presented here may be out of date by the time you read it.

Endometrial Aspiration

Also called *menstrual regulation*, and *pre-emptive abortion* (means: done before verification of pregnancy just in case you are pregnant). Improperly called "menstrual extraction" (see below).

WHEN. Done any time after menstrual period is due until positive pregnancy is determined (4-6 weeks LMP—up to 72 days LMP).

METHOD. A small, flexible plastic tube is inserted through the cervix into the uterus without any dilation (stretching) of the cervix. The outside end of the tube is attached to a source of suction—an electric or mechanical pump, or in very early pregnancy, a syringe—which gently sucks out the tissue from the wall of the uterus. What comes out is the "endometrium," or lining, that has built up over the four weeks of the menstrual cycle, plus the tiny bit of fetal tissue if the woman is pregnant. It takes only a few minutes. Cramping can be mildly painful but is brief. Anesthesia (local) rarely necessary.

ORIGIN OF METHOD. The development of this flexible-tube method is a fine example of medical research done by women for women. The technique has been pioneered in large part by women in the self-help movement at the Feminist Women's Health Center in Los Angeles. They have practiced on each other in order to develop safe instruments and techniques for removing the lining of the uterus just about the time the menstrual period is due. As done on this experimental-research basis by women in advanced self-help groups, the procedure is called *menstrual extraction*. The aim of menstrual extraction is to help women to avoid the discomfort or inconvenience of a monthly period. In this context it is *not* intended to be an abortion. More research needs to be done before we know whether extraction of the uterine lining on a monthly basis is a safe thing.

AVAILABILITY. As a method of pre-emptive abortion done in case the woman might be pregnant, this technique is being used in a number of women's clinics, Planned Parenthood clinics and doctor's offices around the country. It is not, however, widely available at present.

COST. From $60 to $90. In some clinics, however, it costs as much as a "very early abortion" (see below).

RISKS AND COMPLICATIONS. Not much data available yet, but seems to have a very low rate of complications, risks, side effects. The flexibility of the tube means less risk of scarring or perforating the uterus. Since it is done without dilating the cervix there is probably less risk than there is in later abortions of adversely affecting the cervix's ability to perform properly in subsequent pregnancies.

ADVANTAGES. Can be done by a trained paraprofessional; expense and waiting of pregnancy testing eliminated; minimal complications; takes little time; relatively cheap; early emotional relief for the woman. Some women, however, would prefer to wait to know for sure whether they are pregnant, so as to deal with their feelings about it.

DISADVANTAGES. In many cases it may be done unnecessarily: many women with a period a week overdue are not in fact pregnant. Secondly, perhaps because the fetal tissue at this stage is so tiny, it is hard for the abortionist to be totally certain that it was removed: it is occasionally missed and the woman remains pregnant. Because of this slight risk of continued pregnancy it is advisable to get a pregnancy test a week or so afterward.

CONTRAINDICATIONS. A pre-emptive abortion probably should not be done if you have Rh negative blood, because of the remote possibility of Rh sensitization (see p. 229 and Chapter 16).

Very Early Abortion
Also called *early uterine evacuation*.

WHEN. Done after a positive pregnancy test, up to 7–8 weeks LMP.

WHERE. Doctor's office or clinic.

METHOD. Same as above—no cervical dilation; flexible tube used. During these early weeks of pregnancy the more standard abortion procedure, the Dilation and Evacuation (see "D & E," below), is not generally used. This is because the D & E, involving as it does a non-flexible tube (usually) and dilation of the cervix, has a slightly higher complication rate during these early weeks when the cervix is so tight.

AVAILABILITY. Not yet widely available. In many facilities women are asked to wait until 7–8 weeks LMP for a D & E.

COST. Varies. Often the same as a D & E: $80–$150.

RISKS AND COMPLICATIONS. Same as above.

ADVANTAGES. Minimal complications; takes little time; relatively cheap; early emotional relief; can be done by a trained paraprofessional though this is not legal at present.

DISADVANTAGES. Same slight failure rate as mentioned above.

CONTRAINDICATIONS. Same as above.

Dilation and Evacuation (D & E)
Also called *vacuum suction*, or *vacuum curettage*.

WHEN. From 7 through 12 weeks LMP.

WHERE. Doctor's office, clinic, or hospital.

METHOD. The cervical opening is dilated (stretched) until the tip (*vacurette*) of a non-flexible* tube can be passed through into the uterus. Size of tip goes up to 12mm., depending on duration of pregnancy and size of fetal tissue. The free end of the vacurette (in the vagina) is attached to a flexible tube leading to the vacuum aspirator, an electric or sometimes mechanical pump. The suction of the aspirator frees the fetal tissue from the uterine wall and pulls it through the tube and out of the body into a small container within the aspirator. The procedure takes about 10 minutes. For fuller description, see "Having a Vacuum Suction Abortion," p. 228.

RISKS AND COMPLICATIONS. Minor risk of perforation, infection, hemorrhage, incomplete abortion. Full discussion on page 231.

ADVANTAGES. Quick and easy to perform, can be done by trained paraprofessionals (not legal at this point); low complication rate; little discomfort for most women; relatively cheap; available almost everywhere.

DISADVANTAGES. Slightly more complications than for very early abortion.

AVAILABILITY. The most widely used method of abortion. Generally available except in very rural areas. The Supreme Court declared first trimester abortion to be

---

*The Feminist Women's Health Center in Los Angeles suggests a flexible tube be used in a D & E up to 12 weeks LMP.

the decision of the woman and the doctor, so most areas of the country have medical facilities performing vacuum suction abortions. However, some states, such as Louisiana, Mississippi, Oklahoma, West Virginia, Utah, North Dakota, Wyoming and Maine, have been slow to provide services. Women from these states usually have to go to a nearby state (which adds to the expense and hassle). As a rule, services are more available and costs lower in those areas that had liberal abortion laws before January, 1973—for example, New York, San Francisco, Los Angeles; Madison, Wisconsin; Washington, D.C.; Seattle, Washington. Abortion services vary so much that even when there is a facility easily available it is important to make sure it meets your standards for good health care (see p. 227, "What to Look For").

COST. $150–$175, could be lower at a Planned Parenthood clinic.

Dilation and Curettage (D & C)

WHEN. From 8 through 12 and occasionally 15 weeks LMP.

WHERE. Usually in a hospital, as it requires general anesthesia.

COST. $250 and higher.

AVAILABILITY. The D & C is a standard gynecological procedure used for such conditions as infertility, persistent menstrual irregularity and excessively heavy periods. The D & C used to be the best method for first trimester abortions. Now it has been virtually replaced by the quicker, easier and slightly safer D & E, which can be done with local anesthesia.

A private doctor who does not do abortions frequently may want to do a D & C rather than a D & E because s/he feels more comfortable doing a familiar procedure. A few facilities offer a "late D & C" up to 15 weeks LMP. Though less safe than a pre-twelve-week abortion, a D & C at this time seems to have lower complication and mortality rates than the second trimester induction procedures (see below). But this is a subject on which complete data are not yet available. If you are 13 weeks LMP, it would seem that it would be a whole lot easier on you emotionally if you could terminate the pregnancy with a late D & C rather than waiting until 16 weeks for an induction abortion. But medical opinion is so divided on the subject that a late D & C is rarely available.

METHOD. The cervix is dilated as with the suction method. As a rule, for the D & C slightly more dilation is necessary. After dilation the doctor uses a curette, a metal loop on the end of a long thin handle, to loosen the uterine lining, removing the fetal tissue with forceps.

RISKS AND COMPLICATIONS. Perforation, infection, hemorrhage. Somewhat more bleeding than with D & E.

ADVANTAGES. No advantages over suction method for 7–12 weeks LMP. From 12–15 weeks it's the only method currently used.

DISADVANTAGES. More dilation, more bleeding, more discomfort, general anesthesia, high cost, all put D & C at a disadvantage to the D & E through 12 weeks.

Induced Labor with Intra-amniotic Infusion: Saline Abortion, Prostaglandin Abortion. Also called Late Abortion.

WHEN. From 16 through 24 weeks LMP.

WHERE. In a hospital.

COST. From $800–$1400.

METHOD. As a pregnancy progresses through 12–15 weeks, the uterus expands and tilts and the walls become thinner, softer and more spongy, making perforation and excessive bleeding more likely with the vacuum suction and D & C procedures. The fetus becomes too large to be safely removed by suction or curettage. The preferred technique after 16 weeks is to cause the woman to go into labor so that the abortion occurs through the natural process of uterine contractions and cervical dilation as in full term labor and delivery. An abortion-causing solution is injected ("instilled") into the amniotic sac, or "bag of waters," which surrounds the fetus. (Before 16 weeks LMP this sac is not large enough to be located accurately, so the induction procedure cannot be used until this time.) Several hours later, contractions cause the cervix to dilate and the fetus and placenta to be expelled. (For details, see "Having A Second Trimester Abortion.")

Until recently the most commonly used abortion-causing solution was hypertonic saline (salt) solution. Recently, the prostaglandin $f_2\alpha$ has been FDA approved. Prostaglandins, contraction-causing hormone-like substances found in most body tissue, appear naturally in a woman's body at the time of full term labor and delivery. Comparison of these two abortion-inducers appears in "Having a Second Trimester Abortion," p. 232.

RISKS AND COMPLICATIONS. Higher than for earlier abortions. Very slight risk with saline of emergency shock or bleeding disorder (see page 233). For both, possible hemorrhage (1.77 out of every 100 abortions); retained placenta (29.38/100 abortions); infection.*

CONTRAINDICATIONS. Saline: liver or kidney problems, cardiac failure, hypertension, sickle-cell anemia. Prostaglandin: history of convulsions, epilepsy, asthma.

*Center for Disease Control, Abortion Surveillance Project.

ADVANTAGES. Safer than the other late abortion method, hysterotomy (see below).

DISADVANTAGES. Medically, higher risk and complication rate than for early abortion. Emotionally, can be a harrowing experience: for fuller discussion see "Having a Second Trimester Abortion." Delivery of dead fetus is upsetting to woman and to staff. Delivery of live fetus, possible with prostaglandins and increasingly likely as pregnancy gets later, is even more upsetting. Costly.

AVAILABILITY. Not widely available. Because of all the disadvantages listed above, most doctors and hospitals choose not to offer induction abortion. As someone from Planned Parenthood told us, "Many doctors wish the problem would go away." In February, 1975, a Boston jury convicted Kenneth Edelin, M.D., of manslaughter for performing a routine hysterotomy on a woman who was somewhere between 20 and 28 weeks LMP. Hospitals around the country have reacted by closing down their second trimester abortion services or by bringing in costly equipment to try to keep alive fetuses that show signs of life when expelled (cost to be passed on to the woman). Though the Boston jury's decision was reversed in a higher court and Dr. Edelin was acquitted of the charges, the power of the so-called "right-to-life" movement (see the "Today" section of this chapter) can be intimidating to physicians and health providers.

Even where induction abortion is available, it is usually done only under 20 weeks and with 2 to 3 weeks' delay. Planned Parenthood in New York City and San Francisco, two cities where abortion is available up to 24 weeks at a fairly low cost, would be good places to call. It is a good idea to use a facility that has plenty of experience with late abortions. Because of price variations, local delays and differences in quality of service, it may be worth your while to travel for a late abortion.

Hysterotomy

WHEN. Can be done any time from 10 weeks or so. Usually done from 16 through 24 weeks. Rarely used at all.

WHERE. In a hospital, as it is major surgery.

WHY. Done if induction method is contraindicated or has been tried unsuccessfully several times.

COST. At least $1,000.

METHOD. Like a caesarean section (see p. 287). The fetus is removed through a small abdominal incision, usually below the pubic hairline.

RISKS AND COMPLICATIONS. Highest complication and mortality rate of all abortion methods. General anesthesia, which is used, carries its own risk. Does not affect

reproductive system (unlike hysterectomy, with which it is sometimes confused).

DISADVANTAGES. High risk; several days' hospital stay required; very expensive; can limit woman to caesarean births thereafter.

Comparative Statistics for the Different Abortion Methods

1. Incidence
United States 1972–1975*

1972		1975
65.2%	Vacuum Aspiration	82.6%
23.4%	Sharp D & C	8.4%
10.3%	Intra-amniotic Instillation	6.2%
0.6%	Hysterotomy/Hysterectomy	0.4%

As time goes by and information about abortion gets around, more and more women are able to have abortions in the first 12 weeks, when they are safer.

2. Mortality (deaths related to each procedure)†

Statistics compiled from 1972–1975
- 1.6/100,000 Vacuum Aspiration
- 2.4/100,000 D & C
- 13.7/100,000 Saline
- 42.4/100,000 Hysterotomy
- 26.5/100,000 other, including Prostaglandin Instillation

Total 3.2 deaths per 100,000 abortions. Early abortion is safer. These mortality rates compare favorably to the 12.6 deaths per 100,000 live births for women going through pregnancy and childbirth.‡

3. Rates of complications per 100 legal abortions. This includes major complications, such as perforation, infection, and retained tissue, and minor complications.§

	SUCTION	D & C	SALINE	PROSTA-GLANDIN
under 8 weeks				
9–10 weeks	4.55			
11–12 weeks	4.81			
13–16 weeks	5.47	5.88	41.23	56.32
over 17 weeks	264	5.38	35.87	51.08

*Family Planning Perspectives, Vol. 9, No. 3, May–June 1977.
†It is important to note that these statistics would be better if abortion services were less expensive and more accessible.
‡Family Planning Perspectives, Vol. 10, No. 2, March–April 1978.
§From a JPSA/CDC Survey from 1971–1975, Family Planning Perspectives, Vol. 9, No. 6, Nov.–Dec. 1977.

IF YOU CHOOSE ABORTION—HOW TO FIND THE BEST ABORTION FACILITY FOR YOU

As we have said, although abortion is legal now, it is by no means everywhere available. This in itself is an injustice. How much control you have over where your abortion takes place will depend on a number of factors, such as what part of the country you live in; how far along you are in your pregnancy; how old you are; what referral sources you can get in touch with; how the local prices compare with what you can pay or what your insurance will cover; and how able you are at such a difficult and anxious time to be an "informed consumer" of abortion services. The personal support of a friend or counselor can be invaluable in this matter of finding an abortion service that fits your needs, or if there is only one facility available, of getting your particular needs met there as fully as possible.

Agencies That Can Help You Find an Abortion

There are a number of good, responsible sources of information on where to get an abortion, but there are also profit-making referral agencies that charge exorbitantly for services and/or get kickbacks from the doctors or clinics they refer to. Some rip-off agencies have been exposed, prosecuted and closed, but there are undoubtedly others still around just about everywhere. We suggest that you ignore the splashy newspaper ads for referral agencies, whether or not they mention price, and that you use the more dependable, non-profit referral services listed here.

WOMEN'S CENTERS AND WOMEN'S HEALTH CLINICS usually offer problem pregnancy counseling, and often abortion services themselves. They can be found in the phone book under the name of the city they are in. The women's centers and clinics usually are the most reliable sources for good health care. You can also write to the National Women's Health Network, 2025 Eye Street, Suite 105, Washington, DC 20006, about resources in your area. Examples of good women's health centers may be found in Burlington, VT, Concord, NH, Cambridge, MA, Tallahassee, FL, Iowa City, IA, Portland, OR, Los Angeles, CA, and Santa Cruz, CA.

PLANNED PARENTHOOD has offices in almost every state. If they do not have a clinic of their own to refer you to, they will know what is available in your state for every stage of pregnancy. If you can't find a listing for Planned Parenthood in the phone book, call their central office in New York City (212-541-7800).

What to Look for When Choosing an Abortion Facility for a First Trimester Abortion.

As abortion becomes more widely accepted, more and more abortion facilities will be opening up, with a variety of procedures, prices, atmospheres and attitudes toward women. Whether you are in an area where you have to struggle to find one abortion service or where you have to choose among competing services, it is important to know what you are looking for. Here are some of the different factors to consider in making your choice.*

Type of Facility

DOCTOR'S OFFICE. A number of private doctors have vacuum suction and/or endometrial aspiration equipment. Questions to ask: does s/he have backup services (see below)? Does s/he do enough abortions to keep up on the technique? Some private doctors will offer a D & C, but these are best done in a hospital. Other factors below apply also.

FREESTANDING CLINIC. Most first trimester abortions are being done in clinics, set up for that purpose, which are not part of a hospital. Their single focus *can* bring efficiency, which means prices *can* be lower; high numbers of abortions means practice in doing the procedure, which most often means lower complication rates; sometimes not so much red tape as at a hospital. Clinics vary greatly, so check further guidelines.

HOSPITAL OUTPATIENT ABORTION CLINIC. Some hospitals have vacuum suction abortion services for outpatients (no overnight stay required). Many people feel that hospitals *should* be providing this as part of their regular overall services. One Planned Parenthood person suggested that if your local hospital does not do abortions and you have to go elsewhere to get one, you should *ask* the local hospital anyway, and inform your local ob-gyn society that your need was not met. We must not let our local facilities get away with ignoring the need for abortion.

HOSPITAL WITH OVERNIGHT STAY. This is rarely necessary, except when some health condition makes it safer for the woman to be in a hospital for the abortion. It is done, however, when there is no local abortion clinic and/or when a woman goes to a private doctor who does not have the equipment and whose hospital's policies dictate that abortion is an overnight matter. It is sometimes done because health insurance will pay only in case of hospitalization.

*A helpful checklist of things to look for in an abortion facility can be obtained from the Judson Health Advocacy Project, Judson Memorial Church, 55 Washington Square South, New York, N.Y. 10012.

Profit or Non-profit

There are some profit-making clinics that offer good services at a reasonable price. However, many are organized simply to make a profit for the owners and doctors. These tend to provide no service except abortion; may not be as careful as you'd like about emergency equipment; and are often thoughtless about a woman's needs for information and emotional support. (Not all non-profit clinics are perfect on these counts either.) Licensing regulations in some areas may keep rip-off clinics under control, but money can often buy licenses. Keep a watch out for them.

Backup Services

Does the clinic or doctor's office have a good lab of its own or connections with a good lab? Does it have ample emergency equipment and arrangements with an ambulance and good nearby hospital in case of serious emergency?

Counseling

We believe it is very important to look for a facility which has a woman counselor assigned to each abortion patient or small group of them. The facility should consider her important, pay her well, and give her a role in decision-making. See "Having a Vacuum Suction Abortion" for fuller discussion of counseling.

Procedure

Does the facility provide the procedure that best suits where you are in pregnancy? See "Medical Techniques for Abortion."

Anesthesia

Does the facility offer the kind of anesthesia you want? See "Having a Vacuum Suction Abortion."

Payment

Does the clinic require money in advance? Does it accept Medicaid?* Health insurance?

Consent Regulations

Are there state regulations such as requirement of parents' or spouse's consent? (These are illegal.)

Age Limit

Many clinics have a minimum age limit.

---

*Federal funds are no longer available for Medicaid to pay for abortions. States may or may not be paying for abortions through their own Medicaid programs. The federal government will administer Medicaid funds in cases of rape, incest, or if the health of the woman is endangered. Although this situation is being legally challenged, be sure to check on the current status of Medicaid funds for abortion in your state when making arrangements.

Other Services

Does the facility provide other kinds of gynecological health care? Do they do Pap smear, breast exam? Do they prescribe birth control? Do they test and treat for gonorrhea, syphilis, herpes, venereal warts, vaginal infections? Do they provide aftercare in case of discomfort or emergency?

Further Considerations

Is your medical history screened by telephone prior to your appointment so you won't get there and find you're not eligible? Is the clinic licensed by the state? Is positive pregnancy test required before abortion is performed? Is removed tissue analyzed to verify that the abortion was successful, and do you get a report on this? Will you be informed of blood test results so you will know if post-abortion Rhogam shot (see page 229) is necessary? Is a recovery room available for postoperative rest and monitoring of vital signs? Will you be allowed to wear your street clothes? Many women find that putting on white hospital garb makes them feel like an anonymous "patient" who is sick rather than well.

HAVING A VACUUM SUCTION ABORTION

Since the great majority of abortions performed in this country are 7 to 12 week LMP vacuum suction procedures done in freestanding or hospital outpatient clinics, we want to describe that experience step-by-step. We hope our outline will give you an idea both of what to expect and of what to ask for by way of good medical care and emotional support.

Preparation

Before you go to the clinic on the day of the abortion, you can ask them in person or by telephone how long you should expect to be there (usually 4 to 6 hours); when and in what form they want payment; whether you will have a counselor assigned to you (if not, try to bring a friend). Check also about their services in case of complications or emergency after you leave the clinic: if they do not provide such services, or if you live too far away, you should have the name of a nearby doctor *before* you go for your abortion. Complications are rare, but it's important to be prepared.

Make a plan for getting home from the clinic, as you may feel slightly weak for a few hours after you leave: can a friend come get you? You may be asked not to eat for several hours before you go in, so as to avoid nausea; clinics vary on this.

In a preliminary telephone interview, you should be asked some key questions about your medical history. If you have had several full term pregnancies, a history of caesarean birth, asthma, TB, heart disease, acute kidney disease, bleeding or clotting problems, epilepsy, or a recent major operation, it may be necessary for the abortion to be done in a hospital.

Counseling

If you have been able to find a good clinic, you will have a counselor assigned to you individually or in a small group of women. The counselor can give you the kind of clear information that keeps the experience from being scary; help you talk about your feelings about the pregnancy and the abortion; and she can be with you through the abortion procedure. She will also be able to give you information about birth control.

In addition, we have found that a lot of support and encouragement can come from the other women who are having abortions with us.

The two rooms where the abortions were done opened onto the porch where the six of us were waiting. One girl from our group, who had said she had never had even a pelvic examination in her life, was just coming out of the abortion room. She had just had her abortion, and she looked okay. That was comforting. A seventeen-year-old girl came in. She was very very scared. I held her hand and comforted her. I hadn't had my abortion yet and was scared too (though I'd had one operation, two children, and a D & C with a spinal). Something amazing happened when I held her hand. Any fear I'd had disappeared as if it were drawn out of me from all sides. We were all such different women who for varying reasons were having the identical physical thing done to us.

Medical Preliminaries

A detailed medical history should be taken. Then some tests. A urine test will check once more for pregnancy, and for your general state of health. A blood test is done to check your hematocrit and hemoglobin to see whether you are anemic. If you are anemic, the doctor needs to be extra careful about blood loss. Your blood can also be tested for syphilis. Another blood test determines your Rh factor.

RH FACTOR. Everybody's blood is either Rh positive or Rh negative. When an Rh negative woman carries an Rh positive fetus (which will usually be the case if the father is Rh positive) either birth or abortion can cause antibodies to build up in the woman's blood. These antibodies may react against a fetus in a future Rh positive pregnancy. If you have Rh negative blood and plan to have children in the future, unless the father of the fetus is Rh negative you should be given a shot of a blood

derivative called Rhogam within 72 hours after the abortion. Rhogam will prevent the antibodies from forming in your blood. Rhogam can cost from $40 to $50. Many clinics include it in their single overall charge.

Your blood pressure should be taken before, during and after the procedure. A change in blood pressure during the abortion can indicate internal bleeding.

You should be given a breast exam, pelvic exam, a pap smear and a gonorrhea culture. If this is your first pelvic exam—and for many it is—you can look at Chapter 6 for what to expect and how to make it most comfortable.

Anesthesia

The abortion we will describe uses local anesthesia to numb the cervix. You can choose to have general anesthesia if you want to be asleep for the abortion. Keep in mind, however, that this is more expensive, can make you feel groggy and slow for a day or two afterward, and carries a slight risk of serious complications and even death. General anesthesia is not usually offered at a free-standing clinic.

The Abortion*

You will lie down on the examining table with your feet in stirrups or your legs supported by knee pads.

The doctor performs a bimanual exam, inserting two fingers into the vaginal canal, holding the cervix with her/his fingers, and placing the other hand on the abdomen above to feel the size and position of the uterus.

At this point you may be given a tranquilizing injection to help you relax and/or an intravenous drip (I.V.) into your bloodstream. The drip usually contains a glucose (sugar) mixture or pitocin, a hormone that helps the uterus contract to its original size after the fetal material is removed.

The vaginal area is thoroughly cleaned with antiseptic solution. It is unnecessary to shave off the pubic hair.

The doctor then inserts an instrument called a *specu-*

*This section comes from the Women's Health Forum's pamphlet *Vacuum Aspiration Abortion*. See bibliography for ordering details.

Vacuum suction abortion at Preterm Institute in Washington, D.C. Note that the woman getting the abortion is wearing her street clothing.

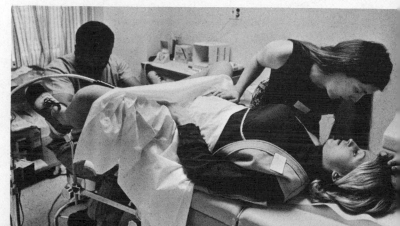

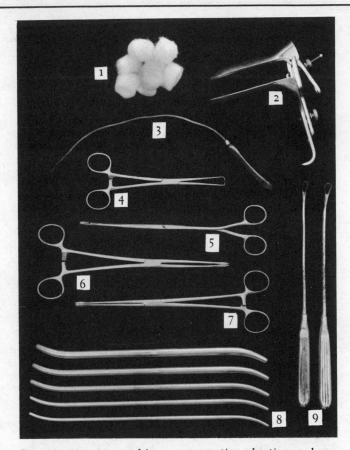

Some instruments used in vacuum suction abortion and D & C: 1. cotton balls; 2. speculum; 3. flexible sound; 4. square-ended, pointed tenaculum; 5., 6. and 7. forceps; 8. graduated dilators; 9. curettes

cervix has been dilated before (e.g., during miscarriage, delivery, or previous abortion), the cramping is usually less. Dilation usually takes less than two minutes.

The aspirator, or suction machine, consists of a vacuum-producing motor connected to two bottles. A hollow tube several feet long is attached to the bottles. A variety of different-sized sterile hollow tips (vacurettes) can fit on the end of this tube. These tips are either stainless steel or disposable plastic and are approximately 6 inches long. The diameter of this tip varies with the length of the pregnancy.

This tip is inserted through the open cervix into the uterus. The machine is turned on. The fetal material is removed by gentle pulling on the uterine walls, and is drawn through the tip, through the plastic tube, and into the bottle. The aspiration takes from 2 to 5 minutes.

Some doctors will then insert a thin metal instrument called a curette and move it around inside the uterus to

lum, which keeps the walls of the vagina apart and allows a good view of the cervix (the mouth or opening of the uterus). This does not hurt, but it can feel like pressure.

The cervix is then grasped with a *tenaculum* (see instrument 4 in photograph above), which feels like a slight pinch. The tenaculum will be held throughout the rest of the procedure to keep the cervix steady.

A paracervical block (local anesthetic), usually Xylocaine or Novocaine (a substance similar to that used in a dentist's office), is injected into the cervix. This numbs the cervix. The injection is relatively painless, as the cervix is a muscle and has few nerve endings in it.

The cervix is then dilated (opened) slowly with sterile, generally stainless steel, instruments called dilators. They are from 6 to 12 inches long and vary in diameter from the size of a matchstick to the width of a piece of chalk, and are slightly curved on the ends. The cervix is dilated with the smallest dilator first and then with larger and larger dilators until it is opened wide enough for the tip of the aspirator to enter the uterus.

You may experience what feel like very heavy menstrual cramps while the cervix is being dilated. If the

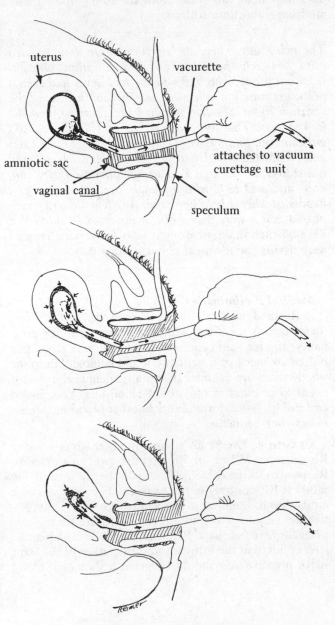

VACUUM SUCTION ABORTION

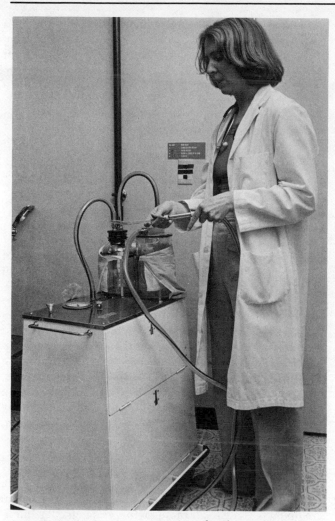

Operating unit for vacuum suction abortion

check that it is completely empty (see "Dilation and Curettage"). Others feel that this extra procedure causes unnecessary extra bleeding, and use tiny forceps to pull out any tissue not taken by the suction.

As the uterus is emptied of fetal material it contracts back to its original size. These muscle contractions may cause quite strong cramps, which generally subside 10 to 30 minutes after the procedure is over.

Recovery

You will lie down (or sit, depending on how you feel) for a half hour to an hour afterward, in a recovery room where clinic staff can check your vital signs, such as blood pressure, temperature, etc. Then in many facilities you will be asked to sit in a lounge or waiting room for a while longer to make sure you are fully recovered, with no excessive bleeding, before you leave.

Complications

Although the instances are very rare, physical complications do sometimes occur after a medically performed legal abortion. Here are the possible complications and

their symptoms so that you will know what to look for. Seek medical help immediately if any of these signs should occur after you leave the clinic.

PERFORATION. Occasionally one of the instruments may poke through the uterine wall, making a small hole or perforation. These generally heal themselves with time. If a large perforation occurs the doctor usually knows right away by the amount of bleeding and pain during the procedure and recovery time.

HEMORRHAGE. A hemorrhage could be caused by laceration of the uterine wall or perforation of the uterus with the dilator, vacurette or curette. A heavy flow of blood accompanied by heavy clotting (not to be confused with the slight spotting that follows most normal abortions) could also indicate that not all the fetal material has been removed or that the uterus has not contracted to normal size.

INFECTION can occur if your resistance is low after the abortion so that an infection present before the abortion can spread. It can occur if the instruments used were not properly sterilized. It is most likely to occur if you douche, use tampons, or have sexual intercourse too soon after the abortion, thereby allowing germs to enter the uterus through the vaginal canal before the uterus has had a chance to heal completely. Nausea, vomiting, heavy cramping, or a temperature of 100.5 degrees Fahrenheit or more are all signs of possible infection.

INCOMPLETE ABORTION. This results when a doctor fails to remove all fetal material from the uterus. The abortion may then have to be completed in a hospital with a D & C (see p. 225). The danger signs to watch for are a foul-smelling vaginal discharge, cramping, nausea, vomiting, or hemorrhage as described above.

UNSUCCESSFUL ABORTION. A very small number of abortions fail to remove the fetus from the uterus. Continued pregnancy symptoms—nausea, breast tenderness, etc.—would be the warning signals. There are also rare cases of ectopic pregnancy (see Chapter 16), in which the pregnancy is not in the uterus at all and continues to develop after the abortion, requiring an emergency operation at a later time.

To minimize the risk of both *incomplete* and *unsuccessful* abortion, abortion facilities should always examine the tissue removed from the uterus. If it isn't clear that all the fetal material has been removed, they should send the tissue to a pathology lab for analysis. Some clinics and doctors are not careful enough about this. One reader reported to us that her clinic, which had otherwise treated her very well, did not inform her that no fetal tissue had been removed. She had an emergency operation for ectopic pregnancy when severe abdominal pains took her to a hospital a few weeks later.

Aftercare

1. Because of the chance of infection, many doctors

prescribe an *antibiotic* such as tetracycline. Some advise you to take it right away, others to use it later if symptoms of infection develop. (Some believe that antibiotics taken right after the abortion can mask infection signs.) When taking tetracycline, do not eat for an hour before or after the medication. (Dairy products are especially to be avoided, as the calcium keeps the body from using the tetracycline properly.) *Ergotrate* is a drug that is sometimes given: it helps contract the uterus to its normal size, thereby diminishing chances of infection or possible hemorrhage.

2. People's recoveries vary, but it is a good idea to rest for the remainder of that day and not to push yourself or do strenuous physical exercise for a day or two afterward.

3. Keep an eye on yourself for danger signs: excessive bleeding or vomiting, fever, bad cramps or a foul smell from your vagina should be reported to the clinic or doctor.

4. To avoid infection: no douching, tampons, tub baths, or sexual intercourse for 2 to 3 weeks after the abortion, so as to avoid getting any infectious germs into your vagina and up into your uterus before you are healed.

5. You will probably have a bloody discharge like a menstrual period for several days. Your period will start about 4 to 6 weeks after your abortion.

6. See a doctor after 2 or 3 weeks for a post-abortion checkup and for birth control if you did not get any at the time of your abortion.

BIRTH CONTROL AFTER AN ABORTION

There is a temptation for us to say after an abortion, "I'm never going to have sex again, so I don't need birth control." Or, if we were in fact *on* some method of birth control when we got pregnant, we may feel angered and confused by the whole business of choosing a method again.

I lost my faith in birth control methods and finally began to take the Pill, which I hadn't wanted to take but which was by now the only thing I felt any sureness with.

Most of us feel that, yes, we will be wanting to have sexual intercourse again, and that despite the drawbacks of the current methods of birth control, we do not want to go through another abortion. So we have to make the choice.

If you are in doubt about a method, you can read Chapter 10, "Birth Control." For some of us, the counselor and staff at the abortion clinic may be the first people who have given us a clear idea of what the methods are and how to use them.

Some clinics will insert a plastic IUD at the time of a first trimester abortion.* If you plan to take birth control pills, it is a good idea to start taking them right after the abortion so that you will be fully protected by the time you have intercourse 2 to 3 weeks later. If you plan to use a diaphragm, wait until your post-abortion checkup to be fitted or re-fitted. You can use a combination of foam and condoms if your checkup is delayed.

HAVING A SECOND TRIMESTER ABORTION BY THE INDUCTION METHOD

Having an induced-miscarriage abortion from 16 to 24 weeks of pregnancy is a more difficult experience both physically and emotionally than a pre-12-weeks abortion. Physically, as described below, you can go through several hours of discomfort as the uterus contracts to open the cervix and expel the fetus. The complication and mortality rates, though no higher than for full term pregnancy and delivery, are higher than for earlier abortions.

Emotionally, too, it tends to be a hard experience, even when you are very sure you do not want to have a baby and are feeling great relief at the prospect of being free of pregnancy after long weeks of worry. The pain, the length of time it takes, the similarity of what you go through to what delivery of a baby would have been like; the fact that you have carried the pregnancy for many weeks and probably even felt the fetus move inside you; the fact that a very vocal part of society says what you are doing is "bad"—all these factors can make late abortion much more upsetting than early abortion.

The very fact that you were not able to have an early abortion probably means that you have had a struggle already. Maybe you had hassles with, or fears about, doctors and hospitals which kept you from getting help until this late; perhaps you ran into opposition or lack of support from someone close to you; perhaps you had felt too confused to make up your mind whether to have an abortion or not; maybe for many weeks you had pretended to yourself that you were not pregnant because you felt you could not face it. So you come into the experience somewhat emotionally exhausted already.

Choosing a Facility

Going through contractions and the expulsion of a fetus with mixed emotions like these can be very hard. It is a time when you most need loving, caring treatment from everyone who touches you. This is an important thing to keep in mind as you look for a hospital in which to have an induction abortion. (For other guidelines, see

---

*Cu-7 instructions indicate it is not to be inserted immediately post-abortion. Some clinics do not insert *any* IUD at this time as IUD side effects of cramping and bleeding might mask the symptoms of an abortion-related infection.

page 227.) Unfortunately, as we discussed on page 226, it is very difficult to find *any* hospital which will do a second trimester abortion.

Induced abortions are usually, though not always, done in a general hospital. There are a few small hospitals that specialize in abortion and usually try to make late abortion as comfortable as possible: but these are too rare.

In a general hospital the quality of care and degree of personal attention vary greatly. If you must go to a general hospital, try to look for one with a special second-trimester abortion unit with counseling and special staff. Some hospitals insensitively and even cruelly place abortion patients in with women who are having babies. In some hospitals you will be left alone a lot, not told clearly enough what is being done to you, not offered enough pain medication (if you want it). Unfortunately, since so few facilities are offering second trimester abortions at all, you will probably have to take whatever kind of care you can get. The only protection in many cases is to call the hospital in advance about their policies, and bring a friend with you if they will allow it. Also talk with the doctor beforehand: s/he has more say in these matters than hospitals will always admit.

A Comparison of Saline and Prostaglandin Abortions

We suggest that you review the brief introduction to the induction abortion procedure on page 225. In an induction abortion a miscarriage-causing solution is injected into the amniotic sac. The solutions used are a saline (salt) solution, which usually causes fetal death, uterine swelling and contractions, or the prostaglandin $f_2\alpha$, which causes contractions. In some hospitals you will, barring medical contraindications, have a choice between the two methods—if you are firm about it. What follows is a discussion of the advantages and drawbacks of each method. For contraindications of each, see page 225.

SALINE SOLUTION, in longest use, currently has the advantage that doctors are more familiar with it. It also has fewer side effects, a lower rate of re-instillation (done if labor fails to begin in 48 hours), and a slightly lower rate of incomplete abortion and consequent D & C. It is cheaper. Disadvantages of saline: labor takes longer to begin and goes on longer before delivery (see below); slight risk of serious emergency:

shock and possibly death if careless instillation allows salt to enter blood vessel;

a bleeding disorder probably caused by the release of material from the injured placenta (this can also occur in cases of fetal death not induced by abortion).

THE PROSTAGLANDIN $f_2\alpha$ has come into use more recently. Advantages: works more quickly; does not have the risk of serious emergency carried by saline. Disadvantages: more side effects like nausea, vomiting and di-

arrhea; higher rate of unsuccessful instillation; slightly higher rate of excessive bleeding and retained placenta (requiring immediate D & C); more expensive at present. There is a likelihood that the fetus will be expelled with signs of life and not expire until shortly afterward—this is why the prostaglandin method is not often used beyond 20 weeks LMP. There is also a risk of the cervix tearing in too-rapid dilation caused by the quick and sharp contractions. To protect the cervix, many doctors cause some dilation in advance, using dried, rounded stems of seaweed, "laminaria digitata," 5 to 7 cm. long and 1 mm. or more in diameter.* Inserted into cervix 12 hours before instillation, the seaweed stems gradually expand as they absorb moisture, dilating the cervix in a gentle and painless way. Laminaria must not be left in longer than 12 hours because of risk of infection.

Preparation

Similar to preparation for vacuum suction abortion (see page 228). Plan to be at the hospital for at least 36 hours. Ask by phone what to bring with you. If you are going out of town for the abortion, make sure before you go that you have the name and phone number of a doctor or clinic to call in case of complications at home.

Medical Preliminaries

Same tests and examinations necessary as for vacuum suction. In taking your medical history, doctor should check for conditions which would contraindicate use of saline or prostaglandin methods (see page 225). If you are to have a prostaglandin abortion, you may be asked to come in 12 hours in advance for insertion of laminaria (see above).

The Procedure

What follows is a step-by-step version of the experience. It should be read along with the introductory description on page 225.

There are five phases in an induced abortion: instillation, waiting, contractions, the expulsion of the fetus and placenta, and the recovery period.

INSTILLATION. The process is started when the doctor cleans your abdomen, numbs a small area with a local anesthetic, then inserts a needle or narrow plastic tube through the abdominal wall a little below the navel and injects the miscarriage-inducing liquid into the amniotic sac. (Often in a saline abortion some amniotic fluid is removed before saline solution is introduced.) This does not hurt, although there may be a bloated feeling. In a saline abortion this instillation procedure must be done very slowly and carefully, because salt injected into a blood vessel by mistake could cause shock and death. You must let the doctor know immediately if you feel waves of heat, dizziness, backache, extreme dryness.

WAITING. It will take several hours for contractions to

*See photo, p. 230.

begin: with saline, at least 8 or 12 and sometimes over 24 hours; with prostaglandins, less. With saline you will feel very thirsty. With prostaglandins you may feel nausea and diarrhea. If the waiting period is too long with saline (or occasionally with prostaglandin method), you may be given an injection of pitocin or oxytocin to bring on contractions or to speed them up.

CONTRACTIONS. As contractions begin they will feel at first like mild cramps. At a certain point you may feel a gushing of liquid—this is the bursting of the amniotic sac. After this, and expecially for the last few hours before the fetus is expelled, contractions will be stronger and more painful. With a prostaglandin abortion or when a drug like pitocin is used, the contractions are quicker and sharper.

As a rule the contractions are not as strong as those of full term labor and delivery, but they can cause you considerable pain. The breathing techniques taught in Chapter 14, "Preparation for Childbirth," should help make the later contractions more tolerable. No general anesthesia is given, but tranquilizers and pain medication should be offered.

EXPULSION. At the end of about 8 to 15 hours of contractions (less for prostaglandins), the fetus, and then in a few minutes the placenta, will be expelled. With saline, the fetus is almost always dead. With prostaglandins, the fetus often will show some signs of life for a few minutes.

RECOVERY. You will generally stay in the hospital for 24 hours or so after the procedure.

Possible Complications

During a saline instillation, slight risk of salt entering blood vessel, and rare chance of bleeding disorder (see above). At the time of expulsion, the placenta or part of it may be retained in the uterus: this necessitates a D & C, which is painful if there is not time for adequate anesthesia. Hemorrhage is possible at time of expulsion. Infection can occur later. See page 231 for discussion of hemorrhage and signs of infection.

Aftercare

The same as for vacuum suction abortion—see page 231.

FEELINGS AFTER THE ABORTION

For most of us the end of an unplanned pregnancy is a tremendous relief. We feel glad to be able to go on with life in the way we need to, and proud that we have made and carried out an important decision. But many of us at the same time experience a return of some of the same mixed feelings we had in deciding whether to have the abortion. Even the most positive feelings afterward tend to be mixed with negative ones.

I left the clinic with my friend, feeling two ways about the whole experience: one, that I'd had as good and supportive an abortion experience as a woman could have; and two, I would never put myself in the position of having to go through it again.

Immediately after the abortion there can be a reaction which, like the depressed feelings a woman often has shortly after a full term delivery, may be related to the lowering in our body of the hormone levels of pregnancy. We may have feelings of inconsolable sadness and periods of crying shortly after the abortion.

It is natural, perhaps even necessary, to feel sadness as we adjust to being no longer pregnant. For now, we have said no to possible parenthood—and often this brings a sense of loss.

I began my mourning during my short pregnancy. I feel there has to be mourning in some form for the life that was never allowed to continue.

I was so relieved not to be pregnant any more that I didn't think I had any sad feelings at all. Then a few days later, on my way to a friend's house, I saw a young couple walking a new baby and I burst out crying right there on the street.

Sometimes our grief is not only because of the lost opportunity to have that child, but because the experience has really brought home to us how hard life can be.

There are sometimes hangover feelings of guilt about what we have done. This is understandable in a society that doesn't totally accept the rightness of abortion. We may occasionally feel an irrational fear that "punishment" will come.

Even after the punishment of the operation itself I expected that in some way the odds would be evened in my life for the presumptuous thing I had done. When my favorite aunt got very sick I took it as a sign that I had done something wrong. I felt a nagging fear that I wouldn't ever be able to conceive again.

A number of studies reported by Osofsky and Osofsky (*op. cit.*) reveal that severe depression after an abortion is very rare. If we have been able to work through our mixed feelings before the abortion by talking them out with a sympathetic and objective friend, relative or counselor, we are unlikely to be seriously depressed afterward. If we do feel depressed, however, this is not a "punishment" that we have to put up with! The clinic we went to, or any of the referral groups mentioned in this chapter, can refer us to someone to talk with—social worker, counselor, clergy person. Or maybe what we most need is a chance to share our feelings with friends.

As we move back into our "real life," the life that was so drastically interrupted by the pregnancy, we can carry a lot of feelings from the experience we've had. Many of us, for instance, feel intense frustration and anger at what we've had to go through. It can take a long time for these feelings to go away.

Even though my husband was very supportive, I felt angry—not so much because he put the sperm in me as because he in no way could understand what I had experienced.

We may feel isolated, even from the people we are close to.

While Bill and my women friends are emotionally supportive, none of them understands the physical aspects of the post-abortion period or the sense of emptiness I sometimes feel. Nor has any of them sheltered and nurtured a fetus.

My boyfriend's attitude afterward was depressingly callous. His idea was: "Well, it's over now, why bother thinking about it." That's when I started to have to pull away from him emotionally.

Sometimes having an abortion marks the end of a relationship, leaving us with all those mixed high and low feelings of being on our own again, in addition to the feelings from the abortion experience. Sometimes the whole episode strengthens the relationship we are in.

Some of us have negative feelings about sex for a while after the abortion.

For a good month or two I felt like sex was repulsive. We'd start to make love and I'd feel, "I hope I don't have to pay for this." Also, we were using a diaphragm for the first time, and I didn't trust it yet. My husband was gentle and tried to help by pulling out to ejaculate outside my vagina. But I never relaxed, and I kept asking him, "Are you going to come soon?"

Afterward I felt very much that my boyfriend was potentially my destroyer, or even my enemy, because he had the capacity to impregnate me again. When I used two applicators full of foam while waiting for the Pill to *become effective, I used to think that I was arming myself against the act itself. This was not the most pleasant feeling to have just before making love.*

On the other hand, some of us had a chance to choose a reliable method of birth control for the first time when we had the abortion, and we feel more relaxed about sex than we ever did. It can be a drag to have to wait two or three weeks to have intercourse—yet this is a good chance to explore ways of pleasuring each other without intercourse (see Chapter 3).

Any of the negative or confused feelings we do have after an abortion tend to pass away with time—for some of us quickly, for some of us more slowly. For a few, feelings of depression and loss can come back again in cycles around the time of year when we had the abortion or when the baby would have been born. This often depends on how good or bad we are feeling about ourselves and our lives at the time.

What's important for us to realize is that positive, negative, ambivalent feelings are all natural after an abortion. We need to accept them all as part of us, give them space in our lives, and not put ourselves down for having them—only then can we make our peace with them. For many of us a crucial part of this process has been the chance to share our feelings with supportive friends.

Fortunately all my conflicts about the abortion were resolved about a year and a half later, when I found the courage to speak of it in a women's group I was in. Because of the calmness and caring the other women shared with me, as well as some of their own experiences with abortion, I came away from that meeting feeling that this thing that had haunted me for so long was finally resolved. I no longer felt bitter about the only choice I could possibly have made in order not to totally wreck my own life and that of others.

TWO PERSONAL EXPERIENCES

1967 (An Illegal Abortion)

Probably the most insidious untruth about abortion concerns the so-called post-abortion guilt feelings on the part of the woman. In fact, many women have been taught to expect and, in some perverse way, may welcome the "cleansing effect" that anticipated post-abortion guilt offers them—as though they have to atone for their crime. For as long as this society fails to recognize and refuses to sanction the right of a woman to have an abortion whenever she chooses to do so, the fear of post-abortion self-recriminations represses her as surely and as effectively as any prohibitive law is capable of doing.

The problem, then, is how to get women to face the reality of post-abortion *feelings* while shaking off the shackles of superimposed guilt feelings. Ironically, guilt, the psychologists tell us, grows out of anger—anger at ourselves for feeling inadequate and unwomanly, but also anger at a society that reveres us as mothers and child-raisers but despises our rights to make the decision not to have a child. Perhaps, then, sharing my personal experience might in some way show my sisters that guilt and its attendant emotions need not follow an abortion.

"I'm sorry," the voice said to me over the phone, "the test was positive." From that moment on I was a changed woman. I was going to become a mother. But was I really, in the true sense of the word? Any woman who has ever conceived understands the mixed emotions I was feeling. Understand, then, the thrill I felt in knowing that life was beginning. My body is constructed to bear children, and it was fulfilling that purpose. But then I was forced to ask myself: Is that *my* purpose as a rational as well as a biological human being, and am I not reacting to a societal stimulus as well as a biological one in feeling good about being pregnant?

For me the answers to these questions resulted in the decision to abort my pregnancy. For I realized that these vague biological stirrings inside of me could never justify giving birth to a child I did not want and was not prepared to raise. Neither was I willing to subject myself to the ordeal of pregnancy and waiting, only to relinquish the child at the end of it all. It's all crystal clear to me now in telling about it. At the time, my decision was not so well thought out, but rather grew out of the conviction that I could not in my circumstances continue with an unwanted pregnancy. For me the fetus represented an undesirable growth that had to be expelled, and with it also any guilt feelings about what I intended to do. Not once did I ever think of the fetus as a human being, but rather as an entity that contained some of the properties and carried the potential for human life in much the same way that a fertilized egg contains the properties and potential for life. If, then, the destruction of a fertilized egg is within our power, why not a fetus?

Finding an illegal abortionist was not easy. The few legal avenues that are open did not even occur to me (I had my abortion in 1967), although I'm sure I would not have qualified for a so-called therapeutic abortion. Like millions of desperate women before me, I went underground. My search led to a registered nurse (I was told) who did illegal abortions. My contact was a woman who had recently undergone an abortion by the R.N. and seemingly had suffered no physical ill effects from it. The negotiating was done entirely through my intermediary, and after settling on the price ($400), the date was fixed. All the while, I was unable to pry out of my contact many details about the procedure, which really panicked me. There was no one else to ask, so I went into the thing "cold turkey," and all of my dreaded fears about the physical pain were realized.

The woman came to my apartment on Friday, spread me out on the kitchen table, and inserted a catheter tube up my vagina into my uterus. This, I was told, would in time start the contractions in the uterus that would lead to the expulsion of the fetus. When I questioned the abortionist further, she put me off as though I were undeserving of anything more than what she had just done for me for $400. I had to be content with her vague instructions about what to do when the bleeding began, while trying to stifle my anxiety about complications. The entire procedure took about 15 minutes, and her attitude was one of "do the abortion and run." It was apparent that with the exception of two friends who remained with me (who were as ignorant of the process as I was), I was strictly on my own.

And so began a 48-hour ordeal of pain and anguished waiting for it to be over. At that point I had little regard for myself as a worthwhile human being: I was someone to be scorned and avoided—I was a walking, bleeding catheter tube. On Sunday the contractions began, and by the middle of the afternoon, it was over. The force of the uterine contractions had dislodged the catheter tube and it slipped out easily, and along with it, the fetus. Looking at the fetus was an experience I will never forget. I had been approximately two months pregnant, and at that stage the fetus had acquired some of the characteristics of a human being as we know it. It was about an inch long, and I am unable to remember its color. I do remember staring at it in a curious, somewhat detached way; it looked so strange, and indeed it was. Its appearance did not shock or repel me, partially because of the fact that by that time I had shut myself down emotionally and was feeling only relief that it was over.

It was only much later that I was able to internalize how I felt—and continue to feel—and then to verbalize, as I have tried to do here. Even now my total emotional reaction to it escapes me, except in one vitally important way. At no time, even in the shadow of societal taboos, did I believe that I was doing something wrong or committing some offense against nature—since, in fact, it is my nature and my right to determine my destiny as a woman. Since that time my confidence in the rightness of my decision has grown, and along with it, a sense of dignity and self-determination about myself as a woman.

1972

It has become very important for me to write about my abortion, yet it is difficult to know where the beginning is. I am at a place in time where my life, by my own efforts, is beginning to change. After having two children (ages six and seven and a half) reach a point of some adjustment in school, I began to feel I needed and wanted more from life. I decided to return to school, to a plan that had been interrupted by my marriage and children. As many women who have gone or will go back to school know, that is a process of awakening within ourselves that is incredibly exciting. After one marvelous year (with at least one to go) I found myself pregnant. I couldn't believe it. It seemed somewhat like a very bad dream that I would wake up from at any time. The idea of a third pregnancy was suffocating. I just couldn't go through another five or six years of intensive child rearing.

I couldn't—didn't want to—talk to anyone about my pregnancy, and I felt really alone. The burden of every anxiety and fear of childbirth, unwanted babies, guilt about abortion, death, life—everything I could possibly lay on myself, I did. I tried to accept the fact that I was pregnant so that I could make plans for my life that included a baby, but all the while I kept hoping for a miscarriage. The idea of abortion—the word—came in and out of my head but was quickly dismissed. I felt strongly that abortion was not a choice for me. I, as a person I thought I had begun to know, did not have the freedom to make that choice. I had believed abortion was every woman's right, but those were hollow, liberal thoughts for me. It's so easy to be a liberal when you're comfortable. For me abortion was a whole life-death question that I could not bear to settle.

I simply couldn't make a choice. I neither wanted to bear another child nor felt I could allow myself the alternative of an abortion, which I believe so strongly was a destructive, violent act. It's important to say that my husband was adamantly opposed to a third child, which didn't help me at all in making a decision. We argued bitterly—I defending anything he was against. We really turned our backs completely on each other, and the support we had so often given to each other was gone. The situation was hopelessly deadening. It's so hard to describe those feelings. I really just wished I could die.

I went to bed at night hoping to wake up to a miscarriage, and I guess it was at this point—when I was down very low—that I realized that I was actually considering an abortion. I saw that my problem was not so much that I was having difficulty adjusting to the idea of a third child, but that somewhere in the back of my mind I understood I could make a choice—and that realization was really mind-blowing.

I tried to be really honest with myself, and it seemed that to hope for a miscarriage was about the same as wanting a guilt-free abortion. That's really the way I looked at it. If nature would only expel this fetus, everything would be all right.

I began to talk to other women about myself—my feelings, my life, everything. They were really supportive. I started thinking about myself and what I really wanted. I tried to sort out my feelings—what was real, what were the influences of my Catholic upbringing, society, my husband, myself. I couldn't stop thinking of a fetus as a child—as my six- or seven-year-old playing in the yard. I kept getting very entangled in the sanctity of life: this fetus was growing within me whether I was awake or asleep, all the time. When does one have the

right to destroy life, potential or real? When is life real? I wanted to just stop and search a bit for an identity that I thought I had found but that had become confused by the realization that I could consider aborting a fetus. Fetus—to me a child.

I was completely muddled—and I had nowhere to go. But friends kept helping and supporting—women supporting no decision, just me as I was. At about the point when I felt completely spent and done in, I began to think about the responsibility of making a decision. It became clear to me that my confusion was a result of my unconscious desire to avoid making a real decision. I couldn't come around to the reality of the situation. I had to take on the responsibility of saying "I want to have this child and I will accept that" or "I do not want another child and I must accept the responsibility for aborting this fetus." I had to say that I was real, that my life was real and mine and important. Those feelings were very hard to come to. I don't think I believe in them fully even now, but I did begin to think of myself in a direct way, and I began to feel more sure of myself. There was a certain strength in knowing that I could make a choice that was mine alone and be entirely responsible to myself. It became very clear to me that this was not the way to have a child, that in thinking about the sanctity of life I had to think about the outcome of my pregnancy, which would be a human being/child that was not wanted. On the strength that I had begun to feel as a woman I made the decision to have an abortion. There was no decision of right or wrong or morality—it simply seemed the most responsible choice to make. It is still upsetting to me—the logic of it all—but somewhere within me it is still very clear, and I'm still very sure of that decision.

After I made my decision to have the abortion I had a great deal of support from some beautiful women who helped me over a lot of bumps. That support became very crucial to me—I'll never forget it.

My feelings the day of the abortion were in some ways very much numbed and at the same time quite clear. I was very sure of my decision that day, much more than at any other time, but my emotions were somewhat shut down. Perhaps it was in self-defense; I had questioned my decision so many times that I just had to stop. I remember thinking the next day that what had happened to me had nothing to do with my concept of the word "abortion" and all the images that word brings into one's head. What in reality had happened was that I had become a person I control—someone who is able to say, "This is the way my life must go." I was fully awake during my abortion, and although it was difficult to go through, it was especially important because I felt in control of the situation. I had made my decision and was able to carry it through without losing touch with what was happening to my body. (Also, being awake and aware alleviates some of those fantasies about what has happened to you, what a fetus may look like, and so on.)

I also had a woman friend with me throughout the abortion, which was a really beautiful thing. Mentioning her in one sentence can give no indication of the feelings we shared, but because of her and because of two very loving friends who accompanied me to New York, I remember that day as one of strength.

In retrospect, my feelings are very contrary and complex—some high, some low. I do not feel guilt—almost rather guilty over my astonishing (to me) lack of guilt. I have felt at many times very strong and sure in my identity as a woman—a very real person.

FURTHER READINGS

The Abortion Experience

Lyvely, Chin, and Joyce Sutton. *Abortion Eve* (1973). Nanny Goat Productions, P.O. Box 845, Laguna Beach, CA 92652.
  A wonderful cartoon book depiction of several abortion experiences (65¢).

Montreal Health Press. *Birth Control Handbook*. See Chapter 10 bibliography for ordering instructions.

Planned Parenthood of New York City. *Abortion: A Woman's Guide* (written by Beth Richardson Gutcheon). New York: Abelard-Schuman, 1973.
  Clear, friendly, thorough. Highly recommended.

Tietze, C. *Induced Abortion: 1977 Supplement*. 75¢. Available from Population Council, 1 Dag Hammarskjöld Plaza, New York, NY 10017.

Women's Research Action Project. *The Abortion Business: A Report on Free-Standing Abortion Clinics*. Cambridge, MA: Goddard-Cambridge Graduate Program, 1975. Rev. ed., 1977. Available for $1.00 from the Boston Women's Health Book Collective, Box 192, W. Somerville, MA 02144.

History and Legal Aspects

Abortion Praxis Collective. *Abortion: A Critical Analysis*. c/o Women's Studies, Kresge College, U.S.S.C.
  Practical and political discussion about abortion in this country.

Ambrose, Linda. "The McRae Case: A Record of the Hyde Amendment's Impact on Religious Freedom and Health Care," *Family Planning Population Reporter*, Vol. 7, No. 2, 1978, pp. 26-30.

Bart, Pauline. *Seizing the Means of Reproduction: An Illegal Feminist Abortion Collective—How and Why It Worked*. 14 pp. Available for 50¢ plus stamped self-addressed envelope from the Boston Women's Health Book Collective, Box 192, West Somerville, MA 02144.

Bygdeman, M., and S. Bergstrom. "Clinical use of prostaglandins for pregnancy termination," *Population Reports: Prostaglandins*, Series G, No. 7, 1976, p. G-65.

Callahan, Daniel. *Abortion: Law, Choice and Morality*. New York: Macmillan, 1970.
  Long and careful examination.

Cates, Willard, Jr., Kenneth F. Schulz, David A. Grimes and Carl W. Tyler, Jr. "Abortion Methods: Morbidity Costs and Emotional Impact," *Family Planning Perspectives*, Vol. 9, No. 6, 1977.

Cohen, Marshall, Thomas Nagel and Thomas Scanlon, eds. *The Rights and Wrongs of Abortion*. Princeton: Princeton University Press, 1974.

Committee on Psychiatry and Law. *The Right to Abortion: A Psychiatric View*. New York: Charles Scribner's Sons, 1970.

Darling, J. R., and I. Emanuel. "Induced abortion and subsequent outcome of pregnancy," *Lancet*, 1, 1975, pp. 170-172.

Golditch, I. M., and M. H. Glasser. "The use of laminaria tents for cervical dilation prior to vacuum aspiration abortion," *American Journal of Obstetrics and Gynecology*, 119, 1974, pp. 481-485.

Hodgson, J. E., et al. "Menstrual extraction: putting it and all its synonyms into proper perspective as pseudonyms," *Journal of the American Medical Association*, 228, 1974, pp. 849-850.

Lader, Lawrence. *Abortion*. Boston: Beacon Press, 1967.
———. *Abortion II: Making the Revolution*. Boston: Beacon Press, 1973.

Muller, Charlotte F. "Insurance Coverage of Abortion, Contraception and Sterilization," *Family Planning Perspectives*, Vol. 10, No. 2 (March/April 1978), pp. 71-77.

Pakter, J. "Legal abortion: a half-decade of experience," *Family Planning Perspectives*, 7, 1975, pp. 248-255.

Rapping, Elayne, "The Small City with the Big Law," *Moving On*, May 1978.
  History of the restrictive Akron, Ohio, Ordinance.

Schulder, Diane, and Florynce Kennedy. *Abortion Rap*. New York: McGraw-Hill, 1971.

Sullivan, Ellen, Christopher Tietze and Joy Dryfoos. "Legal Abortion in the United States, 1975-76," *Family Planning Perspectives*, Vol. 9, No. 3, 1978.

Willis, Ellen, "Abortion Backlash: Women Lose," *Rolling Stone*, November 3, 1977.
  Concise discussion of the recent legislative changes that make abortion more difficult to obtain.

Films

Abortion. Boston Women's Film Collective, c/o BWHBC, Box 192, W. Somerville, MA 02144.
  Women-made, noncommercial b&w, made in 1971; how things used to be and still are for many women. Excellent sterilization abuse discussion.

It Happens to Us. New Day Films, Box 315, Franklin Lakes, NJ 07417.

CHAPTER 12
CONSIDERING PARENTHOOD: SHALL I BECOME A MOTHER?

INTRODUCTION

What is it like for us now, in 1979, to think about whether we want to become mothers? It is not a question that was often asked by our grandmothers' generation, when women took it for granted that they would get married and have children. There was ineffective birth control and there were few other acceptable choices. Womanhood was equated with maternity, and maternity was the natural course of events. By our mothers' generation, women had better birth control, but still the vast majority did not question the fact that they would have children. Now maternity is no longer seen as absolute, an inevitability. Because of our own changing ideas of what it is to be a woman, largely stimulated by the consciousness-raising of the women's movement, we are increasingly able to accept ourselves as people whether or not we have children. Some of us are shifting our priorities and pursuing many interests along with, or instead of, child-rearing. Available birth control and abortion procedures make it physically possible to remain sexually active yet control our pregnancies. There are also many reasons which create new pressures on us to have smaller families or no children—the current economic crisis, population explosion, increased expectations of women to be employed, and nuclear family mobility among them. Since it is more socially acceptable not to have children, becoming a parent is more the option it should be.

When we ask ourselves whether we want to be a mother we fortunately face a range of life options of which motherhood is only one. Our collective has a somewhat complicated point of view on this question. Most of us are mothers, and those among us who are feel that children have enriched our lives immeasurably and that parenthood is an extremely attractive life option, even though there are those among us who became mothers because it was the thing to do, and regret either that we did not see a range of options then or that we had unrealistic expectations. Some of us were more fully aware of our options when we got pregnant, and had a more realistic sense of what it would be like. But although we all think that parenting is an extremely gratifying life choice, we also feel there are very good reasons for not having children.

The Decision-Making Process

When we ask ourselves the question, "Shall I become a mother?" we face a major life decision. Either we will have children or we will not; each choice has its problems and joys. Unlike most decisions, the one to have children is irrevocable and carries deep implications for the rest of our lives. The decision not to have children is made during the limited span of time we have to deal with it during our childbearing years, and in the end the commitment is also final. There is no way of knowing beforehand, of course, what it's like to be a mother. We do not know what our children will be like, nor how we will respond to them. We don't know if we will enjoy parenting or be good at it.

As young women we are primarily involved with leaving the world of our parents and guardians. During this time the thought of having children is probably in the background (we may not think much about it) or it is a future possibility we do not feel ready for yet. Then for many of us there is a shift in balance and we begin to feel that we want a child or children. Where it comes from we don't know. Is it instinctive? Is it learned? Whichever, the feeling takes hold. Some of us make the decision to try to become pregnant.* Those of us who have not felt a shift of balance, or whose feelings have not coalesced, keep the question open. We do not want a child now, possibly later, maybe never. A few of us

*If you want to become pregnant and are either black or Ashkenazi Jewish, have yourself and your partner tested for sickle cell disease (if black) and Tay-Sachs disease (if Jewish). It's advisable to test yourself before becoming pregnant because these diseases are much more difficult to detect in carriers when pregnant. Most cities have screening programs, so consult your local public health agency.

take the steps to be sterilized; that decision, too, is irrevocable.

In this chapter we want to help women who are trying to decide whether or not to have children to understand their options by discussing what motherhood is, and why some women do and others don't choose it. Although we know the decision is emotional in large part and not reducible to formula, it should not be uninformed. Knowing what is involved and preparing ourselves for this decision is important.

WHAT HAPPENS WHEN WE BECOME PARENTS?

We experience many changes as we participate in this basic life event.

"It's a boy" (somehow I expected my first baby to be a girl). All of a sudden I heard him cry. The cry was not a cry of pain but the cry of life. The baby was alive and well and they brought him to me. I was amazed that this tiny human being, fully equipped for life and very beautiful, could come out of me. I was now a mother and how exciting that was.

Becoming a parent puts us in touch with the passage of time and marks a stage in our growing up.

I just had my thirty-first birthday. It was lovely—family and friends spanning three generations were there. We took home movies as we used to do when I was a child, and I realized that although I was the "birthday person" I was also one of the grown-ups on the film and no longer a child.

Some of us have mixed feelings about our own aging process.

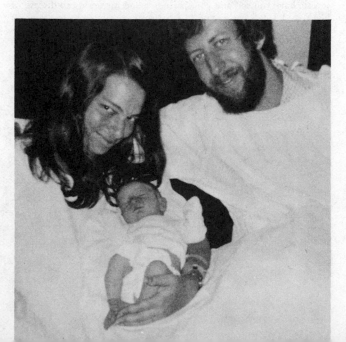

Seven months after my baby was born I went to a gala family Christmas pageant. A joyous singing and dancing event structured a lot around the participation of children. I loved it but felt a sense of sadness. It reminded me of pleasures of my childhood, and that it was over. I spent a lot of time thinking of my son, what his childhood will be like, and how much I wish to give him as wonderful a childhood as possible.

In a sense, having a child becomes a time both to say goodbye to our childhood and to see it from a new perspective.

My daughter loves school. When I see her doing well in reading and math, areas in which I did well, I feel proud of my influences on her. When she is poor in athletics, as I was, I relive my own sense of inadequacy and also feel frustrated that I can't help her. Recently my daughter learned how to swim. Watching her struggle to learn something difficult for her inspired me to learn how to swim myself. So at age thirty-four I took lessons and learned myself.

Seeing my little girl grow to be five and watching her go to her closet to choose what to wear is touching to me. She asks me if I'll be wearing a dress or pants and then wears the same. The event brings back a pleasant childhood memory of when my mother and I had the same dress and I remember how much I loved that.

As parents, we are responsible for our children in a way we had previously been responsible only for ourselves. This intensely intimate relationship is quite unlike any we've experienced before. Some people find this a burden, and being a parent does have its burdens. At the same time, parenting gives us the opportunity to grow—to learn, for instance, to love and accept another person unreservedly, and to observe first hand and help a tiny infant to grow into an adult. It is crucial to see parenting as a process and not as an end to our own growth.

Care for Babies Takes Time and Energy

Loving care for a baby takes a lot of time and energy. The responsibility of parenthood can be overwhelming during the first year.

The first week home with my baby was both fascinating and overwhelming. I was unfamiliar with infant behavior. I did not know how much she would want to eat, and when, what her crying meant—fatigue, discomfort, pain, exercise. I was totally obsessed by this stranger and thought about her all the time. I felt this intense phys-

ical and emotional bonding with her. It was as if I was breathing with every breath and crying with every cry.

The helpless, relentlessly needy, dynamically growing infant requires 24-hour active care and passive presence of adults. Although it is possible for us to establish a rather predictable schedule for our child, fairly soon unexpected needs are always arising.

I hear Charlie cry for what seems like the fiftieth time today. It's that dry, piercing, persistent cry of a newborn. Although I often can figure out what he is saying and enjoy comforting him, this time I cannot. I find myself feeling numb and a bit resentful.

We, too, need mothering more acutely when we are new parents, because of all the memories of being cared for in our own childhoods and because so much of our physical energy goes into nurturing the new baby. We also need mothering because we often feel shaky as we face the responsibility of caring for a helpless infant. It's not surprising that, along with the exhilaration we feel with our new status as parents, we feel overwhelmed by an incredible sense of dependency on our partners, parents, friends and relatives.

Right after I had my baby I missed my parents intensely in ways I had not felt since I was a child. Embarrassing! Friends who were parents reassured me that they had felt the same. I wanted to crawl back to my parents' home and be taken care of.

One afternoon, sitting in John's room nursing him, I had a rush of feeling unbearably lonely. Intensely, I felt, "I need to be mothered." My husband, who needed reas- *surance himself, couldn't mother me. My own mother could not mother me. My need was profound and, except in snatches, unmeetable by any one human being.*

As long as our children stay relatively healthy, parenting will never again be as intensely demanding as it is during the first few years. And some of us will have more than one small child to care for. With time, naturally, the relationship(s) between us and our children becomes more reciprocal, and what our growing children bring into our lives as lively people in their own right cannot be measured. But although older children need less physical care, we are going to be called on throughout our lives and theirs to give them emotional support, guidance, limits and affirmation.

Our Relationship with Our Partner Changes

Having a baby often complicates and changes our relationship with our partners. It's difficult to anticipate what is involved when we add a new member to our family. In addition to feeling excited about becoming a family and proud of our baby, both partners—but especially the man—may feel jealousy at being divided or excluded, and may doubt their parenting abilities. As women, especially, we feel that we are expected to know what to do as mothers, and that we are not allowed to make any mistakes. But ease and competency in mothering is learned only over time; it is not something we are born with. We all need reassurance from our partners as we try to establish ourselves in this new role. But our

partners are often anxious about their fathering abilities and need reassurance equally as much. Our culture makes it hard for men to become fathers. They receive scant support from the societal structure, in which they are most often asked to prove themselves by performance. Fearing that they will be judged inadequate, they often cannot allow themselves to ask for help from friends or relatives.

Both of us may be so preoccupied with caring for the baby and so needy ourselves that we cannot give each other the support we need. It is important to recognize this and try to be as communicative as possible—even to set aside special time to talk about it. If each partner has not had a sense of identity and confidence independent of the other, as well as good communication and the ability to offer support and acceptance to the other, the added stress of child care and financial responsibilities can magnify existing problems. A child can become a football between two people who are not supportive of one another. On the other hand, many couples have found that becoming parents is a turning point; that the act itself increases their sense of confidence in themselves and each other and that sharing in the raising of their children enriches their relationship immeasurably.

During the time a couple has a small baby it's important to set aside time to be together and this requires planning and structuring. Our sex life might become less spontaneous, but we can plan for sex if we choose to—we don't have to try to make love when we're exhausted.

Sharing Parenthood

Having a child brings us tremendous responsibility. Having the support of the people around us—whether with partners, with friends, or in communes—gives us both emotional strength and physical help. As mothers we do not want to feel we are in it alone. We ask ourselves who will take care of our babies when we want to be by our-

selves, when we are working, or when we want to rest. Do we have the support of the person or persons we live with? Will they share responsibility with us? Can we rely on friends, relatives and/or baby-sitters? Even in good situations it takes time to work out a comfortable balance between time with and time away from our child, and even then the balance keeps changing.

There are days I love to spend with Sandy. She is so lovely and responsive and learning all the time. This is such a precious period for both of us.

But on other days we want time for our work.

My part-time teaching job allows me to work in the world outside my family. When I return home I find I love and cherish my baby even more.

Some of us take out a few years to do mothering exclusively; some of us try to work for a balance between child care and part-time work either at home or outside; others of us return to work fairly soon. If we are married, our husbands may feel similar pulls and pressures. Some men can decrease their work load or change their hours to be closer to their children. For many men this is impossible, and they try to do their best to make up for it. Some men will feel they have to increase their work load because of financial worries, and others simply do so to avoid domestic duties. Clearly then, certain external factors are out of our control—our own work options, our partners, part-time work possibilities, our financial situation, availability of sitters and family friends to fill in determine in part what is possible. Working out satisfactory arrangements in a spirit of good will and balancing the child's and our needs is hard. It requires thought and compromises on both sides. It is important to face our feelings about all this and come, as best we can, to some mutually satisfactory agreement about how we will approach child care before we have children.

Our culture has traditionally emphasized the differences and minimized the similarities between the sexes, so we are not likely to feel much support as we try to work these conflicts out with our partners, nor they with us. Women are expected to raise children; men are expected to find it demeaning and assume it's not their job. Along with men, we are in the process of rethinking our priorities between our work and our families. As we begin to think of men as child-rearers along with women, both sexes can begin to share functions in the family and society. Our society pretends to be supportive of parents but it often is not, at least not in any profound or meaningful way. We should not have to choose between commitment to motherhood and other serious work, or between earning enough money to support our children and having enough time to feel like their parents. If we need to continue work we are penalized by a society that expects its mothers to be home and so provides little or no good child care. Often if we choose to stop or reduce our work involvements we are penalized in future employment possibilities. Child care facilities in our communities and at work, paternity leaves for fathers, decent pay for part-time jobs, and the option of two people sharing a full-time job part time, some sort of payment for child-rearing—these are all changes we would like to see. Still, living with the current realities, we must try to do the best we can cooperatively.

Parenting in a Commune

Communes are often attractive places for single or married parents to live in because child-rearing can be shared with others.

Lisa has become such a warm, open, self-sufficient girl. She doesn't cling to me as she used to. She seeks attention from other adults almost as much as from me. She has her own world with the other children here. . . . And then there's me. I have more time for myself. It's a new freedom I still have trouble getting used to although we've been here over a year. I sometimes forget that I don't have to run to meet Lisa's needs; she can and will turn to others here. My time with her has been much "better-quality" time.

Communal child-rearing challenges our ability to move out of some of the accepted restrictive ways of approaching parenthood. How do we begin to share the responsibility for raising our children? How do we trust other adults to do right by them? How do we encourage our children to turn to and respond to others? And whether or not we have children of our own, what do we

risk by becoming very close to another's child? How will we and the child feel if the commune breaks up and we must separate? How do we deal with deep-seated feelings about "interfering" and begin to share in a whole new responsibility for raising a child we didn't give birth to? There are no easy answers, but some of us feel that our lives and the lives of our children will be better if we can adapt to the challenge of communal living. However, it is an important warning to keep in mind that communal living situations are often temporary and short-lived.

In this section we've tried to give you some idea of what problems and pleasures we face when we become mothers. Contrary to sentimental myths, becoming a mother, like having a relationship with a man or getting married, does not solve all one's problems.

Ideally, thinking and talking about the issues we've discussed will make us feel more informed about what is involved in parenting and more confident as we try to make our decision.

SHALL I BECOME A MOTHER— I DO NOT KNOW

Perhaps, even after giving this issue a good deal of thought, you are deeply undecided about whether or not you want to become a mother. Again, many of us want to be parents at some point—but not now.

It feels good to be clear about my priorities. Though I have a fine relationship with a man I love very much, I know I won't choose to live with him on a long-term basis if he doesn't want to share parenthood with me. I want very much to be a parent, though I don't want to take on that responsibility alone.

I need space for myself—to work, to make music, to be alone, to be with friends—and this is pretty hard to do without sharing parental responsibilities. I also want someone else to be as important to and as involved with my children as I am—for their sake as well as my own.

I keep hearing everyone has children and loves it, wouldn't give them back and so on—but I do not comprehend it. I need a real good reason for having a child.

Others of us are not sure whether we ever want to be parents. It is important for the rest of us to offer support for this point of view. Women have been socialized so strongly to become mothers that we often feel guilty, unfeminine or a failure if we are not sure whether we want children. We have to protect our right to be undecided and help people to understand it as legitimate.

I hear two conflicting points of view. One that it is ter-

rific to be a mother and the other—you'll regret it; your life will change! I am just beginning to find myself and grow. Having a child might stop that process, and I would feel so resentful. Everyone in my family is pressuring me to have a child, "Have one before I die," my grandmother says to me. I have to fight so hard not to give in to the pressures.

It is important to accept our feelings, understand our own point of view, and not apologize. Only then can we act with any sense of freedom.

Many of us want to do things in the near future that we could not do if we had children. We want to have children in our late twenties or early thirties, after we have had a chance to be on our own and have a variety of experiences with work, relationships and travel. Some of us want to understand ourselves better emotionally before we become parents.

I want to have children when I can appreciate them and love them for what they are: separate people who will develop their own ways. . . . I'm afraid I would not be able to relate to them without imposing my neurotic needs on them. . . . I want to be strong, so that my daughter will see that a woman can be strong. Being strong means working out my feelings of passivity and masochism. It means being able to be alone without fear. It means separating my sexual powers from my total life energy, so that I don't use my sexuality in an aggressive way toward my child. . . . I know that I'm not strong enough now to fulfill infant needs for love, nourishment, protection, limits and guidance.

Our mothering will be better if we feel comfortable with ourselves. But one danger is that cultural definitions of mothering and our own expectations of ourselves as mothers are so impossibly idealized that we may never feel ready.

When you decide to enter a contest, you do the best you can and either win or lose . . . for me motherhood looms like a big contest waiting for me to enter. But this is an event to be won, period. Obviously I cannot risk the motherhood game while hosting thoughts of being a losing contestant. I have to be a great, winning mother, but I have never approached any event in my life with that kind of self-assurance and/or arrogance. I am never sure of the successful outcome of my morning soft-boiled egg. Nevertheless, here I am with unfathomable control over my ova and his sperms and an outrageous inability to declare to the world that, yes, I am ready, able and strong enough to provide love, security and guidance to our creation.

But as we said, the decision to have children is irrevocable and the decision not to have them, even though that is made over a certain number of years, is, in the end, equally so. Those of us who postpone the decision to our late twenties or early thirties have a certain valuable perspective which helps us to be more realistic about parenting. But as we approach our mid-thirties, our fertility decreases and the risks to the child increase. Still, having a child and embarking on the unknown of motherhood is scary—and time and age do not change that. What we can hope for is to be honest and clear enough with ourselves that our decisions are not made by default. We are trying to develop support structures to help us consider parenthood in a balanced way. We do not want to be pressured to become parents before we are ready and comfortable, and yet we do not want to postpone the decision until it's too late.

SHALL I BECOME A MOTHER—NO

More women than before are thinking seriously of not having children. Since maternity is now not our only option, we can look more critically at "motherhood." It's always been culturally assumed that maternity is intrinsically gratifying and is a vital step in all women's maturation. Now some women ask what maternity deprives us of. For one, it requires that we shelve or reduce our involvement in non-family interests. Some of us feel that the gratifications of maternity are not sufficient compensation.

I like kids and like my friends to have kids . . . but not me. My mother gave up a career to have us, and acted like she was in prison the whole time. Now that we're grown up, she's back to work and finally enjoys her marriage. I know a lot of women have kids and interesting work, but it's hard. My work demands most of my time and hardly pays at all—but I love it. My boyfriend is in the same situation. We just wouldn't risk it all to have a kid.

Secondly, maternity can shift the balance in our equitable marital or couple relationships. Some of us have established relationships in which both partners have satisfying careers, share many common experiences, and share equally in decision-making and household responsibilities. We want to be competent mothers, and we think this means taking on a more traditional role, which may create distance between us and our partners and slow our occupational growth.

[A WOMAN.] *People say, "But when you get older, you'll*

be sorry you didn't have children." If they mean that I'll have no one to take care of me, I wouldn't want my children to baby-sit me in my senility. If they mean that in my old age I'll have only my children to spark up my life, then what about my friends, my interests, my work? As for immortality, I've never craved it. If some of my ideas live on in people's memories, fine. If they don't, fine.

When I state my reasons for not having children, everything starts sounding egocentric—until I realize that my honest feelings and anxieties are going to affect the child in many ways. My relationship with my husband, my teaching career, and my plans to pursue a Ph.D. are my most important considerations. A child simply would not get enough attention or even "quality time" with me. Some women fulfill their personal goals while the children are being brought up by day-care centers or live-in baby-sitters. I do not trust any kind of surrogate parent to bring up my child with the atmosphere and ideals that I would want the child to have.

---

*[*HER HUSBAND.*] When my wife and I decided to marry, it was with the idea that we would not have children. We believe that it is hard enough to maintain a viable, working marriage, and in order to keep it lively, we have to have the time to work at it. With a child, our time together would probably be reduced by eighty percent. We also want to make sure that both of us fulfill our own personal dreams, which do not include having a child. We hear so much about people who always wanted to do something but never did because they had the responsibility of caring for their children.*

Neither of us wants the sole responsibility of supporting the child and the other parent. And neither can take five years out of our careers. We entered marriage intending to share everything, including the finances.

The funny thing is that people have told us that we would be great parents, but that doesn't mean that we would be. We both know that we would transfer many of our phobias and worries, and our lack of confidence to our children.

Thirdly, the additional responsibilities of maternity sometimes cause us to regress rather than mature. Social pressure to have children has been so great that it has been hard for us to assess our actual desire for children and our ability to perform as parents. Although our culture is rather resistant to the image of a non-nurturant woman, some of us feel we are not interested nor cut out to be mothers.

The fact of being an only child makes it hard for me to choose not to have children. My parents have been very understanding, but in many ways they let me see how much they would like a grandchild. I would like to make

them happy, but I do not want that to be a prime reason for bearing a child—I see my decision as very much my own to make, because mothers have so much responsibility for care of the young in this society, and are required to give so much of their emotional lives to children. Women have been processed to put other people's needs before their own. I have always had trouble doing this—I have always seen my life as my own. When I lived with three other family units in a commune for a year, I became very upset by the quality and emotional content of much of the parent-child interaction. I saw the high levels of anxiety that these parents had, and their inability to deal with their own emotions openly with their children. I think I got a glimpse of the nightmare that some women experience when they have to cope with meeting the emotional needs of several children. . . .

After I made the decision not to have children, I felt an enormous sense of control over my life. . . . I could pursue my life goals as a stronger person because I had come to terms with myself.

It's possible to incorporate children into our lives even if we choose not to have any.

It's too bad that young women think that they have to have children in order to be a "fulfilled" woman. I'm fifty-six, never had kids, and feel as "fulfilled" as I could possibly be. Our lives can be rich with work, friends, other people's children, and many other things. I don't think that motherhood is the right choice for every woman.

SHALL I BECOME A MOTHER—YES

Although it is difficult to keep our sense of individuality, even of personhood, intact as we embark upon motherhood, it's worth working on. Deciding to become a mother is basically an emotional decision, no matter how much thought goes into it. We viscerally wish for a

baby and delight in our own fertility. Although we will encounter many problems, we feel the joys outweigh them. When we become a mother our response to our child borders on the sentimental, or cliché, since it involves us in the universal experience of childbearing and child-rearing, and there is obviously little new to be said. Still, when it is our experience and our baby, it's a new miracle, and familiar words take on new meanings.

Before I had a child, although I loved being with other people's children, any time something went wrong or the child irritated me, I would think to myself, How could I ever stand the full-time responsibility of being a mother? I guess it is not for me. Somehow becoming a mother changed that. There is an intangible, indescribable bond intrinsic to the relationship, which mothers talk about, that in the long run transcends the petty, everyday irritating occurrences.

Raising our children is extremely intimate and can be creative and challenging work—and satisfying work, paid or unpaid, is difficult to find in this fast-paced, highly technological culture.

I heard a squeal of delight across the room and turned around to see my seven-month-old pulling himself up with the support of a box to a standing position for the first time. It was miraculous to see him growing before my eyes. What a tender moment for me!

The dynamic relationship between ourselves and our children changes as we grow and our children grow.

I have learned to stop and watch my kids. All the energy I have put into getting in touch with the child in me I use now to stop and just listen to all the messages my children are giving me. . . . I feel like it's taken me a good part of my kid's lives to enjoy them. It's as if one day I woke up and said, "Hey, there are two people here." I feel I don't have to be doing all the giving; they have been giving me a lot of attention all the time, but I have not been seeing that. The giving and receiving between parent and child is different from that between me and my friends.

Having and raising our children gives us an opportunity to continue life and extend our spirits and our ways into the future.

One reason I had children was I wanted to take my place in the history of mankind. It's one of those basic, universal life experiences. I wanted so much to feel a part of the continuity of life. I like to think that people have had children for generations before me and will for generations after me.

We can learn so much from our children as we watch them experience life so directly.

Child of mine, child of mine
Oh yes, sweet darling, so glad you are a child of mine.

Although you see the world different than me
Sometimes I can touch upon the wonders that you see
And all the new colors and pictures you've designed
Oh yes, sweet darling, so glad you are a child of mine.

Nobody's going to kill your dreams
Or tell you how to live your life
There'll always be people who make it hard for a while
But you'll change their heads when they see you smile.

The times you were born in may not have been the best
But you can make the times to come better than the rest
You know you will be honest if you can't always be kind
Oh yes, sweet darling, so glad you are a child of mine.*

I feel a real old-fashioned possessive pride in them as MY kids—I want to say, "Look, everybody, aren't they great?" Other times it's almost a detached kind of wonder or curiosity that the helpless little babies I cared for such a short time ago are developing into separate human beings, whom I genuinely like and enjoy.

When they were little, my husband and I had total responsibility for them. We could structure their experience, teach them, select their friends, etc.

Now they are in school, which is not only freeing for me but freeing for them. They are learning things that I remember learning myself, and sometimes they come home with new ideas that they want to tell me about. I feel very excited when they want to share their new interests and their school life with me. It is a little like when a woman who has always been very home-centered goes out to a job or community work. She has new interests to share in her own work. At the same time, my kids take an interest in my work and seem to have a strong identification with our political involvements, particularly feminism.

So some of us have said and are saying, Yes, I shall become a mother—I want to know what mothering is all about.

FURTHER READINGS

Books

There are a lot of books about parenthood. Many of them deal with how to be better parents and how to raise better children. Here is a list of some that talk instead, in a non-judgmental way, about how it feels to be a parent, as a member of a couple or as a single parent. In addition there are books that discuss non-parenthood as a positive option.

Aries, Philippe. *Centuries of Childhood: A Social History of Family Life.* New York: Vintage, 1962. Suggests that our notion of childhood is a fairly recent social invention.

Bernard, Jessie. *The Future of Motherhood.* New York: Penguin, 1975. Highly readable sociological analysis with a deep awareness of the feminist issues.

Bel Geddes, Joan. *How to Parent Alone.* A Continuum Book. New York: The Seabury Press, 1974.
This book focuses on the single parent's experience and presents some good ideas on how to cope emotionally.

Biller, Henry, and Dennis Meredith. *Father Power.* New York: David McKay Co., Inc., 1974.
Two fathers write an account of fatherhood.

Boston Women's Health Book Collective. *Ourselves and Our Children. A Book by and for Parents.* New York: Random House, 1978, paperback.
This comes out of our own life experience and tells of our feelings and needs as people who are parents. It is useful to those wondering if they want to become parents; are about to become parents; or are parents of children of all ages. It describes different forms families take; shared parentings and the way society affects them; support we can find ourselves and through others; and resources parents can turn to.

Brazelton, T. Berry. *Toddlers and Parents.* New York: Delacorte Press/Seymour Lawrence, 1974.
This book is the sequel to *Infants and Mothers* and focuses on the toddler. Deals with special problems of working parents, single parents and day-care centers.

Callahan, Sidney Cornelia. *Parenting: The Principles and Politics of Parenthood.* Baltimore, MD.: Penguin Books, 1974.
Author draws on own experience as mother of six and on theoretical literature about American parenting in an attempt to clarify and define parental roles.

Group for the Advancement of Psychiatry. *Joys and Sorrows of Parenthood.* New York: Scribner's, 1975. Mental-health professionals focus on parents.

Howell, Mary. *Helping Ourselves: Families and the Human Network.* Boston: Beacon Press, 1975.
Describes the relationship between families and professionals. Author argues that if we continue these relationships as they exist, we encourage families' dependency, incompetency and inadequacy.

Hawke, Sharryl, and David Knox. *One Child by Choice.* Englewood Cliffs, NJ: Prentice-Hall, 1977.

Lankin, Patricia. "Marriage Without Children Becoming a Chosen Lifestyle," *Boston Sunday Globe, New England Magazine,* April 10, 1977.

Lazzare, Jane. *The Mother Knot.* New York: McGraw-Hill, 1976. Funny, passionate, human, uncompromisingly honest account of the author's early years of motherhood. Must reading for new parents.

LeShan, Eda J. *How to Survive Parenthood.* New York: Random House, 1965. Easy-to-read, commonsense approach to parenthood and family life.

Levine, James A. *Who Will Raise the Children? New Options for Fathers (and Mothers).* New York: Lippincott, 1976. Looks at fathers who have chosen child care and householding as at least half their work.

MacBride, Angela. *The Growth and Development of Mothers.* New York: Harper & Row, 1973.
A very real account of motherhood.

McCauley, Carole Spearing. *Pregnancy After 35.* New York: Dutton, 1976.

Menning, Barbara Eck. *Infertility—A Guide for the Childless Couple.* Englewood Cliffs, NJ: Prentice-Hall, 1977.

Peck, Ellen. *The Baby Trap.* New York: Bernard Geis Associates, 1971.
This book contains the author's arguments against parenthood.

Peck, Ellen, and Judy Senderowitz, eds. *Pronatalism: The Myth of Mom and Apple Pie.* New York: T. Y. Crowell Company, 1974.
An anthology of articles that examine pronatalist biases in society and discuss the advantages of non-parenthood.

Pleck, Joseph H., and Jack Sawyer, eds. *Men and Masculinity.* Englewood Cliffs, NJ: Spectrum Books, 1974.

Rapaport, Rhona and Robert, and Ziona Strelitz. *Fathers, Mothers and Society.* New York: Basic Books, 1977.
Surveys the research in a wide variety of academic disciplines toward a new understanding of parenthood in modern society. Excellent discussions of some of the more controversial parenting issues.

Rich, Adrienne. *Of Woman Born: Motherhood as Experience and Institution.* New York: Norton, 1976.
Written with passion and insight, this is a basic feminist book on motherhood. Focuses very little on men.

Rozdilsky, Mary-Lou, and Barbara Banet. *What Now?* Send $1.50 to the Boston Association for Childbirth Education, P.O. Box 29, Newtonville, MA 02160.
This is a pamphlet on the adjustment to new parenthood.

Silverman, Anna and Arnold. *The Case Against Having Children.* New York: David McKay Co., Inc., 1971.
A number of reasons for not having children are presented in this book.

Spinner, Stephanie, ed. *Motherlove: Stories by Women about Motherhood.* New York: Dell, 1978.
Fiction. A pleasure to read.

Sullivan, Judy. *Mama Doesn't Live Here Anymore.* New York: Arthur Fields Books, Inc., 1974.
A personal account of a woman who broke one of the strongest of cultural taboos and left her daughter and husband.

Whelan, Elizabeth M., Sc.D. *A Baby? . . . Maybe.* New York: Bobbs-Merrill, 1976.
Well-researched and helpful guide to deciding about parenthood.

Magazine Articles

Morrone, Wanda Wardell. "Motherhood: How much chance for personal growth?" *Glamour* Magazine, December 1974.
A good personal account of a contemporary woman's experience of the transition into motherhood.

Willis, Ellen. "To Be or Not to Be a Mother," *Ms.* Magazine (October 1974).
In this book review Ellen Willis articulates her own conflicts as a radical feminist "non-mother" on the issue of having children.

Other Resources

NON (The National Organization for Non-Parents), 8 Sudbrook Ln., Baltimore, MD 21208.
This organization supports those of us who want to wait before having children or who do not want to have children at all.

Joyce at 34. Film by Joyce Chopra and Claudia Weill. 28 min., 16mm., color. New Day Films, P.O. Box 815, Franklin Lakes, NJ 07417. Film sells for $350 and rents for $39 (handling fees included).
Study of a woman, who at 34 becomes a mother and faces conflicts between motherhood and a career.

CHILDBEARING UNIT

INTRODUCTION TO CHAPTERS 13, 14 AND 15

There are as many different ways of experiencing childbearing as there are women having babies. Our social, cultural, economic and family circumstances affect us, and within those networks we are each an individual. We may be single or married, in our teens or in our thirties. We may have other children, or this may be our first. We may work full time, care for a family, or be in school. The pregnancy may have come as a surprise, perhaps unwelcome; or it may be an event for which we hoped and planned.

Given the broad range of differences among us, there are many things we share in the process of having a baby. At times, we find ourselves preoccupied with practicalities. We may be concerned about losing our jobs or about arranging good care for the baby. We might be wondering what doctor or clinic to choose; how to pay for the birth; whether or where to take classes in preparation for childbirth. And when we have a moment to dream we may wonder what the baby will be like.

Often our preparation for childbirth is marred by fears, misinformation and a feeling of helplessness as we cope with a medical system that can quickly dehumanize us during this most deeply human of experiences. The aim of this section is to affirm childbearing as a dignified and creative act; to educate ourselves both physically and psychologically for pregnancy, childbirth and the postpartum period; to underline the vital importance of good nutrition; to explain the risks involved in such common hospital procedures as administration of anesthesia and fetal monitoring; and to discuss the alternative of home birth. We stress that this kind of childbearing information must become easily available to all women. We encourage women health consumers to work for woman-controlled, woman-oriented health care and to pressure medical institutions to respond more flexibly to our needs.

It is magnificent to be able to create a new human being. During pregnancy, as we go to work, prepare meals, figure out our budget and cope with the thousands of ordinary concerns that make up a usual day, we may also touch another level of existence from time to time. As we think of our fetus growing in us we may revert to our own childlike and dependent feelings and even wish to be back in a womb again ourselves. We'll think about what motherhood means to us; who our mothers were in relation to us; what kind of mother we want to be. We might have strange and vivid dreams and fantasies. Things we hadn't thought of since adolescence or childhood might come to mind: What is the meaning of existence, of my existence, of bringing a child into the world? We might want more strongly than usual to make the world a better place for our child to grow up in. We may feel ourselves as one of hundreds of millions of mothers, part of a vast history, living one of the most common and yet unique human events. Labor itself is a vivid example: It can be an extraordinary time—both physically intense, as we experience powerful contractions, and mystical, as we are in touch with the awe of giving birth.

Sometimes it is helpful to think of each childbearing year as a period having several phases of change and growth. (Not every woman will feel this way; we offer it as one model). Before becoming pregnant I am a separate individual. I have ties of varying strengths to others, but basically I am independent. When I first become aware of my pregnancy, I have to incorporate my consciousness of it into my self-image. I am no longer myself alone, but myself plus another. At times I will feel my baby as a part of me. Then I feel it move and realize it is going to be separate from me with a life of its own. Later, before I give birth I will prepare for a physical separation, the "delivery" of my child into the world. I will lose a part of my being; it will be apart from my body for the first time. I might feel grief, relief or gladness, or all three. Finally I spend the next year—the next eighteen years!—learning how to preserve my connections with my child in the most positive and most loving way, while I also learn to give it a firm basis for becoming independent, and learn to feel my own independence again.

Our society does not have language rich enough for honoring these rites of passage. Rarely are we allowed to experience the dignity and universality of our childbearing times. Our present socioeconomic system refuses many of us the right to be well-nourished and well-educated and secure so that we can more fully celebrate the joy of childbearing. (If I have been malnourished for years, work long hours at a difficult job, become pregnant and don't have the money to buy adequate food, can I confidently expect my child to be born in the best of health?*) Our present medical system, with its increasingly centralized institutions, its abuse of technological devices, and its crisis-intervention mentality, does not cope adequately with the humanness, naturalness and continuity of our childbearing year.

We have needs that are not being met. One great need we have is to experience our childbearing year as a continuum. This continuum begins physically with conception and psychologically with our decision to carry our child to term. It includes pregnancy, labor, delivery, the period immediately after our child is born, and the postpartum adjustment period, which may last a year or more after birth.

We need to receive knowledgeable medical care from one person or set of persons during this continuum. With the present medical system, each phase of childbearing is handled rather mechanically by a different set of "experts." During pregnancy we see a series of doctors and nurses in a clinic or we have a private doctor. We might deliver our baby with a doctor we know or with one we've never seen before. After the birth we're cared for by a new set of attendants and nurses, while our baby has his or her own doctor. When we come home we have no doctor at all. We take care of ourselves or depend on family and friends. An experience that could be a unified one is all broken up.

An example of this fragmentation is the childbirth experience. Childbirth could be as much a part of our everyday lives as pregnancy and child care. Instead, we are removed to an unfamiliar place for sick people† and separated at a crucial time from family and friends. We and our children suffer from this sudden removal; to our children it's a mysterious absence. In the hospital we are depersonalized; usually our clothes and personal effects, down to glasses and hairpins, are taken away. We lose our identity. We are expected to be passive and acquiescent and to make no trouble (passivity is considered a

sign of maturity). We are expected to depend not on ourselves but on doctors. For the doctor's convenience we are often given drugs to "ease" our labor. We often let ourselves be convinced by doctors who have never experienced labor and by our unprepared, frightened mothers and grandmothers that our labor will be too painful to bear. After our baby is born s/he is taken away for an hour, for a day. We pay a lot of money for our hospital space, sometimes more than we can afford.

Obstetricians are trained mainly to deal with complications of childbirth. "Well," we say, "you never know. Something might happen. We need our doctor." We are afraid on many levels. We have been taught to have very little confidence in ourselves, in our bodies. In fact, 95 percent of our deliveries have no complications. Most of us could very easily give birth with the help of a trained, experienced midwife, in a hospital, a special maternity house, or at home among family and friends if emergency equipment were present or nearby.

During the childbearing continuum we need one or more people to provide personal support from beginning to end. This support could come from a parent, friend, or partner. At times we will have to rely emotionally on someone else. We are going through changes and will have ups and downs. Some of us mistakenly rely on our doctors for this support and are disappointed when he (it's usually a he) doesn't meet our expectations. If we have our baby in a hospital we have a right to have our friends by our side during labor and birth. No other society isolates laboring mothers as we do. And we will need help afterward as we get used to being a mother, or as we work at fitting our child in with our existing family.

There are many steps we can take to become more active, conscious and critical participants in our childbearing experience. We must learn all we can about pregnancy, childbirth and care of ourselves and our children after birth. With this knowledge we can make certain choices. Too often in a critical situation we're not aware of the choices we have. With this knowledge we can sometimes prevent certain complications from arising. We must work on, and along with, doctors and nurses to demystify and deprofessionalize medicine, and persuade them to share their information with us so that we can mutually decide what steps to take if problems arise. We must work to make hospitals more humane places in which to have our babies—i.e., less medication (which can be harmful to our babies and ourselves); no experimentation during labor or childbirth without our informed consent; more rooming-in. We desperately need more good, humane doctors, and especially more women obstetricians. We must work for the development and legalization of midwifery services; for maternity homes; for the development of neighborhood clin-

---

*"'I wish we had more vegetables and fruit . . . but right now it takes nearly all our money for food and I have to buy clothing for the children.' Sadie Yazzie, Navaho Indian. Every poverty population is hungry. . . . We see the evidence all the time, eye diseases, respiratory diseases. . . . Sadie Yazzie is probably getting one-third the protein she needs. . . . As nutritionists, we'll never make inroads till we convince the politicians that they deprive the nation of a great natural resource by allowing malnutrition to exist." Pat Roseleigh, federal nutritionist at Window Rock, Arizona, quoted in *The Boston Globe*, January 27, 1975.

†Lester Hazell states: "Pregnancy, labor and delivery are states unto themselves but they are by no means illnesses." (*Commonsense Childbirth*, p. xxxiv. See bibliography p. 313, under "General Childbirth Books.").

ics; for efficient mobile medical emergency units so we could have our babies more naturally and inexpensively at home.

These are long-range goals. We are not naive enough to expect the medical system to change easily or quickly. It's a fact that many advances which were brought about over the past thirty years by women dedicated to improving childbirth care—advances such as prepared, unmedicated labor and childbirth, husbands or friends in the delivery room, and family-centered childbirth—are now being undermined by the trend toward centralization of hospital services in large cities; by the increasing use of epidurals (see p. 282) and fetal monitoring (see p. 285); and by the emphasis on treating every woman in labor as a "high risk" patient, thereby subjecting her to "precautionary" measures that interfere with her childbirth experience. (See Appendix, pp. 368–370.)

It's a fact that 98 percent of us have our children in hospitals (though home births are increasing in number, see p. 269). If we try beforehand to let medical personnel know which procedures we want and which we don't want, we are more likely to get our way; but chances are that our preferences will be ignored and little or no deviation from hospital routine will be permitted. Some of us might be subtly "punished" for wanting to have some say in the management of our experience ("You don't want a fetal monitor? Don't you care about the well-being of your child?"). We stress again that it is a strength to be active, to question and criticize procedures; that we have certain rights as patients (see "Our Rights As Patients," in Chapter 18); and that we need constant support from our husband or friend if we're faced with an important decision while in the midst of labor contractions. It would be wonderful indeed if it became common practice for each of us to draw up a careful contract with our doctor or clinic. Together we would plan the management of our labor and childbirth, put it in writing, and both do our best to abide by the terms of the contract.

It is clear from the foregoing that our definition of "good medical care" differs from that of most doctors. Most obstetricians are educated basically to have not our interests at heart but their own. Our value systems are very different: we emphasize teaching ourselves to participate wisely and strongly in our childbirth experience; they emphasize "what might go wrong" and make us almost totally dependent on them. We want more than the token communication with them that we have already, if indeed we communicate at all. We urge women who aren't in the vulnerable position of being in labor or giving birth to organize in a systematic way as consumers and evaluate the medical treatment most women receive. We urge you to investigate hospitals in your area; to assess the real needs of women in your area; to insist on whatever changes and improvements in the medical system may be indicated; and to publicize your concerns throughout your community.

Doctors, hospitals and other medical institutions are powerful and unresponsive. Forcing them to become responsive to our health needs (to do in fact what they are supposed to do!) involves a difficult struggle, one which will be successful when our health care system is no longer based solely on the profit motive. Meanwhile, we must do what we can.

We want to re-own our childbearing experience. In this childbearing unit we divide our discussion into three chapters, pregnancy, childbirth and postpartum care, because there are specific things we need to know and do during each period. It's crucial to remember that each phase is interconnected with the others.

CHAPTER 13
PREGNANCY

A PREVENTIVE PROGRAM: WHAT YOU CAN DO TO PREPARE YOURSELF

Taking Care of Yourself: Choice, Commitment, Preparation, Feelings, Emotional Needs

Some of you decide to have a child and soon afterward become pregnant. Clearly you have chosen to become pregnant before conceiving.

I was thirty and a half. I had on and off thoughts about when would be the best time to have children. Then I asked myself, Do I want children in my life or not? I realized I had a deep wish to have a family and children. Children had been loved and respected in my family and I wanted some of my own. It was a pleasure I wanted for myself.

I had a gut desire to have a child. It took me so long to have a successful pregnancy. I was lonely. A desire for a life-style change.

Some of you become pregnant unexpectedly, without feeling ready, without being ready. You haven't chosen to conceive.

In either case pregnancy begins physiologically at the moment of conception.

If you have planned your pregnancy, when you find you are pregnant you know you have already chosen to keep your baby. If you haven't planned your pregnancy, when you find you are pregnant you have to decide whether or not you will continue your pregnancy. When you decide to continue it you have made your first crucial choice—to be pregnant. Sometimes it takes a few months to make this choice. Some women let time decide.

After three months I knew my pregnancy was irrevocable, I wasn't going to end it. I felt it was taken out of my hands.

I didn't want to have another abortion, I really was amused by the idea of having a kid; I wanted a kid. I didn't feel I could ever consciously decide to have a kid, I didn't know what grounds to base that decision on.

The pregnancy is established now in each case. You have chosen to let the pregnancy run its course.

You make a second kind of choice when you think of how you want to be pregnant, when you decide to deal with all the kinds of changes that childbearing involves. This commitment can come at any point—at the beginning, middle, or even toward the end of your pregnancy. If your pregnancy was unexpected, you might be so confused and so hassled that for a long time you drift along not being able to think clearly. It's not uncommon during pregnancy to often feel out of control. It's to your advantage that you take on/assume/choose your pregnancy as early as possible, for the more you know about the process (what's happening in and to your body) and about your feelings, the more you can be in control of what happens during pregnancy, childbirth and the postpartum time. (See p. 325 on birth defects screening.)

The first step in planning to have your first child begins with planning for a fundamental change in your life. It's not easy to experience beforehand what that change will mean. Your body and mind will change during your pregnancy; your life will change with the birth of your child. A new being will enter your home, someone unknown, whose temperament may be totally unlike yours, and whose needs and demands remain constant day in and day out. For the next eighteen years or so, you will be responsible for a dependent being.

Begin to think of these changes and then take advantage of every tool and every scrap of information available. Use what used to be thought of as a time of "waiting," of simple passivity, to prepare for the changes ahead.

For many of us it has been important to spend time with sympathetic people during our pregnancy—to be in contact, talking, sharing work, checking feelings and questions. But some of us find it can be hard to move out of isolation. Some of us marry and move away from our families and friends. We are often isolated in our apartments and houses. In our isolation it's hard to find other pregnant women to talk to. It's frustrating, because we have lots to talk about.

It can be hard to bring up our questions and anxieties, because our bodily functions have traditionally been taboo subjects. If we save our questions for doctors or nurses, most often they can't answer us satisfactorily. They might not know the things we need to know, or be aware of feelings we may be having, or be able to take the time to speak with us. So we have to make an effort to talk among ourselves. (One thing to be a little careful about as we turn to each other for information and support is that some people who offer information and advice can misinform us or frighten us needlessly with stories of their own pregnancies and births, which they themselves didn't understand.)

During pregnancy we need to depend on someone.

You have to know how to ask for help. It's all right to ask, even for a cup of tea. Most of the time I had a lot of energy and was able to do things for myself, but there were times when I was really tired and I really didn't want to do physical things. The thing to aim for is instead of denying that the pregnancy makes a difference, just admit it. It made me aware of my own physical limitations.

At the beginning I felt independent. But toward the fifth month, when we came back from vacation, Dick went to work, and I felt very isolated from the "real" world. Then I had no one. I needed to be able to talk to people, and I wasn't talking to people.

Pregnancy shatters the illusion of our separateness and reminds us of our interconnectedness with others.

You need to make a continuity for yourself. If you can, find one or more supportive women or men to share your whole experience with, to lean on at times of need and stress, to whom you can easily say, "I need you."

I depended on my mother and two friends. One friend had factual information that I trusted.

Often you can ask for help from the man you're close to. Sometimes you can't. He might be too busy, not able to cope too helpfully with your problems—and then too, he's not a woman. But it's good to have him involved as much as possible in your pregnancy, as he will be living with all the joys and problems of your childbearing and he'll need preparation too.

Some of you will be isolated on farms, in mountains, in suburbs. Maybe you feel more isolated than you need to feel. Maybe close by there are people to talk to. If you do have only your doctor or your clinic to depend

on, try to find out as much as possible about all that is happening to you.

This emphasis on preparation may begin to sound repetitious. But one thing we don't concentrate on enough—our society doesn't teach us to do so intelligently—is the fact that establishing a new human being, especially during the early weeks and months of its life, is an extremely complicated, demanding piece of work. So keeping your health and sanity is vitally important.

It's also important to realize that no matter how well prepared and ready you feel at each step, something unexpected will usually happen. At least the knowledge you have will help you be more open, more flexible, more able to meet new situations with confidence.

And, finally, don't knock yourself out as you learn about yourself. There will be enough time. Take it easy. Wherever your learning begins, you have taken a first step.

Taking Care of Your Physical Needs

There are three crucial ways for you to take care of your physical needs during pregnancy (thus helping yourself feel better emotionally). First you must see a doctor as early in your pregnancy as possible so that s/he can give you a complete physical checkup. Most serious complications can be prevented by a combination of your knowledge and his/hers. Those of us who work all day or who live far from hospitals or who can't find or afford baby-sitters have a hard time getting prenatal health care. But given the present health care system in this country, we know that it is up to us to seek and find the care we need. For guidelines for this search, see the section "Choosing and Using Health and Medical Care" in Chapter 18. *Prenatal care is a form of preventive medicine, for when we are pregnant we are not sick. Our goal in seeing our doctor is to prevent sickness.*

Second, it is good to exercise to develop and strengthen your body. Develop your perineal muscles (see "Pelvic Floor [Kegel] Exercises," p. 101). Strengthen your back muscles to prevent backache by (1) bending and touching your toes, (2) sit-ups, (3) bicycling.

Third, you must eat well throughout your pregnancy. This is what we're going to discuss next.

Nutrition *(Also see Chapter 6, "Nutrition")*

EATING WELL AS AN EXAMPLE OF PREVENTION. You are pregnant now. You have to eat nutritious food. By eating well you'll help prevent some minor discomforts and help guard against some major illnesses in yourself and your baby. Studies in progress and studies made over the past forty years show that eating well is vitally important to ensure the health of your growing body. In this section we'll talk about (1) good nutrition (some facts and figures); (2) a good diet for your pregnancy; (3) why these foods are important; (4) controversy about nutrition; (5) gaining weight; (6) toxemia; (7) edema; (8) diuretics; (9) diet pills; (10) salt; (11) the effects of drugs on pregnancy and birth; (12) nutrition as a political issue.

GOOD NUTRITION—SOME FACTS AND FIGURES. In general, doctors and obstetricians know very little about the role of nutrition in pregnancy. Many studies have been made and much is known about nutrition, but this knowledge is not applied. In the ob/gyn examinations medical students have to take before becoming doctors there is no question relating to nutrition. We urge medical schools to pay attention to the subject of nutrition, as it is vitally important, and to de-emphasize drugs.

There is strong evidence that if we eat well, we bear strong, large, lively babies. During World War II in Great Britain pregnant women were given priority in food-rationing programs, and even under adverse conditions the stillbirth rate fell from 38 per 1,000 live births to 28—a decrease of about 25 percent.

If women eat well during pregnancy and gain weight, there's much more chance that the baby's weight will be adequate. It should be obvious that if the baby's birth weight is adequate, the baby is less apt to die or get sick after birth.* Women and babies from poor homes are most vulnerable to disease and complications, never having had adequate medical care or adequate diet. Low-birth-weight infants are more often born to women who don't have much money; who are under seventeen years of age; who don't gain much weight during pregnancy; who are poorly nourished; who have infections and chronic disease.† Good nutrition, then, helps prevent stillbirth, low birth weight, and prematurity from low birth weight. It also helps prevent infections, anemia in mothers, and brain damage and retardation in babies.‡

A GOOD DIET FOR YOUR PREGNANCY. Every day you must eat: (a) one quart (four glasses) of milk—low-fat, whole, or buttermilk (equivalents such as cottage cheese and yogurt are fine; skim milk is also good); (b) two eggs; (c) one serving of fish, chicken, lean beef, lamb, pork, or cheese (alternatives are dried beans, peas, or peanuts); (d) one or two servings of fresh green leafy vegetables—mustard, collard, or turnip greens, spinach, lettuce, or cabbage, or fresh-frozen vegetables; (e) whole-wheat bread; (f) one citrus fruit or glass of lemon, lime, orange, or grapefruit juice (not "drink"). Also (a) four times a week a serving of whole-grain cereal—Wheatena, farina, or oatmeal; (b) five times a week a yellow- or orange-colored vegetable; (c) a baked potato three times a week. Equivalent variations are possible.*

WHY THESE FOODS ARE IMPORTANT. All these foods together combine proteins, vitamins and minerals that are crucial to your health and which must remain in a certain balance in order for your body to function well and provide good materials for the growth of your baby.

Protein (meat, fish, eggs, milk, beans, cheese and soybeans in all their forms). Protein contributes to the building of tissue, a solid placenta, and a strong uterus. It keeps the blood sugar (the immediate source of body energy) at a high level. It furnishes amino acids.

Vitamin A (vegetables, whole milk, fortified milk) builds resistance to infection, strengthens mucous membranes, and has a vital function in your vision. Vegetables are good laxatives.

Vitamin B (bread, whole grains, liver, brewer's yeast, wheat germ) is said to help prevent nervousness, skin problems, lack of energy, constipation, and changes of pigmentation in your skin.

Vitamin C (citrus fruits) detoxifies the junk foods you eat; takes care of poisons produced by bacteria and viruses; keeps capillary and cell walls strong; and builds a strong placenta. It helps absorb iron from the gut and acidifies urine.

Vitamin D (sunshine, vitamin-D-fortified milk, or fish-liver oil) works with calcium to strengthen bones and tissues, helping the calcium to be absorbed from the blood into tissue and bone cells.

Vitamin E (whole grains, corn, peanuts, eggs) governs the amount of oxygen your body uses. You use more oxygen than you need to if you lack vitamin E. It promotes healing and helps the metabolism of vitamin A.

Vitamin K is necessary to the clotting mechanism. Vitamin K is synthesized by gut bacteria and doesn't come directly from food.

Folic acid (leafy green vegetables). Symptoms of folic-acid deficiency are anemia and fatigue. Our bodies don't store folic acid, so if we are anemic we need daily supplements. Excessive folic-acid deficiency can lead to nerve damage. Orally administered folic acid can remedy the deficiency. Essential for protein synthesis in early pregnancy; also for formation of blood and new cells.

Iron† (raisins, blackstrap molasses, fish, egg yolks, meat). You need vitamin B to use properly the iron you get. Iron is a main component of hemoglobin, and the blood hemoglobin, composed of complex molecules of

---

*In a study made in Toronto: ". . . Four times as many of the poor-diet mothers were considered to have serious health problems in pregnancy when compared to the mothers whose diets were supplemented with extra-nutritious foods. The poor-diet group had seven times as many threatened miscarriages and three times as many stillbirths. Their labors were recorded as lasting about five hours longer. . . ." (Niles Anne Newton, "Childbearing in Broad Perspective," in Boston Children's Medical Center, *Pregnancy, Birth and the Newborn Baby,* p. 19). It is upsetting to reflect on the immorality of this study. It is clear that mothers and babies in the control group will be sicker and die, when this sickness and death could be prevented.

†*Maternal Nutrition and the Course of Pregnancy,* p. 4. (See bibliography, p. 313.)

‡A federally funded nutrition program called WIC provides eggs, cheese, orange juice and milk to low-income families with children.

*See Frances Moore Lappe, *Diet for a Small Planet.*

† Liver, traditionally a good iron source, is not included because it often contains DES (see pp. 146–47), which is used to fatten animals.

protein and iron, carries oxygen to your baby and your cells. The baby also draws on your iron reserve to store iron in its liver to last for the duration of her/his milk diet after birth. Also during labor you'll need a lot of oxygen (supplied by hemoglobin) for your uterus; the baby's brain cells need oxygen, too. Your own iron stores are seldom large enough to meet the requirements of pregnancy, and many young women are already iron-deficient before pregnancy. Food rarely provides enough iron. Most doctors prescribe ferrous sulfate as an iron supplement. Vegetarians also need vitamin B_{12}.

Calcium (milk, stone-ground grain). Sleeplessness, irritability, muscle cramps, nerve pains, and uterine ligament pains can be signs of lack of calcium. You can take extra pills—calcium gluconate or calcium lactate. They should be taken on an empty stomach with sour milk or yogurt. Vitamin C (acid fruit or juice) helps in the absorption of calcium and iron. *All of us must insist that our doctors give us iron, calcium and folic-acid supplements in the form of pills.* By taking them we are sure to prevent serious deficiencies.

Zinc and Cobalt (seafoods) are trace minerals, which are necessary to the building of certain enzymes that speed chemical reactions.

Calories. You need calories to carry on your life and your pregnancy. You can't get good nutrition without calories, but it's calories without nutrition that you need to avoid, e.g., sweets (candies and cakes). Severe caloric restriction is potentially harmful. Women under seventeen especially need a lot of calories as they are still growing. And toward the end of pregnancy everyone needs more calories.

Fluids. Drink a variety of fluids daily. Water aids the circulation of blood and body fluids. It helps the distribution of mineral salts and stimulates the digestion and assimilation of foods. Caffeine, however, is toxic.

It's important to know that the nearer most foods are to their native state, the higher their food value. (See "Nutrition" in Chapter 6.

CONTROVERSY ABOUT NUTRITION. Our doctors don't agree with one another about the role of nutrition in pregnancy. While all doctors agree that we should drink milk, eat eggs, leafy green vegetables and fruit, they disagree about our intake of salt, our weight gain, the number of calories we need, the value or harmfulness of diet pills. Up till now we have accepted our doctors' words as truth. For example, many of us who had children in the sixties were advised not to gain much weight and were put on low-salt, low-calorie diets. We accepted these restrictions without question. We didn't question our doctors intelligently because we didn't have enough information. Now we're learning about a large and growing body of research that criticizes the traditional pregnancy diets we had. We are becoming acquainted with the findings of this research. We have learned that many of these dietary restrictions were imposed on us because doctors believed that weight gain and salt somehow *caused* a condition called toxemia (see below and p. 261). It is being discovered that they are not the cause of toxemia.

GAINING WEIGHT. Now you are eating well, and you find you are gaining weight. As your pregnancy advances you might feel voracious. There has been much controversy over whether or not it's okay to gain much weight beyond the weight of the uterus, placenta, fetus and amniotic fluid. Some studies show that as long as your diet is well balanced you may gain extra weight. Again, there is a positive correlation between weight gained during pregnancy by the mother and high weight of the newborn baby. The pattern of your weight gain is more important than the total amount: that is, some women might gain one pound every week, other women two pounds every week. If the pattern remains fairly regular, everything is all right. A sudden large gain after the twentieth to twenty-fourth week, especially if you haven't been eating well, might mean excessive water retention (edema) and should be checked by a doctor. Be attentive: check your own weight weekly. Weight loss or no gain should be checked by a doctor too.

The main thing to remember is to balance your diet over the whole course of your pregnancy. Even if your doctor has limited you to a twenty-pound weight gain for the entire pregnancy and you have already gained twenty pounds by your seventh month, it's important that you continue to eat well rather than restrict your diet radically. You'll need vitamins, minerals, proteins and other nutrients even more toward the end of your pregnancy. Weight gain restriction is outdated.*

There are two important arguments against gaining *a lot* of extra weight. One is that excessive weight gain can put too great a strain on your circulation and your heart. The other is that many women find it very hard to get rid of all that extra weight after the baby is born; and sometimes not being as light as you want can be depressing after all those months of heaviness.

TOXEMIA. (See also "Toxemia," p. 261.) Many of us were cautioned by our doctors not to gain much weight during pregnancy so that we wouldn't swell up and get toxemia. Most of us have never known exactly what toxemia is.

During my pregnancy I thought that if my hands or ankles started to swell, something would happen—I

*"Substantial weight gain during pregnancy is normal. Pregnant women should take supplements of iron and folic acid, but other vitamin supplementation is unnecessary for women eating a balanced diet, and overdoses of some vitamins may be harmful to the fetus." *The Medical Letter,* a nonprofit publication on drugs and therapeutics, Vol. 20, No. 15, July 28, 1978.

*would suddenly be in some kind of danger, a danger that
I didn't understand.*

[From a description of a clinic] Women . . . were threatened with frightening stories about deaths from toxemia.

What is toxemia? Metabolic toxemia of late pregnancy (MTLP) is a condition that has several stages: The first stage, pre-eclampsia, is characterized by edema (swelling due to water retention), high blood pressure, and protein in the urine. It usually happens anytime after the twentieth to twenty-fourth week of pregnancy, usually late in pregnancy. Pre-eclampsia may be mild or severe. In the second stage a woman might have trouble with her vision, abdominal pains, mental dullness, or severe headaches. In the most severe stage, the eclamptic stage, she might have convulsions and go into a coma. Usually women don't advance into the eclamptic stage if they are receiving medical care.

Whereas the majority of doctors are unsure of the causes of toxemia (in one major obstetrics textbook* there's a long chapter on the subject of eclampsia that contains at least eighteen theories about how the illness is caused, and a related bibliography of one hundred and eighty articles, only three of which deal with nutrition), Dr. Thomas Brewer, who ran a clinic for poor women in California, is convinced after twenty years of study and clinic work that toxemia of pregnancy is caused mainly by malnutrition. When women in his clinic were placed on good diets, the incidence of toxemia dropped radically. M. Bertha Brandt states that "Toxemia may be associated with undernutrition and low total serum proteins."†

Maternal Nutrition and the Course of Pregnancy points out that the lower a state's per capita income, the higher the incidence of toxemia and the higher the maternal mortality from toxemia. Mississippi and South Carolina rank fifty-first and fiftieth in per capita income. Whereas the rate of mothers dying from toxemia is 6.2 per 100,000 live births nationwide, in Mississippi it is 30.2, and in South Carolina 20.3. The author of the above-mentioned textbook, Nicholson J. Eastman, has written a letter to Brewer admitting that malnutrition plays an important, and possibly *the* most important, part in causing toxemia.

We don't have the medical expertise to evaluate Dr. Brewer's findings, but the facts seem to establish the credibility of his argument. We also cannot say too strongly that if toxemia has already been systematically prevented by good nutrition, then it's clear that all preg-

*N. J. Eastman and L. M. Hellman, *Williams Obstetrics*, 13th edition (New York: Appleton-Century-Crofts, 1966).
†Nancy A. Lytle, ed., *Maternal Health Nursing* (see bibliography, p. 314), p. 75.

nant women should be well nourished *at the very least*. Whatever symptoms and sicknesses remain, one known cause of this sickness would be eliminated. Perhaps toxemia itself will disappear—one of those "diseases" that need never have been; one of the diseases of an economically unequal society.

EDEMA. (See also "Edema," p. 261.) Associated with weight gain during pregnancy is a condition called edema. In edema your body tissues retain water, and this retention causes face, hands, legs, or feet to swell, usually at the end of the day. Doctors in the past and present immediately connect weight gain with toxemia. However, they must make distinctions. They must not confuse accumulation of fat with weight gained as a result of edema. They must not confuse regular edema with the edema which is a manifestation of toxemia, and which will be accompanied by other symptoms of toxemia.

DIURETICS. Too often doctors will automatically give you diuretics (water pills) if you have edema. These diuretics may be harmful. They can cause many undesirable side effects in mother and fetus. The immediate effect of these pills is to cause your body to eliminate water excessively. You urinate more. Diuretics are dehydrating. Among other things, they cause nausea, vomiting, diarrhea, jaundice, muscle spasms, dizziness, headache and loss of appetite. These diuretics appeared in 1958 and have been pushed by the drug industry, regardless of their effects. They can be lethal to both mothers and babies.

DIET PILLS. Diet pills are "speed" (amphetamines). They are drugs. Women who gain weight are sometimes given these pills. They go straight through the placenta to the fetus. They are given to you to kill your appetite, to make you feel good for the moment even when your diet isn't as good as it should be. They only serve to mask problems of poor nutrition. You shouldn't be taking these pills. And if you are eating adequately, you won't need to take them. There are other ways to stop eating too much if you find you are indeed eating too many of the wrong kinds of foods. Don't ask your doctor for diet pills. Your baby will be born addicted.

SALT. When you are pregnant you need a certain amount of salt. Salt is stored in fluids outside your cells, and it leaves your body as you perspire. So you need to replenish it. For instance, if you happen to lose some blood and you have adequate salt in your system, then extra salt and water can move into your bloodstream and you don't readily go into shock. Also, if you are preparing to nurse, salt and water mean less dehydration, which is better for milk production. Margaret Robinson did a study in which she found that women on low-salt diets developed leg cramps, and increased salt intake relieved them. You should not avoid salt in ordinary amounts, though it's necessary to avoid oversalted foods, since too much salt can lead to excessive fluid retention. In cases of toxemia, salt can be harmful. It increases hypertension and blood pressure, fluid retention and edema. If you have cardiac edema, your salt intake might need to be restricted.

EFFECT OF MEDICATION, DRUGS, X RAYS AND VITAMINS. Your decision about whether to use a drug must be a compromise between possible good effects (to you) and possible bad effects (to you, to your baby). *It is essential that you know that any drug you take gets through the placental barrier to your fetus.* Some drugs produce malformations of the fetus (they have *teratogenic* effects). Some drugs alter the level of hormones in the maternal/fetal circulation and thus alter the functioning of the placenta.

Lately studies have been coming out which show that drugs taken by pregnant women have harmful effects on their babies. A study reported in *The New England Journal of Medicine* reveals that two of the most commonly prescribed tranquilizers—Librium (chlordiazepoxide hydrochloride) and Equanil/Miltown (meprobamate)—may cause defects when taken early in pregnancy.* The pill also causes them.†

If you have been on narcotics, especially heroin, your fetus will possibly become addicted before birth. Your doctor must know if you are taking narcotics (including methadone), for withdrawal symptoms in a newborn infant will be dangerous if not recognized immediately. Babies born to women addicted to alcohol can also suffer withdrawal symptoms, and fetal alcohol syndrome.‡

Some antihistamines may produce malformations. General anesthetics at high concentrations may produce malformations. Cortisone reaches fetus and placenta and may cause alterations. Antithyroid may cause goiter in infants. And tetracycline may cause deformities in babies' bones and stain their teeth.

In general, if you are affected by a drug it will get through to your baby. Try as hard as you can to know what drugs you're taking and what effects they might have, and take no drugs unless you are convinced they are absolutely needed. This also includes simple over-the-counter "drugs" such as aspirin and sleeping preparations. The less medication you take, the better.§

The New York Times, December 12, 1974.
†See bibliography under "Articles"; also Ch. 10.
‡E. M. Ouellette, et al. *NEJM*, 297:528, 1977. Also *JAMA*, April 5, 1976.
§"Among drugs known to damage the human fetus are the antibiotics streptomycin, tetracycline and sulfonamides taken near the end of pregnancy; excessive amounts of vitamins A, D, B₆ and K; certain barbiturates, opiates and other central nervous system depressants when taken near the time of delivery, and the synthetic hormone progestin, which can masculinize the female fetus.

"In addition, animal studies have implicated such common drugs as aspirin, antinausea compounds, phenobarbital and the tranquilizer chlorpromazine as possible causes of fetal abnormalities." [*The New York Times*, December 12, 1974.]

X rays can be harmful to a fetus, especially during the 42-day period after conception. There are at least sixty-three X-ray diagnostic procedures that can expose a developing child to some radiation.*

Routine multivitamin supplementation is not necessary during pregnancy if your diet is well balanced. Vitamin A in excessive dosage may cause malformations; nor is too much vitamin C healthy (too much = more than 1 gm. per day). (*Medical Letter*, Vol. 20, No. 15, 1978.)

NUTRITION—A POLITICAL ISSUE. All of us, rich and poor, have to struggle separately and together against ignorance, our own and our doctors'. Our struggle is much greater if we don't have enough money to buy needed foods; if good fresh foods aren't available; if we aren't getting good continuous medical care. We all quickly have to learn what we need and why.

We asked Dr. Brewer how the women he works with manage to get enough of the right foods. He answers:

The women I work with manage because out here in California there is a "welfare system"; vicious as it is, it does provide something . . . as differentiated from many parts of the rural Deep South. Once a woman learns the life-and-death importance of eating enough, she usually manages. The fact that women in my clinic have healthy babies is the best evidence that they do manage. There are exceptions . . . such as a young woman with twins who fell behind in her protein intake and got sick because of it.

We must work for a social and medical system which educates its doctors to provide basic positive preventive services for pregnant women (indeed for all women and men), with an emphasis on good nutrition. We must work for a social and economic system which educates its pregnant women to expect good health and which makes good food easily available. It is clear that we can't have healthy babies unless mothers and fathers have eaten decent natural food and are healthy themselves. We must work for changes in attitudes of doctors and drug companies so that drugs are not pushed on women regardless of their harmful effects. We must be very careful about what we take into our bodies when we are pregnant.

THE PREGNANCY ITSELF

Introduction

During your pregnancy there are two kinds of development: (1) the physical and emotional changes you are going through, and (2) the growth of the fetus within you—two stories going on at once.

Though your pregnancy will have much in common with other women's, it is yours and unique. (And each

*Drs. Robert Rugh and William Leach, in a paper presented to The International Radiation Protection Association, quoted in the *Boston Globe*, November 13, 1974.

pregnancy you go through will differ from the others.) In talking to women who have been pregnant and who are pregnant at the same time you are, you will discover that there's no one, right way to be pregnant. Also realize that when we talk about experiencing changes and emotions, there are many exceptions and many combinations.

For instance, many changes will take place in your body as the fetus develops in you. Some of these changes are just changes; some can lead to discomfort. For though we are adapted to bearing children, discomforts can arise, and complications too.* You'll all have changes to deal with. You might feel many discomforts, few, or none at all. You'll want to know what the changes will be, why they occur, when they occur, and any discomforts you might feel. Some minor discomforts, if neglected, can lead to major complications. And you might want to know that in every pregnancy there's a possibility of miscarriage, so that if it happens to you, you won't be totally unprepared. (See p. 321.)

As for your feelings, they will vary tremendously according to who you are; how you feel about having children; how you feel about your own childhood, your parents, or the people who reared you; whether or not you are with a man—and if you are, how you feel about your man. At each stage you may feel conflicts as well as harmonies. Sometimes you'll feel positive, sometimes negative. You'll have doubts and fears. It's important to know that these doubts and fears occur during a "good" pregnancy too, for in a very real sense your body has been taken over by a process out of your control. You can come to terms with that takeover actively and consciously by knowing what's happening to your body, by identifying your specific feelings (especially the negative ones, because they are the most difficult to deal with), and also by learning what the fetus looks like as it grows. Its growth is dramatic and exciting.

The length of a normal pregnancy can vary from 240 to 300 days. We'll divide our discussion into trimesters (approximately three three-month periods). This division will be relevant for some of you and not for others. Your feelings will ebb and flow and not always follow predictable courses. But since we have so many changes and feelings to talk about, it's more convenient to talk within the framework of trimesters.

First Trimester (First Twelve Weeks)

Physical changes

You might have none, some, or many of the following

*"Regardless of the fact that from a biological point of view childbearing is considered a normal reproductive process, the borderline between health and illness is less distinctly marked during this time because of the numerous physiologic changes that occur in the mother's body during the course of parturition" (Elise Fitzpatrick, *Maternity Nursing*, p. 443).

early signs of pregnancy. If you have had regular periods, you will probably miss a period (amenorrhea). However, some women do bleed for the first two or three months even when they are pregnant, but these periods are usually short and there's scant blood. Also, about seven days or so after conception, the *blastocyst*, the tiny group of cells to become the embryo, attaches itself to the uterine wall, and you might have slight vaginal spotting, called implantation bleeding, for new blood vessels are being formed.

You might have to urinate more often because of increased hormonal changes; pituitary hormones affect the adrenals, which change the water balance in your body, and you retain more body water. Also, your growing uterus presses against your bladder.

Your breasts will probably swell. They might tingle, throb, or hurt. Your milk glands begin to develop. Because of an increased blood supply to your breasts, veins become more prominent. Your nipples and the area around them (areola) may darken and become broader.

You might feel nauseated, mildly or enough to vomit, partly because your system is changing. One theory is that the higher level of estrogen accumulates even in the cells of the stomach and causes irritation as acids tend to accumulate. The rapid expansion of the uterus may be involved. If you feel nauseated, eat lightly throughout the day rather than taking large meals. Munching crackers or dry toast slowly before you get up in the morning can really help. Avoid greasy, spiced food. Avoid fasting. Apricot nectar helps.

You might feel constantly tired.

You might have increased vaginal secretions, either clear and non-irritating, or white, yellow, foamy, or itchy. The chemical makeup, as well as the amount, of your vaginal fluids is changing. If you are uncomfortable for any reason or if you have questions, see your doctor. (See also "Vaginal Infections" in Chapter 6.)

The joints between your pelvic bones widen and become movable about the tenth or eleventh week. Occasionally the separating bones come together and pinch the sciatic nerve, which runs from your buttocks down through the back of your legs.

Your bowel movements might become irregular, both because of the pressure of your growing uterus and again because the heightened amount of progesterone relaxes smooth muscle; therefore your bowels might not function as efficiently as they did. Also, if you are resting often, your decreased activity might cause some constipation.

During the first ten weeks you'll feel relatively few body changes. All those above are fairly common, not too annoying.

Early pregnancy surprised me. I was expecting to feel very different and instead was feeling things I'd felt before. It was like premenstrual tension. I was a little nau-

seous. But it's amazing, once I realized I was pregnant the symptoms were tolerable, because they are not signs of sickness, but life-producing.

Procedures for detecting pregnancy

TESTS. You will see the doctor when you recognize some of the above as pregnancy signs; or you might discover you are pregnant while being checked for something else. Some women can become pregnant and not be aware of it for the first few months.

There are tests to determine whether or not you are pregnant. These tests may be given by your doctor or by the nurses at your clinic. Or you might go first to a pregnancy lab. Some labs charge $8 for their services. Some charge less. At some you can get results in a few hours; at others you have to wait overnight. You can look up pregnancy labs in the Yellow Pages of your phone book, and perhaps check their prices, promptness and accuracy through local women's groups. In some towns you can only have pregnancy tests made through local doctors or hospitals.

There are two main kinds of pregnancy test, biologic and immunologic. Both use a hormone (HCG—human chorionic gonadotropin) secreted by the developing embryo and found in the urine of pregnant women. Pregnancy can be detected as early as three weeks after conception. Both kinds of tests use urine. In the biologic tests, when the urine containing this hormone is injected into laboratory animals—rats, mice, rabbits, or frogs—it causes them to ovulate. This process takes a few days, whereas the fastest immunologic test takes only two minutes. In the latter test, most commonly used now, a drop of urine is mixed on a slide with a drop of serum sensitized to it and two drops of another substance; if the hormone HCG from the placenta is present, the mixture won't coagulate.

These tests are 95 to 98 percent accurate, but can be false if they are performed too early (before there's enough hormone in the urine), if there are technical errors in handling or storing the urine, or if the test animal doesn't respond as it should. Sometimes even if you are pregnant, your first or second tests will be negative. Keep testing. Some women don't show positive signs at all in tests. There are also rare occasions when a pregnancy test can be falsely positive. Usually a diagnosis of pregnancy can be made independent of these tests. If the test is positive, if you want to keep your baby, and you haven't yet seen a doctor, it's a good idea to see one or go to a clinic as soon as you find out. It's a good precautionary measure.

Another test was developed at Cornell. It is called the beta subunit HCG radio-immunoassay. It specifically measures HCG, and is sensitive enough to detect a pregnancy eight days after ovulation, or approximately five days before the first missed period. It involves taking a drop of blood and measuring the level of human HCG. Avoid hormonal tests. EPTs (early pregnancy tests) are expensive and unreliable.*

PELVIC EXAM. If you are pregnant (1) the doctor can feel that the tip of the cervix has become softened, (2) he can see that the cervix has changed from a pale pink to a bluish hue because of increased venous blood circulation, (3) the uterus feels softer, and (4) the shape of the uterus changes: where the embryo attaches itself to the inside of the uterus it makes a bulge, which can sometimes be felt on the outside of the uterus.

SOME WOMEN JUST KNOW THEY ARE PREGNANT. Some of us feel we know the moment we become pregnant. Or from one sign—a missed period, tender breasts—we become tuned in to the fact that our bodies feel different. Or we find out at the doctor's.

With my first child I missed a period and my breasts hurt. With Jesse, I knew the moment I conceived him. There's no way of pinning that down, no way of explaining how I felt. I just knew.

I realized I was pregnant the same night I became pregnant. I lay there all night. I'd had a very active sex life, and it was the first time I had ever felt this way. I wasn't expecting to get pregnant, but I felt different that night.

EXAM SCHEDULE. Doctors and clinics usually set up a fairly routine examination schedule.

The first visit should consist of a complete general physical exam: (1) Medical history: menstrual history; previous babies, pregnancies, operations, abortions, illnesses (have you had German measles—rubella?), drugs taken; history of family illnesses, such as heart disease, kidney disease, diabetes, sickle-cell anemia. (2) General physical exam. It's important that you either bring any previous records that you have, or try to be complete in your description of what's happened to you physically. (3) Exam for pregnancy, which includes (a) examination of your breasts to see if there are changes in the glands; (b) a pelvic examination, as described above, which shows the position and consistency of the uterus, condition of ovaries and fallopian tubes, consistency and color of the cervix; (c) taking a blood sample to determine its type and Rh factor (see p. 324) and to provide blood for a blood count, hemoglobin analysis, syphilis checkup, and a hematocrit to see if you're anemic; (d) herpes and gonorrhea smears; (e) urinalysis to check for urinary in-

---

*The Medical Letter, 20:8, April 21, 1978.

fections*; (f) weight and blood pressure checks.

Insist that your doctor give you complete information about the results of all these tests. Also insist on a Pap smear, an HAI test to see if you have had German measles (rubella),† and a blood sugar test. Diabetics should get frequent tests of blood and urine.

Your next visits will be monthly and much shorter. The heartbeat and position of your fetus will be checked, as well as your urine, weight and blood pressure.

At the beginning of your eighth month you'll see the doctor every two weeks.

During the ninth month you'll see him or her once a week. S/he will take internal measurements (if s/he hasn't already) to see if your pelvis is large enough for the baby to come through; s/he will check the thinning of the cervix wall (*effacement*), the width of the opening of the cervix (*dilation*), and the position of the baby. S/he will keep checking the heartbeat.

If you can, try to find a pediatrician or family doctor early, and try to check his or her competence.

We describe the schedule above as an ideal schedule, ideal only in the context of our present system, and not really ideal at all, because it stops with childbirth and doesn't deal with your emotions. At the other extreme of exam scheduling are many women from poor areas who never see a doctor until it's time to deliver. Or conditions in some hospitals and clinics are so bad—crowded, long waits, careless medical people, lack of respect for patients—that some of us feel discouraged and don't want to take the time to come for appointments.

Your feelings about yourself and your pregnancy

At the beginning of a first pregnancy, of any pregnancy, there are so many variations in feeling, from delirious joy to deep depression.

SOME POSITIVE FEELINGS. You might feel an increased sensuality, a kind of sexual opening out toward the world, heightened perceptions, like being in love. A lot of new energy. A feeling of being really special, fertile,

*When you are pregnant you become more susceptible to urinary tract infections. Five percent of women have latent urinary tract infections. Because the hormone progesterone relaxes smooth (involuntary) muscle, the collecting area in the kidneys and the tube connecting kidneys to bladder becomes larger. Urine tends to stagnate there, aggravating any latent infection. Signs of infection are increased urination, hurting or burning. More extreme signs of infection are: back pain, chills and fever, bloody urine. You must get a urine culture made, and drink lots of water. In the first trimester of pregnancy your infection should be treated with sulfa drugs.

†If you are not immune to German measles, try to avoid exposure. When you have it, you might have a rash, tenderness of the lymph nodes in the back of your neck, and possibly mild joint pains. If you are exposed in the first trimester of pregnancy, and if you get the disease, chances are high that the fetus will be deformed. At this point you will have to make a decision about whether or not to continue your pregnancy. A blood test will tell you if you have rubella.

potent, creative. Expectation. Great excitement. Impatience.

Being pregnant meant I was a woman. I was enthralled with my belly growing. I went out right away and got maternity clothes.

It gave me a sense that I was actually a woman. I had never felt sexy before. I went through a lot of changes. It was a very sexual thing. I felt very voluptuous.

It meant I could get pregnant finally after a lot of trying, that I could do something I wanted to do. It meant going into a new stage of life. I felt filled up.

SOME QUESTIONS. What's going to happen to me? How will being pregnant change me? Will I be able to cope well? Can I physically handle birth? Will I miscarry? How long can I keep my job? Who am I? What image can I form of who I want to be? What is my baby going to be like? What about my man?

SOME NEGATIVE FEELINGS. Shock. I'm losing my individuality. I'm not the same any more. I'm a pregnant woman; I'm in this new category, and I don't want to be. I don't want to be a vessel, a carrier. I won't matter to people now, only my baby will. I can't feel anything for this thing growing in me. I can't feel any love. I'm scared. I'm tired. I feel sick.* I wish I weren't pregnant. I'm not ready. I don't understand motherhood.

Negative feelings are all relevant and natural. They should be dealt with, not avoided or ignored. The deeper you go into these feelings, the better prepared you'll be to handle them close to the birth and afterward.

Sometimes it seemed like I had gotten pregnant on a whim—and it was a hell of a responsibility to take on a whim. Sometimes I was overwhelmed by what I'd done. A lot of that came from realizing that I had chosen to have the baby without the support of a man. I was scared up until the third trimester that I wasn't going to make it.

Some of you will be too busy to think often about your pregnancy. Others will have more leisure. Some of you will be interested in your pregnancies in different

* There are many theories about the nausea that accompanies pregnancy: that it is peculiar to Western culture; that on some deep level, though we are raised in a society that adulates motherhood, we are disgusted by the animal fact that we have conceived and are now pregnant; that by vomiting we are trying to get rid of the fetus in a symbolic way; that nausea is a result of anxiety and tension, of the many pressures we feel.

degrees, your awareness switched inward at different times. You might be interested and involved in pregnancy without coming to terms with what it means to have a baby.

When I first felt her move, I knew there was life inside me. But I didn't realize I was having a baby until my doctors literally pulled her out of me upside down and she sneezed, and then she lay next to me and I felt her tiny breath on my fingers.

Maybe the last three weeks I started looking at other babies.

At the beginning of pregnancy it's sometimes a relief not to think about it, and you can even forget it if you want to. At some point during pregnancy you might want to escape from the inevitability of what is happening to you.

If pregnancy meant anything, it meant being married. I no longer felt it was easy to get out. It was like a seal on the marriage.

Growth of the fetus

You can't feel the changes going on inside you. Both the placental systems and the complicated systems of your fetus are developing on a miniature scale. This is fantastically exciting to learn about. Knowing what's going on inside our bodies at each stage makes pregnancy a much less alienating and frightening experience than it has often been in the past.

We regret that we don't have enough space to describe the step-by-step development of the fetus. But there are several good books on the subject. We especially recommend Geraldine Lux Flanagan's *The First Nine Months of Life* (see bibliography, p. 312) and Anthony Smith's *The Body*, which are available in paperback.

Second Trimester (Thirteenth to Twenty-sixth Week)

Physical changes

At about the fourth month the fetus begins its bulkier growth. Your waist becomes thicker, your clothes no longer fit you, your womb starts to swell below your waist, and beginning with the fourth or fifth month you can begin to feel light movements. The fetus has been moving for months, but it's only now that you can feel it. Often you will feel it first just before you fall asleep.

You are probably gaining weight now. Eat as well as you can. (See "Nutrition," p. 252.)

Your circulatory system has been changing, your total blood volume increasing, as your bone marrow produces more blood corpuscles and you drink and retain more liquid. Because of the increase in blood production, you need more iron. Your heart is changing position and increasing slightly in size.

In some women the area around the nipple, the areola, becomes very dark, due to hormonal changes. The line from the navel to the pubic region gets dark too, and sometimes pigment in the face becomes dark, making a kind of mask. The mask goes away after pregnancy, but usually the increased color around your nipples and in the line on your abdomen doesn't go away.

Some women salivate more. You might sweat more, which is helpful in eliminating waste material from your body. Sometimes you'll get cramps in your legs and feet when you wake up, perhaps because of disturbed circulation. It's believed that calcium relieves these cramps. Just relax—the cramps will go away. Or rub them if you want to, or keep your feet elevated and warm.

Your uterus is changing too. It's growing. Its weight increases twenty times, and the greater part of this weight is gained before the twentieth week.

As your abdomen grows larger the skin over it will stretch, and lines may appear, pink or reddish streaks. Your skin may become very dry; add oil to your bath and rub your skin with oil.

By mid-pregnancy your breasts, stimulated by hormones, are functionally complete for nursing purposes. After about the nineteenth week a thin amber or yellow substance called *colostrum* may come out of your nipples; there's no milk yet. Your breasts are probably larger and heavier than before. If you are planning to breast-feed, some experts feel it's a good idea to begin gently massaging your nipples. If your nipples are inverted (turned in), pull them out gently several times a day by putting your thumbs on each side of your nipples, pressing down into the breasts and away from the nipple. You should wash your breasts daily with mild soap or clean water. It's also a good idea to support them by wearing a good supportive bra, as they can begin to feel very heavy.

Your bowels and your entire digestive system might move more slowly. Indigestion and constipation can occur. You might have heartburn because of too much acid in your stomach. Again, a good diet eases these situations. Eat frequent small meals if possible. Avoid greasy foods and coffee. Dried fruit helps constipation, also fresh fruits and vegetables. Drink a lot of fluids. Avoid choosing medicines yourself and taking strong, oily laxatives. Avoid laxatives containing sodium, such as baking soda, or Alka-Seltzer.

Also, as a result of pressure of pelvic organs, veins in your rectum (hemorrhoidal veins) may become dilated and sometimes painful. Lie down with your rectum high and apply ice packs. Tucks Pads and "Preparation H" are okay. Or take warm baths and apply Vaseline.

Proper diet, liquids and exercise will be helpful. Varicose veins are veins in your legs that have become enlarged and can hurt. Again because of pressure, the veins and blood vessels that carry blood from your legs to your heart aren't working as smoothly as before. A tendency to varicose veins can be hereditary. Many women find it very helpful to wear support stockings a half size larger than their ordinary stockings. And lots of rest, with legs elevated, is good.

Many women have nosebleeds because of the increased volume of blood and increased nasal congestion, or perhaps because of increased hormone levels (it's also possible to have sympathetic nosebleeds during periods). Put a little Vaseline in each nostril, and that will stop the bleeding.

We want to speak of edema here again (we discussed it in the section on nutrition). Edema is swelling of the face, hands, ankles, wrists, or feet as a result of water retention by the body tissues. Some edema during pregnancy is normal. Exercise helps squeeze water from the tissue spaces in your blood vessels. If you are uncomfortable, try to lie down with your feet raised several times a day. Cut down on refined carbohydrates and get more physical rest. See if this helps. If edema persists, check with your doctor.

Toxemia (see "Nutrition," p. 255)—after the twenty-fourth week of pregnancy you might develop high blood pressure, edema, or protein in your urine.* You might have mild pre-eclampsia, with the symptoms mentioned in the paragraph above. You should check with your doctor. Your blood pressure should be observed on at least two occasions at least six hours apart, and the amount of albumin (a protein) in your urine must be checked at least two times. Toward the third trimester of pregnancy you might have severe pre-eclampsia, indicated by very high blood pressure, a large amount of protein in your urine with a decrease in the amount of urine, blurred vision, a severe continuous headache, or swelling of your face and fingers. Severe pre-eclamptic conditions can develop in a few hours. Unless these pre-eclamptic stages are checked immediately, eclampsia—convulsions and coma—might occur. (Pre-eclamptic conditions *must* be treated in the hospital; your life and your baby's are at stake.) There is disagreement about the treatment of pre-eclampsia, with various claims made for the restriction of weight gain, curtailment of salt, hormonal treatments, and the use of diuretics. *It's essential to repeat that all medical people agree that incidence of toxemia of pregnancy is much lessened by constant prenatal care and supervision, and good diet.*

What about smoking tobacco? The 1971 Surgeon General's report, *The Health Consequences of Smok-*

*Toxemia develops mainly in very young (under sixteen) women, older women, and women with their first pregnancy. Women with diabetes, high blood pressure and chronic kidney disease are most susceptible, as are women who carry twins, or have too much fluid in their uteri.

ing, analyzes over 100,000 births showing that the infants of smoking mothers weigh an average of 6.1 ounces less than infants born to nonsmoking mothers. Low birth-weight newborns have more survival difficulties than fatter babies do. In the area of premature births, more than fifteen different studies have shown a significantly higher number of premature births in smoking mothers. In its 1973 report on smoking, the Public Health Service calculates that each year 5,000 babies are stillborn because of mothers' smoking habits.

Caffeine is in Coke, tea and coffee. It is toxic. It crosses the placenta and is implicated in birth defects. You may actually feel less fatigue if you cut out coffee, tea and Coke altogether. Try fruit juices instead.

Alcohol is a depressant drug which can lead to fetal alcohol syndrome. Even a brief overindulgence, especially in early pregnancy, can damage the fetus. (See p. 256.)

Your clothes should be loose and comfortable, warm in winter and cool in summer. Many women modify their own pants by piecing in an elastic stretch panel in the front. Simple unbelted smocks are useful as dresses. Large men's shirts are useful too. Maternity clothes in stores are often ugly and expensive. Ask your friends for any clothes they might have.

Get as much rest as you possibly can.

Your feelings about yourself

How will you feel about your changing, changed body?

_____

I was excited and delighted. I really got into eating well, caring for myself, getting enough sleep. I liked walking through the streets and having people notice my pregnancy.

_____

But many of us watch ourselves growing outward so quickly (when for years we hadn't grown too much in any direction) with mixed emotions. Our confusion is legitimate. We have been brought up to be mothers eventually. During pregnancy we change from the slim wraiths we were (supposed to be) to large-bellied women. We are making a visible transition from one role to another, moving from one myth to another. Some women try to hide their pregnancies from the world and even from themselves either by continuing for a time to wear the same clothes as before, though they no longer fit, or by wearing clothes so baggy that no one can see what is happening underneath.

You've got to find yourself beyond and in spite of these myths. It's possible to feel comfortable and happy with the changes you are going through.

Your feelings about your baby

If you are feeling really good, or ambivalent, or even

bad, the first movements you feel your baby make can be very beautiful and very moving.

I was lying on my stomach and felt—something, like someone lightly touching my deep insides. Then I just sat very still and for an alive moment felt the hugeness of having something living growing in me. Then I said, No, it's not possible, it's too early yet, and then I started to cry. . . . That one moment was my first body awareness of another living thing inside me.

And after the first movement—in the fourth or fifth month—you might wait days for another sign of quickening.* Then the movements will become frequent and familiar. The baby begins to feel real. You can feel from the outside the hard shape of your uterus.

If you are feeling angry, upset, or threatened by pregnancy, then your baby's movements serve to focus your anger. You might feel increasingly taken over.

Last night its kicking made me dizzy and gave me a terrible feeling of solitude. I wanted to tell it, Stop, stop, stop, let me alone. I want to lie still and whole and all single, catch my breath. But I have no control over this new part of my being, and this lack of control scares me. I felt as if I were rushing downhill at such a great speed that I'd never be able to stop.

Perhaps feeling the baby move for the first time will change you.

Sitting on a rock overlooking the domesite, trees growing right out of the rock. They cling and flourish on nothing. Images of the growing life inside me, also coming from nothing, getting nutrition from my body the way the tree does from the rock. . . . Occasionally I give it warmth, mostly when it moves. The more it moves, the more I like it. I also resent it an awful lot; I feel big, ugly and uncomfortable, and in spite of Len's protestations, I feel alone.

It's important again to say that even during the most positive pregnancies there may be moments, hours and days of depression, anxiety and confusion. These depressions are probably connected to all the underground anxieties you have in relation to your own mother and your childhood; doubts that come from our society's ignorance about pregnancy and childbirth; doubts you have about your own identity; economic problems; having too many children already; and problems in your relationship with your man.

*If you aren't sure when you conceived your baby, you can be almost certain that quickening occurs between the eighteenth to twentieth week of pregnancy, earlier in second pregnancies.

It seems that my feelings about my pregnancy, my body, the coming of the baby, were inextricably wound into my feelings, problems, hopes and fears for our relationship. . . . It's hard to separate which feelings were a result of my unhappiness about us (a lot of the bad feelings about my body arose because Bob showed very little interest in my enlarged, changing body); which ones were my own negative feelings about having a less functional body (I wanted to keep working and active, but my body was so cumbersome that I was always worn out and tired); and which ones were just moods caused by pregnancy.

We all have general fears too. Fear of the unknown, especially if it's a first pregnancy. No matter how much we do know about the physiological changes in our bodies, there's something incomprehensible about the beginnings of life. And by becoming pregnant we open ourselves to possible changes, complications and events that are risks in a sense. We become much more vulnerable.

I remember feeling overwhelmed by sad things I saw, and was overwhelmed by things that could happen to innocence. I'd wake in the night and think people were going to come in and take things, take the baby from me. I was beginning to be out of control. I was terribly afraid of chance. I've always been afraid of irrationality, of fate.

For two nights now my falling asleep has given rise to that old childhood dream image of falling down a deep, dark, square hole ever diminishing in size.

We fear that our babies will be deformed. Four percent of babies are born with diseases and one percent with physical malformations.* Some of us have dreams, fantasies and nightmares about deformity. These are normal, universal, international.

When I was about six months pregnant and Dick was starting school again, I was home alone, isolated for days at a time. My nightmares and daydreams started around then. Really terrible fears of the baby being deformed. All my life I've always been the good girl. I knew I wasn't really good. I knew I had bad thoughts, but I was never allowed to express them. So I thought that my baby's deformities would be the living proof of the ugliness and badness in me.

We fear our own death, the child's death.

*See p. 325, for the facts about diagnosis of birth defects in early pregnancy.

In fact, we do have to face the fact that some women miscarry, and some babies die. (See p. 323.) While it's difficult, threatening and sad to think of, we know it happens. Though it's not usually useful, and is also very hard, to prepare ourselves for death, it helps to know what has happened to some of us, so that if we or our friends experience such tragedy, we can in some way be acquainted with the event. This knowledge is a kind of preparation. It's vitally important to be able to reach out to friends when tragic things happen, and to help break down their feelings of isolation. It also helps us to know that we can and need to ask for help if such a thing happens to us.

I went into the hospital for the birth of my first child. . . . The child's lungs became infected and he died two days later. I never saw him. When I began to return to myself I found that despite all those times I had told myself that nothing could really happen, I had nothing but an empty belly. I don't know if we should be warned ahead of time to worry needlessly about something that happens to a very few women, but as one of those women, I definitely needed to feel some sense of sharing with others in the same position—not to cry over what had happened, but to work out how to face other people. That's the hardest part—nobody wants to deal with death, especially when your friends are at the childbearing age themselves and can't help being afraid of you for what you stand for. I found that my friends wanted me to pretend nothing had happened—that there had been no pregnancy even. I don't think it was just my particular friends—it's natural to want to avoid those things. And so my fantastic pregnancy, in which a lot of things went on in my head and body that helped me to change and get myself together, had to be buried. Even now, after a year, I can see their pain and fear for me as I start into my eighth month of pregnancy with my second child. I have to be the one who keeps them calm, and I especially must assure everyone that this one will be okay.

To deny that unpleasant things happen is to deny to ourselves and to our friends the reality and totality of our experience. Recognition of misfortune is an affirmation.

And then, we feel guilty about having fears. Don't they in some way suggest that as mothers we will be weak and inadequate? The myth is that we can't allow ourselves these depressions, because we are supposed to be strong, mature, maternal, accepting, loving all the time.

It's vital to us to realize that our feelings are legitimate. We should feel free and right in expressing them.

Men's feelings about you and your pregnancy

How will the man you are involved with feel about you? That depends on how you feel about yourself; on the relationship between you; on how he feels about himself, and what he feels his part to be in your pregnancy. If he feels like getting involved, it's a very good idea to prepare with him and learn together, especially if he lives with you after your baby is born. He might feel attracted to you and close, and fascinated by your growing body. Or, for reasons having to do with his own background and upbringing, with his hang-ups, he might feel repelled, confused and threatened by all your changes and your impending motherhood (his impending fatherhood). Or he might feel positive sometimes, negative sometimes. One man says:

Sometimes I thought you were very beautiful and your belly was beautiful. And sometimes you looked like a ridiculous pregnant insect. Your navel bulging out looked strange.

If you are having problems it's certainly best if you can talk together and realize that often your and his complex feelings are changeable. Talk can also lead to some deep, good questioning about the conventional ideas of beauty we are all brainwashed with. It's possible that he won't be able to talk about or to cope at all with the changes and responsibilities that your pregnancy implies. He might be jealous or resentful. Some men for many reasons seek out women other than the pregnant women they are living with, whether they're married or unmarried. Some men, while not actually leaving you, may withdraw from you emotionally at this crucial time.

If you are single and get involved with men during your pregnancy, these men will all have different kinds of attitudes toward you as a person, as a pregnant woman, and as a sexual being.

Intercourse

What about making love during pregnancy? There are two things to talk about: medical fact and fiction, and your own feelings.

MEDICAL FACT AND FICTION. Traditionally, doctors have asked that we abstain from intercourse for four to six weeks before giving birth and up to six weeks after: altogether we were told to abstain for three months. According to a fairly recent Siecus study guide, this abstention was based on four unproven beliefs: (1) the thrusts of the penis against the cervix induce labor; (2) the uterine contractions of orgasm induce labor; (3) membranes may rupture, leading to infection; and (4) the sex act is physically uncomfortable.

It's tempting here to wonder how uncomfortable doctors are with the idea that we can be sexually active and potential mothers at the same time (don't mix sex with motherhood). These unscientific, cautious beliefs can deny us our sexuality and prevent us from maintaining a closeness to the man we're involved with when that closeness is much needed, before and after our child's birth.

Some of you will get strong uterine contractions when you make love or when you masturbate. These contractions are valuable and useful. They strengthen the uterine muscles. You know when they happen. Your uterus becomes harder. If you lie quietly and relax, they will nearly always die down. Labor will start only if it's time. (There is a substance in a man's semen, called prostaglandin, and possibly a like substance created by a woman's orgasm, which may induce labor a little earlier than it might ordinarily occur.)

Intercourse can be a good exercise for the muscles of the pelvic floor. Also note how completely you can relax after making love. It's helpful to know how it feels to relax, because later, during labor contractions, that kind of complete relaxation can be useful.

Toward the end of pregnancy, when the baby's head has moved down, an erect penis can cause discomfort, for there's not a lot of room in there.

Later in your pregnancy the "traditional" position (man on top) can be uncomfortable. The pressure on your abdomen makes you feel that you're going to pop, and pressure on your breasts causes them to leak. Pillows under your back can make you more comfortable. But at no time should the man's whole weight rest on you, nor should great pressure be put upon your uterus. You can use other positions more happily: you can be on top, or he behind you. Sheila Kitzinger says men and women should make love "with emphasis upon a careful tenderness" (*The Experience of Childbirth*, Copyright © 1962, 1967, 1978 by Sheila Kitzinger. Published by Taplinger Publishing Company, Inc., New York.

What are the problems? Masters and Johnson have some evidence that the contractions of orgasm could set off labor, but the women in their study were close to term anyway. (In some cultures women ready to go into labor make love to induce labor.) The SIECUS pamphlet concludes that intercourse toward the end of preg-

nancy is usually not dangerous. But you should not make love at any time during your pregnancy (1) if you have vaginal or abdominal pain, (2) if you have any uterine bleeding, (3) if your membranes have already ruptured (then there *is* danger of infection), or (4) if you have been warned or think that miscarriage might occur. That's important for you psychologically, so if a miscarriage should occur, you won't consider yourself responsible. And throughout your pregnancy, be aware that during oral-genital contact, air blown into your vagina may be dangerous, causing air embolism.

All these remarks refer to unusual circumstances. It's useful to be aware of them, for our main worries are that we will harm the baby in some (unknown) way. The truth is that intercourse during pregnancy is almost always harmless. (See Chapter 15, "Postpartum," for intercourse after pregnancy.)

YOUR FEELINGS ABOUT MAKING LOVE. You'll each have many different feelings about making love.

I wanted to make love more than ever.

I remember feeling very sexy. We were trying all these different positions. Now that we were having a baby, I felt a lot looser, a lot freer. I used to feel uptight about sex for its own sake, but when I was pregnant I felt a lot freer.

I felt very ambivalent about making love. I had miscarried several times. I wanted to make love and I was scared to make love. As a single woman it was hard to find men who found me attractive with my belly so big. I had no sexual contact at all the last two months.

Some of you might have times when you really turn inward, when you won't want or be able to "give" to a man.

Masters and Johnson report an increase in sexual desire during the second trimester and a decrease during the third.

If you are living with a group of people

It's a good idea to think about how you want them to relate to your child. In an ideal situation most everyone wants to help care for her/him. Some communities exist that are themselves large extended families. But many groups are composed of people who will have very different commitments to your child. Often people don't want to have anything much to do with taking care of children. They either don't want to or don't feel ready to. Try to figure out just what you are expecting of each person and whether your expectations are realistic. Talk to each person if you can and find out how s/he feels about your coming child. Do it early.

You can't assume that people will automatically help on their own and know you need help. Also, with people who don't have children you have to be explicit and tell them what to do. I don't think it's a good thing to have a lot of people take care of the baby at first, but I was glad that people helped me out. Also find out how they feel about you. Having chosen these people as your new family, you might expect to be cared for and nurtured, and you might find that people won't be able to meet your increased needs.

Third Trimester
(Twenty-seventh to Thirty-eighth Week)

Physical changes
Your uterus is becoming very large. It feels hard when you touch it.

I remember my friends' surprise when they put their hands on my belly to feel it. They expected it to be soft and somehow jellylike and were amazed at its hardness and bulk.

It's a strong muscular container. You can feel and see the movements of your fetus from the outside now too, as it changes position, turns somersaults, hiccups. Sometimes it puts pressure on your bladder, which makes you feel that you need to urinate even when you don't, and which can hurt a little, or sometimes a lot, for very brief periods. Sometimes, toward the very end of pregnancy, it puts pressure on the nerves at the top of your legs, which can be painful too.

Your baby will be lying in a particular position, sometimes head down, back to your front, sometimes lying crossways. It moves around often. Your doctor can help you discover which position the baby is in.

Sometimes your baby lies still. It's known that babies sleep in utero. If you don't feel movement for three to four days and you're wondering, call your doctor if you can and ask whether s/he thinks it's a good idea to check the fetal heartbeat. Usually these are periods of "rest" for the baby and can last several days.

You will feel your uterus tighten every now and then. These are painless contractions called Braxton-Hicks contractions. They are believed to strengthen uterine muscles, preparing them for eventual labor. (See p. 270.)

It becomes increasingly uncomfortable for you to lie on your stomach. You might experience shortness of breath. There's pressure on your lungs from your uterus,

and your diaphragm may be moved up as much as an inch. Even so, because your thoracic (chest) cage widens, you breathe in more air when you are pregnant than when you are not. Sometimes when you lie down you might not be able to breathe well for a moment. Prop yourself up with pillows and the pressure on your diaphragm will be lessened.

The peak load on your heart occurs in about the thirtieth week. After that the heart doesn't have to work so hard, usually, until delivery.

You are still gaining weight. If you have hemorrhoids or varicose veins, try to avoid standing up for long periods of time, and when you sit or lie down, be sure your feet are raised.

Your stomach is pushed up by your uterus and flattened. Indigestion is common. Eat small amounts. Don't take mineral oil—it causes you to excrete necessary vitamins. Avoid indigestion remedies that contain sodium.

If you have insomnia, or trouble sleeping because the baby moving around in you makes you uncomfortable, take walks, hot baths, or some wine at bedtime. Avoid sleeping pills.

Your navel will probably be pushed out.

Since your body has gotten heavier, you'll tend to walk differently for balance, often leaning back to counteract a heavier front. This can cause backaches, for which there are exercises. Your pelvic joints are also much more separated.

At about four to two weeks before birth, and sometimes as early as the seventh month, the baby's head settles into your pelvis. This is called "lightening," or "dropping" or "engagement." It takes pressure off your stomach. Some women do feel much lighter. And if you have been having trouble breathing, pressure is now off your diaphragm. This "dropping" can cause constipation; your bowels are more obstructed than they were.

As for water retention, an average pregnant woman retains from six and a half to thirteen pints of liquid, half of this in the last ten weeks. Ankle swelling is common.

Your feelings about yourself and your pregnancy

I had a feeling of waiting at the end, of nothing else being terrifically important.

I thought it would never end. I was enormous. I couldn't bend over and wash my feet. And it was incredibly hot.

At the end I started to feel it was too long. Dick took pictures of me during the eighth month. I saw my face as faraway and sad.

I had insomnia. I couldn't get comfortable. I couldn't sleep, he'd kick so much.

I wonder what it looks like. How fantastic that it only has to travel one and a half feet down to get born.

My kid is dancing inside under my heart.

The relationship of mother carrying child is most beautiful and simplest.
I pity a baby who must come out of the womb.

Fairly confidently and calmly awaiting the baby—quite set on a home delivery. Doctor said Thursday I was already dilated two and a half centimeters, so it must be getting close. Getting a bit anxious, listening to every Braxton-Hicks contraction, awaiting with hope, and fear too, its change into the real thing.

I feel exultant and tired and rich inside. My belly is large, and last night the baby beat around inside it like a wild tempest. I thought the time had come and was panicked and nauseated, then very excited. I woke Gene up. Then at five I fell asleep. Meanwhile I move in slow motion and wait.

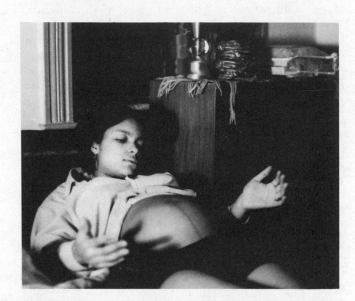

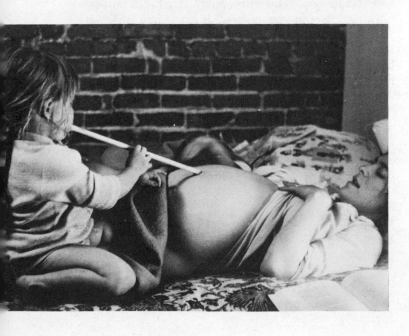

CHAPTER 14
PREPARATION FOR CHILDBIRTH

In our own ways, we all prepare for our baby's birth. We think about the hospital we'll be using or whether we'll use a hospital at all. We choose names for our baby-to-be, and we might start wondering where our baby will sleep or what s/he will wear after s/he's born. Even if we haven't had a baby before, most of us have heard or read something about labor and delivery, so we may spend some time imagining how it will be. If our expectations are based on scary stories or on our own unhappy past experiences, we may be afraid of labor and delivery. We may fear that labor will be hard for us to endure; we may find ourselves wishing that we didn't have to go through it. Our fear of pain remains a central issue.

Much of our fear comes from not knowing what the coming labor will be like for us, or from remembering our last labor, in which we felt out of control and alone.

Giving birth does not have to be lonely and frightening. In fact, preparation for childbirth means finding ways to make childbirth less frightening and more understandable, and finding someone to share the entire birth experience with us. We can prepare ourselves by attending childbirth classes, which are offered free in many hospitals and clinics or for a fee by private organizations. We can teach one another and read some of the books mentioned in the bibliography on page 313. Usually it is a good idea both to read and to attend classes.

Through such preparation we learn what labor and delivery are really like; what will happen to our bodies physically during labor; what goes on in the maternity ward of a hospital; and what we can do to make our birth experience a good one. We will learn some simple breathing exercises to help us get through even the most intense parts of labor, and we will learn how to avoid the drugs and instruments, so commonly used in labor and delivery, which have risks that might affect our babies and ourselves. Most important, by preparing ourselves for childbirth we will be giving ourselves more control over our experience. We will be able to make educated choices about the way we want to deliver our babies. We will understand why and how our labor is progressing, and we will be able to experience the full excitement and joy that are part of the birth of a baby.

If you don't prepare for childbirth you probably won't be able to resist the hospital routine of medication and interventions. If you have never thought about preparation before, we hope you will read this chapter as a description of a way to make an important choice in your life as a woman. If you have been considering preparation, we hope the chapter will be a useful overview.

The concept of preparation for labor and delivery was made popular in Europe and the United States by two obstetricians. In 1932 Dr. Grantly Dick-Read, an Englishman, first introduced a method of concentrated relaxation during labor with the publication of his book *Childbirth Without Fear*, which is still available in book stores today in a revised and updated American edition. Dick-Read learned from watching his patients that fear causes tension, and tension adds to pain. His approach was to try to eliminate the fear of labor through education and the teaching of relaxation and exercise techniques. A French doctor, Fernand Lamaze, offered a different idea, which he learned in Russia, where he saw large numbers of women laboring with what appeared to be no pain at all. He called his technique the "psychoprophylactic method for childbirth" (*psycho*—mind, *prophylactic*—prevention). Lamaze asked his patients to respond actively to labor contractions with a set of pre-learned breathing exercises. As the intensity of the contractions increased, so did the woman's rate of breathing. The laboring woman's whole posture and attitude changed. She was no longer flat on her back, pitied by all onlookers; now she was active, altering her positions and breathing patterns according to the progress of her labor. The onlookers cheered. Marjorie Karmel, who had her first baby in Paris with Dr. Lamaze, introduced the Lamaze method to the United States with her book, *Thank You, Dr. Lamaze*, published first in 1959. Now childbirth preparation classes are available in every part of the United States.

As women giving birth, we are connected through time and space to all other women who have ever given birth. Rather than being ordinary, it is a profound experience, worthy of respect. That the process of labor and delivery is universal to all mothers, everywhere and at all times, dignifies our experience even further.

When we are going to have a baby we usually hope and even expect that the people close to us will understand the significance of the event and will give us support. We also tend to expect this from those whose professional help we seek; we look to them for answers to our questions and for reassurance if we need it. Under the best of circumstances our family, friends, relatives and workplace acquaintances come through for us, even though their efforts may not be perfect. But with doctors, nurses and clinic staff we are likely to be disappointed in our expectations for personal support and reassurance. We may at first just feel insignificant as we wait and wait to be seen by the doctor; then we may feel silly for asking questions which he or she brushes aside or answers sketchily. We may even be made to feel that we are downright annoying to the doctor. Inside ourselves we may feel angry and yet powerless to do anything about what we know to be an affront to our dignity. There are many of us who have experienced these feelings of disappointment and anger, although individually we may feel isolated. What we want from the obstetrician is thorough prenatal care, and competent technical assistance if we really need it at the time of delivery. Moreover, we would like to include the doctor as an ally who respects our entire birth process. This, however, is rarely possible.

If it were only that doctors were too busy to respond to us with the respect we deserve, we might criticize them for taking on more patients than they should, putting economic considerations before human ones. However, it is more than just economics. Most doctors have been taught throughout their entire medical education to see patients as a class rather than as individual people with special needs. They have learned to treat us paternally; they have been taught that we want them to take care of us, and we as patients often play into that dependent role. The strength and anger that we may feel have no opportunity for expression in the usual doctor-patient relationship. We, as pregnant women, are expected to put ourselves in the doctor's hands, and he or she expects to take control of our birth experience.

In actuality the doctor or midwife should have very little part to play in a normal delivery. S/he checks the progress of labor and how the baby's heart is responding to it; looks to see if we have entered second stage (explained later) and can thus begin to push our baby out; and helps to ease our baby out during the birth. After birth the baby sometimes needs a little encouragement to take the first breath or needs to have mucus drained from his or her nose and mouth, but usually these procedures are taken care of by a nurse. Seldom is a baby born to an unanesthetized mother in as much need of medical assistance as a baby born to a mother who has had medication in labor.

What really worries us is that, despite the whole childbirth education movement over the last twenty years, obstetricians and anesthesiologists intervene more and more in our birth experience. The reasons for this may be:

1. Doctors have their own myths about how painful labor is, and they see it as an ordeal from which they can rescue us. (Most of them are men, who of course have never experienced childbirth themselves.)

2. Doctors are trained to think in terms of complications. They see each one of us as potentially a "high-risk" case needing emergency care. Normal births are seen as "boring"; complicated births are considered "challenging."

3. In medicine, the American worship of technology is carried to an extreme. Few doctors want to take the chance that the patient might be deprived or even harmed if they don't use the latest drug or machine.

4. Doctors are very afraid of being accused of malpractice. They want to use the latest drugs and instruments so that they can prove, if necessary, that they gave the patient "the very best care available."

5. Hospitals are understaffed and doctors are overloaded, which makes it impossible for each patient to be given the time and personal attention she deserves. So there is a tendency to treat all laboring women alike, using routine procedures and monitoring machines to take the place of continuous personal supervision.

We are not ungrateful for the medical advances that have saved many lives. We simply don't want our childbirth experience *unnecessarily* mechanized and interfered with. At least 90 percent of us will have perfectly normal, healthy deliveries if our labors are not in some way tampered with by the doctor.

As we have said throughout this book, the emphasis in medicine is almost always placed on making medical intervention more reliable rather than on making medical intervention unnecessary. Already in most big teaching centers, doctors and staff think in terms of intervention from beginning to end and plan for complications as the "normal" course of events. Many prenatal childbirth classes, especially those offered by hospitals, are in fact preparing women to accept drugs and instruments as a regular part of a prepared childbirth.

In some of the largest and richest maternity hospitals, labor rooms are full of women lying or sitting still, with tubes and wires coming out of their vaginas connected to fetal monitors attached to their unborn babies scalps; tubes coming out of their backs connected to epidural anesthesia units; and tubes coming out of their arms connected to an intravenous solution unit, which usually contains a drug to speed up their labor. Each of these procedures has merit if it is used judiciously and when there is a real medical necessity, but each carries with it a number of serious potential risks. (For a detailed discussion, see "Drugs and Obstetrical Interventions," p. 278.) Hospitals are not proven safe for normal births.

If we don't like to picture ourselves wired up that way in labor, if we think we would rather try having our babies in a simple, dignified manner, we will probably have to fight hospital routines and doctors' orders to get what we want. But even so, if we have our baby in a hospital we must be prepared for the fact that the doctor is ultimately in control. Medical training, pressures from the hospital to use the latest equipment, the need to learn or practice a new technique, their desire to use us as data for their research, or simply timing and convenience often influence our doctors to intervene in our labors when intervention may be both risky and unnecessary. If we as consumers of health care do not want the medical industry to control our childbirth experience, now is the time to make our ideas heard. Here are four proposals we can make:

1. Education, about all aspects of sexuality and reproduction, starting in elementary school, so that people can approach labor and delivery with as many facts and as few superstitions as possible.
2. More women in medicine, as obstetricians and as midwives, so that "obstetric" can regain its original meaning, which is "a female who stands near."
3. More home deliveries, which if funded and supported, could be made safe and popular. Then there would be some competition for the big maternity hospitals, and competition is the consumer's best weapon.
4. Family-centered maternity centers which are not parts of hospitals, which would be community clinics where women could have their babies in comfort and safety, knowing that emergency equipment is available if the need should arise. High-risk cases would be screened prenatally and sent to special high-risk hospitals.

Since, for the time being, most women in the United States are going to be having their babies in hospitals that are high-risk oriented, we are going to spend a good deal of this chapter talking about what that experience is like and how to handle it. However, there are growing numbers of women who don't want to have to fight the hospital and the doctor just to have a normal, untampered-with childbirth. Many women are choosing to have their babies at home. Whichever you choose, home or hospital, you owe it to yourself and to your baby to learn as much as you can about the process of labor and the means of preparing for it.

HOME BIRTH

Home birth offers us the opportunity to labor in familiar surroundings; to choose our own attendants; to follow rituals and actions which soothe and encourage us. At home we avoid the annoying, and sometimes dangerous, hospital routines. At home, birth is a family event, with the father, grandparents, older children and friends all welcome to share the wonder of birth and greet the new baby. Once the baby is born, we can relax in our own way, eat the food we like, and get to know our new baby without regard for an institution's schedules. (See also p. 367.)

We are also concerned with the safety of home birth. The outcome of childbirth is determined primarily by the care we give ourselves and the training of our birth attendant rather than by the place of birth. We should be screened prenatally for contraindications to home birth (toxemia, kidney disease, severe anemia, heart disease, hypertension, diabetes, drug addiction, severe infection, cephalo-pelvic disproportion (pelvis too small for baby), abnormal presentations, multiple births, Rh sensitization, placenta previa). However, this screening should not be confused with or interpreted as a substitute for the care we give ourselves throughout pregnancy. If genuine high-risk conditions are identified, then we should plan for the birth to take place in facilities equipped to deal with possible complications. Most birth attendants will not agree to attend a woman at home who has any of these conditions.

Once you've decided to have your baby at home, preventing complications and handling unexpected problems is your next concern. The best single preventive is to eat a sufficient quantity of high-quality food (see pp. 252–256). However, exercise, general life-style, and attitudes also play an integral part.

Most complications of childbirth are minor and can be handled without difficulty by an attendant experienced in normal births at home. Training to attend home births includes: an apprenticeship with an experienced home birth attendant; a complete understanding of all the processes of normal conception, pregnancy, labor, delivery and postpartum in the mother's body; learning to recognize when things are wrong with either mother or baby. In addition, competence in resuscitation of newborns and control of maternal hemorrhage is essential. Even in the cases of more serious complications, however, there is almost always enough time to get more specialized help. The number of cases where hospital care unexpectedly becomes necessary instantaneously is extremely small. A matched, controlled study

A home delivery

by Mehl et al., comparing the outcomes of 1000 home births vs. 1000 hospital births, found no significant difference in maternal or infant mortality or morbidity.

While hospital emergency rooms are required by law to accept anyone who appears for emergency care, both parents and birth attendants feel more comfortable knowing that they have made arrangements for such an emergency transfer in case it becomes necessary. Sometimes parents are asked to make their own backup arrangements.

Birth attendants have differing criteria for transferring a birth to the hospital. Their decisions may vary depending on: the nature of the problem; their training; the available equipment; their agreements with supporting physicians; and the nature of the emergency backup facility as well as its distance from the birth.

In this country the woman who wants to give birth at home has to take a great deal of initiative. The first hurdle is to find a doctor or midwife willing to help screen for any high-risk factors and then to supply emergency backup if no contraindications to home birth are present. Most doctors oppose home birth outright. They may frighten you with horrible tales of what "might" happen without discussing ways of making home birth safe. Pre-screening for risks, emergency backups, and the excellent statistics from Europe and our own Kentucky Frontier Nursing Service will be ignored.* Behind this smoke screen lie other, probably unspoken, factors: it is inconvenient for doctors; it is frightening for them to be away from all their hospital equipment; it is psychologically threatening for them to be the invited guest in your home, where you set the tone and they are not in complete control. For midwives, legality and medical backup are added issues.

Once you find one, you can expect the doctor to charge $0 to $900, depending on local rates and his/her devotion to the idea of home birth. Most insurance policies will pay all or part of a doctor's fee regardless of where the birth takes place, but not the midwife's.

There is still more to be done. Here is what you have to do though there is great variation:

The room should be clean.

The bed should be made up with clean sheets. Then cover it with a rubber sheet (a clean shower curtain liner is fine). Put on a second set of clean sheets. After the birth, simply peel off everything from the rubber up and have a nice clean bed to settle into.

The baby will need receiving blankets, shirts, nighties, diapers. A large basket, box, or drawer is fine to put the baby in.

Pain is eased by the relaxation of being at home, but it does not disappear, and labor is hard work. But discomfort is bearable with the support of friends and loved ones. Breathing techniques and comfort-

*Founded in 1925, Frontier Nursing Service provides medical care to a 1,000-square-mile territory.

ing rituals are also useful. Most women find courses in preparation for childbirth at home very helpful.

Emergency plans include: phone number and location of hospital; stand-by transportation; and person to stay with older children if you have to leave.

Reading is important. The better informed you are, the better you can make informed decisions. However, talking with other parents who have given birth at home may be even more important.

Companions are your choice: the baby's father, friends, relatives, older children, whoever you want. You can give them useful tasks such as preparing food, answering the phone, taking care of older children, taking pictures, chanting, making music, preserving silence, leading prayer, celebrating a new life. However, you may prefer just one or two loved persons at your side.

It was a really beautiful thing to do—not only to be freed from the atmosphere and personnel of the hospital (and who knows what it means for a newborn to see wood walls and carpeted floor, to smell real human smells, to feel wool and cotton and flannel clothes instead of starchy, white, deodorized . . .) but also to know that my body and her body knew what to do, and probably did it better than any doctors could. She was crying before the push that sent her into the world had faded, and was wide awake from the start.

Now that it's over I can think of the risks we took—being an hour and a half from the hospital on a cold night if we needed help—and I can get angry again at the system and the attitudes that forced me to choose this risk. But still, the pride, the joy, the beauty, the wonder of it all overshadow the anger and fear. I hope lots more women do this—I feel strangely stronger (in terms of self, not physically) than ever before.

WHAT IS LABOR?

Labor and delivery are named and understood differently by mothers and by medical people. We present a simplified technical description of the process through which the baby moves from the mother's uterus to the outside world. Later (pp. 289–295) we describe a woman's lived experience of giving birth.

Delivery comes only after the *effacement* (thinning) and *dilation* (opening up) of the *cervix* (neck of the uterus). Effacement is measured in percentages. For example, at one of the last prenatal examinations your doctor might say that you are already 80 percent effaced.

That means that the neck of your uterus is almost totally thinned out or "taken up." Dilation is the term used to refer to the size of the round opening of the cervix, which is exposing more and more of the baby's head. It is measured in centimeters, or sometimes in finger widths. When the cervix is ten centimeters, or five fingers, open, the first stage of labor is over and the baby is ready to come down the birth canal to be born.

Many women start to dilate even before labor begins. All through your pregnancy you'll probably feel occasional tightenings of your uterus. Sometimes these preliminary contractions are strong enough to make you catch your breath, but they are rarely painful. Although these so-called Braxton-Hicks contractions are painless, they aren't useless. Each contraction is exercising the uterus, getting it ready to function with utmost efficiency during actual labor. Also, these pre-labor contractions are working to start the effacement and dilation of the cervix. It is not unusual for a woman to begin labor already 90 percent effaced and one or two centimeters dilated.

Which brings us to the question, when does labor really begin? There is no general answer. The only guide is that when labor finally does really get under way, one will feel contractions that are stronger and more regular than Braxton-Hicks contractions. They will begin with a gradual tightening of the uterine muscles and slowly rise in intensity. Then a peak will be reached, and the tightening will slowly relax. It reminds some women of the rising, breaking, and falling of waves on the shore. The first contractions are usually not too uncomfortable; they last anywhere from forty-five seconds to a minute. Then when the contraction is over, you feel nothing until the next contraction begins. What is happening is that the lengthwise muscles of the uterus are involuntarily working to pull open the circular muscles around the cervix. This first stage of labor may take anywhere from two to twenty-four hours, or more, depending on the size of the baby, the position in which the baby is lying, the size of the mother's pelvic area, and the behavior of the uterus. The average length for first-stage labor in a mother who is having her first baby (primipara) is twelve hours. But, remember, not one of us is average.

The entire birth process is divided into three stages.

FIRST-STAGE LABOR is itself split into three categories: *early, late,* and *transition.* Again, for each of us the experience of these stages will be very different. But it is usually the case that early first-stage labor is easily handled, sometimes without any discomfort. Late first-stage labor occurs when the cervix is opening from five to eight centimeters. This segment of labor is often shorter in duration and more intense in feeling than early first-stage. Most prepared women rely on a mixture of deep- and shallow-breathing techniques—which are described later—to overcome the discomfort of these contractions. After eight centimeters comes the hardest and the shortest part of your labor. It is called transition, and it

is the time just before the cervix opens to a full ten centimeters. These contractions are usually very discouraging, the part of labor that many of us felt was painful. This stage rarely lasts for one hour, or more than fifteen contractions (see p. 290).

A good analogy to this first stage of labor is trying to pull on a turtleneck sweater. At first your head fits easily. Then, as you get closer to the neck opening, it becomes harder to push your head out. You tug at it and stretch it, and finally your head comes through. Similarly, the uterus is stretching and pulling open the cervix, until finally, when the cervix opens to its limit, the delivery of the baby begins. This is called second-stage labor.

SECOND-STAGE LABOR begins when the cervix is completely dilated and the baby's head (or presenting part) moves into the birth canal; it ends when the baby is born. It is during this stage that many women will experience a tremendous force inside their bodies. If a woman has learned to bear down correctly, she can help to push her baby down and out at this point. Doctors very frequently anesthetize women for the second stage of labor, possibly because a woman pushing during this phase of labor looks as if she is in great pain. However, with preparation and encouragement, second-stage labor is joyful, not painful, to the overwhelming majority of women. Many women have described second-stage as "the fun part," since it is at this point that we can actually work with our contractions and use all our strength for our baby's benefit.

Another reason for choosing second-stage to anesthetize a laboring woman is that the doctor may want her desensitized so that s/he can perform interventions to speed up the delivery. Once again, we believe that second-stage labor should be allowed to take its normal course, usually lasting from one half hour to two hours,

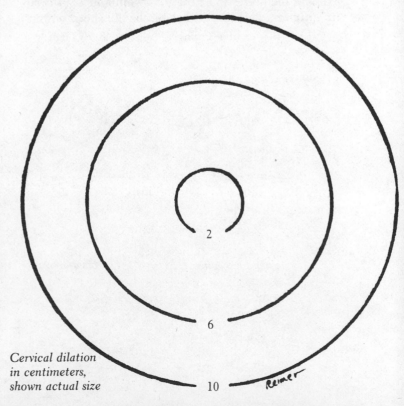

Cervical dilation in centimeters, shown actual size

without unnecessary intervention. If a mother is unanesthetized and prepared, she will know when to push and how long to push, without anyone telling her.

The birth of the baby under normal circumstances is gradual—head first, then shoulders, then body. With each of the last few contractions a new part emerges. The baby may take a breath and cry before being completely born, especially if the mother has not been anesthetized. Almost all drugs given to the mother during labor reach the baby *in utero*, and a drugged baby usually takes longer to breathe than one who has not been drugged. The less medication the mother takes during labor, the better off the baby will be at and immediately after delivery.

At this point the baby will still be attached to the mother by the umbilical cord, which shouldn't be clipped until all the blood has emptied from it into the baby's system, except if there is an emergency. The umbilical cord is attached at one end to the baby's navel, and at the other end to the placenta.

THIRD-STAGE LABOR is the delivery of the placenta, the life-supplying organ that has kept the baby healthy and nourished during the first nine months of life. There may be one or two more contractions before the placenta is released. Third-stage may take no more than a few minutes, or it may take half an hour. After its birth, the placenta must be examined by the doctor to make sure it is intact; if a piece of it is left in the uterus, the mother may subsequently experience hemorrhage due to the blood vessels torn by the only partial removal of the placenta.

Less Usual Presentations

In the above discussion we have assumed the baby's position in the uterus to be the most common—*left occipito anterior*. This means that the baby is head down in the uterus, lying on the left side, with the occiput, or back part of the skull, toward the mother's front. It is the most efficient way for a baby to slip past the pubic bone and into the birth canal. A baby in this position faces the floor at birth if the mother is lying flat on the delivery table.

Another position is head first but faced the opposite way, with the baby's face toward the mother's front. This is called *posterior presentation*. It often means a more tedious and more uncomfortable labor, since the baby will try to turn around during first-stage labor in order to be born in the more favorable way, facing the mother's back. This type of presentation usually means that the mother will experience labor pains in her back, and she should have this explained to her beforehand so she can prepare herself.

Some babies are born buttocks down or feet first, in what is called *breech presentation*. This, too, can cause a longer labor, with contractions felt in your back. A danger in breech birth is that the baby will take its first breath as soon as its bottom is born, while the head is still inside the birth canal. To avoid this the baby's emerging body can be wrapped in a warm, clean blanket to keep the colder air from shocking her or him into a breathful of mucus. Also, the attendant may insert a finger into the birth canal to clear a passageway for air to reach the baby's face. These days, cesareans are too often (unnecessarily) performed with breech babies (see p. 287).

Some Signs of Abnormal Labor and Delivery

If complications should arise during labor, our bodies will usually give us some warnings. It is, of course, of vital importance that we be aware of them and make our doctor aware of them. A woman who is awake and not medicated will have a much clearer sense of what is going on than one who is anesthetized.

Before labor begins   *Early labor*

Transition: just before the baby's head enters the birth canal   *The baby's head before crowning*

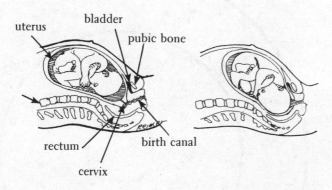

uterus
bladder
pubic bone
birth canal
rectum
cervix

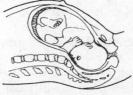

The head crowning   *The head emerging*

The third stage of labor: the placenta coming loose and about to emerge   *The pelvis after delivery*

placenta

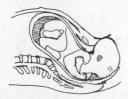  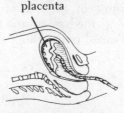 

Here are a few signals that should warn you to notify your doctor immediately:

A CONTINUOUS AND SEVERE LOWER ABDOMINAL PAIN, OFTEN ACCOMPANIED BY UTERINE TENDERNESS. This is different from the pain of normal labor contractions, which comes on with increasing intensity and then gradually disappears completely until the next contraction. Also, during normal contractions the uterus and entire abdomen become very hard and distended.

DISCONTINUANCE OF GOOD, STRONG CONTRACTIONS DURING FIRST-STAGE LABOR. Labor contractions usually get more and more intense and are spaced closer and closer together as you approach second-stage. When second-stage labor is reached, however, contractions come less frequently again, though they do not cease to be effective.

EXCESSIVE VAGINAL BLEEDING. There are a number of reasons for this, such as cervical laceration, placenta abruptio (when the placenta becomes detached from the uterus), delivery before the cervix is fully dilated. It is not uncommon, however, to have a bloody mucous discharge during transition, especially if the cervix is opening up very quickly.

ABNORMALITY IN FETAL HEARTBEAT. This condition is a sign that the baby may be in trouble. Fetal heartbeat should be checked regularly throughout labor. If an abnormality is picked up, the mother ought to be turned on her left side to take the pressure off her major blood vessels, which are midline and slightly to the right. Immediate delivery may be advised in some instances. For safety and comfort a mother might want to be on her side during much of her labor. (See "Positions for Labor and Delivery," p. 277.)

ABNORMALLY SLOW DILATION OF THE CERVIX. If contractions are severe and still the cervix is not dilating with regularity, then the dysfunctional contractions may be creating undue stress on the fetus, the mother, or both. This is a particularly hard condition to diagnose, since pain is subjective and many labors last much longer than others. In this case, use of a monitor to measure the intensity of contractions might be indicated.

AN ABNORMAL PRESENTATION OR PROLAPSE OF CORD, PLACENTA, OR EXTREMITY. If any of these occurs, an experienced obstetrician or midwife must decide if a caesarean is required (see p. 287). Prolapsed cord and placenta previa (placenta first instead of baby first) generally call for a caesarean section.

ANY ADVERSE CHANGE IN CONDITION OF MOTHER OR BABY. If the pattern of heartbeat and/or blood pressure changes; if the woman develops a fever; or if some other difficulty arises, the presence of an experienced doctor or midwife is essential to interpret the signs. (See "Cesarean Section," p. 287.)

Premature Labor and Delivery

A premature baby is one who is born in or before the thirty-seventh week of pregnancy. Until recently a baby of five and one-half pounds or less was considered premature, but now doctors are more concerned with the maturity and functional development of the baby than with his or her birth weight. Seventy percent of deaths of newborn babies in the United States are due to low birth weight. This is a tragedy, since much prematurity can be prevented by good nutrition (see Chapter 13), competent prenatal medical care, and adequate birth control for those who may be unable to carry a fetus to term (e.g., young teenagers whose bodies are not yet developed enough).*

There is little known about the cause of prematurity in nearly half the cases. Poor health, inadequate nutrition, and heavy smoking all increase one's chances of having a premature delivery. Some specific causes of premature labor are infectious diseases (such as syphilis), toxemia of pregnancy, diabetes, thyroid disturbances, fetal abnormalities, placental abnormalities (placenta previa, abruptio placenta, etc.) and multiple pregnancies. Some of these problems can themselves be avoided through adequate health care and nutrition. Statistics show that poorer women receive poorer prenatal care and thus are more likely to deliver prematurely than middle-class women, as are young teens.

Premature labor proceeds as does normal, full-term labor, although it may be a little slower owing to weaker contractions. *Premature babies are extremely susceptible to the dangerous side effects of the drugs used during labor,* so if you are prepared to handle labor without drugs you will be doing your premature baby a great service.

There is often much more anxiety involved in a premature labor, since the mother may be wondering if her baby will survive. Most premature babies who do not live are victims of hyaline membrane disease.† This is a lung disease which frequently affects premature babies and, less often, those delivered by cesarean section. Apparently a good, strong labor is good for the baby. In general, the premature infant is much more susceptible to all infections.

The smaller and more feeble the baby, the more need there is for immediate care. Premature infants are placed in oxygen-, temperature-, and humidity-con-

*DHEW Publication (NIH), No. 77-1079 (1977).

†"Hyaline membrane disease is a syndrome of neonatal respiratory distress in which the alveoli and the alveolar ducts are filled with a sticky exudate, a hyaline material, which prevents aeration" (*ibid.*, p. 532). It is seen mostly in premature babies and those delivered by cesarean section. There is recent evidence to suggest that hyaline membrane disease may be preventable before birth.

trolled incubators, and they must be constantly watched and carefully protected from every possible source of infection, since infection epidemics are common hospital problems. Often parents are not even allowed to touch their own baby until his or her chances of survival are clear. This usually adds to the already high level of anxiety the parents may feel.*

Feeding the premature infant may be a problem because of the baby's underdeveloped intestinal tract. A study by V. Crosse and others showed that "premature infants fed human milk not only had the lowest incidence of major infection and mortality during the hospital stay but also proved free from infection after leaving the hospital when breast-fed at home."† A mother can pump her own colostrum and milk with an electric or hand breast pump, and this milk can be supplied to her infant in the nursery incubator. Human colostrum, the liquid that fills the mother's breasts before her milk comes in, is so full of antibodies to fight the very infections to which the premature infant might succumb that it seems foolish not to insist that colostrum be an integral part of the premature baby's diet.

Another important reason to feed the premature infant breast milk is the mother's need for contact with her newborn. The birth of a premature baby comes usually before the mother has prepared herself psychologically for delivery and motherhood. Guilt feelings and emotional uncertainty are an almost inevitable aspect of prematurity. This anxiety is normal and healthy. A recent study indicates that mothers who were open in their expression of anxiety for their premature babies were better able to cope with mothering.‡ The hospital staff, nurses and doctors alike, should be aware of this and should encourage the mother and father to visit their baby, hold the baby and even feed it whenever possible. If the mother feels that it is her milk that is sustaining the infant and her efforts that are helping the baby to grow stronger, then she will begin the postpartum period with a much stronger and more confident attitude.

HOW TO PREPARE FOR CHILDBIRTH

There are three basic aspects of a prepared childbirth: education, companionship and techniques. We have already spoken about the physical process of labor, and we will discuss drugs, hospital procedures and what it feels

*See "Prematurity," by Dr. Richard I. Feinbloom, in *Pregnancy, Birth and the Newborn Baby.*

†V. Crosse, *et al.,* "The Value of Human Milk Compared with Other Feeds for Premature Infants," as discussed in Haire and Haire, *Implementing Family-Centered Maternity Care,* pp. V, 42–43.

‡Edward A. Mason, M.D., "A Method of Predicting Crisis Outcome for Mothers of Premature Babies," *Public Health Reports,* Public Health Service, U.S. Dept. of Health, Education and Welfare, Vol. 78, No. 12 (December 1963), pp. 1031–35.

like to have a baby in the following sections. Here we shall concentrate on the techniques and exercises you and the companion you choose will learn to help you manage the course of your labor.

A basic part of our preparation is to find someone—husband, friend, or relative—to share our childbirth experience with us. The companion we choose, early in our pregnancy, will want to read some of the same books, attend the same classes, and learn the same exercises and breathing techniques that we do. This person will serve as our coach during labor and will stay with us through the entire birth process. Often our baby's father will be our coach. Sharing the labor experience and witnessing the birth together is an important beginning for sharing the responsibilities and joys of parenthood.

On the other hand, some of us may want to be with another woman during labor. We will find it most helpful to have as coach a woman who has already given birth. She will be able to support us with her firsthand knowledge, and her presence is a testament to the fact that it can be done.

Whether or not our companion has been through labor, s/he must attend the childbirth classes with us so that s/he will know how to use the breathing techniques and how to time our contractions.

If you have trouble finding someone to be with you, contact one of the prepared childbirth associations listed in the appendix to this section, or in your phone book. Also be sure to explain to your doctor and hospital that you expect to have a companion with you during labor and delivery. If they are not willing to honor your request, your choices are to find another doctor, go to another clinic, or fight the system with community pressure. These days many hospitals will welcome a trained labor companion—the result of a long, hard battle over the past twenty years, a battle not yet over.

Your companion will be comfort and support to you during labor. S/he will keep you from being lonely or afraid and will help to boost your morale if and when your labor becomes trying. The exercises we are about to describe will be the tools you will both use to keep you in control during labor and delivery.

Exercises

The work of labor centers in the pelvis and the uterus, so the object of our preparation is to help these parts work most effectively. We have to learn two basic things: first, how to breathe in a way that will give our body the oxygen it needs to function most efficiently; and second, how to allow one part of our body to work while the rest is relaxed.

One idea behind these two techniques is efficiency. If we can teach ourselves to pace our breathing according to how vigorously our body is working, we can help it do its work well. Controlled breathing, sending the right amount of oxygen to our laboring muscles, will give those muscles the fuel they need to keep functioning. At the same time, by voluntarily relaxing all muscles except those of the uterus, we will not take needed energy away from our laboring parts.

Another idea behind the techniques is selective attention. We all have experienced selective attention. If we receive too many outside stimuli at once, we can't incorporate them all into our consciousness, and so some go unnoticed. It's like trying to listen to two conversations at once; we either confuse them or let one surface to the disadvantage of the other. Well, by concentrating as hard as we can on what our response to the contractions will be, we don't give our minds time or room to register that we might be feeling pain. As a result, some women say they never really felt any pain during labor; others say that feelings of pain kept surfacing but that they were almost always able to control those feelings with increased concentration on the breathing techniques. One woman wrote that there was a kind of beauty in her acceptance of the pain she felt:

I don't think pain is necessarily bad. I had a short, hard labor, and it was clear to me that the incredible euphoria that I experienced afterward was in part a function of the fact that it was very painful. It really was almost positive pain, really worth it in retrospect.

The way each of us will experience her own labor is impossible to predict, but it is certainly true that we needn't be afraid of labor.

It can only be to our advantage to learn how to use the tools that can help us during labor. There are many exercises that we can do to get our bodies into condition, even before our pregnancies begin, and there are many others that we can practice during pregnancy. You can find exercises in some of the books in the bibliography. Four books are particularly helpful: *Commonsense Childbirth*, by Lester Hazell (a woman); *The Experience of Childbirth*, by Sheila Kitzinger; *The New Childbirth*, by Erna Wright; and *Six Practical Lessons for an Easier Childbirth*, by Elisabeth Bing.

Here we will be concerned mainly with *dissociation techniques* and with *controlled breathing*. First, however, there is one very simple exercise, called the Kegel exercise or the "elevator" (see Chapter 6, p. 101), that can be done at any time and in any place. It involves gradually tightening the muscles around your vagina, the perineal area, and then loosening them just as gradually. You can really feel this working during urination. If you can stop the flow of your urine by tightening your vaginal muscles then you will know how this exercise is supposed to feel. Do it first to a count of six, then work up to a count of ten. Once you become proficient at this, try to imagine the muscles up farther inside you, those on the pelvic floor. See if you can repeat this exercise using those muscles.

Try to do it whenever you think of it. It's an important exercise, for it teaches you how to relax the muscles of the pelvic floor and perineum—which have to be relaxed for the baby to pass through at birth—and it also teaches you how to tighten those muscles so that after the birth you can return to your naturally firm condition.

We shall now describe some dissociation techniques. Since we have learned to use muscles not singly but in combination, we have to learn to dissociate the muscles from one another if we are going to be able to let the activity of the uterus be as unhampered as possible. We do not want any muscles other than those that work automatically to be using up energy during labor. Our goal in these exercises is to learn what a tight muscle feels like and how to relax it. Try doing these exercises with someone around to check your relaxation.

Lie flat on the floor with pillows comfortably under your head and knees. First relax all your muscles as much as you can. Then, starting with your toes, begin to tighten them one at a time: first your toes, then your feet, then your calves, then your knees, thighs, vagina, rectum, abdomen, chest, shoulders, neck and face. By the time you reach your scalp you should be one mass of tensed muscle. At this point we want to reverse the process: starting at the top of your head, begin to relax one muscle at a time until, when you relax your toes, you feel totally limp. This exercise should be done at least once a day—before bed is a perfect time—and perhaps two or three times a day if you can comfortably manage it.

A variation on that exercise is to lie comfortably relaxed, then think of one part of your body and tense it. Make sure that all your other muscles stay loose. Then relax again and tense another part.

Another variation is trying to tighten two parts on opposite sides of your body while keeping all your other muscles relaxed. Lie on the floor again, with pillows arranged for your comfort. Make sure all your muscles are relaxed by checking them from head to toe in a mental rundown. Then tense your left leg and your right arm at the same time while everything else is relaxed. After a slow count of five, loosen up and switch to your right leg and left arm.

Try doing these exercises in different positions. During labor you may be on your back very little, and you should be able to keep your muscles relaxed no matter what your position. Also, check yourself from time to time when you're not doing these exercises to see which parts of you tend to tense up without your knowing it. If you locate specific areas, such as your mouth or your hands, you can concentrate especially on keeping them relaxed during labor.

Before we describe the four main types of breathing we should state that these have evolved over the years and are still subject to change. For that reason it is worthwhile to check with a childbirth education class to find out the newest techniques. To find a class near you, contact the national childbirth association offices listed in the Appendix, or look in the phone book.

The first type of breathing is a deep, full abdominal breathing. You breathe in through your nose and out through your mouth, trying to make your abdomen rise as you inhale and fall as you exhale. Do this slowly and rhythmically, counting forward (to five or eight or even ten) as you breathe in, and backward as you breathe out. This type of breathing will be very helpful during early first-stage labor. It will help to relieve some of the pressure around your abdomen.

The second type is a chest breathing. This is also a very deep breathing, but it takes all the air into your chest. Place your hands under your breasts on your ribcage as you breathe this way, and feel your ribs rise and fall. Again breathe in through your nose and out through your mouth, just as in the abdominal breathing. Make sure your abdominal muscles are as relaxed as you can make them. During early and late first-stage labor you will use this second technique to meet the contractions which make your abdominal wall go involuntarily rigid. You needn't keep your hands on your ribs during this exercise once you are sure you are doing it properly. Breathe evenly and rhythmically.

The third type of breathing is a shallow chest breathing. It is sometimes called the "out" technique. Take a short breath in through your mouth and then push it out by making the sound "out" in a whisper (in some classes the word is "hut"). Try doing this exercise for thirty seconds at a time. Pace yourself comfortably, and try not to breathe too quickly. During labor this exercise will be very helpful. Some women use it from the moment labor begins to get serious until the baby is ready to be pushed out. You will probably not be using "out" throughout an entire contraction. It is more likely that you will begin with a few deep chest breaths and then, as the contraction becomes more intense, switch to this more rapid breathing. Then as the contraction eases, so will your breathing. At the end of each contraction you should remember to take a long, deep breath and exhale it fully. This will help you to relax while awaiting the next contraction.*

It's very useful to practice this shallow chest breathing with someone there to time you with a clock or stop watch. Your companion can give you the signal: "Contraction begins." You take a deep breath and exhale it completely. Then you breathe deeply as described in the second technique. When your companion calls fifteen seconds, switch to the "out" breathing and keep that up until s/he calls forty-five seconds. At this point your breathing should return to a deeper, chest-centered breathing. After one minute is reached, finish your practice with a deep breath and exhale it completely. When

they occur, use Braxton-Hicks contractions for practice purposes.

The fourth type of breathing is a very shallow, mouth-centered panting. It takes a lot of practice to learn this technique well; some of us never master it in practice, but find that it often comes naturally during labor. Actually, it doesn't matter—do what you can and what keeps you comfortable for as long as possible. Panting will be most useful during transition, when you might vary it by a combination of panting and blowing. To learn the pant, relax your body, drop open your jaw, and breathe in and out through your mouth so that you feel the air going only to the back of your throat and then out again. You will probably hear a very quiet panting noise during this, but it should not become too loud. Try to keep the breaths regularly spaced, perhaps three or four a second, and don't pant too rapidly or you might become hyperventilated. The best way to avoid *hyperventilation** is to make sure that for every breath you inhale, you exhale completely. To pant correctly requires a certain amount of concentration, and that is helpful to take your mind off your uterus. Sometimes, however, even panting might not be sufficient—for example, when you are trying to control the urge to push at the end of transition. Here are two techniques to help you through those times:

Pant-pant-blow: Many women who have trouble panting have no difficulty at all with this technique. All you do is take two, three, or four panting breaths and on the last one blow out. In-out, in-out, in-out, in-*blow*. Make sure to blow out with force.

Whoo-ha: This is a rapid, shallow pant done saying the word "whoo-ha" and moving your head slightly from side to side (another thing to keep your mind busy) at the same time.

There are some other tools that you or your labor coach can use to make labor manageable. One of these is *effleurage*. Elisabeth Bing describes it in *Six Practical Lessons:* "Cup your hands lightly, place them under your abdomen. Then massage gently with your fingertips, leading your arms out and up while you inhale, completing the circle down again as you exhale."† This light massage helps you to relax, it relieves some of the tension you might feel in your abdomen, it gives you something to do, and it feels good.

It is often very helpful to you if your coach gives you a gentle massage on your legs, usually around your thighs, or on your back. Some women with backache labor rely on this massage to keep them comfortable. Unfortunately, during transition you may be so irritable—a common symptom of transition—that you won't

---

*Contractions are different for everyone, and even within the course of your own labor your contractions may follow different patterns.

*Hyperventilation is caused by an improper oxygen-carbon dioxide balance. If you become hyperventilated you will feel dizzy and your fingers and toes will tingle. You may even faint.

†Bring along some corn starch to rub on your stomach. It makes effleurage easier.

allow anyone to touch you. This, of course, may not be at all what happens to you, so remember massage as an effective technique. Sheila Kitzinger gives a detailed account of massage in *The Experience of Childbirth* (pp. 94–95).

Finally there are many ways you can be made to feel more comfortable during the intervals between contractions. Sucking ice chips or a wet washcloth, sipping water, licking a candy stick, or feeling a cool washcloth on your forehead can all help to relax you and give you the confidence you need to keep on working.

The preceding discussion applies to the first stage of labor. It suggests ways to keep yourself comfortable during the tedious process of dilation. Now we can talk about the much more exciting work of labor, the expulsion of the baby. Once second-stage begins you'll probably feel terrific, because finally you'll be able to help actively in your baby's birth.

To push effectively you should be in a semi-sitting position, or if you are in the delivery room, with your feet in stirrups, your back should be raised off the table at about a 45-degree angle. Either your coach can support your back or you can prop yourself up on two pillows, brought from the labor room for this purpose. As soon as you feel the contraction coming on, get into the pushing position by curving your back, holding your legs

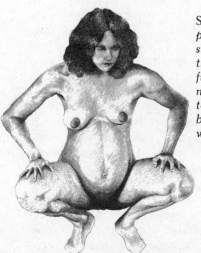

SQUATTING—*a good position for second-stage labor; helps open the perineal area to its fullest for delivery. You need strong leg muscles to maintain it for long, but it can be alternated with other positions.*

SITTING UP—*with heels close to body or legs crossed; especially good for transition and as a stretching exercise during pregnancy.*

up under the knees, pointing your elbows out, and bending your head down with your chin on your chest. Then take two deep, cleansing breaths and exhale each one completely. Take a third deep breath in and hold it. At the same time bear down with all your might, thinking about how you are helping to push the baby through the birth canal. Continue bearing down with this first breath for as long as you can comfortably; then lift your head, blow the air out, take another deep breath, and bear down again. Keep your legs up while you change breaths. You will probably have to take at least three breaths during each second-stage contraction. Try to keep your vagina and perineum relaxed. (*Note:* While you are learning the pushing technique during pregnancy, practice the position and the breathing sequence, but *do not push or bear down very hard.*)

There are some women who have reported that they never felt the urge to push. If this happens you will have to be directed when to push by your doctor or coach, who will have a hand on your abdomen to feel when the contraction begins its tightening. Keep pushing until they tell you the contraction is over.

As the baby's head crowns, you will have to stop pushing, and you can use the pant-pant-blow technique to control your urge. You want to ease the baby out without tearing your perineum.

It is of course best to be as awake and aware as possible during labor. If you can feel your contractions, you will know how to work with them. During first-stage you will know when to switch from one breathing level to another, and you will be able to feel your contractions increasing in intensity as second-stage approaches. When, finally, the urge to push becomes utterly uncontrollable, you will be in second-stage, and you will be able to start pushing your baby out.

Positions for Labor and Delivery

When we close our eyes and think of a woman in labor, our picture is probably of a woman flat on her back. Although this is a common position for a woman to take, it is neither the most efficient nor the most comfortable position during labor, and it is quite possibly the most dangerous one. When we are lying flat, the uterus presses on the *inferior vena cava* and the aorta, the major sources of blood to and from the uterus, cutting off oxygen, which in turn may cause shock-like symptoms in the mother and distress in the fetus. Furthermore, by lying flat, we are not allowing gravity to

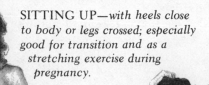

LYING ON SIDE ("RUNNING POSITION")—*used by many women throughout first-stage labor. Some women like a pillow under their head as well as their knee. Also great for sleeping, especially in late pregnancy.*

help us. Sitting up, standing, squatting, in a knee-hand position, or lying on our side, all keep the pressure off the *inferior vena cava* and aorta. Any upright or semi-upright position works with gravity to help the baby move downward and out naturally, with least risk.

During second-stage labor it is especially important to push in a sitting or semi-sitting position. Some hospitals are now equipped with birth tables, the backs of which can be raised to support the mother's back while she pushes. (See drawings below.)

Remember, labor is a time to do everything you can to make yourself as comfortable as possible. Move around, change positions, do anything you have to do to keep on top of your contractions. Lying or sitting in a comfortable way and being able to change your position when you feel like it both help to keep your spirits high during labor and delivery and increase your chances of having a normal birth.

How to Choose a Childbirth Class

A good course in childbirth preparation, along with good prenatal medical care, is one of the most valuable investments a pregnant woman can make.

1. Make sure the class is small—although it's hard to find one with fewer than ten couples.
2. Compare the prices of the classes with the quality of teaching and attention to your needs as an individual.
3. Make sure the class will include adequate discussion, detailed information, plenty of rehearsal to learn physical techniques. Six weeks is minimal; eight to ten weeks better. Usually classes are two hours long.
4. Be sure the class encourages fathers and/or friends to participate. The class should be built around the expectation that someone who is as trained as you are will always be with you throughout labor and delivery.
5. The class should discuss feelings and attitudes as well as techniques. It should not only prepare you for labor but also for parenthood, breast-feeding, etc.
6. Find out as much as you can about the organization that sponsors the classes. If it is a hospital class, make sure they aren't simply trying to get you to accept all hospital procedures as normal and in-

evitable. If the organization is profit-making, find out why. Most classes are too expensive as it is.
7. If your class is to be part of any research study, find out as much as you can about it. Don't consent to anything you don't feel comfortable with.
8. Look at the qualifications of the instructor. A reputable teacher needn't be an R.N. (registered nurse), but she should have a detailed list of her qualifications and experience ready to give you. She should be able to provide references (students who have taken her classes previously), and she should have had either personal or professional experience with prepared childbirth during delivery. Find out how the instructor is supervised. Be cautious of independent instructors.
9. Find out whether any professional board is affiliated with the class program and who is on it. Both doctors and nonmedical professionals should be represented, especially mental-health workers. Psychological and emotional problems are too often overlooked.

DRUGS AND OBSTETRICAL INTERVENTIONS

Every drug, every method of anesthesia, and every instrument used in childbirth has possible risks or side effects for ourselves and our babies. Every single drug given to the mother during labor crosses the placenta and reaches her baby, some in greater amounts and with greater rapidity than others. If the baby is premature, smaller than average, or in poor health, the consequences can be dangerous (usually there is no way of knowing the exact weight, maturity, or relative health of the fetus before delivery). Even a normal baby can suffer from the effects of maternal medication, and we mothers can sometimes suffer more from the aftereffects of the drugs used in our labor than we might have from the labor itself. The problem is compounded because along with each drug often come two or three other procedures designed by the hospital to insure, as much as possible, the safety of the medication used. Each of these procedures carries its own potential risks and side effects, and by definition interferes with the natural process of our labor.

One major reason so many of us prepare for child-

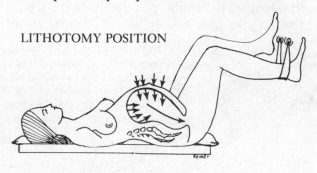

LITHOTOMY POSITION

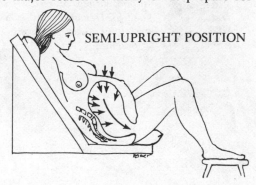

SEMI-UPRIGHT POSITION

birth is to learn how to handle labor without using medication. The exercises described in the previous section and the methods taught in childbirth classes are appropriate, safe and simple-to-use tools which will help us overcome the discomfort or pain that we might experience during labor. Just by reading this chapter you have started to prepare yourself.

Even when we are prepared for labor, however, there is always the chance, however slight, that we will have to be anesthetized so that the doctor can perform a necessary intervention.

I was in labor for twelve hours, keeping in control by breathing according to the childbirth exercises, but toward the end my doctor told me that my cervix didn't seem to be dilating properly. He said I might have to have a cesarean section. After another fifteen minutes I was wheeled into the operating room and given a spinal; my baby was delivered by cesarean twenty minutes later.

When there is a complication, we must trust the doctor's judgment and assume that s/he has weighed all the alternatives. We can ask the doctor to share the possible alternatives with us, and some doctors will. Ultimately, however, in the hospital, the doctor has the final say.

We have a legal right to know the names of the drugs given to us and to know what procedures the doctor will use in his or her intervention and why. The hospital staff is obliged to tell us if we ask. Furthermore, we have a right to be told, without asking, what the possible risks and side effects are of all drugs and procedures used on us, although very few hospitals actually honor that duty. There sometimes is an attempt to intimidate or cajole a patient who stands up for her right to be consulted, so that is a very important reason to have a companion educated in childbirth procedures with you in labor, someone who can watch the performance of the hospital staff with a more objective eye. It is a good idea also to discuss drugs with our doctors before delivery to find out their favorite drugs, their tendency to rely on drugs, the dosages they prefer, and what choices they will allow us to make. Go over each one of the medications and procedures described in this section with your doctor at a prenatal visit and find out his or her opinions and preferences. If you have any preferences, make them known to your doctor or clinic then. (See pp. 355–357.)

Obstetrical Medication

Childbirth drugs are divided into two major categories: analgesia and anesthesia. Analgesics are drugs which decrease our sensation of pain, and anesthesia agents remove our sensation of pain altogether by creating sleep or a temporary loss of feeling in the specific area affected. In this section we will first describe the various

analgesics and then discuss the different types of anesthesia available to a woman in labor.

A study completed in 1970 by Brackbill and Conway, two child psychologists, showed that infants whose mothers had received analgesia and anesthesia during labor and delivery had retarded muscular, visual and neural development in the first four weeks of life.* This doesn't mean all babies will be so affected, nor will the babies affected be permanently retarded in development, but four weeks is a very long time in the life of a newborn infant. Many imprinting patterns can be set during that time, both for mother and for baby.† The way the baby and the mother respond to each other during the first few days and even the first few hours after birth can have an important effect on their relationship.‡

I was really doped up when my baby was delivered and barely got to see that she was alive before she was whisked away to the nursery. When I finally woke up and she was able to be brought to me, I remember thinking, "Is this really my baby? Do I really want to take her home with me?" It took me awhile to feel connected to her.

Analgesia

TRANQUILIZERS AND NARCOTICS. As soon as labor begins to become serious business, and you find you have to work hard to keep yourself in control, you will probably be offered a tranquilizer or narcotic "to take the edge off your contractions." All tranquilizers and narcotics cross the placenta and reach the fetus. Tranquilizers may have a depressant effect on some newborn functions. For example, Valium is thought to interfere with

*In Haire and Haire, *Implementing Family-Centered Maternity Care*, pp. iii–10; from W. Bowes, Y. Brackbill, E. Conway and A. Steinschneider; *The Effects of Obstetrical Medication on Fetus and Infant*, Monograph of the Society of Research in Child Development, Vol. 35, No. 4 (1970), University of Chicago Press. Control groups showed that this effect was directly related to the obstetrical medication used. Furthermore, R. Kron, M. Stein and K. Goddard show in "Newborn Sucking Behavior Affected by Obstetrical Sedation" (*Pediatrics*, 37:1012–16, 1966) that newborn sucking behavior may be depressed for as long as four days after delivery by barbiturates used routinely on the laboring mother.

†Imprinting refers to certain bonds of a psychological nature that create patterns for future action and that either take place at a specific time or do not take place at all. Also called "bonding." (See Klaus and Kennel.)

‡*The Cultural Warping of Childbirth*, by Doris Haire, a special report to the International Childbirth Education Association, 1972, pp. 27–28. Mrs. Haire cites two articles which demonstrate that the first twenty-four hours after birth are extremely important for the development of infant-mother bonds.

a newborn's ability to cope with cold stress,* and since most delivery rooms are kept very cool, this can affect the baby's health at birth. Other tranquilizers, such as Sparine (which is given commonly in conjunction with Nisentil, a narcotic) may cause labor to slow down or even cease altogether.†

Tranquilizers may be helpful in allowing the mother to relax between contractions. However, she may find herself falling asleep until the contraction reaches its peak, and then she may panic, forget to breathe properly, and actually experience more pain than she would have without the drug. A good coach should remind the mother to use controlled breathing techniques from the beginning of the contraction until the end.

Narcotics have a similarly relaxing effect on the mother, but all narcotics—such as Demerol, Dolophine, or Nisentil, for example—have a serious depressant effect on fetal respiration, and the newborn's behavioral responsiveness may be significantly decreased by these drugs.

Even small amounts of meperidine (Demerol) given to the mother in labor affect the baby. According to an article by John W. Scanlon, M.D., the newborn's behavior can be especially inhibited in terms of responsiveness to mothering stimuli such as cuddling, consoling and startling.‡ So besides inhibiting vital physical functions in the newborn, narcotics depress the infant's behavior as well.

BARBITURATES, derivatives of barbituric acid, have been used to produce sleep in the laboring mother. Nembutal and Seconal fall into this category, as do Luminal, sodium Amytal and barbital, to name a few. These drugs are dangerous to the fetus; they cross the placental barrier readily, and they can depress fetal respiration and responsiveness. Furthermore, a study by Ploman and Persson found that

. . . the selective tissue storage of depressant drugs such as barbiturates was many times higher in the midbrain than in the circulating blood [of the newborn]. This selective storage lasted for as much as a week in the immature brain, affecting the midbrain-mediated behavior of the newborn for the entire time. Since the newborn's behavior is primarily midbrain in origin, this means that his behavioral repertoire is influenced for the entire important first week of his life by medication given innocently to the mother in the few hours just prior to delivery.§

*Conversation between this author and John W. Scanlon, M.D., Perinatologist, Beth Israel Hospital and Boston Hospital for Women. Boston, March 1975.

†John J. Bonica, *Principles and Practice of Obstetric Analgesia and Anesthesia*, vols. 1 & 2. (Philadelphia: F.A. Davis Company, 1972), p. 268.

‡"Obstetric Anesthesia as a Neonatal Risk Factor in Normal Labor and Delivery." by John W. Scanlon, M.D., in *Clinics in Perinatology*, Vol. 1, No. 2 (September 1974), pp. 465–82.

§L. Ploman and B. Persson, "On the Transfer of Barbiturates to the Human Fetus and Their Accumulation in Some of Its Vital Organs,"

It is often the case that barbiturates are given early in labor in combination with a small amount of scopolamine. Scopolamine, sometimes called "twilight sleep," is an amnesiac and a hallucinogen that has the effect of making the woman forget what she experienced during labor, but it does not stop her sensations at the time. In other words, she goes through labor in a kind of nightmarish sleep, and then when she wakes up, her conscious mind forgets what she has felt. Like other hallucinogens, scopolamine can cause some women to become physically violent and others to become stuporous. A woman under the influence of scopolamine can cause herself physical damage by thrashing about wildly during contractions, and as a result, she must be constantly watched. This is how one obstetrical text describes the use of scopolamine:

This method can be properly used only in a hospital in a quiet, darkened room; the mother must be watched carefully to guard against injury or falling from the bed if she becomes excited. Some physicians believe that a woman who is spared the recollection of her labor may be harmed psychologically and may even reject her offspring. This method has very largely fallen into disfavor because of the associated pulmonary edema, swallowing of the tongue, and maternal excitement.*

According to Scanlon's article (cited earlier), "The combination of scopolamine and methadone given to the mother causes severe neonatal [newborn] depression." He then adds that scopolamine both "prolongs the second stage of labor and increases the rate of Caesarean section." There is no excuse for the continued use of scopolamine, and yet it is still given.†

Anesthesia

In still another category of medication are general analgesic/anesthesic agents which are inhaled by the mother. According to Scanlon, all such inhalation agents reach the fetus and serve as a depressant to newborn responsiveness. Ether, for example, can retard labor and may "provoke vomiting, excessive uterine relaxation, and bleeding in the mother."‡ Inhalation gases are administered with each contraction to ease the discomfort associated with it. The trick is to breathe in the right

J. Obstet. and Gynaecol. Brit. Emp., 64:706–11 (1967), as discussed in Brazelton, *op. cit.*

*Charles E. McLennan with collaboration of Eugene C. Sandberg, *Synopsis of Obstetrics*, ed. 8. (St. Louis: The C.V. Mosby Co., 1970), p. 175.

†"Labor and Delivery," by Arthur Gorbach, M.D., in *Pregnancy, Birth and the Newborn Baby*, p. 185. Dr. Gorbach writes that in spite of the known drawbacks, scopolamine, in combination with barbiturates and tranquilizers, is a satisfactory method of pain relief. On the contrary, every study we have read indicates that the combination of scopolamine and barbiturates has a seriously depressant effect on the newborn as well as possible negative psychological effects on the mother.

‡*Synopsis of Obstetrics*, p. 176.

amount of the vapor just in time to have it working when it is most needed, during the peak of the contraction. Because of its tendency to slow down labor, its negative effect on the newborn, and its potentially fatal complications if too much is inhaled general anesthesia is being replaced. In view of these serious risks, it is appalling to note that inhalation anesthesia is still being used in one-third of U.S. deliveries.*

GENERAL ANESTHESIA, which puts the woman completely to sleep, should not be used during first-stage labor because it slows down the process of labor, and it has a severely depressant effect on the baby. Furthermore, there are serious dangers from the injudicious use of general anesthetics, which can lead to death. General anesthesia is most often given during the very last minutes of labor, by those doctors who like their patients to be totally unaware of the obstetrical procedures used (see "Episiotomy," "Forceps"). Sometimes, after special preparation of the mother, general anesthesia will be used during a cesarean section. (See fn. p. 129.)

REGIONAL ANESTHESIA, on the other hand, is widely used. It is injected into the woman's body at a specific point, and it is expected to anesthetize only a particular part of the body. If the doctor decides the numbing effect is needed only during delivery, to perform an episiotomy (see p. 286), or to use mid or low forceps (see p. 287), then local infiltration or a pudendal block might be given.† Of course, if everything has gone normally and no drugs have been administered up until this point, the actual delivery is the worst time to give the mother anesthesia. If she has learned how to push and if her doctor is willing to coach her by telling her when to stop pushing, then she can experience the thrill of delivery fully, without an anesthetic to cut off her sensations and make her recovery that much more annoying.

The *pudendal block* anesthetizes only the vulva, or external female organs. Even this relatively minor anesthetic can cause "a persistent decrease in oxygen saturation in the newborn during the first thirty minutes of postpartum observation."‡ Here again, if the baby is healthy the effect will probably be insignificant, but if the baby's health is less than normal, serious effects could result from the drugged baby's inability to make full use of the oxygen available.

Another form of anesthesia, the *paracervical block,* is being questioned by many anesthesiologists who consider it dangerous to both fetus and mother. Maternal

complications such as convulsions and severe hypotension are common.* Since the injection is made into the area around the cervix, there is the possibility that the anesthetic will accidentally be injected into the presenting part of the fetus. Moreover, the injection site is very close to the main artery of the uterus, which increases the chance of its being absorbed rapidly by the placenta and depressing the fetus. Some infants have died.†

Spinal anesthesia is used during delivery to anesthetize the entire birth area (from belly to thighs or knees). Spinals, or subarachnoid blocks, are injected into the subarachnoid space around the spinal column. Usually they are given only at the very end of labor, since there is some evidence that they slow down labor if given too early.‡ Spinal anesthesia obliterates our urge to bear down during second-stage, so instead of our pushing the baby out, the obstetrician often uses forceps (see p. 287).

A common and serious complication of spinal anesthesia is maternal hypotension (drop in blood pressure). Some effects of hypotension on the mother may be shock-like symptoms, altered pulse rate, nausea and vomiting. The effects on the fetus are slowed heart rate, decreased flow of blood through the placenta, and insufficient oxygen intake. This is true of all spinals.

Hypotension can be avoided, or at least contained, in most cases by the generous use of an intravenous hydrating solution, as well as continuous care by an attendant, preferably an experienced anesthesiologist. If the woman becomes hypotensive she should be turned on her side immediately to take the pressure off the inferior vena cava, the major source of blood to the uterus.

A number of women who have spinals suffer aftereffects in the form of severe headache, stiff neck and backache.

Spinals can and should be avoided, except when necessary for an emergency delivery.

Continuous Regional Anesthesia: Two forms of regional anesthesia can be given to the woman during the first stage of labor and can be readministered until delivery. They are caudal block and lumbar epidural block.

The *caudal block* is injected into the sacral canal at the base of the back. For a continuous caudal block a catheter is introduced into the lower back and the anesthetic is injected into the catheter. Continuous caudal blocks can be given from about eight centimeters dilation on. A caudal block requires a significantly larger dose of anesthetic than does either a spinal or an epidural (explained below), and it therefore carries a greater risk to both mother and baby. Furthermore, the failure rate for caudals is higher than for epidurals, owing to the greater chance of improper needle placement. Maternal hypotension and subsequent lack of oxygen to the baby is a potential problem that must be carefully guarded

---

*Symposium on Obstetric Anesthesia, San Francisco, Univ. of Calif., *OB-Gyn News*, Dec. 1, 1977.

†Pudendal block anesthesia is named for the pudendum, or external female genitalia. Pudendum in Latin means "that of which one ought to be ashamed." Obviously, we can't imagine a more inappropriate name!

‡*Implementing Family-Centered Maternity Care with a Central Nursery*, pp. iii–13.

---

*Bonica, *op. cit.*, p. 510.

†Rosefsky, J., et al., "Perinatal Deaths Associated with Mepiracaine Paracervical Block Anesthesia in Labor," *NEJM* (1968), 278:530.

‡Bonica, *op. cit.*, p. 546.

against by the anesthesiologist. A very rare, but extremely serious complication of the caudal technique is injection of the anesthetic directly into the baby's head.* This disastrous mistake can result in severe neonatal (newborn) depression, failure to breathe, and possibly death.

For most of us, the end of the first stage of labor, from eight centimeters to ten centimeters—the part called transition—is very intense, and it is the time when we may feel like taking some medication to tide us over. One thing we have to remember though is that transition is for the great majority of us the shortest part of labor. So when we are considering anesthesia we ought to weigh the possible risks and aftereffects of the technique against our ability to withstand this very last bit of first-stage labor. Anesthesia given to us during transition will in almost every case last through second-stage labor, and it may in fact prolong our labor.

Epidural anesthesia can be administered to the laboring woman from about four centimeters dilation on. For this reason many obstetricians and anesthesiologists, and some new mothers as well, would have us believe that the epidural is the answer to our labor problems.

Epidurals are administered like continuous caudal blocks through a catheter placed in the back. An injection is made in the middle of the woman's back, into her epidural space, the space around the dura mater of the spinal cord. An experienced anesthesiologist should administer the anesthetic, since a mistake in placement can lead to serious consequences—in the extreme, paralysis, death, or fetal injection. Less anesthesia has to be used in epidurals than in caudals, which makes them safer for mother and baby. However, both epidurals and caudals often cause maternal hypotension (discussed above).

Epidurals, when administered properly, will eliminate the sensations of labor in most cases. However, if we choose this form of anesthesia we are also choosing a number of interlocking procedures which increase the risks of the method:

1. An intravenous hydrating solution—necessary to avoid or counteract hypotension. This will be attached to one arm. Infections sometimes occur.
2. Blood pressure gauging—your blood pressure will probably be checked about every fifteen to thirty minutes, since a drop in blood pressure can have serious effects on the fetus, as well as on the mother. As a result, you may be asked to wear a blood pressure cuff on the other arm.
3. Artificial rupture of the membranes (see p. 283)—if your membranes have not already ruptured by themselves they will probably be ruptured before you are given an epidural or caudal. This is to make sure that the baby's presenting part is firmly

positioned in the birth outlet. There is some evidence that transverse arrest (the baby's getting stuck in a sideways position in the uterus) is a possible complication of epidurals, due to uterine relaxation brought on by the anesthesia.
4. Oxytocin—many doctors give the labor stimulant oxytocin (usually in its artificial form, Pitocin) to women receiving continuous regional anesthesia. One reason is to speed up labor; another is to counter the possible slowing down of contractions which some doctors associate with regional anesthesia. The combination of ruptured membranes plus Pitocin can create very strong uterine contractions, which *must* be monitored, since their strength will not be felt by the anesthetized mother (see p. 284), and the uterus might rupture.*
5. A fetal monitor—if they are used by your hospital, will be either attached around your waist or inserted into your vagina (see p. 285). It is especially important during continuous anesthesia (caudal or epidural) to check the baby's reactions to it by means of his or her heart rate.

The direct effect of the anesthetic on the baby has been studied by a number of doctors. Scanlon found that behavioral changes in newborns whose mothers received epidural anesthesia included decreased rooting activity (a basic food-searching survival technique) and muscular floppiness.† Conway and Brackbill also found negative behavior changes after continuous regional anesthesia, but they concluded that the effects on the baby were less than those suffered by babies whose mothers had received high doses of labor medication or general anesthesia.‡ One particular epidural anesthetic, Marcaine (bupivacaine), seems to have the least adverse effect on the newborn's condition of all epidural anesthesia.§

---

*Ibid., p. 607.

*E. Daw, "Oxytocin-induced Rupture of the Primigravid Uterus," Journal of Obstetrics and Gynecology of the British Commonwealth, Vol. 80 (April, 1973), pp. 374-75. The uterus of a first-time mother ruptured due to excessive contractions caused by oxytocin, and the rupture was not discovered until after the baby had died, since the strength of the contractions was masked by the epidural anesthesia and the fetal heart was monitored only intermittently.

†Scanlon, op. cit., p. 479.

‡Ibid., p. 478.

§*Obstetrics and Gynecology News*, December 1, 1974, "Lidocaine Use in Epidural Anesthesia is Criticized," p. 2. Also, in same edition, "Anesthesia Advances Cut Obstetric Risks," p. 3. Studies conducted at Boston Hospital for Women by Scanlon, Ostheimer, Weiss, and Alper indicate that bupivacaine has the least observable-measurable effect on the newborn. However, Dr. R. Bryan Roberts of the Mount Sinai School of Medicine said that bupivacaine may have a significant depressant effect on uterine contractions. Consequently, a labor stimulant is often needed when bupivacaine is used. There is some evidence that the mixture of epidural anesthesia and oxytocin (labor stimulant) altered fetal heart rate patterns.

It is probable that women are subjected to more cesareans these days *because* the above interventions disrupt an otherwise normal labor, causing the fetus unnecessary (hospital-caused) difficulties and the mother unnecessary risks. (See p. 287.)

When we choose epidural anesthesia we are choosing a doctor/hospital-controlled labor and delivery; we are accepting the risks and possible side effects of many procedures and drugs; and we are too casually taking for granted the competence and skill of the doctors and attendants.

Obstetrical Interventions and Procedures

There are a great number of interventions and procedures connected with labor and delivery in the hospital. Here we shall list them and discuss the reasons for their use, their effects and risks, and their relationship to the use of other procedures.

Shaving Pubic Hair: The "Prep"

This procedure is carried out routinely in all American hospitals. After we enter the hospital we are taken up to the labor room, where we are asked to undress and put on a hospital gown. Then a nurse either shaves off all our pubic hair or shaves off all the hair around our vagina and cuts the rest short. Doctors say that prepping is done to decrease the risk of infection, since germs may be carried in the hair. However, Doris Haire, in *The Cultural Warping of Childbirth*, cites two articles stating that the incidence of infection is in fact a little higher in mothers whose pubic area was shaved. Furthermore, some of us may not feel comfortable with this procedure. We might feel embarrassed or we might feel that prepping is an affront to our dignity. On the other hand, we might think nothing of the shaving but then find that as our hair grows back it causes us to itch and feel annoyed.*

Enema

Another part of the preliminary labor room preparation is the administration of an enema to laboring women. Since there is very often a natural diarrhea for a few days before labor begins, many of us are already pretty well empty anyway. Furthermore, if we are in the middle of labor an enema can cause our contractions to become stronger and harder to control, which in turn might make us feel like asking for drugs. Then we set off the chain of procedures and risks related to the use of drugs. If we are not in labor when we enter the hospital, sometimes the enema will cause our contractions to begin. If we are concerned about either the prepping or the enema, we ought to speak to our doctors or the hospital staff before labor to find out what options are available to us.

Rupturing the Amniotic Sac (Membrane)

The bag of amniotic fluid in which our baby has been floating throughout our pregnancy normally does not break until the very end of first-stage labor or during second stage. Ten percent of all amniotic sacs which are allowed to break spontaneously are still intact up until birth. According to research that is being conducted in Latin America by Dr. Roberto Caldeyro-Barcia, the amniotic membranes may be a beneficial buffer for the infant's head as it passes against the mother's pelvic floor during labor contractions.* About ten percent of us will experience a premature rupture of the membranes before our labors begin. Once the membranes rupture there is an increased chance of infection, so mothers are usually advised to stay in bed and not to bathe at that time. You will probably know if your membranes rupture because water will trickle out of your vagina quite uncontrollably. If your membranes rupture, call your doctor. If labor has begun you will be asked to come to the hospital. If labor has not started, you may be asked to come to the hospital anyway to have your labor induced (see "Induction of Labor," p. 284). Weigh your options carefully before choosing induction. Remember, just because the membranes have ruptured, it does not mean that all the fluid will empty from the sac permanently; your body will continue to produce amniotic fluid, but the fluid will no longer be caught, so it will continue to dribble out. The baby may be premature.

Doctors often artificially rupture the membranes of their patients to stimulate and speed up labor although some studies disagree that rupture of the membranes has this effect.† Sometimes after the membranes have ruptured, or been ruptured, our labors become so intense that we feel like taking some medication to ease our discomfort. It is helpful to realize that this intense part of our labor usually won't last too long, unless the entire labor process has been induced artificially. In that case we might experience strong contractions for a longer period of time.

No one knows whether the rupturing of the membranes in itself causes stress to the infant. If it does, then medication would just be added stress. With support from our labor companion or from a helpful nurse who can breathe with us and try to keep us relaxed, we are more able to get through this part of labor without drugs.

Infrequently, after the membranes rupture, the umbilical cord or the placenta is able to slip into a position under the baby, so that when the baby pushes down s/he

---

*(See Doris Haire, *The Cultural Warping of Childbirth*, p. 18.) Try some soothing cream on the area when your hair begins to grow back. Ask your doctor to give you some.

*Roberto Caldeyro-Barcia, M.D., in his talk before the conference, "Obstetrical Management and Infant Outcome," March 1974, New York. As reported by Margaret Worrall in the newsletter of the Boston Association for Childbirth Education, May-June, 1974.

†Emanuel A. Friedman, M.D., *Labor: Clinical Evaluation and Management* (New York: Appleton-Century-Crofts, 1967), p. 256.

is pushing against the umbilical cord or placenta and cutting off his or her own oxygen supply. In this case an emergency cesarean section will probably have to be performed.*

Depending on what s/he has been taught, each doctor will have a particular feeling about how long labor should be allowed to go on after the membranes have ruptured. Since the risk of infection is greater without the amniotic sac, some doctors will try to shorten labor in a woman whose membranes have ruptured if it seems to be progressing slowly. They will often administer an intravenous pitocin drip, which has the effect of speeding up labor. It causes some women to experience extremely intense contractions (see "Induction of Labor," below), which, added to the increased strength of contractions without the membranes, may be harmful to the uterus and fetus, very difficult for the woman to control, and can lead to the use of further drugs and interventions to weaken the contractions.†

Intravenous glucose solution

Doctors usually advise us not to eat once labor begins. The idea is that if our stomach is empty we will be less likely to vomit during labor or during the administration of anesthesia. To substitute for light eating and to keep us from becoming dehydrated, American doctors usually administer an intravenous glucose (sugar) solution to a laboring woman by attaching an I.V. unit to a vein in her arm. Many childbirth educators feel that this I.V. adds to our apprehension and fear by making us feel as if there is something wrong with our labor and by limiting our mobility. Some doctors, anesthesiologists in particular, believe that an intravenous solution should be started in every laboring woman so that her veins will be open just in case any emergency anesthesia has to be administered, or to prevent hypotension (epidurals).

Elective induction of labor

Induction is the term used to refer to a pre-planned delivery in which labor is artificially started. There are a number of methods used to induce labor, some more effective than others. The first step in induction usually involves artificial rupture of the membranes (see above). Once the bag of waters is ruptured, labor will very frequently begin within a few hours. Sometimes rather than rupturing the membranes the doctor will "strip" the membranes during an internal examination. Using a finger, s/he will separate the amnion (bag of waters) from the wall of the uterus, and thus stimulate the beginning of labor. No one knows exactly why this causes labor to begin in some cases. The procedure is performed by many obstetricians without informed consent‡—just considered part of routine practice during an internal exam in the labor room—although if there is an unrec-

ognized placenta previa (placenta nearer to the cervix than the baby) the placenta could be stripped away from the uterus, with harmful and possibly catastrophic effect to the baby.

If labor does not begin within a given amount of time (each doctor and hospital has a particular policy) then a chemical substance will be given to the mother to substitute for the hormones present in natural labor. The name of the hormone is oxytocin and its chemical substitute is pitocin. Pitocin is most successfully administered intravenously, although it has been injected intramuscularly and at times given by mouth. Intravenously, the dosage of pitocin is more easily controlled—which is important, since pitocin can cause very strong contractions, creating potential dangers for both the baby and the mother. No one knows what, if any, direct effect pitocin, or the combination of pitocin and other drugs, has on the baby, although it is known that the baby can suffer distress and oxygen loss from sustained, stronger than normal contractions. Prostaglandin is also used.

There is still considerable controversy over induction, and in some hospitals elective induction (for convenience—the mother's or the doctor's or both) is not permitted. Nevertheless, unfortunately, induction for convenience is growing more and more common. Some obstetricians have their delivery schedules arranged in advance. One of the reasons for the controversy over induction is that it is often difficult to tell the true maturity of the fetus, since the time of conception can rarely be pinpointed. Without knowing the true age of the baby, it is difficult to know if s/he is ready to endure extrauterine life or the stresses of labor and delivery. Furthermore, induction before the mother's body is ready for labor can be dangerous.* (Some signs of readiness are considerable effacement of the cervix and a certain amount of dilation.)

On the other hand, induction may be considered necessary if there is some question about the baby's chances for survival, as in the case of toxemia of pregnancy, hemolytic disease (Rh factor), or maternal diabetes. These and other indications might require emergency mobilization of the hospital team, which would be easier if labor were planned. Furthermore, if the mother has a previous history of extremely short labors and if she lives some distance from the hospital, induction might be chosen rather than risking the baby's birth en route to the hospital.

However, induced labor poses a special problem for the laboring mother because of the peculiar character of induced contractions. They frequently do not follow the normal wave-like course but reach intensity instantly and remain intense for a long period. They are often de-

---

Pregnancy, Birth and the Newborn Baby, p. 175.
†Bonica, *op. cit.*, p. 1315.
‡Bonica, *Ibid.*, p. 1315.

*Maisels, Rees, Marks and Friedman, "Elective Delivery of the Term Fetus: An Obstetrical Hazard," *JAMA*, Nov. 7, 1977, Vol. 238, No. 19.

scribed by women who have experienced both as much more painful than normal, non-induced contractions. If the mother is not prepared for this, it can prove very discouraging; she may give up hope and rely on more drugs to ease or eliminate her pain.

A mother whose labor is induced will probably require extra support and definitely needs good information on the progress of her labor. Naturally, she must be closely monitored to make sure that the uterus is not overstimulated or the baby distressed by the use of the drug.

Contractions of too great an intensity (*tumultuous labor*) which may result from the use of chemical stimulants such as pitocin (but which might also occur in non-induced labors) can lead to decreased blood supply to the uterus and the placenta (*uteroplacental ischemia*). Also, hyperactive contractions can lead to dips in the fetal heart rate owing to oxygen deficiency and the increased pressure on the baby's head. This pressure is further exaggerated by the fact that the membranes will probably have been ruptured as part of the induction process.

Some of the risks involved with induction are uterine rupture, hypertension, possible water intoxication, prolapse of the umbilical cord, and fetal distress. Careful and judicious administration of the oxytocin drip greatly reduces the chance of these potentially fatal complications. Oxytocin may also cause jaundice. As we go to press, the FDA has banned oxytocin for elective induction.

The following is the story of one woman whose first labor was induced.

At the hospital I got some injections of what I thought was pitocin. My labor was very intense and unexpectedly short—four hours. I felt pretty much in control. My daughter had to be delivered by forceps because her heartbeat was slowing down and I couldn't push her out quickly enough. I was told her life had been endangered because my contractions were too strong and the placenta had separated from the uterine wall too early. My doctors were heroes! They had saved her life.

Three years later, seven months pregnant, I asked my doctor a casual question about my first labor and delivery. He began reading my record to me. He read about injections of Demerol. I was amazed and said, "That doesn't sound like my labor." It turned out that I had gotten pitocin to induce my labor for a time, then Demerol to slow my contractions down, because they were going too fast.

Now that I look back, I think that perhaps the pitocin stimulated my labor too strongly so that indeed it wasn't natural, and was even dangerous. And I think that my strong contractions made the placenta separate early. I'm sure that the Demerol slowed my daughter's heartbeat and oxygen intake. It also explains why she was so sleepy the first three days and didn't immediately nurse.

Labor in hospital

Now I know that unmedicated babies are not sleepy at birth.

In other words, now I don't feel the dangers would have happened if I hadn't been induced and then slowed down. My doctors gave me the feeling that they were responsible for saving my daughter's life, and if they hadn't been there . . . ! Now I feel they were responsible for the dangers to my daughter's life—if not completely, at least in great part. Induction complicated my labor and delivery.

When there is medical necessity, induction may be less hazardous to the mother and her baby than the alternative, waiting until labor begins spontaneously. When induction is chosen merely for the mother's or the doctor's convenience, the risks and complications are too great.*

Fetal Monitors

Fetal monitors are machines which electronically record the fetus' heart rate during labor. There are two basic kinds of monitors: external (non-invasive) and internal (invasive). A variety of external monitors exist, some a good deal less accurate than others. The most accurate monitor is applied by temporarily sticking gummy electrodes onto the laboring woman's chest. The electrodes pick up and record the fetal heartbeat. In addition, two straps, about two to three inches wide, are placed around the woman's abdomen. The upper belt holds the tocodynamometer, which records the intensity of the uterine contractions, and the lower strap holds an ultrasonic transducer, which monitors and records the fetal heart rate. Sometimes the machines don't work well, causing fetal signs to be misinterpreted, and confusing birth attendants and parents. Studies conducted in Japan and Britain indicate that the ultrasonic device may be a factor in brain damage and birth defects when used early in pregnancy.† There is no evidence which clearly proves that the ultrasonic transducer has no adverse long-range effect on the baby when used during labor. This is another instance of doctors' eagerness to use technology before the complete range of its effects is known. When the ultrasonic device is not used, the external monitor is only about 57 percent accurate.

*Immature infants may develop hyaline membrane disease (see p. 273).

†See also p. 325.

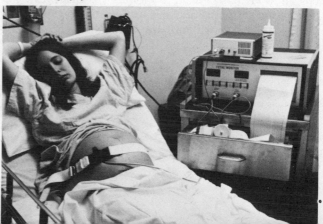

Some women feel that the straps are too snug and increase their discomfort during labor. Many have stated that the monitors limit their mobility. Other women have said that the external monitor did not inhibit their labor at all.

Internal fetal monitors are almost routinely used now. They have electrodes connected to wires within a plastic tube, and are introduced into the woman's vagina and attached directly to the baby's presenting part (usually the head) by means of metal clips or screws. No one has bothered to find out if this causes pain to the fetus, but we would assume it must, and we find it appalling that that has not been considered. The wires coming out of the vagina are held in place by an elastic strap around the woman's thigh. These electrodes measure the baby's heartbeat. The woman's contractions are measured by either a catheter designed for that purpose, introduced into her uterus through her vagina, or by the same external tocodynamometer strap described above. The internal monitor is newer than the external and is now used extensively. There is much more risk of infection with the internal monitor, especially when the uterine catheter is used as well, and there are of course serious potential risks to the baby, considering the possibility of bleeding due to the way the screw or clip is attached.* More common side effects of the internal monitor are a post-delivery rash on the baby where the electrodes were attached, and possibly scalp abscesses (infected areas). The long-range physical or psychological effects are not known. Fetal scalp blood sampling is increasingly used to attempt to improve accuracy.

In order for the internal electrodes to be applied, the mother's amniotic sac must first be ruptured. This adds to the possibility of infection and, as we stated previously, usually leads to further interventions and possible complications.

With both the internal and the external monitors the mother's blood pressure is intermittently measured by means of a blood pressure cuff attached to one of her arms. The other arm is very frequently attached to an intravenous solution unit, depending on the doctor's policy. It is not hard to imagine that all these procedures during heavy labor can leave the mother feeling very restricted, immobile and apprehensive.

I had a belt around my abdomen to monitor my contractions and a monitor inserted into my vagina attached to my baby's head to monitor her heartbeat. The belt kept slipping off and felt very uncomfortable. I felt like I couldn't move and was annoyed by that restriction.

---

*John W. Scanlon, M.D., and Edward I. Walkley, M.D., "Neonatal Blood Loss as a Complication of Fetal Monitoring," *Pediatrics*, 50:6 (December, 1972), p. 934.

There are studies which indicate that the use of fetal monitors has not significantly decreased the newborn death rate nor the number of brain-damaged children. Also, women at higher risk are less likely to be monitored than low-risk women.*

We now have evidence that some of the fetal stress picked up by the monitor might itself be a product of the placement and operation of the monitor, or other hospital procedures, such as artificial rupture of the membranes; injudicious use of pitocin to induce or stimulate labor; sedation of the mother, which reaches the baby in proportionally much higher doses; and use of the forms of regional anesthesia that often result in maternal hypotension and consequently create oxygen problems for the baby.† Haverkamp demonstrated in a controlled study of high-risk women that the use of fetal monitoring, as compared with supervision of labor by nurses with stethoscopes, did not improve fetal outcome at all. Monitored patients had three times the C-section rate and more infection than unmonitored patients.

Episiotomy

Just before the baby's head is born, the doctor will probably perform an *episiotomy* on the mother. This is an incision in the perineum, the area between the vagina and the anus, to enlarge the opening through which the baby will pass (see diagram). Although episiotomies are done routinely in the United States, there is often no need for them. If the mother is unanesthetized she will feel when to stop pushing and when to start easing her baby gently out. Her attendants can direct her. The vaginal opening can stretch to very wide proportions without tearing.

We question the practice of performing episiotomies on all women before delivery. Some babies need more

*Raymond Neutra, et al., "Effect of Fetal Monitoring on Neonatal Death Rates," *NEJM*, Vol. 299, No. 7 (Aug. 17, 1978), pp. 324–326.

†A. D. Haverkamp, et al., "The evaluation of continuous fetal heart-rate monitoring in high-risk pregnancy," *Am. J. Obst. Gyn.* 125:310–320, 1976; and R. Caldeyro-Barca, "Some Consequences of Obstetrical Interference," *Birth and the Family Journal*, Vol. 2, No. 2 (1975), 34–38.

AN EPISIOTOMY

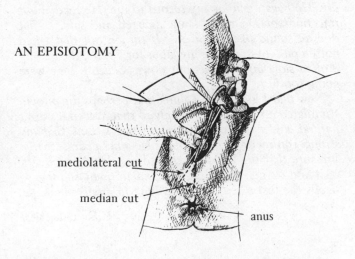

mediolateral cut

median cut

anus

room to get out, and some lie in a position that calls for an episiotomy. Then it makes sense for a doctor to cut a straight incision, either to avoid a possible ragged-edged tear in the perineum or to ensure the birth of the baby as speedily as possible. Yet if a woman learns how to control her pushing, and if her perineum is carefully massaged, softened and supported while she pushes during second-stage contractions and rests in between (mild oils and warm wet compresses are used), there will be little if any tearing, minor and easily stitched. Unfortunately, most medical students are not taught this patient, caring method, and instead are taught to cut routinely.

Often male doctors are concerned that the woman's "looser" vagina will interfere with the man's sexual pleasure during intercourse.

I saw my doctor at the checkup six weeks after my baby was born. Full of male pride, he told me during my pelvic exam, "I did a beautiful job sewing you up. You're as tight as a virgin; your husband should thank me."

The episiotomy stitches are uncomfortable and they often itch. Many times the healing of an episiotomy is painful and debilitating for several weeks.*

After the baby and the placenta are born, the doctor will sew up the episiotomy. If the woman is unanesthetized, the doctor will probably use a local anesthetic to eliminate the pain of the stitching. Many doctors give this local anesthesia even before they perform the episiotomy, and thus the drug reaches the baby. Since the pressure of the baby's head on the perineum creates a natural numbing of the area, the episiotomy can be performed without anesthetics. After the birth, when the numbing has worn off, a pain-killer can be injected into the area to make the stitching-up easier on the mother.

Forceps

A deviation from the normal spontaneous vaginal delivery is delivery by forceps. Instead of the mother pushing the baby out, in a forceps delivery the doctor pulls the baby out with a double-bladed instrument. There are many varieties of obstetric forceps, but in general they resemble salad tongs, except that the blades are longer and curved to fit the shape of a baby's head. Each blade is introduced into the vagina separately and placed carefully on the side of the baby's head, usually over the ear, but sometimes at the temples. Then the two blades are clamped together outside the vagina. Depending on

where the baby's head lies at the time of delivery, the doctor will use high or low forceps. The higher the forceps, the more dangerous the delivery, since that indicates that the baby will have to be pulled out a longer distance and through a more contorted angle.

We know that delivery by forceps has saved the lives of many infants and mothers, but we also know that many forceps deliveries are performed simply for the sake of teaching young obstetricians the technique. Discuss forceps with your doctor before delivery and find out his or her views on the subject.

The usual reasons for a forceps delivery are:

1. To speed up second-stage labor if there is severe fetal distress.
2. If the umbilical cord is wrapped tightly around the baby's neck or if the cord prolapses.*
3. In case of unusual presentations.
4. If regional anesthesia doesn't allow the mother to push out her baby.
5. To shorten a very long second-stage labor.

It is uncommon for a prepared, unanesthetized mother to have to have her baby delivered by forceps, but should the occasion arise, the breathing techniques may be enough to carry you through without anesthesia.

According to the book *Pregnancy, Birth and the Newborn Baby*, ". . . since the early 1900's American obstetricians have come to use forceps for most of their deliveries, even the uncomplicated ones."† The major purpose of forceps in uncomplicated labors is to shorten second-stage, which the doctor believes to be "exhausting" to the mother and possibly dangerous to the baby. Normal second-stage can go from one half hour to three hours, and unless there is some indication that the baby is having trouble getting out, there is no medical reason for introducing forceps. Women are designed to be able to give birth to babies. Today cesarean sections are replacing forceps in most situations.

Cesarean Section

Cesarean sections used to be undertaken *only* in emergencies—i.e., when mother or baby suddenly had an adverse change of condition, or when the baby's head was too big to pass through the mother's pelvis (cephalopelvic disproportion). These days, "elective" cesareans are the rule; one in every four women will be delivered this way (these figures are the highest in the world and rising). Two of the most common reasons are that hospi-

---

*As the stitches heal you might experience itchiness or extreme pain. Some women we know were allergic to the stitching material, and some had stitches that didn't dissolve. If you have trouble, notify your doctor or clinic.

*"The cord around the neck is common and occurs in 25 or 30 percent of deliveries" (C. E. McLennan with collaboration of E. C. Sandberg, *Synopsis of Obstetrics*, ed. 8; St. Louis: C. V. Mosby Co., 1970, p. 166). Usually the doctor can loosen it and slip it over the baby's head. If the cord is prolapsed and falls into the vagina, there is danger of the cord being compressed between the presenting part of the baby and the bony structure of the mother, cutting off the baby's circulation.

†*Pregnancy, Birth and the Newborn Baby*, p. 183.

tal procedures and interventions hinder the normal course of labor, causing a baby distress and obliging the doctor to save it; and also, now that malpractice suits are common, doctors want to make sure they have done everything medically possible, so as not to be sued for negligence. With just the slightest indications of questionable monitor tracings, cesareans are done; routine cesareans are considered all right. This practice of "defensive obstetrics" (taught to medical students) leads to cesareans being scheduled and performed when neither mother nor fetus is in danger or compromised. One great objection to elective cesareans is that a baby may not be fully developed in utero, its lungs not adequate, and it may have hyaline membrane disease.*

During a cesarean the mother gets anesthetized. She may request a spinal in order to be awake when her baby is delivered. The actual operation may be hidden from her behind sterile drapes. An incision is made through the abdominal wall and into the uterus. The baby is then removed from the uterus by the doctor's hands. After baby and placenta are out, both incisions, uterine and abdominal, are repaired by stitches.

The following is a discussion of cesarean section by two women whose first babies were delivered that way.

My doctor knew when he first examined me that there was a chance that I'd have to have a cesarean, but he didn't tell me. He didn't want to scare me. So I wasn't at all prepared for it. He did tell me that I'd have a long labor, and toward the end of my pregnancy he said he was worried because the baby's head was so big, but he didn't tell me why he was worried. Then after eighteen hours of labor he told me I'd have to have a cesarean because I wasn't big enough. I thought there was something wrong with the baby. Part of me believed it was because I hadn't labored hard enough. Part of me believed I had failed because I hadn't been able to deliver normally (that's one thing Lamaze training doesn't prepare you for, how to deal with a childbirth that doesn't work out normally).

I saw my baby being lifted from my stomach in the reflection of a lamp over me. That was very nice. I think my operation took longer, too, because I had a punctured bladder. I found out later that that was a fairly common thing to happen. They flashed my baby past me, and because cesarean babies are more susceptible, they put him in intensive care for twenty-four hours in an incubator. I didn't understand why they took him away so quickly, because they kept telling me he was very healthy. They didn't tell me before the surgery that

he would automatically be put in intensive care, so I didn't understand why I couldn't see him the next day. I thought something was wrong. Finally I got to see him that night, and he was put into the regular nursery.

Afterward I had a lot of happy, normal birth feelings. I was very proud. I got over being ashamed. The day after he was born I had to walk, and my stomach hurt. One thing that helped me was that I was in a bed next to another woman who had had a cesarean six days before. Breast-feeding was a little hard, because I had to have this thing to prop him up, and for the first few days I couldn't turn on my side. After that I could put him next to me while I nursed.

Part of my easy postpartum adjustment was that I stayed in the hospital for eight days and was well taken care of because I'd had surgery. Also, I had no episiotomy, and I was well rested. And when I got home, people took good care of me.

Two days after my due date, my waters broke and my labor was induced with pitocin. After twelve hours of labor and one hour of transition, my cervix was only seven centimeters dilated. The doctor recommended that I go on a half hour more before he would decide about an emergency delivery. I had been exhilarated by my labor and by the fact that I could control my rather strong contractions, but after he said that, my motivation started to decrease. One half hour later my doctor told me that I still wasn't dilating and that he would have to perform a cesarean. I was so physically involved in labor that this felt like an interruption and a disappointment, and I began to cry. But of course, anything that interfered with the safe delivery of my baby was unthinkable, and I agreed to the operation. I was wheeled to the operating room, given a spinal, and became numb from my upper waist down. A cloth was draped in front of me so I couldn't see anything. My husband was not allowed in the operating room. (According to hospital procedure, such arrangements had to be made three months prior to delivery. We wish we had been informed of this so we could have protected my husband's right to attend our childbirth.) In contrast to my intense involvement with labor, I felt passive, numb, and I wished only for a healthy baby. I was surprised at how little discomfort I felt. I did feel slight strokes on my abdomen as the incisions were made, and after a half hour I felt a slight tug on my abdomen. Someone said, "It's a boy." I was so touched. His cry was not one of pain, but of life. They brought him to me: he was beautiful, and mine.

----

*Delivery by cesarean section is a factor that in itself increases the incidence of HMD. . . . One third of the cases of HMD can be prevented simply by avoiding iatrogenic prematurity." Bruce D. Ackerman, M.D., "Prevention of Hyaline Membrane Disease," *Perinatal Medicine*, March 1978, p. 196. (See also Marieskind in bibliography.)

We have a right to know beforehand if the doctor suspects there might be complications in our delivery, but often the doctor will keep that information from us for fear of scaring us.

Be sure to discuss the operation with your doctor before labor so that you understand all aspects of it, including postoperative recovery for both mother and baby. Many hospitals are beginning to allow coaches or fathers into the operating room during a cesarean. Talk this possibility over with your doctor, too. Usually a cesarean birth is a last-minute decision; if, however, a woman has delivered once that way, all future births may have to be conducted by cesarean, although each successive pregnancy should be judged individually.

A hysterectomy should be performed during a cesarean only in an emergency, when the uterus has become seriously infected or ruptured, and never without the fully informed consent and understanding of the mother. Routine hysterectomies during C-sections are deplorable (and even criminal without informed consent). This also applies to appendectomies.

A cesarean delivery is not as safe for the mother or baby as a normal delivery.* It is a major abdominal operation, and as such carries with it the risks that any major operation involves. However, if complications during labor call for a cesarean, the operation is usually safer for the mother and/or baby than a vaginal delivery would be under the circumstances. Support groups for cesarean parents exist (see p. 316).

BEING IN LABOR IN THE HOSPITAL

You'll have a few signs at the end of your pregnancy that labor is about to begin. Sometimes you'll find some blood-tinged mucus on your underclothes. This is the mucus plug that has been in the end of the cervix (like a cork in a bottle), whose purpose it was to keep the uterus free from germs that might have entered through the vagina. Many women never notice or never have a bloody show, as it's called, before labor. Others have an increasing amount of show all the way through the first stage of labor. This is another indication that each labor is unique.

Some women begin labor when their membranes rupture. Once the bag of waters has burst there is a good chance that the baby will be born soon. For that reason it is very important to contact your doctor or hospital if you think your membranes have ruptured.

Diarrhea is another sign that labor is approaching. Many women have a diarrhea-like urge for about three days before labor begins. This is nature's way of emptying the rectum before the birth process, so that there will be no unnecessary pressure on the birth canal. Frequently women feel an increased number of Braxton-

*There are 0.31 maternal deaths per 1000 sections (Evrard, Gold, Edwin, "Cesarean section and maternal mortality in Rhode Island," *Ob. Gyn. Survey*, Vol. 32, No. 7, Sept. 1977, 590–592). Also, the current rate of infections following C-sections is close to 40% (see bibliography, Marieskind).

Hicks contractions for some time before labor actually begins, and often these contractions are confused with real labor contractions. Most books say that the difference between false and real contractions is that the former are erratic and the latter are regular, lasting for a specific amount of time, with a regular interval between them. This isn't the case for some of us.

I didn't begin to feel regularly spaced contractions until I was four centimeters dilated. My doctor had told me to call him as soon as my contractions were lasting about forty-five seconds and spaced about five to ten minutes apart. That just never happened. My contractions from the beginning were anywhere from two to five minutes apart, and the spacing stayed that way throughout much of my first stage. Only the intensity of the contractions changed.

Probably the best sign that you are in labor is that you have to do your breathing techniques to stay comfortable during a contraction. If you suspect you are beginning labor, *eat very lightly*, perhaps some clear bouillon and some gelatine. This will give you a little extra energy, but it won't fill your stomach enough to make you nauseated as labor progresses. Bring some barley-sugar lollipops with you to the hospital to suck on for added quick energy between contractions. If you live far from the hospital, check with your doctor about the clues you'll need to get you there on time. By the way, it's a good idea to register at the hospital early, so that you won't have to go through all the impossible red tape while you're in heavy labor. Most hospitals have forms that you can fill out ahead of time and bring with you when you enter; some also arrange "tours."

When you arrive at the labor room the nurse will prep you and give you an enema. You will probably then be given a vaginal or rectal exam to see how far your cervix has dilated. The person doing this may be the resident doctor and not your own doctor at all. Your doctor may not show up until forty-five minutes before your baby is born, as mine did! But don't let this stop you from asking questions. You have to let them know from the beginning that you are very much interested in what your body is doing, and that you are going to be actively involved in your labor from start to finish. Be sure the doctor or nurse checks the vital signs, such as fetal heart rate and your temperature, blood pressure and pulse. Remember, you have learned what should be happening during labor, and you are aware of what is happening to you. Putting these two together should give you enough indication that your labor is going normally, or that something is seriously wrong. If you suspect the latter, keep complaining until someone listens to you!

Although your contractions up until now have probably been fairly easy to handle, they may get stronger after your enema. Often your contractions will fall into a pattern and you will be able to anticipate the intensity of the next one from that of the previous one. However, you must constantly be on guard so you can switch to another kind of breathing without forewarning. If you practice breathing for weeks beforehand it makes this easier. Relax between contractions, but keep very alert during them.

By this time you are probably four or five centimeters dilated. That means soon you'll be meeting heavier contractions of longer duration with shorter spaces between. Deep abdominal breathing may not work for you now, and you should switch to another level, ribcage or "out," to keep yourself comfortable. Again, remember the point of the exercises is to keep you feeling okay, so do whatever breathing you feel meets your needs. You may still be able to read, sing, play cards and talk to people around you if that helps you to relax between contractions. You may just want to sleep. Sleeping can be a hindrance, however, unless you are alert enough to jump into your breathing as soon as the next contraction starts. Usually if you don't ride the contraction from the start it is difficult to remain in control when it reaches its peak. If the people in your room are bothering you or keeping you from relaxing between contractions, ask them to leave. If, because of sleep or someone annoying you, you lose control in the middle of a contraction, do the following: relax, pant rapidly, and use the time after the contraction to relax completely. At this point a back rub or leg massage can help immensely to give you confidence.

By the time you are six centimeters dilated your contractions will in most cases be very strong, and you will probably feel a definitely uncomfortable rise of pressure and tension at the peak of the contractions, and then a gradual lessening of the tension until the contraction is completely over. You should take full advantage of your vacation time between contractions to rest, but be sure to start your breathing as soon as the next contraction begins. Many women ask for medication at this point. Whether or not we use drugs in our labor is a choice we all must make for ourselves. (See "Obstetrical Medication," p. 279.)

The closer you get to transition, the more intense your contractions will become, and the more help you'll need to cope with them. But that help doesn't necessarily mean medication. A good coach will be sensitive to your needs and will remind you gently that a change of position might do some good, or perhaps a temporary switch to a deeper breathing. Even better s/he could begin to breathe with you throughout the contraction. That helps you to pace yourself and to keep alert. Unfortunately, you may resent any suggestion from someone else and stubbornly remain fixed to a certain position or breathing style. This irritability is very normal and probably indicates that you're entering transition, the very end of the first stage of labor. The more you begin to worry that you'll never make it, the closer you are to making it. The long middle phase of labor is over. Now you are about eight centimeters dilated, and you will feel the most intense contractions of all. But be encouraged! If you've come all this way without drugs, you can overcome transition on your own too. It is the shortest part of a normal labor, and it means that very soon you'll be in second-stage labor, during which you will want to be wide awake.

Transition is different for everyone, but some common signs are nausea and vomiting, leg cramps, shaking, severe low backache, pressure deep in the pelvis, increasing apprehension, irritability, frustration, and an inability to cope with contractions if left alone. It is during transition more than at any other time that your coach's presence is essential. Your coach should actively participate in your labor by breathing with you, comforting you, and continually reminding you that this is the most difficult and the shortest part of your labor. Try to change your position if you remember. Try sitting almost upright, with the soles of your feet together and your legs relaxed. Prop pillows behind you to support your back. Use your most comfortable rapid breathing techniques—pant-pant-blow, or four pants and a blow, or anything else you've practiced and can do automatically. A sip of water or some ice chips to suck between contractions may be the thing to lift your spirits.

You will feel very vulnerable during transition, and you'll be very tempted to accept medication at this point. Be careful—because by the time you ask for it, and by the time it is administered and takes effect (depending on which type of anesthesia you are given), you'll be very near to second-stage. And you don't want to be asleep when it's time to push. Also, the closer to delivery a drug is given, the more effect it has on the baby's responsiveness.

My legs shook all the way through transition, not just during a contraction. My husband gently held them, and that really helped. He also offered me ice chips after each contraction and wiped my forehead with a cool washcloth. I couldn't have made it without his being there every minute.

Someone should be with you throughout transition. If you are alone, call the nurse and make her stay until transition is over. Sometimes your doctor will come in time to help you through. You'll have a hard time concentrating on your breathing now unless someone is being very directive and doing the rapid breathing with you. Be careful not to become hyperventilated. If it happens, slow down and breathe into a paper bag (brought from home for this occasion) or into your cupped hands. If your oxygen–carbon dioxide balance is off, so may be your baby's, so try to avoid hyperventilation by being sure to breathe out fully for every time you breathe in.

Just when it seems that transition will go on forever

and all you want to do is leave the hospital and your coach and forget completely about this baby business, something remarkable will happen. You will begin to feel, slightly at first and then with more and more urgency, the need to push, or bear down. It's a hard feeling to explain, but it is amazingly different from anything in the preceding contractions. Actually, it feels like what it is, a tremendous pressure inside you, trying to push its way out.

It would be terrific if at this point we could simply follow our body's demand and *push*. However, unless the doctor or midwife tells you your cervix is completely dilated (a full ten centimeters open) you must not push or you might tear your cervix (however, opinions vary on this question).

With the onset of pushing, second-stage has begun, and within two hours or less of pushing you'll be holding your baby. The delivery of the baby will probably be done in the delivery room of the hospital, and to get there you'll be wheeled on a kind of movable bed-table. Ask the nurse not to transfer you from one bed to another in the middle of a contraction.* In the delivery room your bed will have stirrups and arm straps and many other medieval-looking contraptions that may scare the wits out of you. Don't panic. The arm straps are completely unnecessary, since you are awake and not thrashing about wildly as you might be if you were totally drugged. Also, the stirrups are not too uncomfortable if you insist they be adjusted to your satisfaction, and they can in fact make pushing a little easier, since you won't be supporting the full weight of your legs any more. Be sure you or your coach brings some pillows along to keep your back propped up. Pushing while lying flat on your back is nearly impossible. Your coach, too, can help support your back during contractions.

For almost everyone the second stage of labor is thrilling and not painful. Once you are allowed to push along with your body, you will finally be able to help actively in your baby's birth. It feels great, and you feel exhilarated. You push only during contractions—your body will give you no choice then—and between contractions you relax. Make sure you blow out all your air at the end of the contraction, and try to remain as limp as possible.

If everything is going normally, there'll probably be a lot of laughing and exciting chatter during the rest intervals. There are about five minutes between these second-stage contractions, and soon the next one will come. Breathe in, breathe out, breathe in, breathe out, breathe in and hold. Sometimes your obstetrician or your coach

may keep up a running commentary as you're pushing: "Good, good, keep it up. Push, push, push, come on, come on, push, push. Good." Although some women appreciate this encouragement, others resent it and find it interferes with their concentration. Tell everyone to keep quiet if you have to. Or perhaps, since you'll be working so hard, your coach can tell them all for you.

By now you're probably very tired, and perhaps you're beginning to feel a burning sensation around your perineum. This means the baby's head is about to crown and the birth is imminent. It's your body's way of saying, "Don't push so hard; ease the baby out." Try to keep your perineum relaxed by releasing those muscles. Also, keep your mouth loose between contractions; you may find this influences the relaxation of your vagina.

When the last contraction comes, the doctor will tell you to stop pushing and to use some rapid breathing to control your urge to push. Then, in the middle of the contraction, out will come your baby's head, usually facing the floor and then rotating to the side. Before you know it, the body will come sliding out.

Although there was no mirror, so I couldn't see my baby emerge, I could feel everything. It was the most thrilling experience I'd ever had—a perfectly formed baby slithering out of my body.

There he was, our new son, facing us for the first time. He breathed in some of our worldly air and began to cry, loudly and unremittingly. We cheered to hear him and to know that he was really, finally, alive.

If your baby breathes before s/he is completely out, s/he may be born with a normal flush. Otherwise s/he will probably look bluish-yellow. Soon his or her breathing will become regular and sustained. No one knows for certain the cause of the onset of respiration in the newborn,* but whatever the reason, the first real breath is a time for rejoicing!

An evaluation of heart rate, respiration, cry, muscle tone, color and reflexes of the newborn is expressed as the 1 and 5 minute Apgar score (1-10). Most babies score between 7 and 10.* Some infants, however, will require help. The doctor in a hospital has various instruments and equipment at hand to encourage the baby's respiratory functions to begin. This is vital, since lack of oxygen can cause brain damage to the infant.

Your baby will be wet-looking, possibly covered with a

---

*There is really no reason why women should be asked to labor in one bed and deliver in another. In the Netherlands the delivery takes place on the labor bed, and of course in home births one does not change beds for delivery. There is a labor-delivery bed being used in at least one major American hospital; more are being planned.

*Ibid., p. 101, Irving and associates showed that while less than 2 percent of infants delivered of mothers having no sedation had a delayed onset of respiration, 35 to 67 percent had delayed respiration if sedation was used.

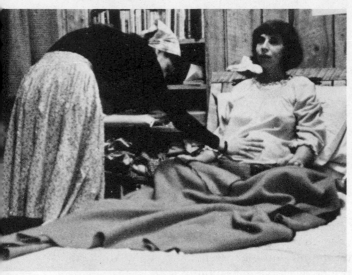
Labor at home

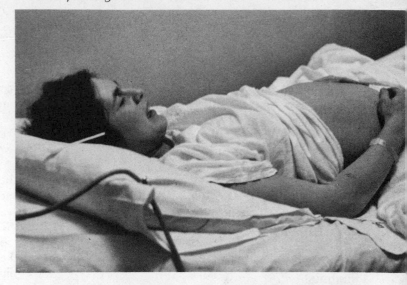
Late first stage

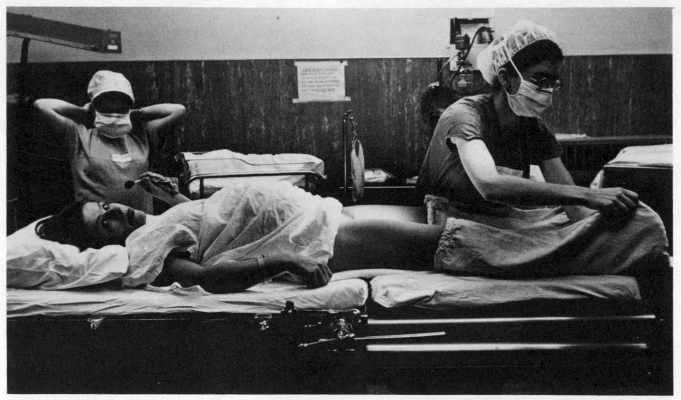
In the delivery room

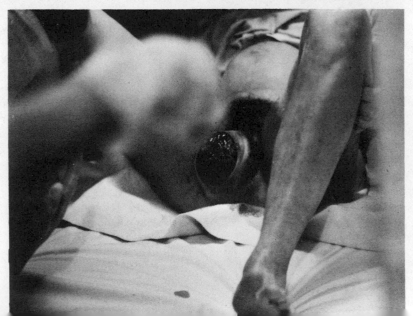
The baby's head crowning

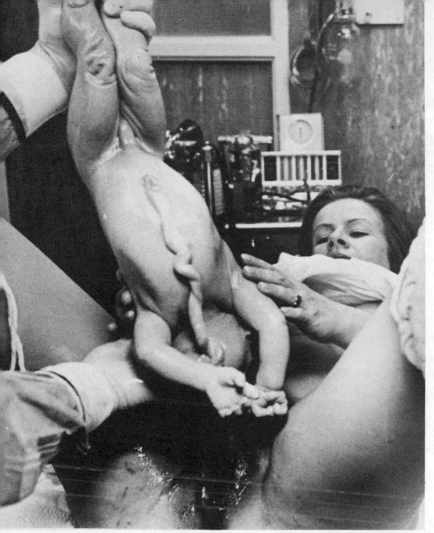

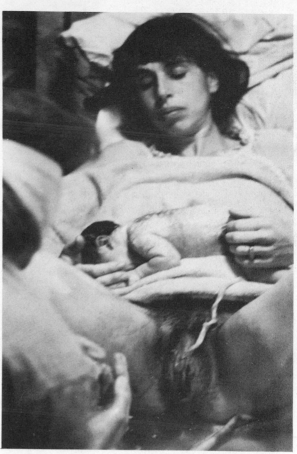

The cord still connecting baby to placenta (home delivery)

The baby is born

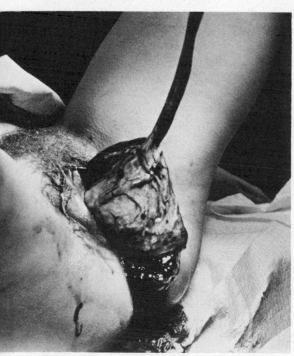

The emergence of the placenta

The tiny newborn nursing (home delivery)

milky substance called vernix, and usually not very bloody. Her/his head may look very strange at first, due to its molding during the birth. This odd shape is temporary, and the baby's head will look normal soon. You may want to reach down and touch her/him immediately, but the delivery room staff may try to stop you due to hospital rules.*

The umbilical cord is still connecting you to your baby via the placenta, which is still inside you (except in the case of placenta previa). As soon as the blood is emptied from the cord, the doctor will clamp it, and then he will cut it a few inches from the baby's navel. In a week or so the cord will dry out completely and fall off, leaving the baby with a normal navel.

The cord struck me as exceedingly strong and beautiful—translucent, blue, and in the shape of a telephone cord, but thicker. The doctor gave my baby to the nurse to suck out more mucus, wipe and wrap her, and only then did I get her. I was shaky, chilly, exhausted and happy. I wanted to hold and nurse my baby but had no energy left. So my husband held her close to me. I felt so close to him at that moment, and also to the woman who had been my monitress.

After a short interval you will begin to feel a contraction coming. This is the third stage of labor, the birth of the placenta. After a few minutes the placenta will separate from you completely, and you will push it into your vagina and out. The whole process might take from five minutes to forty minutes. Sometimes the placenta will actually follow the baby almost immediately, and sometimes the placenta will have to be extracted manually by the doctor. With the birth of the placenta, labor is ended.

The doctor will examine the placenta carefully to make certain it is whole. If there is any doubt, he may explore inside your uterus to see that no fragments are remaining. Then, if you had an episiotomy it will be sewn up.

I didn't have any medication whatsoever, and that was

Delivery rooms are often cool, for the comfort of the adults. The baby, however, needs a warmer environment, so s/he is usually wrapped and placed in a heated crib and then transferred to the nursery. The object is to keep the baby from losing too much heat. A study conducted by Celeste R. Nagel Phillips indicates that a well-dried, covered baby could be given to her/his mother at birth without significant heat loss. This immediate mother-child contact is important both for their future relationship and for the mother's sense of accomplishment.

*A new book, *Birth Without Violence*, by the French obstetrician Frederick Leboyer, introduces a method of childbirth which tries to make the birth experience peaceful, warm and gentle. Leboyer believes the tiny newborn can be traumatized by the bright lights, cold temperature and loud noises of the modern delivery room.*

---

the only thing that hurt me. It could have been less painful if he [the doctor] had put in the stitches loosely before the numbness of the area wore off, and therefore before the placenta was even removed. It was a sensation of pin pricks. It was especially bothersome because by that time I didn't want anyone to touch my body.

You will probably then feel afterpains, which are caused by the uterus beginning to return to its normal shape and size (involution). The whole process takes, on the average, six weeks. In addition to these cramps, which are strongest during the first few days, you'll have a bloody discharge lasting for several weeks. This is called *lochia.* Have a good supply of sanitary napkins at home waiting for your arrival.*

If you are planning to breast-feed your baby, now is a good time to start if you feel up to it. The sucking reflex of a baby born to an unanesthetized mother is very strong indeed, and the colostrum in your breasts is full of protein, minerals, vitamin A and nitrogen, as well as antibodies that help to keep the newborn immune to harmful germs, such as several staphylococci and *E. coli.* It is the most desirable thing to do: let your baby suckle right on the delivery table. Your milk won't come in for a few days, but the newborn can certainly benefit from the colostrum so soon after birth.

In most hospitals the baby will be taken from you very soon after birth and placed in a separate nursery room for anywhere from six to twenty-four hours.

I remember feeling very strange, to have experienced the most remarkable of all things, the birth of my first child, and then to be left all alone. First they took the baby into the nursery. Then I was wheeled into my room, where my husband was able to stay and chat for a while. But he had to work the next day, so he needed some sleep. I was tired but too excited to sleep. So there I was, alone, full of wonder and amazement, remembering the experience we had all shared. But for the next few hours we were not sharing. The hospital had separated us.

MODIFIED ROOMING-IN (Sometimes called family-centered maternity care). When you are looking for a hospital, be sure to find out about its rooming-in policy, if that interests you. In some hospitals the mother is allowed to keep her baby in her room whenever she desires and for as long as she desires. When she is too tired to be entirely responsible for the baby, the baby can be brought back to the nursery. This is called modified rooming-in. Some hospitals, however, work on an all-or-nothing plan, meaning that if the mother chooses rooming-in she must keep the baby with her in her room at all

*For the first few weeks at least, don't use tampons.

times. This can prove to be a tremendous burden, especially for a new mother. Also, some hospitals do not allow the father or other family members to visit except during the regular, restricted visiting hours, even if the mother and baby are in the same room.

Rooming-in provides the right atmosphere for breast-feeding and feeding on demand rather than according to a rigid schedule. The baby usually cries less and gains weight faster if s/he is fed when s/he feels hungry and not when the hospital staff thinks s/he should be hungry.

THE IMMEDIATE POSTPARTUM PERIOD

During the first few hours after the birth of your baby your body will already be beginning to get itself back into its normal condition. Your uterus will be firm and contracting, reducing its size, so that by the tenth day after delivery it will have descended from your abdomen into your pelvis again. Breast-feeding your baby will naturally speed up this involution process by releasing the hormones you need to trigger the uterine contractions and keep them working. These post-delivery contractions of the uterus are often strong and may startle you. Your doctor can prescribe drugs, such as Darvon, to reduce the pain, but remember, if you are breast-feeding, all drugs you take will reach the baby through your milk.

While you are in the hospital they will be checking your temperature often to make sure you are not developing a puerperal (*puer*, "child" + *parere*, "to bear" = *puerperal:* "pertaining to childbirth") infection. Also, your pulse will be checked, and you will be given a blood test after a day or so.

As we have already mentioned, you will have a postpartum uterine discharge called *lochia*, which will change in color over the first couple of weeks from red to pinkish-brown to yellowish-white. This lochia should not smell bad. If it does, that is a sign that an infection is developing, so warn your doctor. Sometimes bits of the placental tissue are left inside the uterine area, so if you experience persistent bloody lochia, inform your doctor, because it generally indicates that something is in the uterus that shouldn't be there.

One thing many of us worry about during the immediate postpartum period is how we will ever be able to move our bowels. As long as you don't strain, you won't tear your stitches or dislodge your recovering organs (a common fear). Drink a lot of liquids to keep your bowel movements soft. Hospitals worry a lot more than they ought to about your bowel functions. Don't you worry. Relax and let your body take over. If necessary, you can always have an enema or a suppository to stimulate your bowels.

Urinating should not prove difficult, but if you experience pain, tell your doctor about it. For that matter, if you experience pain anywhere, let your doctor know, and make sure s/he checks it. The immediate postpartum period is a time when infection can occur easily, and you must be on the lookout for signs that something might be wrong. Depend on the hospital and the doctor only so far; they are busy supervising the recovery of many women and may overlook the very thing that might bother you later on. Women who experience the most bowel and bladder trouble after delivery are those who were totally anesthetized. In this case, it takes a lot longer to get back to normal functioning.

Your breasts may become markedly engorged when your milk first comes in, during the second or third day after delivery. Breast-feeding on demand should relieve this situation quickly.* If you do not plan to breast-feed your baby, the hospital staff will be around to suppress your milk supply with shots of DES or androgen (male hormone). Tell your doctor and the hospital if you would like to breast-feed so they'll know not to give you the shots, which are often given routinely.†

After your baby's birth in a hospital, s/he may be subjected to certain risks you were not informed about beforehand. For instance, infections are a significant risk for newborns in both ordinary and intensive-care nurseries, sources of infection being ordinary hospital procedures and equipment.‡ And babies with (and without) jaundice may be routinely given phototherapy, a light treatment of which the exact mechanism and side effects are not understood, but which is suspected by some microbiologists to be dangerous.§ Learn as much as possible in advance about hospital procedures. It is helpful if you write a letter in advance stipulating all you want to have done (or *not* have done) to/for you and your baby. Send one copy to the head of your hospital, to the head of nursing, to your own doctor, and keep a copy for yourself.

Your baby will be given a thorough medical checkup by either your own private pediatrician or one assigned to you by the hospital. This pediatrician should spend time with you after the examination to inform you of your baby's health and to answer any questions you might have concerning your baby's well-being. You will be asked to bring your baby in for her/his next checkup in two to six weeks.

---

*If you nurse your baby from birth onward without the usual twelve-to-twenty-four-hour wait, and if you nurse according to the baby's demand for food, engorgement will probably not occur.

†DES may soon be banned for this purpose. Even if you are given the shots to suppress your milk, you can nurse. Just put your baby to your breasts regularly and persistently, and the suckling will cause your milk to come in. However, the hormones will reach the baby. Mothers are also at risk from DES (breast cancer, thromboembolism).

‡Martin G. Myers, M.D., "Neonatal Infections from Routine Hospital Procedures," *Modern Medicine*, May 15, 1978, p. 98.

§"Potential Hazards for Newborns Cited," *New York Medical College Alumnus Magazine*, May 3, 1978.

When you are released from the hospital you will probably be given instructions about what you should and shouldn't do in the next few weeks. Remember, don't overexert yourself, and don't try to return to your normal routine until you feel absolutely ready for it. Many women continue to feel tired and lethargic for six months or more. Trust yourself and try to accept postpartum as the total readjustment period it is.

Some important things to remember are:

1. Get plenty of rest.
2. If you are breast-feeding, drink a lot. Usually a quart of milk (or two cups of milk and two cups of another liquid) per day is recommended.
3. Take frequent warm-to-hot baths to help your stitches dissolve. To avoid infection, only put a few inches of water into the tub or basin so the water won't flow into your vagina and up to your uterus.
4. Overexerting yourself can be dangerous. Take advantage of this short time to pamper yourself for a while and concentrate on your new baby.
5. If you have any sign that something is wrong, call your doctor immediately, especially if there is a marked increase in vaginal bleeding.
6. Try to share your fears (they're just about inevitable). Talk to your husband, your friends, your doctor, your mother, or whoever is available and willing to listen, about what may be bothering you. If you don't feel any better, call your prepared-childbirth instructor for help. There may be postpartum groups organized in your area.
7. Most doctors say sexual intercourse can be resumed after six weeks, but this is an individual thing. You may be ready before then, or you may not feel like making love for a while after that time.

Your baby is born. You have done all in your power to give her/him the healthiest and safest birth possible. You may feel delighted with the labor and birth—high, fulfilled, ecstatic and immensely close to your partner. But often, especially if you have had unexpected complications and medical interventions (induction, cesarean, etc.), you may find that your experience leaves you with conflicting feelings—joy and disappointment, confidence and a sense of inadequacy.

Birth is such a powerful event that to participate in it often isn't enough: We relive the birth of our child many times over during the following days, weeks and months; thinking and talking about it, feeling it in our heart. This reenactment is a natural and sometimes essential means of understanding what has happened. Those of us, men and women, who experience birth in the setting of our choice, with no, or few, complications, relive the event in a relatively clear, happy way. Those of us whose experience was altered so that we were not the active participants we planned to be may feel confusion, less satisfaction, less closure.

All that we learned before the birth of our child can help us afterward to assimilate its complexities and depths. Even with our knowledge we are sometimes unable to find a language adequate and powerful enough either to express our wonder and sense of accomplishment, or to exorcise any frustration, anger or outrage we may feel.

Still, as our knowledge about ourselves, childbearing, and current medical practices increases, it becomes possible to be really *present* during childbirth, and to understand it afterward.

Our goal must be to work for the most informed, deep and joyful experience possible and to struggle (it has become a struggle indeed!) for the kind of childbirth each of us wants—safe and satisfying for ourselves and healthy for our children.

CHAPTER 15
POSTPARTUM—AFTER THE BABY IS BORN

COPING WITH POSTPARTUM

The post- (after) partum (birth) period is that time which encompasses the moments after our baby's birth, the days in the hospital, and the weeks and months of adjusting to our new role as mother. We will be faced with many adjustments: getting used to our body in its non-pregnant state, our role with our new baby, and our changed role with the baby's father, older children, housemates and others. This adjustment period is marked by intense highs and lows. The wonderful highs: "I've done it" . . . "I've given birth to this beautiful, perfect being" . . . "This is the first time it's been done" . . . "it's over" . . . "I'm thankful" . . . "She's perfect" . . . "I'm terrific" . . . "I DID IT"—to the lows: "Help" . . . "What have I done?" . . . "I can't take responsibility for a baby" . . . "I'm a baby myself" . . . "I don't want to be a mother" . . . "I can't be a mother, I'm not equipped, I'm not prepared" . . . "I WANT OUT," accompanied by the cosmic realization that this utterly dependent newborn is our responsibility—for keeps.

We all experience some of these sentiments in varying degrees. We all have to adapt and cope with our new role as parent. We can talk about this postpartum adjustment period as having three stages, but it is well to remember this does not mean we will experience it as defined stages. More likely, we will have some of these feelings at various times and at various levels of intensity. For some women this adjustment period may be calmer and easier than for others.

The First Stage

The first stage is the immediate postpartum feelings which we have during our hospital stay. We may feel incredibly high about the actual birth of our baby, and tremendously relieved that there is nothing wrong with her/him (after we've minutely examined her/him), and then we come down with a crash, aching from stitches and general weariness. Some of us may not mind the achiness, it being a constant reminder of the hard work we have just completed and felt so good about.

I had my baby through prepared childbirth. It was the most physical experience I'd ever had. I worked so hard and my work was so amply rewarded—a real baby. I was so pleased with myself. I had the feeling that I had just done a piece of good work. I lay in bed savoring my triumph, and memories of my own childhood flooded me. I felt connected with all womankind.

By the third day, most women have the by now familiar "baby blues." We may cry; have frightening dreams and fantasies; feel scared or worried by our lack of "maternal feelings." These blues last only a day or so (usually), and are accompanied by the milk letdown reflex (breast milk comes in) and may be due to the sudden hormonal changes in our bodies. Usually as we get to know our baby our positive maternal feelings begin to grow; the more experience we gain with our baby, the more these feelings are nurtured. The "letdown" feelings may also be connected with having this exciting event—the birth, for which we've spent nine months preparing—over, and with the full impact of our baby's reality.

Immediately after the birth of my first baby I felt high and exhilarated. But that night I got sad. I cried all night long. During the next few days I lay on my bed thinking of how I would kill myself. I looked at how the windows opened and I concentrated on figuring out times when no nurses were on duty. I couldn't sleep at all. I tried to tell them I was depressed, and all they gave me were sleeping pills. I felt like I'd never feel anything again but this incredible despair, that it would never end. I had nightmares. The one I remember best is where I would be feeding the baby. I would fall asleep and the baby would fall off the bed and be killed. I don't know why I had these dreams and impulses. I have a happy marriage and it was a wanted pregnancy.

Many women have vivid dreams and fantasies after having a baby. It is important to talk about our feelings and fears and to share our pain. We're not alone and we can support each other.

The Second Stage

The second stage of postpartum, which may last from one to three months, is the actual coping with ourselves and our new baby once we get home. There is the incredible fatigue that comes from not having an uninterrupted night of sleep; the stress of incorporating this new person into our existing family; our changing role with our mate; along with our baby's constant needs. In addition to exhaustion, we may feel fragmentation, disorientation and chaos. Life seems a blur; we feel little control at this time.

There are enormous physical changes occurring in the postpartum period. Though they are popularly considered natural, "under no other circumstances does such marked and rapid tissue breakdown (catabolism) take place without a departure from a condition of health," says the author of a widely used textbook on obstetrics.* Under any other circumstances the drastic reduction in blood volume (30 percent) that takes place during this period would be felt as exhaustion, but many women feel exhilarated instead.† Most of the blood and metabolic alterations of pregnancy disappear within the first two weeks postpartum. In a study of one thousand deliveries, 20 percent of the patients had anemia on the fourth day postpartum. In 15 percent it was mild, but in 5 percent it was severe. If you feel unusually weak or tired during the first two weeks, anemia may be the cause. It is very important to continue taking your prenatal iron pills through the first six weeks postpartum.

We should be aware that such changes are taking place and that they can affect us physically as well as emotionally. It is important to note here that feelings, particularly of depression, are intensified and last longer if we permit ourselves to get run-down physically. Some of us have stubborn virus infections that may lead to depression, or substitute for it (in those of us who cannot acknowledge depression).

After a normal delivery the new mother is out of bed in twelve to forty-eight hours. Those of us who get up soon after delivery feel better and stronger sooner and have fewer bladder and bowel problems. Getting up and walking as soon as possible seems to prevent severe constipation. By getting on our feet earlier it has been possible to reduce the recommended hospital stay to two to four days, as compared to the customary ten days of the recent past.

However, it should be emphasized that just because we are able to get up out of bed and move about, and because those of us who have had prepared childbirth feel better sooner, this does not mean that we should expect to resume all of our former responsibilities immediately. It is important to get enough sleep and to set aside some time in the afternoon to make up sleep lost in night feedings. For six weeks—or longer if you find it helpful—time should be set aside for exercise and rest.

Special postpartum exercises are needed to get your abdomen back in shape. If these are not provided by your doctor or clinic, call your local childbirth education group (see bibliography, p. 316). After the first six weeks see "Women in Motion," in Chapter 6, for ideas on exercise.

As in pregnancy, some women will experience a number of discomforts, while others will hardly have any at all. Some common ones are sweating (especially at night), loss of appetite, thirst (due to loss of fluids), and constipation. You may feel great, you may have few or no discomforts, you may have many: you will not know until the time comes. Being aware of the range of possibilities, you are better equipped to cope with them when they occur.

In a study of childbearing stresses, women who were asked which experiences they found most stressful mentioned fatigue more often during postpartum than during pregnancy. Mothers of three children mentioned fatigue both before and after delivery and said that they had difficulty adjusting to the needs of their families.*

The first six months of my third baby's life are a blur to me. Constantly tired and irritable, I somehow got through each day, but it certainly was no fun for us all. The older children (ages six and three) suffered from not getting enough attention. Because the baby was breast-feeding six times a day, there was almost no time to take the kids out—or even get through the daily housekeeping.

Having three little people dependent on you is very demanding emotionally. The middle child especially needs extra attention. She came into our bed almost every night for two months, and wet her bed for two weeks after the baby came home, and still has tantrums occasionally. I still feel spread thin most of the time.

Studies have shown that in the last weeks of pregnancy women experience a loss of REM (rapid-eye-movement) sleep. Rapid eye movements are associated with dreaming, which occurs in deepest sleep, and some scientists believe this deep sleep is needed for both physical and psychological replenishment. The loss of REM sleep and the associated disturbance in dream patterns may be related to the impending crisis of childbirth. Loss of sleep can and should be made up. If the postpartum woman continues to lose sleep, she builds up a backlog of REM sleep loss, which can lead to emotional and physical disturbances.†

*N. Eastman, *Williams Obstetrics*, 11th edition, 1956.

†Reva Rubin, "Puerperal Change," in Nancy A. Lytle, ed., *Maternal Health Nursing* (see bibliography, p. 314, under "General Childbirth Books").

*Virginia Larsen, *et al.*, *Attitudes and Stresses Affecting Perinatal Adjustment*, pp. 7 and 8 (see bibliography, p. 315).

†Barbara Williams, "Sleep Needs During the Maternity Cycle," *Nursing Outlook* (February, 1967), pp. 53-55. For more on REM sleep, see Sharon Golub, "Rapid Eye Movement Sleep," pp. 56-58.

Whether one can get enough REM sleep during the period when the baby is waking at night depends on the individual. Some women feel fine even though their usual sleep pattern is disrupted. If you are someone who sleeps most soundly in your sixth or seventh hour of sleep (you can tell if you feel sleepy during the day), the baby's father or someone else can feed the baby during the night, early in the morning, or during your afternoon nap, so that you can sleep for a longer stretch than the three or four hours between feedings. If you are breast-feeding, the baby can be given a relief bottle for one

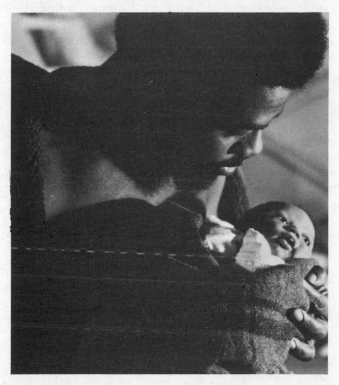

feeding each day. (See "Some Notes on Feeding and Taking Care of Your Baby," p. 311, for more on breast-feeding). Unless family responsibilities can be shared and/or day care can be provided for older children, telling a mother of several small children to nap during the day is "little more than a sick joke."* A first-time mother can try to nap when her baby sleeps.

Housework should be kept to an absolute minimum during this time. It should be shared by all family members, but if you have no help during your first week at home, plan on carry-outs, frozen dinners, paper plates and every possible shortcut. (Do not feel guilty about the legitimate use of paper products. This is the industry's way of shifting the blame for pollution onto the consumer.) If you use a lot of frozen dinners and ready-prepared foods, be sure to supplement your diet with lots of fresh fruits and vegetables, cheese and whole

*Beverly Jones, "The Dynamics of Marriage and Motherhood," in Robin Morgan, ed., *Sisterhood Is Powerful* (New York: Vintage, 1970), pp. 57-58.

grains. If you are nursing, your diet should be the same as during pregnancy, with the addition of a pint of milk, bringing the milk total to a quart and a half a day. You need at least 80 to 100 grams of protein per day when nursing. Nursing mothers ordinarily do not menstruate as long as the child is completely fed by nursing; but there is great variation, with menstruation recurring sometimes as early as two months postpartum, but most commonly at four months. (It usually happens in eight weeks in women who do not nurse.) Most women do not ovulate while nursing, but a substantial number do, so it is essential to employ reliable birth control.

A great deal of attention is given to the pregnant woman's diet and vitamin supplements, attention which usually ceases with delivery. Whether you are breast-feeding or not, you need good nutrition to get *your* strength back. Good appetite may be an indication of postpartum adjustment.* If you are not eating well, you should try to get some help. Continue taking your vitamins and iron supplements throughout the first six weeks postpartum. (See "Nutrition" in Chapter 6.)

You may want to limit stair-climbing to once a day for the first week. Be careful of heavy lifting. Try to tune into signs your body gives you to tell you you are tired; don't ignore them.

Some of the signs of postpartum physical problems are: unusually heavy bleeding, heavier than your period on any day; strongly unpleasant odor of vaginal discharge; temperature 101 degrees or higher; breasts red, feeling hot or painful. If you have any of these symptoms, start immediately to get more rest, and call your doctor.

Feelings About the Baby

The full impact of having a child often doesn't hit us until we're home from the hospital and faced with the reality of caring for that new, helpless human being. Many feelings, thoughts and fears come to mind: I am supposed to be fulfilled because now I am a mother, but I feel ambivalent; I have to be around all the time just to care for my baby's needs, so I don't have any time for my other interests—I've lost my independence; I feel scared—what if I do something wrong? I'm even afraid to bathe the baby for fear I might drop her.

All these feelings are common to so many of us. We don't instinctively know how to care for children just because we're women. Experience is essential; we *learn* how to be good mothers.

Talking over our ambivalent feelings and fears with other women helps us to put those thoughts in proper perspective. We realize that we don't have to perform perfectly right from the beginning; everyone feels uneasy at first.

*Virginia Larsen, *op. cit.*, pp. 91-93.

Once your child is born, s/he is a separate being whom you have to get to know and who has to get to know you. S/he's not really as fragile as it might seem to you, and s/he has a built-in will to live. But don't let that stop you from calling your doctor or clinic anytime you have a question about your baby's health or welfare. Even if you haven't seen the pediatrician yet, the doctor is there to help you. You don't have to feel satisfied until all your questions are answered.

———————————

The first month was awful. I loved my baby, but felt apprehensive about my ability to satisfy this totally dependent tiny creature. Every time she cried I could feel myself tense up and panic. What should I do? Can I make her stop—can I help her? I called the pediatrician daily for advice. One day I called to ask whether it was too hot to put an undershirt on the baby. He said, "For Christ's sake, didn't they teach you anything at the hospital?"

After the first month I got the hang of it, partly because I had such an easy child. She rarely cried. She slept a lot, and when she was awake she was responsive—she'd look at me alertly and smile. Gradually my love feelings for her overcame my panic feelings, and I relaxed, stopped thinking so much about my inadequacies, and was just myself. It was pretty clear from her responses that I was doing something right.

———————————

A word here about the kind of baby you have. If your baby sleeps a lot, wakes up for feedings, smiles at you, and goes back to sleep again, you might feel that this baby business is a breeze. But if your baby is colicky (a catchword to describe baby discomfort, fussiness, crankiness) and cries sixteen hours out of twenty-four (that is not an exaggeration; one couple we know just went

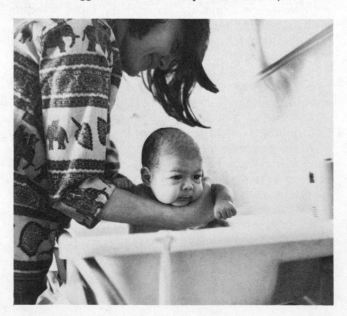

through forty-eight hours of constant wailing), your physical and mental powers will be stretched to their limits. There is nothing quite so jarring to the nerves as a baby's cries—especially if the baby is yours. First there is the feeling of impotence at watching your baby writhe in discomfort or pain; then there is anger at being so helpless to do anything about the situation. It used to be thought that a baby's colic reflected his parents maladjustment to him (if you really wanted the child it would be a good baby). Now we know that sometimes a milk allergy is responsible for the colic, and if this is the cause, your doctor will put the baby on a substitute formula. More often, colic is due to the immature digestive system of the baby. This is developmental, so by two months most babies will outgrow it. That's little comfort while you are going through it, but there it is. No amount of preparation can really equip you to withstand this time calmly. The only advice we can offer is to try to have lots of people around to hold and walk the baby so you can get away for a period each day.

Another interesting factor is the mesh between baby and mother. It seems that an active mother who has an active baby gets along fine; and a calm mother who has a calm baby does too; but an active mother with a calm baby seems to have some conflict and the same is true of a calm mother with an active child.

Our Changed Role with Our Mate

To My Husband

I mothered you,
then weaned you,
so we could parent
together.
Children grow so tellingly.
And who will dare
share this startling
gut
tenderness
when my son (soon)
moves on beyond where I
can pull him on my lap
and smell his hair?
I've lost the smell of your grown-up hair.
Will this parenting lose us
each other?

w. s. 1973

It is important to realize just how stressful our relationship with our mate may be at this time. He may feel jealous of our ability to give birth and may feel we are neglecting him in favor of the baby. Some new fathers feel inadequate to comfort a crying baby who is being breast-fed, and some fathers experience sexual jealousy when the baby is breast-fed. We may need mothering and support ourselves and may find that we have little emotional reserves for being supportive to our men. Both parents may feel jealous of the other's attention to the baby. And the new mother may feel conflicted about sharing the baby with others.

I hadn't known what to expect—what it would be like to be a mother. I experienced watching myself take care of David as if I were two people. . . . Though Mark was willing to help, it took some time before I felt okay about letting him. Becoming a mother for the first time, I really felt legitimate as a person. I was threatened by sharing the responsibility. I was hard on myself, too. I felt I ought to know what to do as a mother instinctively.

When my second child was born I felt lots more comfortable in knowing how to take care of her. I had wanted a girl child. There were a lot of hassles in my marriage. I really wanted her to be my child. I had a lot of anger at my husband. After she was born I was tired and depressed. It took me six months to realize what I was doing. I wasn't sharing taking care of her.

After Ruth was born I was feeling so many strains, marriage problems, fatigue, David's needs. He needed me so much, and I had so little energy for him. It just took time to work out. When I nursed Ruth I would read to David, holding the book on my lap, or David would hold it and turn the pages. He was very interested in the nursing. I took out pictures of me nursing him and told him how much fun it had been.

Some of us may have little or no interest in sex soon after childbirth. Others of us resume sexual activity fairly quickly. We each need to set our own pace. If the vaginal area feels okay and the bleeding (lochia) has stopped, there is no medical risk in having intercourse. Masters and Johnson report that many women resume sexual intercourse within three weeks following delivery.* The taboo period varies from culture to culture throughout the world. U.S. doctors make the six-week rule ostensibly to prevent infection, but today it is largely for their convenience, so that the end of the celibate period coincides with the six-week checkup. (This rule originated in the days before antibiotics.) If you sleep with one person regularly, you probably already share the same germs and have a tolerance for them.

However, some women do experience discomforts and/or low sexual interest which are physically caused and certainly legitimate reason to avoid intercourse until you feel ready. Some women who are breast-feeding ex-

perience painful cramps during intercourse. In some women the stitches in the episiotomy (see Chapter 14, p. 286) continue to be painful for several weeks. Ask your doctor about sitzbaths (*very* shallow warm baths) to help dissolve the stitches. Intercourse can be painful until the stitches dissolve.

Low sexual interest may be associated with lowered estrogen levels in your body. This is fairly common and does not mean you've become "frigid." If you do have sexual interest but find that your vagina does not lubricate easily, this again is physical (related to low estrogen levels) and more common in nursing mothers. Just use an unscented lubricant such as K-Y Jelly or ask your doctor to prescribe Estrogen Cream.

Low sexual interest may also be caused by the trauma of having your life tipped upside down; of having the needs of a new baby, a mate, possibly other children, to consider while your needs go unmet. We then may need to feel nurtured and cared for for a while, without the expectation of sexual intercourse. Remember too that sexual expression need not always include intercourse. (See Chapter 3.)

You must use reliable birth control from the time you begin intercourse. Your old diaphragm will not fit. You can use condoms with lots of foam or jelly. No pills while breast-feeding. Do not rely on breast-feeding or the absence of menstruation to protect you. You can get pregnant the first time you ovulate *before* you begin to menstruate again. (See Chapter 2.)

Masters and Johnson examined a limited number of postpartum women during intercourse and found marked changes from the normal. The physiologic reactions of most parts of the genitals were reduced in rapidity and intensity.*

It was different—I knew I was guilty of putting the baby before my husband all the time. I often used the baby as an excuse for him to do a lot of things for me. He really was wonderful. His sexual desire increased after the baby, and my desire was nil. This was a complete reversal of our situation before the baby.

During this time it is important to keep communications as open as possible. Talking to other couples who have recently had babies may help too.

We think the following story captures with humor the feelings of bringing home a new baby.

We are surviving. Just. Why don't they give Croix de Guerres to people who can go without more than two hours total daily sleep for five weeks? I mean, after this, fighting a war would be fun—I thought babies ate at 6-10-2-6-10-2—mine does. He also eats at 5-7-9-11,

*William H. Masters and Virginia E. Johnson, *Human Sexual Response,* p. 163.

*Ibid., p. 151.

and 4-8-12. I am getting rather used to going around with my breasts hanging out—they are either drying from the last feed or getting ready for the next one. But the love! I really never knew—never ever imagined I would love him like this. This incredible feeling of boundless, endless love—wish to protect his innocence from ever being hurt or wounded or scratched. And that awful, horrible, mad feeling in the first week that you'll never, ever be able to keep anything so precious and so vulnerable alive.

The Third Stage

The third stage, coping with the long-term adjustments of becoming a parent, may last up to one year or more.

Giving birth to our baby may bring back our own childhood feelings of love and rejection; the experience may trigger in us feelings about death, our own, or the death of close older relatives, our parents or our grandparents. It can recall all sorts of jealous and angry feelings we may have toward our sisters and brothers. We may have strong feelings about its meaning to our love relationship with our man.

Often we remain upset months after the baby's birth because we expected at some point to get our lives and feelings back to "normal." It is important to understand that once we become mothers we will never again lead altogether the same lives. Thus, ideally, deciding to become pregnant ideally involves a conscious decision to change one's life forever. For the next two decades we will have to consider the child's needs in making our own plans. (Of course the special tie and caring exist even when the child is independent.) If the experiences of the childbearing year (pregnancy, childbirth, and postpartum) are resolved in a positive way, we will have grown in strength and maturity and feel good about our new responsibilities most of the time.

It is only natural to yearn occasionally for the freedom of childlessness and to feel angry and resentful toward our kids. We have our own needs as people, and at times we need to be separate from our kids. By recognizing this need we can feel freer when away from our kids and enjoy them more when we are with them.

The first child, particularly, brings completely new experiences for the parents, and each new baby brings new relationships and new family interactions. The husband and wife become mother and father as well. The stresses of the postpartum period may bring clashes of child-care ideas, unfamiliar roles, fatigue and financial strain.*

The six or eight months after Peter was born were hard ones for me and my husband. I had wanted very much to have a baby and I enjoyed taking care of him, but I

*Virginia Larsen et al., Prediction and Improvement of Postpartum Adjustment (see bibliography, p. 315), p. 1.

didn't seem to have any energy. My physical energy started to return when he slept through the night and more when he stopped needing a 10 P.M. feeding. But my mental and emotional energy seemed to have disappeared for good. It sometimes felt like it was all I could do to get through a day. I took long naps and I cried often. I got jealous about women my husband saw at work. I felt out of touch with the me who had been an interesting, active and humorous person. Love him as I did, in some moods I resented Peter for even existing. To most people I pretended to be a "happy, young mother," but I was actually quite depressed. Because I didn't know about postpartum depression, I blamed what I was feeling on my own failure to be a good mother. I think I also blamed my husband, as though he could have made me feel better. He, for his part, was feeling worried about his job and resentful that I was too low to give him any comfort. He accused me of having wanted a child and now "not wanting one." (He didn't know about postpartum either.)

A lot of things contributed to my feeling better. I began admitting to friends how bad I was feeling; I began a cooperative play group with four other mothers. Most important, I went to an OBOS course and learned that many women feel depressed for several months after childbirth. All of a sudden I knew it wasn't all my fault. I wasn't a bad person for what I was feeling. Unfortunately, even then my husband and I were not able to talk clearly about postpartum depression together. A lot of damage was done to our relationship during those months of confusion.

Perhaps contributing to our depression may be our expectations of what a good mother is or should be. Our expectations depend in part on the kind of mother we had, and in part on our fantasies of what a mother should be. The disparity between the fantasy mother within us (spotless house, floors we can eat from; serene, looking lovely when our man comes home; feeling fulfilled with full-time baby care) and the feelings we have as real mothers may cause us anxiety. If our fantasy

mother is kind we may find it easier to be good to ourselves—to get enough rest and to feel legitimate in concentrating on our own needs. If our fantasy mother is demanding we may feel guilty much of the time—the house is a mess, there are always chores to be done, and we are busy with the baby. We may often feel undeserving of special care after we've given birth. Some studies suggest that the woman who recognizes the fantasy mother within her and chooses to listen to the good messages and discard the unsupportive ones is likely to be more realistic about her capacities and to get along better with her own mother.* It is important at this time to get help from our own mothers, if possible, but only if they can be supportive and loving to us. We do not need to be undermined in our efforts to adjust to our new baby. We have to be strong enough to assess realistically just what kind of help we will be getting if we ask our mothers. This is not a time for us to "prove" to ourselves or our mothers how well we can cope.

Many women feel lethargic and vaguely upset for the first year after their baby's birth. It is confusing to sort out our feelings during postpartum. There are so many of them; they sometimes change quickly and seem to come from deep within us.

I am a psychiatric nurse and therefore was aware of how angry thoughts about the baby postpartum are a normal part of the adjustment process. But I was unprepared for the enormous amount of anger I felt. I was angry about everything, it seemed. First, we had so carefully planned the conception (scientifically) of a baby girl, and I gave birth to a boy; then my sister-in-law, who had given birth six weeks before me, used the name I had reserved for my child for her baby. Then I realized how much my son resembled my father, who thirty years ago had rejected me. I also heavily identified with my oldest child about his displacement as kingpin. When I attempted to share child care with my husband, who worked at home, I found myself at the mercy of two schedules, the baby's and his. It wasn't until six months later that I felt my anger dissipating and it was a full two years before I felt myself again. During this time I had obsessive fantasies about hurting the baby, how fragile he was, how easily I could drop him, how maybe I would forget him and leave the house, etc. I hated myself for such thoughts, but they persisted. It wasn't until I finally accepted the fact that a "nice woman like me" could have such anger that the fantasies abated. Postpartum for me was learning to deal with more anger than I've ever felt in my entire life. It felt like one long temper tantrum—unscreamed.

Many feelings are related to the kind of mothering we ourselves received, and to our ambivalent feelings about

*Margot Edwards, R.N., "The Crises of the Fourth Trimester," *Birth and the Family Journal*, Vol. 1, No. 1 (Winter 1973-74), p. 9.

it. Many other feelings have to do with our deep, basic fear that we won't be able to be good mothers. Societal pressures on new mothers to drop their major areas of interest in order to be with their babies constantly seem to us to be a major cause of postpartum depression. In becoming a mother for the first time, we experience an abrupt social discontinuity. If we drop out of work, we may exchange a fairly egalitarian relationship with our mate (both working, both sharing decisions and household chores) for a more traditional relationship in which the expectations for us are more stereotyped. We are deprived of adult company for six to eight hours a day or more in order to carry out full-time child care.* Yet the society has no adequate built-in system of support for new mothers. We have no place to share our confusing feelings, the strangeness of our new roles, the newfound satisfactions. The sad fact is that parenthood is not highly valued in our society. We pay lip service to its importance, but we do not talk seriously about it the way we do about other work. Parenting is not considered a career, although the thought, time and energy invested by most women would rival the most taxing of careers. The new mother's work is interesting and challenging; even with its boring aspects (like any other work), shaping the growth and development of a human being is exciting in so many ways. Still, mothers do not get recognition for doing this important work. The motherhood role is one society encourages a woman to take, but once she does, society leaves her alone. Furthermore, it blames her for every possible problem her child may have and even excuses adult behavior on the grounds of faulty mothering.

Many of us feel that sole responsibility for a newborn infant is harder than we have been prepared for. We need to have other people around right from the start to share the work, and the fun, of parenthood.

We have learned that our independence and emotional well-being are as important for our children as for ourselves—we must remain people in spite of the fact that we're now mothers! Therefore, in thinking about child care we have to talk about our own needs as well as the needs of our baby.

Even though we have physically borne the baby alone, we know that we cannot for our own sakes, and should not for our children's sakes, rear them alone. Depending on our own living situations, we have to find the easiest way to share baby care from the very beginning. Sharing, to us, means joint responsibility, not just a division of tasks. We expect the other adults who are constantly part of our children's lives to know how to take care of the baby without having to turn to us as "the expert."

*Alice S. Rossi, "Transition to Parenthood," *Journal of Marriage and the Family*, 30 (1968), pp. 26-39. Also see Arlene S. and Jerome H. Skolnick, eds., *Family in Transition: Rethinking Marriage, Sexuality, Childrearing and Family Organization* (Boston: Little, Brown & Co., 1971).

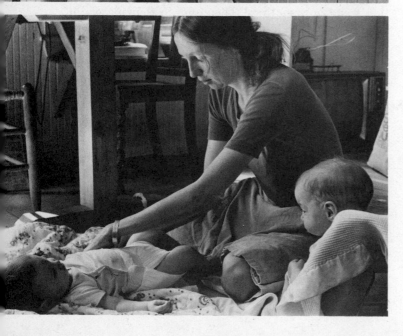

I didn't know how to change a diaper any more than my husband did. In fact, I may have been more nervous about it, since as a woman I was supposed to know how. I learned to do it because I had to learn, and my husband learned too. I always resent those fathers who pride themselves on never having changed their baby's diaper.

Our children need intimate, loving care from more than just one adult. That care can come from ourselves, the child's father, friends with whom we might be living collectively, relatives, good child-care centers, and close family friends. The important thing to remember is that if we as mothers allow ourselves to think that we are the only adults able to care for and love our children, we will almost always come to think of our children as exclusively our possessions and exclusively our responsibility.

We women don't want to feel pushed out of the home, but we do want to leave the door wide open— both for ourselves and our children—to grow and develop as independent people.

The Childbearing Year as Maturational Crisis

Most doctors treat pregnancy and postpartum from a purely physiological point of view. They dismiss most of the psychological and emotional reactions as "natural." But Grete Bibring, a psychoanalyst, in cooperation with a multidisciplinary team including obstetricians, pediatricians and mental-health workers, has completed a ten-year longitudinal study of pregnant women which shows that some far-reaching psychological changes take place during and after pregnancy.

Despite the modern myth that pregnancy is a time of pure harmony and bliss, the social workers in the Bibring team found that pregnant women who had *not* sought psychiatric counseling consistently revealed severely disturbed dreams, thoughts and mental imagery.* However, these women were helped by some simple suggestions or sometimes merely a display of interest from the therapist. Eventually the researchers concluded that the symptoms were characteristic of pregnancy and were not individual disturbances. They came to see pregnancy as a maturational crisis similar to puberty and menopause, an "intrinsically psychosomatic developmental step"† in which biological and endocrine changes bring accompanying psychological disequilibrium, which, *when resolved*, results in emotional growth. The bodily and emotional changes are interdependent, and Bibring sees

*Bibring, *et al.*, "A Study of the Psychological Processes in Pregnancy and of the Earliest Mother-Child Relationship" (see bibliography, p. 315), pp. 9–72.

†Grete L. Bibring, "Recognition of Psychological Stresses Often Neglected in OB Care" (see bibliography, p. 315).

them as equally responsible for the successful resolution of this developmental step.*

The maturational crisis begun by pregnancy does not come to resolution with delivery but continues into the postpartum period, and the "essential maturational changes" come well after the child is born. Thus, often during the early weeks and sometimes months of the child's life we are still in a state of psychological disequilibrium.† This raises the question of what effect our still-unresolved emotional state has on the earliest mother-child relationship. It was suggested by the research team that, instead of taking the traditional psychoanalytic route of blaming mothers for being rejecting, hostile, narcissistic, or smothering, child-development specialists should turn their attention to this period of crisis and maturation in the mother's life. By doing so, a cycle of mutual frustration, resulting in a disturbed relationship, could be prevented.‡

In some instances postpartum disturbance is acute: more than 4,000 women (one in every thousand who give birth) are hospitalized each year in the United States because of postpartum disturbances. At least 20 percent, or 800 women, are permanently incapacitated.§ Twelve and a half percent of the women admitted to a state hospital in Washington were admitted within six months of a delivery or had previously been admitted within six months of a delivery. Of this group of 47 women, 36 were first admissions. The largest number of postpartum admissions were third-time mothers.‖

SOME THEORIES

Because so many of us experience some form of mild or severe postpartum depression or emotional stress we want to discuss at some length various reasons for postpartum disturbances and what can be done about them.

The "traditional" and first serious theory (forty years ago) # was that women who suffered from severe postpartum depression had deep-seated mental illness and the birth of the baby was merely the trigger that brought the pre-existing psychic disturbance to the surface. Women suffering from psychotic postpartum distur-

bances used to be diagnosed as schizophrenic, manic depressive, or whatever clinical syndrome their behavior was thought to resemble. In many cases they were hospitalized for years, in some cases for life.

Today, psychological theories are being supplemented by stress-triggering theories. These can be broken down into two schools of thought: (1) The depression is caused by physical stress—that is, hormonal imbalance and the bodily shock of labor; (2) The depression is caused by social stress, including one's background and one's current environment.

Physical-Stress Theories

In 1962 a study found postpartum depression analogous to combat fatigue.* Women who exhibited severe symptoms were sometimes found to have thyroid difficulties, and made dramatic recoveries when treated with thyroid compounds. Hypothyroidism of itself will not cause psychosis, but may help to trigger it in combination with psychological factors.† It is known that there is normally a change in the amounts of 17-hydroxycorticoids—steroids related to the adrenal gland—in the blood whenever there is a general emotional arousal. Perhaps the imbalance in the sex hormones, the dramatic reduction in estrogen and progesterone, that occurs at the end of pregnancy can help to trigger the depressed feeling so often encountered. Those who favor the physical-stress theories emphasize hormonal treatments, drugs such as tranquilizers or antidepressants, and sometimes hospitalization in severe cases.

After subsequent deliveries the incidence of recurrence of acute postpartum psychosis is high without intervention, estimated at 20 to 50 percent. One current attempt at preventing recurrence uses hormone treatment and drugs: tapering dosages of estrogen and progesterone, as well as tapering dosages of cortisone, are given over a period of about two months following delivery, so that the hormonal changes will not be so dramatic as to trigger a psychosis. Tranquilizers are administered when necessary. The only criterion of success is that the subjects do not require hospitalization.

I agreed to participate in the hormonal study because I feared a repetition of the experience which had resulted in my hospitalization after the birth of my first baby. Whenever I expressed anxiety over this possibility I was told to put my trust in the experiment and the doctors and "not to get in a flap over it." When I asked to see

*Bibring, *et al.*, *op. cit.*, pp. 9–72.
†*Ibid.*
‡*Ibid.*
§Hugh F. Butts, "Postpartum Psychiatric Problems; A Review of the Literature Dealing with Etiological Theories" (see bibliography, p. 315).
‖Virginia L. Larsen, *et al.*, *Attitudes and Stresses Affecting Perinatal Adjustment*, p. 6.
#G. Zilboorg, "Post-Partum Schizophrenias," *Journal of Nervous and Mental Disorders*, 68 (1928), pp. 370–83. Quoted in Hugh F. Butts, *op. cit.*

*J. A. Hamilton, *Postpartum Psychiatric Illness* (St. Louis: C. V. Mosby Co., 1962), quoted in Butts, "Psychodynamic and Endocrine Factors in Postpartum Psychosis" (see bibliography, p. 315), pp. 224–27.
†*Ibid.*

the psychiatrist who was supposed to be associated with the project my obstetrician told me to call and set up the appointment myself. I called the psychiatrist and was told that I could see him only as a private fee-paying patient.

I went to a clinic and got some help from a social worker. After my baby was born I was occasionally depressed and sometimes agitated, but as long as I took the pills and didn't become sick enough to be hospitalized, I was counted as a success for the hormonal experiment.

Social Stress Theories and Prevention

Other reports show that the social factors, including background and current environment, can be major contributors to depression in most people.* Reports of depression in fathers† and adoptive mothers‡ indicate that the causes are not *purely* physical.

A questionnaire developed by Richard and Katherine Gordon was successfully used to predict the likelihood of postpartum difficulties.§

The fourteen stress factors listed by Gordon, Kapostins, and Gordon:

1. Primipara (woman having first baby).
2. No relatives available for help with baby care.
3. Complications of pregnancy in family history.
4. Husband's father dead.
5. Wife's mother dead.
6. Wife ill apart from pregnancy.
7. Wife ill during pregnancy.
8. Wife's education higher than her parents'.
9. Husband's education higher than his parents'.
10. Wife's education incomplete.
11. Husband's occupation higher than his parents'.
12. Husband's occupation higher than wife's parents'.
13. Husband often away from home.
14. Wife has had no previous experience with babies.||

The fourteen stress factors are divided into two categories: Category I, "Conflict with the Motherhood Role," consists of factors indicating a desire for social

and economic mobility, such as both the man's and the woman's education being higher than that of their respective parents. It also includes the woman's preparation for achievement outside the home. Category I is associated with living far from close relatives who could provide practical help and emotional support, and a husband who is often away from home. Category II is related to unfortunate past experiences of failure, fear and loss, such as the death of the wife's mother or the husband's father; the wife's formal education being incomplete; a history of pregnancy complications in the wife's family. Inexperience with babies is included. (Is this an instance of failure or loss? Only for women, presumably.)

The Gordons found that the more stresses, past and present, the more difficulty women had in coping with postpartum. Of 95 women with higher scores (five or more out of fourteen stress factors) 40 percent developed emotional difficulties at six weeks and 29 percent continued to have trouble after six months. Of the 211 women with lower scores (less than four out of fourteen) only 6 percent had emotional problems, and these tended to last for fewer than six months.

Current environmental factors, such as lack of emotional support and assistance, the husband often away from home, and other relatives not available to help, were significant in cases where problems persisted for longer than six months.*

If you are pregnant and many of the above factors are present in your life, first of all do not be alarmed. Remember, 60 percent of the 95 women with high scores did *not* develop problems. We have included this information in the hope that it may help pregnant women to sort out which aspects of our lives are likely to give rise to conflicting feelings and roles following childbirth. We want to suggest fruitful areas for discussion with the baby's father, the doctor, woman friends, prenatal classes, etc., and to suggest some alternatives for minimizing the stress.

Present environmental stresses could be lessened if new fathers could arrange to spend more time at home during the early months and years. Many couples today feel it important to share both the income-producing role and the domestic role, thus cutting down on the woman's isolation during the early parenting years. Also couples or single women with infants and small children can develop a network of friends to exchange baby-sitting and share concerns or possibly try living with other people.

The findings of the Gordon study are an invaluable advance in our understanding of the many-faceted triggers of postpartum difficulties. A questionnaire similar to that developed by the Gordons could be routinely used by obstetricians and clinics as a screening device

*Rita F. Stein, "Social Orientation to Mental Illness in Pregnancy and Childbirth" (see bibliography, p. 316).

†Beatrice Liebenberg, "Expectant Fathers," presented at annual meeting of American Orthopsychiatric Association, Washington, D.C., March 1967.

‡F. T. Melges, "Postpartum Psychiatric Syndromes," *Psychosomatic Medicine*, 30 (January–February, 1968), pp. 95–108.

§Gordon, Kapostins, and Gordon, "Factors in Postpartum Emotional Adjustment" (see bibliography, p. 315); see also Virginia Larsen, *et al., op. cit.*

||Gordon, Kapostins, and Gordon.

Ibid.

early in pregnancy, and women with high-stress scores could be referred to whatever special help is appropriate and desired—financial aid, baby care classes, baby-sitting exchanges, counseling and/or support groups for women or couples. Some of us may want to talk with an abortion counselor to explore whether or not we want to continue the pregnancy.

Though we applaud any approach that stresses prevention and takes the social milieu into account, it is important to look carefully at the inherent biases of even the best-intentioned researchers. It would be interesting to see a list of stress factors compiled by a group of women. For example, is the category labeled "Conflict with the Motherhood Role" caused by preparation for achievement outside the home, or is it the lack of good child-care facilities and the mystique of the full-time mother that are really the causes of stress? (See "Some Proposals for Change," below, for ways that childbearing and child-rearing can be made less stressful—and more joyful!)

Unfortunately, our society encourages us to fuse and confuse ourselves as people with our roles as mothers. We are taught to believe that we and *only* we can best raise our children, and that it must be a twenty-four-hour-a-day commitment. We are in conflict with ourselves because our society makes it so difficult for us to pursue our own goals while providing good care for our children.

Possible Connections Between Physical and Social Factors

A preliminary study of new mothers hospitalized for psychiatric problems showed that they had lower thyroid activity than is normal following childbirth. Interviews showed these women to have more negative attitudes toward motherhood and different kinds of social stress in their lives than a control group of unhospitalized new mothers. This suggests that there may be a relationship between emotional and social stress and lowered thyroid function. Also, third-time mothers had significantly lower postpartum thyroid activity than first-time mothers. The researchers recommend that thyroid activity in the postpartum months should be explored with respect to age, number of children, nutrition and emotional stress.*

Clearly a great deal more needs to be done by the medical profession and the mental-health professions to recognize mind-body connections, as in thyroid function, and more broadly, the "psychosomatic" nature of pregnancy. They should be prepared to work with us as whole people rather than focusing on that which their

limited training and fragmented medical practices make convenient, lucrative and ego-gratifying.

Education and Preparation for Child Care

Even the visiting nurse seems to have gone out of style as women become "better educated." That our education rarely touches on baby or child care is taken into account by no existing public or private institution.*

Although there are classes that help us to deal with the physical side of pregnancy and childbirth,† there is little readily available instruction that prepares us emotionally and experientially for parenthood. Child care is demanding and becomes more so if we expect ourselves to know instinctively things which are learned skills. We can learn how to take care of our babies through our own experiences, through watching or listening to friends or relatives, and through reading or classes.

I feel ecstatic about this baby. I don't have any of the fears and trepidations I had the first time. I feel very adequate to meet my baby's needs and make him happy. I enjoy this baby so much. With my first baby I kept looking forward to the next stage even when she was going through a great stage. With this baby I appreciate each day. I find myself wishing they wouldn't go so fast. I'm acutely aware that he'll only be a baby for a short time.

A study of women who attended prenatal classes during pregnancy showed that those who attended two extra sessions of discussion focusing on *helpful suggestions for new parents* (see box) took more of the recommended suggestions and had significantly less emotional upset postpartum. *When husbands attended special instruction classes, fewer than half as many of the wives developed emotional disturbances compared to the women who participated alone.* Six months later those mothers who had attended the child-care discussions had fewer problems that still persisted. Their babies were less irritable and had fewer problems with sleeping and feeding.‡ The instruction emphasized that the responsibilities of mothers are learned and are not inborn. This confirms our conviction that knowing what to do with a newborn does not get into our heads by "maternal instinct."

---

*We are by no means advocating a return to the kind of education that prepared women to be "educated companions" and mothers and little else. What we want is free education for those men and women who want to learn about becoming parents.

†Education for childbirth (prepared or "natural" childbirth) may improve the postpartum adjustment of women with stressful life histories. Such women often cope better than women with more favorable histories who do not prepare for childbirth. (Leon Chertok, *Motherhood and Personality* [Philadelphia: J. B. Lippincott Co., 1969].)

‡Gordon, Kapostins, and Gordon, pp. 158-66.

*Virginia L. Larsen, *et al.*, "Attitudes and Stresses Affecting Perinatal Adjustment," pp. 66-72, 94.

Helpful Suggestions For New Parents

The responsibilities of motherhood are learned; hence get informed.

Get help from mate and dependable friends and relatives.

Get to know other couples who are experienced with child rearing.

Don't overload yourself with unimportant tasks.

Don't move soon after the baby arrives.

Don't be overconcerned with keeping up appearances.

Get plenty of rest and sleep.

Don't be a nurse to relatives and others during this period.

Confer and consult with husband, family and experienced friends, and discuss your plans and worries.

Don't give up outside interests, but cut down on responsibilities and rearrange schedules.

Arrange for baby-sitters early.

Get a family doctor early.*

Ibid., pp. 158–66.

HOW MEDICAL INSTITUTIONS SHAPE OUR CHILDBEARING EXPERIENCE

There is no medical professional whose specialty includes facilitating the adjustment of the new mother. There is little research that attempts to address early maternal adaptation—and we need such research badly.* We don't know enough about the earliest signs of a mother's inability to parent. No medical professional is trained, and few have taken the trouble, to watch for these early signs. Yet the distance between disturbed mother-child relations and the battered child syndrome is not so great. (We know that there are things past which we cannot change; a mother has her own genetic endowment, her relations with her family, the care she got from her own mother, the experience of her pregnancy.)† We can change some of the negative influences during the first days of life; the unnecessary and harmful separation of mother and infant in the hospital, the insensitive behavior of doctors, nurses and hospital personnel, as well as other practices of the hospital. Childbirth used to be a magnificent sharing experience and has now

*Marian Gennaria Morris, "Psychological Miscarriage: An End to Mother Love," *Transaction* (January–February, 1967).

†Marshall H. Klaus, and John H. Kannel, "Mothers Separated from Their Newborn Infants," *Pediatric Clinics of North America*, Vol. 17, No. 4 (November, 1970).

increasingly become a technical event.* In the hospital, administrative and physical needs get priority; emotional needs and personalities get in the way of efficiency. There is evidence that prompt presentation of the baby to the mother after birth (on the delivery table) is important for the mental health of the mother.† Studies of other mammals indicate a delay interrupts mothering impulses and may bring on rejection. Yet the normal hospital routine is such that mothers are immediately separated from their babies for 12 to 24 hours.‡ The staff may see it as cute, amusing or inconvenient that mothers wish to hold and examine their babies at birth, but they don't see it as a crucial step in the mother-child relationship. It is at this time that a mother "claims" (emotionally makes the baby her own) her baby. Babies now are presented briefly, pinned and blanketed tightly so that intimate fondling (for women who have carried these infants for months) is difficult and sometimes guilt producing.§ This is a travesty! The hospital staff acts as if the baby belonged to them. The concept that close contact between mother and child during the first days of life may facilitate mothering behavior is supported by observations at a hospital where rooming-in was made compulsory. Breast-feeding rose from 35 percent to 58.5 percent, while phone calls from anxious mothers after discharge dropped by 90 percent.‖ It may well be that our hospital routines are partially responsible for the depression women feel after birth. In cultures where there are many women around at birth and after to help with the baby there are fewer reports of postpartum depression. Nurses and doctors and aides should come to know and treat pregnancy, labor, delivery and early growth as one continuing process rather than in bits and pieces, a series of techniques.# They need to see it and understand it from the mother's point of view. There is nothing more important than the experience with which parenthood begins. Hospitals must stop the depersonalization of mothers. After all, the ultimate cause of maladaptation is lack of human sympathy, contact, or support. We must therefore offer that support to new

*Morris, "Psychological Miscarriage."

†*Ibid.*

‡In one recent study, fourteen primiparas (women having first babies) who had more than the usual contact with their babies in the three days following delivery (one hour with their babies within the first three hours following birth, and five additional hours during each of the first three days) were matched with fourteen primiparas whose hospital stay followed usual hospital procedures. Twenty-eight to thirty-two days later, the mothers who had more contact with their infants during the hospital stay displayed more motherly behavior and more intensive interest in eye contact with their babies, who in turn were more attentive. Marshall H. Klaus, *et al.*, "Maternal Attachment: Importance of the First Postpartum Days," *New England Journal of Medicine*, Vol. 286, No. 9 (March 2, 1972), pp. 460–63.

§Morris, "Psychological Miscarriage."

‖Klaus and Kannel, "Mothers Separated from Their Newborn Infants."

#Morris, "Psychological Miscarriage."

mothers, especially those who are isolated from contact with adults, and thereby stop a potential national health problem (mothers' inability to parent, babies' failure to thrive [grow], battered child syndrome) which perpetuates itself in a vicious cycle.*

SOME PROPOSALS FOR CHANGE

We as women can begin to organize ourselves to fight those aspects of our society that make childbearing and child-rearing stressful rather than fulfilling experiences: the fragmentation and regimentation of medical services, the lack of education for parenthood, the mystique of the full-time mother. We need paid maternity and paternity leave and good child-care facilities so that women need not choose between family and career. We must fight the male supremacist mystique that requires women to be responsible for the greater part of home and child care even when both parents work.

We must free ourselves from these equations: woman–passive, man–active, woman–child-rearer, man–provider. We are all human beings, all one species. Our reproductive organs determine complementary roles in reproduction. They need not and should not determine our roles in society.

Some of the changes we need are:

1. Adequate federal subsidies for the diet of *all* pregnant and postpartum women. The government should also subsidize each child, so that better nutrition and a more healthful and stimulating environment would be guaranteed to each child.†

2. Timely help for pregnant women who are likely to be upset postpartum. A questionnaire similar to the Gordons' could be widely distributed to obstetricians and clinics, with follow-up provided for women who showed five or more stress factors. Or women's groups could invite women to come to meetings to talk about women's needs, infant care, and the effects of social stress on pregnancy and postpartum. Group counseling could be organized for women already experiencing emotional upset or who just want to talk to other women. Given the findings of the study by Grete Bibring *et al.*,‡ it does not seem unreasonable over the long term to expect hospitals and clinics to provide group and individual counseling sessions as part of routine obstetrical care. We pay enough for it anyway.*

3. Groups for expectant parents to explore feelings, fears and hopes about pregnancy, childbirth and parenthood and to provide instruction in the skills of infant care. (The groups can take many forms depending on the needs and preferences of the participants—couples' groups, women's groups, possibly other kinds of groupings.) Those who currently teach such classes (usually nurses) should get some training to be able to deal with feelings and group interaction. Midwives, as well as psychiatrists, social workers, marriage counselors and other mental health workers, should be available for consultation with individuals or couples. The government should subsidize these too, to be sure they are available at all income levels.†

4. Prenatal and postnatal "hot-line" telephone services set up and staffed by women. Any woman with a problem could call for advice or just to talk. Women who wanted to be in groups could be brought together. Serious problems would be referred to qualified people.

5. New organizations of visiting laywomen to help with postnatal problems and baby care.

6. A nurse-midwife approach as in England. The midwife sees the woman throughout her pregnancy, stays with her during *all* of the delivery, and helps with child care for the first few months of the child's life. She can handle all routine procedures competently and can recognize complications. Then the obstetrician would be on call for all difficult pregnancies and births, and pediatricians could be on call for all serious infant illnesses, without distinctions made for private and clinic patients. American nurse-midwives have this training and capability already, but the ob-gyns have restricted their use.

7. More females in obstetrics-gynecology. Only 2 percent are women! Ob-gyn is listed as a surgical specialty, and because there is a bias in the medical profession against female surgeons, women have a hard time if they want to be in that field.

8. Safe home delivery for those of us who want it. Mobile emergency units could be equipped as delivery rooms to stand by with whatever may be needed should complications arise. This would have the dual benefit of removing the birth process from the hospital setting, with its associations of sickness and trauma, and at the same time,

*Klaus and Kennel, "Mothers Separated from Their Newborn Infants."

†Pregnant mothers and mothers of children four and under should be aware of the WIC Program. It is a federal food supplement program available in some states, regardless of income. Contact the public health dept. in your city or town. If this program is not available in your state, fight for it. It is your right!

‡"A Study of the Psychological Processes in Pregnancy and of the Earliest Mother-Child Relationship."

*COPE ("Coping with the Overall Pregnancy Experience") groups have been started privately in many communities. Write to COPE, 2 Hanson St., Boston, Mass. 02118.

†Write ICEA (p. 316) for names of local groups already providing all these services, including postpartum discussion groups.

freeing hospital beds and medical personnel for sick people. Specially trained practical nurses could be provided to care for mother and baby where needed.

9. Realistic and up-to-date community-resource information in every clinic and doctor's office, where it will be readily available to patients.

10. Maternity leave for mothers and paternity leave for fathers, with full pay provided by all places of employment, as in Sweden. Subsidized day care or baby-sitting for older children. Both parents need time to learn together to meet their baby's needs as well as to readjust their family relationships.

11. Day care to be provided by all places of employment (as well as in the community) so both parents can return to work when they need or want to. Day care must be provided by *all* places of employment, not just those that employ large numbers of women. Parents should have the option of deciding which parent will take the child to day care, and employers should not be able to claim that provision of child care makes it more expensive to hire women rather than men. Mothers should be able to nurse the child on the job if they choose to. This would have the added benefit of breaking down puritanical prejudices against public breast-feeding, a natural function of a woman's body. It is ridiculous that a woman cannot feed her child in public without breaking a law or being accused of exhibitionism. (Fathers, likewise, should be able to bottle-feed their babies on the job, breaking down conventional prejudices against fathering!)

12. Paid consumer and citizen involvement by women in planning, monitoring, delivering and evaluating maternity and child health services. Our U.S. Public Health Service provides for *no* consumer/user input into policy and practice at the local level, and neither do tax-supported hospitals. Almost all decisions about maternity care, public and private, are made by male physicians and their specialty societies, who hire full-time physician lobbyists to effect legislation, not only in Washington but in every state in the union. This area of health care above all others should have a majority involvement of those who receive services, *all* of whom are women.

13. Contact any of the organizations listed on p. 296 and find out how you can help locally.

APPENDIX: FEELINGS WHEN THE BABY DIES

There are more deaths during the first few days of life than at any subsequent time during childhood, and almost all occur in a hospital. Hospital staff have little knowledge of how to be-

have toward parents whose babies may die or have died. Little research has been done, and so medical personnel just follow customary medical procedures and relate to the parents according to their own personal reactions and common cultural assumptions.

In Latin America all the relatives come to mourn the death of a newborn with the parents. In the United States all traces of the baby's existence are wiped out, largely for the peace of mind of others.

Until recently mothers were not permitted to touch their premature infants because of the fear of infection and also because women were thought to have more of an emotional reaction if the baby died after they had held it. Now that aseptic techniques have reduced the risk of infection, some hospitals are letting the mother, scrubbed and gowned, handle her baby in the incubator. The authors of the Kennel study* seem to feel that having held or touched the baby before it died may have increased the initial grieving to a minimal extent, but helped women in the long run to work through the mourning experience.

In one hospital certain changes in procedure were made following a study of parents whose babies had died. Room assignments were changed so that bereaved mothers did not have to watch other women's babies being brought to them. Staff communication was improved so that parents were given consistent reports as to their babies' chances. Discussions and interviews were held to inform the parents about common reactions to loss and how long they are likely to last. The couples were advised to talk freely to each other about their feelings,† and follow-up interviews were held three to 'four months later to help work through feelings of grief.‡

This is the experience of a woman who lost a baby for the second time. The first time the cord was wrapped around the baby's neck. The next baby died of hyaline membrane disease.

The physical recovery, even after a caesarean, went quickly, but the emotional recovery of pulling myself together to function every day took much longer than anyone, even those closest to me, could comprehend. Such a large part of me had died, not once, but twice—all the hopes, plans, proffered love, with no one to give it to. My arms, my belly were empty. I felt like an empty shell, making only the motions required by the rest of my family.

Everyone said, "Be grateful for the two sons you do have," and I was, but they weren't the right size or shape to be the baby that my body had been preparing for. A year later at a physical exam, when I got weepy talking about losing the baby, the doctor said, "Oh, you're overreacting. After all, you never held him." And all the rage and frustration rose again. I had held him, the baby, minute by minute for nine long months close inside, ready to offer him life with us as part of our family and all I could give him as a mother. And then nothing.

I wanted to adopt a baby immediately, but my husband said, and everyone said, that we had to wait until I was more

*John H. Kennel, *et al.*, "The Mourning Response of Parents to the Death of a Newborn Infant," *New England Journal of Medicine*, Vol. 283 (August 13, 1970), pp. 344–49.

†Men in our society seem to need extra help in expressing feelings, and those sessions with both parents present seemed to be most valuable. Some men tended to repress their grief and bury themselves in extra work.

‡Kennel, *et al., op. cit.*

rational—and that angered me. The reasons were valid. My husband said that the wanting in me was so strong that I'd devour the child emotionally, and that he wouldn't go ahead until I could truly say that if we were turned down by the agency, I could learn to be content with our two sons and let the rage and sorrow wither away. We talked and talked, did apply for a child, and received a five-month-old daughter about a year after the last loss. She is wonderful, and she speeded up the process of recovery by being a baby for us and by becoming far more important to us than what might have been.

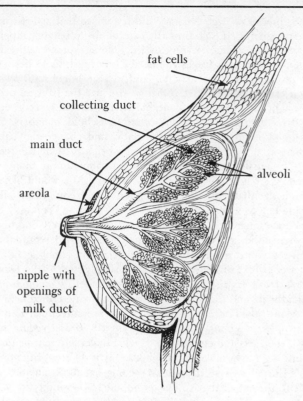

SOME NOTES ON FEEDING AND TAKING CARE OF YOUR BABY

When you decide how to feed your baby, whether to use breast or bottle, you may want to consider how that method fits in with the idea of sharing infant care. Most of us in our group who have children breast-fed our babies. We did it because we wanted that experience, and also because we were feeling proud of our bodies and glad as women that our bodies can provide nourishment for our children. However, it is no wonder that many women in America feel ambivalent about breast-feeding. We are told that our breasts are our sexiest parts, and we are whistled at and winked at until we begin to think of ourselves as little more than sex objects for men. Consequently, many of us feel embarrassed or uncomfortable using our breasts to feed our babies.

Breast-feeding is a kind of sexual thing, but not because men tell us our breasts are sexy. Breast-feeding is sexual because it is satisfying, sensual and fulfilling. It is a pleasant and relaxing way for both mother and baby to enjoy feedings, and it is an affirmation of our bodies.

Also, human milk is ideally suited to a baby's needs. Often

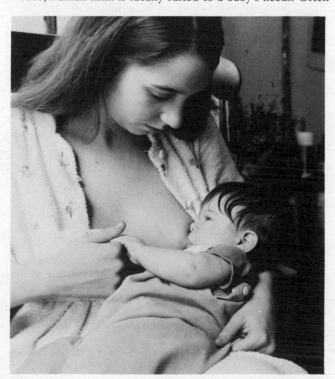

babies who cannot tolerate any other food will have no trouble digesting breast milk. Furthermore, breast-feeding helps to strengthen the infant's resistance to infection and disease. Colostrum, the liquid in a new mother's breasts before the milk actually comes in, is especially high in antibodies that protect the tiny newborn against staphylococcus infections, polio virus, Coxsackie B. virus, infant diarrhea, and *E. coli* infections. These are the very germs to which infants are usually most susceptible. Breast-feeding also gives our babies a natural immunity to almost all common childhood diseases for at least six months, and usually until we stop breast-feeding completely. Moreover, the physical closeness of mother and baby during breast-feeding is important to the baby's future emotional health. If you've chosen bottle feeding, or if you find that you want to switch from breast to bottle feeding, don't feel that you can't be close to your baby. Whatever the method of feeding, babies like to be held close and cuddled by the person doing the feeding.

Sharing child care is easier with bottle feeding but can be very compatible with breast-feeding, especially when the baby gets a little older. It's difficult to establish a successful part-time breast-feeding arrangement, but if you want to have time for yourself away from your baby, it's worth the effort. Also, it's important for the other members of your family not to feel that you have the exclusive power to meet your baby's needs.

Don't try to impose a schedule for feeding on your newborn at first. Feed the baby whenever s/he cries for food during the early weeks. S/he will gain faster and be happier, and your milk supply will grow. Of course, after a few weeks or at most a couple of months, a modified schedule will work itself out. Then you can begin to move about more freely and leave other people in full charge more often.

Our milk supply and the baby's growth needs are perfectly coordinated. The more the baby nurses, the more milk our breasts will produce. It's just that simple. Feed the baby from both breasts at each feeding, and try to see that at least one breast is emptied each time. Be careful not to let your nipples get too sore; whenever you can, leave them exposed to the air.

During the early weeks you need a lot of rest, so it's best not to resume too many activities outside the home right away. You can, of course, have someone else give the baby an occasional bottle when you go out, but try not to miss two consecutive feedings. At this point other household members can bathe the baby, play with the baby, and change the baby. Then, after a month or two, you can begin to share the feedings by missing one regularly. Try not to miss more than one feeding a day during the first two months. We would like to emphasize that regularity, missing the same feedings every day, is the key to successful part-time breast-feeding. You may experience some problems at first, but don't give up. Good high-protein food, lots of liquid, enough sleep, and determination will see you through. (For some special hints, such as taking brewer's yeast to increase your milk supply, see Adelle Davis, *Let's Have Healthy Children*; Lester Hazell, *Commonsense Childbirth*, and the La Leche League book described below.)

Many books have been written about breast-feeding. The La Leche League book, *The Womanly Art of Breastfeeding*, will give you facts and confidence. It will answer any specific questions you might have, but its philosophy is different from ours. We do not believe that breast-feeding has to dominate your life to the extent that you have the sole responsibility for your new baby. The baby's father, or another household member who will be sharing child care, wants to feel that s/he too can have a part in satisfying the baby's needs, the most prominent of which is food.

We have learned that there are no final rules to follow regarding infant care; our children are as different from each other as we are from our friends. The key thing is to try to relax and enjoy our children; they can be great fun as long as we don't have exclusive responsibility for them twenty-four hours a day.

Here are some ideas for making motherhood a little easier:

1. Very few books are adequate, because they rarely take into account the mother as an independent person. Talking to friends is more helpful. Dr. Benjamin Spock's *Baby and Child Care* can be reassuring at times with specific information.
2. Time for yourself alone is essential—awake and asleep. You'd be surprised to learn to what extent getting enough sleep determines your ability to cope. When you're away from your baby, enjoy being yourself; motherhood is only one part of you.
3. If you're planning to breast-feed, read some good, supportive books about it first. We recommend Lester Hazell, *Commonsense Childbirth*; Sheila Kitzinger, *The Experience of Childbirth*; Karen Pryor, *Nursing Your Baby*; La Leche League, *The Womanly Art of Breastfeeding*; Alice Gerard, *Please Breast Feed Your Baby*; and Eiger and Olds, *The Complete Book of Breastfeeding*. Check the bibliography for others and for the publishing information about these.
4. Check with family and friends; their experiences will give you support as well as information.
5. Here is a list of some of the products we have found helpful. You may want to try some of these.
    Disposable diapers. Good for traveling especially, but lots of women use them instead of cloth diapers all the time.
    Pacifiers. Some babies won't take them, and probably don't need them, but it's useful to introduce pacifiers during the first week to see how your baby feels about them. After a while the baby may reject the pacifier completely, so don't force it on her or him at that point.
    Baby carriers, infant seats, portable beds—anything that increases your mobility. A baby can sleep anywhere and under most circumstances. Security comes more from adult reassurance than from a bed or a place.
    Other equipment that gives the baby mobility and variety: jump seats, swings, jumpers, mobiles, and so on.
    A baby-food grinder. You can buy a grinder for about a dollar, or a special baby-food grinder for under ten dollars. A blender will work too, but it's a more expensive purchase if you don't already own one. This will allow you to grind all adult food into baby food, thus almost eliminating the need to buy baby food.

We can't emphasize enough that caring for a baby is a learned skill, and one that we are continually learning. It also seems clear to us that successful infant care is as much political as it is physical and emotional. Paid maternity and paternity leaves, adequate housing, and excellent child-care facilities are nothing more than reasonable demands which we can rightfully expect to have fulfilled. We can't hope to be "naturally" good mothers without preparation, education, determination and help.

Childbearing Readings and Resources

Pregnancy

General

Brewer, Gail Sforza, ed. *The Pregnancy-After-30 Workbook.* Emmaus, PA: Rodale Press, 1978.
    Practical guide, illustrated.
11 Million Teenagers. 1976. $2.50. Available from Guttmacher Institute, R and D, 515 Madison Avenue, New York, NY 10022.
    Documents scope of pregnancy problem.
"E.P.T. Do-It-Yourself Pregnancy Test," *The Medical Letter* 20, No. 8 (21 April 1978).

Ingelman-Sundberg, Axel, Claes Wirsen, and Lennart Nillson. *A Child Is Born.* New York: Dell Publishing Co., Inc., 1969 (pb.).
    Fine, detailed color photographs of the growth of the fetus, and photo story of a couple during pregnancy and birth in Sweden.
Lichtendorf, Susan S., and Phyllis Gillis. *The New Pregnancy.* New York: Random House, forthcoming, Fall 1979.
    First complete guide for pregnant working women.
McCauley, Carole Spearin. *Pregnancy After 35.* New York: Dutton, 1976.
Menning, Barbara Eck. *Infertility: A Guide for the Childless Couple.* Englewood Cliffs, NJ: Prentice-Hall, Inc., 1977 (pb.).

Clear, compassionate discussion of medical, psychological and social issues surrounding infertility. Written by founder of Resolve, support group for infertile people.

Scales, Peter. *Teenage Pregnancy: A Selected Bibliography.* February 1978. Available from National Organization of Non-Parents, 3 No. Liberty Street, Baltimore, MD 21201.

Stellman, Jeanne Mager. *Women's Work, Women's Health: Myths and Realities.* New York: Pantheon, 1978 (pb.).

Contains several excellent chapters on environmental and occupational hazards to both men and women of childbearing age.

Nutrition in Pregnancy

Brewer, Gail Sforza, and Tom Brewer, M.D. *What Every Pregnant Woman Should Know: The Truth About Diets and Drugs in Pregnancy.* New York: Random House, 1977.

Excellent and convincing arguments on the relationship between prenatal nutrition and newborn health.

Corruccini, Carol G., and Patricia E. Cruskie. *Nutrition During Lactation and Pregnancy.* California State Department of Health, 1975.

Special concerns for diets of Mexicans, Blacks, Chinese, Japanese, Filipinos, native Americans and vegetarians.

Kenda, Margaret E., and Phyllis Williams. *The Natural Baby Foods Cookbook.* New York: Avon, 1973.

Maternal Nutrition and the Course of Pregnancy. Washington, DC: National Academy of Sciences, 1970.

Williams, Phyllis. *Nourishing Your Unborn Child.* Los Angeles: Nash Publishing Corp., 1974.

Basic information on good nutrition, including scores of recipes.

Pregnancy and Sexual Intercourse

Bing, Elisabeth, and Libby Colman. *Making Love During Pregnancy.* New York: Bantam, 1977.

Brecher, Ruth, and Edward Brecher. *An Analysis of Human Sexual Response.* New York: Signet Books, 1966.

Demystification of Masters and Johnson.

Israel and Rubin. *SIECUS Study Guide No. 6, 1967.* SIECUS Publications Office, 1855 Broadway, New York, NY 10023 (Sex Information and Education Council of the U.S.).

Pregnancy and Exercise

Medvin, Jeannine O'Brien. *Prenatal Yoga and Natural Birth.* Albion, CA: Freestone Publishing, 1974 (pb.).

Helpful photographs accompany description of yoga postures.

Noble, Elizabeth. *Essential Exercises for the Childbearing Year: A Guide to Health and Comfort Before and After Your Baby Is Born.* Boston: Houghton Mifflin Co., 1976 (pb.).

Easy to understand and well-illustrated.

Preparation for Childbearing. New York: Maternity Center Association.

Inexpensive, well-illustrated booklet showing how to exercise, walk, stand, sit and function, as well as how to prepare for childbirth when you are pregnant. Available in Spanish.

Childbirth

General

Arms, Suzanne. *Immaculate Deception: A New Look at Women and Childbirth in America.* Boston: Houghton Mifflin; San Francisco: San Francisco Book Co., 1975.

The first systematic exposure of the abuse of technology and intervention in normal childbirth and how women have lost their power over normal childbearing to male doctors. Beautiful tribute to midwives.

Ashdown-Sharp, Patricia. *Guide to Pregnancy and Parenthood for Women on Their Own.* New York: Random House, 1977.

Bean, Constance A. *Labor and Delivery: An Observer's Diary. What You Should Know about Today's Childbirth.* New York: Doubleday, 1977.

A real eye-opener for anyone who thinks "natural childbirth" is the norm today.

Beels, Christine. *The Childbirth Book.* London: Turnstone Books, 1978.

Bing, Elisabeth. *Six Practical Lessons for an Easier Childbirth.* New York: Bantam Books, 1977.

One of the best step-by-step guides to the American Lamaze method, especially for people who cannot attend class.

Bradley, Robert A. *Husband-Coached Childbirth.* New York: Harper & Row, rev. ed., 1974.

Dick-Read, Grantly. *Childbirth Without Fear,* 2nd ed. New York: Harper & Row, 1959, 1972 (pb.).

By the English doctor who originated "natural childbirth." More stress on education and relaxation, less on activity and breathing.

Donovan, Bonnie. *The Cesarean Birth Experience.* Boston: Beacon Press, 1978.

Useful resource guide for parents and professionals.

Elkins, Valmai Howe. *The Rights of the Pregnant Parent.* New York: Two Continents, 1976.

An empowering book for those planning hospital birth.

Eloesser, Leo, Edith J. Galt, and Isabel Hemingway. *A Manual for Rural Midwives.* Instituto Indigenista Interamericano, Ninos-Heroes 139, Mexico 7, D.F. Also in Spanish.

Third edition of a book written by midwives. Used to train women to do thorough prenatal care and home deliveries.

Fitzpatrick, Elise, et al. *Maternity Nursing,* 12th ed. Philadelphia: J. B. Lippincott Co., 1971.

Interesting, readable, comprehensive textbook written for nurses.

Fitzpatrick, Dorothy, et al. *Home Oriented Maternity Experience: A Comprehensive Guide to Home Birth.* Washington, DC: H.O.M.E., Inc., 1977.

Excellent pamphlet for home-birth preparation.

Gaskin, Ina May. *Spiritual Midwifery.* Summertown, TN: The Book Publishing Company, 1978 (rev. ed.).

Haire, Doris. *The Cultural Warping of Childbirth.* Hillside, NJ: International Childbirth Education Association, 1974.

Thoroughly documented critique of American hospital maternity practices in comparison with the best-ranked nations. Indispensable. Write to 251 Nottingham Way, Hillside, NJ 07205. (Send $1.)

Hausknecht, Richard, M.D., and Joan Rattner Heilman. *Having a Cesarian Baby.* New York: Dutton, 1978.

One of the best on the subject.

Hazell, Lester. *Birth Goes Home* (Home Birth Study). Available from ICEA Supplies Center (see "Resources").

———. *Commonsense Childbirth.* New York: Berkeley Medallion, 1976 (pb.).

Best overall book: good reading, complete, sensible approach to childbirth. Author has had four children and conveys what it feels like to give birth and lose a child. Excellent critique of childbirth problems caused by medical profession. Encouraging view of home birth.

Jordan, Brigitte. *Birth in Four Cultures.* St. Albans, VT: Eden Press, 1978.

Anthropologist who truly understands birth compares U.S. with Danish, Dutch and Yucatecan customs. Fascinating reading.

Karmel, Marjorie. *Thank You, Dr. Lamaze.* Philadelphia: J. B. Lippincott Co., 1959; New York: Doubleday Dolphin (pb.).

Kitzinger, Sheila. *The Experience of Childbirth.* New York: International Publications Service, 1964.

English childbirth educator and anthropologist who combines Read, Lamaze and Method Acting to prepare women for birth.

An excellent book incorporating the psychological with the physical. One of the best.

Kitzinger, Sheila, and John A. Davis, eds. *The Place of Birth: A Study of the Environment in Which Birth ,Takes Place.* Oxford: Oxford University Press, 1978.

Drawn from meetings among British health care providers. Raises critical current issues: safety of home versus hospital birth, routine obstetrical intervention, father participation, etc.

Lang, Raven. *Birth Book.* Palo Alto, CA: Genesis Press, 1972 (pb.). Available from Genesis, P.O. Box 11457, Palo Alto, CA 94306.

A moving, personal book about home deliveries, with descriptions of births by women and men involved in them.

Leboyer, Frederick. *Birth Without Violence.* New York: Alfred A. Knopf, 1975.

Meltzer, David, ed. *Birth.* New York: Ballantine, 1973.

Unusual collection of birth myths, prayers, poems, rituals, stories.

Mothering Magazine. P.O. Box 2046, Albuquerque, NM 87103. $8/ year.

Counterculture quarterly with useful ideas about birth and kids.

Myles, Margaret. *Textbook for Midwives,* 8th ed. Edinburgh, London and New York: Churchill Livingstone, 1975.

The midwives "bible."

NAPSAC Directory of Safe Alternatives in Childbirth. Write NAPSAC (see "Associations") for current edition, listing physicians, midwives and birth centers.

Parfitt, Rebecca Rowe. *The Birth Primer: A Source Book of Traditional and Alternative Methods in Labor and Delivery.* Philadelphia: Running Press, 1977 (pb.).

Contains numerous explanatory drawings and charts, comprehensive list of childbirth education resources, films, acronyms, abbreviations, superb glossary and excellent annotated bibliography.

Rich, Adrienne. *Of Woman Born.* New York: Bantam Books, 1977 (pb.).

The poet turns her power to birth and motherhood, combining her own experiences with fiction, mythology and history. Painful, enlightening and sometimes frustrating.

Shaw, Nancy. *Forced Labor: Maternity Care in the United States.* New York: Pergamon Press, 1974.

Powerful sociological analysis of how women of different classes are treated by doctors and nurses during pregnancy and childbirth.

Stewart, David, and Lee Stewart, eds. *Freedom of Choice vs. Compulsory Hospitalization.* Report of 1978 Atlanta Conference of NAPSAC. Forthcoming, early 1979. Available from NAPSAC, P.O. Box 267, Marble Hill, MO 63764.

———. *Safe Alternatives in Childbirth.* Available from NAPSAC. A transcript of the NAPSAC National Conference proceedings.

———. *21st Century Obstetrics Now!,* Vols. I and II. Available from NAPSAC.

Vellay, Pierre, et al. *Childbirth Without Pain.* Trans. by Denise Lloyd. New York: E. P. Dutton & Co., 1959.

Ward, Charlotte, and Fred Ward. *The Homebirth Book.* New York: Doubleday, 1977 (pb.).

Essays on the medical, psychological, sociological and practical benefits of giving birth at home. Beautiful photographs.

Wertz, Richard W., and Dorothy C. Wertz. *Lying-In: A History of Childbirth in America.* New York: The Free Press, 1977.

Only complete social, legal and cultural history of childbirth in U.S. Scholarly and readable. Inadequate history of the 1970s alternative birth movement. Many little-known facts.

Wessell, Helen. *Natural Childbirth and the Family.* New York: Harper & Row, rev. ed., 1973.

Has chapters on history of childbirth, mistranslation of the Bible, and accounts of anesthetic death statistics.

White, Gregory. *Emergency Childbirth,* rev. ed., 1968. ICEA Supplies Center (see "Associations").

Indispensable for people living in deep country or for anyone who might have to deliver a baby unexpectedly. If you aren't having your baby in a hospital, this is must reading.

Wiener, Joan, and Joyce Glick. *A Motherhood Book.* New York: Macmillan, 1974 (pb.).

A personal look at motherhood by two awake young mothers.

Wright, Erna. *The New Childbirth.* New York: Pocket Books, 1968.

Anesthesiology, Gynecology, and Obstetrics Textbooks

Aladjem, S., ed. *Risks in the Practice of Modern Obstetrics.* St. Louis: C. V. Mosby, 1975.

Bonica, John J. *Principles and Practice of Obstetric Analgesia and Anesthesia,* Vols. 1 and 2. Philadelphia: F. A. Davis Company, 1972.

Chard, Tim, and Martin Richards, eds. *Benefits and Hazards of the New Obstetrics.* London: Heinemann, 1977; U.S. distributor: J. B. Lippincott, Philadelphia.

Collection of technical articles by leading obstetrical authorities. Challenges routine obstetrical interference with facts and figures. "Must" reading for all concerned with childbirth.

Douglas, R. Gordon, and William B. Stromme. *Operative Obstetrics,* 3rd ed., 1976.

Eastman, Nicholson, and Louis Hellman. *Williams Obstetrics,* 15th ed. New York: Appleton-Century-Crofts, 1976.

Ericson, Avis J. *Medications Used During Labor and Birth.* ICEA, 1977.

Much-needed guide to the benefits and risks to mother and baby of all obstetrical medication.

Articles

Ad Hoc Committee on Maternity and Newborn Care, HSA IV, Massachusetts. *The Proposed Plan for Regionalization of Maternity and Newborn Care in Massachusetts: Preliminary Analysis and Recommendations.* February 1977, updated May 1978.

Write for above, plus related materials to OBOS, Box 192, W. Somerville, MA 02144.

"Amniocentesis in the Second Trimester," *The Medical Letter,* 20, No. 21, (20 October 1978).

Barry, Kathleen, et al. "Birth: Suffering for Science," *Off Our Backs,* September/October 1975.

Caldeyro-Barcia, Roberto. "Some Consequences of Obstetrical Interference. Part I," *Birth and the Family Journal,* March 1974.

Introduction to the medical case against the use of a variety of routine medical procedures.

Daniels, Pamela, and Kathy Weingarten. "A New Look at the Medical Risks of Late Childbearing," *Women and Health,* Vol. 4, No. 1 (Spring 1979).

Dunn, Peter. "Obstetric Delivery Today: For Better or For Worse?" Editorial, *Lancet,* 10 April 1976.

FDA Bureau of Radiological Health. "Draft of preliminary notice of intent to develop regulations for diagnostic ultra sound." HFX-440. Available from Melvyn R. Altman, 5600 Fishers Lane, Rockville, MD 02857.

Fleck, Andrew. "Hospital Size and the Outcome of Pregnancy." 1977. Available from Commissioner for Child Health, New York Department of Public Health, Albany, NY.

Fremont Birth Collective (Seattle). "Lay Midwifery—Still an 'Illegal Profession.'" *Women and Health* 2 (November/December 1977): 3.

Haverkamp, A., et al. "The Evaluation of Continuous Fetal Heart Rate Monitoring in High Risk Pregnancy," *American Journal of Obstetrics and Gynecology* 125 (June 1976).

Heinonen, Olli P. "Cardiovascular Birth Defects and Antenatal Exposure to Female Sex Hormones," *New England Journal of Medicine* 296 (1977): 67-70.

Pregnant women taking oral contraceptives have a higher incidence of offspring with cardiovascular birth defects.

Holmes, Lewis B. "Genetic Counseling for the Older Pregnant Woman: New Data and Questions," *New England Journal of Medicine* 298, No. 25 (22 June 1978).

Kay, C. R., et al. "Oral Contraceptives and Congenital Limb Reduction Defects," *New England Journal of Medicine* 292 (January 1975): 267.

Lake, Alice. "Childbirth in America," *McCalls*, January 1976.

Lipnack, Jessica. "Birth: A Special Report," *New Age*, October 1977, pp. 27-39, 86-89.

Lubic, Ruth, and Eunice Ernst. "The Out-of-Hospital Setting as an Alternative for Meeting the Needs of Childbearing Families: Assumptions and Operating Principles," *Nursing Outlook*, forthcoming, 1979.

Marieskind, Helen. *Report on Cesarian Section Rate Rise, 1965-1978.* Forthcoming from HEW (U.S. Government Printing Office). Write: Clara Schiffer, Office of the Secretary, HEW, Planning and Evaluation, 200 Independence Avenue, SW, Washington, DC 20201.

Mehl, Lewis E. "Home Delivery Research Today—A Review," *Women and Health* 1, No. 5 (1976).

National Women's Health Network. *Resource Guide on Maternal and Child Health.*

NICHD National Registry for Amniocentesis Study Group. "Midtrimester Amniocentesis for Prenatal Diagnosis: Safety and Accuracy," *Journal of the American Medical Association* 236 (1976): 1471-76.

Randal, Judith. "Is Fetal Monitoring Safe? Widely Used Technique Needs More Testing," *Washington Post*, 16 April 1978, p. B3.

Scanlon, John W. "Obstetric Anesthesia as a Neonatal Risk Factor in Normal Labor and Delivery," *Clinics in Perinatology* 1, No. 2 (September 1974): 465-482.

Shearer, Madeleine H. "Fetal Monitoring: Do the Benefits Outweigh the Drawbacks?" *Birth and the Family Journal* 1, No. 1 (Winter 1973-74): 12-18.

————. "Some Deterrents to Objective Evaluation of Fetal Monitors," *Birth and the Family Journal*, Spring 1975.

Shearer, Madeleine, et al. "A Survey of California Ob-Gyn Malpractice Verdicts in 1975 with Recommendations for Expediting Informed Consent," *Birth and the Family Journal* 3, No. 2 (Summer 1976).

Silver, George, "Childbirth Without Hospitals," *Washington Post*, 3 April 1977.

Simpson, Nancy E., et al. "Prenatal Diagnosis of Genetic Disease in Canada: Report of a Collaborative Study,"*Canadian Medical Association Journal* 115 (1976): 739-740.

Sugarman, Muriel. "Regionalization of Maternity and Newborn Care: How Can We Make a Good Thing Better?" *Journal of Perinatology/Neonatology*, May/June 1978.

U.S. Senate Subcommittee on Health and Scientific Research of the Committee on Human Resources. *Hearing on Obstetric Practices in the U.S., 17 April 1978.* U.S. Government Printing Office.

Yanover, Mark, et al. "Perinatal Care of Low-Risk Mothers and Infants: Early Discharge with Home Care," *New England Journal of Medicine* 294, No. 13 (25 March 1976).

Breast-Feeding

Corruccini, Carol G., and Patricia E. Cruskie. *Nutrition during Lactation and Pregnancy.* See above, "Nutrition in Pregnancy."

Eiger, Marion S., M.D., and Sally Wnedkos Olds. *The Complete Book of Breastfeeding.* New York: The Workman Publishing Company, Inc., 1972.

Gerard, Alice. *Please Breast Feed Your Baby.* New York: New American Library, 1971.

Gerard, J. W. "Breastfeeding: Second Thoughts," *Pediatrics* 54 (December 1974): 757-764.

> Documentation of the protection against disease which colostrum and breast milk give, especially if the infant is fed exclusively by breast for six months.

Jelliffe, Derrick B., and E. F. Jelliffe. *Human Milk in the Modern World: Psychosocial, Nutritional, and Economic Significance.* New York: Oxford University Press, 1977.

> A "general systems" view of mother's milk. Covers psychophysiology, biochemistry, nutrition, economics, weaning and cultural attitudes. Extensive appendices.

————. "The Uniqueness of Human Milk," a symposium, *American Journal of Clinical Nutrition*, August 1971. Available from La Leche League, 9616 Minneapolis Avenue, Franklin Park, IL 60131. (Send $2.25.)

> Articles by many leading authorities on all aspects of lactation.

Pryor, Karen. *Nursing Your Baby.* New York: Harper & Row, 1963; Pocket Books, 1973 (pb.).

> One of the best books on nursing, an updated classic handbook.

Raphael, Dana. *The Tender Gift.* Englewood Cliffs, NJ: Prentice Hall, 1973.

White Paper on Infant Feeding Practices (see below, "Infant and Child Care").

The Womanly Art of Breastfeeding. Franklin Park: La Leche League International.

> Does give a woman lots of support for breast-feeding. Also in Spanish.

Postpartum

Bibring, Grete I. "Some Considerations of the Psychological Processes in Pregnancy," *The Psychoanalytic Study of the Child* 14 (1959): 113-121.

Bibring, Grete, et al. "A Study of the Psychological Processes in Pregnancy and of the Earliest Mother-Child Relationship," *The Psychoanalytic Study of the Child* 16 (1961): 9-72.

Chertok, Leon. *Motherhood and Personality.* Philadelphia: J. B. Lippincott Co., 1969.

Gordon, R. E., E. E. Kapostins, and K. K. Gordon. "Factors in Postpartum Emotional Adjustment," *Obstetrics and Gynecology* 25, No. 2 (February 1965): 158-166.

Jones, Beverly. "The Dynamics of Marriage and Motherhood." In *Sisterhood Is Powerful*, ed. by Robin Morgan; New York: Random House (Vintage), 1970, pp. 57-58.

Kennel, John H., et al. "The Mourning Response of Parents to the Death of a Newborn Infant," *New England Journal of Medicine* 283 (13 August 1970): 344-349.

Rozdilsky, Mary Lou, and Barbara Banet. *What Now?* Send $1 to 341 NE 50th Street, Seattle, WA 98105.

Rossi, Alice. "Transition to Parenthood." In *Family in Transition*, ed. by Skolnick and Skolnick; Boston: Little, Brown & Co., 1971.

Wortis, Rochelle P. "The Acceptance of the Concept of Maternal Role by Behavioral Scientists: Its Effects on Women." *American Journal of Orthopsychiatry* 41, No. 5 (October 1971): 221-236.

Infant and Child Care

Berends, Polly Berrien. *Whole Parents/Whole Child.* New York: Harper's Magazine Press, 1975.

> A mother discusses the parent-child relationship during the first four years.

Boston Women's Health Book Collective. *Ourselves and Our Children.* New York: Random House, 1978. (See bibliography, Chapter 12.)

Brazelton, T. Berry. *Infants and Mothers: Differences in Development.* New York: Delacorte Press, 1969; Dell (pb.).

> Follows three "typical" infants from birth through the first year, with emphasis on the effects the infant can have on his/her environment and the mother-infant interaction.

Fraiberg, Selma. *The Magic Years.* New York: Charles Scribner's Sons, 1959 (pb.).

Hope, Karol, and Nancy Young, eds. *MOMMA: The Sourcebook for Single Mothers.* New York: New American Library, 1976.

From the MOMMA Collective. Excellent sourcebook, support book for single mothers. Contains literary writing and practical information about successful survival.

Kelly, Marguerite, and Elia Parsons. *The Mothers' Almanac.* New York: Doubleday, 1975.

Klaus, Marshall H., and John H. Kennel. *Maternal-Infant Bonding.* St. Louis: C.V. Mosby Co., 1976.

Slightly mistitled. Sensitive, provocative, theoretical and practical treatment of adult/infant attachment. A rare book.

Leach, Penelope. *Babyhood.* New York: Knopf, 1976.

Lessing, Doris. *A Man and Two Women.* New York: Popular Libary, 1963.

The title story focuses on the behavior of a new mother.

Marzollo, Jean. *9 Months, 1 Day, 1 Year: A Guide to Pregnancy, Birth, and Baby Care.* New York: Harper & Row, 1976.

Personal experiences of a group of parents.

Montagu, Ashley. *Touching: The Human Significance of the Skin.* New York: Columbia University Press, 1971.

Fascinating account of human needs and emotions relating to physical contact at all ages; includes some animal studies, etc. Especially shows artificiality of society in the United States.

Prenatal Care; Infant and Child Care; Your Child from 6 to 17. U.S. Department of Health, Education and Welfare, Children's Bureau pamphlets.

Spock, Benjamin. *Baby and Child Care.* New York: Pocket Books, rev. ed., 1968.

Still a classic (it's much misquoted). Not good on breast-feeding or socialization, but good for basic everyday troubles.

Stern, Daniel. *The First Relationship.* Cambridge, MA: Harvard University Press, 1976.

One psychologist's view of how the relationship between child and caregiver builds up.

Thevenin, Tine. *The Family Bed: An Age-Old Concept in Child Rearing.* Minneapolis, MN, 1976.

A book that says it's OK to sleep with your kids.

White Paper on Infant Feeding Practices. Write to Center for Science in the Public Interest, 1779 Church Street, Washington, DC (Send $1.00.)

Vital reading for all expectant and new mothers; scientific documentation opposing prevailing U.S. infant-feeding customs.

Winnicott, D. P. *The Child, the Family, and the Outside World.* Pelican, 1964.

A psychiatrist talks about the family as an emotional unit.

N.B.: Also worthwhile, really helpful reading: books by R. D. Laing, Fritz Perls, David Cooper, Arthur Janov and other modern "existential" psychiatrists, and books by educators John Holt, A. S. Neill, Sylvia Ashton-Warner, George Denison, Jonathan Kozol and Herbert Kohl. Especially useful to new parents are books by family therapists. Virginia Satir's *Peoplemaking* (Palo Alto: Science & Behavior Books, Inc., 1974) has an excellent chapter on parenting.

Films

Arms, Suzanne. *Five Women, Five Births.* Available from Suzanne Arms Productions, 151 Lytton Avenue, Palo Alto, CA 94301.

Women speak for themselves about their babies' births: two at home, three in hospital. Teaching manual accompanies film.

Baldwin, Rahima. *Informed Homebirth* (Audiotape series). Available from Informed Homebirth, Inc., P.O. Box 788, Boulder, CO 80302.

Superb lecture series covering necessary knowledge for those planning home birth. Comes with useful workbook.

Emergency Childbirth. Available from Perennial Education Films, 477 Roger Williams, Box 855, Ravinia, Highland Park, IL 60035.

Dramatization not credible, but expulsion scenes and instructions are outstandingly well done. Information everyone should have.

Associations Concerned with Childbirth Education and Childbearing Resource Centers

American College of Nurse-Midwives. 1012 Fourteenth Street, NW, Suite 801, Washington, DC 20005.

American Foundation for Maternal and Child Health, Inc. 30 Beekman Place, New York, NY 10022.

Concerned with public protection against abuses of drugs, interventions, and other obstetric procedures which could cause damage to the fetus, infant or child in later life. Write for proceedings of two outstanding conferences.

American Society for Psychoprophylaxis in Obstetrics (Lamaze). 1523 L Street, NW, Suite 410, Washington, DC 20005.

Association for Childbirth at Home International (A.C.H.I.) Bookstore. C/o Sue Crockett, R.D. 9 Fair Street, Carmel, NY 10512.

Good resource for childbirth books by mail.

Birth Day. Box 388, Cambridge, MA 02138.

A group devoted to helping parents who want to have a home birth experience.

Cesarian Support. 414 N. Cass Avenue, Westmont, IL 60559, and 14 E. 60th Street, Downer's Grove, IL 60515.

Parent information and support group serving the Midwest.

C/SEC: Cesareans/Support, Education, and Concern. C/o Melissa Foley, 15 Maynard Road, Dedham, MA 02026.

An organization that provides support and information for couples whose children are born by cesarean section. Also, it works to bring about changes in the attitudes and policies of doctors and hospitals so that each cesarean birth may be as fulfilling an experience as possible. Literature and slide/tape available.

H.O.M.E. 511 New York Avenue, Takoma Park, Washington, DC 20012.

ICEA: International Childbirth Education Association. P.O. Box 20852, Milwaukee, WI 53220.

An interdisciplinary organization, founded in 1960, which represents a federation of groups and individuals, both parents and professionals, who share a genuine interest in education for childbearing and family-centered maternity care (FCMC). ICEA has a Supplies Center with a very large stock of books and publications on prepared childbirth, infant nutrition and feeding, and related topics: 1414 NW 85th Street, Seattle, WA 98117.

Informed Homebirth. Box 788, Boulder, CO 80306.

Membership, newsletter, tape series.

La Leche League International (concerned with breast-feeding). 9616 Minneapolis Avenue, Franklin Park, IL 60131.

Materials also in Spanish.

Maternity Center Association. 48 E. 92nd Street, New York, NY 10028.

Literature; domiciliary childbearing center; midwifery programs. Materials also in Spanish.

NAPSAC: National Association of Parents and Professionals for Safe Alternatives in Childbirth. P.O. Box 267, Marble Hill, MO 63764.

Goals are: to promote education about the principles of natural childbirth; to act as a forum facilitating communication and cooperation among parents, childbirth educators and medical professionals; to encourage and aid in the implementation of family-centered maternity care in hospitals; to assist in the establishment of maternity and childbearing centers; to help establish safe home-birth programs; and to provide educational opportunities to parents and parents-to-be that will enable them to assume more personal responsibility for pregnancy, childbearing, infant care and child rearing. Send for current directory.

Society for the Protection of the Unborn through Nutrition (SPUN). 17 North Wabash Avenue, Suite 603, Chicago, IL 60602.

Devoted to improving pregnancy and birth outcomes by improving nutrition and eliminating dangerous diuretic drugs in prenatal care. Has literature, bulletins.

CHAPTER 16
SOME EXCEPTIONS TO THE NORMAL CHILDBEARING EXPERIENCE

Many of us have childbearing problems which cause us difficulty and emotional pain. We might find we aren't able to conceive a child, or that when we do conceive, we miscarry, have a tubal pregnancy, or our child is stillborn. Those of us who have Rh factor, a family history of birth defects, or sickle-cell anemia might have to take extra precautions when we plan to have children.

These problems are not uncommon, yet most of us are taken by surprise when something happens. Why are we so unprepared? One possible reason is that the *majority* of women have few serious problems, so the myth is that few problems occur. Secondly, if something goes wrong, it is often hushed up because many people are superstitious, hesitant to talk about things related to sexuality, or simply want to keep their privacy. Thirdly, many of us don't live in extended families or close communities, so we remain ignorant that certain problems are facts of life for some women.

Even when we are generally healthy, things can and do go wrong:

[From a description of a totally unexpected miscarriage in the 13th week.] *My husband held me and we cried together. It is not hard to remember what we were feeling. The deepest and most obvious was the sense of loss. Almost as strong was the fear. We did not understand what was happening and why, why it was happening to us. Did this mean something was wrong with one of us? Did this mean we could never have children? Had I done something wrong during the early months to cause the miscarriage? We were also frightened by the amount and look of what was pouring out of me . . . it was terribly bloody. It wasn't bad enough that we were losing our baby, but in the midst of all that pain, we had to stay strong enough to deal with all that blood. Why hadn't anyone given us any preparation? Since no one had ever told us about miscarriage, we had no healthy tools to deal with it while it was happening.*

We can learn to deal with potential problems and actual crises in two ways. First we will want to have a general awareness that things might go wrong. We can tuck away such information to be used if necessary. It can't hurt us. If this knowledge upsets us, we can hold dialogues with ourselves, our partners, or our friends. Secondly, if we do suspect we can't conceive, if we do miscarry, or if we have a problem not of crisis proportions, we will want a more specific kind of information to answer our questions: What is happening? What shall I do? Where shall I get help? How shall I cope? What is my next step? What other questions shall I ask?

Often when we ask our doctors for help, either before we are pregnant or in early pregnancy, they brush aside our questions and worries:

I was told by a doctor that he does not discuss miscarriage so that he will not frighten women who (he thinks) are not going to have them.

This kind of attitude insults our intelligence and undermines our emotional strength. We and our doctors are practicing sound preventive medicine when we ask our questions as strongly as we can and they answer them respectfully to the best of their knowledge.

We can also seek out with our doctors the physiological causes of our problems, and we can read all the available literature. We can learn about diagnostic procedures and available treatments. We can ask for test results and insist on further tests if we are not satisfied.

We can learn to develop emotional strengths to cope with what we are living through. Crisis may produce feelings of isolation, fear, anger, grief, guilt and helplessness, as well as obsessions and fantasies. During such times we need sympathetic support from our partners, friends and others who have had similar experiences. We need to be able to reach out to others.

This chapter is meant to be a first tool to help us acquire some of the information we need.

INFERTILITY

When we decide to have our first child, we never expect to be infertile. We know it might take a few months, that we might have some "trouble," but we are not prepared for infertility. We're even less prepared when we already have a child or two and can't get pregnant again.

Infertility is defined by most doctors as the inability to conceive after a year or more of sexual relations without contraception. The category includes women who conceive but can't maintain a pregnancy long enough for the fetus to become viable (able to live outside of the mother). You have the right to consider yourself infertile whenever you begin to feel concerned that you are not pregnant. Infertility may be a temporary or permanent state, depending on your problem and on the available treatments. Many people are surprised to learn that (1) infertility is fairly common, and (2) male factors as well as female factors can be responsible. Between 10 and 15 percent of the couples in the United States are infertile. In 35 percent of these cases, male factors are responsible. In another 35 percent, female factors are responsible. And in 30 percent, combined factors are responsible.

Though up until now the myth has held that infertility is the woman's problem, it has become clear that the man and woman must be diagnosed and treated together. If it's the man who has the problem, then treatment of the woman alone has little value and usually involves many needless, painful and expensive tests. A man, by his very anatomy, is easier to diagnose: the semen analysis is one of the logical tests to perform first.

As new research and techniques become available the cure rate for infertility is improving. Infertile couples are putting a lot more pressure on doctors and researchers, especially because it's becoming very difficult to adopt a child these days. Some problems respond easily to treatment, while others are incurable or respond in less than 20 percent of cases. Infertility appears to be increasing rapidly in the United States, possibly because little is known about the effect of prolonged use of birth control—the pill and the IUD—on fertility, and because the higher VD rate (see Chapter 9) is causing more long-term infections women may not be aware of.

Infertility, a problem in itself, may create many unexpected feelings: isolation, despair, helplessness and anger. It may create problems with our partner, family and friends. Not all people feel the pain of infertility with equal intensity. Certain feelings will appear, disappear and reappear.

It was a shock and a sadness to hear I'm not ovulating. That means I'm not fertile. I feel bitter toward those doctors who said "nothing to worry about" and "have a baby." So now I shall undergo all kinds of tests. Today I feel optimistic, I know (I hope) my body will be set right in some way.

Every time we make love, I hope. Then, my period— blood—no child.

If you seek help for infertility, it's *crucial* to have a good relationship with your doctor. Ideally, find someone who specializes in infertility. If you don't have confidence in a doctor's methods, go elsewhere if possible. It's important that your doctor be respectful of your body, mind and feelings; aware of your pain and other emotions; and accessible to you when you need him or her. It's the responsibility of your nurse and doctor to explain words and procedures so that you can fully understand—it might take you a while, because you are learning a new language and may at times be under stress. You may need help from your partner, close friends or an infertility support group to demand the necessary tests and diagnostic procedures you have learned about. It's a good idea for you to become as familiar with your own body's functions as you can.

Diagnosis and Treatment

Fertility is based on several physiological events and their timing. Your partner must produce sperm of sufficient quantity, quality and motility (ability to swim). You must produce a healthy ovum. Sperm must be deposited in your vagina and move upward through cervical mucus to meet the ovum while it is still in the tube (timing of sexual relations is important, since an ovum may live as little as 12 or 24 hours, a sperm as little as one or two days). Once the sperm and ovum have united, the resulting group of cells must implant properly in the uterine lining and proceed to grow. The usual order of tests done in an infertility checkup is based on an organized attempt to check all the links in this chain of events.

Possible Causes of Infertility

A man might be infertile because of: (1) *No sperm or low sperm production*. The most common cause of male infertility is varicocele—a varicose vein of the testicle (usually on the left side) which may impair sperm production and motility by a mechanism still not fully understood; an infection after puberty accompanied by high fever; unrepaired undescended testicles; taking of certain drugs; exposure to large amounts of X ray; trauma to testicles; congenital malformation or absence of testicles. (2) *Inability of sperm to swim (low motility)*. This may be due to chronic prostatitis, surgical removal of the prostate, or hormonal factors. (3) *Inability to deposit sperm in the vagina near the cervix*. This may be due to impotence; the opening of the penis being either on the underside or the top side of the penis; premature ejaculation; obesity (causing inability to penetrate); or lack of knowledge of the most effective sexual techniques. (4) *Blockage of the passageway carrying the sperm*. May be caused by untreated VD or other infection, varicocele, or vasectomy. (5) *Other factors*. Emotional stress, poor nutrition, or psychological problems.

A woman might be infertile because of: (1) *Pelvic in-*

flammatory disease (PID). Be sure to see p. 141. (2) *Endometriosis.* See p. 141. (3) *Venereal disease* (gonorrhea—see Chapter 9). If not properly treated, gonorrhea can cause tubal blockage. (4) *Endocrine problems.* Failure to ovulate may be due to any malfunction of the glands that influence the menstrual cycle—pituitary, thyroid, or adrenals. (5) *Cervical factors.* Cervical infection; cervical mucus which repels the sperm for some reason; polyps (growths) all might keep sperm from entering the uterus. (6) *Other factors.* Congenital malformation; absence of any of the reproductive organs; premature aging of the ovaries; polycystic ovaries (Stein-Levinthal's syndrome); poor nutrition (e.g., inadequate iodine during adolescence, long-standing folic acid deficiencies); obesity; emotional stress.

A couple may have a combination of problems which results in infertility. Some shared causes are: (1) *Immunologic response.* There may be sperm antibodies present in either the man or woman which tend to destroy the sperms' action by immobilizing them or causing them to clump. (2) *Simple lack of knowledge.* Neither of you might know when you are fertile, how often to have intercourse during this time, or what to do during intercourse to make pregnancy more possible.

In a recent article, Masters and Johnson say that 1 out of 8 couples who have attended their infertility clinic over the past 25 years have conceived within 3 months with no treatment other than this basic information.* If your menstrual cycle is regular, whether it be long or short, you will probably ovulate 14 days (give or take 24 hours either way) before the beginning of your next period. In other words, you will try to become pregnant the thirteenth, fourteenth and fifteenth days before your next period. During these three days, spacing your lovemaking is important. A man's sperm production decreases if he makes love too often, so you should have intercourse no more than once every 30 to 36 hours, if possible, to keep active sperm in your genital tract during that period of time. (Again, one way of finding out when you ovulate is to check the consistency of your vaginal discharge—cervical mucus: see p. 208.)

If your uterus is in a normal position (not tilted back) the most effective position for intercourse will be with your partner above and facing you, and a folded pillow under your hips to raise them. Make love in the ways that give you pleasure, and when he penetrates you, draw your knees up to your chest and make room for him between your legs. He should penetrate as deeply as possible, and when he has an orgasm he will stop thrusting and hold quite still deep in your vagina. Approximately 60 to 70 percent of the sperm are contained in the first few drops of ejaculate. It's best if he withdraws

*William H. Masters and Virginia E. Johnson, "Advice for Women Who Want to Have a Baby," *Redbook* (March, 1975), pp. 70-73.

immediately after ejaculation, and gently props the pillow underneath your hips if it has become flattened. Remain there for an hour, if possible, with your knees still close to your chest. This way you are more likely to retain seminal fluid until the sperm make their way up through your cervix.

Use no artificial lubricant, such as jellies or creams, and never douche afterward.

Though these methods may at times seem too mechanical and make you tense, try to keep in your minds and hearts your good feelings for each other.

If your menstrual cycle is very irregular, ask your doctor for help to find out when you ovulate, or use a basal temperature chart (see p. 208).

Diagnosis

Though a sequence of diagnostic studies will vary with both doctors and individuals, it will include some or all of the following: (1) *A general physical exam and medical history of both man and woman.* (2) *A pelvic examination of the woman.* Your reproductive tract, your breasts and your general development will be checked. You will want to tell your doctor about your menstrual history, its onset and pattern; about any previous pregnancies, episodes of VD, or abortions; about your use of birth control; about your sexual relations (frequency, position and related feelings). (3) *A basal temperature chart.* You will take your temperature daily with a special thermometer and record it on the chart given to you. Unfortunately, the chart gives information only in hindsight: by the time you see the rise in temperature, ovulation *has* occurred. If you are ovulating normally, from the time of your last period until your ovulation you'll have a fluctuating, low temperature (around 98 degrees or less). About the time of ovulation there's usually a sharp dip followed by a rise of half a degree or more. Some cycles show just a rise with no preceding dip. The higher plateau (usually around 98.4 degrees) is maintained until the day before your next period, when it drops again. Your doctor will give you a chart, or you can get one from your nearest Planned Parenthood Association.

The chart, while very useful, can make us feel as if we are scheduling sex, especially if we have to use it over a long period of time.

I started with the temperature charts. This is quite taxing for me and really mentally depressing. I felt very regulated and calculating, both with my own body and in my relationship with my husband. I need not say what it did to our natural sexual impulses. But a child at all cost. That's how we felt.

You must wait at least two cycles to begin to interpret the chart.

(4) *Semen analysis for the man.* Your partner will ejaculate a sample of his semen into a clean container. It

must be examined as soon as possible under a microscope to find out the sperm count and motility. It is now believed that any sperm count above 20 million, in presence of good motility (about 50%) and morphology (70–80% normal forms) can result in pregnancy. Volume is also measured and should be between 2–5 cc. A semen analysis is usually repeated at least once, since a man's sperm can fluctuate in count and motility for many reasons. If the semen analysis is abnormal, your partner will want to pursue his own diagnosis before further tests are done on you.

Any diagnosis of infertility can make things difficult for both man and woman.

My husband's sperm count was very low; we were both crushed. I don't think my husband believed it was actually happening. In fact he often talked in the third person, not truly accepting the results. I love him and therefore hurt for him. I didn't know what to say. I couldn't say the typical "Oh, it's all right" because we both knew it really wasn't all right. For some reason, I found I could handle a problem with myself but found it very difficult to handle my reaction to his problem. I was even more concerned that he couldn't handle his problem. Then we started seeing doctors for him.

If all male factors are normal, study of the woman continues. You may need to have a (5) *post-coital test (Hühner test)*. Just before you expect to ovulate you will make love with your partner and within several hours will arrive at your doctor's without washing or douching. The doctor will take a small amount of mucus from your vagina and cervix to be studied for the number of live, active sperm. A normal test shows that sperm have the ability to penetrate cervical mucus and live in this environment. This test may be combined with another, also done at this time in your cycle, called (6) *tubal insufflation (Rubin test)*. A gas, carbon dioxide, is blown under carefully monitored pressure into your uterus, through the cervix. In a normal situation it will escape out the tubes into the surrounding cavity, causing shoulder pain when you sit up (it is eventually absorbed into your body). If the gas doesn't pass readily, pressure will be increased within safe limits. If the test is abnormal, it may be repeated or confirmed by X-ray studies. It is often difficult to tell the difference between tubes that are blocked permanently and those which are only in spasm. An old-fashioned diagnostic tool, this test is being replaced by the more comprehensive uterotubogram.

(7) If your tubes appear blocked, your doctor might order a *uterotubogram (hysterosalpingogram)*, usually done in an outpatient X-ray department. It involves injecting a dye that shows up on X rays into your uterus and tubes. If the tubes are open, the dye passes into the surrounding cavity to be harmlessly reabsorbed by your body. This test can be painful, especially if pressure is needed to get the dye to pass.

(8) At this point your *basal temperature chart* is studied to check whether you are ovulating or not.

(9) Another test to determine whether you are ovulating is called an *endometrial biopsy*. It can be done anytime from a week after ovulation is suspected to the first day of your period.* A small instrument is inserted into your uterus after your cervix has been partially dilated (this will cause some unpleasant cramping). The instrument scrapes a tiny piece of tissue from the lining of the uterus (endometrium), and this is sent to be examined microscopically. Tissue formed while progesterone is being produced (after ovulation) is different from tissue formed under the influence of estrogen (before ovulation) or under no hormonal influence. Hormonal levels in urine and blood serum can also be helpful in diagnosis of ovulation and the total hormone picture.

(10) If no problem has been found, your doctor might want to do *culdoscopy* or *laparoscopy* (see glossary, Chapter 6), hospital procedures which allow direct visualization of tubes, ovaries, exterior of uterus and surrounding cavities. In culdoscopy, a small incision is made in the back wall of your vagina; and in laparoscopy, an incision is made near your naval. Both tests are done under anesthesia and yield a great deal of information.†

When you are going through these tests, you may temporarily have to give up some of the privacy of your sex life. In the first place, you are under "scientific scrutiny."

We were supposed to make love at seven o'clock in the morning and then I had to run to my doctor's for the post-coital test. Who feels like making love at seven in the morning during a busy week anyway? It was not exactly what you'd call spontaneous.

Secondly, you become a "public" figure. Relatives ask you, "Well, has it happened yet?" Or worse, they don't say anything, but they look at you and sigh a lot. People you don't know well might comment on your problem. Hopefully, during these times you can support each other and learn to keep both your sense of humor and your sense of the awesomeness and privacy of sexuality.

*Doctors differ greatly in their thinking on the timing. Many feel that taking such a minute piece of tissue presents no danger to a new conceptus. Others refuse to risk hazard to a possible pregnancy by having the woman come in on the day her temperature drops, or even at the moment her period starts. Some doctors advise using a condom during relations of this cycle so there is no worry over a possible pregnancy.

†Some doctors prefer to do these procedures first, and others do them as a last resort.

Treatment

After all diagnosis has been carried out, a problem is often found and appropriate treatment can begin.

In general, male problems respond poorly to treatment. In low sperm counts which are motile, you can be artificially inseminated with your partner's sperm. Collecting and concentrating semen specimens is also being tried currently, but without much success. If the problem is a blocked passageway or a varicocele, surgery may be indicated. Some motility problems respond to steroid treatment, and male hormones may help to increase a count temporarily.

For women, the highest degree of success is currently with endocrine disorders, such as failure to ovulate, short luteal (post-ovulatory) phase, or problems of implantation. Cervical problems, such as cervicitis, hostile mucus, or incompetent (weak) cervix, also respond well to treatment. If uterine adhesions are found, dilatation and curettage (D & C) may be performed. Surgery on polycystic ovaries may produce normal ovulation. Tubal adhesions and blockages respond at a low rate of success to tubal surgery or medical irrigations with antibiotics and steroids. If you are found to have many adhesions due to long-term pelvic infection, you may require abdominal surgery to "clean out" scar tissue, suspend the uterus, and improve chances of conception. Success in all treatment is highly individual.

Shared infertility problems are usually treated by separate doctors. The man gets sent to a urologist while the woman is treated by a gynecologist or infertility specialist. It is very important that your doctors communicate with each other. The potential for any couple with a shared problem to achieve a pregnancy is improved dramatically if even one member of the couple can be treated and helped. If both of you can be helped, then your chances are excellent.

In over 10 percent of all infertile couples no reason for infertility is found. This is called "normal infertility." You might be told your problems are all in your heads. This kind of attitude is not helpful at all. Often you may be victims of a condition whose cause or cure has yet to be discovered. We all must press for more research.

In all cases, a 5 percent spontaneous cure rate exists. This means a cure without any treatment whatever. Often after many years of trying pregnancy will finally occur. We do not understand these spontaneous cures very well, but they are a source of hope when all else fails.

When you are finally persuaded that you can't have children, you will probably feel grief, and this can be a terrible thing to go through. It may feel as if the death of "all your babies" has occurred. Grief may be felt for the loss of a part of womanhood or manhood. Grief is felt for the parts of you that don't work or have been cut out of you. To deny or repress this feeling of grief can prolong its resolution process. Somewhere inside you the experience gets dealt with. You have the choice of living it as consciously and directly as you can or suppressing these very natural but painful emotions. Sometimes the pain of infertility is never completely resolved but is accepted as a familiar ache which may recur, unpredictably, throughout life. Grieving often takes a long time.

If You Are an Infertile Couple, How Can You Be Parents?

If you are fertile, you may be artificially inseminated with sperm, either from your partner, or from an anonymous donor if your partner is infertile. Artificial insemination is still very controversial. Although more than 14,000 couples conceive this way annually in the United States (statistics are hard to verify), they usually prefer to remain anonymous. There are important legal, moral, religious and philosophical aspects to consider. It is a choice, and often a difficult one.

Adoption is satisfactory for many couples. But new abortion legislation, use of birth control, and the fact that 60 percent or more of single mothers now keep their babies all mean that there are very few infants available for adoption. Babies are obtainable, with difficulty and often great expense, from some foreign countries. Children over six years, black children, sibling groups, emotionally disturbed children, children with major handicaps, and a few multi-racial children are available. The situation varies dramatically from city to city, state to state.

MISCARRIAGE (NATURAL ABORTION)

It is a surprising statistic that about one in six pregnancies ends in miscarriage. Seventy-five percent of these miscarriages occur in the first trimester of pregnancy (weeks 1 to 12). These are usually the result of a failure of the fertilized egg (therefore both egg and sperm) to undergo its first important chromosomal divisions correctly, producing a conceptus which cannot grow or survive beyond 10 or 12 weeks. The germ plasm dies, and in the second or third month your body expels this matter.

Twenty-five percent of all miscarriages occur in the second trimester of pregnancy (weeks 13 to 24). They are more often due to the inability of the growing fetus to maintain its placental attachment, either because of some mechanical or hormonal problem, or because a weak (incompetent) cervix dilates too early, expelling the fetus. (Any fetus delivered between the twenty-fourth and twenty-eighth weeks is called a premature delivery and not a miscarriage. Such a baby has a statistical chance of surviving which improves for every week in utero after this point.)

Miscarriage, then, is a fairly common event. We want to be at least minimally prepared in order to know how it feels and what to expect. Miscarriage is both a physical event for a woman and a serious emotional crisis which may be shared by both of you or experienced by each of you in very different ways. Miscarriages are usually unexpected the first time. They come at a joyful time of beginning pregnancy, and thus are all the more of a shock.

When I found out I was pregnant I danced around the house. My pregnancy was an easy one . . . my body was slowly and pleasantly changing. Because it was a conscious and well-thought-out decision to have a child, I felt free to revel in my pregnancy and motherhood. It was a special time. I mention all of this because having a miscarriage has to do with the loss of something so deeply ingrained for so long that it is partially by understanding the depth of the joy that one can understand the depth of the loss.

Early miscarriage can feel no worse physically than a very heavy menstrual period. With late first-trimester miscarriages there can be bleeding and cramping lasting for a few days, sometimes starting and stopping irregularly, until the contents are completely expelled. Afterward there is a period of bleeding until the uterine lining heals. Second trimester miscarriages are in fact a kind of mini-labor, with regular strong uterine contractions dilating the cervix. Miscarriage is frightening because it is so unexpected and so unwanted.

Miscarriages are characterized by stages, each of which has an official name. *Threatened abortion.* You might have bleeding or spotting, which may or may not be accompanied by minor cramps. Your cervix is closed. The process may stop by itself, with bed rest or hormone treatment, or it might continue. Your doctor will usually advise you to stay in bed for 24 hours, to see what happens. *Inevitable abortions.* The process has gone so far that miscarriage cannot be prevented by any medical means. Bleeding becomes profuse; is usually brighter red as the placenta begins its separation from the uterine wall; and cramps are more intense. The fetus, amniotic sac and placenta, along with a lot of blood, may be expelled completely intact. You'll probably know when this is happening. It's very important to say here that if you are not in a hospital you must do the difficult task of collecting fetus and afterbirth, putting it in a clean container, and taking it to a laboratory for examination. It will yield important information as to why you miscarried. You can ask that both routine and specialized tests be done on it. If tests show you have lost a "blighted pregnancy" (where egg and sperm together have failed to divide correctly) then you can try to be more at ease, knowing that this has been a random event and that your chances of having it happen again

are as random as before. If a study of the fetal tissue shows genetic abnormalities or suggests that you had an illness or infection, you'll work together with your doctor on how to proceed. If the fetal tissue is normal, you might learn that your hormone levels were insufficient, or that a weak cervix was at fault. Both of these conditions can be treated.

An *incomplete abortion* means that only part of the "products of conception" has been passed. Part remains within, and bleeding will continue. Usually a doctor will do a dilatation and curettage to clean your uterus so it will heal. A *complete abortion* means that everything in your uterus has been expelled. You will continue to bleed, but less and less. If you think you are bleeding for too long, ask your doctor. (Perhaps a D & C will be necessary after all.)

Another kind of abortion is a *missed abortion*. In this case, a fetus dies in the uterus but is not expelled. It can remain within for several months. Signs are no periods, cessation of signs of pregnancy, and sometimes occasional spotting. Treatment is either a D & C or induction of labor.

After you miscarry, it is usually medically permissible to resume sexual relations in 4 to 6 weeks, or after your cervix has closed (to prevent infection), and to attempt another pregnancy after one or two normal menstrual cycles. Check with your doctor.

After a miscarriage you will be dealing with two things: (1) Your feelings, both physical and emotional, and (2) your effort to find out why you miscarried.

We went home from the hospital dazed and tired. I was weak and enormously sad. I don't know that I've ever experienced such deep emotional pain. The loss was so great and so complete in the way that only death is. For the first few days I couldn't talk to anyone, but at the same time it was painful to be alone. I just would cry and cry without stopping. One of the clearest reminders that I was no longer pregnant were all the speedy changes my body went through. Within two days my breasts, which had grown quite swollen, were back to their normal size. My stomach, which had grown hard, was now soft again. My body was no longer preparing for the birth of a child. It was simple and blatant. Tiredness was replaced with weakness. And then there was the bleeding. My body would not let me forget. I knew things would improve once we could make love again and would be even better when we were full of hope. But it seemed so far away.

Almost always you will feel grief and anger. You will need the support of friends.

Most people didn't know how to give me support and perhaps I didn't really know how to ask for it. People were more comfortable talking about the physical and not the emotional side of miscarriage. I needed to talk about both. It was also difficult for my husband, because people could at least ask how my body was doing. Unfortunately he would sometimes be completely bypassed when someone called to talk with us, despite the fact that he too was in deep emotional pain.

———————————

Feelings of grief are often complicated by guilt, which can cause tension between you and your partner.

———————————

My husband said it was so hard to be supportive because he had such strong feelings: Anger: "God damn that woman! How could she have done that!" And misery— he wanted to crawl into a corner—and self-doubts: "Can I have any children at all?" Maybe if we could have talked about it during the days I was beginning to miscarry, we could be less tense now.

———————————

You might wonder if either of you did something "wrong" (too much activity, too much sex, not enough good food, etc). You will be blaming each other unnecessarily, for such factors rarely cause miscarriage. Dispelling the tension will take awhile, and longer for some than for others. It is best if your feelings are acknowledged and talked out.

Another common feeling is fear: You have lost control over your body. It could happen again.

Try to learn why you had a miscarriage. Some of the diagnostic procedures described above for infertility will be useful here. Ask to see the pathology report, and ask that all terminology be explained fully. If you are not satisfied with the explanation, ask if there are other tests that could be done. It is your right to learn as much as is medically possible to find out about your miscarriage.

One miscarriage does not mean you are infertile. However, if you have two or more in a row you might want to begin investigating. Make a contract with your doctor to plan each detail of your next pregnancy as it progresses, including possible reasons for any spotting or cramps, definite ways to deal with contingencies, tests to be made as they become necessary, and so forth. You will need support in this project from your partner, possibly friends, or a support group, maybe even one geared to childbearing problems.

The rate of miscarriage for couples who have had difficulty conceiving is much higher than for other couples. It's probable that the reasons involved in your infertility are also the ones which cause a "high risk" pregnancy. Again, working with a competent and careful specialist will be essential for both woman and man, as hopes run high. Precautions must be taken step by step, with a great deal of consideration for the fragile feelings involved. To go from the despair of endless cycles without conception to the absolute joy of having finally conceived only to come crashing down to the reality of a miscarriage is emotionally devastating.

STILLBIRTH

Stillbirth is, fortunately, a rare occurrence. But if it happens to you, statistics mean nothing. Usually it is the result of the baby's oxygen support system failing before it can be safely born, or failure of its lungs or heart to oxygenate its system after the cord is cut.

Your body knows nothing about stillbirth. It is elaborately prepared for the close contact and physical nurturing of a baby. Your breasts are filled with milk, never to be used. (It's an interesting fact that in some cultures, women who lose babies at birth frequently hire out as wet nurses to nurture other babies in place of the one they have lost. The wet nurse is an esteemed person in those cultures.) Your mind is also prepared for the event of a new baby, and the same is true of members of your family.

Some considerations are in order if you suffer a stillbirth, beginning with the moment the death is expected or known. If the baby's death takes place before delivery, anesthesia and delivery in the quickest and least hazardous way possible are desirable. Your partner should be included as long as he feels he can be supportive. The baby, once delivered, should be handled in a reverent and careful manner—especially when autopsy is indicated to find the cause of death. It would be best if you could be put in a room away from the nursery and if hospital personnel could be told that you have lost your baby. Above all, if possible, you and your family must be allowed your grief, in privacy if you need and want it. You might need to withdraw at first and not confront the reality which may be too much to bear. There might be a period of numbness. If you ask for help in grieving, we hope it will be intelligently and humanely extended.*
Platitudes such as, "You'll have another baby before you know it," or, "Think of your wonderful children at home," have no place in grief. The death of this particular child is being experienced—no other actual or potential children have any relevance to the situation. Perhaps the best help others can offer is sympathetic listening and close physical comforting.

It is important for you to understand what has happened physically with the baby. Most likely whatever happened was totally beyond your control or the doctor's. If you do suspect malpractice by your doctor, legal counsel should be sought quickly and the facts analyzed.

When either miscarriage or stillbirth occurs, a process

———————————

*Drugs and sedatives are often prescribed routinely by many doctors caring for grieving patients. This practice can actively interfere with the healthy resolution of grief. Unless doctors have had special training in helping people to deal with grief, the advice of most physicians at this time is not expert advice.

is stopped abruptly, never to be completed. Grief may focus on the completion of that process. A couple might need to grieve for a long time. Anniversaries such as expected due date, date of conception, or of the loss itself are often painfully remembered for years to come. (See Menning, in "Pregnancy" bibliography.)

ECTOPIC (MISPLACED) PREGNANCY

If you're old enough to bear a child, have had intercourse, and feel abdominal pains you don't understand, it's possible you have an ectopic pregnancy, a pregnancy that is out of place.* In ectopic pregnancy the fertilized egg implants itself, not in the wall of the uterus, but most often in the fallopian tube; or much more rarely, in the abdominal cavity, the ovary, or the cervix.

TUBAL PREGNANCY. Fertilization of the egg by the sperm almost always occurs in the fallopian tube. If the function of the tube is impaired in any way—if the cilia (hairs) don't move as they should to propel the egg into the uterus; if the tube's structure has been changed by pelvic inflammatory disease so that there are "pockets" in it; if the tube is genetically malformed—then it's possible that the fertilized egg might attach itself to some part of the tube instead of proceeding on into the uterus. The egg implants itself in the tubal lining. It establishes a beginning placenta and space for itself just as if it were in the womb. The fetus begins to grow. Because placenta and fetus are growing, both producing and using the usual pregnancy hormones, all the usual changes of a beginning normal pregnancy might occur. So early symptoms of an ectopic pregnancy can be a missed period, breast tenderness, nausea and fatigue. The uterus may also be slightly enlarged and softened because of the influence on it of placental hormones, as in a normal pregnancy. If you go to a doctor, s/he might diagnose a normal pregnancy after examining you internally and listening to your symptoms. It's difficult to discover an unruptured early tubal pregnancy.

As the pregnancy enlarges, the tube will stretch slightly. It's not made to expand indefinitely, and eventually, as the placenta burrows into the muscle wall of the tube, it bursts. This usually happens between the eighth and twelfth week.

Now the signs of ectopic pregnancy appear. Just before it bursts you might feel acute (sharp) stabbing pain at the site of implantation, or cramps, or a constant, dull abdominal pain, which is temporarily relieved by the rupture. But then you'll bleed inside and soon feel lower abdominal pain again. Or later you might feel aching pain in your diaphragm and sharp shoulder pain caused

*Dr. Edward Quilligan in his article "Ectopic Pregnancy" speaks of a dictum to the effect that if any woman of reproductive age feels abdominal pain, it has to be first investigated as a possible ectopic pregnancy. *Hospital Medicine*, Vol. 5, No. 4 (March, 1969).

by blood flowing up to your diaphragm. If the bleeding is greater, you might be in shock, with low blood pressure and a high pulse rate. Symptoms of shock are hot and cold flashes, nausea, dizziness, fainting. If you experience any of these symptoms, see your doctor. Try to be especially aware that that first sharp abdominal pain might indicate a rupture, and go quickly to your doctor.

Sometimes, before or after the rupture, you might have a late period with mild, menstrual-type bleeding or fragments from your uterine lining, because the hormones secreted by the fetus are not strong enough to keep up the growth of the lining of your uterus, or the ovum has died and estrogen production has stopped. This bleeding can be misleading, as you and your doctor might think you have had an early "natural" abortion. If the lining of the uterus is passed, it should be examined microscopically, and if there's no evidence of trophoblastic (early fetal) tissue, ectopic pregnancy should be suspected.

Internal bleeding is of two kinds: a sudden acute bleeding, or much more common, a slow trickle of blood into the pelvic cavity. If there has been much bleeding, your abdomen will feel sore, breathing will be painful, and you might have pain in each shoulder.

A pelvic examination might show no findings at all or a number of findings: tenderness or mass in the fallopian tubes or ovaries; enlargement of the uterus; softening of the cervix; fullness behind the uterus. Blood tests might or might not be useful.

It has been found that ectopic pregnancies produce a lower level of HCG (human chorionic gonadotropin) than do normal pregnancies. The beta sub-unit test (see Chapter 13, p. 258) is extremely sensitive to lowered HCG levels and can help to identify an ectopic pregnancy before it becomes dangerous.

Then your doctor might do a culdocentesis, inserting a needle vaginally into the space behind the uterus (pouch of Douglas). If non-clotting blood is found, ruptured ectopic pregnancy is a possibility, because the intraperitoneal blood doesn't readily clot. The doctor might recommend operative diagnostic procedures such as culdoscopy or laparoscopy.

The therapy—treatment—for tubal pregnancy is usually a salpingectomy, in which the entire tube is removed. This must be done under anesthesia in a hospital. There's disagreement over whether the ovary on that side should be removed too.

It's likely that if a woman has had one tubal pregnancy, she'll conceive less readily than if she hadn't had it. (There's a 50 to 60 percent chance of not conceiving.) Chances of another tubal pregnancy are increased.

RH FACTOR IN BLOOD

The Rh factor is a substance in the blood. At least 86

percent of us have this substance coating our red blood cells: we are called Rh positive (Rh+). Those of us who don't have it are Rh negative (Rh−).

If some one with Rh− blood receives transfusions of blood containing Rh+, the Rh− blood gradually builds up antibodies, which defend the blood from the hostile Rh+ factor, causing some red cells to be broken down, and their products spread through the body, thus exerting a poisonous effect. Some Rh− women don't produce antibodies.

When you are pregnant there's a certain amount of blood transference between you and your fetus through the placenta, though each circulatory system remains fairly separate. Most of the exchange goes from the mother to the fetus. At birth, however, because of the separation of the placenta from the uterus, there can be a much larger spillover, and a quantity of the baby's blood can be absorbed by the mother. This does not occur often. If you have Rh− blood and are pregnant for the first time and have not had a transfusion containing Rh+ blood, your first child will probably be all right. But at birth you can absorb your baby's Rh+ blood, and within the next seventy-two hours your own blood reacts and begins developing antibodies. These antibodies will be present in your blood during your next pregnancy, and can get into the blood stream of your second child as it grows, attacking and destroying some red cells. The baby could be stillborn, severely anemic, or retarded.

Thus every woman should have her Rh factor checked early in pregnancy. If you are Rh−, you should pay careful attention to the following: (1) The father's Rh factor should be checked. If he is Rh− too, your offspring will be Rh−, and there's nothing to worry about. If he's Rh+, it should be determined whether he has both Rh+ and Rh− genes, in which case the fetus, having some Rh− genes (like you), and some Rh+ genes, has a 50 percent chance of being affected. If the man has only Rh+ genes, the fetus is much more vulnerable. (2) You should know whether you have had previous blood transfusions. Even matched blood types contain Rh− and Rh+ factors, so that it's possible (though hopefully rare now that people are aware of the Rh factor) for a woman with Rh− blood type B to have received Rh+ blood type B, and thus to have already developed antibodies. (3) You should have your own blood tested for Rh sensitization (the presence of antibodies). (4) A fetal amniotic fluid sample can be taken through a needle to see whether the blood cells of the fetus are being altered. This test can be done at any time in the pregnancy. If the bilirubin level in the fluid is high, it indicates that the fetus is affected, and a blood transfusion may be given to the baby in utero. (5) Recently a shot (Rhogam) has been developed which prevents you from producing antibodies. The solution coagulates all the Rh+ antigens from the fetus so that your system does not begin to produce antibodies.

These coagulated antigens disappear in six weeks. To be effective, this shot must be given within seventy-two hours after a miscarriage from the second month on, and after every abortion or pregnancy. In some states you can get free Rhogam shots. Check with your health department.

What can be done if the blood of the fetus is being invaded by maternal antibodies? There are techniques now for exchanging invaded fetal blood for good blood while the fetus is still in the uterus, and for exchanging the baby's blood after it is born. Check with your doctor about the benefits and risks of these techniques. Compel him or her to tell you everything you want to know. If s/he doesn't, don't pay him or her. Check with other doctors, if you can, to learn even more. Ask for names of other women with Rh factor and find out from them what their experiences were.

EARLY DIAGNOSIS OF BIRTH DEFECTS

You can now be tested early in your pregnancy for an increasing number of inherited disorders in order to determine whether or not your child will be affected.

Parents who are carriers of certain hereditary diseases can be diagnosed before the woman becomes pregnant by studying a blood or skin sample.

The disorders that can be diagnosed in early pregnancy are (1) virtually all chromosomal abnormalities (such as Down's Syndrome—formerly called "mongolism"), (2) certain biochemical diseases (that is, some amino acid disorders), (3) sex-linked diseases, carried by females, but affecting males (hemophilia, muscular dystrophy) and (4) fetal spinal cord or brain disorders.

These diagnoses can be made by studying the amniotic fluid (the water surrounding the fetus) and cells in it which are from the fetus. About two tablespoonsful of amniotic fluid are withdrawn with a needle from the uterus by a procedure called amniocentesis.

Amniocentesis should be done between fourteen and sixteen weeks of pregnancy. There's a one percent risk of losing the baby if this procedure is done early in pregnancy. Later the risk is greater.* It generally takes about fourteen to eighteen days to complete most of the laboratory work needed to make a prenatal diagnosis.

When might you want to have this done? (1) If you have already had a child with one of certain hereditary biochemical diseases. (2) If you are a carrier of serious disorders that affect males only. (3) If you have had a child with a chromosomal abnormality—you may wish to have the test done because of increased risk or because you are anxious during this second pregnancy. (4) If you are over forty, since the risk of having a child with a chromosomal abnormality increases as you get older.

The amniocentesis should be done while undergoing

*Greater than 3%.

or within minutes after undergoing ultrasound examination. (This decreases the risk of puncturing the placenta or fetus itself, and increases the chance of getting fluid on the first try. However, the possible risks of ultrasound to the fetus must also be considered in deciding whether to undergo amniocentesis.*

If you find that there might be a chance of your fetus's having birth defects, it will be your decision, with the advice of your physician, whether or not you will continue your pregnancy. One doctor suggests that if you would continue your pregnancy in either case, it would be wiser to omit the test.

SICKLE-CELL TRAIT AND SICKLE-CELL ANEMIA

One in every twelve black people in the United States has sickle-cell trait. This means that less than half of the hemoglobin (oxygen-carrying red protein of red blood cells) in the blood has undergone a change in the composition of its protein. Cells are normal in appearance. This change came about thousands of years ago in people who lived in Africa and in countries around the Mediterranean Sea, and helped protect them from malaria. It's a genetic trait, meaning that it is inherited from parents. If you have sickle-cell trait, you will be healthy and probably unaware that you have it. Only under very unusual conditions, like mountain climbing at extreme heights, might you have a problem.

Sickle-cell anemia is a disorder resulting from inheritance of the trait for sickle-cell hemoglobin from *both* parents. About 1 in 625 black people is born with sickle-cell anemia. Symptoms are poor physical development, jaundice, weakness, abdominal pains, lowered resistance

---

*Ultrasound is also used to determine fetal size in relation to the duration of the pregnancy, and therefore can assess placental sufficiency. The procedure can help establish a more accurate due date. Single ultrasound readings are inadequate for this purpose, however, so the risks of multiple exposures (weeks apart) to ultrasound must be weighed, balanced against the necessity for the information. There is now evidence in animal and cellular studies to suggest that ultrasound may not be harmless as we have been told. The FDA is now examining the scientific evidence and will soon issue regulations on ultrasound, since no studies exist which document the safety of the procedure, while increasing numbers of women and infants are being exposed. (See bibliography under FDA/Altman.)

to infections, bouts of swelling and pain in muscles and joints. Red blood cells, shaped like a farmer's sickle, don't live as long as normal cells and are destroyed at a faster rate, so movement of oxygen is at a minimum. The clinical picture is variable. Some people who have severe anemia during childhood may find the symptoms becoming milder as they grow older. For others the anemia is tiring at times, but tolerable. It can also be extremely painful.

If you are black or if you are of Mediterranean descent, it is wise for you to be tested for sickle-cell trait. The blood test is simple and you can have the results in thirty minutes.

If you have the trait and your partner doesn't, or vice versa, then your children might or might not inherit the trait. If one of you has the anemia and the other has normal hemoglobin, all your children will have the trait. If you both have the trait, there is a 25 percent chance each child will have normal hemoglobin, a 50 percent chance each child will have the trait, and a 25 percent chance each child will have the anemia. If one of you has the trait and the other has anemia, there is a 50 percent chance each child will have sickle-cell trait, and a 50 percent chance each child will have sickle-cell anemia.

Ideally, your test for sickle-cell trait and anemia should be part of a program which will do several things for you. It will inform you as soon as possible of test results and keep them absolutely confidential. If you and your partner both have the trait, it will provide counseling support if you want it as you decide about having children. If you have the anemia, it will identify which form you have, as some are not as serious as others. It will help you learn the problems and risks of going through a pregnancy: some of your symptoms may be intensified by pregnancy (circulatory problems might become worse, you might be more tired or depressed than usual, and more prone to miscarriage). Finally, a good program will provide counseling and support services to you and your family if your children or your partner have the anemia and you need these services.

To locate a sickle-cell program in your area, check with your local hospital, neighborhood health clinic, or department of health.

For more information about infertility and related childbearing problems contact RESOLVE, a Boston-based organization: Box 474, Belmont, Mass. 02178. Phone: 617-484-2424.

CHAPTER 17
MENOPAUSE

My first sign of menopause was the night sweat. Even though I knew why I was having the sweats, it was a little frightening to wake up in the middle of the night with my sheets all drenched. It was hard not to feel that something was very wrong with me. And I lost a lot of sleep changing sheets and wondering how long the sweats would go on. Sometimes I felt chilled after sweating and had trouble going back to sleep. It was a good thing I could absorb myself in a book at times like that.

I also had hot flashes several times a week for almost six months. I didn't get as embarrassed as some of my friends who also had hot flashes, but I found the "heat wave" sensation most uncomfortable.

I felt generally good around the time of menopause. My children were supportive and patient, particularly when I was irritable from lack of sleep. My husband, unfortunately, was quite insensitive and frequently accused me of "inventing" my "afflictions." Without the help of friends and children who did try to understand what I was going through, it might have been harder for me to be around him.

Even though menopause has been a neutral or positive experience for many women, the physical and emotional changes associated with it are often misunderstood and mystifying. Since lack of knowledge may easily lead to anxiety, it's not surprising that some women have felt that the worst part about menopause was that they did not know what to expect or had no resources to refer to.

I received no emotional support during menopause. It was my fault really. I was too ignorant of the facts, both physical and otherwise, to get the support I could have used.*

I feel that far more education should be done (or did I just happen to miss it?) as to menopause, its onset, what to expect, and more specific help and understanding and explanation of all its aspects. I used to ask my doctor

*Many of the quotes and insights found in this chapter are taken from responses to a menopause questionnaire sent out by the Boston Women's Health Book Collective in 1974. See p. 333.

when I would know I was in menopause, and he would smile benignly and not answer; I would ask if I shouldn't be taking pills, and he'd say he'd tell me when.

This chapter will try to help women reduce the anxiety which results from a lack of knowledge. We will provide factual information about the menopausal experience—its causes, symptoms, and possible alternatives for treatment if this should be necessary. By better understanding menopause and by seeking medical help when appropriate, we women will be better equipped to deal with this phase in our lives. This chapter also seeks to encourage women to research and study menopause, a subject which has been inexcusably neglected by the male-dominated medical profession.

Even when physical symptoms are minimal or under control, menopause is often a more negative experience than it needs to be because of our society's attitude toward us during that time. The popular stereotype of the menopausal woman has been primarily negative: she is exhausted, irritable, unsexy, hard to live with, irrationally depressed, unwillingly suffering a "change" that marks the end of her active (re)productive life.

I usually think of geriatric types: little old white-haired women in wheelchairs in nursing homes. It's such an ugly word and image. Dried-up womb—bloodless insides. I'll never forget a man's description of an elegant hotel in the Virgin Islands as "menopause manor"! It made me glad at that time that I was still menstruating and didn't qualify for his derogatory observation. Now, ten years (and Women's Liberation) later, I can see the folly of his remarks and his machismo. But the word by itself still gives me a chill. It seems so final—as if an important bodily function had ceased, and with it all the fun of youth—which, of course, isn't true.

Our ideas of menopause have often been shaped by ads like the one in a current medical magazine that pictures a harassed, middle-aged man standing by a drab and tired-looking woman. The drug advertised is "for the menopausal symptoms that bother him most." This ad, like many others, presents menopause as an affliction which makes us a burden to our family and friends.

Our youth-oriented culture tends to present menopause as a descent into "uncool" middle and old age. In a society which equates our sexuality with our ability to have children, menopause is wrongly thought to mean the end of our sexuality—the end of our sexual pleasure, or even the total end of our sex lives.

We women are now changing these views. As we value ourselves as more than baby machines; as we increasingly view middle age as a welcome time offering new freedom to pursue activities that interest us; and as we make selective use of hormones, vitamins and drugs to minimize the more severe menopausal discomforts, we can make menopause a more positive experience.

I am constantly amazed and delighted to discover new things about my body, something menstruation did not allow me to do. I have new responses, desires, sensations, freed and apart from the distraction of menses [periods].

I felt physically in better shape—in my prime—unencumbered by the cycle of pain, swelling, discomfort, nuisance, etc.

I was immensely relieved that my periods were ceasing. I hated them and resented their prolongation for so many years after childbearing had ceased. It was a damn nuisance.

I felt better and freer since menopause. I threw that diaphragm away. I love being free of possible pregnancy and birth control. It makes my sex life better.

If we feel good about ourselves and what we are doing at this time in our lives, we will cope better with whatever menopause problems we may have. It is important to be able to talk openly with those who are close to us and to ask for the support we need.

WHAT IS MENOPAUSE?

The menopause is the time when menstruation permanently ceases. Up until menopause a woman's ovaries have periodically released estrogen during the monthly menstrual cycle. But as a woman approaches menopause her ovaries stop producing a monthly ovum (egg) and secrete a smaller supply of estrogen. (Well past the menopause, however, lesser amounts of estrogen continue to be produced by the ovaries and the adrenals.) At the same time there is a decline in the production of the hormone progesterone, which each month has been building up the lining of the uterus in preparation for the fertilized egg (see Chapter 2). These hormonal changes mean that we will no longer be able to conceive and bear children, and that we might experience some uncomfortable physical symptoms as our bodies adjust to the new hormonal balance.

The gradual decrease in the cyclic release of estrogen and progesterone usually begins some years before the end of menstruation. Most women are aware that menopause is coming closer when the menstrual periods become scantier, shorter and farther apart. Sometimes whole months are skipped.

My menses were very regular all my life, every twenty-seven days. Then the intervals between menses gradually lengthened during menopause.

In some women the cycles become shorter and the flow more prolonged and profuse.

My periods ceased abruptly and I was grateful, but for the final two or three years preceding menopause they were excessively lengthy and torrential.

It is not possible to predict the exact age at which a woman will begin menopause, though it usually happens between forty-eight and fifty-two; there is some indication that the age may vary with national or geographic origin. It is not true that the younger a woman starts menstruation the earlier she will go through menopause.

An early menopause can occur when a woman's ovaries are removed (oophorectomy) or as a result of ovarian disease. A hysterectomy, the removal of the uterus, will *not* bring on menopausal symptoms (unless, of course, both ovaries are removed in addition to the

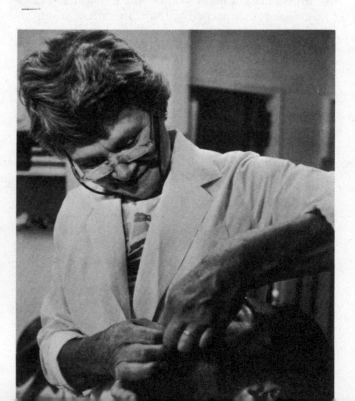

uterus). The removal of one ovary does not bring on menopause, since the remaining ovary continues to produce sufficient estrogen. When the ovaries are removed in a younger woman who still has her uterus, estrogen is usually administered afterward to maintain menstrual periods.

In my case I was glad to have the hysterectomy—no more worry about profuse bleeding, no more heavy feeling, no more muss and fuss. Since I cannot take hormones, I expected much more of a jolt. I was somewhat nervous and excited—but not much. Compared to other things that can happen in life, I think the "problem" of menopause is much overrated.

Symptoms of Menopause

The two predominant symptoms characteristic of the menopausal period are "hot flashes" (also called flushes, flushing, sweats) and a decrease of moisture and elasticity in the vagina. A hot flash is a sudden sensation of heat in the upper body, sometimes accompanied by a patchy redness of skin. It usually lasts from several seconds to a minute and may involve some sweating. When it is over, a woman often feels chilly. These hot flashes may average four or five a day, most often occur at night, and may disturb sleep.

Women who have experienced them describe the hot flash as "an all-over hot feeling with profuse perspiration." "They happen unpredictably and momentarily, as if I had a fleeting fever with perhaps a slight dampness on my forehead." "It is a feeling of heat and sweat flooding one's head without warning."

Hot flashes are not fully understood. They may result from "vasomotor instability," which affects the nerve centers and the flow of blood. One important factor is that the pituitary gland increases its production of the ovary-stimulating hormone FSH (follicle stimulating hormone) in response to the decreased production of estrogen and progesterone. The large amount of FSH in the blood causes an upset in the intricate glandular balance of the body. Symptoms such as the hot flash may occur as a result of the body's attempt to achieve a new hormonal balance. Another explanation is that the hormonal changes taking place in our bodies cause the blood vessels and the nerves to be irritated, thereby causing the blood vessels to overdilate.

The other predominant symptom of the menopausal transition is vaginal dryness and inelasticity. It is the thinning of the mucous membranes which, along with a loss of elasticity in the walls of the vagina, can cause the uncomfortable dryness. When this occurs, it is most often during the latter part of menopause (and more severe cases usually don't develop until five or ten years after menstruation has ended).

The physical discomfort due to the dryness of the vagina was very sexually inhibiting. We were both concerned about the problem with intercourse. I am now using a cream to counteract the dryness. But for a long while ignorance plus poor gynecological care were responsible for a lot of discomfort.

Often vaginal dryness can cause irritation and an increased susceptibility to vaginal infections. During intercourse, a substitute for the missing lubrication may be necessary to prevent uncomfortable friction. A water-soluble lubricant such as K-Y Jelly works well. A woman who experiences painful intercourse should seek medical help, since problems other than vaginal dryness and inelasticity may be the cause (see p. 58 in Chapter 3).

So far, medical research has not proven that symptoms other than these two are clearly linked with menopause. However, a small percentage of women have reported other troubling symptoms during menopause. Like the hot flash, some of these secondary symptoms possibly result from "vasomotor instability." Palpitations, anxiety, dizziness and swollen ankles may be related in some as yet undefined way to the body's readjustment to different hormone levels. Other symptoms, such as sleeplessness, less energy, headaches and fatigue, may be indirect results of the annoying hot flashes.

There is not yet enough clear information about the effects of the changing hormonal levels on our mental health. But it is understandable that a night's sleep disrupted by hot flashes might result the following day in tiredness, irritability and a nervous edge. If hot flashes occur during the day, a woman may feel chagrined, anxious, or tense.

I once saw another woman having a hot flash. Her face reddened, she started to cry, and went to bed.

Hot flashes may be uncomfortable, but if you know what they are you can live with them.

It may be embarrassing to have such an obvious and uncontrollable menopausal symptom, especially since the connotations of menopause in Western culture have been negative. As we women demystify menopause we may see that these negative connotations have been more harmful than the physical symptoms themselves.

Although it is not certain that any symptoms other than hot flashes and vaginal atrophy are related to estrogen deficiency, some doctors treat a whole group of symptoms, ranging from depression, dizziness and headaches to bloatedness, diarrhea and so on as part of the "menopausal syndrome." Since medical viewpoints differ, it is important for us to understand the present controversies as to what are and are not menopausal symptoms and how those symptoms should be treated. We do not need to accept automatically whatever our particular doctor may suggest. We should be especially wary of doctors who put every woman on medication and, equally, of those who tell us that our symptoms are "only in the mind." There are cases when severe symptoms *may* require treatment, and we have a right to medical help that will provide such treatment.

TREATMENT OF MENOPAUSE

About one out of every five women will have no (or just a few) menopausal symptoms. Although most women do experience some bothersome symptoms, many of these will not actually require treatment. We should seek help whenever symptoms significantly interfere with our normal activities, particularly because continuous and unrelieved physical distress may result in depression.

At the time when I felt the hot flash and sweating I also experienced a feeling of tension; it is hard for me to tell which triggered which. At the moment I felt tension, worry about some problem came to mind.

Physicians treat menopausal discomforts in a variety of ways. Some prescribe treatment only on the basis of a woman's symptoms; others prefer to consult laboratory tests first (for example, to check the level of estrogen in a woman's body) and recommend treatment on the basis of these tests.* Neither we women nor our physicians can be guided by imperfect laboratory tests alone to determine hormone levels and the beginning of menopause. We must also consider our medical history, our appearance and all the symptoms we may be experiencing. On the basis of examinations and tests, a number of physicians suggest tranquilizers, sleeping pills, or aspirin to relieve various symptoms. Other physicians prescribe

hormone therapy in the form of injections, or pills containing some form of estrogen, sometimes along with progesterone. This is often called Estrogen Replacement Therapy, although it is not clear that in menopause-age women estrogen *needs* to be *replaced*.

Hormone Therapy

Hormone therapy, often called estrogen replacement therapy (ERT), is dangerous. It has been shown to be related to endometrial cancer, especially among women taking estrogen for longer than a year.* It is wise to consider ERT only in cases of severe menopausal symptoms. Since it can be hard to determine which ailments are menopausal and which are simply related to aging or other life crises, we appreciate how difficult a decision it may be to take ERT.

Estrogen is neither a fountain of youth, nor does it keep us from growing old. It does not change any of the real life crises we may be going through, but under extreme circumstances it may offer temporary relief, especially when alternatives (like vitamin E therapy† or bioflavinoids‡) have failed us.

As a modern liberated woman, the major myth I had to overcome was the one which maintained that menopause was only a problem for neurotic women. I was taught that if a woman was physically active, busy, enjoying life, career-oriented and fulfilled, she would not experience any special discomfort during menopause, as these symptoms are all neurotic and psychosomatic. I am healthy, very busy and active, and was amazed to discover that certain physical menopausal symptoms did indeed occur. Night sweats, joint pains, dreadful nervous instability, terrible feelings of anxiety, impending disaster— This all prompted me to talk to my gynecologist, who prescribed estrogen replacement.

There are at least three groups of women who should not take estrogen at all: women who have a history of cancer, recurrent cysts, or blood clots. Since estrogen has a tendency to cause the retention of salt and water, it is not usually prescribed for patients with kidney or liver

*There are certain laboratory findings which are characteristic of the menopause, such as a higher level of FSH (follicle stimulating hormone) in the blood and urine. This indirectly indicates that there is a change in the base level of estrogen in a woman. Some evidence of the extent can be detected with vaginal smears, but these are not always reliable. More research into ways of establishing the precise quantity of estrogen is needed.

*D. Smith, et al., *New England Journal of Medicine* (Dec. 4, 1975) and Ziel and Finkle, *NEJM*, 293:1167-70 (1975). For best summary see Jack Gordon, et al., "Estrogen and Endometrial Carcinoma: An independent pathology review supporting original risk estimate." (See bibliography.)
†Many women have relieved hot flashes by taking anywhere from 400 to 800 IUs of vitamin E per day.
‡A British study has shown bioflavinoids to be helpful for hot flashes. *Body Forum*, January, 1977.

disease, certain kinds of heart disease, or endometrial hyperplasia (see below). Women who have endometriosis or fibroids (see Chapter 6) usually should not take estrogen. However, exceptions are sometimes made in cases of extreme menopausal symptoms. When doctors make such exceptions in recommending ERT, they should fully explain the risk factors.

There is not yet *one* preferred method for administering ERT: the type, amount, frequency and duration of the dosage will vary, depending on the doctor and the individual woman.*

Most cases of vaginal dryness and hot flashes—both of which may result from lowered levels of estrogen in the body—are relieved by ERT. For many cases of vaginal dryness it is sufficient to use an estrogen cream (applied to the vagina), thus avoiding the possible dangers of orally ingested estrogen, which affects the whole body.

Although ERT is often used to treat other symptoms thought to be related to lower levels of estrogen—such as insomnia, irritability, nervousness, depression, nausea and constipation—there are not yet any medical data to support this practice. It is not clear why or how ERT is effective in such cases or if in fact it is ERT and not something else that is really relieving the symptoms. It does appear, however, that ERT *does* affect many menopausal women by relieving symptoms and imparting a greater sense of well-being, but this must be balanced against the knowledge that ERT should be considered potentially carcinogenic.

How long should hormone therapy continue? Whenever possible the dosage of estrogen should gradually be cut down. This reasoning is based on the fact that so much about estrogen remains unknown, and that the dangers of estrogen therapy may outweigh the benefits (see below). Some women *do* get habituated to a high estrogen level, so that when medication is stopped, hot flashes and other previous symptoms may come back. Some physicians are less concerned with the dangers and believe that hormone therapy once begun should continue throughout a woman's life. Occasionally they will even increase the dosage when an attack of serious infection, surgery, severe emotional stress, flu, or even a pro-

longed heat wave results in a relapse of severe menopausal symptoms. Women must be cautious about taking estrogen replacement therapy, since physicians often aren't.

Side Effects and Risks of ERT

Besides the difficulties involved in gradually reducing dosage, ERT has risks and side effects. As with the pill, taking estrogen increases the risk of blood clots and hypertension. The risk of blood clots increases with age. (See p. 190 in Chapter 10 for important details.)

Usually the goal with ERT is to prescribe as small an amount of estrogen as possible to control the menopausal symptoms without precipitating side effects (such as weight gain and swelling, breast tenderness, nausea and increased cervical secretions) or stimulating the lining of the uterus to proliferate and produce "breakthrough" or "withdrawal" bleeding (see p. 192, in Chapter 10). This bleeding, which occurs in as many as 30 percent of women taking ERT, may happen either during the few days of every cycle when *no* estrogen is being taken (withdrawal bleeding), or irregularly, at any point in the cycle. Such proliferation, caused by too much estrogenic stimulation, may lead to endometrial hyperplasia, a condition in which the uterine lining becomes thick and produces an abnormally large number of cells.

I was satisfied with the estrogen treatment at the time, for it did relieve my symptoms; but I learned (after my hysterectomy) that I had developed hyperplasia of the uterus and should not have been given estrogen replacement because of a higher possibility of developing uterine cancer in my case.

In the women who have this condition, uterine cancer may eventually develop, so it is wise to treat breakthrough bleeding to avoid that possibility. Some doctors recommend a lower dosage of estrogen to prevent such bleeding. If it is not possible to find a dosage small enough to prevent breakthrough bleeding and still high enough to relieve menopausal symptoms, some doctors then recommend a combined estrogen-progesterone therapy in order to produce *regular* bleeding. The progesterone—usually a synthetic progestin—produces a more complete shedding, or "sloughing off," of the uterine lining and usually reverses any hyperplasia that may exist. Some doctors think that such combination therapy should even be used preventively (before any bleeding occurs), while others claim that the benefits of progesterone have not yet been proved, especially its role in preventing uterine cancer. In particular, some pathologists believe that there are small immature areas of the uterine lining which do not respond to the progestational hormones and are not sloughed off periodically. Thus,

---

*The usual dosage is .625 to 1.25 mg. of a conjugated estrogen given daily, orally, in 21- to 25-day cycles. The cyclic use of estrogen is especially important in order to avoid possible harmful effects of prolonged and uninterrupted ERT. In cases where conjugated estrogen is not well-tolerated, natural crystalline estrogen is administered. Ethinyl estradiol (.02 to .05 mg.) and diethylstilbestrol (.25 to .50 mg.) have also been prescribed by some doctors, though for many women both produce more negative side effects than conjugated estrogens. Sometimes progesterone is given along with estrogen toward the end of the cycle. For a discussion of the classifications of different kinds of estrogen, see *A Clinical Guide to the Menopause* (1968), Ayerst Laboratories, Information Publishing Co., 3 West 57th St., New York, N.Y.

these isolated areas would be constantly subjected to estrogen stimulation and its possible harmful effects.

In a woman taking ERT, any abnormal bleeding is probably breakthrough or withdrawal bleeding. However, there is a small chance that endometrial cysts, polyps, or uterine cancer could be the cause. To distinguish ERT-related bleeding from other kinds, most doctors recommend combined estrogen-progesterone therapy (see above). Such therapy will stop ERT-related bleeding, while it usually won't affect other kinds of abnormal bleeding. (To determine the cause of non-ERT-related bleeding, an endometrial biopsy, a D & C, or a suction procedure similar to menstrual extraction—see p. 223— is usually performed in order to examine the endometrial tissue for abnormal cells.) Some doctors think that combined estrogen-progesterone therapy may, in rare cases, stop even bleeding caused by uterine cancer. To rule out this possibility, they always recommend an endometrial biopsy or a D & C in addition to the combined estrogen-progesterone therapy.

Estrogen replacement therapy has other side effects besides breakthrough and withdrawal bleeding. Some women on estrogen experience gastrointestinal disturbances, fluid retention and weight gain. Some have experienced breast and pelvic discomfort due to tissue engorgement. Headache, vaginal discharge and changes in skin pigmentation have also been noted. The kinds of side effects vary with the different oral forms of estrogen; natural conjugated estrogens are the most easily tolerated.

Estrogen Replacement Therapy and Other Diseases: Cancer, Osteoporosis, Heart Disease

Estrogen hormones have a profound and widespread effect on the entire metabolism of the body in addition to their effect on the reproductive system. Perhaps the most consistent worry has been the influence of estrogen on *cancer*. Recent studies indicate that there is a causal relationship between ERT and cancer of the uterine lining. (Evidence now exists linking estrogen to breast cancer.*) Since ERT has been in use only since 1940, we do not as yet have sufficient data concerning other long-term effects. It does seem probable, however, that estrogen stimulates such processes as cystic mastitis, possibly culminating in a true malignancy.

Estrogen's effect on *osteoporosis* is controversial. Osteoporosis is a condition which affects the human skeleton. Gradually, small amounts of bone mass are reabsorbed by the body. The bony mass which remains becomes fragile and susceptible to fracture. There is no evidence as yet that ERT can prevent osteoporosis. ERT apparently keeps osteoporosis from progressing for a limited time (3 to 9 months), but after this time osteo-

porosis usually resumes, sometimes at an even more rapid rate. The high dosages required to stop osteoporosis in these latter cases may induce bleeding and may increase the risk of heart disease (see next paragraph). Since osteoporosis also occurs in the male, a great many people believe it is simply part of the aging process rather than estrogen-related, and that adequate calcium and protein intake along with exercise are the best treatment* (this seems to have preventive value too). It is important to remember that osteoporosis is not just an inevitable aspect of aging, but can also be a consequence of poor calcium and protein intake and insufficient exercise.

Studies have not yet shown any definite benefits of ERT with respect to *heart disease*. There is even a strong statistical indication that heart disease may not be related to the menopause, ovarian function, or estrogen. One study indicates that ERT may contribute to an increase in triglyceride levels in the blood. These higher levels are apparently related to an increased risk of heart disease.

Much more research is needed in the area of ERT, particularly its effect on osteoporosis, heart disease, cancer and mental depression. Because of present uncertainties, many women are very cautious about ERT, choosing it only when symptoms are very severe and when no contraindications are present. In most women, post-menopausal production of estrogen (primarily by the adrenals) is sufficient, and no therapy is indicated. For some women, an alternative is found in carefully planned tranquilizer therapy and the strong psychological support of family, friends and medical personnel. Studies of such substances as anti-hypertensive agents are now in progress to find satisfactory alternatives to

*See DES bibliography, Chapter 6.

Medical World News (June 28, 1974), p. 41.

ERT. As it stands now, the value of ERT must be balanced against the possibility of negative side effects and the real risk of increased susceptibility to uterine cancer.

MENOPAUSE FROM THE WOMAN'S POINT OF VIEW

Those of us looking ahead to menopause or just beginning to experience it can find little material that explores what most women go through during menopause. Most research has been done on "clinical samples"— that is, on the minority of women who have chosen or been forced to seek medical care because of the severity of their symptoms. Consequently we know very little about what menopause is like for all the women who never seek medical help.

At least one woman, the sociologist Bernice Neugarten, has done research on the menopausal experience of the average woman. One of her studies* involved 100 women aged forty-three to fifty-three, from working-class and middle-class backgrounds, all in good health, all married and living with husbands, all mothers of at least one child, and none having had a hysterectomy. These women were asked about their expectations regarding menopause; whether they considered themselves pre-menopausal, menopausal, or post-menopausal (and what the basis of their assessment was); and what changes in their lives they attributed to the menopause.

Interestingly enough, the women in Neugarten's study did not view menopause either more positively or more negatively as a result of their being "pre-menopausal," "menopausal," or "post-menopausal." Also, women with more severe menopausal symptoms did *not* tend to view menopause more negatively than women with less severe symptoms. Only 4 out of the 100 women thought of menopause as a major source of worry. "Losing your husband," "just getting older" and "fear of cancer" were much more frequent concerns.

When asked how menopause affects sexuality, 65 percent of these women maintained that there was no effect. Of the remaining women, "half thought sexual activity becomes less important and half thought sexual relations become more enjoyable because menstruation and fear of pregnancy were removed."†

Those women who reported more negative experiences in the areas of menstruation, first sexual experience, pregnancy and childbirth also reported more severe menopausal symptoms. There could be a variety of explanations for this correlation. Conceivably, the physical cause or causes of previous reproductive or sexual difficulties could also be the cause of menopausal problems. Or maybe negative attitudes that our culture teaches us about our bodies and about our reproductive processes continue throughout our lives to have a negative effect on all our sexual and reproductive experiences.

Our Menopause Questionnaire

Our Collective, unable to find much information about menopause as most women experience it, in 1974 sent out almost 2,000 menopause questionnaires to women all over the United States. Since we wanted to know if certain symptoms did in fact occur more frequently around the time of menopause, we asked women aged twenty-five and up (*not* just older women) to fill out the questionnaire. We asked about personal background, symptoms, medical treatment and, when relevant, the menopausal experience itself.

In this chapter we can present only a small fraction of the information that has been gathered from these questionnaires. We are hoping to prepare a longer publication that will more thoroughly describe and analyze all the responses we have received. Please remember that this study is in no sense a "scientific" one. The women answering the questionnaire do not represent a cross section of women. However, these responses give us a better idea of what research needs to be done and also give us the privilege of hearing the voices of many women talking about this experience which society presents so negatively. In general, our questionnaires corroborate the findings of Bernice Neugarten.

The Sample

Following is a brief description of the 484 women who answered the questionnaire:

Age Range	% of Total Sample
25–40	37%
41–50	26
51–60	26
over 60	11

About two-thirds of the women were married, about one-fifth divorced or widowed, and about one-tenth single. Four-fifths of the married women had been married more than 21 years.

Most of the women who responded were living in large cities or suburbs. Three-fourths had children; of these, about one-half had one or two children, and half had more than two children. Almost all were, or had been at some point in their lives, involved with full-time housework and/or child-rearing. Of the menopausal and post-menopausal women, about two-thirds worked outside the home during their menopause. Including volunteer work, this figure rose to about three-fourths. Post-menopausal women worked outside the home slightly more often than menopausal women.

One-fifth of the women had had a hysterectomy. (See

*Neugarten, *et al.*, "Women's Attitudes toward the Menopause" (see bibliography).

†*Ibid.*, p. 82.

Chapter 6 for information about hysterectomies.) Half of these operations included the removal of both ovaries. Two-thirds of the women had sought a second medical opinion before deciding to have the surgery. Slightly less than two-thirds had primarily positive things to say about having had the operation.

Our Survey: Attitudes Toward Menopause

We were especially interested in finding out more about the different attitudes women have toward menopause, so the first thing we asked on the questionnaire was, "What comes to mind when you first see the word 'menopause'?"

About half the women gave positive or neutral associations, while half referred to negative aspects. In general, younger women were more fearful and felt more negative about menopause. Older women, especially post-menopausal women, were more matter-of-fact about this particular stage in life. This suggests to us that younger women tend to have a distorted view of the menopausal experience, anticipating it as much worse than it usually turns out to be. Is this because of all the myths about menopause that surround us? Is it because younger women especially fear our society's attitude toward aging women and look upon menopause as a key symbol of the aging process? If younger women have such fear, why don't older women answering the questionnaire express as much fear or even extreme frustration with living in a society that treats the aging with so little respect? Possibly the older women in our sample represent a unique group of fairly active women (two-thirds of them had jobs outside the home during and/or after menopause) who have managed to feel basically good about themselves despite society's generally negative attitude toward them. Another possibility is that since most (two-thirds) of these older women felt that they received emotional support from family and/or friends during menopause they were more likely to have positive attitudes toward menopause. There are probably a number of likely explanations, and we would like to encourage more groups to explore these kinds of questions.

Our Survey: "Symptoms" Experienced by Younger and Older Women Alike

One question asked all women (age twenty-five and up) to check off any of 23 various "symptoms" (excluding hot flashes and vaginal dryness) they might have experienced during different decades of their lives. (All of these were symptoms often associated with menopause.) The question had very interesting results. Women twenty-five to forty years old checked more symptoms much more frequently than women in any other age group. And women over sixty checked by far the fewest symptoms. It is not clear what this difference might reflect: Do older women have difficulty remembering and thus recall fewer symptoms than they have actually ex-

perienced? Or do older women tend to see themselves as less "laden" with symptoms? Or do they define a "symptom" differently (that is, would they check off only very severe symptoms)? The checklist results suggested that menopausal women *weren't* more likely than other women to report having symptoms (other than hot flashes and vaginal dryness).

Our Survey: The Experiences of Menopause

Another part of the questionnaire asked older women who were going through or who had gone through menopause to describe their actual experiences at that time.

About two-thirds of the menopausal and post-menopausal women reported hot flashes. Although very few women mentioned vaginal discomfort or painful intercourse, many of them may not have known that this symptom can be related to menopause. The incidence of vaginal dryness therefore may well have been higher than reported.

There were a variety of symptoms experienced during menopause, some more extreme than others. For most women menopause was reported to have lasted about 2 years or less, but for others it seemed to last as many as 4, 5, or 6 years. This is partly due to the 15 percent of the post-menopausal women who resumed their periods after they had not been menstruating for a whole year. It would be interesting to know why this happens to so many women.

Following are some of the emotional and psychological changes women reported having around the time of menopause: "Relief" . . . "Tearfulness" . . . "Unexplainable periods of nervousness and irritation" . . . "Rage at aging" . . . "Disorientation, crying, sense of being 'over the hill,' sense of failure" . . . "Delight that childbearing years were coming to a close" . . . "Happy to anticipate relaxed intercourse without need of contraceptive devices—disappointed because of vaginitis."

Here are some individual feelings and reactions to the various changes that women experienced around the time of menopause: "I merely feel regret at the evidence of aging" . . . "There hasn't been that much change" . . . "I like not needing contraceptives" . . . "I feel much better now. I had feared menopause because I was told that I would go crazy" . . . "The lack of sex desire really bothers me" . . . "I believe that the hot flashes I experi-

enced were milder than most. I was always so busy with my work I didn't have time to think about them" . . . "The changes were not drastic. I have just accepted them. They will stop one of these days" . . . "Most of the problems at this time were due to other causes: aging, role-stereotyping, other people's attitudes toward me" . . .

In general, about two-thirds of the menopausal and post-menopausal women felt neutral or positive about the changes they experienced. One-third felt clearly negative. When asked specifically about the loss of childbearing ability, 90 percent felt either positive or neutral. Although our culture has attached great importance to a woman's ability to reproduce, most women in our sample were not upset by the end of menstruation. Possibly this reflects the fact that, for these women, childbearing ability was only part of their self-image: after menopause they were able to value (and had the opportunity to develop) their talents and capacities beyond childbearing. Perhaps for most of these women it was a simple matter to accept this biological change as an inevitable and natural part of aging.

Our Survey: Sexuality and Menopause

The women also expressed a variety of feelings about their sexuality and sexual desire. About half of the menopausal and post-menopausal women reported no changes in their sexual desires, while the rest indicated about equally often either an increase or decrease in sexual desire. When asked if they felt differently about themselves sexually, two-thirds of these women said no. (Note how similar this is to Neugarten's finding.)

The responses to our questionnaire clearly indicate that many of us need much more accurate information about menopause. We hope that more women will do research in this area, both to improve the medical treatment of menopause and to increase our own knowledge of what menopause really is. On the brighter side, our questionnaire definitely suggests that most women feel positive or neutral about menopause, are untroubled by the loss of fertility, and go through the two years or so with minimal discomfort.

CONCLUSION

The most unpleasant aspects of menopause for many women are not necessarily the specific physical problems. Menopause comes at a time in a woman's life when her relationships may be changing. It is a time when her parents may be starting to get feeble or to fall ill. They may be needing her in new ways, putting new demands on her physical and emotional strength. It may take new inner resources to deal with this problem. If she is married, her husband may be seeking her help

with his own life changes. If this is the case, this could be a time when a couple could find new and more profound ways of offering mutual support. If a woman has children, her children are becoming more independent or have families of their own. This can be a difficult transition, but the delightful bonus of grandchildren is a great joy to many women. (Some communities have adoptive grandparent programs. Investigate, or start one!)

If a woman has spent a large part of her life to date raising a family, she now has some important decisions to make about what to do with her new freedom and the next thirty years of her life. She may find that her options are terribly limited, since the labor market does not value her abilities and potentials. She may want to talk with other women about these problems, and there are groups getting together to discuss just these issues.* The women involved in them recognize that the needs of older people are not separate from the needs of society as a whole. We are all going to grow older, and we must all work to eliminate age discrimination.

We as women must work to change society's negative attitude toward aging. We know that we can be as valuable to others and to ourselves after menopause as before—in fact more so as we grow in wisdom and experience. It may be hard to grow older in a society that worships youth, but we must challenge the stereotypes which minimize our abilities; we must challenge social and economic forces in our culture which falsely glorify youthfulness. Let us reaffirm our potential for personal growth and meaningful contribution to society at every stage in the continuum of life.

*For information, write to: (1) The Gray Panthers, 3700 Chestnut St., Philadelphia, Pa. 19104; (2) Tish Sommers, Coordinator, Now Task Force on Older Women, 434 66th St., Oakland, Calif. 94609; (3) *Prime Time, an Independent Feminist Journal*, 168 W. 86th St., New York, N.Y. 10024.

For Sylvia

I found you warmed and white and peaceful in sunlight
your world increasingly private, unreachable;
    and you smoothed my brow the way you used to
    and remembered the children, their father, and
    asked if I'm well, how it goes with me now.
    I shared my joy and pain, confusion and fears
    weary of struggling with changes.
        Your small chuckle came from deep within
        and you reminded me "It's not over."
           Ancient old woman laughing
               shooing me away to new beginnings . . .
               still.

                    Marcia Kasabian

Dotage Thoughts

I read in the paper about an old lady
who married an Arab at seventy three.
She left all her children astonished, behind her
and galloped off, chuckling and slapping her knee.
        Shall I marry an Arab?

I saw in a movie an elderly person
who bought an old wagon instead of a house.
She drove to the Andes and set up a sawmill
and ran it with her aboriginal spouse.
        Shall I buy an old wagon?

I went to a party and met an old woman
who stood on her head when they passed the dessert.
Descending again, she explained to the people
that if you eat vegetables age doesn't hurt.
        Shall I stand on my head?

I read in a book of an octogenarian
living alone in the top of a tree.
She spent most of her time in the lotus position
and lived to a skittish one hundred and three.
        Shall I live in a tree?

    Not daring to put all my eggs in one basket
    but feeling it urgent to go forth and seek,
    I bought an old wagon and put a tree in it
    and stood on my head while I married a Sheik.

                    Alice Ryerson

FURTHER READINGS

Bart, Pauline B., M.D., and Marlyn Grossman, Ph.D. "Menopause," *Women and Health*, May/June 1976.

Boston Women's Health Book Collective. *Ourselves and Our Children.* (See bibliography, Chapter 12.)

Burke, L., et al. "Estrogen Prescribing in Menopause." Paper presented at American Public Health Association Annual Meeting, 2 November 1977. Available from Drug Use Analysis Branch, FDA, 5600 Fishers Lane, Rockville, MD 20857.

Clay, Vidal S. *Women: Menopause and Middle Age.* Pittsburgh: Know, Inc., 1977. 156 pp. $5.

Gordon, J., et al. "Estrogen and endometrial carcinoma: an independent pathology review supporting original risk estimate," *New England Journal of Medicine* 297 (15 September 1977): 570-571.

"Health in the Middle Years—A Symposium About Women." Report of a conference on 3 November 1975. Feminist Health Project, American Friends Service Committee, 2160 Lake Street, San Francisco, CA 94121. $2.

Hoover, R., et al. "Menopausal estrogens and breast cancer," *New England Journal of Medicine* 295 (1976): 401-405.

Jowsey, J. "Prevention and treatment of osteoporosis," in *Nutrition and Aging*, ed. by M. Winick. New York: Wiley, 1976, pp. 131-144.

Lieberman, Sharon. "But You'll Make Such a Lovely Corpse," *Majority Report* 7, No. 21 (19 February-5 March, 1977).
    Exposé about Ayerst Laboratories marketing of Premarin for estrogen replacement therapy.

Masters, W., and V. Johnson. "Human Sexual Response: The Aging Female and the Aging Male," in *Middle Age and Aging*. Chicago: University of Chicago Press, 1968.

Moira, F. " 'Estrogens forever': marketing youth and death," *Off Our Backs*, March 1977, p. 12.

Morgan, Susanne. *Hysterectomy.* Available from the author, 2921 Walnut Avenue, Manhattan Beach, CA 90266. $1.

National Women's Health Network. *Menopause Resource Guide.* Available from NWHN, 2025 Eye Street, NW, Suite 105, Washington, DC 20006. $2/Network members; $3/nonmembers.

Neugarten, B. L., et al. *Personality in Middle and Late Life.* New York: Atherton Press, 1964.

———. "Women's Attitudes Towards the Menopause," *Vita Humana* 6 (1963): 140.

"Oestrogens as a cause of endometrial carcinoma," *British Medical Journal* 1 (1976): 6013.

Reitz, Rosetta. *Menopause: A Positive Approach.* Radnor, PA: Chilton Books, 1977; New York: Penguin, 1979 (paperback).
    Excellent discussion of all aspects of menopause. Well-documented.

Rose, Louisa, ed. *The Menopause Book.* New York: Hawthorn Books, Inc., 1977. 256 pp. $12.50.
    Written by eight women physicians. Intended to show menopause as "one more stage in the series of biological events that women experience."

Russell, Cristine. "Industry's Bid to Block Estrogen Warning Fails," *Washington Star*, 9 October 1977.
    Concerns Pharmaceutical Manufacturer's Association's attempt to stop patient package inserts from going into estrogen replacement therapy products.

Ryan, Kenneth. "The FDA and the Practice of Medicine," *New England Journal of Medicine* 298 (8 December 1977).
    Editorial about patient package inserts favoring broad disclosure of information.

———. "Cancer risk and estrogen use in menopause," *New England Journal of Medicine* 293 (1975): 1199-1200.

Seaman, Barbara, and Gideon Seaman. *Women and the Crisis in Sex Hormones.* New York: Rawson Associates, 1977 (502 pp. $12.95); New York: Bantam Books, 1978.
    For women experiencing menopause, chapter on "wholesome remedies."

U.S. Department of Health, Education and Welfare. *Menopause and Aging.* DHEW Publ. No. (NIH) 73-319. Available from HEW, National Institute of Child Health and Human Development, 9000 Rockville Pike, Bethesda, MD 20014.

Weideger, Paula. *Menstruation and Menopause: The Physiology and Psychology, the Myth and the Reality*, rev. ed. New York: Dell Publishing Co., Inc., 1977.

Weiss, Noel S., et al. "Increasing Incidence of Endometrial Cancer in the United States," *New England Journal of Medicine* 294 (3 June 1976): 1259-1262.

Ziel, Harry K., and William Finkle. "Increased Risk of Endometrial Carcinoma Among Users of Conjugated Estrogens," *New England Journal of Medicine* 293 (4 December 1975): 1167-1169.

CHAPTER 18

WOMEN AND HEALTH CARE

I: The American Health Care System

This section represents the efforts of several of us to help other women understand their experiences in seeking and receiving health care. We have focused not only on the general and political context in which the system operates in the United States but specifically on how women may deal personally with doctors and hospitals and what they can expect from routine examinations and treatment for common illnesses.

Hundreds of books have been written on various aspects of medicine and medical care, although only a few appear in our bibliography. And many books have been written about women and their health problems, but almost all by men. We have tried to give some basic facts, to discuss the issues that affect women, and to meet the need for support that has been expressed by so many women.

We hope that women will come to feel entitled to more information about their medical care; will demand better care for themselves; and will work for better care for all women. This is a beginning in trying to spare other women the confusion and frustration we have known.

PROBLEMS OF INADEQUATE CARE FOR WOMEN

We cannot hope to discuss fully the failures of the present health system and the reasons for them. The focus on women's relationship to health care, however, is especially appropriate, because we consume the largest proportion of health services; average 25 percent more visits to the doctor each year than men (100 percent more if visits of mothers with children are counted); take 50 percent more prescription drugs than men; and are admitted to hospitals much more frequently than men.* Not only are we the largest consumers, but we make up 70 percent of all health workers in the United States, 75 percent of all hospital workers, and three-fifths of all the medical workers in the world.†

In stark contrast to women's numerical superiority as workers and consumers is the fact that only about 7 percent of the physicians in the United States are women. Only three countries have a lower percentage of female doctors—South Vietnam, Madagascar and Spain.* Given the extraordinary status, wealth, power and prestige that physicians have, it is evident that women as workers and patients occupy the wide base of a pyramid with white male doctors at the narrow top, controlling everything and everyone below them for their own interests.

Naturally some women fare better than others, but all of us suffer as a group from the effects of male-dominated medicine. We have listened to our black, brown and yellow sisters tell us that for them health care is in addition often pervaded by racism—in the poor quality of care, the unavailability of services, and the alienation of the largely white medical personnel they have to deal with, who have little comprehension of their situation or of the community from which their needs arise.

Critics have lately commented on the frequency with which non-white people seem to be chosen as experimental populations. A graphic example of this was a study reported in *Medical World News*, in which seventy-eight multiparous chicano women were given placebos, or "dummy" pills, without their knowledge, in a Texas birth control pill experiment, with the result that ten of the women became pregnant in the first four months of the experiment.† Recent investigation shows that this type of research is still going on, funded by the AID.‡

The use of women as experimental groups for research on population-control measures is now a worldwide problem. According to the highest ethical standards, such experiments should only be carried out when direct benefits to the group involved can be positively demonstrated. In fact, the results of the research on the pill and IUD were passed on, not to Third World

---

Health-PAC Bulletin (March, 1970), p. 1.

†"Woman Power Under-Used Though More Mothers Work," *American Journal of Nursing*, Vol. 71, No. 4 (April, 1971), p. 664.

Ibid.

†Report cited in "Aiding the Poor," *Health-PAC Bulletin*, No. 40 (April, 1972), p. 11.

‡Summary of research activities of Dr. Robert Goldzieher, given by Barbara Seaman at Eastern Sociological Association, Philadelphia, May 4, 1974.

groups and poor women, but to middle-class American women. Women asked to control their fertility in developing countries are not given opportunities to participate in meaningful work or supported in their personal lives but rather are made available as cheap factory labor in dull, repetitive jobs. Families there are not assured that their few remaining children will receive the highest quality of health care which would guarantee their survival. Very often, even in this country, contraceptive devices are available to women where other badly needed types of health care are unavailable. As much as we as individual women may want freedom from unwanted pregnancy, we do not want it at the cost of the health of our Third World sisters or our own unborn children. It is difficult to avoid the conclusion that the men who dominate population policy internationally have decided that reducing the numbers of Third World people is their first priority, even at substantial risk to the health and well-being of the women involved. Here is a quote from one of them, Dr. Frederick Robbins, a Nobel laureate and dean of the Case Western Reserve University School of Medicine, addressing his colleagues (1969):

"The dangers of overpopulation are so great that we may have to use certain techniques of conception control that may entail considerable risk to the individual woman."

If you are a woman and also happen to be poor, your health problems are likely to be greater and your access to proper health care services more difficult than is true for the rest of the population.* In a sense, poverty, with its attendant problem of malnutrition, is the greatest health problem in the nation. This was illustrated by what happened when Tufts University started its health program in Mississippi. It was discovered that the greatest community health need was adequate food. The health center pharmacy that had been set up proceeded to stock and distribute food the way drugs are usually supplied. Eventually the project became involved in a farm co-op in order to help meet the food needs. As one doctor pointed out, "The last time we looked in the book, the specific therapy for malnutrition was food."†

Even though this country spends billions of dollars a year on health care, we do not compare well with other Western nations in some health statistics. For instance, our infant mortality rate in 1972 placed us sixteenth on a scale of modern industrial nations which use the same reporting methods, and all of which spend far less per capita on health and medical care.‡ Our maternal mor-

tality rate in 1968 was twelfth in the world, and both Hong Kong and Bulgaria had fewer maternal deaths per 100,000 births than the United States. The cost of inadequate health services can be counted in part in a needless loss of life. A nationally prominent male gynecologist claimed that 50 percent of all maternal deaths associated with childbirth are potentially avoidable, and nearly half the women delivered in city and county hospitals in this country have no prenatal care.* And if we are to believe the predictions of yet another prominent gynecologist, things will be getting worse, not better. He predicts that by 1980 "40 percent of babies will be born on wards of municipal and community hospitals in which there are not and will not be enough physicians to deliver the babies or even enough to provide adequate supervision."†

The lack of adequate free birth-control information, abortion services, and even of education about reproduction, goes side by side with the moralistic and punitive attitude of many gynecologists toward unmarried and even married women who seek birth control. Most public hospitals still do not offer abortion services. These factors result in the anguish of unwanted pregnancies, and suffering and death from illegal or self-induced abortions (see Chapters 10 and 11).

Women are also extremely vulnerable to needless hysterectomies. (See "Hysterectomy," p. 147.) On the other hand, when a woman wants to be sterilized, it is sometimes difficult to get a physician to perform a tubal ligation if "he" thinks she doesn't have enough children, or isn't "stable," or doesn't have her husband's permission.‡ (See "Our Rights as Patients," p. 355.)

THE ORGANIZATION AND CONTROL OF HEALTH CARE

Some of these problems, and many others, can be traced to inadequate public health programs and the lack of emphasis on preventive medicine. Instead, our present health system relies mainly on haphazardly distributed, crisis-oriented, expensive, hospital-based facilities for dispensing many health services. Thus the present system is disease rather than health oriented, and doctor and hospital dominated. The recent organization of medical power into urban empires based around university teaching hospitals, where the priorities of profit, research and medical education all come before patient care, is an important development of the last two decades, and is

---

*William Richardson, "Poverty, Illness and the Use of Health Services in the U.S.," *Hospitals*, Vol. 43, No. 13 (July 1, 1969), pp. 34-40.

†H. Jack Geiger, "Community Control—or Community Conflict?" *NTDRA Bulletin* (November, 1969).

‡Given by Myron Wegman, M.D., of the University of Michigan School of Public Health, at the second annual meeting of the American Foundation for Maternal and Child Health, New York, April 9, 1975.

*Robert J. Wilson, "Health Care for Women: Present Deficiencies and Future Needs," *Obstetrics and Gynecology*, Vol. 36, No. 2 (August, 1970), p. 178.

†Louis Hellman, quoted in Donna M. Ledney, "Nurse Midwives: Can They Fill the OB Gap?" *RN*, Vol. 33, No. 1 (January, 1970), p. 38.

‡P.C. Steptoe, "Female Sterilization," *Nursing Times* (December 9, 1971), pp. 1529-30.

described in the Health-PAC book *The American Health Empire* (see bibliography).

The Capitalist Theory of Disease Causation

The basic idea of health care with which the public at large and women in particular have been indoctrinated by the medical profession and the media is what we will call the "capitalist theory of disease." This model of illness centers around the private relationship between an individual and his or her physician. The economic basis immediately underlying this model is the fee-for-service system.

The emphasis is on treatment of the symptom, isolated both from the rest of the mind and body and from the social context of the illness. The glamorous image of the doctor in the laboratory making discoveries, or the heroic male surgeon doing technical and difficult operations surrounded by elaborate machines, is a common one. The ideas behind it are that most diseases are exclusively caused by germs, viruses and bacteria—specific, identifiable agents—and that the main problem of health care is to combat the enemy microbe with chemicals, or to repair damage done to parts of the body, which is conceived of as a machine. In *The Wonderful Human Machine*, a book published by the American Medical Association in 1961, this analogy is carried to absurdity with the chapters on nerves, "Nature's Radar and Computer Networks"; the heart, "The Perpetual Motion Pump"; and the digestive system, "Fuel Refinery for a Chemical Engine." It is also interesting to speculate on the effect on doctors of their first contact with the human body in medical school—a corpse, the ultimate passive object.

A Theory of Social Context and Prevention of Disease

We feel that a very different model of disease causation should be developed. On one hand, we must realize the social context of illness and admit that certain diseases seem to be occupational hazards arising from conditions that impair the health of large numbers of workers, and that the responsibility for these conditions rests with those corporations and industries whose manufacturing processes or products are at fault. Some substances used in industry are cancer-causing, or carcinogenic. It is interesting to note that insurance figures show that "death from cancer is 39 percent greater among 'industrial' policy holders [chiefly lower-paid wage earners] than for holders of standard policies [chiefly middle-class salary earners]."* According to the National Cancer Institute, 70 to 90 percent of *all* cancers are environmentally associated.

The need to control the activities of and change the

profit-above-all policies of some American corporations in the interest of public health is illustrated again by iatrogenic diseases—those caused by the *practice* of medicine.* The American drug industry has marketed worthless and dangerous drugs that have had many serious side effects.† Critics have pointed out that there are so many different kinds of drugs on the market under so many different names that it is next to impossible for doctors to be knowledgeable enough about them all to prescribe them with safety. In that sense the marketing practices of drug companies are in themselves a health hazard.

We would like to look more thoroughly at one or two examples of the cost of inadequate preventive health care for women. Twelve thousand women die each year as a result of undetected cervical cancer. The treatment and cure for cervical cancer in its early stages have been known for roughly fifteen years. The Pap smear test involves a relatively simple procedure (see "Neoplasia: Dysplasia and Cervical Cancer," p. 143). Yet only an estimated 20 percent‡ of American women have this test each year.

There is also a test you can give yourself, invented by an American and costing twenty-five cents, which was unavailable in the United States in 1967 and had to be imported from Denmark. While conducting a study on these self-administered tests for cervical cancer, the researchers met with good acceptance but remarked that 53 percent of the women approached had never had a Pap smear.§

Even though these simple diagnostic procedures are known, thousands of women have this kind of cancer and it goes unnoticed until it has spread to other parts of the body, when it is much less treatable and in many cases fatal. There are many factors contributing to this situation, and we can only point out some of them.

The situation with breast cancer is even more serious, since it kills at almost four times the rate of cervical cancer, and even women who do go for physical exams are not routinely examined for breast abnormalities. (See Breast Problems, p. 124).

The Power and Role of Male Doctors∥

Since the Depression, when the incomes of many doctors decreased, the medical profession has practiced

*See also box on p. 362.
†Morton Mintz, *By Prescription Only*. (See bibliography).
‡Richard W. Telinde and Richard F. Mattingly, *Operative Gynecology*, 4th ed. (Philadelphia: J.B. Lippincott Co., 1970), p. 704.
§Jean Maynard, John Tierney, *et al.* "Cervical Screening with the Davis-Pipet on a Door to Door Basis," *Public Health Reports*, Vol. 84, No. 6 (June, 1969), p. 556.
∥Elsewhere in this book we have tried to be consistent in referring to a doctor as "he or she," or "s/he." In many other countries the "s/he" would be accurate; in the United States it is a dream that we are on our way to making a reality. Because this section of the book deals with how things are, and with choices we can make today in the existing health-care system, we have referred to the doctor as "he."

*John A.H. Lee, "Prevention of Cancer," *Postgraduate Medicine*, Vol. 51, No. 1 (January, 1972), p. 86.

what Rick Kunnes has called "professional birth control." The result is that we have fewer doctors per person than we had fifty years ago. This alone might not be such a disaster if doctors were willing, as a profession, to share their skills widely and train paramedical personnel or give more responsibility to nurses for routine procedures. The facts seem to be to the contrary. One doctor in a community south of Boston told a friend of ours he objected even to public health nurses' giving Pap smears. Instead of sharing its skills, the medical profession has kept its knowledge restricted, and only very recently has it permitted other health workers to assume roles that alleviate the crisis of the doctor shortage. In many cases it is not even a matter of skill but of simple procedures which not only waste the doctor's time, but could often be done by the patient herself.

Another result of this imperialism of knowledge is that many women have not learned enough about their health needs to demand Pap smears or breast self-examination instruction as a public service. This kind of ignorance about our bodies, and particularly those parts related to reproduction and sexuality, is connected with the alienation and shame and fear that have been imposed on us as women. Some people feel that this is an internalization of male values, of the male fear and envy of the generative and sexual powers of women.

The American doctor has been given unusually broad powers. It is "he" who decides which patients are treated and where; the cost of treatment; who goes to the hospital; which treatment is given and for how long; and which drugs are administered and in what quantities. In fact, all health care has become equated in the public mind with the practice of medicine by physicians. This has enormous implications. One result has been that the roles of other health workers—nurses, for example—have been unnecessarily limited by licensing and tradition.* Through its organizational representatives, chiefly the AMA, the medical profession has jealously guarded the prerogative of being the exclusive access route for health care by the threat of legal punishment of paramedical people and nurses who practice medicine. For example, lay midwives in Santa Cruz, California, were arrested and charged with practicing *medicine* without a license in 1974. (In most modern countries childbirth is not considered a *medical* event.)

The physician is the gatekeeper of the health-care system. . . . not only does he control the entry into the health-care system, he provides the only pathway through the system. Other health professionals who might offer great relief or meaningful benefits to the patient may never see her because, from the doctor's perspective, she is not sick or her health needs are not the kind the doctor recognizes or understands. No matter how many other professionals are available, patients must wait until the doctor screens, refers, or "writes orders."*

The consequences of this power and control are not simply frustrating for other health workers and for patients. They are the basis for the unusually high income which doctors enjoy. Doctors are still the highest paid of any profession in the United States. (See also "Managing the Obstetrician-Gynecologist," p. 351.)

Women as Workers in the Health System

The restriction of women in health care to the most menial and lowest-paying status seems to be further evidence of the dominance of male doctors. The financial rewards of being a doctor are high, while the salaries of other health workers, nurses and hospital workers in general—predominantly female—have been notoriously low. One nurse told us that, having had several years of experience as an R.N., she went back to school, and after she had received her college degree her salary was increased by about four dollars a week.

Recent figures show that over 75 percent of federal funds allocated for training health workers went for the training of physicians and less than 20 percent for nursing, despite the fact that the average M.D. regularly makes four times the annual earnings of a nurse.† (See "Choosing and Using Health and Medical Care," p. 344.)

The fact that nursing has been an overwhelmingly female profession, with little autonomy and molded to serve the needs of the mostly male medical profession, has probably frustrated many talented nurses and deprived the people at large of the benefits of skilled independent nursing care.

Currently feminist voices are being heard in the nursing profession, challenging the traditional subordination of women in our system of male medicine. In the *American Journal of Medicine*, Virginia Cleland stated:

There is no doubt in my mind that our most fundamental problem in nursing is that we are members of a women's occupation in a male-dominated culture.

She goes on to point out the lack of overall administrative power that plagues nursing.

I am appalled every time I recognize that the vast majority of directors of nursing do not control their departmental budget even though the nursing department frequently spends 80 to 85% of the total personnel budget of the institution. I cannot imagine a man accepting a similar title with such absence of corresponding authority.‡

*For a provocative historical study of the rise of male medical professionals, the suppression and decline of women healers, and the resulting decline in the quantity and quality of health care, see the pamphlet *Witches, Midwives, and Nurses—A History of Women Healers*, by Barbara Ehrenreich and Deirdre English (listed in bibliography).

*Catherine M. Norris, "Direct Access to the Patient," *American Journal of Nursing*, Vol. 70, No. 5 (May, 1970), pp. 1006–1007.
†Personal communication, Nancy Milio, 1974. (From her book, *The Care of Health in Communities*. See bibliography.)
‡Virginia Cleland, "Sex Discrimination: Nursing's Most Pervasive Problem," *American Journal of Nursing*, Vol. 71, No. 8 (August 1970), pp. 1542, 1545.

Nursing is a profession in which the sex role is confused with the occupational role in a particularly profound way. The general image of the nurse involves so many of the traditional female virtues. Dr. Cleland points out further evidence of sex-role confusion in the advertisements that hospitals use to recruit nursing personnel. After looking at ads obviously designed to make getting a man the most attractive aspect of working at certain hospitals, Dr. Cleland says, "I can only conclude that they would rather entice nurses by cheap sexual inducement than pay an honest salary. Could this common practice be called 'procuring'?"*

Innovations such as pediatric nurse-practitioner, nurse-colleague and nurse-midwife give nurses so-called "expanded roles" and slightly more money but restrict their function to whatever the doctor chooses to delegate. In this way, many more patients can be seen routinely, thus increasing his income several times over.

Women have usually been excluded from the elite institution of medical school on the grounds that they are not strong enough to survive the rigors of training, or that they will drop out of the profession to marry and have families. Many women never even consider going to medical school because of the generally prevalent idea that they are not good at science and couldn't (or shouldn't) compete intellectually with men in male professions. So they are channeled by counselors into nursing or other fields.

Once inside the sacred circle, women have usually been encouraged to specialize in areas in which they are thought to have, as one doctor put it, "intuitive understanding."† Thirty-three point six percent of the female graduates of medical school who passed specialty board requirements from 1931 to 1956 were in pediatrics.‡ Once again we are presented with our biological and predetermined nature. After all, women care for children, so pediatrics is a good place for them. Surgery, which occupies the opposite end of the medical status ladder from pediatrics, has very few women in it. Less

than 4 percent of all obstetrician-gynecologists are women.

Medical schools are now taking in increasing numbers of women (currently as high as 40 percent of incoming classes at Tufts and Harvard),* and these women, theoretically at least, have one another for support. However, they undergo considerable stress and harassment from both male professors and male fellow students. Contemptuous remarks about women as patients, nudie slides in lectures, and dirty jokes are only the most obvious kind of discomfort women medical students experience.† Many of these women are deeply interested in community medicine and family practice at a time when the super-specialties are dominant in all the elite medical schools. Some hope to be able to improve medical care for women and families, and will be looking for communities in which to do this work.

The Profit Motive in Health Care

Over the last two decades, and especially since government funding of Medicare and Medicaid, the health business has become a huge growth industry involving drugs, hospital supplies, and construction and insurance companies. In the sixties the total dollars spent for all health care in the United States doubled, reaching $62 billion in 1969. The figure was expected to climb to over $94 billion by 1975, but instead it reached $104.2 billion, in fiscal 1974, making the health industry the nation's largest in dollar volume and number of people employed.‡

It is not simply that there are profits of millions each year made out of our illnesses§ but that the impact of the marketing, advertising and product development of large corporations on our health care system as it is presently organized tends to get in the way of effective general and preventive health care for those of us who depend on the system for our survival.

A good way to become aware of the influence of marketing and advertising in medicine is to scan the medical journals, in which the results of the most recent research in various fields are made available to the medical profession. Drug ads in these journals generally portray helpless, passive women as nuisances to be managed via drugs, roughly two women for each male patient shown.¶ (See also box, p. 343.)

---

*Ibid., p. 1545.

†"Women MD's: An Extraordinary Accomplishment," *MGH News* (Bulletin of Massachusetts General Hospital), Vol. 31, No. 3 (March 1972), p. 7.

‡*Ibid.*

*It is estimated that within a few years one quarter of all doctors will be women. (*American Family Physician*, 2/77.)

†For an outstanding, detailed survey of women in medical schools, see *Why Would a Girl Go into Medicine?* by Margaret Campbell (listed in bibliography).

‡See box, p. 342, "Where Does All the Money Go?"

§Harold B. Myers, "The Medical-Industrial Complex," *Fortune* (January 1970), pp. 90–95.

¶See also *Taking Our Bodies Back*, a film by Margaret Lazarus of Cambridge Documentary Films, Box 385, Cambridge, Mass. 02139.

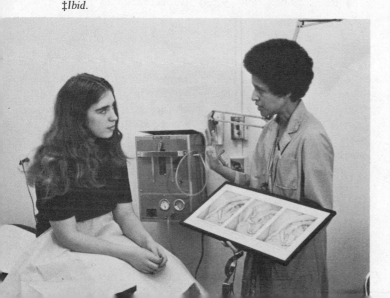

Where Does All the Money Go?*

by Naomi Fatt

The total American health bill for fiscal 1974 was $104.2 billion or 7.7 per cent of the Gross National Product. That is an average cost of $485 per person, up 10.6 per cent from 1973. Where does all the money go?

The biggest chunk or 39 per cent goes to hospitals. Hospital costs for fiscal 1974 were $40.9 billion. Hospitals, with an average 75 per cent occupancy rate, reported a 2.7 increase in in-patient days. Doctors also get their "share." They grossed $19 billion last year. While the per doctor figures for 1974 are not yet out, in 1972 the median *net* earnings for doctors were $40,730. That is an 84 percent increase over the 1959 net of $22,100. Some of the best paid include ob-gyns at $47,000 and general surgeons at $45,340.

The cost of drugs was almost $10 billion for fiscal 1974. Drug company profits between 1972 and 1973 rose 16.6 percent for an average rate of 9 percent (twice the average net for other industries).

Or, looking at it another way—in 1972, the cost of health care for the average person under age 19 was $148. For the adult between 19 and 64, it cost an average of $456. The cost of care for the average adult 65 and older ran to $982. Health costs for women tend to be higher than for men. In 1970, the average woman paid roughly half again as much as men overall. One of the highest costs is the price of being born, up 54 percent from 1959, to $550 in 1970.

Who pays for all this? For one thing, the patient pays out of his/her pocket for approximately 8 percent of hospital costs, 41 percent of physician costs and a whopping 68 percent of other health expenses. Despite Medicare, older people are shelling out an average of one-third of their medical expenses. Estimated out-of-pocket expenses in 1973 equaled 36.4 percent of the total bill, higher in most categories for women than for men.

Through taxes, the government pays 37.1 percent of health costs. To pay for patient care, the government often hires Blue Cross and Blue Shield (private, non-profit companies) to set the reimbursement rates to health providers and maintain quality care. Blue Cross is presently paying the going rate for 20 million people on Medicaid/Medicare and Blue Shield for 13 million. The government also finances one-third of hospital construction costs and part of the medical research bill.

Private insurance pays about 25.2 percent of the total health bill. This includes Blue Cross and Blue Shield and private profit-making companies. Blue Cross collects $10 billion in premiums, Blue Shield $22 billion and the profit-making companies $8.7 billion. While Blue Cross and Blue Shield are ostensibly not making money, they spend about $560 million per year on salaries and other "administrative" costs. Private companies, which pay out approximately 90 percent of group policy premiums in claims, say they are losing money. However, they also have high "administrative" expenses and often sell insurance packages to companies and unions where they take losses on health premiums in order to get bigger profits on life insurance.

Who's getting healthy on this regimen? It is not clear that the public is. People in more than 25 other countries have longer life expectancies than Americans and at least 12 other countries have lower infant mortality rates. For blacks, it is even more unhealthy. Infant mortality for black babies runs 29/1,000 compared to a national rate of 18.5/1,000, while maternal mortality is 55.9/100,000 versus 21.5/100,000 respectively.

Hospitals and doctors aren't doing badly; the insurance companies are just beginning to feel the pinch, but the people know, "This ain't healthy at all."

For additional information, see U.S. Government Printing Office Publications, including Statistical Abstracts of the U.S.; Social Security Bulletin, and other H.E.W. materials. These are often available in public library reference sections.

HealthRight (The Women's Health Forum, N.Y.), Vol. 1, No. 3 (1975), p. 4.

The aggressive marketing of expensive electronic instruments and complex equipment for crisis care in such unusual and sophisticated treatments as kidney dialysis (a process of cleaning the blood when the kidneys have failed), or open-heart surgery, tends to produce a wasteful duplication of facilities, many of which are underused. The market dynamic is to sell as many machines as possible, not to encourage the careful centralization of complex equipment for maximum use. Pouring money into therapeutic medical instruments related to the care of uncommon conditions diverts funds and attention from much more common, basic needs for preventive care. Some of the machines are life-saving, but many lives are lost because resources are sacrificed to the interests of the marketplace.

The medical supply industry, geared to inpatient care in hospitals, benefits from an increased number of hospital stays. Although it would be more reasonable to de-

Quotes on Drugs*

In 1970, the American pharmaceutical industry manufactured enough amphetamines to provide a month's supply to every man, woman and child in the country. This, despite the fact that amphetamines are justified for the treatment of only two very rare diseases.

MORE THAN 2 BILLION PRESCRIPTIONS ARE WRITTEN EACH YEAR. THIS ENORMOUS CONSUMPTION OF THE PRODUCTS OF THE DRUG INDUSTRY HAS ALREADY CREATED A MAJOR HEALTH HAZARD. UP TO ONE AND A HALF MILLION PEOPLE ARE ADMITTED EACH YEAR TO HOSPITALS FOR ADVERSE DRUG REACTIONS. ONCE IN HOSPITAL, BETWEEN 18 AND 30 PERCENT OF ALL PATIENTS HAVE A DRUG REACTION.

In 1971, the pharmaceutical industry showed a return on equity of 15.1 percent, far higher than the return of 9.1 percent showed by the rest of American industry.

"An American, buying prescription drugs, is like no other American at any other counter of any other store in the country. . . . Although he is the consumer, he is not the shopper; he buys (on faith) what his doctor has prescribed. He is like a child who goes to the store with his mother's shopping list, which he cannot even read. He is totally unsophisticated as to the workings of the $5,000,000,000 industry to which he is contributing and which his tax money is already helping to support. The consumer of drugs pays up and takes his medicine, and the Drug Establishment, about which he knows nothing, scores again."

Dr. James L. Goddard,
a former commissioner of the FDA

"Contraception is not merely a medical procedure; it is also a social convenience, and if a technique carried a mortality several hundreds of times greater than that now believed to be associated with the Pill, its use might still be justified on social if not medical grounds."

Textbook of Contraceptive Practice,
John Peel and Dr. Malcolm Potts

"Almost all studies show that generic name drugs and brand name drugs are indistinguishable in therapeutic effectiveness, purity, or accuracy of labeling. The exaggerated and probably false distinction between brand name and generic drugs is regrettable."

Dr. Robert Ebert,
Dean of Harvard Medical School

By 1967, Parke, Davis & Co. was reported to be deriving one-third of its net profits from the sale of the drug Chloromycetin [chloramphenicol]. By 1967, 3½ to 4 million Americans were being prescribed Chloromycetin each year—partly as a result of an aggressive and successful advertising campaign. Yet this drug's limited usefulness and potential toxicity had been known to the medical profession and the drug industry since the early 1950s. Death from aplastic anemia was the fate of thousands of Americans due to the widespread use of this drug.

By 1968, the drug industry had an annual advertising and promotion bill of $800,000,000. This amounted to $3000 spent per doctor in an all-out attempt to increase drug usage in this country.

"*. . . medical care in this country is not a public responsibility, it's a private business operating for the convenience of the practitioner—and not the needs of the sick. . . .*"

John H. Knowles, M.D.

*Portions reprinted from Science for the People, Science and Society Series, Number One (November, 1973), 9 Walden St., Jamaica Plain, Me. 02130.

liver some health services on an outpatient basis, the influence of this industry causes too many people to be treated as inpatients. Another reason many people go to the hospital when their problems could be dealt with in a well-equipped outpatient clinic is that their health insurance is hospital-oriented and won't pay for outpatient services. The construction industry has benefited from the building of many modern hospital plants. In some cases these have resulted in an edifice complex, producing as a by-product increasing transportation problems for women with children and for the aged, who have to travel long distances to get to a large hospital. Regionalization promises to aggravate this problem even further (see p. 368). Accessibility of service is an important concept which is not necessarily served by making the hospital the only place to go for care.

Perhaps we have to rethink the idea that health is a commodity to be bought like any other item in the marketplace. We feel it is time to assert that the health of all the people in the broadest sense is a basic right and a high social priority, and that we should work to eliminate the profit motive from health care and develop a planned, decentralized system, funded by public money, that is responsible to the community.

The Hoax of National Health Insurance*

by Tom Bodenheimer

National health insurance is supposed to be an idea whose "time has come." But for whom? For the tens of millions of patients who pay too much, have a hard time getting appointments, receive fragmented specialized care without a personal doctor, are bombarded with overpriced and dangerous drugs, and have nowhere to complain? No. National health insurance does not speak directly to the health care crisis of the American patient.

National health insurance is designed to meet another health care crisis: the financial instability of influential providers and payers of health care.

Local Blue Cross plans bemoan their fiscal state and ask for huge rate increases: the majority of Blue Cross plans reported losses in 1970; Blue Cross–Blue Shield showed a $51 million 1970 deficit in their Federal Employee Program; in 1970 Blue Cross raised rates 43% in New York and 25% in Philadelphia while Michigan Blue Shield rates increased by 47%.

Commercial insurance carriers also claim to pay out more than they collect in premiums; underwriting losses were reported as $600 million in 1970.

Labor leaders see their hard-bargained health benefit packages eaten up by health cost inflation.

Voluntary hospitals, whose uncertain financial position was improved by Medicare and Medicaid, need national health insurance to further stabilize hospital revenue.

Nursing home profits are largely a product of Medicare and Medicaid, and can be expected to go up with national health insurance.

Local and state governments are cutting back municipal hospital and Medicaid services.

Medical schools approach economic collapse, begging for government assistance. In the words of Association of American Medical Colleges President Cooper, "The perilous financial structure of our medical schools has now reached such a degree of instability that the whole structure is gravely threatened."

Among health providers only doctors, drug manufacturers and medical supply companies are satisfied with the present situation.

National health insurance, then, is not a massive popular movement toward better health care. It is, rather, a creation of the financially shaky elements of the health power structure. These elements are calling for a well-known American remedy: public subsidy.

National health insurance plans differ on the methods of subsidizing health institutions. Nixon's plan mixes direct government subsidy in Medicare, Medicaid and the Family Health Insurance Plan with compulsory employer-employee payments to insurance companies. Kennedy's bill relies purely on tax supported subsidy to health providers. Common to all national health insurance plans is the transfer of money from working Americans to powerful health payers and providers.

*Bodenheimer, et al., *Billions for Band-Aids* (see bibliography under "Pamphlets"). From the Introduction.

II. Choosing and Using Health and Medical Care

INTRODUCTION

As we mentioned in the last section, health care has become equated in the public mind with the care and services of a physician. Most of us can't make a clear distinction between health care and medical care. As women and as mothers we use the medical care system for health care—for maintaining our health when we are essentially normal—most of the time and more than any other group. Part of the frustration and resentment we feel toward the system derives from this fact, and from the realization that both the system of care and the training of most doctors are unsuitable and inadequate for these needs.

To explain why things are so bad and how they might be changed is partly the purpose of the preceding section, "The American Health Care System." While the legislative process will clearly be bringing some changes in the delivery of basic health care within the next few years, from the patient's viewpoint, and especially the woman's, the problems of attitude, communication, information and continuity in dealings with physicians will probably remain for a long time to come. For women who need medical care and doctor's care today, who can't wait for the revolution to get here, we've tried to bring together some thoughts and experiences that may be helpful. (See also Section III., "Coping, Organizing and Developing Alternatives.")

The idea that we "choose" medical care is in itself a myth. For a number of important reasons, most of us do not have unlimited choices, and many of us have no choice at all. First, we are limited by our economic status. If we are at the bottom of the ladder or on welfare there are only certain clinics and certain doctors that will accept the Medicaid or Medicare fees as adequate reimbursement. If you are not on welfare you may still be able to afford only clinic care.* If you have some form of health insurance you will probably discover that it will pay only a portion of any hospitalization costs associated with clinic care and still may not include the cost of the outpatient care itself. If you are a private patient seeking private care, these same insurance terms may apply. In fact, there are hardly any health-insurance programs in existence that will pay for office visits to a doctor.† Only if you are a private patient with a health-insurance policy and a considerable amount of money to spare are you in the "right" income bracket to get good care. But even this is not a guarantee.

Second, apart from the fact that there is a doctor shortage, there is a severe maldistribution of doctors and hospitals, so your choice of both is determined by where you live. This limits both the number of doctors and hospitals that you may choose from, and it also defines their quality. If you live in the deep country, only one doctor may be available, with a hospital even farther away. If you live in a big city, on the other hand, the number of hospitals and doctors is so great that it may be a matter of pure chance that you get satisfactory care.

Third, you are limited by your education and social class, which also determine how well informed you are likely to be about the health care non-system—the training and qualifications of doctors and nurses; the drugs and procedures they use; the settings in which this care is given; and the state of the art and science in general. There is no other area of American life in which so little consumer information is available in proportion to the amount spent for services. Discrimination according to social class is also more widespread than in other areas of consumer spending.

Fourth, you are limited by your own personal values and value system. If you insist on having only doctors and hospitals associated with academic medicine, or if you refuse to go to a large, busy hospital or clinic, then these kinds of convictions will in themselves affect the quality of your care and often the attitude with which

you are treated. The fact that some doctors have large, busy practices may convince you that they are superior, and if some doctors charge less and seem to have more time for you, you may feel you are getting a bargain. Many people, including the doctors themselves, can be influenced by the fact that a certain doctor or hospital cares for prominent local or national citizens. All of these ideas are true and false, for different reasons at different times. Some of the least able doctors have the highest incomes.*

Fifth, you are limited by time. Because there is no plan of preventive care, most of our contacts with the non-system are emergency contacts, made when a problem or even a crisis is already apparent. This is the most difficult time to try to negotiate, to argue, to ask questions and demand answers. Paradoxically, however, it is when you are sickest that you may get the very best possible care and service from people in the medical world. You can almost get real love from them if you are sick enough. But if you are basically healthy and need their services to maintain your health or simply prevent disease, the treatment can be very different. Somehow your wanting information and answers to questions and your wanting to feel a sense of cooperation in developing a philosophy of preventive care for yourself can inspire outright hostility. Medical people, especially in hospitals, are simply not trained to deal with normal people who have a sense of entitlement and have expectations of give and take about their care. Often they label healthy curiosity or determination "uptight" or "making waves." If we want to have what seems to us a normal and reasonable amount of control, we are categorized as aggressive or difficult patients, and of course we are wasting their time. While the profession has always put great emphasis on getting medical information from only the most authoritative sources, it has set very sharp limits on both the length of time we spend with the doctor and what we have a right to know, so time becomes one of the limiting factors in our ability to negotiate the system. Also, most of us don't have time to "shop" for care.

Finally, even if you are in an ideal position with respect to all the above limitations, you are limited irrevocably in what you can get from the system because you are a woman. The value placed on your health, the respect given your complaints or requests, the general way in which treatment is prescribed and administered are not the same as for male patients, and a United States Health Education and Welfare report has documented this. Women's complaints are even labeled "neurotic" and dismissed, "sometimes until physical diseases are beyond treatment."†

In other words, if you live in a sizable city that has

---

*This is changing in some areas. In a recent survey in Boston it was shown that some clinic fees surpassed those of private specialists in the area. Investigate! (See *The Boston Sunday Globe Magazine* for February 9, 1975, article by Sue Mittenthal.)

†Exceptions are big health plans such as Kaiser-Permanente, HIP of New York and other prepaid group practice or health maintenance organizations (HMOs). See page 347.

*Fred Cook, *The Plot Against the Patient*, p. 24. (See bibliography).

†Beth Fallon, "Feminists in a Fever over Medical Care," New York *Daily News* (April 25, 1972), p. 48.

many hospitals and doctors, are a man, have health insurance and can also pay the inevitable extra costs, are well educated and somewhat informed about health care, are flexible in your values and have time to develop a relationship before a crisis by interviewing doctors and hospitals, you are in the best position to choose good care. Only if you are a doctor or are related or married to someone who is a health professional could you have a greater advantage. But the most that can be said is that all this would help you to avoid the worst; it still doesn't guarantee you the very best.*

The following is an attempt to give a brief guide to some of the background information every woman consumer should have when making health decisions.

CHOOSING THE DOCTOR

The Doctor

A doctor is any person who has completed four years of medical school and has received an M.D. degree from a recognized institution. Doctors may also be Doctors of Osteopathy (D.O.) or Chiropractic (D.C.).

Most of us have been brought up to think of osteopaths and chiropractors as "quacks" who should be avoided by sensible, modern, scientifically enlightened people. Some of us have been pleasantly surprised by our encounters with these doctors, however, particularly after our contacts with conventionally trained M.D.s.

I had suffered from lower back pain for years. Most doctors to whom I mentioned it weren't interested, so I always assumed nothing could be done. When I complained of my discomfort to a friend, she gave me the name of a chiropractor who turned out to be both helpful and interested. The most impressive part of the experience was not that the pain went away (it did almost as soon as treatment was started), but that over the weeks of treatment I was involved in every aspect of planning the care. X rays were shared with me, and I was also helped to give certain parts of the treatment to myself between visits—a form of self-help—and to recognize the difference between tension and pain everywhere in my body. The whole encounter was so different from the usual medical experience, where passive dependency and drugs are encouraged and you are almost never treated like an adult. There was a deep respect for the power of the body to heal itself; it helped me to evaluate other types of care.

In order to practice, a doctor is required to have a

license for each specific state. The license is acquired for life unless he commits an act that causes the license to be revoked (extremely rare). "A license to practice permits any M.D. to prescribe for any case. He may also perform any operation (short of an illegal abortion)."* Only hospitals, and only a few of them, have imposed limits on the procedures that doctors may perform, usually on the basis of training and, occasionally, experience. Therefore, all any doctor needs is your willingness to have his care. The only other limitations on a doctor derive from the regulations of the hospital where he practices, or from the code of a specialty society if he is a specialist. The hospital *can* impose strict requirements as to which procedures a doctor may carry out; for this reason it may be wiser to choose a hospital first, then choose the doctor from their list. The specialty society requirements are less valuable since they are almost entirely voluntary, rarely enforced and easily ignored. (See "Hospitals," p. 358.)

Basically there are two types of physicians available to the private consumer: (1) the general practitioner and (2) the specialist.

The General Practitioner

The general practitioner, or G.P., is a doctor who has completed four years of medical school and a year of internship and then has set up a "solo" practice, much the way a businessman sets up a small self-operated business. He sets his own hours, hangs out his shingle, and collects his own fees, which are usually set after he has conferred with colleagues in his own county medical society (a practice that would be called price-fixing in any other industry). Fortunately or unfortunately, G.P.s are a declining group in medicine as the rise of the specialist and subspecialist has continued, and fewer and fewer medical school graduates choose general practice. As a result, G.P.s tend to be found in small towns or in private-home offices in city and suburb. They are held in ill-concealed contempt by the specialists, and it has been estimated that probably only a quarter of G.P.s are really giving good-quality care; an equally large percentage are probably totally incompetent owing to overwork, old age, or a general failure to keep themselves informed about the latest medical developments. These last are the ones who never open a journal and are the darlings of the drug detail men. Members of the American Academy of Family Practice, on the other hand, have high standards and are expected to spend a certain amount of time on a regular basis studying, attending postgraduate courses, and otherwise keeping up, something that is a voluntary matter even among specialists.† For these reasons members of the AAFP are sometimes quicker to

---

*Edward M. Kennedy, *In Critical Condition*, pp. 168-69. (See bibliography).

*Cook, *The Plot Against the Patient*, p. 24.
†"Education for Family Practice," Commission on Education, AAFP (January, 1972), pp. 1-3. Also AAFP Reprints, Nos. 101, 104.

make appropriate referrals to a specialist than the specialists themselves, because they try to know and respect the limitations of their own competence, whereas the specialist sometimes is tempted to play psychiatrist or even endocrinologist or surgeon himself, rather than pass the patient on for another opinion. However, both groups are guilty of this tendency.

The loss of the G.P. has meant the loss of an easily accessible doctor with whom a family and all its members could have a relationship over time, and also the loss of a general outlook on health rather than a narrow, isolated focus on a single body part or system. These are considerations you need to weigh in terms of your own value system, and all the other factors listed in the Introduction, when you consider going to a G.P.

The Specialist

One tremendous problem confronting the laywoman today is the complicated and disorganized way in which the medical specialties have developed. It is estimated that there are now over fifty medical specialties and subspecialties, and not only is there a doctor shortage and a maldistribution of doctors, but there are not enough of some specialists and too many of others.* As might be expected, there are far too many surgeons altogether, and in some communities too many psychiatrists, while other areas go without the type of doctor needed most.

In a big city, where there are practically no G.P.s and sometimes even no hospitals with which they are allowed to affiliate, patients are literally forced into making their own diagnoses in order to get care—something the doctors are adamant about not wanting patients to do. But the system forces us all into it.† While internists have been chosen by many patients and doctors to replace the G.P.s, the general public is not well-informed about the role they should play in coordinating care.‡ If you go to the emergency ward of a suburban hospital you will be asked who your family physician is. In the emergency room of a big-city hospital you will often be asked if you are a patient of the hospital, or who your doctor is, or whether you are a resident of the city, and what means you have to pay for your care. Not that there is anything inappropriate about these questions— only that the wrong answers can be a barrier to care.

When trying to choose a specialist, then, it might seem somewhat reasonable to assume that one is as good as another who has passed the same specialty board examination. Much depends on the quality of the residency training, which is very uneven,§ but the examination is expected to be the standard. Some experts feel

that the hospital a doctor works in after residency has more to do with his continuing quality, partly because of the stimulation of contact with other specialists and partly because of the use of the technology available in it. But keeping up with developments elsewhere through the literature can also be important, and in some teaching centers a dangerous competitive smugness develops, which is based on the assumption that only what is done "right here" is really top-notch or worth doing. Even more alarming is the fact that any doctor can announce himself as a specialist of any type, even if he has not passed the boards.*

Group Practice

All other things being equal, choose a doctor who is in group practice rather than solo practice. In some places now group practice is almost as rushed and crowded as a clinic, where you may never see the same doctor twice, and so much more is charged for group practice care than for clinic care that it may not seem much more desirable. The whole attitude and approach in private care is still class-oriented. You are seen as having the money if you seek private care, whether you really can afford it or not, and this does to a large extent define the attitude with which you are treated. This slightly more respectful attitude, however, is often based on respect for the man (husband or father) who is assumed to be paying your bills rather than respect for you as a woman and a person.

There are two kinds of group practice, with important differences. One kind is simply a group of the same type of specialists who have banded together to share the load and better manage their time and profits by seeing many more patients. (Most obstetrician-gynecologists in metropolitan areas are in this type of practice.) The other is a collection of different specialists who are trying to offer families and individuals more comprehensive care through both general and specific perspectives, such as internal medicine, pediatrics and so on. Quite new and somewhat rare, this latter type seems to offer the best hope of working one's way through the specialist maze, usually through prepaid systems. Both types are still specialty medicine for those who can afford the fees or prepayment plan supporting it, though some multispecialty, prepaid groups have shown substantial cost reductions. One reason for these lower costs is the avoidance of unnecessary tests and repeated visits and emphasis on thorough preventive care. Salaried doctors gain no financial rewards from extra, unneeded services.

HMOs

The term "health maintenance organization," or HMO, has been coined to describe some of these newer, prepaid systems for delivering care. Recently the federal

---

*The Graduate Education of Physicians, report of the Citizen's Commission on Graduate Medical Education, Council on Medical Education of the AMA, p. 111.

†Ibid., p. 34.

‡For a moving account of one man's experience, see "With a Life at Stake," by Edward Brecher, McCall's (October, 1967) p. 96.

§Ibid., pp. 57-59.

*Edward Kennedy. In Critical Condition, pp. 160-61.

government has allocated funds to help HMOs to get started in states which allow group practice (several states still have protective laws against group practice). Those HMOs begun in California and some other states and designed for profit rather than as nonprofit organizations have already shown that shady and misleading practices can result—such as offering "free" radios for new enrollees, like banks or insurance companies, promising benefits and then not offering adequate services. From too much doctoring for profit, the system may shift to too little doctoring for profit. From individual, solo profit, medicine is moving now to corporate profit. As indicated earlier, the profit motive in health care has not existed side by side with the very best health care for patients. In the case of HMOs, the profits are generally split between insurance companies and doctors. Even nonprofit HMOs have problems.

We interviewed a number of families in the Boston area who are or have been patients in an HMO. Most of them agreed that it is a far better system with respect to convenience (one-stop shopping), care during mild illnesses, and price than trying to coordinate a whole group of specialist doctors on their own—the system many younger families had given up for the HMO. (As mentioned earlier, many clinic patients now pay as much or more for crisis care.) However, almost all HMO patients described unpleasant or even frightening incidents in which they had tried to get treatment during a crisis and were discouraged by receptionists or doctors by telephone, only to discover later that important medical conditions had been ignored. Several others deplored their loss of choice and leverage as consumers when they tried to get some flexibility in procedure during hospitalization for maternity or pediatric care. Still others who had felt obliged to seek emergency care at other than designated hospitals were denied coverage by the plan, even though the emergencies were justified, because they had "violated the terms of the agreement."

These are just a few of the more obvious problems of trying to get care in an HMO. The federal guidelines are unfortunately not requiring that HMOs be nonprofit, simply because the private insurance industry lobbies in so many states are too powerful to be opposed. The result will be that few nonprofit HMOs will be started, and those that are will face overwhelming competition from the profit-making ones. Your state government is now or soon will be determining how HMOs can operate in your state. If you can, try to outlaw profit-making HMOs. Try to get it established that each HMO in your state must take its share of high-risk, low-income patients so that the burden of caring for these patients will not continue to fall exclusively on overworked, crisis-oriented, tax-supported public facilities. Especially try to insist that consumers of these services—representative of all age groups and socioeconomic groups, and particularly representative of the proportion of women and parents of children users, get elected to positions of control in the HMO corporations.* Since HMOs are recipients of our federal tax money, nothing less is equitable. The excesses that can result from abuses of the HMO are already visible, but we as women can try to prevent the grossest of them. (See Section III., *"Coping, Organizing and Developing Alternatives."*)

Family and Primary Care Physicians

Two other important new developments are worth looking into when you are choosing a physician. The first is the recent creation of an approved residency-training program in family practice. These doctors are members of the AAFP, just as the G.P.s may be (as we mentioned earlier), but unlike the AAFP G.P.s, who commit themselves to keeping abreast of medical developments after their internships, these doctors go on to a full, approved residency training, which is followed by board examinations and certification. In other words, they are specialists like other specialists, but their training is in so-called family medicine. This term, incidentally, does not mean that a doctor sees only families but that he is able to give basic, comprehensive care to any person of any age, who may or may not be a member of a nuclear family. In medical circles this kind of doctor is frequently called a "primary-care" physician, someone you would turn to first with any kind of problem, who would then refer you to a specific type of specialist if that became necessary. The question of ob-gyns as primary-care physicians for women is important. (See "Managing the Obstetrician-Gynecologist," p. 351.)

A few medical schools in the country have recently established whole new medical curricula designed to train from scratch the kind of doctor who will become a primary-care physician. There seems to be a high possibility that some of these doctors will provide many people with more satisfactory medical care than they would get from clinics or their own chosen specialists. Ask at local clinics and look up newer doctors in the community with this idea in mind.

What to Look For

Once you know your doctor's qualifications, you at least know how competent he is supposed to be. However, we cannot really rate a doctor's performance because we have almost no frame of reference—nor has anyone else really. Doctors admit that even they are not sure how to find out how competent another doctor is if they do not work with him every day. Asking a doctor's peers for an opinion, however, is like asking a blood relative for an objective opinion of a member of the family. Unless he is medically dangerous or behaving in a way that colleagues find politically threatening, the recommenda-

*See Andy Schneider, "Model Consumer Health Maintenance Organization Act Commentary," Health Law Project, University of Pennsylvania, revised, May, 1974.

tions will usually be enthusiastic.* In most cases doctors make referrals the way they give other kinds of non-medical opinions; they select on the basis of friendship and their own experiences, or because an exchange of referrals has become profitable. The competitiveness of big-city, university-linked specialists should work in the consumer's favor, but most of the time it doesn't, because these doctors often behave like small boys on rival football teams.

In a strange way, a doctor often feels personally attacked or threatened when he cannot find any physical cause for the symptoms you report, and this can cause him to become hostile and use a label of "neurotic" or "psychosomatic" as a weapon when in fact he has no evidence of psychological symptoms and isn't qualified to diagnose them anyway. In other words, it is false reasoning to diagnose a problem as psychological merely by ruling out other, physical causes. It becomes a weapon of convenience, used whenever the doctor cannot deal with the situation in his accustomed way, and frees him from having to take the complaints seriously any longer.

What about "shopping". for doctors? Doctors don't like it, of course, and neither do clinics. Some psychiatric clinics even have a blackball system whereby they will not give you treatment in their setting once you admit that you have been to another system even for a preliminary intake. Thus you either have to go back to the first clinic or do without help. However, private "shopping" for doctors is becoming more common, and to some extent the profession is learning to live with it. The AMA has always given lip-service support to the practice because it upholds the myth that only under the present "fee-for-service," private-enterprise system does the consumer truly have a "choice." Actually there is some truth in this, but the myth is that all people have a choice and that they know what they are choosing. In fact, only private patients—never clinic patients—have such a possibility of choice.

Some doctors charge for an exploratory talking interview, others do not. Some, but not all, will answer a few basic questions about their practice and how they handle patients in a phone call, without charge. "Shopping" takes a lot of time and may even cost a lot of money, but some people feel it's worth it. They track down every lead they have, try to get some feeling for the reputation of the hospital in which the doctor practices, and have some trial interviews. They ask questions about the decision-making process; they ask about honest answers to straight questions in the future, and about the sharing of information generally. They sometimes also ask how

*Recent scandals involving the failure of colleagues to restrict incompetent physicians may produce new legislation. See "Physician, Heal Thyself" (editorial), *Boston Sunday Globe* (August 24, 1975), p. A6; Judith Randal, "Why Did Cornell Let Twin Drug Addicts Practice Medicine?" *Boston Sunday Globe* (August 17, 1975), p. 1; Boyce Rensberger, "Medical Profession Acting on Addict-Doctor Problem," *The New York Times* (August 31, 1975), p. 1ff.

the doctor would feel if his advice were not followed on some occasion; because unless the doctor recognizes a patient's right to disagree, he may not recognize a patient's right to know. (See p. 355.)

When you are actually in the process of trying to get a doctor to give you information about your functioning, you can discover just how willing he is to spend time making sure you have the information you want, need and have a right to and whether you really understand what he is saying—in other words, whether the doctor is willing to make you a partner in the process of caring for yourself, or prefers to do it all. However, apart from the tests he performs himself, with which most of us are reasonably familiar, the modern doctor depends for much of his information on increasingly sophisticated laboratory work. Some doctors are overly dependent on laboratory tests when they should be taking more careful histories and examinations. Others dismiss symptoms without testing to check their reasoning. Both types of error force patients to keep close watch on a doctor's judgments, which in turn is apt to make the doctor defensive.

Some doctors obviously prefer to control all the information they have about you; others let you know in subtle or not so subtle ways that they think you are not bright enough to understand it, or present it in such a way that you couldn't anyway, thus fulfilling their own estimate of you. If you question the doctor in a matter-of-fact and non-threatening way, conveying your feeling that you are entitled to know, he should be able and willing to tell you what he is looking for, and what are the norms of the tests he is ordering, so that when the results come in, you will understand their significance. One doctor we know sends at least some of his patients Xerox copies of all their test results and discusses these openly with them.

It is difficult to think of any other area in American life where we pay such high prices for information to which we are denied access. When a doctor orders tests from a laboratory or special office outside his own, he expects you to pay for these tests. Yet if you ever try to learn the results of such tests directly from the labora-

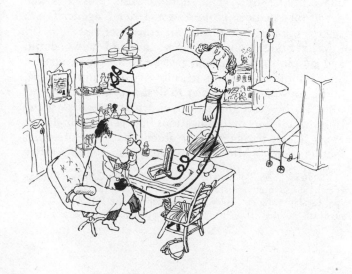

tory, you are told that only the doctor can release the information because he ordered the test. Someday there will be a legal test to determine who owns this information; in the meantime we can try to get both laboratories and doctors to be quicker and more open about test results and any other kind of information.

Information about risks is even harder to get. Many people thought that the object of the 1969 hearings on oral contraceptive risks was to determine once again the safety of the pill. But the hearings were rather an effort to discover for the first time whether or not women were being adequately informed about the *risks* of oral contraceptives. No more direct challenge has ever been presented to the sanctity of the doctor-patient relationship and, as might be expected, there was indignation and outrage from the doctors, particularly obstetrician-gynecologists, who were among those most frequently prescribing the pill. But the hearings concluded with a recommendation that women had a guaranteed right to information from the manufacturers that there were side effects and possible risks in some cases.

The hearings tried to establish that a woman need not be dependent exclusively on her doctor for this knowledge, even though the final package insert was much watered down from the original proposed by the Food and Drug Administration. It contained repeated warnings to report any unusual signs to the doctor and to take the pills only under a doctor's care, and stated that a woman had to go to her doctor in order to obtain the information booklet. To the last, the society of specialists in ob-gyn opposed *any* package insert, later falling back to the position that they wanted to be involved in planning the wording and the distribution (which they ultimately were). The reasons they gave were the usual: that the patient might become unduly alarmed reading about the hazards, that she might not take the pill even though it was indicated, and so on and so on.* The essential principle of the patient's right to know and even decide against a procedure if she chooses escaped them right to the end. The paternalistic mode still prevails in their thinking, and the concept of patient as partner in her own health care remains a threatening and unacceptable one. This episode also illustrates the power of medical groups over federal agencies and against the best interests of the consumer.†

What about women doctors? It would be wonderful and simple to believe that just being a woman made a doctor more compassionate, more flexible, more sympathetic to women and easier to deal with than male doctors. To be sure, the sexual undercurrents that sometimes cloud the communications between a male doctor and a female patient may be absent, but there are other factors present. Most mature women in active practice

today came of age in medicine during a time when prejudice against career women at all levels in our society, and especially against women in medicine, was at an all-time high. They had to "outman the men," so to speak—to be more conservative, more rigid, "better" in every way than their male colleagues, or even renounce the mother-wife role altogether, just to survive. It has also been suggested that as women they had problems with their sexuality, and perhaps in that day in the United States they did, having absorbed so much contempt for their sex from doctors and from society and yet still wanting to be doctors. At any rate, young women doctors today stand a far better chance of being at least liberal (that now dirty word) if not liberated, radical and innovative, and of feeling more entitled to be women and doctors too than their senior counterparts ever did. Your doctor should be chosen not only because she is a woman but because you have rated her as you would any doctor—for skill, honesty, quality of communication, flexibility, intellectual curiosity, ability to really listen, and respect for you as a person. (See also "Women as Workers in the Health System," p. 340.)

THE DOCTOR-PATIENT RELATIONSHIP

In the private setting, or even in a clinic, the fact that a woman asks for or even begs for advice and guidance with non-physiological problems may be seen by either the woman or the doctor as a sufficient excuse for him to give it. But it is very hard to measure the impact that this advice sometimes has on a woman, given as it is in the name of medical care, with all of the authority that seems to imply. Often a woman ends up being utterly dependent on her doctor, and then is freed from neither her problems nor her dependency. It is this kind of relationship that doctors are eventually tempted to resolve through the use of barbiturates and tranquilizers, and much of the so-called "housewife" drug addiction syndrome begins this way.* (See "Drugs Women Should Know About," p. 150.)

For many medical specialists the development of this special kind of dependency, or "transference," as it is called by psychiatrists, is seen as a deliberate goal of the doctor-patient relationship, about which so much romantic nonsense has been written. Eliciting this transference is specially taught as a technique in many medical schools—with a few vague cautions thrown in—as a useful tool for "managing" patients. When the doctor re-

---

*"Statement on 'Pill' Insert," *ACOG* [American College of Obstetricians and Gynecologists] *Bulletin*, Vol. 14, No. 5 (May, 1970), p. 12.

†See also Anthony Ripley, "11 on Staff Accuse F.D.A. of Harassment on Studies," *The New York Times* (August 16, 1974).

*Roland Berg, "The Over-Medicated Woman," *McCall's* (September, 1972), p. 67 ff.; also, Muriel Davidson, "How 'Nice' Drugs Killed My Sister," *Good Housekeeping* (September, 1970), pp. 96–97; also, Sam Blum, "Pills That Make You Feel Good," *Redbook* (August, 1969), p. 70 ff. Valium abuse has risen dramatically; its mention in overdose fatalities alone has doubled since 1973, according to the National Drug Abuse Council (UPI release, Chicago, October 19, 1975).

fers to this dependency, or transference, however, he calls it trust, at least when speaking to the patient (especially a woman). The parent-child relationship seems to be the model. Whenever there are real, matter-of-fact questions raised by the patient, a doctor is apt to say, "What's the matter, don't you trust me?" Also, for most doctors the fact that the transference develops is justification for it—that is, if a woman becomes overly dependent it's because she "needs" or wants to be. It is this expectation that accounts for the reflex behavior of so many doctors who constantly try to play a paternalistic role, calling patients by their first names from the first visit (while we must use "Doctor") or telling them, "Don't worry your pretty head, my dear. Just leave everything to me." In the past, or perhaps even today at some levels of our society, there may be women who find this treatment appropriate and reassuring, but their numbers are fast dwindling.

Especially in regard to sexual problems, most doctors are dangerously ignorant, even though the public continues to see them as knowledgeable.* Until very recently most medical schools did not even have any courses on human sexuality, and the majority of schools still do not require such courses, merely offering them as optional.† There is nothing like making a course optional to convey to a medical student that it is not important. The courses that do exist have often been designed by urologists or gynecologists rather than by behavioral scientists and reflect a mechanistic rather than a humanistic bias. Many patients whom these future doctors will meet will have read more widely and have a far deeper knowledge of the subject. This same discussion applies to nutrition as well.‡

Managing the Obstetrician-Gynecologist

While doing the research for this book several of us came upon certain sections in medical texts—the kind that medical students study and doctors use as references—which offer medical opinions about the character of female patients. In one text on gynecology there is a long section on the psychology of women in which the doctor is advised to interview the woman patient when he first sees her and to measure what might be called her "femininity" quotient. He is told to pay attention to how the patient responds to his questions, whether "in a feminine way or whether she is domineering, demanding, masculine, aggressive or passive in her attitude."§

What these value-laden terms mean exactly is not clear. Is being demanding the same as asking the doctor to explain what he is doing?

This text states: "The traits that compose the core of the female personality are feminine narcissism, masochism and passivity," and that a woman "bases an increased sense of her own value on her image of the person who loves her. She says, 'I am valuable, important, etc., because he loves me.'" Listed in an accompanying table of "components of mature feminine personality" are such traits as "allows male to conquer" and "sacrifices own personality to build up that of husband."*

Another text† points out that the only real way to happiness for women is marriage: "The full potentialities of feminine psychosexual maturity are seldom achieved except in a marriage relationship based upon love." What follows from this line of reasoning is that other settings are not considered appropriate for the expression of female sexuality.

Coital participation and experimentation by the adolescent or adult woman in settings other than marriage not only seldom resolves her personal problems, but more often results in guilt, shame, and loss of self-respect. Few unwed pregnant women have extolled the pleasures of the event or events which led to the conception.‡

The moralistic, puritanical, and judgmental tone of this comment only encourages our doctors to think that they have the obligation and right to be our moral guardians. Furthermore, it is not factually up-to-date. As indicated elsewhere, medicine is often forty years behind times in applying knowledge.§ Nowhere is this more evident than in the area of female sexuality. Many unmarried women have written in vivid detail of their sexual pleasure, which has also been studied scientifically.

There is great irony in the fact that doctors are socially sanctioned as sexual counselors and advisors, and yet are astoundingly ignorant of female sexuality. In one obstetrics book, in discussing female orgasm, the author-doctor says that "it is as variegated as thumbprints and not at all contingent on mechanical and muscular stimuli but rather on how a woman feels about her husband." He goes on to say that the only important question to ask a woman with regard to her lack of sexual satisfaction is, "Does she really love her husband?"‖ That certainly simplifies the counseling process for the doctor.

These attitudes toward women remind us again that many male doctors, like many other men, have created

*Harold Leif, "What Your Doctor Probably Doesn't Know About Sex," *Harper's Magazine* (December, 1964), pp. 92–96.

†J.D. Cade and W.F. Jessee, "Sex Education in American Medical Schools," *Journal of Medical Education*, Vol. 46 (January, 1971), pp. 64–68.

‡M.G. Phillips, "The Nutrition Knowledge of Medical Students," *Ibid.*, pp. 86–90.

§Willson, J. Robert, Clayton T. Beecham, and Elsie Reid Carrington, *Obstetrics and Gynecology*, 4th ed. (St. Louis, The C. V. Mosby Company, 1971), pp. 43–44.

Op. cit.

†Sprague Gardiner, "The Psychosomatic Aspects of Obstetrics," in Nicholson Eastman and and Louis Hellman, *Williams Obstetrics*, 13th ed. (New York: Appleton-Century-Crofts, 1966), p. 341.

‡*Ibid*, p. 335.

§John Millis, in J. Knowles, ed., *Views of Medical Education and Medical Care*, (see bibliography).

‖J. P. Greenhill, *Obstetrics*, 13th ed. (Philadelphia: Saunders & Co. 1965), p. 481.

myths about the female character and personality which blind them to us as a group and as individuals. What is frightening is how much power male doctors hold over many aspects of our lives, and how their *official* ideas about women affect the medical care we get and thus our very survival. We must not forget, however, that many of these ideas and characteristics are taken from the language of psychiatry, and psychoanalysis in particular, to which some obstetrician-gynecologists have turned as a kind of final authority.

The notion that there are some ob-gyn specialists who are greatly superior to others is often a myth. The fact that many of us have a need to believe that we are in the hands of superior physicians is one of the problems we need to be liberated from.

I knew that my doctor had a reputation for being one of the best in the city, and it made me feel good when I said his name and other people would say, "Oh, right, I've heard of him." I felt he was great and I was one of his lucky patients, even though I was rarely comfortable with him and always felt belittled when I went to him.

The first time I met him I thought he was so cold, clinical and businesslike. Then all his "charm" made me feel dependent on him. I respected that he was going to do the best job he could possibly do. If he criticized me I shrank inside. Sometimes I'd be annoyed that I had to travel so far for him to look at my stomach. But the mysteries still held. He was going to give me the baby. Once he confused me with someone else and I was very depressed.

Remember: Obstetricians don't provide continuity. Don't choose them to depend on emotionally. During pregnancy you really need to lean on someone who will also be there after the baby is born. Find someone else to share the whole experience with, for the doctor disappears from the scene right after your baby is born, and you don't see him again for six weeks or so.

Many of us may still be looking for an authoritarian figure, for a father, in our doctor. And doctors foster our dependency.* One well-known medical textbook discusses a woman's "strong need" for an emotional attachment to her obstetrician, speaking of this dependence as "healthy and therapeutically beneficial" (to whom?). The author speaks of a woman's need to be recognized and accepted and approved of by "an authoritarian figure into whose care she has placed *completely* herself and her baby-to-be." The obstetrician, he says, will advise her regarding her every activity, and he adds that it's

little wonder that he becomes identified in her mind with other masculine figures of her life. In other cases he "may fulfill an idealized image in [her] mind when authoritarian . . . male figures in her past life were disappointing, inadequate or absent altogether."* The ultimate in this line of reasoning is the passage in one text which suggests that through her relationship with her obstetrician-gynecologist a woman "may catch a glimpse of God."†

The fact that the specialized field of obstetrics-gynecology is now claiming that it wishes to be identified as *the* resource for all the health needs of women must be looked at closely. It implies that women can expect to have all their needs for psychological as well as physical care met by the obstetrician-gynecologist. Yet there are no standing requirements either in the residencies or as part of the specialty board examinations that an ob-gyn demonstrate any competence in any aspect of behavioral science, human development, psychology of women, or even psychology in general. Every woman should understand that what this means is that just because a doctor is a certified ob-gyn doesn't mean that he is qualified or trained or prepared in any way to give advice or counsel or any other sort of help in any human-relations area of a woman's life. He is only competent to assess the state of our organs and treat them if necessary, or prescribe contraceptives and fit them. If he does more than that he is simply guessing, or worse, answering out of his own beliefs and experience. Occasionally, of course, he may have taken some human-behavior courses, or rarely, a psychiatric residency, but these are simply not enough to qualify him for the delicate work of therapy or counseling about sexual adjustments. Many college-educated liberal-arts majors know as much, sometimes more. Even here, however, psychological and physiological factors are so closely interwoven that even the most skilled and knowledgeable people are reluctant to separate them. In the light of these facts it is shocking to realize that some 93 percent of physicians are treating the marital and sexual problems of their patients and only about 15 percent *felt* that their medical training had prepared them; 90 to 95 percent felt that additional training was needed.‡

At one level it is possible to think of the ob-gyn as a friend who is helping to protect you against unwanted pregnancy or venereal disease or death and disaster in childbirth. But at another level it's possible to see him as someone whose main concern is to keep you healthy and maintain you in your place as a sex object for your man, or for men; or as "housing" for unborn children and mother-servants to them afterward—"clean," the right

---

*This dependency has dangerous consequences for many women, who are persuaded to sleep with their physicians. See Betty Fier, "Masters Blasts M.D.s Who Rape Patients," *Moneysworth* (October 27, 1975), pp. 1, 12 ff.

*Sprague Gardiner, *op. cit.*, p. 342.

†Diana Scully and Pauline Bart, "A Funny Thing Happened on the Way to the Orifice." (See bibliography.)

‡Ethel M. Nash, "Divorce, Marriage Counseling" in Allan C. Barnes, ed., *The Social Responsibility of Obstetrics and Gynecology* (Baltimore: Johns Hopkins University Press, 1965), pp. 117–18.

size, in good working order and free from fear of disease or pregnancy, or pregnant but to be returned to the non-pregnant state "as good as new" and as quickly as possible, almost as if the pregnancy had never happened. Sometimes it seems as if one reason why many ob-gyn men are negative (subtly or not so subtly) about breast-feeding, for example, is that they have identified with a man's sense of sexual possessiveness about the breasts and want to preserve these exclusively for him, and in nearly virginal condition for as much of the time as possible. The same may be true for the use of forceps and the practice of routine episiotomies, or the oft-repeated caution that a woman should not get overtired (which can, on the surface, seem so solicitous).

Certainly, we may want all of these things, too, for our own reasons. When we want sex we want to feel ready for it in every way and protected against pregnancy if we choose to be—but not because we see this as our exclusive or even our primary function as women, and especially not because our first "duty" is to be in shape for a man whenever he might want us. Similarly, we know that children have needs too, but so do we as women have our own special needs. The doctor, and the ob-gyn in particular, can be viewed as society's representative in identifying us to ourselves and to others as creatures whose only needs appear to be meeting the needs of others. Our medical care thus sometimes seems directed toward those purposes. (See Zola, Irving under "Articles" in bibliography.)

The other problem for women, however, is that we have been taught to assume that the ob-gyn can at least meet all of our needs for basic medical care, even if we do finally realize that he isn't competent to help with feelings or sexual matters. Because of this, many women fail to have a thorough adult checkup by a competent specialist in internal medicine. While the ob-gyn does give routine checkups, they are usually very sketchy affairs, as any woman can testify, and the possibility is always present that he will not look for or will ignore certain problems that might result from treatment that he himself has given or is giving, such as the effects of the pill or other drugs, or the aftereffects of surgery or childbirth. (See also "Breast Problems," p. 124.)

With the kind of sophisticated tinkering going on today with our female endocrine systems, before half the knowledge is even available, and with the heavily operative, manipulative interference that is routine even in normal childbirth, all of us should be a lot more careful. A once-a-year checkup with a good internist is a bit of insurance against any pet biases or enthusiasms of the ob-gyn or any other narrow specialist, and you may find that some of the complaints and symptoms that are being brushed aside or dismissed in one office may be listened to with great care and respect in another. Many internists, by the way, will also do Pap smears and prescribe and fit contraceptives if you ask them to.

In other words, a woman's habit of seeing herself ex-

clusively in terms of her genital or reproductive functioning may prevent her from seeking medical care from other specialists for her other problems. By default, the ob-gyn has become the primary-care physician for women, a role for which he is not trained. Several health bills pending in Congress as we go to press have designated the ob-gyn as a primary-care physician, despite opposition from other experts.

Many ob-gyn specialists get involved with the treatment of breast lumps, including mastectomy, and other cancer and surgery problems, when these procedures should ideally be carried out by full surgeons or in consultation with cancer experts. While ob-gyn is considered a subspecialty of surgery, it is not synonymous with the surgical specialty. Again, be sure to ask about the special interests or subspecialty of any doctor you see.

All these warnings should not discourage us from ever seeing an obstetrician-gynocologist. This specialist has many valuable skills which we have a right to take advantage of whenever we need them. However, we should know when to go elsewhere for other kinds of help. We should also bear in mind that ob-gyns make more money than any other specialty group, including surgeons (median income $50,000).*

Doctors: Summary

In many a doctor's view he is being a "good" doctor when he is best able to shut out human considerations and can focus narrowly on technical, scientific, or pathological factors. At the other extreme, some doctors use their position to allow them to give a lot of purely personal advice. The image and myth of the doctor as humanitarian, which has been so assiduously sold to the American public for the last fifty years, is out-of-date. If there ever were such doctors, they are mostly all gone now. A few with such leanings do get into medical school occasionally, but oftentimes they quit fairly quickly or finally end up in psychiatry. There are reports that a new breed of doctor is now coming into medicine, but the psychological profile of most men in practice today more closely resembles the American business-

*"Doctor Income Rises . . ." (AMA Report), *The Boston Globe* (November 9, 1974), Edward Edelson from the New York *Daily News*.

The obstetrician-gynecologist's view of women

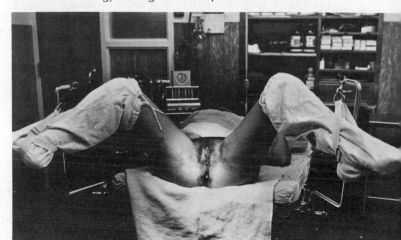

Iatrogenesis

An aspect of medical care we all need to be aware of is *iatrogenic* disease. These are diseases that are caused by the medical treatment itself, by the surgery or drug treatment or whatever other kind of procedure we have undergone. There is now a whole category of diseases resulting from drug treatment, not only severe reactions to a particular drug, so-called side effects, but also diseases that are caused by certain combinations of drugs which by themselves would be well tolerated.* Other examples are emotional illness caused by arbitrary separation of a child from its parents during hospitalization for treatment of some physical condition; violent or even fatal reactions to an anesthetic given for a surgical procedure that may be unnecessary or that would otherwise be safely tolerated; and problems caused by many, many of the obstetrical procedures that are either routine or unnecessarily interfering, from which the mother or the baby then has to be rescued. The average woman and consumer is quite insulated from this kind of information.

*Robert H. Moser, "Diseases Due to Drug Treatment," in *The Medicated Society* (Lowell Lectures, Boston, March, 1967).

man: repressed, compulsive, and more interested in money (and the disease process) than in people. Medical students are usually very carefully selected by men who are attempting to reproduce themselves and usually succeed. After four years of training students have almost invariably become somewhat cynical and even more detached and mechanistic than they were to start with. As a group they are also more immature emotionally and sexually than their peers or the rest of the population of contemporaries, who have taken the time to do the living and loving that brings them closer to maturity. Most doctors finishing their training are in late adolescence, psychologically speaking.*

The purpose of this section is not to single out the doctor as essentially malevolent. He is only one representative of a number of largely male professions. The point is to understand better what it is we are dealing with when we try to work with doctors or get them to work with us. It takes considerable maturity to see clearly enough or to feel free to identify with the person of the opposite sex in any given situation, unless it is an habitual perspective. In medicine there is scarcely any woman's viewpoint, and very little—if any—language for that viewpoint as yet. But given the personalities and

*Leif, "What Your Doctor Probably Doesn't Know About Sex," *op. cit.*

the prejudices they have to work with, it is particularly difficult for doctors to develop this viewpoint, and nothing in the system they work with motivates them to do so.

We can be angry about this and we should be, but it is perhaps a mistake to look to the doctor for confirmation of our feelings and identity as women in the first place. That is where only a group of women, being honest with themselves and one another, can hope to sort it all out. But just sharing horror stories is not enough, even though it is usually helpful. Learning about why things are the way they are and why things that have happened to us did happen, and getting the facts so that perhaps we can change our understanding of what actually happened, are equally important. Over and over again women who were miserably treated, just on the evidence, defend their doctors and even glorify them, saying, "He was so *good* to me. He was just marvelous." Only slowly, after a long time and gradually looking at the facts, can we face what really happened. People, and perhaps especially women, have a way of being very loyal to their concept of whatever happened to them in a medical context, and to the people who were there. When we do finally face the reality of an experience, we get very angry, of course, or even totally disillusioned for a time. We expected too much; we looked for something that perhaps never existed in American society—a "good" doctor.

If the picture of things as they are is discouraging, we mean it to be. Doctors are not gods but human beings with serious problems, both as people and as professionals.* But so, of course, are we all. The uncomfortable difference is that the system has taught the doctor never to reveal his problems and weaknesses to us, but to present himself as perfect and all-wise, whereas the essence of patienthood is that we reveal all of our doubts and vulnerabilities to him. Not to aggravate or take advantage of that essential inequality should be seen as an ethical challenge to the physician just as severe as all of the other points in the Hippocratic oath now going out of fashion. But it is rarely even recognized as an issue by most doctors, or understood if it is pointed out. The myth still persists that we meet one another as parent and child, and that you as patient must obey and pay money for the privilege. How long it will take and how possible it will be to convey fully to both parties the sense of consumer and employee, which is the reality of the relationship, is hard to imagine. If you cannot present yourself with conviction as an adult, and if you don't really feel fully entitled to argue or protest or get information and open communication, you will probably be treated accordingly. Maybe there will always be something about the "laying on of hands" that calls up

*See E. Shapiro, H. Pinsker, and J. Shale, "The Mentally Ill Physician as Practitioner," *Journal of the American Medical Association,* Vol. 232, No. 7 (May 19, 1975), pp. 725-27.

the child in us. And when pain and fear are added, perhaps it is inevitable.

This book is a start in helping us to assume more responsibility for our health care, but we've only been able to touch briefly on the simplest aspects, the common medical events of a woman's life. The real toughies—the complicated diseases, the rare surgeries, death and dying—will have to be coped with and worked out individually over a longer time. But everything we've said here applies: Don't let yourself be stampeded into any sudden decisions or forced to accept any medications or procedures you don't understand or want. It's your body.

OUR RIGHTS AS PATIENTS

Each of us, when we become patients at a hospital or clinic (or with a private doctor), has definite legal rights. We would need no discussion of patients' rights if doctors were taught to be in touch with their patients and if institutions made it the rule to be humane. (We define humaneness as respect for the worth and dignity of every human being, recognition of everyone's capacity for choice and ability to understand what is happening.) Many institutions are impersonal and alienating. When we enter a large hospital we are swallowed up by a huge machine that functions sometimes badly, sometimes well. We are vulnerable, in need of care. We have no guarantee that procedures done on us are in our best interests. We are expected to take most things on faith without too many questions. We aren't expected to know much. If we protest or ask for explanations, the burden of insisting on our rights falls on us as individuals. Sometimes we are heeded, often we are ignored, and sometimes we are punished for our persistence. We can quickly lose our sense of worth in such places.

Many doctors still do not recognize a patient's right to refuse any procedure, life-giving or otherwise. The familiar "ether permit" of the past—which generally gave permission to administer ether and then perform "any needed procedure"—still exists in some places, but it does not stand up legally. Similarly, a nurse can no longer hide behind "doctor's orders." She herself can be held liable if she administers a drug without the patient's consent, even if a doctor did order it.*

It is still common to hear reports of women who refused drugs, for example, and were told, "You're going to get it anyway." There is also increasing evidence that patients frequently do not understand what they are agreeing to when they do give consent or sign a permis-

sion form. There are still reports of procedures that were carried out without the patient's knowledge.* It is essential to read very carefully any consent form and to inquire about any vague or technical terms you don't clearly understand. Some hospitals have resorted to asking patients to write out their understanding in their own words. If you have any questions about the need for a procedure which requires signing a consent form, or for the need for the removal of an organ or tissue, get another opinion.

As we learn about our rights, we can begin to exercise our choice. To do so, we need the immediate support of friends and relatives, and the help of patients' advocates when we come in contact with the medical world.

The legal study of patients' rights is relatively new. Present statements of rights often do not make clear the distinction between legal rights and rights which we feel *should* be ours but which are as yet the result of no legal decision. We believe it is important (1) to make the above distinction between legal rights and "human" rights, for the sake of clarity, and (2) never to forget that the legal rights we have now are pitifully few compared to the rights we should have. We insist that institutions recognize all our rights and not just the ones legally defined.

Following is a *model* patients' bill of rights developed by George Annas for the American Civil Liberties Union. This bill applies to hospitals and clinics, not to doctors in private offices. Its language is precise: where the phrase "legal right" is used, the right is one well recognized by case law or statute. The term "right" refers to one that probably would be recognized if the case were brought to court. "We recognize the right" refers to "what ought to be."

The model bill is set out as it would apply to a patient in his or her chronological relations with the hospital: sections 1–4 for a person not hospitalized but a *potential* patient; 5 for emergency admission; 6–15 for inpatients; 16–22 for discharge and after discharge; and 23 relating back to all 22 rights.

A Model Patients' Bill of Rights

Preamble: *As you enter this health care facility, it is our duty to remind you that your health care is a cooperative effort between you as a patient and the doctors and hospital staff. During your stay a patients' rights advocate will be available to you. The duty of the advocate is to assist you in all the decisions you must make and in all situations in which your health and welfare are at stake. The advocate's first responsibility is to help you understand the role of all who will be working with you, and to help you understand what your rights as a patient are. Your advocate can be reached at any time of the day by dialing———. The following is a list of your rights as a patient. Your advocate's duty is to see to it that you are afforded these rights. You should call your advo-*

*John Haire, "Consumerism in Maternity Care," address at convention of International Childbirth Education Association, Inc., Milwaukee, Wisc., May 23, 1972. (Published in ICEA Convention report. See Childbearing bibliography, p. 316, for address.)

*Carl Cobb, "Students Charge BCH's Obstetrics Unit with Excessive Surgery," *The Boston Globe* (April 29, 1972), p. 1.

cate whenever you have any questions or concerns about any of these rights.

1. The patient has a legal right to informed participation in all decisions involving his/her health care program.

2. We recognize the right of all potential patients to know what research and experimental protocols are being used in our facility and what alternatives are available in the community.

3. The patient has a legal right to privacy regarding the source of payment for treatment and care. This right includes access to the highest degree of care without regard to the source of payment for that treatment and care.

4. We recognize the right of a potential patient to complete and accurate information concerning medical care and procedures.

5. The patient has a legal right to prompt attention, especially in an emergency situation.

6. The patient has a legal right to a clear, concise explanation in layperson's terms of all proposed procedures, including the possibilities of any risk of mortality or serious side effects, problems related to recuperation, and probability of success, and will not be subjected to any procedure without his/her voluntary, competent and understanding consent. The specifics of such consent shall be set out in a written consent form, signed by the patient.

7. The patient has a legal right to a clear, complete, and accurate evaluation of his/her condition and prognosis without treatment before being asked to consent to any test or procedure.

8. We recognize the right of the patient to know the identity and professional status of all those providing service. All personnel have been instructed to introduce themselves, state their status, and explain their role in the health care of the patient. Part of this right is the right of the patient to know the identity of the physician responsible for his/her care.

9. We recognize the right of any patient who does not speak English to have access to an interpreter.

10. The patient has a right to all the information contained in his/her medical record while in the health care facility, and to examine the record on request.

11. We recognize the right of a patient to discuss his/her condition with a consultant specialist, at the patient's request and expense.

12. The patient has a legal right not to have any test or procedure, designed for educational purposes rather than his/her direct personal benefit, performed on him/her.

13. The patient has a legal right to refuse any particular drug, test, procedure, or treatment.

14. The patient has a legal right to privacy of both person and information with respect to: the hospital staff, other doctors, residents, interns and medical students, researchers, nurses, other hospital personnel, and other patients.

15. We recognize the patient's right of access to people outside the health care facility by means of visitors and the telephone. Parents may stay with their children and relatives with terminally ill patients 24 hours a day.

16. The patient has a legal right to leave the health care facility regardless of his/her physical condition or financial status, although the patient may be requested to sign a release stating that he/she is leaving against the medical judgment of his/her doctor or the hospital.

17. The patient has a right not to be transferred to another facility unless he/she has received a complete explanation of the desirability and need for the transfer, the other facility has accepted the patient for transfer, and the patient has agreed to transfer. If the patient does not agree to transfer, the patient has the right to a consultant's opinion on the desirability of transfer.

18. A patient has a right to be notified of his/her impending discharge at least one day before it is accomplished, to insist on a consultation by an expert on the desirability of discharge, and to have a person of the patient's choice notified in advance.

19. The patient has a right, regardless of the source of payment, to examine and receive an itemized and detailed explanation of the total bill for services rendered in the facility.

20. The patient has a right to competent counseling from the hospital staff to help in obtaining financial assistance from public or private sources to meet the expense of services received in the institution.

21. The patient has a right to timely prior notice of the termination of his/her eligibility for reimbursement by any third-part payor for the expense of hospital care.

22. At the termination of his/her stay at the health care facility we recognize the right of a patient to a complete copy of the information contained in his/her medical record.

23. We recognize the right of all patients to have 24-hour-a-day access to a patient's rights advocate who may act on behalf of the patient to assert or protect the rights set out in this document.

As is apparent from the preamble of this document, it is my view that a statement of rights alone is insufficient. What is needed in addition is someone, whom I term an advocate, to assist patients in asserting their rights. As indicated previously, this advocate is necessary because a sick person's first concern is to regain health, and in pursuit of health patients are willing to give up rights that they otherwise would vigorously assert.

The patients' rights advocate

Until institutions, doctors and nurses can recognize our rights as patients as a matter of course, some mechanism must be set up to see that when we go to hospitals our rights are protected. A patients' rights advocacy system is one way to do this.

A patients' rights advocate should be defined as an individual whose primary responsibility is to assist the patient in learning about, protecting and asserting . . . her rights within the health care context. It is essential that the specific rights of patients be *spelled out in a bill of rights that the hospital adopts as policy and which the advocate has power to enforce. . . .* The word advocate is used in its classical sense, *advocate,* "to summon to one's assistance, to defend, to call to one's aid."*

*George Annas, Director of Boston University's Center for Law and the Health Sciences. See bibliography.

It is important that advocates have a basic knowledge of law and medicine and be able to communicate with doctors, nurses and hospital administrators. It is helpful to a patient if the advocate is acquainted with her background outside the hospital and sees her as a whole person.

Currently, some community clinics support patients who must go into hospitals for tests or operations by sending someone along with them to represent their interests. Women have been accompanying each other to doctors' offices. People from childbirth education groups give support to women in labor and help them to make decisions at crucial times. Some hospitals employ patient advocates, yet these people are often "management representatives" and are not always free to represent the patient's medical interests if these conflict with the interests of the hospital. It is best when advocates are salaried, if they are paid by some agency other than the hospital.

What if a community itself could generate a patient advocacy group, perhaps around the nearest hospital? Both laypeople and interested medical people could take part in the group. We are all past, present and future medical consumers. It makes a lot more sense to define our goals for humane medical care when we are healthy and all together than when we are sick, vulnerable and isolated from each other. A community patient advocacy group would form a strong consumer bloc, publicizing within the community and outside both improvements in the hospital and injustices that are not righted. It would be exciting for such a group to educate itself about law, medicine and communication, all the while keeping in touch with the needs of community people and communicating these needs to the hospital.

We are under no illusion that such groups would be easy to form and maintain; nor would it always be easy for them to gain the kind of access to the hospital that they would need to be effective. Yet we must develop ways to mediate between patient and institution.

THE CLINIC

The poorest people still in the medical system, at the clinic level, while they may be quick to know when they are being ill-treated as human beings, have so little health and medical information that they are almost completely at the mercy of their so-called providers of health care. They can only feel enraged and helpless at their dependency, their ill-treatment and their ignorance. It is this combination of emotions that armchair medical experts are fond of referring to as the "apathy" of the lower classes. Not to seek medical care under these conditions can thus be seen as an act of integrity and dignity, even if it ultimately risks health or even life.* This position is incomprehensible to large num-

*Michael Halberstam, "The M.D. Should Not Try to Cure Society," *The New York Times Magazine* (November 9, 1969), p. 32 ff.

Malpractice Suits

The failure of so many doctors to communicate with their patients on an even barely adequate and honest level is partly responsible for the recent reported upsurge in malpractice suits. A lawsuit is literally the only form of communication some doctors seem capable of responding to. One expert has even suggested that without the legal process standards of medical practice would deteriorate.* This statement implies, of course, that other existing mechanisms for keeping a doctor on his toes and making him justify his actions and decisions are not working very well. The much-touted "peer review" is clearly not reaching the issues concerning the patient. We know that there are many, many women whose stories make it clear that they had ample grounds for suing their doctors and should have done so. They either didn't know how or didn't have records, or they didn't want to, but most of all they couldn't afford it: a lawsuit is a recourse of the affluent, who know how to negotiate the system. There was a presidential commission to investigate the rise in malpractice suits,† largely because they increase the cost of malpractice insurance premiums—a cost that the doctor predictably passes on to his patients, thus driving up the cost of medical care for all of us. As we go to press, New York has passed legislation to abolish the right to sue for failure to gain informed consent! This monstrous provision would allow hospital attendants to commit assault and battery without patients' having recourse to suit! Women everywhere can improve their chances of satisfaction through the courts by keeping better personal medical records and working with lawyers to set up better guidelines for suits.

*"Injury Prevention a Steady Concern," *ACOG Bulletin*, Vol. 15, No. 5 (May, 1971), pp. 6-7.

†HEW News Release (A86), U.S. Department of Health, Education and Welfare, Office of Public Affairs, August 22, 1971.

---

bers of doctors and health workers. Most of them even find it contemptible that there are some people who will not accept health care under any conditions.

Poorer women who demand their right to be as much in control as possible of their pregnancy, labor and childbirth, for example, run risks that richer women don't run, and can be threatened by dehumanization and dangers to themselves and their babies, whereas a private patient might suffer, at the worst, minor personal indignity.

However, a recent study of maternal care in the hospitals and clinics of some major United States cities states in a formal way the things that many poor women learn from bitter experience. The quality of medical and personal attention we get in hospitals and clinics is determined by the following factors and combinations of them: our background, race, religion, marital status, education, income level and source, the number of times we have become pregnant, and the number of children we have. If we are rich, married, white and Protestant, we obviously get better care than if we are poor, black and unmarried.* While a well-off woman in a private labor room can "get away" with rightful demands to know what medication she is being given, a poor woman rightfully voicing these same demands might end up ignored or maltreated.

The word "doctor" to middle-class or private patients often means something drastically different from what it means to most clinic patients. Only in some settings does the clinic patient see anyone but residents or house officers, those incredibly bright but dangerously insensitive young men who try their wings here as doctors before becoming full-fledged, practicing specialists.

The clinic is also the place where residents, and some of the nurses too, can act on the stereotyped thinking and prejudices they have acquired in relation to whatever population they work with.† Trained, to begin with, not to see patients as people but rather as whatever part of the body they may be presenting, they add to this peculiar perspective any fantasies they may have about blacks, unwed mothers, Spanish-speaking people, or any other group. There is nothing in their training that requires them to recognize these people as human beings like themselves, whose need for respect and help is as great, or greater, than their own.

It's hard to know whether things are better or worse for patients in clinics staffed by "regular" doctors (whose training is finished and who give time to staff clinics for those who cannot afford private care). Often such clinics are the settings for perhaps the most moralistic kind of charity, which confirms the doctor in his wish to believe that we are still living in the nineteenth century, and helps to keep him, in many cases, a Republican. Here he can tell himself, "Why, they are damn lucky to get me," and in exchange for the donated care, he can feel entitled to give paternalistic advice about how to manage one's life, or make decisions that infringe on a patient's human rights.

Not having a choice of doctor and not feeling entitled to make demands or ask questions even if they did know what to ask, clinic patients seem to feel doubly impotent if the funds that pay the clinic fees are derived from welfare or other assistance programs. If you feel you must go to a clinic, do some homework first. Some clinic care is more expensive than private care from either a G.P. or a specialist who is at a smaller hospital. While there are many private doctors—maybe a majority—who are very outspoken and not at all defensive about not taking welfare patients, there are doctors who will

*Nancy Stoller Shaw, *Forced Labor* (see bibliography).
†*Prelude to Action*, Maternity Center Association (50th anniversary seminar report, Princeton, 1968), 48 E. 92nd St., New York, N.Y. 10025, 1969, pp. 5-7.

accept and care for welfare patients for whatever fee welfare will pay, just as if they were private patients. It's worthwhile to try to hunt out the doctors who will take people on welfare and at least make some comparisons of fees, travel, hours and attitudes. On the other hand, the worst of the Medicaid scandals involved private doctors who became wealthy, though they were incompetent, because they would accept this form of payment when others wouldn't.

Sociologists have found plenty of evidence that if you are white, college-educated, and not noticeably ethnic, you will get the best possible care from your attendants in the clinic setting. Accept your clinic care with some awareness that you are also doing them a favor. Don't ever forget that teaching hospital clinics "need" their patients. They need you and your medical problems in order to teach doctors and nurses in training and to give them experience that would otherwise be hard to get, since a private doctor does not usually allow his own patients to be "used" for teaching purposes. In spite of the fact that you may be seen by many different doctors in a clinic setting, you do have a right to insist on the identity of one doctor who is primarily responsible for you and to talk with him about your overall care. From him, as from any other doctors, you have a right to expect certain kinds of information (See p. 355, "Our Rights as Patients").

THE HOSPITAL

Whenever you decide to accept treatment from a particular doctor or clinic it is important to realize that you are at the same time choosing potential hospital care. In other words, the doctor or clinic is your key, your "entry point" into the system. If something comes up that requires hospitalization, you may be upset to discover, if you have not thought about it beforehand, that you are in a big, impersonal place that will not permit you to visit your sick child when you can, or that there are no facilities or personnel to help with an emotional crisis if one should develop for you or someone you love. Most hospital rules are not made for the benefit of the patients or families but for the staff's convenience, and some of these rules are not only arbitrary and unreasonable but may actually be dangerous to mental or physical health.

Hospitals are rated in a number of ways, differently by different people. First of all, there are 858 so-called private proprietary hospitals, which are owned and operated for private profit.* Some people feel that these should not be allowed to exist, while others feel they are a perfectly appropriate expression of the American Way. In any case, all such institutions need in order to stay in business is to fill their beds with patients who present themselves, and there is clearly no shortage of

*Kennedy, *In Critical Condition*, pp. 182-83.

patients. There are very few efforts to monitor the quality of medical care or check the quality of the training of doctors at these hospitals. Many are owned and operated by doctors as profitable private businesses.

Second, there are the private voluntary hospitals, run by a board of trustees and usually nonprofit, which makes them eligible for various state and federal benefits (although some of them may actually make a small margin of profit). They usually practice a kind of Robin Hood socialism, through which the payments by affluent patients actually are used in part toward the costs of low-paying or nonpaying patients.* This is not only done within the hospital as a whole, but also within the clinic itself. Clinic fees are set higher than necessary so that routine clinic patients help to pay for the care of complicated, more expensive cases.

Within the voluntary, private group are the small community hospitals, the big teaching centers and some religious-affiliated institutions. Some of these institutions are ruthless in their pursuit of unpaid bills, even to the point of causing families actual bankruptcy.†

Third, there are the public hospitals—city, state, or county—which usually operate at a loss of some kind because of the large numbers of nonpaying citizens they handle, for which they are inadequately reimbursed by the various governmental budgets.

Doctors usually rate a hospital by the caliber and training of its personnel, by its academic affiliations, if any, and by its technological facilities—that is, modern, expensive equipment for treatment, anesthesia, or life-saving, and the sophisticated laboratories that back them up. The presence of this kind of technology is one of the factors driving up the price at such hospitals, even though sometimes it is acquired just for the purpose of attracting prestigious physicians and not because it is really needed. Most specialists prefer not to be associated with a hospital which permits general practitioners to perform surgery or obstetrics there. Some hospitals are therefore specialty hospitals, where only specialists practice. Still others are single-specialty hospitals, e.g., maternity, pediatric, or cancer hospitals. This is a growing trend which has both advantages and disadvantages to women and other health consumers. (See "Regionalization," p. 368.)

Beyond this, most hospitals want to be "accredited," that is, to meet the minimum standards set by the Joint Commission on Accreditation of Hospitals. It is important to remember that this does mean *minimum*, and is not a badge of excellence.‡

*Cook, *The Plot Against the Patient*, pp. 17-25. "Robin Hood" generally means that private patients pay more, to cover losses on clinic patients. What also happens is that within a clinic, patients with lesser problems pay more than those with greater problems, to help cover losses.

†Kennedy, *In Critical Condition*, pp. 91-93.

‡See "The Accreditation of Hospitals: A Guide for Health Consumers and Workers, by The Health Law Project. See bibliography, under "Resources."

Most health experts believe that the "best" hospitals today are the larger, private, voluntary, accredited, specialty hospitals that are affiliated with medical schools, that is, the "teaching" hospitals. We have already mentioned many of the reasons for this. It needs to be borne in mind that the distortions of specialization have helped create the distorted structure and services of the hospital. Paradoxical as it may appear, it seems to be the large teaching hospitals devoted to a single specialty that are the least interested in the patient's emotional needs. They are also the most devoted to research and are most often involved in what are really experiments designed to yield information about new drugs or procedures, or to provide training experiences for residents. Where there are so many doctors, almost all of the same mind and very narrowly oriented, it is extremely difficult for an administration to become powerful enough to make rules of its own and be sufficiently responsive to the community and to patients' needs and rights.

Most hospital administrators do not have very much power to begin with, but the single-specialty hospital administrator sometimes seems to have even less in this area. Patients who come to these centers usually come either because they have an unusual problem or because they fear that one might arise, and that particular fear and anxiety makes them less inclined to argue. Teaching hospitals depend on large, trusting patient populations to stay in business, and usually will make only the token concessions that will assure them this steady flow.

The general hospital, on the other hand, usually offers a whole range of services, some of them interlocking, and no one specialty voice is likely to be given precedence over another, though some are obviously more powerful than others. Some administrators of such hospitals are very aware of the importance of the atmosphere and emotional tone of the hospital, and can make rules or take leadership steps to ensure that the hospital remains responsive to the consumer and the community. If you have a choice, consider a general hospital, teaching or otherwise, rather than a single-specialty hospital. This can also be a basis for selecting a physician. Look the hospitals over, talk with friends who have been to different places,* and then ask for a staff list from your choices. If you have never been in a hospital, or if it's a long time since you've been in one, or even if you have expectations based on a very recent experience somewhere else, you really have no frame of reference for assessing another institution. It pays to investigate in advance, if possible. Don't be overly impressed with hospital brochures put out by the P.R. department, however. (See Section III., "Coping, Organizing and Developing Alternatives.")

Hospital Size

Because large teaching hospitals are so crowded and so

*Talk to nurses too. In a recent survey, 38% said they would not like to be patients in their own hospitals. (*New York Post*, 1/5/77.)

busy, they are often dehumanizing. Many of us who live in big cities have had a lot of experience with them, as both private and clinic patients, and this is part of the reason why some of us have sought out smaller community hospitals. In some of these places the atmosphere is warm and quite different from other hospitals even on a casual visit, and the way you are treated during your stay becomes an identifiable and central part of your medical care. For some of us this is more important than the prestige of the big, impersonal centers, and often we find here a respect for our feelings, or our ideas about food, or our different life styles. Many establishment hospitals seem to be filled with people who are hostile to all differences and can be warm and accepting only to people exactly like themselves.

There are unusually fine community hospitals, but there are still others that really should be closed, in which the procedures, the medical care and the rules are hopelessly antiquated and the administration is merely a figurehead, without any sense of responsibility to the community and its needs, acting as housekeeper to a group of physicians who are responsible to no one. It takes looking into. (See Section III., "Coping, Organizing and Developing Alternatives.")

Nursing care in big-city hospitals today, even in the "best" places, is often very disappointing, and it is tempting to believe, as we are so often told, that "It's the same everywhere." There is so much transience in most places, especially in the academic centers, that it's hard to keep any program of patient care alive and in the same hands for more than a year or two at most; and transience also leads to errors in care and medication (as high as 25 percent in some studies!). Six-month turnovers are common. When they feel it is safe to talk, some nurses are frank about their frustrations in working with uncommunicative, unappreciative and rigid doctors, who handle relationships poorly with everyone, but especially with patients. These nurses sometimes have a tremendous idealism, which drives them to make proposals and create programs to improve things, only to have them voted down, under-budgeted or summarily scrapped by a group of doctors or even one doctor with the power to do so. The best way to describe the problem is as an absentee-landlord situation in which the doctor has all of the authority but none of the ongoing responsibility; is rarely available to the patient; and is only to be contacted in a crisis by the nurse. The nurse, on the other hand, has all of the ongoing responsibility and virtually no authority. She sees real needs but has no authority to establish ways to meet them.* Under these conditions it is not surprising that she often becomes cynical or takes on the closed, nonresponsive style of the doctors or the older nurses she works with, finally becoming shut off altogether.

Nursing is undergoing a revolution of its own that will hopefully take its place as part of the revolution of women, but thus far the patient feels very little of its impact, and new "technicians" are being created each day to supplant nurses as a way of both saving on nurses' salaries and reducing the sharing of responsibility beyond the doctor's own decisions.

Physicians in smaller hospitals often have more stable relationships with their nurses, depend on them more, and therefore sometimes treat them better, even (occasionally) listening to their advice. But the quality of nursing care is still uneven, and a lot of "shopping" is required. Don't hesitate to ask for a tour of the hospital, or for a chance to discuss the nursing care there with the Nursing Director or head nurse. They don't get many such investigative interviews, but they should be prepared to receive many more and to answer questions about how their programs for patient care are planned. Hospitals in which nurses have little or no domain of their own where they can make decisions, or have no budget with which to improve things, are much less likely to be satisfactory to patients.

Hospital Maternity Care

Some obstetricians have affiliations with only one hospital; others may have one or more additional affiliations, so you can choose. There are a number of ways to rate hospital maternity care. You want to be sure the hospital is equipped to handle an emergency. If board-certified obstetrician-gynecologists are willing to go there, the chances are good that it is equipped to handle an emergency. But remember, many more obstetrical emergencies are preventable than is commonly believed. And remember also that complications still occur in at most only 5 to 7 percent of all maternity cases. Chances are good that if you have given yourself excellent prenatal care and screening you will be among the roughly 95 percent who deliver normally without complications.

Another way to rate a hospital is to find out how babies are cared for there after they arrive. Most of us are so used to the central nursery system that keeps babies segregated from their mothers except for four-hour feedings that we tend to suspect any other system of being unsafe. In fact, the new Massachusetts code for medical care practice specifically states that it is medically safe for mothers and fathers to care for their own babies at the bedside whenever they wish, provided certain simple precautions are taken.* Most hospitals, in spite of their best efforts, and even in spite of the liberal use of pHisoHex (in the years before its use was restricted in hospital nurseries), have recurrent outbreaks of staphylococcus infections. Though rarely fatal, the infection can make babies very sick and can infect a whole family or even a

*Constance Bean, "Hospital Administration and Implications for Patient Education: A Proposed Program for Maternity Patients," unpublished report (Harvard School of Health, January, 1966).

*"Regulations Concerning Newborn Care in Hospitals," Department of Public Health, Commonwealth of Massachusetts, January 12, 1971.

whole community once the baby and mother are at home. The incubation period is such that the infection sometimes does not show up until then. A mother more or less continuously caring for her own baby (and breast-feeding) in the hospital offers the only preventive that has ever been shown to work consistently. This procedure is routine in most military hospitals, where the luxury of an epidemic is something they don't feel they can afford.

Staph is a hospital disease for the most part, carried mainly by hospital workers. While it is possible to treat staph, most of the current strains are highly resistant to antibiotics, and for a newborn infant both the treatment and the illness are better prevented.* It is a tragic fact that some of the largest and "best" maternity hospitals have constant problems with staph. Because they are large, they are believed to be safer, but the risks of epidemic are actually greater. Other increasing hospital risks are salmonella and strep.

The same questions about hospital rules and conditions are involved in evaluating a hospital for newborn emergency care. Selecting a pediatrician in advance of birth really helps, and while many of the larger hospitals may not permit local G.P.s or pediatricians to come in to examine your baby, most of the smaller hospitals will allow a pediatrician to do so. Most important is early and accurate diagnosis of any difficulties, so that the baby can either be treated or moved for treatment immediately. Find out if the hospital will transfer you with your baby, if that is necessary, and how distant the transfer unit is.

If you go to a teaching hospital you must assume—particularly if you are a clinic patient—that some tests or experimental treatment may be given either to you or your newborn baby.† Ethical medical rules require your informed consent, but as we said earlier, you may not always be informed in an unbiased way.

People in academic medicine insist that they are the best in medicine because they have access to all the latest knowledge and equipment. While this may mean that you become one in a series of experimental cases involving something new that is later abandoned because of complications or side effects, it may also mean that certain improvements and discoveries may not be used on you. Doctors in academe may read the study or know about the new method as reported by highly reputable colleagues in another setting, but they are under no obligation to apply this knowledge, and sometimes they even refuse.

For instance, it has been known for a long, long time that there are risks to both mother and baby if labor and delivery go on for many hours while the mother is lying flat on her back.* Several confirmatory studies have recently been carried out demonstrating more clearly than ever, via fetal monitors, that the back position in labor is a distinct hazard.† Yet in most United States hospitals women are still required to labor and deliver on their backs for the doctors' and nurses' convenience. One doctor we know insists on this practice to such an extent that his patients may not change their positions in labor even when they ask to do so, although the dangers have been directly and repeatedly brought to his attention! (For alternatives, see Chapter 14.)

Continue to find out about the hospital. Does it give a really adequate tour of the maternity unit, including labor and delivery area? Is it willing to discuss its practices regarding care of the baby and the presence of a friend or the father in the labor room, delivery room and afterward? Does it provide adequate referrals to good childbirth classes and to physicians who work with prepared couples? A hospital should have enough links with the community to be knowledgeable in these areas.

*Doris Haire, *The Cultural Warping of Childbirth*, International Childbirth Education Association special report (May, 1972), references 61, 68-71 on pp. 21-22 of the report. (See p. 316 for ICEA address.)
†L. D. Longo and G. D. Power (Loma Linda Medical School), paper presented at the Society of Gynecologic Investigation, April, 1970. Also evidence cited by Dr. Roberto Caldeyro-Barcia of the World Health Organization at the second annual meeting of the American Foundation for Maternal and Child Health, April 9, 1975.

*Doris and John Haire, *Implementing Family-Centered Maternity Care with a Central Nursery*, 3rd ed. (1971), International Childbirth Education Association, Box 22, Hillside, N.J. 07205. Pp. 4-12.
†See "Our Rights as Patients," p. 355.

III. Coping, Organizing and Developing Alternatives

SOME BASIC POINTS

From all that we've said, it can be seen that the way for women to begin getting better care is to learn to negotiate this non-system while they are still reasonably well and healthy. One reason for choosing a doctor before you really need one is to be in contact with someone who can refer to your medical record (if not to a relationship) when you are ill, someone who can also get you into a hospital in a hurry if you should need one. But that someone should be as close to a generalist as possible—someone who understands as much about the entire body system and its interrelationships as possible—and not a doctor with a narrow interest in one body part or system. See box, "What Can One Woman Do."

Form Groups

There are some other ways of approaching the situation. One is to make a concerted effort with your friends to tackle the common problems you may have

WHAT CAN ONE WOMAN DO?*
3 Steps to Begin to Get Better Health Care

1. Before Your Visit

Talk to many other women about individual doctors and clinics. Contact women's groups or consumer groups to get more information about costs, attitudes, and medical competence of a number of doctors or clinics.

Call up the doctor's office, the clinic, or the hospital to ask about:
   Fees: Find out if the standard tests like the Pap and gonorrhea tests are included in the fee for the visit. If not, ask how much they cost.
   The doctor's expertise: Is s/he a gynecologist, an internist, a general practitioner? If the doctor is not a gynecologist, find out if s/he does routine gyn work.
   Which hospitals the doctor works in.

If you can, ask nurses, doctors, or other health workers what they know about different doctors or clinics.

Also, you can check a doctor's credentials by writing the local Medical Society or looking in *The Directory of Medical Specialists* which might be in your local library.

No single source of information will guarantee finding a good doctor. So keep on checking, asking questions, and sharing information with other women.

2. At Your Visit

Know your own and your family's medical history. If possible, bring a written record of your own.†

*Adapted from HealthRight, Inc., by permission. (See "Resources.")

†See "Resources." Both HealthRight and FWHC have sample forms.

If you have a problem, write down when it began, symptoms, etc. In the waiting room, or before that, write down any questions that you want to ask about it.

If you like, bring a friend along with you.

Be sure that the doctor explains your problem and the treatment so you understand it.

Be sure that the doctor explains tests and the reasons for them, and make sure all necessary tests are done.

Make sure that the doctor tells you the name of a prescribed drug and its possible side effects, as well as any alternative treatments that may be available.

Ask the doctor to prescribe drugs by their generic name rather than the brand name (for example, aspirin, *not* Bayer's). This will save you money.

Talk to nurses and assistants. They are sources of valuable information and support and may explain things better than the doctor.

Ask for a written summary of the results of your visit.

Write down in your health record information about the visit for future reference.

Remember you have a RIGHT to a second opinion. If a series of expensive tests or surgery is recommended, you can tell the doctor to wait until you consult another doctor. This may prevent unnecessary treatments.

DON'T FORGET—It's your life and your body. You have a right to make decisions about drugs, treatments, methods of birth control, etc.

3. Afterward

Whenever you can, insist on being billed for medical care, and if you do pay in cash, always insist on having a receipt.

with particular doctors or hospitals, and also the problems that you may need resolved that perhaps a doctor will not or cannot help you with.

Keep records of everything that happens to you and also to other women you know. Form groups to learn facts and share experiences.

The only other possible method is to organize on the community level—form women's groups, welfare-rights groups, church groups, students' associations and so on—and agree to form subgroups of patients at the same hospital or clinic or even of the same group of

physicians. In no other way can women get any kind of reasonable grip on what is really rotten in the system that claims it is serving them. Even now there are some new health care plans that purport to give a single standard of care to a whole population, but almost none of them have provided any mechanisms for the consumers to take action as consumers or as members of a community. There is no way of knowing whether the care is single-standard or not, since the recipients are purposely kept isolated from one another and their token representatives are selected by the care-givers rather than by the

After the visit, write down an accurate account of the facts of what happened. Be sure you know the name of the doctor and/or the other people involved, the date, the place, etc.

"Shop" drugstores too. Studies have shown that many drugstores in poorer neighborhoods charge more than those in richer neighborhoods.*

Also, a recent survey showed no law preventing pharmacists from giving patients the package inserts listing medical indications and contraindications.† Ask for them.

Have clear instructions written on the label, because of the risk to others who may take it in error, and also because when traveling you may be challenged for possession of pills.

If you get poor treatment, if you are given the wrong drugs, if you are not listened to, it is important for your own care and that of other women that you PROTEST.

Then write a letter describing the incident to one or several of the following.

> The doctor involved.
> The doctor who referred you.
> The administrator or director of the clinic or hospital.
> The Director of Community Relations of the clinic or hospital.
> The local medical society.
> The organization that would pay for your visit or treatment (For example, your union, your insurance plan, or Medicare.)
> Organizations that might be paying this doctor for treating other patients. (Such as Medicaid or Medicare.)
> The local health department.
> The neighborhood health council or community boards.
> Community agencies.
> Local women's groups, women's centers, magazines, newspapers.
> HealthRight, Inc.

*Alex Gerber, *The Gerber Report* (New York: David McKay Co., Inc., 1971), pp. 158-59.
†Annual meeting, AFMCH, New York, April 9, 1975.

And, about a hospital:

> Joint Commission on Accreditation of Hospitals, 875 N. Michigan Ave., Chicago, Ill. 60611.
> American Hospital Association, 840 N. Lake Shore Drive, Chicago, Ill. 60611.

However, it is hard for one woman to keep working alone. The medical profession and the health institutions are very strong and powerful and will always defend themselves against complaints from the outside. Patients must work together to get the treatment and services they need.

So, to get changes made . . .
WORK WITH A GROUP . . .
FIND ONE OR START ONE.

We Have the Right to

Low cost quality health care
Considerate and respectful medical treatment
Non-discrimination
Be accompanied by a friend or family member through a medical experience
Full information about our bodies, tests, treatment, and prescribed drugs
Be fully informed before we consent to a medical procedure
Refuse treatment and know the consequences
See another doctor for a second medical opinion
Action or complaints about poor or inadequate treatment
Refuse to have our bodies used for research or teaching purposes
Have our medical records kept private
Access to our complete medical records
Transfer medical records
Complete data on hospital costs and fees *before* a hospital stay
Access to information on the outcome of a hospital stay and records of it

BUT, we must fight for these rights. Join us in the struggle for quality health care.

---

consumers themselves. Under this system there is no mechanism whatever whereby consumers can either rate or affect the quality of the care they receive.*

There are very few patients' associations as yet, although welfare-rights groups and neighborhood health associations have made some efforts. As long as the system encourages people to see health care as a private matter there is no real way that patients can collectivize or organize. Hospitals and doctors will not release the names of patients for reasons of "confidentiality" (except to such commercial interests as diaper services or baby photographers), although they are notoriously poor at protecting patients' privacy and records.

HEALTH EDUCATION

There should be programs in health information and

*Another federal program puts all standards for care into the hands of physicians' organizations, PSROs (Professional Standards Review Organizations). See "PSRO, Doctor Accountability or Consumer Disaster?" memorandum from Health Research Group (in bibliography under "Resources").

WHAT A GROUP CAN DO*

Start a self-help group or a Bodies course.

Work to change a local health care facility.

Get child care/day care into clinics and hospitals.

Start a local health project which will work in education, outreach, preventive health care for women and their children (or families) and begin to give simple training to local workers.

Create a women's counseling center or feminist therapy collective staffed by trained women who have personal experience with the problems of being a woman in today's society.

Start a hot line (abortion, rape crisis center, community sex information, postpartum support, community health resources information directory).

Publish, cheaply and simply: surveys of local practices regarding abortion, children in hospitals, childbirth, breast cancer treatment modalities, birth control options, sterilization, etc.

Support a woman medical student from the community who will return and deliver primary care in that community.

Start a childbirth education group which will educate people to issues of childbirth through public involvement, giving information about all risks and alternatives and not just preparation for hospital delivery.

Start a parents' group to mobilize around certain issues concerning children's health (e.g., immunizations, cost of drugs, violence on TV and in local films, availability of a well-baby facility or children's clinic, comprehensive health care in the community, HMOs, etc.)

Other Issues:

Know organizations nationally which can be resources (see bibliography).

Know materials (books, articles, pamphlets and films) which can be used to teach, support and encourage all levels of action listed above.

Go to a medical library or ask your local library to locate medical books and articles for you through inter-library loan. The general public is not supposed to be denied access to these materials provided there is a sincere purpose. The National Library of Medicine has regional branches throughout the United States, and citizens are entitled to consult them. (There is usually a small charge for subject matter searches by computer.)

Get a copy of the Physician's Desk Reference (PDR), which lists usual treatments for routine conditions. Share costs with others if necessary.

Know local resources in your community and elsewhere, including alternative health care and education settings (and also the politics and limitations of established settings—with hard evidence).

Know Patients' Rights, legal and psychological, and talk about them to anyone who will listen.

Be an advocate for others, for the community or for an individual or family, but do it in such a way that they learn how to get the strength to become independent of you and do this for themselves (maternalism) rather than always doing it for them and becoming a permanent spokesman (paternalism).

Know the value of the legal machinery and how to use it (e.g., suits vs. threats of suits; the responsibilities to consumers and community of agencies and institutions receiving large sums in federal programs; medical ethics in research, experimentation, etc.).

*Adapted from an outline prepared by Mary Howell and Norma Swenson for the workshop "Politics of Health Care for Women," given at the *Women in Health* Conference co-sponsored by the Pennsylvania Commission on the Status of Women and the Pennsylvania Department of Health, Southeast Region, June, 1974, at Temple Law School. See also "What Can One Woman Do?" from the New York Women's Health Forum, reprinted on p. 362.

education—even whole centers devoted to this purpose—as well as instruction in repairing your own automobile engine and re-covering a sofa, in all adult and school-age educational systems. But what passes for health education today has little value. Courses taught by people who are part of the "health" system have rarely given really honest consumer information or unbiased weighing of advantages and disadvantages. For the most part they are highly partisan offerings designed to defend the system and frighten you. Most of these programs are concerned with several factors: what the disease or problem is, how to recognize it, how widespread it is, and how much money is still needed for research.

And they usually offer one overall answer: trust your hospital and get regular checkups from your doctor.

Only when health education is based in the community and run by the community will women be able to get completely truthful information about the risks they take and the decisions they are making concerning everything from nutrition to surgery. And if these centers are well run they will offer all kinds of people the resources and the sense of initiative to keep up with their own health education instead of waiting to be told what the experts consider fit for them to know. Never has the responsibility for maintaining health and avoiding disease been so squarely up to the women in our society.

Therefore, our need for the tools of genuine health care and disease prevention will remain the greatest.*

In fantasy we jump to a Yellow Pages for doctors, hospitals and clinics, compiled by both women and men, rating people and institutions on their humaneness, efficiency, medical excellence, openness and responsiveness to the surrounding community. And we envision medical "clearing houses" in each community, run by and composed of community people, doctors, medical students and nurses, to match up peoples' needs and medical services; to handle complaints and more severe cases of malpractice; to educate community people from childhood up in preventive, commonsense medicine; to fight for equal medical care; and finally to keep doctors and nurses really in touch with the people they are caring for.

SOME MODELS FOR ORGANIZING

Over the past twenty years efforts have been made by different groups to try to improve health care for themselves or to change the system for everyone's benefit. Some of these groups look at one another with suspicion or hostility.

Volunteers and Fund Raisers

One type is essentially committed to working within the system as it now exists, without challenging the profit motive in health, the structure of care, or the unrestricted power and income of doctors. They are usually not consumer-oriented. By forming a pressure group or voluntary special interest group to compete with other interest groups for the attention and sympathy of the public or congressmen, they hope to gain enough money or influence to change, at least slightly, the way things are done for the next individual to be affected. Examples are: the National Foundation/March of Dimes (concerned with birth defects), the Heart Association, the American Cancer Society, etc. They usually have a broad base of volunteers, most of whom are committed to raising money for doctors to continue research.

Information, Referral and Counseling

Another type of group could be called the information and referral agency. Many of these simply help to keep track of the haphazard maze of human and special medical services and make this information available to any consumer lucky enough to know that the information and referral agency exists and what it does. The most conservative of such groups simply describe existing services without any systematic attempt to rate or compare them. The value judgments they do make are almost

*See Lowell Levin, in bibliography under "Articles."

always positive and usually based on professional rather than consumer evaluations and geared to private patient care. Such groups often offer counseling on an individual basis, focusing on personal problems.

For years Planned Parenthood has provided birth control information and clinics, as well as telephone information and referral. Many "hot lines" have been of this type, e.g., suicide prevention and drug dependency services, or community sex information.

In recent years, particularly during the period when abortion was legal in New York but not legal nationally, a wide variety of pregnancy and abortion services, offering information, counseling and referral, were set up in New York and other states. These varied tremendously: some charged large fees and received kickbacks from abortion services. Others attempted to rate price and quality on a nonprofit basis, as a service to women, and by controlling the referrals were able to limit the exorbitant profits to doctors and improve services. They also provided advocates. In the two years since abortion became legal, the need for these services has shifted to other states and communities, but the basic need for consumer ratings and advocates has not changed, especially since many facilities offering abortions have been drastically cutting or even eliminating counseling services in order to maximize profits.* The concept of referral has now been extended to affect all types of agency and institutional care.

Environmental Groups

As more and more toxic substances accumulate in our land, water and air, primarily as a result of the irresponsible, often unregulated practices of industrial and manufacturing corporations, many of us are forming environmental concern groups. Among other things, these groups are working to stop the dangerous use of pesticides and herbicides; to halt the pollution of our country's waters; to stop industrial air pollution; to close or restrict nuclear power plants. They often lobby for legislation and may create watchdog programs to try to en-

*See "The Abortion Business," in bibliography under "Pamphlets."

sure enforcement of current laws, so often flouted by big business and industry.

Unfortunately, many of these attempts fail or are successful only briefly. One of the most glaring examples has been our failure to bring about a complete ban of the use of phenoxy herbicides (notably 2,4-D and 2,4,5-T, also used in the Vietnam War under the label "Agent Organge"—it is ironic and at the same time predictable that one of our powerful biological weapons now has come home to roost). Dioxin, a chlorine compound always present in 2,4-D and 2,4,5-T, is possibly the most toxic substance in existence (one drop can kill 1200 people). Among other things, it has caused stillbirths and birth defects in a number of rural areas. Moreover, it is fast accumulating in our environment, as it will not decompose naturally even after many years. Recently the Environmental Protection Agency found unsafe levels of dioxin in one half of beef-fat samples derived from cattle grazed on land previously treated with 2,4,5-T.* (And many scientists think there is no such thing as a "safe" level of dioxin.) For more information on phenoxy herbicides, read *Sue the Bastards* and Esther Ritter's excellent article (see bibliography).

Some groups, such as Urban Planning Aid in Cambridge, Mass. (see bibliography), have focused on the health hazards of certain work environments. As more women workers are becoming better informed and increasingly alarmed about occupational hazards, they are often the ones who take collective action to improve working conditions.

Groups working on environmental issues include Nader's Health Research Group (Pesticide Project), Environmental Action, and many local women's centers (see bibliography).

Mutual Help Groups

"Mutual help," "self-help," or "mutual support" groups† are usually formed of people who have experienced, or whose children have experienced, the same fate and who offer one another the kind of support only a fellow sufferer could understand. Many arose in response to the failure of the medical profession to understand their needs. Examples are: widows, victims of cancer surgery (the Ostomy Society), parents of children who died of sudden infant death (SID) or of burned children or any hospitalized child. Some of these groups have been more active than others in analyzing their experience and trying to challenge and change procedures and prevent the more destructive practices of the medical or socio-legal system. All have used the principle of group support. Some abortion groups clearly have done this, as have Childbirth Education Associations and La Leche League members.

Chemical and Engineering News (August 25, 1975).
†As described by Dr. Phyllis Silverman of Harvard's Laboratory of Community Psychiatry.

Prevention for "Normal" Experiences

The nearer to normal the experience is, the greater the courage of the group seems to be to challenge the authority of whatever system is involved. Childbirth groups, abortion groups, breast-feeding groups and parent support groups have generally been the most active in the past. They were also among the first to use referral as an instrument of change. The most elaborate of the information, referral and counseling services have involved the use of groups for "courses"—systematic presentation of information and teaching of negotiating skills for use in dealing with institutions—as well as for sharing, support and the teaching of physical techniques that may prevent a normal experience from becoming complicated or producing problems. Childbirth education classes are the older examples of this model, and the community of consumer-controlled Childbirth Education Association classes is still one of the best examples of a grass-roots service which also offers advocacy training so that each person can have a trained companion during hospitalization (usually the father, but not always).

Women's Groups

In recent years courses based on this book, called "Bodies" courses or "Know Your Body" courses, have been given everywhere—in adult education programs, high schools, by town boards of health, in YWCAs and simply in people's living rooms. Similar to childbirth classes, these have usually been limited to the presentation of information; sharing of feelings, knowledge and experiences; and formal or informal referral. Unlike childbirth classes, these courses have usually been restricted to women only.

It now seems like a logical sequence for every woman to begin with a consciousness-raising (CR) group and a

Know Your Body course, and to learn there how to find specialized help for events in her life as they come up.

Self-help Groups

There is nothing new about self-help. People have always banded together to help one another to deal with everyday problems. Currently, self-help groups are among the many kinds of groups that have arisen in response to the failure of many professions to meet our needs adequately. In particular, they have formed in response to the failure of the medical profession.

What is self-help? According to one women's self-help group:

Self-help is women sharing experiences, knowledge, and feelings—women supporting each other and learning together. Self-help begins by working from a practical base, starting with learning from physical self-examination [see p. 122], finding out what we DO know, what we do NOT know, what we WANT to know and exploring from there.

Self-help groups are action-oriented. One self-help group might investigate menopause, another human sexuality, another lesbian health issues, another might train as paramedics and health counselors. The possibilities are endless, depending only on our own creativity and needs.

Self-help is women relating to ourselves in order to demystify health care, the professionals and our own bodies; it involves being able to make personal choices based on our own very valid experiences and knowledge. Self-help is a positive action by which we can change our own lives and those of our sisters.

Self-help is a political act. It is deeply challenging to the existing health care system. Through sharing our knowledge collectively we have developed skills—we, not only the "professionals," will know what is done to us medically and why it is done. We do not take the place of the doctor, but we DO reverse the patriarchal-authority-doctor-over-"patient" roles.*

Self-help represents a wide range of activities. Here are a few examples:

• A group of teenage women getting together for the first time to discuss many of the issues in this book.

• A group of women committed over a period of time to trying to change medical and health care practices at a local hospital.

• A group of women doing original research in areas vital to better health care for women.

• A group of new mothers getting together weekly to help one another cope with postpartum problems and experiences.

Home Birth and Birth Centers Movement

As the technology and interventions of hospital child-

*Women's Community Health Center, 639 Massachusetts Avenue, Room 210, Cambridge, Mass. 02139.

birth have escalated and as the childbirth education movement's effort to humanize hospitals has become increasingly stagnated, many couples are deciding to have their babies at home. As more and more couples do this, the benefits are being more widely discussed and the risks are being put into more reasonable perspective. Another movement has begun and is already separating itself from those groups that prepare couples for hospital birth. So much of the time and energy in hospital childbirth preparation classes is spent in teaching you how to negotiate carefully and politely with cantankerous doctors; teaching you your rights and how to exercise them without antagonizing or offending anyone; how to avoid the more risky hospital interventions and then how to cajole, wheedle and persuade hospital personnel into giving you your own baby when you want it afterward, that many of today's women, instead of being grateful for the information, are offended by it. As they become more aware of the risks of childbirth in the hospital they begin to balance these risks against home birth risks. Home birth groups are now setting up their own classes to give people the special knowledge they will need.

The variety of these groups depends on the local community and the local medical community. On the West Coast there are several birth centers where people give birth in a communal setting with many friends and a lay midwife in attendance. From these experiences, new knowledge about the uninterrupted birth process and the feelings surrounding it is being gathered. In parts of the Midwest there are small networks of families and couples who are quietly giving birth at home without any special attendance at all. In some midwestern and eastern cities groups have been forming around the willingness of one or two doctors to deliver at home, usually within a very limited geographic area surrounding the hospital. Many of these groups are teaching their own classes and are once again trying to humanize local hospitals so that parents will not have to take the risks of inadequate medical backup but can spend only a few hours in a hospital with a minimum of interference.

Often these newer programs have a uniquely feminist perspective, in contrast to the implicit or explicit dependency of women on male doctors or male companions in the older movements.

THE WOMEN'S HEALTH MOVEMENT

As the ideas and actions of referral, mutual help, Know Your Body courses, self-help, paramedical training, home birth and patients' rights groups gain momentum, the challenges to the existing health care system fall into two categories. One directs itself to consumers, helping patients as individuals or in groups to try to gain knowledge and alter their individual experiences or to reform the system. The other is deeply influenced by the limitations and failures of efforts to reform women's health care (some of which go back over twenty years) and is coming to believe that women will have to take over their own health care and the system of women's health care in order to return a sense of dignity and adequacy to these services. These two approaches, and all the shades of political persuasion in between, are united in the conviction of women who identify with other women. We have concluded that the pervasive male bias and control of all our social institutions, particularly health and medicine, at worst has damaging and destructive consequences and at best is not fostering optimum health care for women or anyone else. These common interests are bringing all these different groups of women into contact with one another to the point that we can be called collectively the women's health movement, sharing a perspective on health and health care. We are deeply conscious of linking up with our lost identity as healers in the distant past and of our resemblance to the people's health movement and those women who ran institutions in the last century.

Developing An Alternative Health System: Women's Clinics

Through this movement, in addition to the types of effort already described, the variety of alternatives to the present health system is being extended. Women's clinics are springing up. Some of them are already part of a national network of Feminist Women's Health Centers which offer basic gynecological services, self-help, paramedical training, and which are beginning to get involved with childbirth issues. Others are grass-roots community clinics formed by local women who didn't start out as identified feminists but were simply frustrated and fed up with the lack of helpful health services for women, and who became radicalized by the hostility of local male doctors toward their efforts to improve health care. The growth of all these women-run clinics has revealed the need for a new type of training, geared to this setting, and a new type of hospital care, directed by women for women. Some clinics have already begun more formal training programs, and in some cities plans are being made for a women's health school or a women's hospital. The increasing conflict which these efforts will produce with the medical profession has already been foreshadowed by the early arrests for self-help and lay midwifery. But these arrests, like those of Margaret Sanger and other revolutionaries in the past, are simply the foreshadowing of an idea whose time has come.

Future Demands

Lots of changes are coming, and women's clinics, health

schools, health centers and hospitals will be part of them, but for a long time for most of us doctors and hospitals as they are now will be part of our lives. Our outrage at the system shouldn't keep us from trying to get the very best medical care that money can buy right now, for the very least that we can pay, whenever we need it. But there is at present almost no way that we can get perspective on the system or the care we receive, even in a women's clinic, without study. This doesn't mean, as the doctors like to interpret it, that we all want to learn in order to become nurses or doctors or amateur specialists. For some of us that may be the case, but for others it is simply and rightfully having something to say about what happens to our bodies. Also, it is a hunger after those approaches and understandings that preserve health and prevent disease, rather than a fascination with the drama of emergency curative care.

Medicine in the United States has been arrested for too long at the level of symptoms and mechanisms and chemical tinkering, when it should be pushing on to causes—which will require integration and coordination of all of the fragmented specialties, now so disparate and competitive. Health* is more than just the absence of disease, whether physical or mental or a blend of both, and the concept of homeostasis,† which is still operating in the minds of most men of medicine, is not enough of a goal any more in this age of knowledge explosion, instant communication, and virtually unlimited technological capability. Attaining a broader goal, however, will require an altogether new responsibility from the patient, and a partnership between patient and doctor that bears almost no resemblance to the romanticized model still held in the hearts of so many doctors and perhaps patients too. Health will be the full-time responsibility of the patient, but not health as it is identified today, which is really synonymous with disease. The tools for prevention belong in the hands of the patients.

APPENDIX

Regionalization

The trend today is toward bigger and bigger specialty hospitals, and proponents of academic medicine have worked hard to sell this notion to the public. It is easy to get the feeling that they are talking about a manufacturing plant, or perhaps, more appropriately, a meat-processing plant. What academic and public health physicians are saying is that the industrialization of human care is a more "efficient" way of using the resources we have, such as ultra-expensive technology and the ultra-specialist; and they are suggesting that this efficiency will also produce better care for patients, because only people who exercise

---

*See M. Howell, *Healing at Home*, for an attempt to assess health as a positive state.

†A notion of the body being in balance between negative and positive forces.

their skills on a regular basis can perform adequately, utilizing the best and latest equipment. They are also saying that hospital care should be regionalized by specialty, as modern transportation makes many small local units unnecessary duplications.*

What they have not considered, and may not if they aren't obliged to, is that human services do not always work best if they are bigger, and in fact may only be able to reach a certain size before their very bigness becomes counterproductive, tending more to compound and increase errors than to reduce them, while communication begins to break down altogether. Especially in the realm of family health, or family medicine, or health maintenance there is reason to believe that the bigger, more distant hospitals are more of a hindrance, to say nothing of exposing people unnecessarily to the risks of such special, hospital-based infections as, for example, staphylococcus. Until there is better coordination among the specialists and better conditions for nurses—and even then—there will be a definite place for the small, high-quality community hospital. These are all factors that we as women and as consumers should consider carefully when making decisions about a doctor.

We should also apply pressure on our own state agencies as they respond to doctors and medical groups proposing regionalization. Regionalization as it has been planned for maternity, newborn and pediatric services, and as it is being practiced in some areas, is an excellent illustration of how consumers lose power and how medical care inadequacy is protected at an enormous cost which the patient eventually pays.

No woman—or couple—wants to listen to the condemnation that they are risking the life of their unborn or newborn infant (or the mother's life) by choosing to have their baby at home or in a small local hospital rather than traveling long distances to give birth in a very large medical center. This is generally the basis on which regionalization is presented to young parents and other health consumers. The program proposes, reasonably enough, that every hospital have at least the capability to recognize when a newborn infant needs help and to transfer the infant to a high-risk center where it can receive that help. It also proposes that every hospital involved with maternity care have the highest quality anesthesia services and blood bank capability in the event that an emergency occurs. Given the falling birth rate and the rising cost of both specialized equipment and specially trained personnel, it seems reasonable not to duplicate all of these in every local hospital. Therefore, two additional propositions have been made: *first*, that all mothers should be screened according to two categories: high risk or not high risk; *second*, that only those hospitals which have the highest number of births annually (2,000 or more) would have personnel whose skills are exercised often enough to meet the challenge of the predicted or unpredicted high-risk case.

From these assumptions flow several consequences. First, all hospitals whose birth rates fall below the specified range become suspect; and particularly if they do not meet the other criteria of emergency capability, they may be asked to close. Second, all mothers who are identified as high risk (who have previously developed or develop during pregnancy any

conditions such as diabetes, high blood pressure or cardiac problems, or who have a history of prematurity, etc.) deliver in the high-risk center. These hospitals will be designated as follows: high risk with neonatal intensive-care capability: *Level III* hospital; capability to recognize and transfer to Level III hospital any unpredicted newborns in trouble: *Level II*; no special capability, but geographic isolation prevents additional specialization: *Level I*.

On paper this still sounds reasonable. However, no matter how many expected and unexpected emergencies may occur, a Level III hospital could not by itself reach the rate of births necessary to maintain the skills desired by the regionalization planners. To do this it therefore becomes necessary to have Level II hospitals *within* the Level III hospitals. In other words, in order to have enough patients, the Level III hospital must attract a sufficient number of Level II patients. Since the Level III hospital already has all of the capability asked of Level II hospitals it is no problem to care for these patients. The Level II hospital without these capabilities therefore is at risk of losing its patients to the Level III hospital, and finally of being closed so that the Level III hospital can meet its quota. Since the Level III hospitals are almost always teaching hospitals and also provide the consultation and outreach needed by the Level II hospitals, they also can control the supply of expert specialists which the Level II hospitals need in order to compete.

The regionalization plan thus becomes a mechanism by which Level III teaching and research hospitals can control competition in a shrinking market through policymaking in state agencies, forcing out those Level II hospitals which they find undesirable or unsuitable on medical or any other grounds. Another major question is the appropriateness of caring for normal women with high-risk methods.

Let us look now at costs and benefits to patients. Regionalization is based on the assumption of pre-gasoline-shortage travel time, on good highways in good weather, of one hour. Translated, this can mean as much as fifty or sixty miles distance between the patient's home and the regional center. In post-gas-shortage terms, this can mean an hour and a half or more of travel after labor begins. If an infant is transferred, this can mean an agonizing triangle of commuting for a new father, for example, between the home (where presumably other children may be), the hospital where the mother is, and the distant hospital where the infant is. There are no plans and there is no budget for transferring the mother with the infant, nor are any services being planned to help with the social, psychological and logistical problems which such a splitting of the new family can produce. The transferred infant becomes literally a foster-care infant.

What about the benefits to the infant itself? Aren't all these problems worth it for the benefit to the infant? Unquestionably, an infant in trouble deserves the best that modern science has to offer. Who would argue otherwise? But given the trauma of transfer and intensive care, wouldn't one suppose that everything known or possible would have been done to *prevent* the crisis from ever happening in the first place?

The answer is that everything known which could prevent a crisis is not being done. The prenatal care which is supposed to lead to the screening and the preventive care is in the hands of the obstetrician-gynecologist. As indicated elsewhere, his knowledge of the importance of nutrition during pregnancy is

*Richard Knox, "Hospital Beds," *The Boston Globe* (October 10, 1971), p. 1.

in most cases uneven or inadequate. No systematic effort is made to see that all pregnant women are thoroughly watched for both the quality and quantity of their food intake, or their exercise habits. There are no controls over the private office practice of obstetricians. They may prescribe dangerous diuretics or other questionable drugs still on the market if they choose. They may dangerously restrict weight gain if they wish. They may artificially induce labor for convenience if they wish, without knowing whether or not the fetus is large enough or mature enough to endure labor, delivery and life outside the uterus without difficulties. In other words, the screening mothers get during pregnancy is not quality-controlled. Regionalization for all thus protects against the inadequate care which any one (or more) obstetrician may give. This protection is massive, crisis/emergency, heavily expensive care. Such care now usually involves electronic fetal monitoring, which can pick up infant distress (see "Obstetrical Medications and Interventions," in Chapter 15), and is routine in all high-risk cases. The monitor is also the means by which the "unpredictable" complications are picked up, and for this reason the use of fetal monitors is tending to become routine. However, there is reason to believe that a large percentage of these sudden complications are the result of procedures associated with the use of regional anesthesia, especially the continuous epidural, which is now being so intensively researched in most major teaching centers. Continuous regional anesthesia has a series of considerable risks to both mother and infant which ideally require monitoring and entail rescue costs which must be paid by all of us who pay hospital bills (or pay local or federal taxes). Yet regional anesthesia is rarely necessary. (See Chapter 14.)

"Risking"—procedures for predicting high-risk cases and getting them to appropriate facilities—was not even begun in the United States until recently, almost two decades after such systems had become routine in Europe. Unlike European systems, however, U.S. risking is both too crude and too weak, only picking out the most glaring complications and failing to apply principles of low-risking—that is, screening out those cases which do not require intervention and giving them every support possible to keep them in the low-risk group* with minimal intervention. In other words, the newborn in trouble whose difficulties were not predicted by the high-risk condition of the mother might have been protected from the crisis by more careful prenatal care and fewer interventions in labor and delivery. These interventions in turn might have been prevented by more systematic and thorough preparation of parents for labor and delivery, minimizing the need for surgical and interventive procedures. Careful application of the

---

*Two efforts to introduce low-risking in the United States are presently under way or planned. One is the Booth Maternity Hospital in Philadelphia, where there is a single standard of care for all mothers—high-risk, low-risk and unwed mothers—all for the same lower-than-average fee. Nurse-midwives deliver the babies, with an obstetrician in attendance in case of complications, and there is an intensive patient preparation and education component. Patients are flocking there, and births have doubled in one year. The second effort is at the Maternity Center Association in New York, where a "domiciliary" service has been opened for low-risk patients, with a backup hospital nearby. Patients delivered by midwives with an obstetrician nearby go home in 12 to 24 hours, followed up at home by a public health nurse. Similar out-of-hospital birth centers are in operation now throughout the U.S., and more are being planned. (See bibliography, p. 313.)

knowledge we have about the risks of many routine obstetric practices (such as rupturing of the membrane; immobility and back position during labor; and use of drugs to speed labor) could prevent still other crises from arising.

None of these preventive approaches is being systematically used because to do so would be to interfere with the private practice of obstetrician-gynecologists. In other words, American maternity care has no philosophy of prevention as regards private patients. Instead we have a proposed program called regionalization, which is the most expensive and stressful that could be devised, and we, the public, are blamed for refusing to pay for it!*

Consumers lose under regionalization because they lose competitive leverage. The campaign of the 1960s for prepared childbirth, father and labor coach participation in labor and delivery, and flexible access to the new baby progressed because consumers could pit one hospital against another and drain off desired clientele. Now this leverage is being lost and, between HMOs and regionalization, consumers who feel they must have a hospital delivery are already experiencing a narrowing of options in terms of where they will deliver and who will deliver them, and what the quality of the experience will be. This is in fact how the current home birth movement has been created: when options have become too narrow, so consumers are opting out.

Both inside and outside the "establishment" of the university-linked or accredited system there are doctors and hospitals which do not give good care. Until all hospitals and all medical practitioners have consumer ratings, at least partial consumer control, and systems of consumer evaluation readily available to other potential consumers, the most dangerous assumption you can make is that you will automatically receive the "best" care in a particular place or from a particular doctor just because all the right credentials seem to be there.

READINGS AND RESOURCES

Books

Ann Arbor Science for the People Editorial Collective. *Biology as a Social Weapon.* Minneapolis: Burgess Pub., 1977.
    Good historical survey of how biological determinism was and is used to uphold the status quo. Includes chapter on sex roles.
Annas, George. *The Rights of Hospital Patients: The Basic Guide to a Hospital Patient's Rights.* New York: Avon Books, 1974.
    One in a series of ACLU handbooks; has a chapter on women written by a man. Basic information valuable though, including model patients' bill of rights. (See "Our Rights as Patients," p. 355.)
Barker-Benfield, G. J. *The Horrors of the Half-Known Life: Male Attitudes Toward Women and Sexuality in 19th-century America.* New York: Harper & Row (Harper Colophon Books), 1977.
    Excellent documentation of medical misogyny.
Becker, H. S., E. C. Geer, E. C. Hughes, and A. L. Straus. *Boys in White.* Chicago: University of Chicago Press, 1961.
    Sociological profile of the doctor as student in medical school and residency.

---

*See Saul Kent, "Perinatology: New Science of Childbirth," *Saturday Review/World* (July 13, 1974), pp. 55, 58.

Campbell, Margaret. *Why Would a Girl Go into Medicine?* The Feminist Press, Box 334, Old Westbury, NY 11568. 1974.
> Systematic study of discriminatory practices against women medical students and women patients in major schools, by a woman physician.

Corea, Gena. *The Hidden Malpractice: How American Medicine Treats Women as Patients and Professionals.* New York: William Morrow & Co., 1977; New York: Jove Publications, Inc. (Harcourt Brace Jovanovich), 1978 (pb.).

Donnison, Jean. *Midwives and Medical Men: A History of Inter-Professional Rivalries and Women's Rights.* New York: Schocken Books, 1978.

Dreifus, Claudia. *Seizing Our Bodies.* New York: Vintage Books, 1977 (pb.).
> Good selection of articles on women's health.

Ehrenreich, Barbara, and Deirdre English. *For Her Own Good: 150 Years of the Experts' Advice to Women.* New York: Anchor Press/ Doubleday, 1978.
> Brilliant demystification of scientific theories. A must.

Gordon, Linda. *Woman's Body, Woman's Right.* New York: Viking, 1976; Penguin, 1977 (pb.).
> History of birth control movement from feminist perspective.

Greiner, Ted. *The Promotion of Bottle Feeding by Multinational Corporations: How Advertising and Health Professionals Have Contributed.* Cornell International Nutrition Monograph Series #2, 1975. Available from the editor, Prof. Michael Latham, Division of Nutritional Sciences, Savage Hall, Cornell University, Ithaca, NY 14850.

The Health Policy Advisory Committee (Health-PAC). *The American Health Empire: Power, Profit and Politics.* New York: Random House, Inc., 1970; 1971 (pb.).
> An excellent analysis of who controls American medicine today.
———. *Prognosis Negative.* Ed. by David Kotelchuk. New York: Vintage, 1976.

Howell, Mary. *Helping Ourselves.* Boston: Beacon Press, 1975 (pb.).

Hricko, Andrea, with Melanie Brunt. *Working for Your Life: A Woman's Guide to Job Health Hazards* 1976. Available from Labor Occupational Health Program, University of California, Berkeley, CA 94720.

Hunt, Vilma R. *The Health of Women at Work.* 1977. $6. Available from Program on Women. 619 Emerson Street, Evanston, IL 60201.
> Bibliography and comprehensive review of the scientific literature on health hazards for women in the workplace.

Illich, Ivan. *Medical Nemesis.* New York: Bantam Books, 1977 (pb.).
> Powerful, well-documented critique of the medical establishment.

Institute for the Study of Medical Ethics. *Human Experimentation Without Informed Consent: The Abuses Continue.* 1978. $5. Available from the Institute, Box 17307, Los Angeles, CA 90017.

Kleiber, Nancy, and Linda Light. *Caring for Ourselves: An Alternative Structure for Health Care.* Report of the Vancouver Women's Health Collective. Free. Available from School of Nursing, University of British Columbia, 2075 Wesbrook Place, Vancouver, B.C., Canada, V6T 1W5.
> A description and evaluation of the structure and services of a feminist organization which provides health education and preventive care to women. Report deals extensively with the Collective's non-hierarchical structure, feminist politics, and its emphasis on self-help and the participation of lay women in the delivery of care.

Mass, Bonnie. *Population Target: The Political Economy of Population Control in Latin America.* Latin American Working Group, Box 2207, Station P., Toronto, Ontario, Canada. 1976.
> Solid documentation of population control abuses, especially in Latin America. Marxist orientation.

Milio, Nancy. *The Care of Health in Communities: Access for Outcasts.* New York: Macmillan, 1975.
> Sociological analysis of how health resources and training are and are not allocated to the poor, women and minorities, compared internationally.

Mintz, Morton. *By Prescription Only* (formerly *The Therapeutic Nightmare*). Boston: Beacon Press, 1967. $3.95. In paperback.
> Report on how the drug industry controls the FDA and AMA and knowingly markets worthless, injurious and even lethal drugs.

National Center for Health Services Research. *Women and Their Health: Research Implications for a New Era.* Conference proceedings. USDHEW Pub. No. (HRA) 77-3138. Available from National Technical Information Service, Springfield, VA 22161.

Ruzek, Sheryl. *The Women's Health Movement: Feminist Alternatives to Medical Control.* New York: Praeger Special Studies, Fall 1978.

Seaman, Barbara, and Gideon Seaman. *Women and the Crisis in Sex Hormones.* New York: Bantam Books, 1978.
> Comprehensive, including discussion of links between the government and drug industry.

Society for Occupational and Environmental Health. *Proceedings, Conference on Women and the Workplace,* 17-19 June 1976. Ed. by Eula Bingham, Ph.D. Available from the Society, 1714 Massachusetts Avenue, NW, Washington, DC 20036.

Stellman, Jeanne. *Women's Work, Women's Health: Myths and Realities.* New York: Pantheon, 1977.
> Excellent discussion of myths about working women, workplace health hazards, and fatigue-induced stress resulting from woman's dual role.

Walsh, Mary Roth. *"Doctors Wanted: No Women Need Apply": Sexual Barriers in the Medical Profession, 1835-1975.* New Haven: Yale University Press, 1977.

Articles

Bart, Pauline. *From those wonderful people who brought you the vaginal orgasm: sex education for medical students.* Paper presented at American Sociological Association meeting in New York City, 1976. Copies available from BWHBC, Box 192, West Somerville, MA 02144, for 50¢ plus stamped, self-addressed envelope.

Bates, Barbara. "Physician and Nurse Practitioner," *Annals of Internal Medicine* 82, No. 5 (1975): 702-706.

Bodenheimer, Thomas. "Capitalizing on Illness: The Health Insurance Industry," *International Journal of Health Services* 4, No. 4 (1974).

Caldicott, Helen. *Medical Implications of Nuclear Power.* From Mobilization for Survival, 13 Sellers Street, Cambridge, MA 02139.

Burns, Janice. *The Medical System as a Source of Sexist Ideology.* Paper presented in New Zealand, June 1978. Available from BWHBC, Box 192, West Somerville, MA 02144. (Send stamped, self-addressed envelope with 50¢ in stamps.)

Cousins, Norman. "Anatomy of an Illness (As Perceived by the Patient)," *New England Journal of Medicine* 295 (1976): 1458-1463.

"Crimes in the Clinic: A Report on Boston City Hospital," *Second Wave* (Summer 1973), Box 344 Cambridge A, Cambridge, MA 02139. $6.00.
> Exposé of clinic patients' surgery without consent.

Egbert, Lawrence D., and Ilene L. Rothman. "Relation Between the Race and Economic Status of Patients and Who Performs Their Surgery," *New England Journal of Medicine* 297, No. 2 (1977): 90-91.

Fee, Elizabeth. "Women and Health Care: A Comparison of Theories," *International Journal of Health Services* 5, No. 3 (1975): 397-415.

"Feminist Movement's Impact on Ob-Gyn Care is Not Debatable" *Ob-Gyn News,* 15 June 1975.

Firman, Gregory, et al. "The Future of Chiropractic: A Psychosocial View," *New England Journal of Medicine* 293, No. 13 (1975): 639-642.

Geyman, John P. "Family Practice in Evolution," *New England Journal of Medicine* 298, No. 11 (1978): 593-601.

Gray, Mary Jane, and Jayne Ackerman. "Attitudes of Women Medical Students Toward Obstetrics and Gynecology," *JAMWA* 33, No. 4 (1978): 162–164.

Greenfield, Sheldon, et al. "Efficiency and Cost of Primary Care by Nurses and Physician Assistants," *New England Journal of Medicine* 298, No. 6 (1978): 305–309.

HealthRight Collective. "Prognosis Positive. The Women's Health Movement 1978: Where We Were, Where We Are, Where We're Going," *HealthRight*, Winter 1978.

Heins, Marilyn, et al. "Comparison of the Productivity of Women and Men Physicians," *Journal of the American Medical Association* 237, No. 23 (1977): 2514–2517.

Hirsh, Harold, and Edward White. "The Pathologic Anatomy of Medical Malpractice Claims," *Legal Aspects of Medical Practice*, January 1978, pp. 25–92.

Hornstein, Frances. "An Interview on Women's Health Politics," Parts I and II, *Quest* 1, No. 1 (Summer 1974) and No. 2 (Fall 1974). A discussion of aspects of the political consciousness of feminist women's health centers.

Howell, Mary. "Can We Be Feminists and Professionals?" *Women's Studies International*, quarterly, 1978.

———. "Health Care and Healing: A Womanly Tradition." Paper presented at the American Medical Student Association Conference, Atlanta, GA, 3 March 1978. Available from BWHBC, Box 192, West Somerville, MA 02144. (Send stamped, self-addressed envelope and $1.)

———. "The New Feminism and the Medical School Milieu," *The Annals of the New York Academy of Sciences*, Fall 1978.

———. "What Medical Schools Teach About Women" ("Sounding Board"), *New England Journal of Medicine* 291, No. 6 (8 August 1974): 304–307. Excellent summary of specific attitudes toward women as expressed through teaching and behavior of medical faculty toward women, by a former Harvard Dean.

Lennane, K. Jean, and R. John Lennane. "Alleged Psychogenic Disorders in Women—A Possible Manifestation of Sexual Prejudice" (special article), *New England Journal of Medicine* 288, No. 6 (8 February 1973): 288–292.

Lewis, Charles E., and Mary Ann Lewis. "The Potential Impact of Sexual Equality on Health," *New England Journal of Medicine*, 20 October 1977.

Lewis, Deborah. "Insuring Women's Health," *Social Policy*, May/June 1976.

Luft, Harold. "How Do Health-Maintenance Organizations Achieve Their 'Savings'?" *New England Journal of Medicine* 298, No. 24 (1978): 1336–1343.

Malone, Patrick. "Socialized Medicine at 30: A British Pattern for America," *Washington Post*, 25 June 1978.

Margulies, Leah. "Exporting Infant Malnutrition," *HealthRight*, Spring 1977.

Marieskind, Helen. "Helping One's Self to Health," *Social Policy* 7, No. 2 (September/October 1976): 63–66.

McKinlay, John B. "The Limits of Human Services," *Social Policy*, January/February 1978, pp. 29–36.

Meyer, Lawrence. "New U.S. Problem: Too Many Doctors," *Washington Post*, 6 July 1977.

———. "Prepaid Medical Plan Reaps Millions," *Washington Post*, 2 February 1977.

Moyer, Linda. "What obstetrical journal advertising tells about doctors and women," *Birth and the Family Journal* 2, No. 4 (1975–76).

Navarro, Vicente. "Women in Health Care" (special article), *New England Journal of Medicine* 292, No. 8 (20 February 1975): 398–402. Documents sex discrimination in the health sector; suggests "institutional democracy" as remedy. Marxist analysis.

New York Times Special Series. "Unfit Doctors Create Worry in Profession," "Incompetent Surgery Is Not Found Isolated," "Bad Prescriptions Kill Thousands a Year," "Few Doctors Ever Report Colleagues' Incompetence," *The New York Times*, 26–29 January 1978.

"On the Imminent Death of Freedom for Poor Women," *Village Voice*, 11 July 1977.

"Physicians and the Making of Money," *Washington Post*, 12 June 1977.

Ritter, Esther. *Effects of Herbicide Use on Food Production, People, and the Planet.* National Organic Farmers Association, c/o Ritter, RD 1, Vergennes, VT 05491. Send 50¢.

Ruzek, Sheryl. "Emergent Modes of Utilization: Gynecological Self-Help," in *Women and Their Health: Research Implications for a New Era.* Proceedings of a conference, August 1975. DHEW Pub. No. (HRA) 77-3138. Available from National Technical Information Service, Springfield, VA 22161.

Ryan, George M., Jr. "Improving Pregnancy Outcome via Regionalization of Prenatal Care," *JOGN Nursing* 3, No. 4 (July–August 1974): 38–40. Standard arguments in favor of regionalization.

Sandmaier, Marian. "Fighting for Our Lives: Women and U.S. Health Care," *AAUW Journal*, April 1976.

Scully, Diana, and Pauline Bart. "A Funny Thing Happened on the Way to the Orifice: A Study of Women in Gynecology Textbooks," *American Journal of Sociology* 78, No. 4 (November 1973). Devastating evidence of sexism and paternalism in the experts' own words.

Seaman, Barbara. "Pelvic Autonomy: Four Proposals," *Social Policy*, September/October 1975, pp. 48–49.

Smith, Michael. "The Lilly Connection: Drug Abuse and the Medical Profession," *Science for the People*, January/February, 1978, pp. 8–15.

Soskis, Carole. "Who's on the Hospital Board?" *Region*, January 1976, pp. 6–8.

"10,000 Nurses Speak Out: A Startling Report on Hospitals and Doctors," condensed in *Family Health/Today's Health*, August 1977, pp. 36–38.

Townsend, Susan, and Marcy Rein. "Nurse Power!" *Off Our Backs*, June 1978.

Vaccarino, James M. "Consent, Informed Consent, and the Consent Form," *New England Journal of Medicine* 209, No. 8 (1978): 455.

Wagman, Paul. "U.S. Goal: Sterilize Millions of World's Women," *St. Louis Post-Dispatch*, 22 April 1977.

Walsh, Mary Roth. "Feminism: A Support System for Women Physicians," *Journal of the American Medical Women's Association* 31, No. 6 (1976).

Weiss, Kay. "What Medical Students Learn About Women," *Off Our Backs*, April/May 1975, pp. 24–25.

Wilson, Angela. "Black Women's Health," *HealthRight*, Winter 1976–77.

Zola, Erving Kenneth. "Medicine as an Institution of Social Control," in *Sociology of Medical Practice*, ed. by Carolyn Cox and Adrienne Mead. New York: Collier Macmillan, 1975 (pp. 170–185). Multi-disciplinary overview of the professionals' creation of client dependency and institutions of social control.

Pamphlets

Committee for a National Health Service. *Questions and Answers About a National Health Service.* Available from the Committee, 377 Park Avenue South, New York, NY 10018.

Ehrenreich, Barbara, and Deirdre English. *Complaints and Disorders.* Glass Mountain Pamphlet #2, 1974. $2.50. Available from The Feminist Press, Box 334, Old Westbury, NY 11568. Study of the social and historical continuity of medical care in the

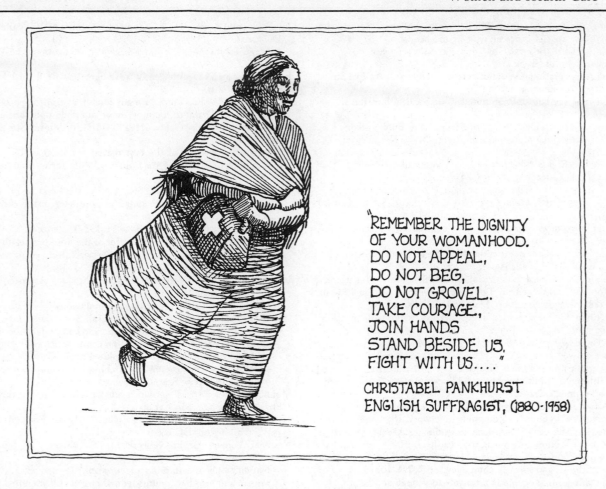

"REMEMBER THE DIGNITY
OF YOUR WOMANHOOD.
DO NOT APPEAL,
DO NOT BEG,
DO NOT GROVEL.
TAKE COURAGE,
JOIN HANDS
STAND BESIDE US.
FIGHT WITH US...."

CHRISTABEL PANKHURST
ENGLISH SUFFRAGIST, (1880-1958)

United States. Concentrates on the social class biases of the 19th century and their expression, much persisting to this day, in health and medical care for women. Must reading.

———. *Witches, Midwives, and Nurses—A History of Women Healers*. Glass Mountain Pamphlets; 2nd ed., 1972. $1.95. Available from The Feminist Press, Box 334, Old Westbury, NY 11568.

An indispensable pamphlet on the rise of male medical professionals and the suppression of women healers since the 14th century.

Hunt, Vilma. *Occupational Health Problems of Pregnant Women*. Department of Health, Education, and Welfare, Washington, DC, 1975. Order No. 5A-5304-75.

ISIS. *Bottle Babies: A Guide to the Baby Foods Issue*. March 1976. (See "Resource" section.)

Examines impact of multinational companies' sales techniques on women and children in the Third World. Includes many resources.

New American Movement. *National Health Insurance and/or National Health Service: Strategic Dilemmas*. Reprinted from discussion bulletins numbers 18 and 21 of the Health Commission of the New American Movement, 19920 Lichfield, Detroit, MI 48221.

Periodicals

Advance Data. Vital and Health Statistics of the National Center for Health Statistics, USDHEW, Public Health Service, National Center for Health Statistics, 3700 East-West Highway, Hyattsville, MD 20782.

Alternatives in Health Care. C/o Siuslaw Rural Health Center, 12326 Tide Route, Swisshome, OR 97480. $5 year or what you can afford. Good resource, especially for rural areas.

Coalition News. Coalition for the Medical Rights of Women, 4079A 24th Street, San Francisco, CA 94114.
West Coast advocacy action by women.

Health Activists' Digest. New American Movement, Health Commission, 19920 Lichfield, Detroit, MI 48221. (Also see "Resources" below.) $3 year.

Health Facts. The Center for Medical Consumers and Health Care Information, Inc., 237 Thompson Street, New York, NY 10012.
Excellent consumer viewpoint on many issues.

Health Newsletter. Health Writers, 306 N. Brooks Street, Madison, WI 53715.
Covers wide range of consumer health issues, including nutrition, sterilization abuse and HSAs.

Health-PAC Bulletin. 17 Murray Street, New York, NY 10007.
The only radical publication on health statistics. Should be read regularly by anyone who considers herself a health activist. (Also see "Resources," below.)

Health Watch. Women's Health Concerns Committee, 112 South 16th Street, Suite 1012, Philadelphia, PA 19102.
Local advocacy group's activities.

HealthRight. 175 Fifth Avenue, New York, NY 10010.
A newsletter of the women's health movement covering all aspects of the struggle to improve health care for women.

ISIS International Bulletin. (See "Resources" section below.)
Covers activities of women from different countries working to

bring about social and political change. Bulletins #7 and #8 (1978) are special issues on women and health.

Medical Self-Care. Box 718, Inverness, CA 94937. $7 year.
    General consumer view.

Network News. National Women's Health Network, 2025 Eye Street, Suite 105, Washington, DC 20006.
    Activities and information about women's health at the federal level.

Population Reports. Department of Medical and Public Affairs, University Medical Center, 2001 S Street, NW, Washington, DC 20009.

Reproductive Rights Newsletter. New American Movement, 3244 North Clark, Chicago, IL 60657. $3/year.
    Vol. 1, No. 2, on right-wing backlash, is excellent.

Seven Days. 206 Fifth Avenue, New York, NY 10010. $12.60/year (21 issues).
    Alternative newsmagazine. Regular column on women's health. See 5 May 1978 issue: "Our Bodies, Their Sales."

The Examiner. Tallahassee Feminist Women's Health Center, 1017 Thomasville Road, Tallahassee, FL 32303.
    Politics and service issues of alternative health care for women.

The Monthly Extract, ed. by Lolly Hirsh. New Moon Publications, Box 3488, Ridgeway Station, Stamford, CT 06905.
    A forum for ideas on self-help. Back issues probably available, even if no longer published.

WIN Magazine. 503 Atlantic Avenue, Brooklyn, NY 11217.
    Special issue on health, July/August 1978 ($1), includes interesting articles on National Health Service, a collectively run rural health center, health feminism. Bibliography inadequate, especially on women's health.

WIN News. International quarterly by, for and about women, ed. by Fran Hosken. Women's International Network, 187 Grant Avenue, Lexington, MA 02173. $15/year, individual; $25/year, institution.
    Extensive section on women and health.

Women and Health, ed. by Helen Marieskind and Ellie Engler. The Haworth Press, 149 Fifth Avenue, New York, NY 10010.
    Scholarly journal devoted exclusively to women and health.

Women and Health Roundtable Reports. Federation of Organizations for Professional Women, 2000 P Street, NW, Suite 403, Washington, DC 20036.

Women in Medicine Committee Newsletter. American Medical Student Association, 1171 Tower Road, Schaumburg, IL 60195.

Women's Washington Report. Women's Washington Representative, 324 C Street, SE, Washington, DC 20003. $25/year, individuals; $37/year, institutions.

Bibliographies

Cowan, Belita. *Women and Health Care: Resources, Writings, Bibliographies.* Revised 1978. $4. Available from the author, 3821 T Street, NW, Washington, DC 20007. (Make checks payable to Belita Cowan.)

Ruzek, Sheryl. *Women and Health Care: A Bibliography with Selective Annotation.* July 1976. $3.50. The Program on Women, Northwestern University, 619 Emerson Street, Evanston, IL 60201.

Resources

American Foundation for Homeopathy. 6231 Leesburg Pike, Falls Church, VA 22044.
    Write for general literature on homeopathy.

Committee to End Sterilization Abuse (CESA). Box A244, Cooper Station, New York, NY 10003.
    Distributes useful literature (e.g., *Sterilization Abuse: The Facts,* 1977), and works actively against sterilization abuse.

Consumer Coalition for Health. 1511 K Street, NW, Suite 220, Washington, DC 20005.

Environmental Action. 1346 Connecticut Avenue, NW, Washington, DC 20036.
    Major environmental group working in occupational health and safety.

Feminist Women's Health Center. 1112 Crenshaw Boulevard, Los Angeles, CA 10019.
    The first FWHC, source of many ideas for organizing and teaching materials basic to the movement and philosophy of self-help.

Health Policy Advisory Center (Health-PAC). 17 Murray Street, New York, NY 10007.
    Publishers of some of the best materials critical of U.S. health care; also the *Health-PAC Bulletin.* Write for information and literature list.

Health Research Group. 2000 P Street, NW, Washington, DC 20036.
    Actively working on wide range of consumer health problems. Send for extensive literature list.

HealthRight. 175 Fifth Avenue, New York, NY 10010.
    Publishes *HealthRight,* a newsletter of the women's health movement, and numerous other pamphlets and flyers giving valuable health information.

Interfaith Center for Corporate Responsibility. 475 Riverside Drive, New York, NY 10027.
    Resource for materials on infant formula abuse.

ISIS. Box 301, CH-1227, Carouge (Geneva), Switzerland.
    A women's international information and communication service. Staffs a resource and documentation center which collects materials from women's groups and makes these and other resources available to women everywhere. Publishes *ISIS Bulletin* (see periodicals) and special Resource Guides.

Mobilization for Survival (group against nuclear power). 13 Sellers Street, Cambridge, MA 02139.

National Abortion Rights Action League (NARAL). 825 15th Street, NW, Washington, DC 20005.

National Women's Health Network. 2025 Eye Street, NW, Suite 105, Washington, DC 20006.
    Nation's only membership organization devoted exclusively to women and health. Monitors federal health policies, provides testimony in Congress, offers resource guides and regular newsletter.

New England Free Press. 60 Union Square, Somerville, MA 02143.
    Send for excellent literature list which has a section on health.

The Feminist Press. P.O. Box 334, Old Westbury, NY 11568.
    Publishers of feminist books, reprints, bibliographies and pamphlets. Catalog on request.

The Institute for the Study of Medical Ethics. P.O. Box 17307, Los Angeles, CA 90017.
    Consumer advocacy activist research group.

Urban Planning Aid. 120 Boylston St., Boston, MA 02116.
    Send for literature list, including resources on occupational health and safety.

Films

American Health Empire (slide show). Available from American Friends Service Committee, 104 Inman Street, Cambridge, MA 02139.

Cambridge Documentary Films. Box 385, Cambridge, MA 02139.
    Good films on women's issues, including *Taking Our Bodies Back: The Women's Health Movement* and *Rape Culture.*

Do No Harm. Serious Business Co., 1145 Mandana Boulevard, Oakland, CA 94610.

Green Mountain Post Films. P.O. Box 177, Montague, MA 01351.
    Films on the dangers of nuclear power.

Nursing: The Politics of Caring. Ilex Films, Box 226, Cambridge, MA 02138. $350/purchase; $35/rental, plus $4 handling.

Song of the Canary, film on occupational health and safety. Available from Josh Hanig, 308 11th Street, San Francisco, CA 94103.

INDEX